W9-BZP-909

Library and Book Trade Almanac™

formerly **The Bowker Annual**

2020 | 65th Edition

Library and Book Trade Almanac™

formerly **The Bowker Annual**

2020 | 65th Edition

Editor John B. Bryans

Published by Information Today, Inc.

International Standard Book Number 978-1-57387-563-9
International Standard Serial Number 2150-5446
Library of Congress Catalog Card Number 55-12434

Information Today, Inc.
143 Old Marlton Pike
Medford, NJ 08055-8750
Phone: 800-300-9868 (customer service)
800-409-4929 (editorial queries)
Fax: 609-654-4309
E-mail (orders): custserv@infotoday.com
Web Site: http://www.infotoday.com

Printed and bound in the United States of America

Contents

International Reports

Part 2
Legislation, Funding, and Grants

Legislation

Funding Programs and Grant-Making Agencies

Part 3
Library/Information Science Education, Placement, and Salaries

Part 4
Research and Statistics

Library Research and Statistics

Directory of Book Trade and Related Organizations

Preface and Acknowledgments

Welcome to the 65th edition of *Library and Book Trade Almanac* (*LBTA*), which each year reports on and updates a wide range of industry facts, figures, activities, and trends. For this volume, *LBTA* staff and contributors compiled and distilled information principally from and about 2019, adding 2020 data that became available as we worked toward our spring deadline.

The coverage in *LBTA* revolves largely around libraries and the critical roles and services they perform, and we were vexed to learn this February that—for the fourth time in as many years—the Trump Administration has targeted the Institute of Museum and Library Services (IMLS) for elimination through its annual budget proposal process. (The very basic table on page 229 may serve as a starting point, but the American Library Association is the place to go for thoughtful reporting on the issue.)

The president's ongoing effort to rip funding from public libraries, museums, and other vital educational and cultural institutions should outrage most Americans, but the story has been under the radar since a deadly new coronavirus became a global health and economic crisis—named a pandemic by the World Health Organization on March 11, 2020. As *LBTA* goes to press, more than 2 million people worldwide have been diagnosed with the COVID-19 disease; some 140,000 lives have been lost and counting.

Unaccustomed as we are to introducing a new edition at such a grave and consequential moment, we recognize that life goes on. We've striven to create a quality reference that we trust will aid your work as an information, publishing, or research professional. In addition to reports from key government agencies, federal libraries, trade associations, and library-centric organizations in Part 1, you'll find a wealth of useful reporting, research, statistics, and reference information in Parts 2 through 5, and a multifaceted directory of organizations in Part 6.

Three special reports lead off the volume; our goal in commissioning them was to offer something for everyone—that is, every *LBTA* reader should find at least one report of relevance or of significant interest. We begin with "They Resisted: How Pushback on Changes to E-book Licensing Terms for Libraries Went Viral," by Shawnda Hines and Alan Inouye, two leading lights within the American Library Association. Their compelling presentation is followed by "How Do I Copyright My Name? The Perils (and Pleasures) of Working with Legal Information," by Anthony Aycock, a law librarian and information industry journalist par excellence. Concluding this year's section of special reports is "Disruptive Technologies in Libraries: Case Studies from the Field," a timely survey by librarian, author, and tech maven Cheryl Peltier-Davis.

I wish to thank the contributors to our 2020 edition for delivering everything they promised, on schedule, even as many of their jobs and lives were being turned upside down by COVID-19. There could be no *LBTA* without them. I would especially like to acknowledge Shawnda Hines, George Aulisio, John Chrastka, Connie Harbison, Erica Jaros, Susanne Markgren, Liz Page, Narda Tafuri, and Steve Zalusky—gifted scribes and experts all, but more than that, individuals who hold their results up to the highest standards. Meredith Schwartz was instrumental (and most gracious) in opening the doors to crucial information that could only be found in *Library Journal*.

Once again, my *LBTA* team members Christine McNaull, Sonya Manes, Nan Badgett, and Owen O'Donnell have brought inspiring skill and dedication to the project. They have my gratitude. To our readers, thank you for perusing and using this reference. Stay safe and healthy in the challenging days ahead, and drop a line any time to jbryans@infotoday.com and let me know how we can make *LBTA* more useful and relevant to your work.

John B. Bryans
Editor

Part 1
Reports from the Field

Special Reports

They Resisted: How Pushback on Changes to E-book Licensing Terms for Libraries Went Viral

Shawnda Hines and Alan Inouye

An explosion took place in the world of library e-book lending in 2019. Macmillan Publishers, one of the "Big Five" U.S. publishers, announced on July 25, 2019, that it would allow libraries to purchase only one copy of each new e-book title for the first eight weeks after a book's release.

Librarians nearly universally were outraged. The embargo itself violates a central tenet of librarianship: providing equitable access to information. Delayed access to works in digital format particularly deprives library patrons with disabilities or learning issues. E-books can become large-print books with only a few clicks, and most e-book reading devices offer fonts, line spacing, and other features that make reading easier for people who have dyslexia or other visual challenges.

The library community saw Macmillan's embargo as an arbitrary decision that could set a dangerous precedent. While the publisher's planned embargo applied only to new titles, what might they embargo next? The embargo was set for eight weeks, but how long might the next embargo delay access for library e-book borrowers? Macmillan's policy was also disconcerting to libraries because it could influence other publishers.

Although library workers weren't directly notified about Macmillan's new policy, it was clear libraries would be among the first stakeholders directly impacted by the decision. The multiple pricing and licensing terms would add yet another level of complexity to an already burdensome library acquisitions process. As American Library Association (ALA) president Wanda Brown said bluntly in the organization's initial reaction statement, "When a library serving many thousands has only a single copy of a new title in e-book format, it's the library—not the publisher—that feels the heat. It's the local library that's perceived as being unresponsive to community needs."

The Macmillan announcement set off a mighty fuse. But beneath the surface lay a vast store of flammable substance built on years of librarian frustration with library e-book lending terms.

Shawnda Hines is ALA assistant director of communications. Alan Inouye is ALA senior director of public policy and government relations.

Libraries and Publishing: A Volatile History

After many years as a niche product, by 2010 e-books were part of the digital information mainstream. The e-book ecosystem of information producers, intermediaries, and users was rapidly evolving, and provided both great opportunity and challenge for all parties. Libraries faced constraints from a complex array of lending models from numerous publishers, including those known at the time as the "Big Six"—Hachette, HarperCollins, Macmillan, Penguin, Random House, and Simon & Schuster—and newly minted publishers like Amazon. Some publishers sold only a limited collection of e-books to libraries. Some sold e-books to libraries at highly inflated prices. Some wouldn't sell them to libraries at all.

The initial turbulent period began in 2011, when HarperCollins Publishing announced a new licensing arrangement for e-book sales to libraries. Instead of selling e-book titles to libraries, HarperCollins began licensing access to an e-book for 26 loans, after which time the library would lose access to the title unless and until it paid again to renew the license. As reported in a 2013 LBTA article by Sari Feldman, Carrie Russell, and Robert Wolven, the arrangement was highly controversial within the library community.

This same period also saw dramatic price increases into the $80 to $90 range for a single copy of an e-book, albeit for a license that did not expire (in effect, a perpetual license—a popular model at the time). Some publishers, including Macmillan Publishers and Simon & Schuster, did not participate in the library e-book business at all for a period of time.

After advocacy by the library community and experimentation within publishing companies, by 2014 all the Big Five (with the just-completed merger of Penguin and Random House) were engaged in library e-book lending. The business models still varied: some publishers offered perpetual licenses, others offered a term license of one or two years, and HarperCollins continued its 26-checkout model. Overall, pricing remained much higher for libraries as compared to consumers, with bestsellers approaching $90 per copy as compared to a consumer price in the low teens.

Following the initial melee were several years of relative stability in the library e-book market, though pressure continued to mount over licensing terms that librarians saw as excessively expensive and unfavorable. Publishers veered away from the perpetual licensing model. By the end of 2019, four of the Big Five had a license term of two years, with HarperCollins continuing its 26-loan license. Pricing remained high, as perceived by librarians, at the $50 to $60 price point for a two-year license for bestselling titles. Just weeks before Macmillan decided to change its library sales model in July 2019, Hachette Book Group and Simon & Schuster both announced a transition of their library e-book lending models to a two-year license at a $40–$60 price point. While movement toward a standardized model was welcomed, the continuing unfavorable terms were not.

In July 2018 Tor, a division of Macmillan, announced without warning or any discussion with libraries that it was immediately beginning to embargo e-book sales of new titles to libraries for four months. The change by Tor came as a shock in large part because of Macmillan's involvement in the newly launched Panorama Project—a large-scale, data-driven research endeavor focused on understanding the impact of library holdings on book discovery, author brand development, and sales. The library community was concerned that the embargo in the Tor pilot would become standard practice and spread to other Macmillan titles. ALA resolved to ramp up engagement on the library e-book lending front and in 2019 reestablished a digital content working group with representation from the library community broadly.

Macmillan's Embargo: Friction with Libraries

Given the fraught history with libraries, one would wonder what concerns weighed heavily enough on Macmillan to warrant instituting an embargo (or "windowing" policy, as some publishers prefer to call it) that would likely set negotiations back by years. The short answer that Macmillan CEO John Sargent gave to its authors, illustrators, and agents in a July 2019 memo was that libraries, in his words, were "cannibalizing" sales and actively "marketing . . . to turn purchasers into borrowers." The longer explanation came in Sargent's open letter to librarians in October, days before the embargo went into effect:

> In the pre-digital world reading for free from libraries was part of the business model . . . In today's digital world there is no such friction in the market. As the development of apps and extensions continues, and as libraries extend their reach statewide as well as nationally, it is becoming ever easier to borrow rather than buy. This is causing book-buying customers to change habits, and they are fueling the tremendous growth in e-book lending.

Macmillan and a number of other publishers are concerned about the loss of friction in the lending process. The process of borrowing and returning a print book involves a labor cost for the patron, and a delay between the return of a book and the loan of the subsequent borrower. These are all but eliminated with e-books, rendering a higher turnover than print books. Moreover, e-books do not wear out, so there is a loss of sales from replacement copies that become lost, damaged, or worn out beyond repair.

Publishers are also concerned about the similar processes for purchasing an e-book and borrowing one from a library. Side by side on a web browser, why would people click to purchase an e-book that they could borrow for "free" (no direct payment) from a library? The theory is that at least some library e-book loans displace consumer sales that would have otherwise occurred.

Libraries counter that there is indeed friction in the market: the lengthy holds lists for bestselling titles. A patron can purchase an e-book now or wait months for a library e-book, which must then be read within two or three weeks.

Furthermore, libraries argue, publishers neglect to factor in the considerable value of marketing that libraries directly undertake, provided for no charge to publishers. While consumer sales for e-books have leveled off, sales to libraries (at quadruple the prices consumers pay) have increased. And while there is no data to support Macmillan's claim that increased e-book checkouts result in lost sales, there are data showing that library borrowers are the same people who buy books.

Libraries are invested in making sure millions of people can discover new authors and explore new books through digital and print collections. The value libraries add in free marketing alone, from website impressions to social media engagement to book purchases, is significant. In an analysis of its 2019 marketing activities, Ohio's Cuyahoga County Public Library estimated the value of its marketing of one new title to be $13,367—an amount worth 955 consumer e-book purchases at the going rate of $13.99.

Macmillan and libraries see the library e-book lending market in materially different ways. Whatever the perspective, one thing is clear: libraries are not likely to promote products that they cannot offer in their collections. The change in Macmillan's terms led to an unprecedented pushback by the U.S. library community, sparking a national campaign, #eBooksForAll.

Libraries Fire Back: #eBooksForAll

As soon as Macmillan announced its new e-book lending model, the library community shot back with unequivocal opposition to the policy, which is contradictory to the library mission of equitable access to information. Librarians of all stripes reacted on every social media platform within reach and penned opinions published in a range of outlets, from CNN to the *Wall Street Journal*. ALA vehemently denounced the decision and called on Macmillan's library customers to tell CEO John Sargent they objected to the new policy. The library community flooded the phone lines and e-mail inboxes of Macmillan Publishers, urging them to cancel the embargo, and dozens of state associations made public statements condemning it.

The appetite for an organized mobilization effort to rally public support for access to e-books became evident. In September 2019 ALA launched the #eBooksForAll campaign in conjunction with the Digital Book World conference in Nashville. At the Nashville Public Library, ALA held a press conference to unveil the #eBooksForAll online petition as the centerpiece for public advocacy, encouraging libraries, library organizations, and the general public to speak out against the Macmillan embargo. And they did.

Countless library systems across the nation, large and small, employed initiatives to increase awareness and petition signatures from among their patron bases. Some libraries sent e-mails to their user bases or featured information in their newsletters about the importance of equitable e-book access for libraries. Some library systems posted notices on their e-books landing pages, alerting library users that access to Macmillan titles would be limited beginning November 1 and directing patrons to sign the #eBooksForAll petition. Librarians produced videos and infographics and wrote letters to the editors of their local papers. The titles of proliferating editorials illustrate the range of perspectives:

"Limiting Library E-books a Blow to Literacy"

"Public Libraries across the Country Face a Different Type of Censorship"

"I'm a School Librarian Whose Students Are Digital Natives, but Their Access to E-books Is Limited"

"Ebook Publisher Takes Shortsighted Approach to Role Libraries Have in Developing New Book Consumers"

Remarkably, the petition became more than an opposition campaign. Advocates from every corner of the country leveraged the public attention to educate their communities about the overall value of libraries, well beyond the matter of access to e-books.

> Public libraries provide open access to books, materials, programs, technology and first-rate customer service. Public libraries are unique institutions because they exist solely to further the common good and to serve you regardless of how you look, what you believe, where you were born, what language you speak, who you love or any other way that you identify.
>
> —Vailey Oehlke, the *Oregonian*

> Public libraries are the best marketing tool publishers have. We provide suggestions to browsers, refer customers to bookstores, host author visits (often for substantial fees), assist new writers with publishing aspirations and market books by displaying covers face-out throughout our libraries. Believe it or not, we provide these services at no cost to authors and publishers. Why would Macmillan turn its back on its allies and friends? What answer should we provide to the student who needs an e-book for a school assignment or a senior citizen confined to a care facility who relies on e-books to stay connected to the outside world?
>
> —Patrick Losinski, the *Columbus Dispatch*

> An embargo against libraries . . . closes doors and deepens the digital divide that already exists in this country. It shouts out that you can only have knowledge if you are privileged or wealthy enough to buy it . . . Corporations should not be able to undermine the social contract of equal access to information through our public libraries. When they do, the power of our democracy diminishes.
>
> —Heidi Daniel and Paula Miller, the *Baltimore Sun*

With the Macmillan embargo set to take effect on November 1, 2019, ALA organized a site visit to the new Macmillan headquarters on Wall Street to deliver the petition with more than 150,000 signatures (which would rise to 250,000 by February 2020). On October 30, a delegation of ALA officials, librarians, and representatives of other library organizations marched to the company. Three ALA officials—Alan Inouye, senior director of public policy and government relations; Barb Macikas, executive director, Public Library Association (PLA); and Sari Feldman, senior policy fellow—met with CEO John Sargent and other executives. Unfortunately, while the conversation was substantive, it did not lead to a path forward.

Negotiations reached an impasse when the embargo went into effect as planned on November 1. However, neither Macmillan nor libraries left the table, to the credit of both. At the national level, meetings between Macmillan and various subsets of librarians, ALA officials, and leadership of the Chief Officers of State Library Agencies and PLA (a unit of ALA) continued. Libraries braced for change, and, for scores of them, change meant to discontinue purchasing e-books from Macmillan altogether.

From Embargo to Antitrust: A Legislative Approach

Meanwhile, in addition to direct engagement with Macmillan and the public #eBooksForAll campaign, ALA began reaching out to members of Congress. On September 13 the House Judiciary Subcommittee on Antitrust, Commercial, and Administrative Law asked ALA to provide input for its investigation into competition in digital markets. Concerns were rising about the power of certain large platforms—notably, Facebook, Google, and Amazon—over information access, and particularly on their influence on elections and political discourse. Given these concerns, the subcommittee launched a bipartisan investigation, led by Chairman David Cicilline (D-R.I.-1) and Ranking Member James Sensenbrenner (R-Wisc.-5), focusing on: (1) competition problems in digital markets; (2) whether dominant firms are engaging in anticompetitive conduct online; and (3) whether existing antitrust laws, competition policies, and current enforcement levels are adequate to address these issues.

The report submitted to the Subcommittee by ALA warned that "unfair behavior by digital market actors—and the outdated public policies that have enabled them—is doing concrete harm to libraries as consumers in digital markets . . . abuse of the market position by dominant actors in digital markets is impeding essential library activities that are necessary to ensure that all Americans have access to information, both today and for posterity. If these abuses go unchecked, America's competitiveness and our cultural heritage as a nation are at risk."

The submission, which addressed the separate digital markets for popular content and scholarly communications, represented a milestone in a number of respects. Foremostly, it raised what was an industry problem to a public policy problem meriting the attention of the U.S. Congress. The report expanded the breadth of the problem to include industry pricing and terms, as well as the unavailability of e-books from Amazon, which refuses to sell its published content to libraries (effectively, a permanent embargo). The submission highlighted additional problems, including those posed by streaming media and other online content that is generally unavailable to libraries due to individual consumer-oriented license terms.

Parallel to the federal investigation in the House subcommittee, which is expected to release its findings in Spring 2020, state library associations and advocates were taking action. By the end of 2019 several states were actively drafting legislation for their senates and/or houses/assemblies. In general, these efforts focused on according libraries the same access that consumers have. Also at the state level, library advocates were exploring possible investigations by their respective attorneys general.

Trajectory for 2020 and Beyond

The library community continues its advocacy, with the major thrust on public policy. The American Library Association continues to cooperate with inquiries from Congress, the U.S. Department of Justice, and the Federal Trade Commission. State library associations continue to engage legislators and attorneys general at the state level. Library supporters across the nation continue to use every platform at their disposal to speak out against Macmillan's embargo and any efforts to deny or delay library access to e-books.

While Macmillan was indeed the most proximate problem for the library community, there is growing sentiment that focus must broaden beyond this one company. Libraries face many other problems pertaining to the acquisition and preservation of digital content, stemming from the loss of protections and rights in the copyright law. For analog materials, the copyright law affords multiple and important rights. The concepts of ownership of copies and lending derive directly from the first sale doctrine. Use of materials in the classroom or other educational settings is explicitly allowed under copyright law.

By contrast, individuals and libraries have few privileges and rights under the contract regime, where, essentially, one can perform only activities articulated in the contract. As most individuals and libraries do not have the wherewithal to negotiate contracts, it is the publisher, vendor, or copyright holder who writes the contract. For society to enjoy proper public interest rights and provisions in the digital age, changes in the public policy regime are necessary. While libraries may have lost the Macmillan embargo battle, there is yet a chance to win the war for equitable access to information.

How Do I Copyright My Name? The Perils (and Pleasures) of Working with Legal Information

Anthony Aycock

Suppose you, or someone you know, is starting a business. Adopting a child. Getting a divorce. Evicting a tenant (or avoiding eviction by a landlord). Fighting a conviction. Working to reduce a prison sentence. Hoping to get an old offense expunged from the record.

Should you or your friend hire an attorney?

If you said "no," you're not alone. As many as 90 percent of litigants handle their cases *pro se*, a Latin phrase meaning "for oneself."[1] A person may be pro se in a civil case as plaintiff or defendant or as a defendant in a criminal case. The right to act pro se dates back to the beginning of the United States with the Judiciary Act of 1789, which provided that "in all the courts of the United States, the parties may plead and manage their own causes personally or by the assistance of counsel."[2] Later, the Sixth Amendment to the Constitution set forth rights related to criminal prosecution—rights that include pro se representation.

Though born out of financial necessity—you don't have to be poor to be priced out of the legal marketplace—attorney DIYing can be a disaster. "Even the most mundane legal matters," according to one writer, "can require dozens of steps and complex maneuvering."[3] If you do decide to forgo counsel, don't expect a lot of help. Courthouse staff can't or won't answer questions. Legal aid agencies are overwhelmed. Ditto law school clinics. Some fillable forms are available online, but these are useful only for the simplest cases. In the face of such odds, where might a desperate person turn for help?

Their local library, of course.

Librarians answer questions. It's what we do. But things get tricky when those questions involve the law. I have been asked to fill out someone's forms, tell them what to request in court, explain their rights, proofread their documents, and interpret the U.S. Constitution. The stakes are no lower for attorneys, many of whom rely on public libraries. The pressures of legal research make access to information the crux of legal practice. Attorneys who do it poorly might face a malpractice lawsuit. Clients sue for malpractice all the time, but the suit is warranted, and the former client will likely win, if the attorney overlooked a key statute or relied on an overturned case. Judges have even sanctioned attorneys for failing to conduct diligent, thorough legal research, sometimes adding the sanction *on top of* a malpractice award.

Anthony Aycock is the legislative librarian for the North Carolina General Assembly. He has worked in public, academic, and law firm libraries in North and South Carolina. He has also taught legal research in the UNC Charlotte Paralegal Certificate Program. Anthony writes regularly for Medium (https://medium.com/@pisancantos43) and *Information Today*; he has also published in the *Missouri Review*, the *Gettysburg Review*, *Ploughshares*, *Library Journal*, and the *Chronicle of Higher Education*. His first book, *The Accidental Law Librarian*, was published in 2013.

Librarians, of course, are not legal experts. Many have no experience in the law, and those who do are often too afraid of liability to offer much help. Yet there is plenty we *can* do. Developing a good approach to legal information needs is the purpose of this report. I will give an overview of legal information sources, review techniques for legal reference interviews, and explain why those liability fears are overblown. Finally, I will discuss what the future holds for legal information.

The Wonderful World of Legal Information

The way it often works is this: a patron contacts the library, tells their story of how some person or group wronged them, and then asks, "Is that legal?" Many times, they want to know "the law" on their issue. Some need an attorney; their issue is too intricate to sort out on their own, even with librarian support. A lot of patrons, however, can do the research. They simply need guidance, starting with: what are the different sources of legal information?

Primary Sources

What people usually mean by "the law" is *primary sources*, which are "the sum total of the rules governing individual and group behavior that are enforceable in court."[4] There are three major primary sources in legal research.

Statutes. This is legislation enacted by an elected body such as the U.S. Congress or a state legislature. Statutes are first published in the order in which they're passed—these are often called *session laws or public laws*—then republished in subject compilations known as *codes*. (Tip: be prepared to explain the difference between Congress and a state legislature. A surprising number of people can't tell them apart.)

Cases. Also called an *opinion* or *decision*, a case is a written ruling issued by a court on a specific matter. Judges are bound in their rulings by how similar cases in the same jurisdiction were decided in the past. This is called *precedent*, and it is the foundation of American jurisprudence.

As with legislation, there is a dual system: the federal courts, culminating in the U.S. Supreme Court; and each state's courts, culminating in the equivalent of a Supreme Court but which may have another name. In New York, for instance, it's the Court of Appeals. The Supreme Court is the trial court (which confused me when I started watching *Law & Order*).

Regulations. You know the IRS? SEC? Attorney General? Department of Transportation? How about Fannie Mae, Freddie Mac, or the U.S. Board on Geographic Names? These are federal agencies—states have them too—created by statute and charged with overseeing some area of society. Agencies pass regulations, or rules, that are as authoritative as statutes, though a legislature can invalidate a regulation.

Agencies also issue rulings in courtroom-like cases called *administrative hearings*. Technically, these rulings can be reviewed by a court, but judges typically decline to do so except in egregious instances.

Secondary Sources

Secondary sources include books, journals, indexes, encyclopedias, newsletters, pamphlets, or anything else that helps a person find or understand a primary source. They are resources about the law, not the law itself.

Treatises. These are in-depth, multivolume works on one area of law. The most renowned ones are cited by courts, studied by lawyers and law professors, and known by their author and subject: Wigmore on Evidence, Corbin on Contracts, Prosser and Keeton on Torts, Wright's Federal Practice and Procedure.

Practice guides. These works are shorter, less scholarly, and more useful to pro se patrons. (Tip: learn the major practice guide for each area of law in your state, and refer patrons with broad questions to these sources.)

Digital v. Print

A single publisher, Thomson Reuters—formerly known as West Publishing, West Group, or simply "West"—has printed the majority of U.S. law since 1879. A second publisher, LexisNexis, built the first legal database in 1973, which West followed in 1975 with Westlaw.

Most lawyers, and many law libraries, now rely solely on these two databases, no longer collecting statutes, case reporters, and treatises in print. There are good reasons to use print resources—simpler to navigate, access to a human-prepared index, plus a lot of historical information isn't digitized. Yet there is no question that these databases have made legal research faster and cheaper.

A few smaller databases like Fastcase have cropped up. They are less expensive than Westlaw or Lexis, which should make them more attractive to cash-strapped libraries and solo attorneys. However, they have so far struggled to gain a real foothold. No two companies dominate their industry like Thomson Reuters and LexisNexis. This is both scary and convenient.

"How Do I Copyright My Name?"

Patrons say the darnedest things. They ask if the Fifteenth Amendment to the Constitution is going to expire.[5] Or if it's illegal for the government to impose taxes.[6] Jonathan Lee Riches made news in 2007 for suing ex-NFL star Michael Vick for $63,000,000,000,000,000,000—that's 63 quintillion dollars—claiming that Vick stole his pit bulls and sold them, using the money "to purchase missiles from the Iran government."[7] I was once asked, "How do I copyright my name?" Seems the patron wanted to make sure no one—like, say, a bill collector—could send mail addressed to him without his permission (which, I have to say, would be awesome).

Most pro se patrons aren't that outré. They're ordinary people faced with legal action who are looking for information to help them take it. Rather than hesitating for fear of legal liability, librarians should do what we do best: a reference interview, the purpose of which is to suss out what the patron really needs vis-à-vis what they think they need. Questions to help with this winnowing include:

- **Do you have any citations?** The legal profession runs on these identifiers for statutes, case law, regulations, and secondary sources. Official citations are published in *The Bluebook: A Uniform System of Citation* (www.legalbluebook.com), which should be on every public library's ready reference shelf.
- **What do you already know about this topic?** Ask the patron to brainstorm keywords or synonyms, which you can match with index headings in a legal encyclopedia. (Tip: *American Jurisprudence 2d*, often called AmJur, is the best of these encyclopedias, though it's pricy. An online alternative is Cornell Law School's Legal Information Institute, www.law.cornell.edu/).
- **Do you need a summary of a law or the actual law?** Most full text documents are only available via a commercial database like Westlaw. As for summaries, state bar associations are good places to start. For example, the North Carolina Bar Association website (www.ncbar.org) offers free pamphlets on home-buying, domestic violence, worker's compensation, living wills, bankruptcy, auto accidents, and other topics.
- **What is your deadline?** If the patron is due in court tomorrow, they don't have time to do their own research. They need a lawyer, stat.
- **What jurisdiction?** Much patron confusion comes down to the difference between federal law and state law. Knowing which system they're dealing with saves you a lot of research time.
- **Do you need current or previous law?** Suppose the patron is trying to get his brother's ten-year-old drug conviction overturned because the police collected evidence incorrectly. He wouldn't need current statutes, which are available online; he would need statutes *as they read then*, for which he'll probably need to contact a government or law school library.

If you do get what could be called "extreme patrons"[8]—those with odd beliefs, or who seem aggressive or hostile, or disoriented—realize that your goal has changed. It is no longer to find information but to keep the situation calm. Even people who aren't mentally ill can be stressed beyond rational behavior due to the urgency and high stakes of legal research.

So don't argue with the patron. Keep your voice even, your gaze steady. Maintain boundaries—no touching, no personal questions—and call a colleague over if necessary. If library policy prevents you from granting a request, don't just apologize; show empathy. Focus on what you can do rather than on what you can't.

Above all, listen. Many law-seeking patrons don't begin with the library. They try other agencies—legislature, governor, attorney general, courthouse, police, legal aid—and each time they are rebuffed, they grow a little more desperate. By the time they reach you, their legitimate question may have evaporated in a welter of frustration.

I always let such patrons vent—a little. I don't tolerate abuse, but if a few minutes of harangue calms them down, that helps me provide better reference service. In fact, some patrons seem to want nothing more than a willing ear. Having someone listen to them makes them feel valued.

Librarianship is ministerial that way. Learn when to lean into it.

UPL? NBD!

The unauthorized practice of law, or UPL, first appeared in the library literature in the mid-1970s and has been frequently discussed, though infrequently agreed upon, ever since.

As early as 1971, librarians were expressing their reticence to help pro se patrons: "I would not close off our library to lay persons and say, 'no lay person can come in, except that I do not believe I have the same obligation to them that I do to the members of the bar."[9] Robert Begg took this sentiment a step further, arguing that public patrons should pay fees, receive limited service, and be given "the old run-around."[10] More severe still is an article stating that pro se users should not be helped at all unless a specific institutional policy requires it. It notes that law librarians can't "hide the law," but neither should they be "spreading the word."[11]

No matter the reason for librarian aloofness, it is a mistake. We forget that we may be the only "law librarian" a patron ever meets and that the patron's problem is real and scary and all-consuming to that person, even if it is work-a-day to us. We have an ethical obligation to provide all the assistance we can while avoiding UPL.

Which is a cinch, according to Paul Healey, a leading writer on the topic. Healey believes that "no librarian will ever be prosecuted for unauthorized practice of law while engaging in normal reference activities"—i.e., helping patrons find and use sources, interpreting citations, and advising on the research process.[12] He advises librarians to do what we do, use reasonable care, and be clear about boundaries. If we do that, UPL is nothing to worry about.

This doesn't mean we should try to answer *every* question. One of a law librarian's most important skills is knowing what you're qualified to answer and what should be referred to an attorney. Generally, an interpretive question is best referred out. Suppose a patron asks for help locating recent cases on age discrimination. This is perfect for a librarian, the equivalent of asking for books on a subject.

However, if the patron wants to know whether she should sue for age discrimination, she is asking you to *interpret* the law as it applies to her set of facts. In other words, she is asking for advice. Even librarians who happen to be attorneys—often the case in law school libraries—should not answer this question, as they may inadvertently create an attorney-client relationship, which imposes all sorts of obligations on both parties.

Most patrons don't want to be referred to a lawyer. After all, attorneys are expensive. If the patron could have afforded one, they would have hired one to start with. Yet there are cheaper options that librarians should be able to recommend. One is a lawyer referral service, or LRS. Often operated by a state bar association, the LRS connects a caller with an attorney who specializes in the caller's area of need. The caller pays the LRS a small fee, usually around $50, for a 30-minute consultation with that attorney, whom the caller can hire outright for more work at a discounted rate.

There are also pro bono opportunities in most areas. Pro bono, a shortened form of *pro bono publico*, or "for the common good," means working for free. Probono.net and Lawhelp.org are two websites that connect people with affordable legal services. Following this example, some public libraries have partnered with their local bar association on events such as Oakland, California's Lawyers in the Library, where volunteer attorneys give free advice and referrals.[13]

The Future of Legal Information

As you read this, soon-to-be college graduates across America are making plans for law school. When they get out in a few years, what will their information landscape look like? What services will they need, and want, from libraries?

For starters, unlike popular e-books, which were supposed to doom traditional publishing but which now seem doomed themselves,[14] the print-to-electronic trend in legal publications shows no sign of a reversal. I used to think there was a *terminus ad quem* for the loss of print, assuming that some things would always be available in a paper format.

I was wrong.

The news that a couple of law practice staples, *Physician's Desk Reference* and *ABA/BNA Lawyer's Manual on Professional Conduct*, have ceased being published in print is significant. Bloomberg Law, which is trying like mad to overtake Lexis and Westlaw in the legal marketplace, sees its future as "completely digital."[15] Yikes. How long will it be before more government agencies follow the example of the Nebraska Supreme Court, which in 2016 began releasing its opinions online only?[16]

Despite these developments, legal researchers need print research skills. Some things, *a lot* of things, will never exist electronically, things such as local bar association journals, professional newsletters, and certain non-U.S. publications. Government documents, Nebraska notwithstanding, are another example. My library is home to the official minutes of my state's legislative committee meetings. Committees are where the grunt work of drafting bills is done, which makes them an intriguing source for the white whale of statutory research: legislative intent. For this reason, they are requested by attorneys, scholars, and really, *really* curious patrons all the time. We are the only library in the state with these records. Committees give them to us as hard copies. We organize and shelve them, and after a couple of years, we send the minutes to the State Records Center to be converted to microfilm, an electronic medium with the functionality of paper. (It would be nice to convert these records to PDFs and post them online, but I have not yet found a cost-effective way of doing that.)

Librarians know the everything-is-online mentality to be a Google-fueled fiction. So do older attorneys, who shake their heads at the young associates' digital overreliance. "When I am researching in the library," writes attorney Scott Stolley, "I feel as lonely as the Maytag repairman."[17] Holdouts like Stolley will be gone someday, leaving the fate of law libraries in the hands of the Google generation.

Some libraries have already closed from lack of use. In 2008, Tennessee Supreme Court Justice Sharon Lee defended the decision to shutter three court libraries by saying, "We were not getting our money's worth out of it at all. Most of our research is online now."[18] In 2007, county commissioners in Miami, FL voted to end the funding for the county's seventy-year-old public law library.[19] Three years later, Indiana law librarian Zoya Golban turned off the lights at the Marion County Law Library for the last time, sending its patrons and collection to the county public library.[20] That same year, law libraries in the Connecticut towns of Milford, Willimantic, and Norwich were boarded up.[21] Most recently, the San Diego Law Library shut down its courthouse locations in East County and South Bay. In addition to moving its collection, it is partnering with public libraries for database access and working with a legal aid group to relocate its clinics.[22]

Attorneys may be using libraries less, but as I've mentioned, demand from pro se users is growing. To handle this demand, law libraries must adapt, something they are loath, yet well-suited, to do. How can they do this? By opening themselves further. Historically, law libraries have focused on building collections, not doing outreach or creating innovative services. But innovation has become the watchword in legal research. Public libraries may provide access to legal databases, but most offer no training on how to use them. It would be a simple matter to hold one free public seminar per month on electronic legal research. Small firm attorneys would show up in droves, as would pro se litigants.

Another way to innovate is through better public access to legal information. The Maine State Law and Legislative Reference Library is the leader in this area. Years ago, the library began an ambitious project to scan and publish online, free of charge, as many state documents as possible. The collection includes

- Bills and amendments back to 1868
- Full text of laws back to 1820
- Codified statutes back to 1840
- Legislative Record—the transcript of legislative chamber proceedings—back to 1897
- Massachusetts laws (Maine was part of this state until 1820) back to 1806, with plans to delve even farther, to 1628

More impressive is the website's legislative history section. The complete history of a statute is a valuable thing, but it can take weeks to compile one. In Maine, it's already been done: the history "for every Public Law, Private and Special Law, Resolve, Constitutional Resolution, Initiated Bill, Legislative Document, and House or Senate Paper since 1987."[23] There are also subject-themed histories on popular topics such as abortion, casino gambling, constitutional amendments, and same-sex marriage.

Schools of library and information science can contribute to the reinvention. They can do a better job of training librarians in legal reference. Law librarians as well can teach the librarian community the truth about unauthorized practice of law—i.e., that it should not constrain library service. To do this, some law librarians will have to reinvent themselves, dumping their don't-spread-the-word attitude toward pro se library use. In short, law libraries must think of themselves not as buildings of books but as parts—no, as the *hub* of the legal community. Those who do will survive, even prosper.

I have been a law librarian for 19 years. It is rewarding, interesting, sometimes maddening, never boring. Legal research can easily overwhelm nonlawyers: the process is far from intuitive, the publications and language are unfamiliar, and for pro se patrons, the stakes are high. Libraries can be critical resources for them, and librarians shouldn't fear their questions. Relevant professional development can position us to make a real difference—we owe it to our patrons to explore that difference.

Notes

1. Lauren Sudeall Lucas and Darcy Meals, "Every Year, Millions Try to Navigate US Courts without a Lawyer," the *Conversation,* July 26, 2019, https://theconversation.com/every-year-millions-try-to-navigate-us-courts-without-a-lawyer-84159.
2. 1 Stat. 73, 92.
3. Lucas and Meals, "Every Year, Millions Try to Navigate US Courts without a Lawyer."
4. Stephen Elias and Susan Levinkind, *Legal Research: How to Find and Understand the Law,* 11th ed. (Berkeley, CA: Nolo, 2003), 3/2.
5. "Constitutional FAQ Answer #6—The U.S. Constitution Online," Constitutional FAQ Answer #6—The U.S. Constitution Online—USConstitution.net, accessed February 3, 2020, https://www.usconstitution.net/constfaq_q6.html.
6. This is a popular argument among antigovernment extremists known as "sovereign citizens." See Anthony Aycock, "Citizen Bane: A Librarian's Primer on Sovereigns," *Information Today,* December 2014.
7. Mike Holtzclaw, "Inmate Sues Vick for $63,000,000,000,000,000,000," *Daily Press,* August 17, 2019, https://www.dailypress.com/news/dp-now-quintillion.au15-story.html.
8. Rhonda Schwartz, "Say What?! How to Handle Reference Questions from Patrons Who Seemingly Inhabit an Alternate Universe," *AALL Spectrum,* (Sept./Oct. 2004): 20–21.
9. "Reader Services in Law Libraries—A Panel," *Law Library Journal* 64, no. 4 (1971): 486–506.
10. Robert T. Begg, "The Reference Librarian and the Pro Se Patron," *Law Library Journal* 69 (1976): 26–32.
11. C. C. Kirkwood and Tim Watts, "Legal Reference Service: Duties v. Liabilities," *Legal Reference Services Quarterly* 3 (Summer 1983): 67–82.
12. Paul D. Healey, "Pro Se Users, Reference Liability, and the Unauthorized Practice of Law: Twenty-Five Selected Readings," *Law Library Journal* 94, no. 1 (2002): 133.
13. "Oakland Public Library," Lawyers in the Library, accessed February 3, 2020, https://oaklandlibrary.org/services/cards-and-visiting/lawyers-library.
14. Constance Grady, "The 2010s Were Supposed to Bring the Ebook Revolution. It Never Quite Came," *Vox*, December 23, 2019, https://www.vox.com/culture/2019/12/23/20991659/ebook-amazon-kindle-ereader-department-of-justice-publishing-lawsuit-apple-ipad.
15. "ABA/BNA Lawyers' Manual on Professional Conduct," CRIV Blog, accessed February 3, 2020, https://crivblog.com/tag/aba-bna-lawyers-manual-on-professional-conduct.
16. Lori Pilger, "Supreme Court Opinions Going Online Only," JournalStar.com, January 2, 2016, https://journalstar.com/news/local/supreme-court-opinions-going-online-only/article_3aa16195-638d-59b0-a584-58f3c4f1e0ae.html.
17. Scott Stolley, "Corruption of Legal Research," *For The Defense* 39 (April 2004): 40.

18. Hillary Baker, "Battling the Economic Bully: How Tough Times Are Affecting Law Libraries, and How You Can Fight Back," *AALL Spectrum* 13, no. 8 (June 2009): 15.
19. Calvin Godfrey, "Law Library Checks Out," *Miami New Times*, October 18, 2007, www.miaminewtimes.com/2007-10-18/news/law-library-checks-out.
20. Francesca Jarosz, "Budget Cuts Force Law Library to Close," *Indianapolis Star,* January 2, 2010, A21.
21. Amanda Falcone, "State Closes Three Law Libraries," *Hartford Courant*, April 7, 2010, B8.
22. "Law Library Courthouse Locations Have Closed," San Diego Law Library, July 1, 2019, https://sandiegolawlibrary.org/law-library-courthouse-locations-closed/.
23. Maine Legislative History Collections, accessed February 3, 2020, https://www.maine.gov/legis/lawlib/lldl/legishistory.htm.

Disruptive Technologies in Libraries: Case Studies from the Field

Cheryl Peltier-Davis

Artificial intelligence, augmented and virtual reality, the Internet of Things, robotics, drones, 3D printing, blockchain technology, quantum computing, and the quantified self are examples of disruptive technologies that are transforming the way we live, learn, work, and play. As described by Klaus Schwab (2017), founder and executive chairman of the World Economic Forum, such technologies are the drivers of the Fourth Industrial Revolution, often referred to as "4IR" or "IR 4.0."

Librarians have a well-established reputation as enthusiastic and effective early adopters of technology through the centuries, from papyrus to petabytes. The library literature is replete with examples of librarians, employed in institutions of all types and sizes, using emerging technology to provide exceptional information services to diverse, multi-generational clienteles. This report looks at disruptive technologies that are particularly relevant to the work of today's librarians and offers examples of libraries successfully pursuing their selection, integration, and implementation.

The selected case studies are informed by the author's independent, evaluative research of recent library literature. The resulting report, intended as an introduction to disruptive tech trends in the library profession, describes projects that practitioners may take inspiration from and perhaps emulate. For further reading on cases and topics covered, refer to the endnotes, which include an alphabetical listing of references and more than 20 websites numbered within the text.

The Center for the Future of Libraries[1] is an online resource integral to the writing of this report that will be of special interest to librarians in future-focused and future-ready modes. This ALA website was developed to identify emerging trends relevant to libraries and the communities they serve and "to promote futuring and innovation techniques to help librarians and library professionals shape their future." Regularly updated, the site is a treasure trove of useful information for those aiming to implement transformative technologies in their libraries.

The First to the Fourth Industrial Revolution—Technology Pervasiveness and Impact

The Fourth Industrial Revolution—hereinafter IR 4.0—builds on the foundations of three previous periods of significant technological advancement: the introduction of the steam engine (IR 1.0, 18th century); the age of science and mass production (IR 2.0, 19th to early 20th centuries); and the rise of digital technology

Cheryl Peltier-Davis is faculty liaison librarian/Social Sciences at the Alma Jordan Library at the University of the West Indies, St. Augustine, Trinidad and Tobago. Her professional interest in emerging technologies has led to the publication of two editions of *The Cybrarian's Web*, a guide for information professionals who need to keep up to date with social media tools and mobile apps. In 2019 she was a program adviser for the Internet Librarian International conference, London, U.K., and recipient of the 2019 Caribbean Information Professional of the Year Award from the Association of Caribbean University, Research and Institutional Libraries (ACURIL).

(IR 3.0, mid- to late 20th century). While it is generally agreed that these earlier stages of technological growth radically changed how people live, work, and communicate, the IR 4.0 environment is unique in "blurring [the] boundaries between the physical, digital, and biological worlds." Propelled by a fusion of advances in artificial intelligence (AI), robotics, the Internet of Things (IoT), and genetic engineering, among other disruptive technologies, IR 4.0 innovation is challenging the very notion of what it means to be human and is poised to change society like never before (McGinnis 2018).

Through its varied iterations from IR 1.0 through 4.0, technology can be viewed as both progressive and pervasive. *Progressive* in the manner in which it has impacted people's daily lives, worldwide industries and economies ("life went from being all about the farm to all about the factory"; Randyansyah 2019), and how humans work and relate to one other. *Pervasive* as evidenced in all sectors, including libraries, powered by the persistence of software developers in creating new products and services, within relatively short cycles, that quickly influence and invade our homes, offices, and social spaces.

A prime example of the impact of ubiquitous technology may be seen in how advances in mobile communication in the 1990s led to the introduction of a small handheld device, the smartphone. In 2019, the number of smartphone users worldwide surpassed 3 billion, a number forecast to grow by several hundred million over the next few years (O'Dea 2020). The widespread adoption of this singular utilitarian device is indicative of the needs of global consumers, leading hectic lives that demand instantaneous 24/7 access to information and to one another.

Understanding and Implementing Disruptive Technologies in Libraries

The late Clayton Christensen, Harvard Business School professor and author, is widely credited with coining the term "disruptive technology." In his book *The Innovator's Dilemma*, Christensen placed new technology into two categories: *sustaining*, which relies on incremental improvements to an established technology, and *disruptive*, which "displaces an established technology and shakes up the industry" (Christensen 2016). Online tech reference tool WhatIs.com offers a brief introduction to Christensen's work along with examples of some now well-established disruptive technologies including the personal computer, e-mail, cloud computing, and social networking."[2]

The library community is far from immune to technological disruption and shifts, and the roles and functions of information professionals continue to be tried and tested—a situation exacerbated by the challenge of providing responsive service despite shrinking budgets. The hurdles notwithstanding, many librarians working in IR 4.0 have been proactive in experimenting with and embracing disruptive technologies that hold promise for the creation of new and enhanced user services. Rightly so, according to Erik Boekesteijn, senior advisor at the National Library of the Netherlands, who acknowledges the "transformative changes enabled by digital technologies" and wants libraries "to rethink their role as curators and keepers of knowledge and as facilitators of education and dialogue."[3]

Tech innovation is rarely achieved without accompanying anxieties, and legal, security, and privacy concerns are being raised regarding IR 4.0 applications in libraries. The Toronto Public Library Digital Privacy Initiative[4] can be viewed as a practical response to this well-founded set of apprehensions. The library offers digital privacy classes to familiarize clients with best practices, tips, and technologies for enhancing security and safeguarding personal data.

Librarians are also faced with the dilemma of choosing best-fit technology options as they wrestle with the question, "How does one identify the innovations that are going to change the world from the dead ends that are a waste of time and investment?" (Widdowson 2014). One of the most important steps a librarian can take is to review current best practices prior to making any significant investment in new technology. Steph Waite, writing at WebJunction, shares the following hard-earned recommendations from Maryland public librarians (Waite 2018) for the benefit of peers considering VR/AR programs for their libraries:

- *Budget.* Low-budget technology options are available for purchase. Consider applying for grants, as well.
- *Space.* Identify dedicated spaces within the library to house technology devices.
- *Community.* Consider and understand your community's unique needs before making any purchasing decision.
- *Get staff buy-in.* Ensure there are enthusiasm and acceptance among staff members and provide the required training before launching programs.
- *Have an open mind.* Explore and evaluate all viable applications and options available.
- *Start small.* Pick a targeted group of patrons for a small-scale rollout.
- *Collaborate.* Leverage local partnerships and talent.
- *Communicate.* Reach out to online communities on social media for policies, procedures, and problem-solving tips and techniques.

Benefits, challenges, and best practices aside, practitioners agree that technology implementation in the 21st-century library environment must be steadfastly pursued and that "remaining static . . . is not an option if we want to ensure the longevity of our profession." This sentiment was effectively expressed in a blog post written for CILIP six years ago, entitled "Can Libraries Survive Disruptive Technologies?" In the post, Jacquie Widdowson shared the tale, taken from the corporate world, of how Borders, Kodak, and Blockbuster—one-time corporate giants, now dissolved—ignored the risks and threats of new technology, and by doing so "failed to turn disruptions into competence-enhancing influences."

Success Stories

Augmented and Virtual Reality

The rising popularity of Augmented Reality (AR), a "technology available on mobile devices that allows users to experience a layered, computer-generated enhancement to their real-world perception" (Abram 2019), was exemplified by the *Pokémon Go* craze of 2016 in which players attempted to capture mythical creatures appearing on their phone screens. The Ikea Place app, which allows customers to virtually view furniture in their homes before purchase, is another mainstream example of AR in action.

AR in Libraries

Guided library tours are a popular method of orienting new patrons with library spaces, collections, and services, but scheduling and staffing the tours can present challenges. Librarians at Texas A&M University Libraries responded by creating self-guided, interactive AR tours that they piloted successfully for first-year students during the 2016–2017 fall and spring semesters. Offered in partnership with the university's English Department, today these unmediated, self-paced tours allow students to explore the range of library service points including study rooms, media services, course reserves, research services, and the library stacks themselves. LeMire et al. (2018) evaluated the project and reported that the AR tour has proven to be a scalable alternative to the traditional library tour and permits librarians to accommodate large numbers of students without overwhelming staff and service points.

The Harrell Health Sciences Library at Penn State College of Medicine in Hershey, Pennsylvania, also offers virtual library tours that employ AR technology. The interactive click-through tour, available via the library's website,[5] facilitates visual exploration of several library spaces including a Technology Innovation Sandbox—a designated space for experimentation, creation, and collaboration. The Sandbox allows students, faculty, and staff to interact with augmented and virtual reality applications in support of learning and research.

VR in Libraries

Whereas augmented reality alters one's ongoing perception of a real-world environment, virtual reality (VR) presents an opposing landscape, completely replacing the user's real-world environment with a simulated one. VR requires special electronic equipment including computers, headsets, and sensors. Competing producers of VR hardware and platforms include Facebook (Oculus VR), Google (Cardboard, Daydream), Samsung (Gear VR), HTC (Vive), and Sony (PlayStation VR).

Libraries have long served as points for the public's first exposure to emergent technologies, often partnering with tech companies to pilot new products. Oculus VR, a Facebook company, in collaboration with the California State Library, piloted a program in 2017 to place 100 Oculus Rift headsets and Oculus-ready PCs in libraries throughout the state. The San José Public Library accepted Oculus's offer and introduced VR programming at two branches, the Evergreen Branch Library and the Dr. Martin Luther King, Jr. Library.[6] Program offerings at the branches have proven sustainable over time. Today, patrons can participate in programs such as "Afterschool VR" and "VR for Adults" to create works of art, travel to distant planets, and become immersed in 3D gaming environments.

VR also offers significant opportunities in the areas of teaching, learning, and research. The VR Lab in the Waldo Library at Western Michigan University (WMU)[7] is a collaboration between the University Libraries and the Office of Information Technology. Designated as a collaborative creative space, the lab offers VR workshops and online tutorials for students, while faculty learn how to integrate VR content into the curriculum.

Artificial Intelligence

Artificial Intelligence seeks to create "intelligent" machines that work and react more like humans. AI has found mainstream value in offices and homes. At the workplace, collaborative robots, or cobots, interact with humans on the factory floor, delivering parts and performing repetitive or dangerous tasks. In homes, AI increasingly enables appliances to vacuum floors, monitor moisture levels in gardens, reorder laundry detergent, and adjust room temperature settings, among other tasks. In the publishing world, AI is perceived as "an invaluable tool for organizing and making accessible large collections of information" (Bates 2019). Two Google AI projects, Life Tags,[8] a searchable archive of *Life* magazine photographs and Talk to Books,[9] described as "a new way to explore ideas and discover books," are examples of this type of automated organization of knowledge base systems at scale, harnessing the power of natural language processing and machine learning.

Artificial Intelligence in Libraries

Voice assistants Amazon Alexa and Google Assistant rank among today's leading consumer AI applications, and the Worthington Libraries in Ohio are taking advantage of their popularity. Alexa Skill and Google Action[10]—voice assistance tools developed specifically for the Libraries—provide users with real-time information about library programs and events. After invoking the wake words "Alexa" or "Hey Google," respectively, patrons can pose questions like "What's happening today at Old Worthington Library?" and "Are there any events for teens this weekend at Northwest Library?" These useful AI apps consign routine requests to the digital assistants while redirecting complex queries to human library staff.

The University of Rhode Island has taken an ambitious approach to integrating AI into its library services, investing in the construction of a 600-square-foot AI lab at the Robert L. Carothers Library and Learning Commons on its Kingston campus.[11] Revered as the "first of its kind in a college library nationwide" (McKenzie 2018), the lab is a cross-disciplinary facility that boasts an artificial intelligence supercomputer, six specialized laptops for running open-source software and unwieldly data sets, a bank of 3D printers, and an array of makerspace tools and software programs. Faculty use the space for on-site lectures and to introduce AI topics into their syllabi, while students explore projects on robotics, natural language processing, smart cities / smart homes, Big Data, IoT, and more.

Robotics

Robots were initially introduced into industrial and factory settings to accomplish tasks deemed too dangerous or difficult for humans. In IR 4.0, a quantum leap in computing power, advances in AI technology, and the declining cost of sensors are among the factors that allow today's robots to react quickly and intelligently and to assume greater roles alongside humans. The remarkable strides being made almost daily in the field of robotics are inspiring a new generation of information professionals to introduce and expand the use of the technology in their libraries.

Robots in Libraries

The Chicago Public Library (CPL) partnered with Google to circulate programmable Finch Robots via its branch libraries catalogs.[12] The collaboration was prompted by the desire of computer science teachers and community mentors to provide students with access to hands-on experience. The robots can be programmed in more than a dozen computer languages to perform a range of functions, including move, make noise, light up, and draw.

At the Palo Alto City Library in California, patrons learn coding with robots Dewey and Elsie.[13] Dewey, like the Finch Robots in Chicago, is programmed to sing, dance, tell stories, and deliver interactive experiences. Since 2016, robotics programs offered at this library have "demonstrated how a public library can prepare the community for the future, demystifying technology and teaching new skills in an exciting way, while learning and co-creating" (Palo Alto City Library 2019). In 2019 the library received the Urban Libraries Council Innovation Award for its sustained work in robotics programming.

Internet of Things

The Internet of Things (IoT) has led to an explosion in the number of everyday devices that are able to collect and transmit data and improve the function and understanding of internal systems. Examples include wearable technologies such as smart watches that record activities, cochlear implants that stimulate nerves within the inner ear to enhance hearing, home appliances that schedule their own maintenance, and self-monitoring infrastructure. It is believed that the interconnection of these devices and the data they produce will, through automation, create vast improvements in services and the user experience (UX). By some forecasts, as many as 50 billion IoT devices will be in use around the world by 2030 (Statista Research Department 2020).

IoT in Libraries

Translated to the library world, IoT capability in connecting common devices that collect and transmit data can offer improved access to collections and services—from tracking room usage and program attendance to monitoring humidity levels for special collections. How libraries accomplish this interconnection of device and data without compromising patron privacy is a delicate balancing act that can be addressed through "librarians leading the way on educating patrons about what IoT entails, its inner workings, uses, limits, and implications for communities and society" ("Internet of Things" 2014). The Chattanooga Public Library in Tennessee created such an educational opportunity by partnering with the Mozilla Foundation to prototype an IoT Escape Room workshop, which included a session on online privacy and safety (Clarke 2018).

The D. H. Hill, Jr. Library at North Carolina State University (NCSU) embraced IoT as a teaching tool. The library partnered with the NCSU Office of Information Technology to create MakerspaceIOT, an open network for experimenting with IoT. Within this DIY creative space, students have access to tools they can use to experiment with prototyping practical applications—smart watches and energy saving devices, for example—that can be easily implemented in the real world.[14]

Hillsboro Public Library in Oregon introduced the Book-O-Mat, an automated book kiosk, in a high-traffic, high-visibility location—the Civic Center Plaza—to expand access to library resources without increasing staff costs. Stocked with bestsellers and movies for checkout, the Book-O-Mat harnesses IoT technologies to track usage, alert the library when restocking is needed, and identify popular selections for informed collection development.[15]

Drones

Drones—unmanned, remotely controlled aerial vehicles, or UAVs—were initially associated with military use but are today used in a wide range of industries and applications, from civilian search and rescue, surveillance, traffic monitoring, weather monitoring, and firefighting to a variety of personal and business uses including aerial photography and videography, agriculture, and delivery services (KC Protective Services 2018).

Drones in Libraries

Drones can be utilized as a valued source of content for the development of special collections. The University of South Florida Libraries leveraged drone-based mapping tools and visualization strategies—VR, AR, and 3D modeling—to document and provide online access to heritage sites, landscapes, and objects from around the world. This unique collection, showcasing an immersive virtual experience, is a valuable resource used in teaching and learning, outreach, research, and sustainable tourism. Historians and other researchers can browse drone-captured enhanced spatial landscape images on the USF Libraries' Digital Heritage and Humanities Collections website.[16]

The Georgia Highlands College Libraries bolstered its technology outreach efforts by adding drones to a list of technology resources available for circulation.[17] Included in the loan packages are video tutorials, flying safety literature, and a link to the FAA advisory "Know before You Fly." The Arapahoe Libraries in Colorado offer a similar drone-lending program "to satiate their patrons' curiosity [and] desire to learn and play with new and uncommon technologies"[18] (Joiner 2018). No FAA registration is required to use the Libraries' two Hover Camera Passport drones, which have a nine-minute per-flight time limit and are available for seven-day checkout once you've reached the top of the waiting list.

Blockchain Technology

Blockchain technology can simplistically be defined as a "chain of blocks linked together, with each block containing a record of information to be widely and openly distributed" ("Blockchain Technology" 2018). Touted as the technology behind Bitcoin and other cryptocurrencies, blockchain promises a new, decentralized way of recording and storing data that could revolutionize how institutions store personal information. Organizations such as Sony Global Education are exploring the use of blockchain to store student information—registration documents, attendance, grades, and so on—that can be efficiently transferred between schools as students move or graduate to new institutions.[19] Future applications are likely to include securing personal identities—birth and death certificates, marriage licenses, property deeds, titles of ownership, and other life records—in blockchains that allow citizens to control their own data ("Blockchain" 2017).

Blockchain in Libraries

Despite thriving as a commercial application, and its 2018 designation as a trending topic and buzzword (Busby 2018), blockchain technology has only recently undergone experimentation by library practitioners. The San José State University (SJSU) School of Information is a key player in this arena, having secured a $100,000 IMLS grant to investigate the potential use and impact of the technology within the information profession.

According to Dr. Sue Alman, iSchool instructor and co-principal investigator on the project, "it is time to examine the possible ways that libraries can support city/community goals through the use of blockchains while the implementation of the technology is still in the infancy stage." Proposed applications of the technology include "developing a distributed, permission-less metadata archive, creating a protocol for supporting community-based collections, and facilitating better digital rights management" ("Blockchain Technology" 2018). The SJSU project supports a dedicated website, Blockchains for the Information Professionals,[20] that features potential scenarios, a self-paced MOOC for readers seeking to understand distributed ledger technology, a news and events page, a blog on related topics, and access to a LibGuide with links to additional resources.

On the Disruptive Horizon: Changes, Challenges, and Choices

New and emerging technologies have the capacity to drastically change our lives. Virtual and augmented reality, artificial intelligence, robotics, the Internet of Things (IoT), drones, and blockchain are key drivers of these transformational changes, influencing the way our patrons view, interact with, access, and share information. Libraries must work to stay at the public forefront of these innovations, investing and working proactively to meet institutional mandates, represent our core values, keep pace with digital transformation, and maintain relevance. What will work best for many of us is a hybrid approach that steadies the hold on traditional library services while simultaneously pushing in new directions—directions that welcome disruption, encourage experimentation, and support patrons with progressive needs.

The case studies highlighted in this report show that many information professionals are already engaged and in future-ready mode. Through actively rolling out new tech initiatives such as AR tours, AI and VR labs, robots that support programming, digital assistants responding to first-line queries, drone-lending programs, and blockchain research, we are choosing innovation over inertia.

Technology is in constant flux, and the next big wave of technological advancements is already here. A notable trend is the merger of disparate disruptive technologies to create unique user experiences. One example is Amazon Go, a new kind of store that utilizes advanced shopping technology, computer vision, sensor fusion, and deep learning algorithms to give customers a "Just Walk Out" shopping experience.[21] In Chicago, New York, San Francisco, and Seattle, customers walk into these shops, take the products they need off the shelf, and walk out. No waiting in line, no cash registers, no checkout. All that is required for the purchase is the Amazon Go app and an Amazon account. Using similar technology, with strong checks and balances in place to protect patron privacy, library prototypes are sure to follow.

An additional tech trend for every library's watch list is human augmentation: the use of embedded and wearable technology to increase human cognitive and physical ability. One example is the use of exoskeletons—mechanical devices worn outside the body that provide the wearer with artificial strength and endurance. With these devices, an average human worker is able "to lift up to 200 pounds, perform precise operations with heavy machinery, and handle repetitive motions without strain" (Shimoda 2019). It's a given that this technology designed to make us smarter, faster, and stronger brings its own new set of concerns, including how hackers will exploit it. Yet, libraries and information professionals will continue to lead the way, keeping vigilant as we encounter and explore technology—disruptive and invasive as it may first appear—for the ultimate benefit of our clients and communities.

References

Abram, Stephen. 2019. "Augmented Reality in Libraries: Technology Trends that Aren't "Out-There" Anymore!" Lucidea. January 22, 2019. https://lucidea.com/blog/augmented-reality-in-libraries-technology-trends-that-arent-out-there-anymore.

Bates, Mary Ellen. 2019. "Insight as a Service: Info Pros and Artificial Intelligence: White Paper." *Springer Nature*. https://media.springernature.com/full/springer-cms-preview/rest/v1/content/16773852/data/v1.

"Blockchain." 2017. American Library Association. October 18. http://www.ala.org/tools/future/trends/blockchain#Notes and Resources.

"Blockchain Technology." 2018. San José State University School of Information. August 28. https://ischool.sjsu.edu/post/blockchain-technology.

Busby, Mattha. 2018. "Blockchain Is This Year's Buzzword—but Can It Outlive the Hype?" *Guardian News and Media*. January 30. https://www.theguardian.com/technology/2018/jan/30/blockchain-buzzword-hype-open-source-ledger-bitcoin.

Christensen, Clayton M. 2016. *The Innovator's Dilemma: When New Technologies Cause Great Firms to Fail*. Boston, MA: Harvard Business Review Press.

Clarke, Loraine. 2018. "Prototyping an Escape Room Full of Future IoT Interactions." *Medium Blog*. February 21, 2018. https://medium.com/read-write-participate/prototyping-an-escape-room-full-of-future-iot-interactions-e51649cbe4ad.

"Internet of Things." 2014. American Library Association. September 24. http://www.ala.org/tools/future/trends/IoT.

Joiner, Ida Arlene. 2018. "Is There a Drone in Your Library's Future?" *Public Library Quarterly* 37, no. 1:103–110. https://doi.org/10.1080/01616846.2017.1379349.

KC Protective Services. 2018. "Drone Services." Accessed February 16, 2020. https://kcprotect.com/drone-services.

LeMire, Sarah, Stephanie J. Graves, Michael Hawkins, and Shweta Kailani. 2018. "Libr-AR-y Tours: Increasing Engagement and Scalability of Library Tours Using Augmented Reality." *College & Undergraduate Libraries* 25, no. 3:261–279. https://doi.org/10.1080/10691316.2018.1480445.

McGinnis, Devon. 2018. "What Is the Fourth Industrial Revolution?" *Salesforce Blog*, December 20. https://www.salesforce.com/blog/2018/12/what-is-the-fourth-industrial-revolution-4IR.html.

McKenzie, Lindsay. 2018. "A New Home for AI: The Library." *Inside Higher Ed.* January 17. https://www.insidehighered.com/news/2018/01/17/rhode-island-hopes-putting-artificial-intelligence-lab-library-will-expand-ais-reach.

O'Dea, S. 2020. "Smartphone Users Worldwide 2016–2020." *Statista*. February 28. https://www.statista.com/statistics/330695/number-of-smartphone-users-worldwide.

Palo Alto City Library. 2019. "Library Wins Top Innovator Award," October 18. https://library.cityofpaloalto.org/news/library-wins-top-innovator-award.

Randyansyah, Jaka. 2019. "The Four Industrial Revolutions." April 19. http://jakarandyansyah.blogspot.com/2019/04/industrial-revolution.html.

Schwab, Klaus. 2017. *The Fourth Industrial Revolution.* London: Penguin Random House.

Shimoda, Jonathan. 2019. "15 Powerful Examples of Human Augmentation in Everyday Life." November 26. https://www.freshconsulting.com/examples-of-human-augmentation.

Statista Research Department. 2020. "IoT Connected Devices Worldwide 2030." *Statista*. February 19. https://www.statista.com/statistics/802690/worldwide-connected-devices-by-access-technology.

Waite, Steph. 2018. "How Maryland Libraries Are Using Virtual and Augmented Reality (and How Your Library Can Too)." *WebJunction*. May 16. https://www.webjunction.org/news/webjunction/virtual-and-augmented-reality.html.

Widdowson, Jacquie. 2014. "Can Libraries Survive Disruptive Technologies?" Chartered Institute of Library and Information Professionals. December 8. https://archive.cilip.org.uk/blog/can-libraries-survive-disruptive-technologies.

Websites Referenced

1. American Libraries Association, Center for the Future of Libraries, http://www.ala.org/tools/future.
2. WhatIs.com, https://whatis.techtarget.com/definition/disruptive-technology.
3. Erik Boekesteijn Facebook message to author, February 9, 2020. Boekesteijn is senior advisor at the National Library of the Netherlands. The National Library partnered with TUDelft to develop the Future Libraries Lab (https://delftdesignlabs.org/future-libraries-lab), which facilitates the interaction between students, researchers, and practitioners and fosters the development of research and innovation activities.

4. Toronto Public Library, Toronto, Canada, https://www.torontopubliclibrary.ca/search.jsp?N=37867&Ntt=digital+privacy.
5. Harrell Health Sciences Library, Penn State College of Medicine (Pennsylvania), https://hershey.libraries.psu.edu/services/elearning-development/library-virtual-tour.
6. San José Public Library, California, https://www.sjpl.org/virtual-reality.
7. University Libraries, Western Michigan University, https://wmich.edu/vr/learning.
8. Google Life Tags, https://artsexperiments.withgoogle.com/lifetags.
9. Google Talk to Books, https://books.google.com/talktobooks.
10. Worthington Libraries, Worthington, Ohio, https://www.worthingtonlibraries.org/visit/services/voice-assistants.
11. Robert L. Carothers Library and Learning Commons, Universities Libraries, University of Rhode Island, https://web.uri.edu/ai.
12. Chicago Public Library, https://www.chipublib.org/news/finch-robots-land-at-cpl.
13. Palo Alto City Library, California, https://library.cityofpaloalto.org/program-robotics.
14. D. H. Hill, Jr. Library, North Carolina State University Libraries, https://www.lib.ncsu.edu/services/makerspace.
15. Hillsboro Public Library, Oregon, https://www.oregonlive.com/hillsboro/2015/11/book-o-mat_hillsboro_public_li.html.
16. University of South Florida Libraries, Digital Heritage and Humanities Collections, https://dhhc.lib.usf.edu.
17. Georgia Highlands College Libraries, https://getlibraryhelp.highlands.edu/drones.
18. Arapahoe Libraries, Colorado, https://arapahoelibraries.org/borrowing/#nontraditional.
19. Sony Global Education, https://blockchain.sonyged.com.
20. San José State University's (SJSU) School of Information, San José, California, https://ischoolblogs.sjsu.edu/blockchains/conferences/blog.
21. Amazon Go, https://www.amazon.com/b?ie=UTF8&node=16008589011.

Federal Agency and Federal Library Reports

Library of Congress

10 First St. S.E., Washington, DC 20540
202-707-5000
https://loc.gov

Carla Hayden
Librarian of Congress

The Library of Congress is the largest library in the world, with more than 168 million items in various languages, disciplines, and formats. As the world's largest repository of knowledge and creativity, the library's mission is to engage, inspire, and inform the United States Congress and the American people with a universal and enduring source of knowledge and creativity.

The library's collections are housed in its three buildings on Capitol Hill and in climate-controlled facilities for books at Fort Meade, Maryland. Its audiovisual materials are held at the Packard Campus for Audio-Visual Conservation in Culpeper, Virginia. The library also provides global access to its resources through its website, https://loc.gov.

Highlights of 2019

In fiscal year (FY) 2019 the Library of Congress

- Responded to more than 979,000 reference requests from Congress, the public, and other federal agencies
- Welcomed nearly 1.9 million visitors to its Capitol Hill campus and recorded more than 119.2 million visits and 520.8 million page views on its web properties
- Through the U.S. Copyright Office, issued over 547,000 registrations and recorded 12,550 documents containing 457,731 titles
- Circulated more than 21.8 million copies of braille, audio, and large print items to patrons, via the National Library Service for the Blind and Physically Handicapped and its network of state and local libraries
- Circulated more than 1.04 million items for use inside and outside the Library

- Performed 10.4 million preservation actions on items in the Library's physical collections
- Recorded a total of 170,118,152 items in the collections, including
  - 24,863,177 cataloged books in the Library of Congress classification system
  - 15,039,990 items in the nonclassified print collections, including books in large type and raised characters, incunabula (books printed before 1501), monographs and serials, music, bound newspapers, pamphlets, technical reports, and other print material
  - 130,214,985 items in the nonclassified (special) collections, including
    - 4,158,585 audio materials (discs, tapes, talking books, and other recorded formats)
    - 73,908,819 manuscripts
    - 5,617,774 maps
    - 17,376,100 microforms
    - 1,849,175 moving images
    - 8,135,588 items of sheet music
    - 2,018,383 other (including machine-readable items)
    - 17,075,339 visual materials including 14,840,703 photographs, 109,796 posters, and 685,938 prints and drawings
- Operated with a total FY 2019 appropriation of $696.112 million, including the authority to spend $55.818 million in offsetting receipts

Carla Hayden, longtime chief executive of the Enoch Pratt Free Library system in Baltimore and a former president of the American Library Association (ALA), began the fourth year of a renewable ten-year term as the 14th Librarian of Congress.

Serving Congress

The Library of Congress was established in 1800 to provide resources to members of Congress for use in their work. The Joint Committee on the Library—the oldest continuing joint committee of Congress—was created through legislation signed by President John Adams on April 24, 1800. That legislation also created a library for the nation's lawmakers and provided for its congressional oversight. The unique collaboration between these two institutions has allowed both to serve the nation for over two centuries.

In FY 2019 the Library supported members of Congress, their staffs and constituents in a variety of ways, from providing reference, research, and analysis on key issues to supplying surplus books to congressional districts. The Library also continued to implement new technologies to make the legislative process more accessible and transparent to the public.

Legislative Support

The Congressional Research Service (CRS) in the Library of Congress serves Congress with the highest-quality research, analysis, information and confidential consultation to support the exercise of its legislative, representational, and oversight duties in its role as a coequal branch of government. The work of CRS is authoritative, confidential, objective, nonpartisan, and timely.

CRS examines pressing legislative issues facing Congress; identifies and assesses policy options; and provides analysis, consultation, and briefings to support Congress throughout the legislative process across the full range of public policy issues.

In FY 2019 CRS responded to 71,000 congressional requests. The CRS website for Congress, CRS.gov, drew approximately 1.4 million views, including nearly 534,000 views of the service's reports and general-distribution products.

Congress established the Law Library of Congress in 1832 with the mission of making its resources available to Congress and the U.S. Supreme Court—a mission that expanded to include other branches of government and the global legal community. Librarians and lawyers respond to congressional inquiries about U.S., foreign, comparative, and international legal and legislative research, drawing upon the world's largest collection of legal resources. The collection includes more than 2.9 million volumes and global legal materials in various formats.

In FY 2019 the Law Library provided members of Congress with 432 legal research reports, special studies, and memoranda. The Law Library's legal reference librarians assist congressional staff any time either chamber of Congress is in session, no matter the hour.

Copyright Law and Policy

The U.S. Copyright Office, headed by the register of copyrights, administers the nation's copyright laws for the advancement of the public good and for the benefit of authors and users of creative works. The register's duties under the Copyright Act include registering creative works, recording information about copyright ownership, and implementing certain statutory licenses. The register and her staff also provide expert, impartial assistance to Congress, the courts, and executive branch agencies on questions of domestic and international copyright law and policy.

In FY 2019 the office continued assisting Congress in several ways, including engaging in studies and important copyright-related litigation matters, conducting regulatory activities aimed at administering the Copyright Act, and working with the executive branch on foreign copyright law and policy. The office assisted Congress on two important pieces of legislation enacted this year: the Orrin G. Hatch–Bob Goodlatte Music Modernization Act, one of the most significant updates to copyright law in decades, and the Marrakesh Treaty Implementation Act, which includes amendments to the Copyright Act representing years of work by office staff in international negotiations and in domestic consultation on implementing legislation. The office also supported Congress in its consideration of the Copyright Alternative in Small-Claims Enforcement Act of 2019, a bill to create a small claims tribunal in the Copyright Office.

Additionally, the office continued working on its Section 512 study, which evaluates the current impact and effectiveness of the Copyright Act's notice-and-takedown system and safe harbor provisions.

Congressional Preservation Efforts

The Library leads several major preservation initiatives at the behest of Congress to ensure America's history and culture are captured and preserved for generations to come. In its concern for preserving the nation's audiovisual heritage, Congress enacted the National Film Preservation Act of 1988 and the National Recording Preservation Act of 2000. These acts direct the Librarian of Congress to select "culturally, historically, or aesthetically" significant films and sound recordings, respectively, for preservation. To date, 750 films and 525 sound recordings have been selected for preservation. [See the "Preservation" section of this report, following, for a list of the most recently selected films and sound recordings—*Ed.*]

Established by Congress in 2000, the Veterans History Project (VHP) in the Library's American Folklife Center preserves the memories of those in our nation's armed services and others who shared America's wartime experience in the 20th and early 21st centuries. During FY 2019 the Veterans History Project received 3,773 collections and now holds more than 110,000 from veterans across the nation.

Collections

The Library of Congress is both the nation's library and the largest library in the world. The institution's enormous collections encompass virtually all formats, languages, and subjects—the most comprehensive accumulation of human knowledge ever assembled. In FY 2019 the Library's collections grew to more than 170 million items. The Library added close to 2.2 million items to its collections during the year through purchase, gift, exchange, or transfer from other government agencies.

The U.S. Copyright office transferred a total of 727,427 works with an estimated value of more than $52,156,311 to the Library's collections in FY 2019; 497,961 of the transferred items were received from publishers under the mandatory deposit provision of the law. Receipts via eDeposits include 139,657 e-books and 97,735 e-serial issues.

The Acquisitions and Bibliographic Access Directorate (ABA) acquired 1,160,270 items for the Library's collections, including purchase and exchange. In addition, ABA facilitated the acquisition of 646,018 collection items through solicited gifts to the Special Collections Directorate and the General and International Collections Directorate. With the acquisition of additional items through means such as transfers from other government agencies, a total of nearly 2.2 million items were added to the collections.

The Library's six overseas offices (located in Cairo, Islamabad, Jakarta, Nairobi, New Delhi, and Rio de Janeiro) acquired, cataloged, and preserved materials from parts of the world where the book and information industries are not well developed. In FY 2019 those offices acquired 179,138 items for the Library's collections. They also acquired 266,939 collection items, on a cost-recovery basis, for more than 100 U.S. libraries that participated in the Cooperative Acquisitions Program.

Collection Development

The Collection Development Office (CDO) directly supports the Library's strategic goal of acquiring and maintaining a universal collection of knowledge and the record of America's creativity to meet the needs of Congress, researchers, and the American public. It ensures that the Library's analog and digital collections reflect the breadth and depth of knowledge published in all media, languages, and regions of the world.

With implementation of the office's digital collecting plan well into its third year, a formal status check was conducted in August. The plan included 74 targets and actions. The summary status overall found 30 completed, four currently in process, and 30 not yet started. Three had preliminary work done and were waiting on U.S. Copyright Office rulemaking. Seven targets and actions were eliminated.

Preservation

The Preservation Directorate is guided by the Library's mission to provide a "universal and enduring" collection that is format neutral in order to record knowledge and creativity. To that end, the directorate executes millions of preservation actions each year in support of the diverse array of preservation strategies required by the national collection. Expert staff perform preventative and corrective treatments and transfer information from obsolete or at-risk media into new formats. They manage secure, environmentally optimized storage facilities and maintain inventory control. This enables fulfillment of over 130,000 loans each year to support Congress, enables core Library operations, and serves researchers across the nation and around the world. The directorate is a center for fundamental research and professional education, and the Library's insights and innovations set standards and enhance preservation and conservation practices worldwide.

In FY 2019 the directorate continued to assess and treat Library collections using established technologies, practices, and procedures to reduce risks to collection materials. It also engaged in scientific research to explore new approaches to preservation. Preservation staff performed 10.4 million preservation actions on books, serials, prints, photographs, audiovisual materials, and other items. During the fiscal year, 110,340 items were bound into new library bindings; 32,214 were treated or repaired in conservation labs; protective containers or housings were provided for 19,988 items; and 166,750 book equivalents and 1,367,933 sheets were deacidified. In addition to these preservation actions, staff also surveyed the preservation needs of 1,003,016 items from the general and special collections, monitored over 240 environmental data loggers, and continued to play a key role in the Library's security and emergency-response programs.

To protect information at risk from deterioration, staff reformat original media to ensure its informational content is available. Digital transformation was an important focus for the year. The Preservation Reformatting Division initiated a multiyear transition from microfilm production to digitization. The Preservation Directorate reformatted 7,703,708 pages, including 5,340,304 for the custodial divisions and 2,007,999 microfilmed by the overseas offices. Within the space of the current strategic plan, this entire workflow will shift to digital imaging.

Newspapers

The National Digital Newspaper Program (NDNP), jointly sponsored by the Library of Congress and the National Endowment for the Humanities, supports the enhancement of access to American newspapers. Through various partnerships and collaborations, 50 institutions select and digitize representative newspapers from their state or territory for contribution to the Chronicling America website. The website recorded 3,769,072 visits and 45,698,744 page views during FY 2019, an increase of over 20 percent from the previous year. In May 2019 NDNP achieved access to over 15 million pages. The collection now includes more than 2.1 million issues of 2,900 titles from 46 states.

In FY 2019 newspaper collection items, excluding Chronicling America, received 317,219 page views and 1,103,933 visits.

National Film Registry

On December 11, 2019, the Librarian of Congress named 25 films to the National Film Registry, bringing the total to 775.

Amadeus (1984)
Becky Sharp (1935)
Before Stonewall (1984)
Body and Soul (1925)
Boys Don't Cry (1999)
Clerks (1994)
Coal Miner's Daughter (1980)
Emigrants Landing at Ellis Island (1903)
Employees' Entrance (1933)
Fog of War (2003)
Gaslight (1944)
George Washington Carver at Tuskegee Institute (1937)
Girlfriends (1978)
I Am Somebody (1970)
The Last Waltz (1978)
My Name Is Oona (1969)
A New Leaf (1971)
Old Yeller (1957)
The Phenix City Story (1955)
Platoon (1986)
Purple Rain (1984)

Real Women Have Curves (2002)
She's Gotta Have It (1986)
Sleeping Beauty (1959)
Zoot Suit (1981)

National Recording Registry

On March 20, 2019, the Librarian announced the addition of 25 sound recordings to the National Recording Registry, bringing the total to 525.

Yiddish Cylinders from the Standard Phonograph Company of New York and the Thomas Lambert Company (c. 1901–1905)
"Memphis Blues" (single), Victor Military Band (1914)
Melville Jacobs Collection of Native Americans of the American Northwest (1929–1939)
"Minnie the Moocher" (single), Cab Calloway (1931)
Bach Six Cello Suites (album), Pablo Casals (c. 1939)
"They Look Like Men of War" (single), Deep River Boys (1941)
Gunsmoke—Episode: "The Cabin" (Dec. 27, 1952)
Ruth Draper: Complete recorded monologues, Ruth Draper (1954–1956)
"La Bamba" (single), Ritchie Valens (1958)
"Long Black Veil" (single), Lefty Frizzell (1959)
Stan Freberg Presents the United States of America, Vol. 1: The Early Years (album), Stan Freberg (1961)
GO (album), Dexter Gordon (1962)
War Requiem (album), Benjamin Britten (1963)
"Mississippi Goddam" (single), Nina Simone (1964)
"Soul Man" (single), Sam & Dave (1967)
Hair (original Broadway cast recording) (1968)
Speech on the Death of Dr. Martin Luther King, Jr., Robert F. Kennedy (April 4, 1968)
"Sweet Caroline" (single), Neil Diamond (1969)
Ola Belle Reed (album), Ola Belle Reed (1973)
Super Fly (album), Curtis Mayfield (1972)
"September" (single), Earth, Wind & Fire (1978)
"You Make Me Feel (Mighty Real)" (single), Sylvester (1978)
She's So Unusual (album), Cyndi Lauper (1983)
Schoolhouse Rock!: The Box Set (1996)
The Blueprint (album), Jay-Z (2001)

Access

The Library makes its multiformat collections publicly available in multiple reading rooms and research centers on Capitol Hill, in the Packard Campus for Audio-Visual Conservation in Culpeper, Virginia, and through its website. The Library provides global access to its resources through its website. By cataloging its holdings in English and other languages, the Library provides bibliographic access to its vast and growing collections. Through shared and cooperative cataloging, the Library ensures the nation's libraries can provide better access to their collections.

Visitors to all Library buildings on Capitol Hill totaled 1.88 million in FY 2019. Of these, 1.59 million visited the Thomas Jefferson Building. The Visitor Engagement Office and its corps of volunteers led 7,900 guided tours and engaged with 137,100 participants.

Reference Services

During FY 2019 more than 73,293 new reader-identification cards were issued—an increase of more than 3,000 from the previous fiscal year. The Library's staff responded to over 316,706 reference requests. More than 95,518 of these requests were received online, including queries handled through the Ask a Librarian service. The Library circulated 1 million physical items on-site, a 12 percent increase over FY 2018, and more than 74,684 items circulated off-site to authorized borrowers.

Cataloging

The Library managed 51,838,392 MARC records in its Integrated Library System during FY 2019. The Library cataloged 386,853 new titles in addition to 1.25 million manuscript items on 137 bibliographic records. The Cataloging-in-Publication program cataloged 53,121 titles and the Electronic Cataloging-in-Publication E-book Program prepared cataloging, in advance of publication, for 15,843 e-books. The Library established 302,275 name and series authorities, 7,259 subject headings, and 4,307 new Library of Congress Classification numbers.

The Dewey Program supports libraries worldwide that classify their titles in Dewey Decimal Classification (DDC). During FY 2019 it assigned DDC to 116,090 titles.

Access for the Blind and Physically Handicapped

In FY 2019 the National Library Service for the Blind and Physically Handicapped (NLS) circulated more than 21.8 million copies of braille, audio, and large-print items. NLS added 8,449 books and magazines to its Braille and Audio Reading Download service (BARD) during the fiscal year, bringing the total number of available titles there to approximately 130,000 (113,000 books and 17,000 magazines). Patrons downloaded about 4.2 million books and magazines from BARD in FY 2019.

Website and Social Media

The Library's website, loc.gov, provides users with access to the institution's unparalleled resources, such as its online catalogs; selected collections in various formats; copyright, legal, and legislative information; exhibitions; and videos and podcasts of events. In FY 2019 the Library's web properties recorded more than 119.2 million visits and 520.8 million page views.

The Office of the Chief Information Officer (OCIO) collaborated with the Congressional Research Service (CRS), the Law Library and Congress to complete 16 major releases of congress.gov, the online database of U.S. Congress legislative information. Each release included functionality, content, and performance enhancements developed using extensive user feedback. Major features of the new releases included a congressional calendar, new filters for subcommittees and bill type; enhancements to committee schedules; support for multiple YouTube channels for committees; a prototype for indexing of bound Congressional Record PDFs; and new navigation components for bill amendments and the Congressional Record index.

OCIO also worked with CRS' American Law Division to design, develop, and release a new website devoted to the Constitution Annotated, or CONAN, a legal analysis and interpretation of the U.S. Constitution. The new site allows users to search and browse the full text of CONAN, access links to digitized versions of court cases referenced in the text, use facets and sorts to refine searches, and access additional resources and reference materials. The mobile-friendly site replaces the legacy implementation of CONAN on congress.gov and makes readability enhancements.

The Library streamed videos of concerts, lectures, and other events on YouTube and Facebook during each month of FY 2019. Thirty-one livestreamed events included appearances by U.S. Supreme Court justice Sonia Sotomayor, former IMF managing director Christine Lagarde, Kluge Prize–winner Drew Gilpin Faust, 2018 Gershwin Prize co-recipient Emilio Estefan, outgoing U.S. poet laureate Tracy K. Smith, and new poet laureate Joy Harjo. The Library also streamed author appearances on the main stage of the National Book Festival, including that of Supreme Court justice Ruth Bader Ginsburg.

During FY 2019 the Library made 429 new videos available on the Library's main YouTube channel, videos that were liked 37,234 times and viewed 3.5 million times. The channel gained 19,042 subscribers during the fiscal year. In July, the account surpassed 100,000 subscriptions. The Copyright Office also made 16 new videos available on its YouTube Channel.

The Library's Podcast account features selected podcasts, historical films from Library collections, and video and audio recordings from collections and of events at the Library. During FY 2019 the Library added 19 files to iTunes podcasts. The account gained over 8,000 new subscriptions and drew over 58,000 visitors and 122,000 consumptions. Since the account was launched in 2009, the Library has added 4,003 files, attracted 918,965 visitors and 228,527 subscriptions with a total consumption of 4.37 million files.

Photo enthusiasts continued to access and help identify Library photos from the early 1900s through the photo-sharing project on Flickr. During the fiscal year, the Library added 2,510 photos to its main Flickr account, bringing the total to 34,787. Over the account's lifetime, the Library has accumulated 71,099 followers and 345.2 million image views. In June 2019 the Library launched a second Flickr account, Library of Congress Life: Events & Architecture, to share photo and video coverage of Library events and spaces. The Library posted 534 images over the next three-plus months, drawing 250,277 views.

In addition to its main Facebook site, the Library offers Facebook pages for the Law Library, the American Folklife Center, Performing Arts, the National Library Service for the Blind and Physically Handicapped, the Veterans History Project, and the Library's international collections. During FY 2019 the Library posted 3,140 times on those pages, gained 27,520 followers, received 333,312 likes on posts, and earned over 62.3 million impressions. Library Facebook accounts have a total of 535,952 followers, and posts have received a combined 391.2 million lifetime impressions.

In FY 2019 the Library launched two new public-facing Twitter accounts, one for the By the People crowdsourcing initiative and another for the National Audio-Visual Conservation Center. At the end of the fiscal year, the Library maintained 13 public-facing and two Congressional Research Service protected accounts on Twitter for members of Congress and congressional staff. The public-facing accounts issued 8,215 tweets during the fiscal year, gaining 101,410 retweets and 5,675 replies. The public accounts also gained 44,704 followers (for a total of 1.58 million followers) and earned over 54.7 million impressions.

The Library maintains 17 blogs that serve as a vehicle for sharing collection discoveries and engaging with users. During the fiscal year, the Library published 1,340 posts, which drew 3.04 million page views for a lifetime total of 17.3 million page views.

The Library's Instagram account continued to share images from current events, concerts, and exhibitions. The account added 19,798 new followers for a total of 55,729 at the end of FY 2019. It earned 116,617 likes for a lifetime total of 264,633.

Loc.gov offers 61 e-mail alerts, including all Library and copyright-related topics for subscription. The LOC account sent 3,983 bulletins in FY 2019 and recorded 487,202 new subscriptions. The copyright.gov account sent 128 bulletins and recorded 151,941 new subscriptions.

Promoting Creativity, Scholarship, and Lifelong Learning

The Library of Congress collections chronicle centuries of human creativity—a rich, diverse, and enduring source of knowledge for the American public and scholars around the world. During the year, the Library presented hundreds of public programs that promoted creativity, scholarship, and lifelong learning. These programs included exhibitions, lectures, concerts, webinars, symposia, panel discussions, and short-term displays of collection items. Webcasts of many of these events can be viewed on the Library's website.

The Library is a catalyst for promoting scholarship through the John W. Kluge Center and the American Folklife Center, which offer fellowship opportunities in various disciplines and publications that showcase the Library's unparalleled collections.

In addition to its fellowships, research services, and collections access, the Library of Congress promotes lifelong learning and literacy through its Center for the Book and K–12 educational outreach efforts, which assist the nation's teachers in engaging students through the use of primary sources in the classroom.

The Library's Center for the Book was established by Congress in 1977 to "stimulate public interest in books and reading." A public-private partnership, the center sponsors educational programs that reach readers of all ages through its affiliated state centers, collaborations with nonprofit reading promotion partners, and the Young Readers Center and Poetry and Literature Center at the Library of Congress.

Educational Outreach

The mission of the Learning and Innovation Office (previously known as the Educational Outreach Division) and the Young Readers Center is to inform, inspire, and engage learners. Learners include visitors to the Young Readers Center—children, parents, caregivers, and educators—as well as classroom teachers and students who may never visit the Library. Through its Teaching with Primary Sources (TPS) program, the Library provides educators across the grade spectrum and the curriculum with high-quality professional-development programs and classroom materials. These opportunities and tools help educators effectively use primary sources from the Library's digital collections in their teaching. The Library's website for teachers, loc.gov/teachers, which provides teacher professional development and educational resources on a wide range of topics, was visited over 5.5 million times in FY 2019.

Celebrating Achievement: Library Prizes and Awards

Throughout the year, the Library of Congress celebrates the achievements of the nation's creative and scholarly communities. Through the following and other awards and prizes, the Library honors those who have advanced and embodied the ideals of individuality, conviction, dedication, scholarship, and lifelong learning.

Library of Congress Prize for American Fiction

The prize honors an American literary writer whose body of work is distinguished not only for its mastery of the art but also for its originality of thought and imagination. On August 31, 2019, the Library presented the prize to Richard Ford at the National Book Festival. Ford is the Pulitzer Prize–winning author of the novel *Independence Day*, along with six other novels, three short story collections, a memoir, and several novellas.

Poet Laureate Consultant in Poetry

Librarian of Congress Carla Hayden appointed Joy Harjo as the 23rd Poet Laureate Consultant in Poetry to the Library of Congress on June 19, 2019. Harjo, an enrolled member of the Muscogee Creek Nation, is the first Native American poet to serve in the position. She was born in Tulsa, Oklahoma, on May 9, 1951, and is the author of nine books of poetry including *An American Sunrise* (2019); *Conflict Resolution for Holy Beings* (2015); *The Woman Who Fell from the Sky* (1994), which received the Oklahoma Book Arts Award; and *In Mad Love and War* (1990), which received an American Book Award and the Delmore Schwartz Memorial Award. Harjo is also author of a memoir, *Crazy Brave* (W. W. Norton, 2012), which won the 2013 PEN Center USA literary prize for creative nonfiction, and two books for children and young adults.

Gershwin Prize for Popular Song

On October 2, 2019, Carla Hayden announced country music artist Garth Brooks as the 2019 recipient of the Library of Congress Gershwin Prize for Popular Song. According to the Library's announcement, Brooks's first number one single, "If Tomorrow Never Comes," set the stage for him as a songwriter and showed his knack for expressing personal feelings that touch on universal truths. The songs he has written and recorded have often moved beyond traditional subject matter for country music, including "We Shall Be Free," which won a GLADD Media Award in 1993 for addressing homophobia, homelessness, and racism. Brooks is also recognized for his charity work, including through his Teammates for Kids foundation. In 2019 he received the inaugural George H. W. Bush Points of Light Award for Caring and Compassion to celebrate his humanitarian efforts.

Bestowed in recognition of the legendary songwriting team of George and Ira Gershwin, the Gershwin Prize recognizes a living musical artist's lifetime achievement in promoting the genre of song as a vehicle of entertainment, information, inspiration, and cultural understanding. Brooks is the youngest recipient of the prize to date.

Harper Lee Prize

The Harper Lee Prize is awarded annually for a published work of fiction that best illuminates the role of lawyers in society and their power to effect change. The award ceremony has been traditionally held at the Library to coincide with the kickoff celebration for the National Book Festival. The 2019 prize was awarded to Sharon Bala for her debut novel, *The Boat People*.

Literacy Awards

Created and sponsored by philanthropist and Madison council chairman David M. Rubenstein, the Library of Congress Literacy Awards, administered by the Library's Center for the Book, seek to reward organizations that have done exemplary, innovative, and easily replicable work over a sustained period of time to promote literacy in the United States and abroad. The 2019 winners were

David M. Rubenstein Prize ($150,000)

ProLiteracy Worldwide, based in Syracuse, New York, advances and supports programs to help adults acquire literacy skills needed to function more effectively in their daily lives.

American Prize ($50,000)

American Action Fund for Blind Children and Adults, based in Baltimore, Maryland, assists blind and deaf-blind persons in securing reading matter, providing free braille books and calendars as well as free white canes.

International Prize ($50,000)

ConTextos, based in Chicago, Illinois, brings literacy to schools, prisons, and communities in El Salvador via two programs: Soy Lector (I'm a Reader) and Soy Autor (I'm an author).

Leicester B. Holland Prize

The Holland Prize recognizes the best single-sheet, measured drawing of a historic building, site, or structure prepared to the standards of the Historic American Buildings Survey, Historic American Engineering Record, or the Historic American Landscapes Survey. In October 2018 the prize was bestowed on the team of Tenzin Nyandak and Grace Meloy, led by Ashley Wilson of the National Trust for Historic Preservation, for their survey drawing of Daniel Chester French's studio.

FEDLINK Awards

The Federal Library and Information Network (FEDLINK) serves federal libraries and information centers as their purchasing, training, and resource-sharing consortium. Each year, FEDLINK presents the winners of its national awards for federal librarianship, which recognize the innovative ways federal libraries, librarians, and library technicians fulfill the information demands of government, business, scholars, and the public. [For 2019 award winners and other details, see the Federal Library and Information Network (FEDLINK) report immediately following the Library of Congress report in this volume—*Ed.*]

Network Library Awards

The National Library Service for the Blind and Physically Handicapped (NLS) created the Network Library Awards to recognize libraries based on mission support, creativity, innovation in providing service, and demonstrated reader satisfaction. On May 16, 2019, the Carnegie Library of Pittsburgh, Library for the Blind and Physically Handicapped, received the Regional Library of the Year Award, while the Staunton Talking Book Center in Staunton, Virginia, received the Subregional Library/Advisory and Outreach Center of the Year Award.

Library of Congress Additional Sources of Information

Library of Congress website	loc.gov
Main phone number	202-707-5000
Reading room hours and locations	loc.gov/rr/ 202-707-6400

General reference	loc.gov/rr/askalib/ 202-707-4773
Visitor information	loc.gov/visit/ 202-707-8000
Exhibitions	loc.gov/exhibits/ 202-707-4604
Copyright information	copyright.gov 202-707-3000
Copyright hotline (to order forms)	202-707-9100
Library catalogs	catalog.loc.gov/
Cataloging information	loc.gov/aba/
National Library Service for the Blind and Print Disabled	loc.gov/nls/ 202-707-5100 TDD 202-707-0744
Literacy promotion	read.gov
Resources for teachers	loc.gov/teachers/
Legislative information	Congress.gov
Library of Congress Shop (credit card orders)	loc.gov/shop 888-682-3557

Federal Library and Information Network

Laurie Neider
Executive Director

Summary

During fiscal year (FY) 2019 the Federal Library Information Network (FEDLINK) continued its mission to achieve better utilization of federal library and information resources by providing the most cost-effective and efficient administrative mechanism for providing necessary services and materials to federal libraries and information centers. FEDLINK also served as a forum for discussion of federal library and information policies, programs, and procedures to help inform Congress, federal agencies, and others concerned with libraries and information centers.

FEDLINK Executive Report

FEDLINK's Advisory Board (FAB) focused its bimonthly meetings on a variety of broad federal information issues including administrative issues related to market sustainability and system updates for the FEDLINK-assisted acquisition model. At several sessions, board members reviewed current working groups and identified action plans to renew working group charters and strategic planning. The FAB also established FEDLINK's new Electronic Resources Working Group to promote increased transparency between the federal information community and vendors.

The 2018 Fall Expo offered an in-depth program on working with FEDLINK, with special sessions on licensing, Fair Use, and digital repositories. FEDLINK's 2019 Spring Expo, "Embracing Change in Federal Libraries," featured keynote sessions on strategic planning, agency librarians as historians, and FedRAMP for integrated library services. Featured speakers were Dr. Michael F. Huerta, National Library of Medicine, and G. Sayeed Choudhury, Johns Hopkins University.

FEDLINK Working Group Highlights

FEDLINK Awards Committee

To honor the many innovative ways federal libraries, librarians, and library technicians fulfill the information demands of government, business, research, scholarly communities, and the American public, the Awards Committee administered a series of national awards for federal librarianship.

The winners of the FY 2018 awards, awarded in FY 2019, were

2018 Federal Library/Information Center of the Year

Large Library/Information Center (with a staff of 11 or more federal and/or contract employees): The U.S. Military Academy Library, U.S. Military Academy (USMA), West Point, New York, was recognized for empowering more than 4,600 cadets and 650 staff and faculty to be leaders of distinction in scholarship and research. The library further supports the academy through its Liaison Program, which links a librarian directly to each academic department and its Personal Librarian Program, which assigns one librarian to each cadet battalion. This develops ongoing relationships with freshman cadets to introduce them to the library and how to do college-level research. In FY 2018 the library introduced the USMA Digital Commons, an institutional repository with contributions from 15 USMA departments and other research-producing institutions within the Academy, to share the scholarly output of USMA with the world. It includes 26 research centers, the Center for Enhanced Performance, and the USMA Preparatory School.

Small Library/Information Center (with a staff of 10 or fewer federal and/or contract employees): The Naval Undersea Warfare Center (NUWC) Division Newport Corporate Research and Information Center, Newport, Rhode Island, was recognized for its outstanding service as a hub for innovation to expand and enhance digital access via the Research Commons portal. In FY 2018 the information center doubled its digital depository to more than 16,000 full-text items. It also expanded its access to allow other Navy Warfare Center libraries to streamline access to content and increase cross-command research collaboration and knowledge sharing. The Research Common's pilot has become so successful that five of the ten Department of the Navy Warfare Center commands have signed on to use the Research Commons as their primary research knowledge management solution. The information center was recognized as the most progressive library within the ten Navy Warfare Centers.

2018 Federal Librarian of the Year

Michele Mason-Coles, clinical librarian, Darnall Medical Library, Walter Reed National Military Medical Center, Bethesda, Maryland, was recognized for providing innovative patient-centered care and advancing readiness, quality, education, and research. In FY 2018 she implemented an electronic Patient Health Education Portal that provides credible, reliable, and vetted plain language health information resources to educate patients and their family members. Mason-Coles provided instruction on literature searching, information organization, and evidence-based medicine to more than 30 pediatric interns and residents. Mason-Coles also accompanied clinicians to the pediatric inpatient unit and the neonatal intensive care unit, where she responded to clinical questions from the medical and nursing teams and bedside patient care queries. She demonstrated information retrieval techniques to residents on medical rounds. As the lead for the Darnall Medical Library's training program for the National Library of Medicine Associate Fellowship Program, she trained ten associate fellows with an additional five associate fellows currently in training.

2018 Federal Library Technician of the Year

Derek McDowell, reference assistant, National Institutes of Health (NIH) Library, Bethesda, Maryland, was recognized for his innovation and dedication as both the technical lead for library technology projects and his superior customer service to patrons throughout the country. As the primary point of contact and technical lead for the NIH Library's Digital Production Studio, he trained and assisted staff in the production of high-quality audio and video products in support of NIH research. McDowell produced a series of oral histories featuring many notable scientists of the NIH staff, saving the agency more than $50,000 in production costs. His efforts also supported online customer usage of the Library's bioinformatics analysis tools. With the assistance of librarians, McDowell prepared over 450 items for analysis for the CounterACT Program, which identifies better therapeutic medical countermeasures against chemical threat agents. He provided direct support to the Indian Health Service and tribal staff from across the country with document delivery service and other account creation projects to support access for 12 regional offices, over 600 hospitals and clinics, and 4,000 clinical staff and others working in the tribal health centers.

FEDLINK American Indian Libraries Initiative

Continuing to build an information culture among local, regional, and national levels and FEDLINK's member agencies and organizations, the FEDLINK American Indian Libraries Initiative (AILI), along with the Institute of Museum and Library Services (IMLS), cohosted "Making Connections: Meet IMLS Native American Library Grantees." Recent awardees of the IMLS Native American Library Services Enhancement grants identified ways federal libraries can build support for the nation's tribal libraries and information centers.

FEDLINK Education Working Group

The FEDLINK Education Working Group, in concert with FEDLINK staff and other working groups, sponsored seminars, workshops, and brokered conferences for nearly 800 members of the federal library and information center community. The working group also sponsored a series of orientations for libraries and information centers in order to provide an opportunity for federal librarians to become acquainted with a variety of institutions and collections in the Washington, D.C., area. These include libraries at the U.S. Senate, the Smithsonian Portrait Gallery, the Folger Shakespeare Theater, the Phillips Gallery, the National Museum of African American History & Culture Library, and the Library of Congress National Library Service for the Blind and Print Disabled.

FEDLINK Library Leadership Working Group

The FEDLINK Library Leadership Working Group provided a forum for federal library leadership to share best practices and build a strong and sustainable future for federal libraries through collaboration, advocacy, and innovation. The working group presented a session at the FEDLINK Spring Exposition on "Demonstrating the Value of Federal Libraries" and produced a corollary document identifying the top ten reasons federal agencies need libraries. The working group positioned this document to be the foundational piece of a future toolkit for federal libraries to share with agency management when making justifications for allocating funds, space, and staffing.

FEDLINK Publications and Education Office

FEDLINK continued to develop targeted resources to support the FEDLINK program, including governing body and educational programming support; directional, business, and customer service plans; promotional materials; and supporting materials for both exposition programs and working group projects and events. Staff deployed a suite of online assisted acquisition forms for customers and vendors and began work on two FEDLINK Marketplace initiatives: a new online vendor directory and an educational platform for vendor demonstrations. FEDLINK continued its publication program as a digital communication provider and used its website and community listservs for outreach on critical advocacy and program information to more than 2,000 electronic subscribers.

FEDLINK Contracts and Network Operations

FEDLINK provided assisted acquisition services to the federal information community by procuring publications in a wide variety of formats (print and electronic journals, print and electronic books, sound recordings, audiovisual materials, items via document delivery and interlibrary loan, and access to databases of full text, indices, abstracts, and a variety of other data) and library support services (cataloging and related technical processing services, staffing support, information management, resource sharing, integrated library systems, digitization, digital archiving, and preservation services). Through interagency agreements (IAAs), FEDLINK's contracts and network staff members worked on behalf of federal agencies with more than 100 vendors to conduct competitions, issue orders, and resolve issues with vendors.

In FY 2019 FEDLINK initiated a review of its business model to increase efficiencies throughout its processes and workflows. FEDLINK also awarded 68 new Indefinite Delivery/Indefinite Quantity (IDIQ) contracts for electronic resources and foreign language learning vendors and 17 IDIQ contracts for preservation services contractors. FEDLINK promoted these services at a number of national conferences sponsored by the American Libraries Association (ALA) and Special Libraries Association (SLA), and at Computers in Libraries.

FEDLINK Fiscal Operations

FEDLINK continued to enhance its fiscal operations while providing its members with $67.5 million in Transfer Pay services, $7.7 million in Direct Pay services, and an estimated $131.7 million in Direct Express services, saving federal agencies approximately $40 million in vendor volume discounts and an estimated $46.6 million more in cost avoidance.

FEDLINK Fees

The final budget for FY 2019 held membership fees steady for 6.75 percent on Transfer Pay service dollars. Direct Pay fees remained at FY 2009 levels, as did Direct Express fees of 0.75 percent for all participating commercial online information services vendors.

Accounts Receivable and Member Services

FEDLINK processed registrations from 206 federal libraries, information centers, and other federal offices, funding 1,491 IAA amendments for agencies that added, modified, or discontinued service. FEDLINK executed service requests by generating 4,285 delivery orders that FEDLINK Contract staff issued to vendors.

Transfer Pay Accounts Payable Services

FEDLINK continued to maintain open accounts for five prior years to pay invoices for members. FEDLINK has completed the closing of the FY 2014. Statements were issued to members for all open years on schedule. FEDLINK serviced invoice payments for over 13K invoices.

Direct Express Services

The FEDLINK Direct Express Program includes 65 vendors offering database retrieval services. The program is set up to provide customers procurement and payment options similar to the General Services Administration (GSA), in which the vendors pay a quarterly service fee to FEDLINK based on customer billings for usage.

Budget, Revenue, and Risks Reserves

In FY 2019 FEDLINK Fee Revenue was approximately $74K higher than FY 2018. The expenditures for FY 2019 were approximately $1.5M lower than FY 2018. FEDLINK's Reserve requirement for FY 2019 continues to be solvent. The program holds reserves for (1) mandatory requirements for shutdown and bankruptcy risks; (2) continuity of operations requirements for mission-essential systems; and (3) compliance risk mitigation initiatives.

National Agricultural Library

U.S. Department of Agriculture, Agricultural Research Service
Abraham Lincoln Bldg., 10301 Baltimore Ave., Beltsville, MD 20705-2351
E-mail agref@nal.usda.gov
World Wide Web https://www.nal.usda.gov

Paul Wester
Director

The U.S. Department of Agriculture's National Agricultural Library (NAL) is one of the world's largest and most accessible agricultural research libraries, offering service directly to the public either on-site in Beltsville, Maryland, or via its website, https://www.nal.usda.gov.

The library was established in 1862 at the same time as the U.S. Department of Agriculture (USDA). It became a national library in 1962, when Congress established it as the primary agricultural information resource of the United States (7 USCS § 3125a). Congress assigned to the library the responsibilities to

- Acquire, preserve, and manage information resources relating to agriculture and allied sciences
- Organize agricultural information products and services and provide them within the United States and internationally
- Plan, coordinate, and evaluate information and library needs relating to agricultural research and education
- Cooperate with and coordinate efforts toward development of a comprehensive agricultural library and information network
- Coordinate the development of specialized subject information services among the agricultural and library information communities

NAL is located in Beltsville, Maryland, near Washington, D.C., on the grounds of USDA's Henry A. Wallace Beltsville Agricultural Research Center. Its 14-story Abraham Lincoln Building is named in honor of the president who created the Department of Agriculture and signed several of the major U.S. laws affecting agriculture.

The library employs about 100 librarians, information specialists, computer specialists, administrators, and clerical personnel, supplemented by about 50 contract staff and cooperators from NAL partnering organizations.

NAL's reputation as one of the world's foremost agricultural libraries is supported and burnished by its expert staff, ongoing leadership in delivering information services, expanding collaborations with other U.S. and international agricultural research and information organizations, and extensive collection of agricultural information, searchable through AGRICOLA (AGRICultural On-Line Access), the library's bibliographic database.

In 2012 NAL reorganized to better align its functions with its overall strategic plan, which includes simplified access to all NAL content, expansion of digital content, and the integration of scientific data sets and discovery tools.

The Collection

The NAL collection dates to the congressionally approved 1839 purchase of books for the Agricultural Division of the Patent Office, predating the 1862 establishment of USDA itself. Today NAL provides access to billions of pages of agricultural information—an immense collection of scientific books, journals, audiovisuals, reports, theses, artifacts, and images—and to a widening array of digital media, as well as databases and other information resources germane to the broad reach of agriculture-related sciences.

The library's collection contains more than 8 million items, dating from the 15th century to the present, including the most complete repository of USDA publications and the world's most extensive set of materials on the history of U.S. agriculture. Publications are selected for the collection based on the National Agricultural Library Collection Development Policy.

Building the Collection

NAL is the only U.S. national library with a legislated mandate to collect in the following disciplines: plant and animal health, welfare, and production; agricultural economics, products, and education; aquaculture; forestry; rural sociology and rural life; family and consumer science; and food science, safety, and nutrition. In addition to collecting as comprehensively as possible in these core subject areas, NAL collects extensively in many related subjects, such as biology, bioinformatics, biochemistry, chemistry, entomology, environmental science, genetics, invasive species, meteorology, natural resources, physics, soil science, sustainability, water quality, and zoology. The library has primary responsibility for collecting and retaining publications issued by USDA and its agencies. As well, NAL collects publications from around the world.

Special Collections

The NAL Special Collections program emphasizes access to and preservation of rare and unique materials documenting the history of agriculture and related sciences. Items in the library's special collections include rare books, manuscripts, nursery and seed trade catalogs, posters, objects, photographs, and other rare materials documenting agricultural subjects. Materials date from the 1500s to the present and include many international sources. Detailed information about these special collections is available on the NAL website at https://specialcollections.nal.usda.gov.

Special collections of note include the following:

- The U.S. Department of Agriculture History Collection (https://specialcollections.nal.usda.gov/usda-history-collection-introductionindex), assembled over 80 years by USDA historians, includes letters, memoranda, reports, and papers of USDA officials, as well as photographs, oral histories, and clippings covering the activities of the department from its founding through the early 1990s.
- The U.S. Department of Agriculture Pomological Watercolor Collection (http://usdawatercolors.nal.usda.gov) includes more than 7,000 detailed,

botanically accurate watercolor illustrations of fruit and nut varieties developed by growers or introduced by USDA plant explorers. Created between 1886 and the 1940s, the watercolors served as official documentation of the work of the Office of the Pomologist and were used to create chromolithographs in publications distributed widely by the department. Although created for scientific accuracy, the works are artistic treasures in their own right. The full collection has been digitized and is now available online.

- The Henry G. Gilbert Nursery and Seed Trade Catalog Collection (https://specialcollections.nal.usda.gov/guide-collections/henry-g-gilbert-nursery-and-seed-trade-catalog-collection), begun in 1904 by USDA economic botanist Percy L. Ricker, has grown to comprise more than 200,000 U.S. and foreign catalogs. The earliest items date from the late 1700s, but the collection is strongest from the 1890s to the present. Researchers commonly use the collection to document the introduction of plants to the United States, study economic trends, and illustrate early developments in American landscape design.
- The Rare Book Collection (https://specialcollections.nal.usda.gov/guide-collections/rare-book-collection) highlights agriculture's printed historical record. It covers a wide variety of subjects but is particularly strong in botany, natural history, zoology, and entomology. International in scope, the collection documents early agricultural practices in Britain and Europe, as well as the Americas. Manuscript collections (https://specialcollections.nal.usda.gov/guide-collections/index-manuscript-collections), now numbering more than 400, document the story of American agriculture and its influence on the world.

NAL continues to digitize these and other unique materials to share them broadly via its website and has published detailed indexes to the content of many manuscript collections to improve discovery. AGRICOLA, NAL's catalog, includes bibliographic entries for special collection items, manuscripts, and rare books. The library provides in-house research and reference services for its special collections and offers fee-based duplication services.

Preservation/Digitization

NAL is committed to the preservation of its print and nonprint collections. It continues to monitor and improve the environmental quality of its stacks to extend the longevity of all materials in the collection. The library has instituted a long-term strategy to ensure the growing body of agricultural information is systematically identified, preserved, and archived.

NAL's digital conversion program has resulted in a growing digital collection of USDA publications and many non-USDA historical materials not restricted by copyright. NAL is in the midst of a large-scale project to digitize agricultural literature and provide online access to the general public. Important and distinctive items were selected from the NAL collection, with an initial focus on USDA-issued publications and nursery and seed trade catalogs. Publications are accessible at NAL's Internet Archive collection (https://archive.org/details/usdanational agriculturallibrary) and in the National Agricultural Library Digital Collections (https://naldc.nal.usda.gov/)

Library Services

Reference Services

NAL serves the agricultural information needs of customers through a combination of web-based and traditional library services, including reference, document delivery, and information centers. The NAL website offers access to a wide variety of full-text resources, as well as online access to reference and document delivery services.

The main reading room in the library's Beltsville facility features a walk-up service desk, access to an array of digital information resources (including full-text scientific journals), current periodicals, and an on-site request service for materials from NAL's collection. Services are available 8:30 A.M. to 4:30 P.M. Monday through Friday, except federal holidays.

NAL's reference services are accessible online using the Ask a Question form on the NAL webpages; by use of e-mail addressed to agref@ars.usda.gov; by telephone at 301-504-5755; or by mail to Research Services, National Agricultural Library ARS/USDA, 10301 Baltimore Avenue, Beltsville, MD 20705. Requesters receive assistance from Research Services staff in all areas and aspects of agriculture, but staff particularly answer questions, provide research guidance, and make presentations on topics not addressed by the seven subject-focused information centers of the library.

Information Centers

NAL's seven information centers are reliable sources of comprehensive, science-based information on key aspects of U.S. agriculture, providing timely, accurate, and in-depth coverage of their specialized subject areas. Their expert staff offers extensive web-based information resources and advanced reference services:

- The Alternative Farming Systems Information Center (AFSIC) (https://www.nal.usda.gov/afsic) specializes in identifying and accessing information relating to farming methods that maintain the health and productivity of the entire farming enterprise, including natural resources. This focus includes sustainable and alternative agricultural systems, crops, and livestock.
- The Animal Welfare Information Center (AWIC) (https://www.nal.usda.gov/awic) provides scientific information and referrals to help ensure the proper care and treatment of animals used in biomedical research, testing, teaching, and exhibitions, and by animal dealers. Among its varied outreach activities, the center conducts workshops for researchers on meeting the information requirements of the Animal Welfare Act.

- The Food and Nutrition Information Center (FNIC) (https://www.nal.usda.gov/fnic) provides credible, accurate, and practical resources for nutrition and health professionals, educators, government personnel, and consumers. FNIC maintains a staff of registered dietitians who can answer questions on food and human nutrition.
- The Food Safety Research Information Office (FSRIO) (https://www.nal.usda.gov/fsrio) delivers information on publicly funded—and, to the extent possible, privately funded—food safety research initiatives. The Research Projects Database provides more than 12,000 active food safety research projects in a searchable database of U.S. and international agencies. The Research Publications Feed offers access to real-time updates of peer reviewed publications in food safety.
- The National Invasive Species Information Center (NISIC) (https://www.invasivespeciesinfo.gov/subject/educator) delivers accessible, accurate, referenced, up-to-date, and comprehensive information on invasive species drawn from federal, state, local, and international sources.
- The Rural Information Center (RIC) (https://www.nal.usda.gov/ric) assists local officials, organizations, businesses, and rural residents working to maintain the vitality of rural areas. It collects and disseminates information on such diverse topics as community economic development, small business development, health care, finance, housing, environment, quality of life, community leadership, and education.
- The Water and Agriculture Information Center (WAIC) (https://www.nal.usda.gov/waic) collects, organizes, and communicates scientific findings, educational methodologies, and public policy issues related to water and agriculture.

In addition to these information centers, NAL manages the popular Nutrition.gov website (http://www.nutrition.gov) in collaboration with other USDA agencies and the Department of Health and Human Services. This site provides evidence-based nutrition information for the general consumer and highlights the latest in nutrition news and tools from across federal government agencies. A team of registered dietitians at NAL's Food and Nutrition Information Center maintains Nutrition.gov and answers questions on food and nutrition issues.

Document Delivery Services

NAL's document delivery operation responds to thousands of requests each year from USDA employees and from libraries and organizations around the world. NAL uses the Relais Enterprise document request and delivery system to support document delivery. With Relais fully integrated with the Voyager library system, with DigiTop, and with other Open-URL and ISO ILL-compliant systems, NAL customers can request materials or check on the status of their requests via the web, and the needed materials can easily be delivered electronically. Document requests can also be submitted via OCLC (NAL's symbol is AGL) and DOCLINE (NAL's libid is MDUNAL). Visit https://www.nal.usda.gov/services/request.shtml for details.

Digital Products

The NAL websites, which encompass nearly all the content and services described here, collectively receive millions of page views per month from people seeking agricultural information.

AGRICOLA

AGRICOLA comprises an online catalog of NAL collections, and the article citation database delivers worldwide access to agricultural information through its searchable web interface (http://agricola.nal.usda.gov). Alternatively, users can access AGRICOLA on a fee basis through several commercial vendors, or they can subscribe to the complete AGRICOLA file, also on a fee basis, directly from the library by e-mailing AgricolaPublishers@ars.usda.gov.

The AGRICOLA database covers materials in all formats, including printed works from the 15th century onward. Its records describe publications and resources encompassing all aspects of agriculture and allied disciplines. AGRICOLA, updated daily, includes the following two components:

- NAL Public Access Catalog, containing more than 1 million citations to books, audiovisual materials, serial titles, and other materials in the NAL collection. (The catalog also contains some bibliographic records for items cataloged by other libraries but not held in the NAL collection.)
- NAL Article Citation Database, consisting of more than 6 million citations to journal articles, book chapters, reports, and reprints. NAL has implemented automated indexing/text analytics software to produce its Article Citation Database. This application combines semantic analysis, machine learning, and human rules to automatically assign subject terms to journal articles.

DigiTop

DigiTop, USDA's Digital Desktop Library, delivers the full text of 7,000+ journals and 5000+ newspapers worldwide, provides 27 agriculturally significant citation databases including AGRICOLA, BIOSIS Previews, Business Source Premier, CAB Abstracts, GEOBASE, GeoRef, Scopus, and Web of Science. DigiTop also supplies a range of digital reference resources, and offers focused, personalized services. Navigator is a component of DigiTop that allows cross-searching of multiple bibliographic databases. This discovery service includes citations from academic journals, newspapers, magazines, and nonprint sources. DigiTop is available to on-site visitors and to the entire USDA workforce worldwide—more than 100,000 people—around the clock. NAL staff provides help desk and reference services, continuous user education, and training for DigiTop users.

Ag Data Commons

The newly released Ag Data Commons' mission is to serve as USDA's single-point-of-access to open agricultural research data. Its catalog with nearly 2,000 records is a gateway to data from large ongoing USDA research programs, including those listed below. Its repository also publishes and preserves data files from many studies. Standardized records describe datasets in detail and link them with corresponding journal publications. The goal of the Ag Data Commons, https://data.nal.usda.gov, is to enable data reuse for bigger, better science and decision-making.

The Ag Data Commons uses a customized version of the open-source DKAN software, which is compliant with U.S. Project Open Data standards for federal agencies. The system includes both a catalog function describing the data and pointing to its online location, and a repository holding and publishing data not otherwise available.

Specialized data services provided by the National Agricultural Library include the following:

- USDA Food Composition Database—https://ndb.nal.usda.gov
- I5K Workspace@NAL—https://i5k.nal.usda.gov
- Life Cycle Assessment Commons (LCA Commons)—https://www.lcacommons.gov
- Dr. Duke's Phytochemical and Ethnobotanical Databases—https://phytochem.nal.usda.gov
- Long-Term Agroecosystem Research (LTAR)—https://ltar.nal.usda.gov
- Geospatial Data Catalog (GeoData)—https://geodata.nal.usda.gov

NALDC

The National Agricultural Library Digital Collections (NALDC) (https://naldc.nal.usda.gov/naldc/home.xhtml) offers easy access to collection materials available in digital format. NALDC offers rich searching, browsing, and retrieval of digital materials and collections, and provides reliable, long-term online access to selected publications. NALDC includes historical publications, U.S. Department of Agriculture (USDA) research, and more.

The scope of NALDC includes items published by the U.S. Department of Agriculture (USDA) and clearly intended for public consumption, scholarly, and peer-reviewed research outcomes authored by USDA employees while working for USDA, and other items selected in accordance with the subjects identified in the NAL Collection Development Policy.

PubAg

PubAg (https://pubag.nal.usda.gov) contains full-text articles authored by USDA employees and citations to the peer-reviewed journal literature of agriculture. These citations have been enriched through subject analysis and application of terms from NALT (NAL's Agricultural Thesaurus). They also contain links to the full text at publisher websites and other locations.

PubAg was launched originally in late 2014 and was upgraded in 2017 to include the following features: a spell checker to improve users' search quality; a type-ahead feature to suggest search terms; the ability to select records for actions such as formatting citations, printing, and e-mailing records and sending them to a reference manager; filtering retrieved results by journal name, publication year, or subject term; and providing access to a publicly available Application Programming Interface (API); and an Advanced Search function.

National Agricultural Library Thesaurus (English and Spanish)

NAL is known for its expertise in developing and using a thesaurus, or controlled vocabulary, a critical component of effective digital information systems. The National Agricultural Library Thesaurus (NALT) is a hierarchical vocabulary of agricultural and biological terms organized according to 17 subject categories. It comprises primarily biological nomenclature, with additional terminology supporting the physical and social sciences.

The 2020 NALT (https://agclass.nal.usda.gov/agt.shtml), available in English and Spanish, contains 396 new definitions in the thesaurus and a separate glossary. New for 2020 is assigning a taxonomic rank to all taxon names from every biological kingdom. Many virus names were replaced and updated according to 18th report of the International Committee on Taxonomy of Viruses. Latin plant names were added and updated after taxonomic verification by the Germplasm Resources Information Network (GRIN). Other expanded subject areas are plant breeding, agricultural technology, human nutrition and diet, genetics, chemistry, enzymes, food sciences, pathology, and environmental sciences. The 2020 NALT is the 19th edition; it was originally released in 2002.

NALT continues to be available as Linked Open Data. NAL can now connect its vocabulary to other linked data vocabularies, which, in turn, will connect NALT to the larger semantic web. Such interconnections will help programmers create meaningful relationships that will make it easier to locate related content.

Associated with NALT, the NAL Glossary provides definitions of agricultural terms. The 2020 edition contains 6,333 definitions, ranging across agriculture and its many ancillary subjects, an increase of 396 definitions from last year. Most definitions are composed by NALT staff. (Suggestions for new terms or definitions can be sent by e-mail to agref@ars.usda.gov.)

NAL publishes Spanish-language versions of the thesaurus and glossary, which carry the names Tesauro Agrícola and Glosario, respectively. Both are updated concurrently with the annual release of the English-language version. The 2020 edition of the Spanish-language version of NALT contains more than 117,000 terms and 6,330 definitions.

The thesaurus and glossary are primarily used for indexing and for improving the retrieval of agricultural information, but they can also be used by students (from fifth grade up), teachers, writers, translators, and others who are seeking precise definitions of words from the agricultural sciences. Users can download all four publications—English and Spanish thesaurus and glossary—in both machine-readable (MARC, RDF-SKOS, and XML) and human-readable (DOC, PDF) formats at https://agclass.nal.usda.gov/download.shtml.

Networks of Cooperation

The NAL collection and information resources are supplemented by networks of cooperation with other institutions, including arrangements with agricultural libraries at U.S. land-grant universities, other U.S. national libraries, agricultural libraries in other countries, and libraries of the United Nations and other international organizations.

AgNIC

Agriculture Network Information Collaborative (AgNIC) is a voluntary alliance of member institutions, mostly U.S. land-grant university libraries, dedicated to enhancing collective information and services among the members and their partners for all those seeking agricultural information over the Internet.

More information about AgNIC and its activities can be found at https://www.agnic.org.

USAIN

The United States Agricultural Information Network (USAIN) is a professional membership organization that provides a forum for members to discuss food and agricultural issues, and seeks to take a leadership role in the formation of a national information policy as related to food and agriculture. Central to its mission is cooperation with and support of the National Agricultural Library.

Learn more about USAIN at https://usain.org/.

AgLaw

Agricultural Law Information Partnership (AgLaw) is a collaboration between the National Agricultural Library, National Agricultural Law Center (NALC), and the Center for Agriculture and Food Systems (CAFS) at the Vermont Law School. The Partnership supports the dissemination of agricultural and food law information to consumers, researchers, and legal professionals. Agricultural law is defined broadly to include land-based agriculture, food and fiber production and systems, aquaculture, and energy issues.

Explore the AgLaw Partnership at https://www.nal.usda.gov/aglaw/agricultural-law-information-partnership.

AGLINET

Through the Agricultural Libraries Network (AGLINET), NAL serves as the U.S. node of an international agricultural information system that brings together agricultural libraries with strong regional or country coverage and other specialized collections. NAL functions as a gateway to U.S. agricultural libraries and resources, fulfilling requests for information via reciprocal agreements with several other libraries, information centers, and consortia. As an AGLINET member, NAL agrees to provide low-cost interlibrary loan and photocopy service to other AGLINET libraries. Most materials requested through AGLINET are delivered digitally, although reproductions via fiche or photocopy are used when appropriate. AGLINET is administered by the Food and Agriculture Organization of the United Nations.

Information Management and Information Technology

Over the past quarter century, NAL has applied increasingly sophisticated information technology to support the ever more complex and demanding information needs of researchers, practitioners, policymakers, and the general public. Technological developments spearheaded by the library date back to the 1940s and 1950s, when NAL Director Ralph Shaw invented "electronic machines" such as the photo charger, rapid selector, and photo clerk. Over the years NAL has made numerous technological improvements, from automating collections information to delivering full-text and image collections digitally on the Internet.

NAL has fully implemented the Voyager integrated library management system from Ex Libris, Ltd. The system supports ordering, receiving, and invoice processing for purchases; creating and maintaining indexing and cataloging records for AGRICOLA; circulating print holdings; and providing a web-based online catalog for public searching and browsing of the collection. In addition, the system is fully integrated with an automated interlibrary loan and document delivery system by Relais International that streamlines services and provides desktop delivery of needed materials.

National Library of Medicine

8600 Rockville Pike, Bethesda, MD 20894
301-496-6308, 888-346-3656, fax 301-496-4450
E-mail publicinfo@nlm.nih.gov
World Wide Web http://www.nlm.nih.gov

Jody Nurik
Director, Office of Communications and Public Liaison

One of the 27 Institutes and Centers of the National Institutes of Health (NIH), the National Library of Medicine (NLM) is a leader in research in computational health informatics and the world's largest biomedical library. NLM's research and information services support scientific discovery, health care, and public health. NLM pioneers new ways to make biomedical data and information more accessible to those who need it; builds tools for better data management and personal health; creates a more diverse and data-skilled workforce; and engages with stakeholders. NLM enables researchers, clinicians, and the public to use the vast wealth of biomedical data to improve the health of the nation.

NLM's cutting-edge research and training programs—with a focus on artificial intelligence (AI), machine learning, computational biology, and biomedical informatics, health data standards—catalyze basic biomedical science, data-driven discovery, and healthcare delivery. Recent applications of NLM research have enhanced natural language–processing methods to better understand medical text and applied novel processing algorithms to improve detection of macular degeneration and diagnosis of early-stage cervical cancer.

NLM research on health data standards makes it possible to rapidly exchange and use data to improve health and advance biomedical research. NLM research has created new computational approaches to comparative genomics to predict previously unknown protein and gene functions, classify and characterize bacterial toxins, and better understand the roles of individual proteins in the maintenance and function of chromosomes. NLM also develops and deploys novel approaches to data processing to rapidly evaluate, annotate, and publish influenza virus sequences; makes huge datasets quickly available for disease outbreak analysis; and develops tools to make infectious disease data easier to find and understand.

Leveraging its 183-year history, NLM develops and applies innovative approaches to acquire, organize, curate, and deliver current biomedical information across the United States and around the globe. NLM's advanced biomedical information services are among the most visited websites in the Federal Government, providing researchers, healthcare professionals, and the public access to high-quality biomedical information and data, including biomedical literature, genomic data, clinical trial data, and chemical data.

NLM supports evidence-driven discovery for better outcomes in health care and public health by improving data collection and sharing for minority health, women's health, health equity, and health quality, including multilingual health information libraries and innovative clinical records integration for youth emancipating from foster care. NLM's biomedical information systems accelerate science, broaden opportunities for collaboration, provide platforms for private-sector innovation, and increase the return on investments in research.

Delivering Reliable, High-Quality Biomedical and Health Information Services

NLM continues to expand the quantity and range of information available to scientists, health professionals, and the public. Advances in fiscal year (FY) 2019 included

Accelerating Discovery

- Uploading public access SRA (Sequence Read Archive) data to two commercial cloud providers. Publicly accessible SRA data include genomes of viruses, bacteria, and nonhuman higher organisms, as well as gene expression data, metagenomes, and a small amount of human genomic data that is consented to be publicly available. These changes expand the discovery potential of the data and make it possible to customize tools and methods for asking research questions of the data.
- Contributing to the comprehensive characterization of proteins involved in the functions of clustered regularly spaced short palindromic repeats (CRISPR) systems, which enable genome editing.
- Undertaking research that allowed for the development of and application of sophisticated analytical approaches to the study of clinical phenomena, such as the effects of medications on health outcomes, using large clinical datasets. In FY 2019 NLM researchers used such techniques to develop insight into the relationship and risk of seven antibiotics, called fluoroquinolones, for tendon rupture in a cohort of 1.2 million Medicare enrollees, and the effects of estrogens on patient survival in a large population of postmenopausal women.
- Creating a new tool, called single-cell sub-Populations Comparison (scPopCorn), that helps researchers understand the differences between populations of cells from single-cell experiments, a research area of heightened interest.

Building a Workforce

- Training nearly 50 intramural scientists in the investigation of challenges in conducting reproducible biomedical research, and opportunities for fellows cofunded by other NIH Institutes and Centers to apply informatics science to research, education, and clinical care.
- Participating in joint initiatives with the National Science Foundation to engage more scientists with expertise in data science research with biomedical researchers. In FY 2019 NLM awarded ten grants.
- Preparing information professionals for data-driven discovery through NLM's National Network of Libraries of Medicine (NNLM). In FY 2019 more than 32,000 people participated in NNLM data-related classes and events.
- Leading 19 codeathons with approximately 900 non-NLM participants, investigating topics ranging from antimicrobial resistance to discovery of novel splice isoforms in RNA-seq data. NLM codeathons are collaborative

events in which researchers and computer coders create a tool or pipeline for the exploration and analysis of biomedical datasets that will be of use to the larger scientific community.

Enhancing Information Delivery

- Indexing approximately 1.35 million new journal articles for PubMed, NLM's most heavily used database, which contained records for over 30 million articles in biomedical and life sciences journals at the end of FY 2019.
- Growing PubMed Central, the digital archive of full-text biomedical literature, which included the full text of more than 5.5 million research articles at the end of FY 2019.
- Expanding ClinicalTrials.gov, the world's largest clinical trials registry, to include approximately 318,000 registered studies, 39,000 studies of which include study results and adverse events information.
- Enhancing Genetics Home Reference, which provides consumer-level information on more than 2,750 genetic conditions and genes to an average of 2.3 million visitors per month.
- Expanding dbGaP, a genotypes and phenotypes database, which connects individual-level genomic data with individual-level clinical information. By the end of FY 2019 dbGaP contained data from 1,200 studies, and more than 2,000 research papers had been published based on new analyses of these data. dbGaP allows unrestricted access to summary-level genomic results from most NIH-supported genomic studies.
- Growing PubChem, an archive of chemical and biological data on small molecules; PubChem contained information on more than 96 million unique chemical structures and more than 1 million bioassays at the end of FY 2019.
- Expanding the RefSeq database by adding nearly 42 million sequence records (a 26 percent increase) to provide a comprehensive collection of sequence and gene information as well as an integrated and well-annotated view of the genetic elements contributing to the nature and behavior of all studied organisms (e.g., human, model organisms, microbes, and viruses).
- Migrating the NLM AccessGUDID data portal to the cloud. This NLM portal for the FDA's Global Unique Device Identification Database (GUDID) contains FDA unique identifiers and registration information for more than 2.2 million medical devices, supporting improvements in care and patient safety. In FY 2019 AccessGUDID received 9.3 million application program interface (API) calls from computer systems accessing the resource and more than 452,000 downloads of the AccessGUDID dataset.
- Responding to more than 251 million API calls to MedlinePlus Connect from health IT and EHR (Electronic Heath Record) systems requesting patient-specific delivery of consumer health information from MedlinePlus.
- Expanding access to NLM's rare and unique historical collections through digitization partnerships with outside organizations, which complement the scanning and digitization of the NLM collection. In FY 2019 NLM's

external partners provided more than 45,000 digitized manuscript pages scanned from eight of its archival collections. NLM also digitized more than 6,269 printed books, totaling almost 700,000 pages; 2,360 prints and photographs; and digitized more than 700 audiovisual titles. NLM added this new digitized content to NLM's Digital Collections, a free online archive of biomedical texts, images, and videos.

Promoting Public Awareness and Access to Information

NLM offers plain-language, direct-to-consumer information resources, such as MedlinePlus, which includes information about disease, conditions, and wellness issues. In FY 2019 the number of MedlinePlus health topics covered in English and Spanish surpassed 1,020. MedlinePlus information is also available through MedlinePlus Connect, which works with electronic health record systems to bring information to patients and healthcare providers at the point of entry in healthcare systems. Other websites focused on consumer health information related to the environment, drug information, genetics, and specific populations are also offered.

In collaboration with other NIH Institutes and Centers, NLM continues to produce NIH MedlinePlus magazine in print and online, and in both English and Spanish. The magazine is distributed to 50,000 subscribers, as well as to medical offices, health science libraries, Congress, the media, federally supported community health centers, and other locations nationwide.

In FY 2019 NLM established the Office of Engagement and Training (OET) for U.S. and international outreach, training, and capacity-building activities. The office serves as a strategic connector between NLM and its multiple audiences. OET also engages and partners with specific populations, particularly groups experiencing health disparities, and coordinates the National Network of Libraries of Medicine. In FY 2019 NLM funded more than 300 outreach projects across the country to enhance awareness and access to health information and to address health literacy issues.

NLM curates and produces traveling banner exhibitions that connect NLM health information resources and historical collections to communities across America and around the world, including international locales for access by U.S. Armed Forces. The portfolio of available traveling banner exhibitions continues to expand. In FY 2019, with public-private partnerships, NLM's traveling exhibitions appeared in 142 institutions in 124 towns and cities in 41 states, the District of Columbia, and two other countries.

Research and Development for Advanced Information Systems, Standards, and Research Tools

NLM conducts advanced research and development (R&D) on many aspects of biomedical informatics through the Lister Hill National Center for Biomedical Communications (LHC) and the National Center for Biotechnology Information (NCBI), both of which were established by Congress.

NLM conducts and supports R&D in areas such as the development and dissemination of health data standards; the capture, processing, dissemination, and use of high-quality imaging data; medical language processing; high-speed access to biomedical information; and analysis of large databases of clinical and administrative data to determine usefulness in predicting patient outcomes, and in validating findings from relatively small prospective clinical research studies.

In the area of natural language processing, NLM conducts research involving language resources and innovative algorithms. NLM develops tools to help advance the fields of natural language understanding and biomedical text mining and applies them to indexing and information retrieval. Projects include the UMLS (Unified Medical Language System), Medical Text Indexer (MTI), SemRep (Semantic Knowledge Representation Project), MetaMap, and MetaMap Lite, which is a customizable tool for identifying medical symptoms, findings, risk factors, treatments, and diagnoses in free text narrative.

Leveraging extensive machine-learning experience and field-based projects in processing clinical images from parasites to lungs, NLM advances analytical tools that are applied in image analysis research.

In FY 2019 NLM

- Applied machine-learning techniques known as deep learning, or deep neural networks, to develop a new research area, Visual Question Answering (VQA), for answering questions about images. One notable application of this automation is for visually impaired people to describe their environment. NLM is developing clinical and biomedical approaches and applications for VQA. For example, enabled by deep learning, NLM's Consumer Health Information and Question Answering system provides personalized answers from reliable resources to consumers' health-related questions.
- Further developed deep learning techniques for image analysis. This includes application to a dataset of deidentified skin photographs to help classify skin diseases, automated classification of chest X-rays in the field to detect patients with active tuberculosis, and automated detection and counting of parasitic cells in NLM's malaria screener smartphone application for malaria detection in the field. In collaboration with the National Eye Institute (NEI), NLM scientists are studying a set of 51,700 retinal photographs to identify and measure the size of the lesions associated with diagnosing and managing retinal diabetes and age-related macular degeneration.
- Conducted R&D on the representation, integration, and retrieval of molecular biology data and biomedical literature, in addition to providing an integrated genomic information resource consisting of more than 40 databases for biomedical researchers around the world. These databases range from data on human genetic variation and viral pathogens to information on genetic tests. NLM's development of large-scale data integration techniques with advanced information systems is key to expanding the ability to support the accelerated pace of research made possible by new technologies, such as next-generation DNA sequencing, microarrays, and small molecule screening. NLM's GenBank, in collaboration with partners in Europe and Japan, is the world's largest annotated collection of publicly available DNA sequences, with 6.69 trillion bases and 1.68 billion records from more than 458,471 different species.

- Contributed to research on genetic causes of antimicrobial resistance as part of an ongoing collaboration with the National Antimicrobial Resistance Monitoring System, a public health surveillance system that tracks changes in the antimicrobial susceptibility of foodborne pathogens. Using phenotypes obtained by other Federal agencies (i.e., Centers for Disease Control and Prevention, the U.S. Food and Drug Administration, and the U.S. Department of Agriculture) for more than 6,000 pathogen isolates, NLM researchers validated the AMRFinder tool they built for antimicrobial resistance gene and protein predictions. This work resulted in greater than 98 percent consistent predictions. The tool predicts the genes and proteins in the new National Database of Antibiotic Resistant Organisms, which consists of more than 400,000 pathogens and is part of the National Action Plan for Combating Antibiotic-resistant Bacteria. This program builds upon a collaborative project among these same agencies to use whole genome sequencing to more quickly and accurately identify and investigate outbreaks of disease caused by foodborne bacterial pathogens, such as listeria and salmonella.
- Continued collaboration with the National Eye Institute (NEI) to develop novel approaches to assess the severity of age-related macular degeneration (AMD) and predict risk of progression to late stage AMD better than existing clinical standards. By leveraging cutting-edge, deep-learning techniques and repurposing "big" imaging data from two major longitudinal AMD clinical trials, the researchers developed a novel data-driven approach (based on their previous DeepSeeNet system) for automatic AMD risk prediction with performance far exceeding that of human retinal specialists.

NLM has been a major force in health data standards for more than 30 years. NLM supports the development, maintenance, and dissemination of health data standards and associated tools used widely in health care and research, including LOINC® for identifying clinical tests and measurements, SNOMED CT® for identifying health conditions and other features, and RxNorm for identifying medications. The goal is to ensure that EHR data created in one system can be transmitted, interpreted, and aggregated appropriately in other systems to support health care, public health, and research. NLM produces tools that help EHR developers and users implement these standards and makes them available in multiple formats, including via APIs. Importantly, NLM support allows key standards to be used free of charge in U.S. health care, public health, biomedical research, and product development.

NLM's Unified Medical Language System (UMLS) resources connect standard clinical terminologies to billing codes and more than 120 other important biomedical vocabularies, such as those used in information retrieval and gene annotation. By linking many different names for the same concepts and by providing associated natural language–processing tools, UMLS resources help computer programs to interpret biomedical text and health data correctly in NIH-funded research, in commercial product development, and in many electronic information services, including those produced by NLM.

In addition, RxNorm is a widely used drug terminology developed by NLM and used for electronic prescription and exchange of drug information. NLM has developed a graphical user interface (RxNav) and APIs to facilitate access by researchers, industry, and the public. In FY 2019 these drug APIs received one billion queries. Recent developments include a locally installable version of the APIs, integration of SNOMED CT in RxClass, and better interoperability of RxNorm with the SNOMED CT model for medicinal products.

In FY 2019 NLM played a critical role in the development, usage, and utility of a data exchange standard to improve flow and availability of data, the Health Level Seven International (HL7) Fast Healthcare Interoperability Resources (FHIR®). NLM is managing the development and testing of FHIR tools that researchers can use to increase the availability of high-quality, standardized research datasets and phenotypic information for genomic research and genomic medicine.

NLM stewards the NIH Common Data Elements (CDE) Repository, a free, collaborative platform for sharing and discovering standard, structured, human- and machine-readable definitions of data elements, variables, and measures used in NIH-funded clinical research. CDEs in the repository can be linked to existing health data standards and terminologies, improve data quality, and enable exchange and comparison of data across multiple studies and electronic health records (EHR) for clinical research and patient registries. In FY 2019 NLM updated and added new CDEs to the repository from six NIH ICs. NLM also developed training materials, improved exports in standard formats, and supported data exchange with other NLM terminology systems.

Extramural Programs

NLM funds extramural research, resource, and workforce development grants that build important foundations in biomedical informatics and data science, bringing the methods and concepts of computational, informational, quantitative, social/behavioral, and engineering sciences to bear on problems related to basic biomedical/behavioral research, health care, public health, and consumer use of health-related information. NLM offers several types of grants within these three general categories: research grants include research projects grants, grants for small businesses, and small exploratory/developmental research projects; resource grants include scholarly works in the history of science and medicine and information resources to reduce health disparities; and workforce grants include university-based training, fellowships, and career transition grants.

NLM also provides management oversight for a selection of informatics or data science grants funded by the NIH Common Fund, including NIH pioneer and early innovation awards, a transformational research award, predoctoral data science research training, and a digital curation award. In FY 2019 NLM funded 177 awards, including 26 that were cofunded with other NIH Institutes and Centers.

Biomedical Informatics Research

NLM's research project grants (RPGs) support pioneering research and development to advance knowledge in biomedical informatics and data science.

Complementing initiatives at other Institutes and Centers at NIH, NLM research grant programs support investigator-initiated innovation in basic and applied research, ranging from small proof-of-concept projects to larger sustained collaborations, creating and testing approaches and tools that will be valuable to more than one domain of interest.

For example, in 2019 NLM supported grant supplements to four investigators to explore methods that can speed research in the NIH Helping to End Addiction Long-term^{SM} Initiative, or NIH HEAL Initiative$^{SM.}$ In 2019 NLM awarded two new grants with a focus on computational approaches to digital curation at scale. In addition, in FY 2019 NLM issued a Notice of Special Interest inviting applications focused on computational and statistical methods for identifying and reducing the impact of bias and other errors in health data sets.

In FY 2019 NLM issued 33 new RPGs, including six exploratory/developmental awards that reflect current and expanding investments in data science as well as investment in data science applications for patients. Several of these awards address data analytic topics, including collaborative filtering for improved information retrieval, 360-degree automated characterization of the built environment, and evidence-based communication of numbers in health. New awards in translational bioinformatics focus on reconstruction and modeling of dynamical molecular networks, inference of molecular mechanisms of complex disease, and panomic analytics for microbiome data. In support of the NIH Next Generation Researcher initiative, NLM awarded new research project support to 18 early-stage investigators.

NLM sets aside funds to support small business innovation and research and technology transfer (SBIR/STTR). In FY 2019 NLM met its required set-aside by funding five new SBIR/STTR awards; NLM's allocation of funds for SBIR/STTR was more than $1 million. The new projects center on decision support for real-time trauma resuscitation, a block-chain enabled healthcare network for population health data, and a home-based monitoring system for children with cerebral palsy.

Resource Grant Programs to Reach More People in More Ways

Seven new awards were made in NLM's unique "Information Resources to Reduce Health Disparities" program on topics such as information resources for migrant workers, support for communities at risk for Chagas disease, and environmental health literacy resources for Appalachian Kentucky. NLM encourages minority-serving organizations to apply. In the Scholarly Works resource grant program, three new grants were awarded targeted to the interests of biomedical terminology specialists, public health officials, and clinical informaticians.

Some NLM research grants focus on developing tools and resources for consumers and patients. For example, in FY 2019 five new research awards were made through the NLM's Data Science Research Personal Health Libraries for Consumers and Patients program in areas such as Spanish-language smartphone access to health information, personalized web service for epilepsy patients, and personalized health maps for patients with diabetes.

Informatics Workforce Development in Biomedicine and Health

Many informatics researchers and health information technology leaders are graduates of NLM-funded university-based training programs in biomedical informatics. As of July 2017 NLM supported research training in biomedical informatics and data science at 16 active university-based programs, training more than 2,000 individuals each year, including 14 trainees emphasizing environmental exposures funded by the National Institute of Environmental Health Sciences.

NLM also supports individual predoctoral fellowships via the National Research Service Awards program; two new awards were made in this program in FY 2019. Career transition programs are offered to NLM's trainees and others ready to launch their informatics research careers; six career transition awards were made in FY 2019. Taken together, NLM's commitment to training, fellowships, and career transition in FY 2019 represented 33 percent of its extramural grants budget.

In FY 2019 NLM increased funding for its university-based research training programs in biomedical and public health informatics and data science at 16 universities, resulting in support for 200 predoctoral and postdoctoral fellows, plus summer research opportunities at these universities for 100 additional undergraduate and high school students.

Research Management and Support (RMS)

RMS activities provide administrative, budgetary, communications, and logistical support for NLM programs to ensure strategic planning, messaging, and evaluation; regulatory compliance; policy development; international coordination; and partnerships with other federal agencies, Congress, the private sector, and the public. NLM is streamlining its organizational and administrative structure to enhance collaborative leadership, innovation, and customer service.

Administration

The director of NLM, Patricia Flatley Brennan, R.N., Ph.D., is guided in matters of policy by a Board of Regents consisting of ten appointed and nine ex officio members.

United States Government Publishing Office

732 North Capitol St. N.W., Washington, DC 20401
World Wide Web http://www.gpo.gov

Gary Somerset

Chief Public Relations Officer
202-512-1957, e-mail gsomerset@gpo.gov

The U.S. Government Printing Office (GPO) was created when President James Buchanan signed Joint Resolution 25 on June 23, 1860. GPO opened its doors for business nine months later on March 4, 1861, the same day Abraham Lincoln took the oath of office to become the 16th president of the United States. On that day GPO began operation in buildings purchased by Congress, at the same address it occupies today.

A historic moment occurred for GPO in December 2014, when President Barack Obama signed into law a bill changing the agency's name to the U.S. Government Publishing Office. The new name reflects the increasingly prominent role that GPO plays in providing access to government information in digital formats through GPO's govinfo (govinfo.gov), apps, e-books, and related technologies. The information needs of Congress, federal agencies, and the public have evolved beyond only print, and GPO has transformed itself to meet its customers' needs.

Under Title 44 of the United States Code, GPO is responsible for the production and distribution of information products for all three branches of the federal government. These include the official publications of Congress, federal agencies, and the courts. Today GPO provides products in print and a variety of digital forms, all of which are born digital. In addition, GPO produces passports for the Department of State and secure credentials for many government agencies.

As the federal government's official resource for gathering, producing, cataloging, providing access to, and preserving published information in all forms, GPO has disseminated millions of publications to the public. GPO's Superintendent of Documents and its Library Services and Content Management (LSCM) organizations administer and manage the four programs required by Title 44:

- The Federal Depository Library Program (FDLP)
- Cataloging and indexing (C&I)
- Distributing government publications to the International Exchange Service
- The By-Law Program, under which certain government publications are distributed to members of Congress and to other government agencies as mandated by law

The Federal Depository Library Program (FDLP) dates back to 1813, when Congress first authorized legislation to ensure the provision of certain congressional documents to selected universities, historical societies, and state libraries. At that time, the secretary of state was responsible for distributing publications. In 1857 the secretary of the interior assumed oversight of printing and the designation of depositories. In the Printing Act of 1895, the governance of the depository program was transferred to the Office of the Superintendent of Documents at

GPO. Duties remained largely unchanged until 1993, when Public Law 103-40, the Government Printing Office Electronic Information Access Enhancement Act, amended GPO's duties to not only provide public access to printed publications but to Internet-accessible publications as well.

Two centuries after the start of FDLP, the program continues to serve a vital need of the public through the partnership with federal depository libraries located in nearly every congressional district. GPO is obviously a much different agency in the digital age than it was years ago. While its name has changed, its mission—Keeping America Informed—is as important and relevant as ever. The FDLP and GPO's information dissemination programs are examples of the agency's long-standing commitment to permanent public access to U.S. government information.

The Superintendent of Documents and LSCM organizations support GPO's continued digital transformation through initiatives to enhance historic and current content on govinfo.gov and the Catalog of U.S. Government Publications, and through the development of online tools and resources to help FDLP libraries manage their depository library more effectively and efficiently.

Working with Key Stakeholders: The Libraries in the FDLP

GPO Partnerships

Since 1997, GPO has developed strategic partnerships with federal depository libraries, federal agencies, and other institutions to increase public access to electronic U.S. Government information.

GPO's partner categories are

- Preservation Steward
- Digital Preservation Steward
- Digital Content Contributor
- Digital Access Partner
- Cataloging and Metadata Contributor
- Other/Specialized

Partnering is an integral part of how GPO is "Keeping America Informed," and over the past two decades, these partnerships have grown and evolved. At the close of fiscal year (FY) 2019 there were 39 Preservation Stewards, 1 Digital Preservation Steward, 5 Digital Content Contributors, 14 Digital Access Partners, and 1 active Cataloging and Metadata partner.

Through GPO's partnerships, free public access to Government information was enhanced during FY 2019, during which LSCM

- Added 2,170 bibliographic records to the CGP for the electronic versions of the United States Geological Survey (USGS) Water Supply Papers through a partnership with the Colorado School of Mines

- Added eight bibliographic records to the CGP for the electronic versions of the USGS Water Resources Investigations through a partnership with the Colorado School of Mines
- Added 1,077 bibliographic records to the CGP for the electronic versions of the USGS Circulars through a partnership with the Colorado School of Mines
- Added 284 bibliographic records to the CGP for the electronic versions of the USGS Open File Reports through a partnership with the Colorado School of Mines
- Completed adding bibliographic records to the CGP for electronic and print versions of WPA publications through a partnership with the University of Kentucky. During FY 2019 204 records were added
- Continued to process new material available on FRASER (partnership with the Federal Reserve Bank of St. Louis)

Two libraries became Digital Content Contributors in FY 2019:

- Washington State Library contributed seven publications to govinfo
- Boise State University contributed two publications to govinfo

Nine libraries became Preservation Stewards in FY 2019:

- University of Alabama, Huntsville: preserving its collection of the NASA SP series
- Jerome Hall Law Library, Indiana University: preserving its collection of the *Code of Federal Regulations*, the *U.S. Reports*, the *Statutes at Large*, the *Revised Statutes*, the *Weekly Compilation of Presidential Documents*, the *Public Papers of the Presidents*, the *Congressional Record* and its predecessors, and the *Monthly Catalog of U.S. Government Publications*
- Idaho State University Libraries: preserving its collection of the *Handbook of North American Indians* and the *Congressional Record* and its predecessors
- Felix G. Woodward Library, Austin Peay State University: preserving its collection of publications related to the 101st Airborne Division
- Lether E. Frazar Memorial Library, McNeese State University: preserving publications from the EPA
- Paul M. Hebert Law Center, Louisiana State University: preserving its collection of the *Federal Register*
- Syracuse University Libraries: preserving its collection of the *U.S. Statutes at Large*
- Joyner Library, East Carolina University: preserving its collection of cold war and internal-security-related publications
- Georgia Southern University Libraries: preserving its collection of Congressional hearings

GPO Collaborations

In FY 2019 LSCM staff contributed to and collaborated with groups in support of the FDLP and Cataloging & Indexing Programs, including

- In July 2019 GPO completed a collaboration with the National Archives' Office of the Federal Register to digitize and make available on govinfo volumes of the *Public Papers of the Presidents of the United States* for Presidents Herbert Hoover (1929) through George H. W. Bush (1990), with the exception of the Franklin D. Roosevelt presidency. The papers of President Franklin Roosevelt were published privately before the commencement of the official *Public Papers* series. Each volume of the *Public Papers* is comprised of a foreword by the president, public writings, addresses, remarks, and photographs. This digitization effort joined the already digital version of *Public Papers* for Presidents George H. W. Bush (1991–1992), William J. Clinton, George W. Bush, and Barack H. Obama.
- In a collaboration with the Law Library of Congress (LC), LSCM is cataloging Global Legal Research Directorate Reports to increase public access. In FY 2019 LSCM cataloged 40 of these reports.
- Through its partnership in the Civics Renewal Network (CRN), a consortium of organizations committed to strengthening civic life in the United States by increasing the quality of civics education in our nation's schools, LSCM makes available, through the CRN website, K–12 resources that support civics education.
- LSCM continued its partnership in the Technical Report Archive & Image Library (TRAIL). LSCM and TRAIL members work together to ensure that federal technical reports are openly accessible, and participating LSCM staff members offer expertise in cataloging and other areas and participate in the exchange of information about U.S. Government scientific and technical information.
- The Digital Public Library of America (DPLA) and LSCM continued their collaboration to broaden public access to the information made available via the CGP. Through the partnership, over 194,000 records from the CGP are available to the public through the DPLA website. Examples of records include the Federal Budget, laws, federal regulations, and congressional hearings, reports, and documents. LSCM and DPLA also partner to provide eBooks to the DPLA Exchange, making this government content even more widely accessible.
- LSCM continues to be heavily involved in cooperative cataloging and metadata activities with members of the library community. LSCM is an active participant in all components of the Program for Cooperative Cataloging (PCC), which is managed by LC, including BIBCO (Bibliographic Record Cooperative), CONSER (Cooperative Online Serials), NACO (Name Authority Cooperative), and SACO (Subject Authority Cooperative).
- GPO has been a member of OCLC since 1976 and contributes bibliographic records for U.S. government information to the international database daily.

- LSCM is part of the Electronic Cataloging in Publication Program (ECIP). ECIP provides cataloging records for books in advance of publication. The publisher then includes the record on the verso of the publication's title page. Through the ECIP Program, LSCM is creating prepublication bibliographic records for publications from federal agency publishers. LSCM has been a part of ECIP since 2015 and created 28 ECIP records in FY 2019. LSCM staff have created ECIP records for GPO, the Combat Studies Institute, the Air Force Research Institute, the Smithsonian Institution Scholarly Press, USGS, and the National Gallery of Art, to name a few.
- In October 2018, in an agreement with the Library of Congress, LSCM's Library Technical Services (LTS) staff began cataloging CRS reports for the CGP and OCLC. Because these reports are frequently updated, GPO has cataloged each report title as an integrating resource.

FDLP National Collection Services Pilot Initiatives

In October 2018 LSCM announced the intention of conducting pilots for services to depository libraries that will support the National Collection of U.S. Government Public Information. This is being done in accordance with the National Plan for Access to U.S. Government Information.

Pilot projects for various services are being planned, including developing collection plans; cataloging; assessing collection condition; conducting inventories; and developing disaster preparedness, response, and recovery plans. The pilot projects are described in Developing a Multi-State Comprehensive Collection | FDLP Preservation Services Pilot Strategies.

At the close of FY 2019 LSCM is in the pilot development phase, working with nearby depository libraries to establish processes, workflows, and timetables, and estimating costs to catalog and conduct piece-level condition assessments of a sample set of government publications. Thus far, LSCM staff have visited the depository libraries at the College of William and Mary, the Library of Virginia, and the University of Maryland.

FDLP Academy

The FDLP Academy was launched by LSCM in FY 2014 to support the FDLP community's education and training needs and to advance U.S. Government information literacy.

The FDLP Academy enhances U.S. Government information knowledge through events, conferences, webinars, and webcasts coordinated by GPO that cover a variety of government information topics. Many sessions are presented by GPO staff, while others are presented by staff from other federal agencies and from members of the FDLP community, as recruited and hosted by GPO.

In FY 2019 the FDLP Academy hosted 35 webinars with nearly 4,000 combined registrants. Training topics covered government information resources such as data.census.gov, cataloging, collection and depository management, library marketing, and more.

This year, 35 webcasts were produced by GPO staff on topics such as free catalog records available through the CGP on GitHub, how depository libraries can get usage statistics using the FDLP Persistent Uniform Resource Locator (PURL) Usage Report, govinfo, and FDLP eXchange. These recordings are available via the FDLP Academy Training Repository.

Enhancing Content in govinfo

LSCM has worked closely with GPO's Office of Programs, Strategy, & Technology (PST) throughout the development and ongoing enhancement of govinfo.gov. Continuing to add to the collections currently available on govinfo is of the highest priority, with a goal of offering complete and historic holdings to its collections.

A few highlights of content added in FY 2019 include

- Digitized volumes of the *Public Papers* of the Presidents of the United States for President Herbert Hoover (1929)–George H. W. Bush (1991)
- 1,322 digitized Congressional hearings, which can be browsed by Congress and congressional committees
- United States Army in the World War, 1917–1919
- Federal Register Index (1936–1994 digitized indices; 2013–2018 annual cumulative editions; 2019 most recent monthly cumulative edition)
- GPO Style Manuals (pre-2000)
- Historic GPO bill style manuals and type books
- Report on the Investigation into Russian Interference in the 2016 Presidential Election (Mueller Report)
- Additional Statute Compilations, expanding the collection to 319 compilations
- Beta USLM XML for a subset of enrolled bills, public and private laws, and Statutes at Large
- Budget of the U.S. Government (FY 2020)
- Economic Report of the President (2019)
- Constitution of the United States of America: Analysis and Interpretation (CONAN, 2018 Supplement)
- Updates to the Congressional Directory, 115th Congress
- Additional National Institute of Standards and Technology (NIST) digitized publications
- House Rules and Manual, 116th Congress

govinfo Certification as a Trustworthy Digital Repository

Since 2015, GPO has worked to be named as a Trustworthy Digital Repository (TDR) for government information through certification of govinfo under ISO 16363:2012.

Certification under ISO 16363 provides GPO stakeholders, including the FDLP community, assurance that govinfo is a standards-compliant digital archive in which government information shall be preserved, accessible, and usable well into the future.

Certification of govinfo validates GPO's commitment to standards-based digital preservation practices and activities across 109 criteria in the areas of

- Organizational Governance
- Digital Object Management
- Infrastructure and Security Management

Trusted Digital Repository certification has been a key GPO strategic initiative and a joint effort between GPO's LSCM and PST business units.

On December 28, 2018, GPO made history by becoming the first organization in the United States and second organization in the world to achieve ISO 16363:2012 Certification. The Primary Trustworthy Digital Repository Authorisation Body Ltd. awarded GPO ISO 16363:2012 for govinfo and publicly announced the certificate on their website. The final audit report from PTAB and a webinar about the audit process are available on FDLP.gov under the Preservation tab.

Beginning in June 2019, GPO initiated the first of two yearly surveillance audits prior to the prescribed recertification audit scheduled for completion in 2021. The process of surveillance audits and recertification is prescribed by ISO to ensure continued compliance with the ISO 16363 standard.

FDLP LibGuides

FDLP LibGuides is a service provided by GPO for depository libraries and the public. Guides are created by LSCM staff on a variety of topics, including those requested by the FDLP community. All guides are available for free use. Libraries and agencies can also submit their own guides for inclusion on the FDLP LibGuides Community page.

LSCM staff members review the site and make enhancements to the look and content on a continuous basis. FDLP LibGuides had more than 30,000 views to the 82 guides offered.

Catalog of U.S. Government Publications

The Catalog of U.S. Government Publications (CGP) (catalog.gpo.gov) is the finding tool for locating publications produced by the federal government, both current and historic. Students, researchers, community leaders, and anyone who needs to find information published by the U.S. government can get help from a great online resource. You can access library catalog records on a wide range of topics including defense, citizenship, U.S. laws, health, science, and more from CGP. There are also direct links to the documents—unless the publication exists only in print. People who need or prefer a print document can learn where to find the nearest federal depository library from the CGP. The CGP even has a feature called MetaLib that lets you research and retrieve reports, articles, and citations by searching across multiple U.S. government databases at once. What's more, there's a collection of U.S. government e-books from a variety of federal agencies, all free to access.

There were over 29 million (29,030,087) successful searches of the CGP in FY 2019.

A new service was launched in October 2017 to provide sets of bibliographic records from the CGP free of charge on a monthly basis via the GPO's CGP on GitHub repository site. The CGP on GitHub datasets contain records produced by GPO staff according to national standards such as Resource Description and Access (RDA) and Anglo-American Cataloging Rules (AACR2) and include GPO Historic Shelflist project brief bibliographic records and other retrospective records.

Web Archiving

The FDLP Web Archive provides point-in-time captures of U.S. federal agency websites while preserving the functionality of the sites to the extent possible. The aim is to provide permanent public access to federal agency web content. GPO harvests and archives the websites with Archive-It, a subscription-based web harvesting and archiving service offered by the Internet Archive.

LSCM continues to harvest digital publications and websites in order to advance FDLP collection development efforts. Throughout FY 2019, LSCM has

- Increased the size of the FDLP Web Archive collection to 22.1 TB, with over 189,000,000 URLs
- Increased website collections available on the FDLP Web Archive on Archive-It from 201 and 247 records available through the CGP

FDLP Distribution Facilities

At GPO's Distribution Facility in Laurel, Maryland, the GPO staff continues to distribute publications, fulfill claims, and send special mailings of tangible items to federal depository libraries and international libraries participating in the International Exchange Service.

In FY 2019 the staff in Laurel distributed 3,639 titles, totaling 713,616 copies of materials, to FDLP libraries.

At GPO's Distribution Facility in Pueblo, Colorado, the staff distributes FDLP promotional items to FDLP libraries nationwide. As of the end of FY 2019 the Pueblo staff managed the inventory and dissemination of 24 different types of FDLP handouts and promotional items.

Effective March 1, 2019, FDLP boxes distributed from GPO's Distribution Facility in Laurel, Maryland, use only paper made from 100 percent recycled material for box packing. Plastic bubble wrap is no longer being used.

Cataloging Record Distribution Program

The Cataloging Record Distribution Program (CRDP) provides GPO-produced catalog records to participating federal depository libraries at no cost to the libraries, through a contract with MARCIVE, Inc.

The CRDP began in 2009 and has expanded each year. In FY 2019 LSCM served 185 federal depository libraries through the CRDP.

Congressional Research Service Reports

In September 2018 LC launched a new website for CRS reports. The new site met the requirements of Public Law 115-141 to make these reports available to the public. In October 2018, in an agreement with the Library of Congress, LSCM's LTS staff began cataloging CRS reports for the CGP and OCLC. Because these reports are frequently updated, GPO has cataloged each report title as an integrating resource.

At the close of FY 2019, LTS staff had cataloged over 2,800 separate, unique CRS report titles, approximately 40 percent of all reports available on the site. Most publications posted are part of the CRS report series, which provides in-depth research and analysis. The LC/CRS has also been adding reports from four other series: In Focus, Insight, Legal Sidebar, and Testimony. GPO will also be cataloging reports from these series. CRS is adding both new reports and older titles to the site on a continuous basis.

National Technical Information Service

U.S. Department of Commerce, Alexandria, VA 22312

Wayne Strickland

Acting Associate Director, Office of Program Management

The National Technical Information Service (NTIS) is the nation's largest and most comprehensive source of government-funded scientific, technical, engineering, and business information produced or sponsored by U.S. and international government sources. NTIS is a federal agency within the U.S. Department of Commerce.

NTIS maintains a permanent archive of this declassified information for researchers, businesses, and the public to access quickly and easily. Release of the information is intended to promote U.S. economic growth and development and to increase U.S. competitiveness in the world market.

The NTIS collection of more than 2.5 million titles contains products available in various formats. Such information includes reports describing research conducted or sponsored by federal agencies and their contractors; statistical and business information; and technical reports prepared by research organizations worldwide. NTIS maintains a permanent repository of its information products.

More than 200 U.S. government agencies contribute to the NTIS collection, including the National Aeronautics and Space Administration; the Environmental Protection Agency; the Treasury; the departments of Agriculture, Commerce, Defense, Energy, Health and Human Services, Homeland Security, the Interior, Labor, Veterans Affairs, Housing and Urban Development, Education, and Transportation; and numerous other agencies.

NTIS Mission

NTIS offers web-based access to federal information and data on scientific, business, and technical research products at http://www.ntis.gov.

NTIS provides cutting-edge data science services to federal agencies through joint venture partnerships with the private sector, which advance federal data priorities, promote economic growth, and enable operational excellence. With over 3 million historical documents, NTIS continues to operate one of the largest permanent and publicly accessible archives for federal technical, scientific, and engineering publications.

NTIS Database

The NTIS Database offers unparalleled bibliographic coverage of U.S. government and worldwide government-sponsored research information products acquired by NTIS since 1964. Its contents represent hundreds of billions of research dollars and cover a range of important topics including agriculture, biotechnology, business, communication, energy, engineering, the environment, health and safety, medicine, research and development, science, space, technology, and transportation.

Prior to a focus on open access, the NTIS Database had been leased directly from NTIS. The 21st-century shift has moved to greater reliance for access through several commercial services. For more information on the database format, category codes, scope notes and access options, see the NTIS Database Search Guide at https://classic.ntis.gov/assets/pdf/dbguid.pdf.

NTIS National Technical Reports Library

As of 2020, the National Technical Reports Library (NTRL), https://ntrl.ntis.gov/NTRL/, contains approximately 3 million publications, which includes 980,000 documents (representing 3.2 terabytes of data) that have been digitized for online distribution. For publication records, which do not yet include a downloadable document, NTIS will, upon request, convert the archived paper documentation into a publicly available, online digital format. Collectively, the entire clearinghouse process, bibliographic information, and online dissemination are provided at no charge to the public.

Through its stewardship of NTRL, which extends back to the 1950s, NTIS recognizes both its public responsibility as well as the continued desire within research, academic, and government communities to access this vast clearinghouse of historic government research and technical information.

Not surprisingly, today's NTRL program has migrated online after decades as a paper-based collection. NTIS was originally called the Publication Board as established in 1945. In 1964, NTIS set a new precedent by designing the first major computerized database of scientific and technical information. In the 1990s, NTIS began digitizing full-text copies of publications. In 2009, NTIS released its first online subscription service, which provided full-text, downloadable documents. In 2016, NTIS removed its cost-recovery subscription service and began providing free, public access to the entire NTRL clearinghouse.

The current NTRL collection spans a wide variety of topics, including categories for Aeronautics, Chemistry, Energy, Environmental, Health Care, Library & Information Sciences, Mathematics, Medicine & Biology, Physics, and Transportation, among others.

In total, there are 39 major subject categories and 375 subcategories. On a weekly basis, NTIS updates the NTRL database and approximately 10,000 reports are added each year to the NTRL electronic clearinghouse.

Regarding legal authorities, Chapter 23 of Title 15 of the United States Code (15 U.S.C. 1151–1157) codified NTIS's basic authority to operate a permanent clearinghouse of scientific and technical information. This chapter also established NTIS's authority to charge fees for its products and services and to recover all costs through such fees "to the extent feasible." As of October 2016, an update to the legislative mandate required NTIS to no longer provide or collect fees for tangible documents and to ensure free and open access to NTRL content in an online environment.

This authority was restated in the National Technical Information Act of 1988, codified as 15 U.S.C. 3704b. That act gave NTIS the authority to enter joint ventures and declared the clearinghouse to be a permanent federal function that could not be eliminated or privatized without congressional approval.

The American Technology Preeminence Act of 1992 (Public Law 102-245): (1) required all costs associated with bibliographic control to be recovered by fees; (2) required agencies to make copies of their scientific and technical reports available to NTIS; and (3) directed NTIS to focus on developing new electronic methods and media for disseminating information.

Since NTIS discontinued its cost-recovery efforts in 2016 for NTRL (which historically utilized a fee-based subscription model), NTIS has been providing the public NTRL service for free while continuously exploring alternative funding models and partnerships to minimize operating loss and maintain this valued U.S. government-sponsored collection. In recent years, NTIS succeeded in cost-saving efforts that helped dramatically lower operating losses. In fiscal year 2020, NTIS will move NTRL into a cloud infrastructure in order to further reduce costs.

Contacting NTIS/NTRL

Program Control

Effective January 2020 the NTIS call center has been retired and the agency will be responding only to e-mail for customer support. For all questions regarding issues with NTRL, please e-mail NTRLHelpdesk@ntis. E-mail messages will be answered in the order received.

Input: Guidance on Submitting Publications and Reports to NTIS/NTRL

For greater efficiency and expediency of making sure your documents are publicly accessible to the general public free of charge, NTIS recommends that you no longer provide hard-copy products. Input into the National Technical Reports Library (NTRL) can be greatly expedited when documents are provided in digital format.

There are two ways to submit an electronic document for input to NTIS:

1. Provide URL. If the documents exist on an agency website, please notify NTIS in an e-mail message to input@ntis.gov. Please specify the URL address where the documents can be found.
2. E-mail. Please attach pdf- or Word-formatted documents in an e-mail addressed to input@ntis.gov.

Mail

National Technical Information Service
5301 Shawnee Rd.
Alexandria, VA 22312

National Archives and Records Administration

700 Pennsylvania Ave. N.W., Washington, DC 20408
1-86-NARA-NARA or 1-866-272-6272
World Wide Web https://www.archives.gov

The National Archives and Records Administration (NARA), an independent federal agency, is the nation's record keeper. NARA safeguards and preserves the important records of all three branches of the federal government so that the people can discover, use, and learn from this documentary heritage. NARA ensures continuing access to records that document the rights of American citizens, the actions of government officials, and the history of the nation.

NARA carries out its mission through a national network of archives and records centers stretching from Boston to San Francisco and Atlanta to Seattle, in addition to 14 presidential libraries that document administrations back to that of Herbert Hoover—a total of 44 facilities nationwide.

The agency includes the National Historical Publications and Records Commission (NHPRC), the grant-making arm of NARA; the Office of the Federal Register, which publishes the official records of the actions of the government; the Information Security Oversight Office (ISOO), which oversees the government's classification programs; the National Declassification Center (NDC), which is streamlining the declassification process; and the Office of Government Information Services (OGIS), which reviews agencies' Freedom of Information Act (FOIA) administration and practices.

NARA also assists federal agencies, the courts, and Congress in documenting their activities by providing records storage, offering reference service, administering records management programs, scheduling records, and retiring noncurrent records to federal records centers. NARA also provides training, advice, and guidance on many issues relating to records management.

NARA's constituents and stakeholders include educators and their students at all levels, a history-minded public, family historians, the media, the archival community, and a broad spectrum of professional associations and researchers in such fields as history, political science, law, library and information services, and genealogy.

The size and breadth of NARA's holdings are staggering. NARA's electronic records holdings amount to 811 terabytes of data. This consists of records that were "born digital" and managed in a digital form throughout their life cycle.

In addition, NARA maintains traditional holdings that will be converted to digital form for preservation purposes and to ensure access to them far into the future. This, along with the ever-growing quantity of "born digital" records, creates a big data challenge for NARA and the federal government.

NARA's current traditional holdings include more than 15 billion pages and 44 million photographs. In addition, 18 Federal Records Centers (FRCs), located around the country, provide storage for about 27 million cubic feet of noncurrent records for 200 federal agencies.

NARA issued its Strategic Plan for fiscal years (FYs) 2018 through 2022, which sets its long-term objectives. It has four strategic goals: Make Access Happen, Connect with Customers, Maximize NARA's Value to the Nation, and Build

Our Future through Our People. Specific initiatives are underway at NARA to reach each goal.

Records and Access

Information Security Oversight Office

The Information Security Oversight Office (ISOO) is responsible to the president for policy and oversight of the government-wide security classification system, the National Industrial Security Program, and the emerging federal policy on "controlled unclassified information" (CUI). ISOO receives policy and program guidance from the assistant to the president for national security affairs and National Security Council staff in the Executive Office of the President.

ISOO oversees the security classification programs (classification, safeguarding, and declassification) in both government and industry. It is also responsible for exercising NARA's authorities and responsibilities as the executive agent for controlled unclassified information. ISOO contributes materially to the effective implementation of the government-wide security classification program and has a direct impact on the performance of thousands of government employees and contract personnel who work with classified national security information. For more information on ISOO, visit archives.gov/isoo.

National Declassification Center

In December 2009 Executive Order 13526 established the National Declassification Center (NDC) within the National Archives to address declassification of classified federal government records. The focus of this effort was to promote transparency and accountability of records created by the Executive Branch of the U.S. government.

NDC led a process that streamlined the declassification review processes for classified historical records and eliminated a 350-million-page backlog at the National Archives. NDC is committed to completing QA on all accessioned classified records no later than one year after they have been transferred to our custody. To date they have met that goal for records received annually from 2014 through 2016. To facilitate public access to these records, NDC established an "Indexing on Demand" process that allows a researcher to request priority indexing and release for eligible record series.

NDC also processes requests for classified records under the Freedom of Information Act (FOIA) and Mandatory Review Provisions of Executive Order 13526 (MDR). To respond to these requests, NDC works closely with other agencies to ensure exempted records are reviewed by the appropriate equity agency, then processes declassified and redacted records for release. For more information about NDC, go to archives.gov/declassification.

Office of Government Information Services

As the FOIA Ombudsman, OGIS educates stakeholders about the FOIA process, resolves disputes, and assesses agency compliance.

The Open Government Act of 2007 created OGIS within the National Archives. The statute requires that OGIS offer mediation services to help resolve FOIA disputes and review agency FOIA policies and procedures. FOIA also charges OGIS with identifying methods to improve compliance with the statute.

The OGIS director chairs the FOIA Federal Advisory Committee. The Committee brings together FOIA experts from inside and outside of government to identify major issues with the implementation of FOIA and develop consensus solutions. The OGIS director also serves as the co-chair of the Chief FOIA Officers Council.

For more information about OGIS, visit archives.gov/ogis or follow OGIS on Twitter @FOIA_Ombuds.

Electronic Records Archives

NARA uses the Electronic Records Archives (ERA) system to take in and store electronic records from the White House, Congress, and agencies across the federal government. In addition, since 2012, NARA has required all federal agencies to use ERA to submit records schedules to NARA for approval by the Archivist of the United States. The adoption of ERA by federal agencies and the use of ERA to support the transfer of electronic presidential records have led to the transfer of increasing volumes of electronic records to NARA for preservation and eventual access through its public access portal, the National Archives Catalog (NAC).

NARA has launched a new system, ERA 2.0, to update and enhance the agency's capabilities to meet the ever-expanding challenges in preserving born-electronic records and digitized material. ERA 2.0 uses cloud services for greater scalability in terms of storage and computer processing to increase NARA's ability to preserve and provide access to greater amounts of digital material over time.

The ERA 2.0 system consists of three major components: a digital processing environment, a digital object repository, and a business object management component. The processing component provides the capability to upload digital material of all types, gives staff a variety of software tools for verification and processing, supports the creation and editing of metadata, and allows users to submit packages of processed digital material to the repository component for preservation. The repository supports the capability to ingest processed digital material to provide for safe archival storage, delivers advanced staff search and discovery capabilities, provides digital material for further processing for preservation, and makes copies of records available for public access through the NAC. The business object management component, slated for deployment in late 2020, will provide a redesign of the online forms and approval workflows used by NARA and federal agencies to schedule and transfer records to NARA. For more information about ERA, see archives.gov/era.

Applied Research Division

NARA's Applied Research Division serves as the agency's center for advanced and applied research capabilities in the fields of computer science, engineering, and archival science. The division's staff conducts research on new technologies, both for awareness of new types of electronic record formats that will need to be preserved and to evaluate new technologies that might be incorporated into electronic records management and preservation systems at NARA to increase their effectiveness. The staff also helps NARA managers and employees acquire the knowledge and skills they need to function effectively in e-government through presentations on new technologies. For more information, visit archives.gov/applied-research.

NARA's Website

The online entrance to the National Archives is archives.gov, which provides the most widely available means of electronic access to information about and services available from NARA. Links to various sections provide help to the particular needs of researchers, including veterans and their families, educators and students, and the general public—as well as records managers, journalists, historians, and members of Congress.

The NARA website provides the following:

- Directions on how to contact NARA and conduct research at its facilities around the country
- Direct access to certain archived electronic records at archives.gov/aad
- Digital copies of selected archived documents
- A contact form, at archives.gov/contact, for customer questions, reference requests, comments, and complaints
- Electronic versions of *Federal Register* publications
- Online exhibits
- Classroom resources for students and teachers at archives.gov/education
- Online tools such as eVetRecs (archives.gov/veterans/military-service records), which allows veterans and their next-of-kin to complete and print, for mail-in submission, requests for their military service records

Public Access Projects

NARA's Office of Innovation is responsible for oversight of the digitization of NARA's holdings and for ensuring public access through the National Archives Catalog (catalog.archives.gov). The Office of Innovation is constantly developing improved tools, techniques, and workflows to accelerate access. In FY 2019 over 38 million pages were added to the National Archives Catalog resulting in a total of over 93 million pages available to the public. This growth included over 28 million images scanned by NARA's digitization partners, partner digitization being a key component of NARA's overall digitization strategy (https://www.archives.gov/digitization/strategy.html). In the coming years the Office of Innovation will continue to find new ways to improve digitization and access as we work toward our strategic goal of 500 million pages available in the catalog by the end of FY 2024 (for more information see https://www.archives.gov/about/plans-reports/strategic-plan).

Engagement with "citizen archivists" also represents a critical component to improving access. In FY 2019 over 223,000 pages were enhanced by the public through tagging, transcribing, and commenting. These additions from the public help make NARA's holdings more discoverable to researchers through the addition of critical metadata and transcribed text.

The History Hub (History.gov) is another tool that helps expand access to the nation's history and to NARA's holdings. After registering on the History Hub, individuals can submit questions about U.S. history; the platform allows responses from NARA staff, staff at other participating cultural heritage organizations such as the Library of Congress, and the public. This crowdsourced platform helps eliminate the silos that exist between information residing at different organizations and allows researchers, citizen historians, and archival professionals to more easily find answers to their questions.

Social Media

NARA uses multiple social media platforms to increase access to the records in its holdings, which is at the heart of its mission. The main goals of social media at NARA are to increase awareness about archival holdings and programs and to enrich the agency's relationship with the public through conversations about its services and holdings. In addition to expanding access, use of social media creates a more collaborative work environment and increases communication and knowledge sharing both within NARA and externally with other federal agencies.

The National Archives has 18 blogs, including one by the archivist of the United States. NARA also offers historical videos from its holdings and videos of recent public events on the agency's ten YouTube channels. The agency shares photographs and documents from its collections through Flickr Commons. Across the country, more than 200 NARA staff contribute actively to the agency's 130 social media accounts, including Facebook, Twitter, Tumblr, Instagram, and others.

Followers can also use Really Simple Syndication (RSS) feeds of the "Document for Today" feature, NARA news, and press releases. Several mobile apps and e-books have been developed and are available free of charge in the iTunes store and Android Market for Today's Document, DocsTeach, and recent exhibits.

Social media also allow NARA's researchers, friends, and the public to become citizen archivists by tagging, sharing, and transcribing documents. For more information, go to archives.gov/citizen-archivist.

Additional information about NARA's social media projects is available at archives.gov/social-media.

National Archives Museum

The National Archives Museum, a set of interconnected resources made possible by a public–private partnership between NARA and the National Archives Foundation, provides a variety of ways to explore the power and importance of the nation's records.

The Rotunda for the Charters of Freedom at the National Archives Building in Washington, D.C., is the centerpiece of the National Archives Museum.

On display are the Declaration of Independence, the Constitution, and the Bill of Rights—known collectively as the Charters of Freedom. The Public Vaults is a 9,000-square-foot permanent exhibition that conveys the feeling of going beyond the walls of the Rotunda and into the stacks and vaults of the working archives. Dozens of individual exhibits, many of them interactive, reveal the breadth and variety of NARA's holdings.

Complementing the Public Vaults, the Lawrence F. O'Brien Gallery hosts a changing array of topical exhibits based on National Archives records. The 290-seat William G. McGowan Theater is a showplace for NARA's extensive audio-visual holdings and serves as a forum for lectures and discussions.

The David M. Rubenstein Gallery houses a permanent interactive exhibit, "Records of Rights," which documents the struggles and debates over civil rights and liberties throughout American history. The Rubenstein Gallery is also home for a 1297 copy of the Magna Carta, owned by Rubenstein.

Inside the Boeing Learning Center, the ReSource Room is an access point for teachers and parents to explore documents found in the exhibits and to use NARA records as teaching tools. The center's Constitution-in-Action Learning Lab is designed to provide an intense field trip adventure for middle and high school students that links to curriculum in the classroom.

DocsTeach (docsteach.org) is an education website designed to provide instruction to teachers in the best practices of teaching with primary sources. Using documents in NARA's holdings as teachable resources, DocsTeach strongly supports civic literacy. This tool gives all teachers access to primary sources, instruction in best practices, and opportunities to interact with their counterparts across the nation.

When developing the DocsTeach site, the agency established an online community that served as a virtual meeting place for NARA's education team and colleagues from schools, institutions, and organizations nationwide to collaborate and share innovative ideas and best practices for this online resource.

The National Archives' New York City field office is located in the Alexander Hamilton U.S. Custom House at the southern tip of Manhattan. There, NARA has a large research center as well as diverse educational and program activities offered for free in the Learning Center. The new Learning Center incorporates many of the resources and activities found in the Washington, D.C., building but also includes New York–specific offerings.

At its Kansas City, Missouri, field office at 400 West Pershing Road, NARA also has a welcome center, changing exhibitions, workshops, and other public programs.

A set of webpages now makes the National Archives Museum available anywhere. An illustrated history of the Charters of Freedom can be found there, as well as information on educational programs, special events, and current exhibits at the National Archives.

Those traveling to Washington can bypass the public line during peak tourist season by making online reservations at recreation.gov. For more information, see "The National Archives Museum" at https://museum.archives.gov. An online version of the "Records of Rights" exhibition is available at recordsofrights.org.

More than a million individuals visited the National Archives Museum in Washington, D.C., in FY 2019.

National Archives Research Centers

At the Robert M. Warner Research Center in the National Archives Building in Washington, D.C., and the Steny H. Hoyer Research Center at the National Archives at College Park, Maryland, researchers can consult with staff experts on federal records held in each building and submit requests to examine original documents.

The Warner Research Center holds approximately 275,000 rolls of microfilmed records, documenting military service prior to World War I, immigration into the United States, the federal census, the U.S. Congress, federal courts in the District of Columbia, the Bureau of Indian Affairs, and the Freedmen's Bureau. The center also contains an extensive, ever-expanding system of reference reports, helping researchers conduct research in federal documents.

Executive branch records housed in the National Archives Building include those of the Bureau of Indian Affairs and of civilian agencies responsible for maritime affairs. Military records in this building include records of the Army before World War I and the Navy and Marine Corps before World War II. In addition, the National Archives Building holds many records relating to the federal government's interaction with individuals; these are often consulted for genealogical research.

The Steny H. Hoyer Research Center in College Park holds textual records of civilian agencies from 1789; investigative records and military holdings that include records from the Army and Army Air Forces dating from World War I and Navy, Marine Corps, intelligence, defense-related, and seized enemy records dating from World War II. In addition to textual records, special media records include motion pictures, still photographs and posters, sound recordings, maps, architectural drawings, aerial photographs, and electronic records. A research room for accessioned microfilm holds records of the Department of State's Berlin Document Center and other World War II–era captured documents.

Field Archives

NARA has 12 field archives where the public can do research. They are located in or near Boston, New York, Philadelphia, Atlanta, Chicago, St. Louis, Kansas City, Fort Worth, Denver, Riverside (California), San Francisco, and Seattle. Archived records of significance, as well as, in some locations, immigration records, are available for use by the public in these field archives.

Presidential Libraries

NARA operates the libraries and museums of the 14 most recent U.S. presidents, beginning with Herbert Hoover, whose library is in West Branch, Iowa, and maintains the presidential records of the Obama Administration. The others are Franklin D. Roosevelt, Hyde Park, New York; Harry S. Truman, Independence, Missouri; Dwight D. Eisenhower, Abilene, Kansas; John F. Kennedy, Boston; Lyndon Baines Johnson, Austin; Richard Nixon, Yorba Linda, California; Gerald R. Ford, Ann Arbor (library) and Grand Rapids (museum), Michigan; Jimmy Carter, Atlanta; Ronald Reagan, Simi Valley, California; George H. W. Bush, College Station, Texas; William J. Clinton, Little Rock; and George W. Bush, Dallas. Unlike other presidential libraries administered by NARA, the Barack Obama Presidential Library will be a fully digital library. After the records are digitized, NARA will store and preserve the original materials in an existing NARA facility that meets NARA's standards for archival storage. Staff at that location will be responsible for caring for the records and artifacts. Currently, the Obama Administration materials are housed in a temporary facility in Hoffman Estates, Illinois, which is not open to the public.

In FY 2019 more than 2.5 million people visited exhibits in the presidential library museums. At archives.gov/presidential-libraries, visitors can learn about the presidential library system as a whole and link to individual library websites to learn about the lives of the presidents and the times in which they served.

Federal Records Centers Program

NARA also serves federal agencies, the courts, and Congress by providing records storage, reference service, life-cycle management, and guidance on many issues relating to records management.

A network of 18 Federal Records Centers (FRCs) stores 27 million cubic feet (about 52 billion pages) of noncurrent records for 200 agencies. In FY 2019 these records centers replied to nearly 10 million requests for information and records, including more than one million requests for information regarding military and civilian service records provided by the National Personnel Records Center in St. Louis.

The Federal Records Centers Program is nationwide. NARA has records centers in or near Atlanta; Boston; Chicago; Dayton; Denver; Fort Worth; Kansas City; Miamisburg, Ohio; Lee's Summit, Missouri; Lenexa, Kansas; Philadelphia; Pittsfield, Massachusetts; Riverside, California; St. Louis; San Francisco; Seattle; Suitland, Maryland; and Valmeyer, Illinois.

Genealogy Research

Genealogy research brings thousands of people to NARA facilities every year. In its holdings NARA has census records dating back to 1790, records dealing with immigration, land and pension records, and passenger lists from ships arriving from all over the world.

NARA is often considered the first stop in searching for one's ancestry, at its facilities in the Washington, D.C., area or one of its 12 field centers around the country. At these locations, NARA staff offers genealogy workshops to show the public how to look through documents dating back to the Revolutionary period.

NARA also offers an annual Genealogy Fair, which is now a "virtual" event at which NARA staff provides tips and techniques for researching genealogy records at the National Archives. Lectures are designed for experienced genealogy professionals and novices alike. Watch past Fairs online at https://www.archives.gov/calendar/genealogy-fair.

NARA also maintains close relationships with genealogical associations as well as organizations such as Ancestry.com and Fold3, which can be accessed without charge at any NARA location.

The National Archives has the census schedules on microfilm available from 1790 to 1940. (Most of the 1890 Census was destroyed in a Department of Commerce fire, although partial records are available for some states.)

Archives Library Information Center

The Archives Library Information Center (ALIC) provides access to information on American history and government, archival administration, information management, and government documents. ALIC is located in the National Archives at College Park. Customers also can visit ALIC on the Internet at archives.gov/research/alic, where they will find "Reference at Your Desk" Internet links, staff-compiled bibliographies and publications, and an online library catalog. ALIC can be reached by telephone at 301-837-3415.

Government Documents

Government publications are generally available to researchers at many of the 1,250 congressionally designated federal depository libraries throughout the nation. A record set of these publications also is part of NARA's archival holdings. Publications of the U.S. Government (Record Group 287) is a collection of selected publications of government agencies, arranged by the SuDoc classification system devised by the Office of the Superintendent of Documents, U.S. Government Publishing Office (GPO).

The core of the collection is a library established in 1895 by GPO's Public Documents Division. By 1972, when NARA acquired the library, it included official publications dating from the early years of the federal government and selected publications produced for and by federal government agencies. Since 1972 the 25,000-cubic-foot collection has been augmented periodically with accessions of government publications selected by the Office of the Superintendent of Documents as a by-product of its cataloging activity. As with the federal depository library collections, the holdings in NARA's Record Group 287 comprise only a portion of all U.S. government publications.

NARA Publications

Historically NARA has published guides and indexes to various portions of its archival holdings. Many of these are still in print, though the most up-to-date information about NARA holdings now is available almost exclusively through online searches at archives.gov. The agency also publishes informational leaflets and brochures.

Some publications appear on NARA's website, at archives.gov/publications/online, and many are available from NARA's Customer Service Center in College Park by calling 866-272-6272. The NARA website's publications homepage (archives.gov/publications) provides more detailed information about available publications and ordering.

General-interest books about NARA and its holdings that will appeal to anyone with an interest in U.S. history and facsimiles of certain documents are published by the National Archives Foundation. They are for sale at the foundation's myArchives Store in NARA's downtown Washington building and via the NARA website's eStore page at myarchivesstore.org.

Federal Register

The *Federal Register* is the daily gazette of the U.S. government, containing presidential documents, proposed and final federal regulations, and public notices of federal agencies. It is published by the Office of the Federal Register and printed and distributed by GPO. The two agencies collaborate in the same way to produce the annual revisions of the *Code of Federal Regulations* (*CFR*). Free access to the full text of the electronic version of the *Federal Register* and *CFR*, and to an unofficial, daily-updated electronic *CFR* (the *e-CFR*), is available via fdsys.gov. Federal Register documents scheduled for future publication are available for public inspection at the Office of the Federal Register (7 G Street, N.W., Suite A-734, Washington, DC 20401) or online at the electronic Public Inspection Desk (federal register.gov/public-inspection). Federalregister.gov provides access to proposed rules, and rules published in the *Federal Register* are open for public comment (the website federalregister.gov and the multiagency website regulations.gov also provide means to comment on these documents).

The full catalog of other Federal Register publications is posted at http://www.ofr.gov and includes the *Compilation of Presidential Documents, Public Papers of the Presidents*, slip laws, *United States Statutes at Large*, and the *United States Government Manual*. Printed or microfiche editions of Federal Register publications also are maintained at federal depository libraries (gpo.gov/libraries).

The Public Law Electronic Notification Service (PENS) is a free subscription e-mail service for notification of recently enacted public laws. Varied subscriptions to the daily *Federal Register* are available from federalregister.gov. Additional information about Federal Register programs appears on Facebook (facebook.com/federalregister) and Twitter (@FedRegister).

The Office of the Federal Register also publishes information about its ministerial responsibilities associated with the operation of the Electoral College and ratification of constitutional amendments and provides access to related records. Publication information concerning laws, regulations, and presidential documents and services is available from the Office of the Federal Register (telephone 202-741-6070). Information on Federal Register finding aids, the Electoral College, and constitutional amendments is available through archives.gov/federal-register.

Publications can be ordered by contacting GPO at bookstore.gpo.gov, or by toll-free telephone at 866-512-1800. To submit orders by fax or by mail, see https://bookstore.gpo.gov/help-and-contact.

Grants

The National Historical Publications and Records Commission (NHPRC) is the national grants program of the National Archives. The Archivist of the United States chairs the commission and makes grants on its recommendation. NHPRC's 14 other members represent the president (two appointees), the Supreme Court, the Senate and House of Representatives, the departments of State and Defense, the Librarian of Congress, the American Association for State and Local History, the American Historical Association, the Association for Documentary Editing, the National Association of Government Archives and Records Administrators, the Organization of American Historians, and the Society of American Archivists.

The commission's mission is to provide opportunities for the American people to discover and use records that increase understanding of the nation's democracy, history, and culture. Through leadership initiatives, grants, and fostering the creation of new tools and methods, the commission connects the work of the National Archives to the work of the nation's archives. NHPRC grants help archives, universities, historical societies, professional organizations, and other nonprofit organizations to establish or strengthen archival programs, improve training and techniques, preserve and process records collections, and provide access to them through finding aids, digitization of collections, and documentary editions of the papers of significant historical figures and movements in American history. The commission works in partnership with a national network of state archives and state historical records advisory boards to develop a national archival infrastructure. For more information about the commission, visit archives.gov/nhprc. For more information about the projects it supports, go to facebook.com/nhprc.

Administration

The head of NARA is David S. Ferriero, who was appointed archivist of the United States in 2009 by President Obama. As of January 2020 the agency employed 2,597 people working at NARA locations around the country.

National Center for Education Statistics

U.S. Department of Education, Institute of Education Sciences
Potomac Center Plaza, 550 12th St. S.W., 4th fl., Washington, DC 20202

Samuel Barbett and Christopher A. Cody
Academic Libraries, Integrated Postsecondary Education Data System

Maura Spiegelman
School Library Media Centers, Schools and Staffing Survey / National Teacher and Principal Survey

In an effort to collect and disseminate more complete statistical information about libraries, the National Center for Education Statistics (NCES) initiated a formal library statistics program in 1989 that included surveys on academic libraries, school library media centers, public libraries, and state libraries. At the end of December 2006, the Public Libraries Survey and the State Library Agencies Survey were officially transferred to the Institute of Museum and Library Services (IMLS). The Academic Libraries Survey and the School Library Media Centers Survey continued to be administered and funded by NCES. However, the School Library Media Centers Survey was incorporated into the School and Staffing Survey (SASS), and the Academic Libraries Survey was incorporated into the Integrated Postsecondary Education Data System (IPEDS).

The library surveys conducted by NCES are designed to provide comprehensive nationwide data on the status of libraries. Federal, state, and local officials, professional associations, and local practitioners use these surveys for planning, evaluating, and making policy. These data are also available to researchers and educators.

Past information about elementary and secondary public school library media centers is available on the School and Staffing Survey website, http://nces.ed.gov/surveys/sass/. The Library Statistics Program's website, http://nces.ed.gov/surveys/libraries, provides links to data search tools, data files, survey definitions, and survey designs for the complete Academic Libraries Survey files from 1996 to 2012. The IPEDS Academic Libraries Information Center, http://nces.ed.gov/ipeds/Section/Alscenter, contains current survey definitions and designs, and the IPEDS Use the Data Website at https://nces.ed.gov/ipeds/Home/UseTheData contains complete data files for the Academic Libraries component beginning in 2014. The two library surveys conducted by NCES are described below.

Academic Libraries

The IPEDS Academic Libraries (AL) component provides descriptive statistics from academic libraries in the 50 states, the District of Columbia, and, if applicable, other U.S. jurisdictions (Guam, the Commonwealth of the Northern Mariana Islands, Puerto Rico, and the U.S. Virgin Islands).

NCES surveyed academic libraries on a three-year cycle between 1966 and 1988. From 1988 to 1998, AL was a component of IPEDS collected on a two-year cycle. From 2000 to 2012, the Academic Libraries Survey (ALS) separated from IPEDS but remained on a two-year cycle as part of the Library Statistics Program. During this time period, IPEDS and ALS data were still linked by the identification codes of the postsecondary education institutions. In aggregate, these data provide an overview of the status of academic libraries nationally and by state. Beginning with the 2014–2015 collection cycle, AL was reintegrated back into IPEDS, and the AL component became a mandatory, annual survey for all degree-granting Title IV institutions. It was at this time, many questions from the 2012 ALS collections and services sections were removed or revised and survey questions related to library staff were moved to the IPEDS Human Resources (HR) component.

The AL survey collects data on libraries in the entire universe of degree-granting Title IV postsecondary institutions using a web-based data collection system. The survey component collects counts of books, serials, media, and databases, both in physical and electronic formats. Additionally, academic libraries report on interlibrary loan services. Institutions with reported total library expenditures over zero or institutions that have access to a library collection are required to report collections data, while those with expenditures equal to or greater than $100,000 are required to report collections and detailed expenditures data. Academic libraries report expenditures for salaries, wages, and fringe benefits, if paid from the library budget; materials and services expenditures; operations and maintenance expenditures; and total expenditures.

For the final 2012 ALS data collection, a First Look report, "Academic Libraries: 2012" (NCES 2014-038), was released on the NCES website in February 2014, as were the final data file and documentation for the 2012 ALS (NCES 2014-039). NCES also has a web-based peer analysis tool for AL called "Compare Academic Libraries" (https://nces.ed.gov/surveys/libraries/compare/) using AL 2012 data. Beginning with the 2014–2015 IPEDS collection cycle, the following First Look reports were released for Academic Libraries:

- "Enrollment and Employees in Postsecondary Institutions, Fall 2014; and Financial Statistics and Academic Libraries, Fiscal Year 2014" (NCES 2016-005)
- "Enrollment and Employees in Postsecondary Institutions, Fall 2015; and Financial Statistics and Academic Libraries, Fiscal Year 2015" (NCES 2017-024)
- "Enrollment and Employees in Postsecondary Institutions, Fall 2016; and Financial Statistics and Academic Libraries, Fiscal Year 2016" (NCES 2018-002)
- "Enrollment and Employees in Postsecondary Institutions, Fall 2017; and Financial Statistics and Academic Libraries, Fiscal Year 2017" (NCES 2019-021)

Finally, AL data from 2014 and on are available via the IPEDS Use the Data website (https://nces.ed.gov/ipeds/Home/UseTheData). Academic library statistics information can be obtained from Christopher A. Cody, Integrated Postsecondary Education Data System, e-mail IPEDS@ed.gov.

School Library Media Centers

National surveys of school library media centers in elementary and secondary schools in the United States were conducted in 1958, 1962, 1974, 1978, and 1986, 1993–1994, 1999–2000, 2003–2004, 2007–2008, and 2011–2012.

NCES, with the assistance of the U.S. Bureau of the Census, conducted the School Library Media Center Survey as part of the Schools and Staffing Survey (SASS). SASS is the nation's largest sample survey of teachers, schools, and principals in K–12 public and private schools. Data from the school library media center questionnaire provide a national picture of public school library staffing, collections, expenditures, technology, and services. Results from the 2011–2012 survey can be found in "Characteristics of Public Elementary and Secondary School Library Media Centers in the United States: Results from the 2011–12 Schools and Staffing Survey" (NCES 2013-315).

NCES also published a historical report about school libraries titled *Fifty Years of Supporting Children's Learning: A History of Public School Libraries and Federal Legislation from 1953–2000* (NCES 2005-311). Drawn from more than 50 sources, this report gives descriptive data about public school libraries since 1953. Along with key characteristics of school libraries, the report also presents national and regional standards, and federal legislation affecting school library media centers. Data from sample surveys are provided at the national, regional, and school levels, and by state.

NCES recently redesigned the Schools and Staffing Survey as the National Teacher and Principal Survey (NTPS). NTPS focuses on teachers, principals, and the schools in which they work. The 2017–2018 survey counted the number of school library media centers; data on library media center staff was not collected but will be part of the next NTPS. For more information about the NTPS or to review data collected in the 2015–2016 and 2017–2018 school years, visit https://nces.ed.gov/surveys/ntps/.

Additional information on school library media center statistics can be obtained from Maura Spiegelman, e-mail maura.spiegelman@ed.gov.

NCES has included some library-oriented questions relevant to the library usage and skills of the parent and the teacher instruments of the new Early Childhood Longitudinal Study (ECLS). For additional information, visit http://nces.ed.gov/ecls. Library items also appear in National Household Education Survey (NHES) instruments. For more information about that survey, visit http://nces.ed.gov/nhes.

NCES included a questionnaire about high school library media centers in the Education Longitudinal Study of 2002 (ELS: 2002). This survey collected data from tenth graders about their schools, their school library media centers, their communities, and their home life. The report, "School Library Media Centers: Selected Results from the Education Longitudinal Study of 2002" (ELS: 2002) (NCES 2005-302), is available on the NCES website. For more information about this survey, visit http://nces.ed.gov/surveys/els2002.

How to Obtain Printed and Electronic Products

Reports are currently published in the First Look format. First Look reports consist of a short collection of tables presenting state and national totals, a survey description, and data highlights. NCES also publishes separate, more in-depth studies analyzing these data.

Internet Access

Many NCES publications (including out-of-print publications) and edited raw data files from the library surveys are available for viewing or downloading at no charge through the Electronic Catalog on the NCES website at http://nces.ed.gov/pubsearch.

Ordering Printed Products

Many NCES publications are also available in printed format. To order one free copy of recent NCES reports, contact the Education Publications Center (ED Pubs) at https://www.usa.gov/federal-agencies/education-publications-center-edpubs, by e-mail at edpubs@edpubs.ed.gov, by toll-free telephone at 877-4-ED-PUBS (1-877-433-7827) or TTY/TDD 877-576-7734, by fax at 703-605-6794, or by mail at ED Pubs, P.O. Box 22207, Alexandria, VA 22304.

Many publications are available through the Education Resources Information Clearinghouse (ERIC) system. For more information on services and products, visit https://eric.ed.gov.

Out-of-print publications and data files may be available through the NCES Electronic Catalog on the NCES website at http://nces.ed.gov/pubsearch or through one of the 1,250 federal depository libraries throughout the United States (see http://catalog.gpo.gov/fdlpdir/FDLPdir.jsp). Use the NCES publication number included in the citations for publications and data files to quickly locate items in the NCES Electronic Catalog. Use the GPO number to locate items in a federal depository library.

Defense Technical Information Center

Fort Belvoir, VA 22060
World Wide Web https://discover.dtic.mil/

The Defense Technical Information Center (DTIC)—which marks its 75th anniversary in 2020—is a Department of Defense (DoD) field activity, reporting to the Office of the Under Secretary of Defense for Research and Engineering, OUSD(R&E).

DTIC's mission is to aggregate and fuse science and technology data in order to rapidly, accurately, and reliably deliver the knowledge needed to develop the next generation of technologies to support our service members and help assure national security.

DTIC amplifies the DoD's multibillion dollar annual investment in science and technology by collecting scientific and technical information, and enhancing the digital search, analysis, and collaboration tools that make information widely available to decision makers, researchers, engineers, and scientists across the department.

In this capacity, DTIC has three main focus areas. "Collection" entails the gathering, preservation, and management of defense technical information. "Dissemination" involves the distribution of content across the department to facilitate collaboration and discovery. "Research and analysis" occurs via the DoD Information Analysis Centers (DoD IAC) program, which efficiently provides critical, flexible, and cutting-edge research and analysis to produce relevant and reusable scientific and technical information (STI) for acquisition program managers, DoD laboratories, Program Executive Offices (PEOs), and Combatant Commands.

Ultimately, DTIC aims to maximize the availability and use of technical information resulting from defense-funded activities, while safeguarding national security, export control, and intellectual property rights.

Reaching Customers

DTIC offers its capabilities to a broad user base within the defense community. Although some products are publically available on https://discover.dtic.mil, many are restricted to registered federal government and contracted personnel. Federal employees and contractors with a PKI card can access these sites with their credentials. More information about eligibility for restricted access can be found at https://discover.dtic.mil/dtic-registration-benefits/dtic-registration/.

Who uses DTIC tools and services? Among its more than 63,000 registered users are

- Acquisition personnel
- Active duty military personnel
- Congressional staff
- DoD contractors

- Engineers
- Faculty and students at military schools
- Historians
- Information professionals / librarians
- Program analysts
- Program executive offices
- Researchers
- Scientists
- Science and technology advisors
- Security managers
- Small business owners
- Software engineers and developers

Collection

DTIC's holdings include both public and controlled collections. DTIC's information collection activities leverage many sources, including DoD organizations and contractors; other U.S. government organizations and their contractors; nonprofit organizations working on DoD scientific, research, and engineering activities; academia; and foreign governments. DTIC accepts information electronically and, when necessary, in physical print and digital formats, such as CD and DVD. More information about submission and selection is available at https://discover.dtic.mil/submit-documents/.

DTIC's holdings include more than 4.6 million documents, such as technical reports on completed research; research summaries of planned, ongoing, and completed work; independent research and development summaries; defense technology transfer agreements; DoD planning documents; DoD-funded journal articles; DoD international agreements; conference proceedings; security classification guides; command histories; and special collections dating back to World War II.

Dissemination

The Research and Engineering (R&E) Gateway—accessible only to registered users via https://www.dtic.mil—is the entry point to DTIC's full suite of tools, some of which are also available on the public website https://discover.dtic.mil. In an access-controlled environment, these unclassified tools offer access to DoD research, other scientific and technical information, and collaboration with other subject matter experts.

R&E Gateway tools help the defense scientific and technical community build on past work with the highest awareness of relevant information, collaborate on current projects, avoid duplication of effort, and maximize the efficient use of DoD project funds. The broad availability of information in DTIC's collections ensures that technological innovations are tightly linked to defense development and acquisition efforts.

Some of DTIC's tools are

- DTIC Thesaurus—Publicly available at https://discover.dtic.mil/thesaurus/, the Thesaurus provides a broad, multidisciplinary subject-term vocabulary that aids in information search and retrieval. Subject terms, called Descriptors, are organized into hierarchies, where series of narrower terms are linked to broader terms.
- Innovators Information Repository (IIR)—DTIC developed the IIR in response to direction from the National Defense Authorization Act for fiscal year 2019, releasing the tool in late 2019 as a beta application. The IIR is a searchable index of Small Business Innovation Research program and Small Business Technology Transfer program awards. Registered users can research award trends and DoD-funded technologies that match current program needs, and identify vendors with demonstrated abilities by contract award, year, and company contact information.
- Journal of DoD Research and Engineering (JDR&E)—Available to registered users, the JDR&E publishes scientific innovations, commentary, and cutting-edge research from the R&E focus areas. The JDR&E provides a venue for researchers, scientists, and engineers working in our labs on limited and classified projects to gain peer-reviewed status for their work. Through its print and online versions, the JDR&E publishes those papers that are most influential in their fields, or across fields, that will significantly advance scientific understanding. Selected papers present novel and broadly important data, syntheses, or concepts that merit recognition by the wider DoD Science and Technology (S&T) focus areas and address the need to collaborate and share information, recognizing valued contributions from our research community.
- PubDefense—In 2013 the White House Office of Science and Technology Policy mandated that federally funded, scholarly journal articles must be made available and free to the public following a 12-month embargo. PubDefense is DTIC's publicly accessible tool to access journal articles, conference papers, and related materials resulting from research funded by the DoD and Office of the Director of National Intelligence / Intelligence Advanced Research Projects Agency. Public datasets associated with scholarly publications are also available through PubDefense.
- Research Budget and Project Information (RBPI)—DTIC publishes DoD research and engineering budget data shortly after release by Congress and offers both public and access-controlled sites to retrieve and analyze these data. With the new access-controlled RBPI application, registered users can search and analyze congressional budget data across fiscal years. Users can quickly evaluate and forecast trends in DoD budget data, facilitating better execution and planning for Research Development, Test and Evaluation (RDT&E) investments. As a value-added service to ensure accuracy and reliability, DTIC thoroughly checks the budget data prior to posting.

Research and Analysis (R&A)

The DoD Information Analysis Centers (IAC) program provides research and analysis services to, and develops scientific and technical information products for, the DoD S&T community in the broad domains of Cyber Security, Defense Systems, and Homeland Defense. The IACs are staffed by, or have access to, hundreds of scientists, engineers, and information specialists who provide research and analysis to customers with diverse, complex, and challenging requirements.

The DoD IAC program provides a broad variety of R&A products and services, including customer-driven research and analysis, prototyping, answers to scientific and technical inquires, access to the S&T community's subject matter experts, technical training, and wide ranging scientific and technical information products.

The DoD IAC domains encompass 22 technical focus areas: Software and Data Analysis; Cybersecurity; Modeling and Simulation; Knowledge Management and Information Sharing; Advanced Materials; Autonomous Weapon Systems; C4ISR; Directed Energy; Energetics; Military Sensing; Non-Lethal Weapons and Information Operations; RMQSI; Survivability and Vulnerability; Weapons Systems; Homeland Defense and Security; Critical Infrastructure Protection: Weapons of Mass Destruction; CBRN Defense; Biometrics; Medical; Cultural Studies; and Alternative Energy.

The DoD IAC Program Office also provides assisted acquisition solutions to program needs by assisting the development of customer requirements, processing all financial documents in an auditable environment, and monitoring contract performance.

Education Resources

National Library of Education

Knowledge Utilization Division
National Center for Education Evaluation and Regional Assistance
Institute of Education Sciences, U.S. Department of Education
400 Maryland Ave. S.W., Washington, DC 20202
World Wide Web https://ies.ed.gov/ncee/projects/nle

Karen Tate, Director

The U.S. Department of Education's National Library of Education (NLE), created in 1994, is the primary resource center for education information in the federal government, serving the research needs of the Department of Education, the education community, and the public. NLE resides in the National Center for Education Evaluation and Regional Assistance, Institute of Education Sciences.

NLE was created by Public Law 103-227, the Educational Research, Development, Dissemination, and Improvement Act of 1994, and reauthorized under Public Law 107-279, the Education Sciences Reform Act of 2002. The act outlines four primary functions of NLE:

- Collect and archive information, including products and publications developed through, or supported by, the Institute of Education Sciences; and other relevant and useful education-related research, statistics, and evaluation materials and other information, projects, and publications that are consistent with scientifically valid research or the priorities and mission of the institute, and developed by the department, other federal agencies, or entities
- Provide a central location within the federal government for information about education
- Provide comprehensive reference services on matters relating to education to employees of the Department of Education and its contractors and grantees, other federal employees, and the public
- Promote greater cooperation and resource sharing among providers and repositories of education information in the United States

NLE works closely with the Education Resources Information Center (ERIC). ERIC collects and archives information and provides a central location within the federal government for information about education. Because ERIC serves as the major public program, it is covered separately. [See "Education Resources Information Center" beginning on page 102—*Ed.*]

The primary responsibility of NLE is to provide information services to agency staff and contractors, the general public, other government agencies, and other libraries. Located in the agency's headquarters building in Washington, D.C., the library houses current and historical collections and archives of information on education issues, research, statistics, and policy; there is a special emphasis on agency publications and contractor reports, as well as current and historical federal education legislation.

NLE's primary customer base includes about 4,000 department staff nationwide; department contractors performing research; education organizations and media; and academic, special, and government libraries.

Collections

The focus of NLE's collection is on education issues, with an emphasis on research and policy, with some materials on related topics including law, public policy, economics, urban affairs, sociology, history, philosophy, psychology, and cognitive development. In addition to current materials, the collection has books dating from the early 19th century, including approximately 800 books on education research in the United States and more than 25,000 historical textbooks. Some of these books were donated to the library by Henry Barnard, the first U.S. commissioner of education.

NLE maintains collections of historical documents associated with its parent agency, the U.S. Department of Education, having a complete collection of ERIC microfiche; research reports reviewed by the What Works Clearinghouse and special panels; and publications of or relating to the department's predecessor agencies, including the National Institute of Education and the U.S. Office of Education in the Department of Health, Education, and Welfare. These collections include reports, studies, manuals, statistical publications, speeches, and policy papers. NLE also serves as a selective federal depository library under the U.S. Government Publishing Office program.

Services

NLE provides reference and other information services, including legislative reference and statistical information services, to department staff, to the education community at large, and to the general public, as well as offering document delivery services to department staff and interlibrary loan services to other libraries and government agencies.

Contact Information

The U.S. Department of Education Research Library can be contacted by e-mail at askalibrarian@ed.gov. The library's reference desk is available by telephone from 9 A.M. to 5 P.M. weekdays, except federal holidays, at 800-424-1616 (toll free) or 202-205-5015, and by fax at 202-401-0547. For the hearing-impaired, the toll-free number for the Federal Relay Service is 800-877-8339.

Located in the department's headquarters building at 400 Maryland Ave. S.W., the library is open to researchers by appointment from 9 A.M. to 5 P.M. weekdays, except federal holidays.

Education Resources Information Center

Knowledge Utilization Division
National Center for Education Evaluation and Regional Assistance
Institute of Education Sciences, U.S. Department of Education
550 12th St., S.W., Washington, DC 20208
https://eric.ed.gov

Erin Pollard

Program Officer, ERIC
202-245-8344, e-mail erin.pollard@ed.gov

The Education Resources Information Center (ERIC) is the world's largest and most frequently used digital library of education resources. Since its inception in 1966, ERIC has added over 1.8 million records of journal articles, reports, and other materials. About 1 million records are for peer-reviewed work, and 400,000 records have free full text available to download from ERIC. Each ERIC bibliographic record contains an abstract of a journal article or gray literature document (for example, a technical report or conference paper), along with an abstract, audience, type of report, information on the assessment used, location where the research was conducted, and descriptors that work as keywords to guide users to relevant results.

Background

ERIC is a free, online database of education research that serves over 12 million users each year. With more than 50 years of service to the public, ERIC is one of the oldest programs in the U.S. Department of Education. As the world's largest education resource, it is distinguished by two hallmarks: free dissemination of bibliographic records, and the collection of gray literature such as research conference papers and government contractor reports.

The authorizing legislation for ERIC is part of the Education Sciences Reform Act of 2002, Public Law 107-279. This legislation envisioned ERIC subject areas or topics (previously covered by the ERIC Clearinghouses) as part of the totality of enhanced information dissemination to be conducted by the Institute of Education Sciences. In addition, information dissemination includes material on closing the achievement gap and on educational practices that improve academic achievement and promote learning.

Mission of ERIC

ERIC undertakes five major activities:

- *Pursues good sources.* ERIC reviews journal issues and publications from education-focused programs, organizations, and agencies to locate research in the field of education. A unique feature of ERIC is the inclusion of "gray literature," such as work from nonprofits, advocacy organizations, government agencies, or other sources that are typically not indexed by commercial databases. ERIC currently provides content from 1,935 sources, including 1,178 journals and 757 organizations and agencies. Ninety-nine percent of ERIC's journals are peer reviewed.

- *Works to make research publicly available.* ERIC negotiates with publishers to make as much of its content as freely available as possible. For example, ERIC contains 364 journals and 757 gray literature sources that allow full text to be downloaded for free. ERIC also links to freely available content on the publisher's website for 364 journals and 591 nonjournal sources. There are over 89,000 full-text, peer-reviewed articles available for free download. Of these, 975 peer-reviewed journal articles are available as result of the IES Public Access Policy.
- *Creates records with supporting information so users know if resources are a good fit.* ERIC creates about 48,000 records per year that provide users with information about each article. Information in the record includes an abstract, audience, type of report, information on the assessment used, location where the research was conducted, and descriptors that work as keywords to guide users to relevant results. The metadata gives users the information they need to quickly see if the article will be relevant and useful to them.
- *Powers search engines with ERIC metadata to help users find good research, wherever they are searching.* ERIC shares its metadata with the public to enable search engines, academic databases, and other information providers to power their searches with ERIC data.
- *Integrates with other federally funded resources.* As applicable, ERIC records are linked with other federally funded resources, including What Works Clearinghouse study pages, Institute of Education Sciences grant abstracts, and links to federal websites. These interrelationships provide additional information and assist users in finding relevant and valuable IES resources.

Selection Standards

The selection policy provides that all materials added to the ERIC database are rigorous and relevant sources of research directly related to the field of education. The majority of journals indexed in ERIC are peer-reviewed, and peer-reviewed status is indicated for all journals indexed since 2004, when this data began to be documented by the ERIC system. The peer-review status for nonjournals is indicated for all sources with a documented peer-review process. The collection scope includes early childhood education through higher education, vocational education, and special education; it includes teacher education, education administration, assessment and evaluation, counseling, information technology, and the academic areas of reading, mathematics, science, environmental education, languages, and social studies.

To be considered for selection, all submissions must be in digital format and accompanied by author permission for dissemination. For individual document submissions, authors (copyright holders) can upload materials through a link on the ERIC website. Journal publishers, associations, and other entities with multiple documents also submit electronic content following guidance and instructions consistent with provider agreements from ERIC.

ERIC Users

About 12 million users search the ERIC website and download more than 7 million full-text documents each year from users all over the world. Approximately half of ERIC's users are driven from a commercial search engine, while 40 percent are driven from academic search engines.

ERIC can be reached at ERICRequests@ed.gov. Questions can also be transmitted via the message box on the "Contact Us" page on the ERIC website.

National Association and Organization Reports

American Library Association

50 E. Huron St., Chicago, IL 60611
800-545-2433
World Wide Web http://www.ala.org

Wanda Kay Brown
President

The American Library Association (ALA) was founded in 1876 in Philadelphia and later chartered in the Commonwealth of Massachusetts. ALA has approximately 57,000 members, including librarians, library trustees, and other interested people from every state and many nations. The association serves public, state, school, and academic libraries, as well as special libraries for people working in government, prisons, and other institutions.

ALA is a 501(c)(3) charitable and educational organization with a mission "to provide leadership for the development, promotion, and improvement of library and information services and the profession of librarianship in order to enhance learning and ensure access to information for all."

ALA is governed by an elected council, which is its policymaking body, and an executive board, which acts for the council in the administration of established policies and programs. In this context, the executive board is the body that manages the affairs of the association, delegating management of its day-to-day operation to the executive director.

ALA is home to 11 membership divisions, each focused on a type of library or library function. They are the American Association of School Librarians (AASL); the Association for Library Collections and Technical Services (ALCTS); the Association for Library Service to Children (ALSC); the Association of College and Research Libraries (ACRL); the Association of Specialized, Government, and Cooperative Library Agencies (ASGCLA); the Library and Information Technology Association (LITA); the Public Library Association (PLA); the Library Leadership and Management Association (LLAMA); the Reference and User Services Association (RUSA); United for Libraries; and the Young Adult Library Services Association (YALSA).

ALA hosts 20 roundtables for members who share interests that lie outside the scope of any of the divisions. A network of affiliates, chapters, and other organizations enables ALA to reach a broad audience.

Key action areas include advocacy for libraries and the profession, diversity, education and lifelong learning, equitable access to information and library services, intellectual freedom, literacy, organizational excellence, and transforming libraries.

ALA offices address the broad interests and issues of concern to ALA members. They track issues and provide information, services, and products for members and the public. Current ALA offices are the Chapter Relations Office (CRO); the Communications and Marketing Office (CMO); the Development Office; the Executive/ALA Governance Office; the Human Resources Office; the International Relations Office (IRO); the Library and Research Center (LARC); the Office for Accreditation; the Office for Diversity, Literacy and Outreach Services (ODLOS); the Office for Human Resource Development and Recruitment (HRDR); the Office for Intellectual Freedom (OIF); the Public Policy and Advocacy Office (PPAO); the Public Programs Office (PPO); and Publishing.

With headquarters in Chicago, ALA's PPAO is based in Washington, D.C., and United for Libraries is in Exton, Pennsylvania. ALA also has an editorial office for *Choice*, a review journal for academic libraries, in Middletown, Connecticut. In 2020 the association will be relocating its headquarters from 50 E. Huron and 40 E. Huron to 225 N. Michigan Avenue, Chicago.

Leadership and Strategic Planning

Wanda Kay Brown, director of Library Services at the C. G. O'Kelly Library, Winston-Salem State University, Winston-Salem, North Carolina, was inaugurated as ALA president at the association's 2019 Annual Conference in Washington, D.C. A theme of Brown's presidential year is "Finding Your ALA," an effort to connect students and new library staff with ALA and help them find a place within the association that furthers their careers and ambitions.

Julius C. Jefferson, Jr., section head of the Congressional Research Service at the Library of Congress in Washington, D.C., was named ALA president-elect and will be inaugurated at the 2020 Annual Conference in Chicago. Other officers are Maggie Farrell, University of Nevada, Las Vegas, treasurer; and Mary W. Ghikas, executive director. Also providing representation on the board is immediate ALA past-president Loida Garcia-Febo, library consultant and president of Information New Wave in Brooklyn, New York.

Ghikas became interim executive director in August 2017 upon the retirement of Keith Michael Fiels and was named executive director in January 2018. Tracie D. Hall will become ALA's new executive director on February 24, 2020. Hall was among the first cohort of Spectrum Scholars in 1998 and served as the director of the Office of Diversity from 2003 to 2006. Prior to returning to ALA, she was director of the Chicago-based Joyce Foundation's Culture Program. Before that, she served as deputy commissioner of the Department of Cultural Affairs and Special Events (DCASE) for the City of Chicago. Ghikas, who has worked for ALA since 1995, will serve as deputy executive director through June 2020.

Also serving on the executive board along with the officers in 2020 are Trevor A. Dawes, University of Delaware Library; Karen G. Schneider, Sonoma State

University Library; Tamika Barnes, Georgia State University Library; Ed Garcia, Cranston Public Library; Maria Taesil Hudson McCauley, Cambridge Public Library; Eboni M. Henry, D.C. Public Schools; Lessa Kanani'opua Pelayo-Lozada, Palos Verdes Library District; and Patricia M. "Patty" Wong, Santa Monica Public Library.

Conferences and Workshops

2019 Midwinter Meeting

The American Library Association hosted its 2019 ALA Midwinter Meeting & Exhibits in Seattle at the Washington State Convention Center and nearby locations to network with peers and leaders, participate in educational sessions, and connect through social gatherings. The conference drew more than 9,000 attendees, including 2,700-plus exhibitors.

Featured speakers offered sessions fresh with ideas that offered a sense of unity in their delivery and content. The opening session featured philanthropist and author Melinda Gates, who stated that gender equity is the goal, hence her call for women's empowerment across the world. Gates was joined by NPR commentator and former librarian Nancy Pearl to discuss Gates's new book, *Moment of Lift: How Empowering Women Changes the World.* Journalist and author Isha Sesay spoke about the heartbreaking story of 276 Chibok schoolgirls kidnapped by the Boko Haram in Nigeria. She stated that the profound story had to be told, but her book, *Beneath the Tamarind Tree*, was also important to write because she could have been one of those girls. Sesay expressed her hope that the book would encourage the Nigerian government to reopen investigations, in the hope of bringing all the girls home to their families.

Other speakers included travel host and community activist Rick Steves, who passionately called for us to travel more, surrender our fears, and travel to exotic places. He stated that in years past, when someone was off to travel, the well-wisher would respond with a cheerful "Bon Voyage." Today, the well-wisher responds with a cautionary, "Be safe." Eric Klinenberg, sociologist, library champion, and author of *Palaces for the People: How Social Infrastructure Can Help Fight Inequality, Polarization, and the Decline of Civic Life*, was the Arthur Curley Memorial Lecture speaker. CEO of the Girl Scouts of the USA Sylvia Acevedo spoke about giving girls the proverbial "hand in the elevator" last-chance opportunity through her book *Path to the Stars: My Journey from Girl Scout to Rocket Scientist*. The ALA President's Program speaker, Robin DiAngelo, racial and social justice consultant and trainer and author of *White Fragility: Why It's So Hard for White People to Talk about Racism*, offered an interesting session on the dynamics of racism, beckoning us all to ask ourselves the hard questions.

A mainstay of the Midwinter Meeting is the popular ALA Youth Media Awards. Attendees flocked to the convention center early in the morning to discover the winners of the Caldecott and Newbery medals, the Coretta Scott King Book Award, and the Printz Award. Winners and honorees are selected by committees composed of librarians and other literature and media experts. Hundreds attended the live event, while thousands of the #alaleftbehind watched via live webcast. ALA's book and media award announcements are consolidated at Midwinter as the RUSA Book and Media Awards, including the announcement of the winners of the Andrew Carnegie Medals for Excellence in Fiction and Nonfiction.

ALA 2019 Annual Conference

ALA hosted its 138th Annual Conference & Exhibition June 20–25, in Washington, D.C. The conference was attended by more than 21,400 librarians, library workers and library supporters, including some 6,800 exhibitors, from across the world. ALA took advantage of the conference's location in the nation's capital to send #FundLibraries messages to the Senate. During the Opening General Session, ALA president Loida Garcia-Febo asked audience members to pull out their cell phones and text the word "library" to a prearranged number. In less than five minutes more than 4,000 messages were sent to senators, with the number climbing throughout conference.

Attendees heard from such notables as George Takei, actor, activist, and author of *They Called Us Enemy*, and Tomi Adeyemi, author of the book and soon-to-be movie *Children of Blood and Bone*. The ALA President's Program featured speaker Nnedi Okorafor, author of the book and soon-to-be HBO movie *Who Fears Death*. Among the other speakers were Thomas Wheeler and Frank Miller, creators of the illustrated novel *Cursed* and executive producers of a ten-part Netflix series based on the book, and Opening General Session speaker and author of *Long Way Down,* Jason Reynolds. In addition to the Young Adult and science-fiction/fantasy literary genres, these authors shared another common bond: the strong desire to encourage a younger generation by sharing past adversity.

Broadcast journalist and television personality Hoda Kotb, author of *You Are My Happy*, Mariana Atencio, author of *Perfectly You: Embracing the Power of Being Real*, and Mo Rocca, Closing General Session speaker and author of *Mobituaries*, all gave moving presentations. Librarian of Congress Carla Hayden invited Eric Klinenberg, professor of sociology and author of *Palaces for the People*, her special guest, to discuss the importance of libraries and the unique services they provide to their communities.

With more than 2,500 events taking place at the Walter E. Washington Convention Center and nearby locations, much of the program content focused on ALA's four strategic directions: advocacy; information policy; professional and leadership development; and equity, diversity, and inclusion. On the first day of the conference, ALA asked that attendees wear rainbow colors or pick up an inclusive rainbow pin at registration to honor the LGBTQ community, the 50th Anniversary of the Stonewall riots, and World Pride Month. The year 2019 also marked the 50th anniversary of the Coretta Scott King Book Awards, given annually to authors and illustrators of outstanding books that help children and young adults gain an appreciation of African American culture and universal human values. The award commemorates the life and work of Dr. Martin Luther King, Jr., and honors his wife, Coretta Scott King, for her courage and determination in continuing his work for peace and world brotherhood. This year's recipients were Claire Hartfield, author of *A Few Red Drops: The Chicago Race Riot of 1919*, and Ekua Holmes, illustrator of *The Stuff of Stars*. In Holmes's acceptance speech, she said that as a child she and her cousin would make their own books because there weren't books in her library about or for African American children. "These stories deserve to be heard and appreciated," she said.

Loida Garcia-Febo, 2018–2019 ALA president, passed the gavel to newly elected president Wanda Kay Brown at the conclusion of the conference. Over the course of her presidential year, Brown promised to work to promote both the value of libraries and ALA, broadly speaking, through a lens of social justice and inclusion.

ALA association business was conducted throughout the conference, including resolutions discussed by ALA Council, among them the Melvil Dewey Medal name change. The Melvil Dewey Medal is awarded annually by ALA to a person who displays creative leadership of high order in the fields of library management, library training, cataloging and classification, and the tools and techniques of librarianship. ALA Council decided to remove the name from the honor, citing Dewey's legacy of antisemitism, sexual harassment, and racism.

ACRL National Conference

More than 4,000 librarians, exhibitors, and guests gathered to reflect and rethink the role of academic librarians in a changing and challenging society at the Association of College and Research Libraries (ACRL) 2019 Conference, held April 10–13 at the Huntington Convention Center of Cleveland. Themed "Recasting the Narrative," ACRL 2019 featured more than 500 carefully selected programs and exhibits from more than 200 companies. An additional 337 attendees participated remotely through a virtual conference.

AASL National Conference

The 2019 American Association of School Librarians' (AASL) National Conference was held November 14–16 at the Kentucky International Convention Center in Louisville, Kentucky, with more than 2,500 registered attendees empowered with educational resources to strengthen, diversify, and transform teaching and learning in schools across the country. The event brought together school librarians, administrators, authors, and exhibitors at the only national conference dedicated solely to the needs of school librarians. Attendees participated in preconference workshops, author events, and more than 150 concurrent sessions that focused on common beliefs central to the school library profession, including research, literacy, advocacy, and diversity.

Highlights of the Year—Offices

Public Policy and Advocacy Office

ALA's Public Policy and Advocacy Office (PPAO) logged another record year of successes in 2019. [See ALA's report in the "Legislation" section of Part 2 in this volume—*Ed.*] Following a year of intense engagement by ALA members, Congress approved, and the president signed, a spending bill containing the largest increase in Library Services and Technology Act (LSTA) funding in 12 years. The Senate confirmed Kansas City Public Library executive Crosby Kemper III, an ALA and PLA member, as new director of the Institute of Museum and Library

Services (IMLS). During the year, ALA's #eBooksForAll campaign mobilized library advocates to publicly oppose Macmillan Publishers' embargo on new title e-book sales to libraries. [See the Special Report by Shawnda Hines and Alan Inouye on page 3 in this volume—*Ed.*]

Communications and Marketing Office

Media Relations

More than 35,100 articles mentioned ALA during 2019, with a total circulation of more than 24.7 billion. (Circulation rate is calculated using the number of articles/mentions multiplied by the monthly unique visitors for each media outlet's website.)

Libraries Transform

Libraries Transform closed out the year with more than 15,000 libraries and library advocates using the free program in all 50 states, more than 100 countries, and all 6 inhabited continents. Resources include dozens of downloadable "Because" statement graphics for print and digital media, templates and instructions for creating customized public awareness materials, and celebrity PSA videos for sharing on social media.

Office for Diversity, Literacy, and Outreach Services

Jody Gray, director of the Office for Diversity, Literacy and Outreach Services (ODLOS), left ALA effective September 6, 2019, to be replaced by assistant director for Literacy and Continuing Education Kristin Lahurd as interim director. Lahurd, who joined ALA five years earlier as literacy officer, coordinates ODLOS's continuing education efforts, including workshops and webinars on topics surrounding equity, diversity, inclusion, literacy, and outreach.

Equity, Diversity, and Inclusion

ALA's Equity, Diversity, and Inclusion Implementation Working Group (EDI-IWG) submitted a report to the ALA executive board at the 2019 Annual Conference. With the approval of the board, ODLOS shared the report with ALA staff members with the recommendation that staff consider how their units can incorporate its guiding principles and recommendations into their work going forward.

To help ALA Annual Conference attendees navigate the many equity, diversity, and inclusion opportunities at the event, ODLOS curated an EDI page on the conference page. Coverage included ALA's recognition of the indigenous peoples in present-day Washington, D.C., an interactive map of diversely owned businesses near the convention center, and a listing of all conference sessions related to equity, diversity, and inclusion.

Spectrum

The Spectrum Scholarship Program actively recruits and provides scholarships to American Indian/Alaska Native, Asian, Black/African American, Hispanic/Latino, Middle Eastern and North African, and/or Native Hawaiian/Other Pacific Islander students to assist them with obtaining graduate degrees and leadership positions within the profession and ALA. A prestigious committee of 21 jurors selected 60 Spectrum Scholars in 2019 based on commitment to equity and inclusion, demonstrated community outreach, commitment to the library profession, and leadership potential.

Anniversaries

During 2019 the Coretta Scott King Book Awards celebrated 50 years of excellence in honoring the best-of-the-best in African American literature for youth. The ALA Social Responsibilities Round Table (SRRT) also celebrated its 50th anniversary, marking decades of its commitment to fighting for human and economic rights.

International Relations Office

ALA International Relations Office (IRO) director Michael Dowling was elected to the International Federation of Library Associations and Institutions (IFLA) governing board for 2019–2021. IRO continued ALA's partnership with IFLA by hosting such webinars as "Benefits of International Exchange Programs" and "Enhancing Your Strengths through Coaching." In addition to the IFLA webinars, IRO worked with the IRRT Webinar Ad Hoc Committee to present webinars aimed to promote interests, programs, and activities on international librarianship. IRO also developed the professional content for the 6th annual Sharjah International Library Conference, November 5–7. ALA president-elect Wanda Brown served as the keynote speaker, as have previous ALA presidents.

Office for Accreditation

In 2019, during events including the ALA Midwinter Meeting, the Office for Accreditation's (COA) spring meeting in Chicago, and the ALA Annual Conference, COA awarded initial, conditional, and continued accreditation status to a number of master's programs in library and information studies. ALA accreditation indicates that a program has undergone a self-evaluation process, has been externally reviewed, and meets the accreditation standards established by COA and adopted by ALA Council. Standards address issues such as systematic planning, curriculum, faculty, students, administration, finances, and resources.

Office for Intellectual Freedom

In October ALA announced the promotion of Deborah Caldwell-Stone as director of the ALA Office for Intellectual Freedom (OIF), following her ten years of service as OIF deputy director. Caldwell-Stone will also serve as executive director for the Freedom to Read Foundation (FTRF), an allied 501(c)(3) organization that participates in freedom of speech and freedom of the press litigation. After receiving several inquiries, anecdotes, and expressions of concern about "First Amendment Audits" taking place in libraries around the country, Caldwell-Stone published an article that provided information about legal precedents and offered guidance on addressing filming in the library. *American Libraries* magazine published a follow-up article that quoted Caldwell-Stone and drew on librarians' first-hand experiences with such incidents.

Public Programs Office

Margaret "Peggy" Barber, a transformative leader in ALA and the library field who was behind the creation of National Library Week and the Celebrity READ series, passed away on August 25, 2019. Barber served as ALA's associate executive director of communications from 1970–2000. In that role, she established ALA's Public Information Office, the Public Programs Office (PPO), and the ALA Graphics department. After leaving ALA, she was a principal consultant with Library Communication Strategies and served as co-president of Friends of Libraries USA, now known as United for Libraries.

PPO highlights in 2019 included call for Libraries Transform Communities Engagement Grant applicants providing $2,000 for a school, public, academic, tribal, or special library to expand its community engagement efforts.

Publishing

ALA Editions | ALA Neal-Schuman

ALA Editions and ALA Neal-Schuman publish books and resources used worldwide by library and information professionals to improve programs, build on best practices, develop leadership, and enhance personal professional development. Books published in 2019 include *Lessons Inspired by Picture Books for Primary Grades*, by Maureen Schlosser and Rebecca Granatini; *Mother Goose on the Loose—Here, There, and Everywhere*, by Betsy Diamant-Cohen; *Community Technology Projects: Making Them Work*, by Margaret Heller; *Blockchain*, edited by Sandra Hirsh and Susan Alman, in partnership with the ALA's Center for the Future of Libraries; *Libraries and Gardens: Growing Together*, by Carrie Scott Banks and Cindy Mediavilla; *Dynamic Discipline*, by Catherine Hakala-Ausperk; *Book Club Reboot: 71 Creative Twists*, edited by Sarah Ostman and Stephanie Saba, and published in cooperation with ALA's Public Programs Office; *Create, Innovate, and Serve: A Radical Approach to Children's and Youth Programming*, by Kathleen Campana and J. Elizabeth Mills; *Library Management 101*, edited by Lisa K. Hussey and Diane L. Velasquez; *The Newbery and Caldecott Awards: A Guide to the Medal and Honor Books*, published in cooperation with the Association for Library Service to Children (ALSC); *60 Ready-to-Use Coding Projects*, by Ellyssa Kroski; *Assessment Strategies in Technical Services*, a monograph from the Association of Library Collections and Technical Services (ALCTS), edited by Kimberley A. Edwards and Michelle Leonard; *Library Web Development: Beyond Tips and Tricks*, by Jason Bengtson; *Beyond Banned Books: Defending Intellectual Freedom throughout Your Library*, by Kristin Pekoll and the Office for Intellectual Freedom (OIF); *The Public Library Director's Toolkit*, by Kate Hall and Kathy Parker (ALA Editions); and *Foundations of Information Policy*, by Paul T. Jaeger and Natalie Greene Taylor.

Also promoted were several books published by Facet Publishing, UK—including *The Freedom of Information Officer's Handbook*, by Paul Gibbons, *Practical Knowledge and Information Management*, by Katharine Schopflin and Matt Walsh, and *Partners for Preservation: Advancing Digital Preservation through Cross-Community Collaboration*, edited by Jeanne Kramer-Smyth—which are distributed in North America by ALA Editions | ALA Neal-Schuman.

The imprint also published the following ALA TechSource products in 2019: 8 issues of the subscription journal *Library Technology Reports* and 12 of the e-newsletter *Smart Libraries Newsletter.*

An ALA Editions book, *The Stories We Share: A Guide to PreK–12 Books on the Experience of Immigrant Children and Teens in the United States*, by Ladislava N. Khailova, was awarded Best Professional Resource for School or Youth Librarians—2019 SLC/ARBA Best of Reference Awards.

ALA Graphics

In 2019 ALA Graphics produced more than 60 new products, including posters, bookmarks, gifts, and incentives in support of libraries, literacy, and reading. For more than 40 years, ALA Graphics has been the home of the iconic Celebrity READ® poster campaign and exclusive art from award-winning children's book illustrators, and is also the official source of promotional materials for Banned Books Week, National Library Week, National Library Workers Day, and Library Card Sign-up Month, among other events.

Milo Ventimiglia, star of *This Is Us*, *Gilmore Girls*, and *Heroes*, and Karamo Brown, star of *Queer Eye*, joined the Celebrity READ® Campaign in 2019. Children and young adults were treated to new work by illustrator Rafael López and items featuring *Unlimited Squirrels*, *Dog Man*, *Narwhal and Jelly*, Toy Story 4, Minecraft, *Vampirina*, and *Children of Blood and Bone*, among other books and media.

ALA Graphics launched an ancillary gift shop at bit.ly/GraphicsGiftShop to offer a variety of T-shirts, mugs, and other gift items featuring its popular poster designs. The department expanded its licensing with Out of Print Clothing, launching the Star Wars READ® collection showcasing iconic Star Wars READ posters created by ALA in the 1980s and '90s.

Booklist Publications

George Kendall joined *Booklist* in June 2019 as its new editor and publisher, bringing more than 20 years' experience with a variety of publishers, including an extensive background in content strategy, digital innovation, web development, and team leadership. Former editor/publisher Bill Ott retired in April 2019 after 39 years on the *Booklist* staff, 30 of them at the helm.

Booklist's internationally recognized, award-winning staff published 26 issues in 2019. The publication remains one of the most trusted collection development and readers' advisory resources in the field, publishing more than 8,000 original reviews annually. In 2019 *Booklist* offered more than 150 columns, essays, author interviews, lists, read-alikes, and related content. The *Booklist* website, with its array of diverse online products such as e-newsletters, webinars, and podcasts, continues to offer engaging and effective ways for librarians to keep up to date on publishing trends, library topics, and professional development.

Booklist is the sponsor and cosponsor of various ALA media awards including the Andrew Carnegie Medals for Excellence in Fiction and Nonfiction, the Michael L. Printz Award, the William C. Morris Award, and the Odyssey Award.

American Libraries Magazine

American Libraries is the flagship publication of the ALA and its 57,000 members, covering news, trends, professional development, commentary, and product information. It is published six times per year, plus one digital-only issue and occasional supplements. During the year more than 220 online-only features and Scoop blog posts were published at American Libraries Online (americanlibraries.org). The publication's top 2019 stories and topics included Macmillan Publisher's e-book embargo, net neutrality, United States supreme court justice Sonia Sotomayor's support for libraries, librarians going without pay during the 2019 government shutdown, Chicago Public Library's fine-free approach, the Right to be Forgotten, the "Dear Appropriator" letter campaign, Supreme Court blocks Census question, ALA's Dewey Medal name change, librarian Emma Boettcher's Jeopardy wins, and multiple anniversaries including PLA's 75th anniversary and the 50th anniversaries of ALA's Social Responsibility Round Table, the Coretta Scott King Book Awards, and the Stonewall Inn riots.

American Libraries offers digital content including through AL Direct, the publication's award-winning, twice-weekly e-newsletter, delivered to nearly 40,000 library professionals and covering library activities, facilities, events, state and federal legislation, and news; and *Dewey Decibel*, a monthly half-hour podcast featuring conversations with librarians, authors, celebrities, and scholars on topics affecting the library world.

Divisions

Association for Library Collections and Technical Services

Preservation in Action (PiA) is a program sponsored by the Preservation and Reformatting Section (PARS) of the Association for Library Collections and Technical Services (ALCTS) in support of ALA's Libraries Transform initiative. The program is intended to promote an understanding of the importance of preservation while engaging with cultural heritage collections in ALA conference locations. At the 2019 ALA Annual Conference in Washington, D.C., Preservation in Action provided a hands-on opportunity to help preserve local cultural heritage. Participants took part in a day-long preservation project with the District of Columbia Public Library, Special Collections. The day included preservation care and handling training and hands-on rehousing activities. Working with archival collections, primarily with damaged and fragile books from the division's Cutter Collection, participants learned about the preservation needs of these types of materials, appropriate storage, and best practices. ALCTS Monographs included *Sudden Position Guide to Cataloging and Metadata* (ALCTS Sudden Position Series #1), edited by Jeremy Myntti, and *Assessment Strategies in Technical Services*, edited by Kimberley A. Edwards and Michelle Leonard.

American Association of School Librarians

After releasing its National School Library Standards for Learners, School Librarian, and School Libraries in 2018, the American Association of School Librarians (AASL) worked to develop and offer implementation tools for school librarians.

AASL District Kits for the standards, with support of Bound to Stay Bound, were distributed to 100 districts nationwide. In addition, AASL past presidents developed a grant program offering $2,500 per state to school library association recipients in support of the planning and execution of events, initiatives, and activities focused on implementing the AASL standards.

The AASL School Leader Collaborative: Administrators & School Librarians Transforming Teaching and Learning was launched and aims to strengthen AASL's collaboration with school administrators. With support from OverDrive Education, the two-year initiative will engage with an audience vital to the success of school librarian advocacy: school administrators. Seven school administrators were selected to serve on the AASL School Leader Collaborative.

AASL released a new resource, the Developing Inclusive Learners and Citizens Activity Guide, that supports school librarians in nurturing inclusive learning communities, offering reflection activities and resources based on one of the six shared foundations contained within the National School Library Standards.

Association of College and Research Libraries

The Association of College and Research Libraries (ACRL) is dedicated to creating diverse and inclusive communities in the association and in academic and research libraries through the association's core commitment to Equity, Diversity, and Inclusion (EDI). A new ACRL Equity, Diversity, and Inclusion LibGuide launched in 2019, containing a wealth of information on ways ACRL has implemented the association's core commitment, including the ACRL Diversity Alliance; standards and guidelines; information on conference and online learning programming; links to books, articles, and other publications focusing on EDI topics; and a calendar of association activities.

The association released a report entitled "Open and Equitable Scholarly Communications: Creating a More Inclusive Future," by Nancy Maron and Rebecca Kennison with Paul Bracke, Nathan Hall, Isaac Gilman, Kara Malenfant, Charlotte Roh, and Yasmeen Shorish. The report makes an important contribution to ACRL's core commitment to EDI, which includes valuing different ways of knowing and identifying and working to eliminate barriers to equitable services, spaces, resources, and scholarship.

ACRL, ALA, and the Association of Research Libraries (ARL) extended their Joint Advisory Task Force through August 31, 2022, to continue efforts to bring the Integrated Postsecondary Education Data System (IPEDS) Academic Libraries Component up-to-date and in-line with current library practices.

A revised version of the "ACRL Policy Statement on Open Access to Scholarship by Academic Librarians" was approved in 2019. Written by ACRL's Research and Scholarly Environment Committee (ReSEC), the revision addresses the sense of the "across the lifecycle" nature of scholarly communication interest in open access.

Association for Library Service to Children

The Association for Library Service to Children's (ALSC) Public Awareness Committee created the Championing Children's Services Toolkit, which encompasses a variety of easy-to-use advocacy resources to empower children's services staff to engage their communities in building healthy successful futures for children. The suite of materials includes a toolkit formatted as a series of "Because Statements," a video featuring children's author Meg Medina, a customizable PowerPoint template, printable postcards, and an Early Learning and Development Standards infographic.

ALSC awarded fourteen $5,000 Strengthening Communities through Libraries mini-grants to members in public libraries. The grants were made possible by the Dollar General Literacy Foundation to support library efforts to provide learning that focuses on STEAM (Science, Technology, Engineering, the Arts, and Mathematics) for children during breaks and in after-school programs.

Throughout 2019 ALSC produced a variety of free digital booklists to support young readers as they explore STEAM and difficult topics, including Building STEAM with Día, Embracing Gender Identities, Graphic Novels, Summer Reading, and Tough Topics.

Public Library Association

The Public Library Association (PLA) officially turned 75 years old on October 13, 2019. PLA continues to work tirelessly to support the unique and evolving needs of public library professionals through its membership and leadership, advocacy, professional development, and special initiatives.

In 2019 Michelle Jeske, city librarian and executive director of Denver (Colorado) Public Library, was elected to the office of 2020–2021 PLA president, following 2019–2020 president Ramiro S. Salazar of the San Antonio (Texas) Public Library. Also elected to three-year terms on the PLA board, as directors-at-large, were Amita Lonial, assistant library director of the Tacoma (Washington) Public Library and Toby Greenwalt, director of digital strategy at the Carnegie Library of Pittsburgh (Pennsylvania). A ballot measure to add a fiscal officer's position to the PLA board was approved, and Clara Nalli Bohrer of the West Bloomfield Township (Michigan) Public Library was appointed to the seat.

PLA worked closely with ALA and other library organizations to respond to Macmillan Publishers' embargo on library e-book lending. PLA released a statement condemning Macmillan's library lending model, sent by PLA's board of directors to Macmillan CEO John Sargent. PLA members, including 2019–2020 president Ramiro S. Salazar, Kent Oliver of the Nashville (Tennessee) Public Library, and Patrick Losinski of the Columbus (Ohio) Metropolitan Library, spoke at a September 18, 2019, press conference in Nashville announcing the launch of a national campaign against the e-book embargo. Consistent communications including e-newsletter articles, direct e-mails, social media posts, and website updates have motivated PLA members to sign the online petition, submit op-eds to their local newspapers, and inform library patrons about the embargo's impact on e-book availability.

PLA expanded its special initiatives that help libraries tackle challenging community needs such as digital literacy, access to government services, and diversity. Through its health insurance enrollment and education initiative, Libraries Connecting You to Coverage, PLA awarded $500 mini-grants to 57 public libraries to help them encourage enrollment in the Affordable Care Act (ACA). PLA also released a new online tutorial on DigitalLearn.org to help consumers sign up for health insurance.

PLA provided more than 300 public access computers and wifi hotspots to 42 rural public libraries. PLA also supported the ALA program Libraries Lead with Digital Skills and the related Grow with Google tour, which included free, one-day events hosted at dozens of local libraries nationwide and microfunding to libraries to provide programming, outreach, and education on digital skills. PLA's Inclusive Internship Initiative held its third cohort, enlisting 48 public libraries across the United States to host a high-school-aged intern for ten weeks of learning, networking, and career development. Finally, Project Outcome, PLA's platform to help libraries measure the impacts of their programs and services, expanded in two significant ways in 2019: a new set of questions was released to evaluate health-related programming, and a companion product was developed with the Association of College and Research Libraries (ACRL) to serve academic libraries.

As 2019 ended, PLA was putting the finishing touches on the PLA 2020 Conference, taking place February 25–29, 2020, in Nashville, Tennessee. An impressive slate of featured speakers, including Stacey Abrams, Dr. Bettina Love, Haben Girma, Soledad O'Brien, and Samantha Bee, and more than 110 educational programs are planned.

United for Libraries

United for Libraries partnered with ALA Publishing on a new workshop: "Equity, Diversity, Inclusion: What Library Trustees Need to Know." In this event, Anne Phibbs, Ph.D., and founder and president of Strategic Diversity Initiatives, gave a basic introduction to equity, diversity, and inclusion (EDI) and discussed what library trustees and boards need to know about EDI.

Several Literary Landmarks were designated by United for Libraries in 2019. Sites included Ray Bradbury Park in Waukegan, Illinois, the Harvin-Clarendon County Public Library in Manning, South Carolina; Vera's Story Garden in Monticello, New York; the Schenectady County Public Library in Schenectady, New York; the Berkshire Athenaeum in Pittsfield, Massachusetts; the Cannon Free Library in Delhi, New York; and the Arthenia J. Bates Millican Home in Sumter, South Carolina.

Library trustees, directors, and staff from more than 250 public libraries in Alabama and Wyoming now have access to Short Takes for Trustees, a series of ten short videos that can be shown during trustee meetings to stimulate discussion about the important role that trustees play in the governance of their libraries. The videos were made possible by the Alabama Public Library Service and the Wyoming State Library.

Working together, United for Libraries, PLA, and the ALA Development Office supported Library Giving Day through promotion in newsletters, member e-mails, and social media. Building on this successful partnership was the International Public Library Fundraising Conference, held in Calgary, Alberta, Canada, July 28–30, 2019.

Young Adult Library Services Association

Tammy Dillard-Steels, MPH, MBA, CAE joined the Young Adult Library Services Association (YALSA) as executive director in 2019. Dillard previously served as executive director of the American Academy of Matrimonial Lawyers (AAML) and as a regional director at American College of Healthcare Executives (ACHE).

YALSA announced a new nationwide teen celebration, TeenTober, to be hosted by libraries every October. TeenTober replaces YALSA's previous Teen Read Week™ and Teen Tech Week™ celebrations, allowing libraries the flexibility to celebrate all types of literacies according to their library's schedule.

Through funding from the Institute of Museum and Library Services (IMLS) and in partnership with the Chief Officers of State Library Agencies (COSLA), YALSA solicited applicants for the second cohort of its Transforming Teen Services: A Train the Trainer Approach project. This effort brings together state library agency (SLA) youth consultants and frontline library staff for a robust training program. By implementing a training program for and with youth services representative from each of the 50 SLAs, as well as frontline library staff, YALSA and COSLA will achieve the next step toward developing a coordinated, efficient, and effective process for transforming teen services throughout the United States, so that teen programs and services enhance civic and cultural engagement, facilitate lifelong learning, promote digital inclusion, and support economic vitality.

With additional funding from IMLS and in partnership with the Association of Rural and Small Libraries, YALSA solicited applicants for the fourth cohort of the Future Ready with the Library project. This project provides small, rural, and tribal library staff the opportunity to work with a community partner to build services that support middle school college readiness and career awareness.

YALSA also teamed up with Dollar General to offer the YALSA/DGLF Digital Equipment Grant. Funded by the Dollar General Literacy Foundation (DGLF), ten libraries in need were awarded $1,000 each to purchase digital equipment to help engage teen patrons in their communities.

YALSA announced its 2019 Teens' Top Ten, a "teen choice" list developed by teens nominating and choosing their favorite books of the previous year. Nominators are members of teen book groups in 15 school and public libraries around the country. Nominations are posted on the Thursday of National Library Week, and teens across the country vote on their favorite titles each year. Readers ages 12 to 18 voted online between August 15 and October 12 on the Teens' Top Ten site. The winners were announced the following week.

YALSA's 2019 symposium was held November 1–3 in Memphis, Tennessee, with the theme "Show Up and Advocate: Supporting Teens in the Face of Adversity." The Symposium included a Book Blitz where registrants received up to five free books.

Membership Development and Customer Service

Melissa Kay Walling, CAE, IOM began serving as the new director of ALA Membership and Customer Service on June 17, 2019. Walling is an accomplished association executive with nearly 15 years of experience serving members, staff, and volunteers. She comes to ALA most recently having served as vice president of education and membership at the Association Forum of Chicagoland, where she oversaw the execution of the Holiday Showcase.

National Celebrations and Observances

Money Smart Week

From March 30 through April 6, 2019, ALA's Chapter Relations Office (CRO) partnered with the Federal Reserve Bank of Chicago for Money Smart Week©—a national campaign that offers thousands of free events to help consumers better manage their personal finances.

National Library Week

First sponsored in 1958, National Library Week is sponsored by ALA and observed in libraries across the country each April. All types of libraries—school, public, academic, and special—participate.

National Library Week events included the release of the 2019 State of America's Libraries Report on April 8, including OIF's Top 10 Most Challenged Books list, National Library Workers Day on April 9, National Bookmobile Day on April 10, and Take Action for Libraries Day. April also is celebrated as School Library Month.

The theme for 2019 National Library Week, April 7–13, 2019 was "Libraries = Strong Communities," with Gates Foundation cofounder Melinda Gates serving as 2019 National Library Week Honorary Chair.

On April 8 the ALA Office for Intellectual Freedom released the Top 10 Most Challenged Books of 2018 list, highlighting 11 titles opposed to 10, due to a tie in rankings. In 2018 OIF tracked 347 challenges to library, school, and university materials and services and a total of 483 challenged or banned books.

Preservation Week

During Preservation Week, April 21–27, libraries, archives, and museums globally presented events, activities, and resources that highlight what we can do, individually and together, to preserve our personal and shared history. Preservation Week was created in 2010 to address the concern that some 630 million items in collecting institutions require immediate attention and care. Eighty percent of these institutions have no paid staff assigned to collections care, and 22 percent have no collections care personnel at all. Some 2.6 billion items are not protected by an emergency plan. As natural disasters of recent years have taught us, these resources are in jeopardy should a disaster strike. Personal, family, and community collections are equally at risk.

Día (El día de los niños, El día de los libros/Children's Day, Book Day)

Libraries across the country hosted Día events on and around April 30, 2019, to highlight the importance of sharing diverse books with children. ALSC has updated its free downloadable resources, including booklists featuring STEAM-related titles, web graphics, customizable event posters, and program registry on the dia.ala.org website.

Choose Privacy Week

From May 1–7, the Office for Intellectual Freedom joined the IFC Privacy Subcommittee in observing Choose Privacy Week. The theme, "Inclusive Privacy: Closing the Gap," focused on the privacy inequities imposed on vulnerable and historically underrepresented populations and highlighted how libraries can close the privacy gap for persons belonging to these communities. The week included an online symposium that featured commentaries by librarians, educators, and privacy experts addressing disability and privacy, student privacy, library privacy for LGBTQ youth, the privacy concerns of formerly incarcerated persons, immigrants' privacy, government surveillance, and conversations on why privacy matters in the library.

Gay, Lesbian, Bisexual, Transgender Book (GLBT) Month

June marked the fourth GLBT Book Month, celebrating authors and writings that reflect the LGBTQ+ experience. Originally established in the early 1990s by the Publishing Triangle as National Lesbian and Gay Book Month, this occasion is an opportunity for book lovers and libraries to connect with and support the best in GLBT literature.

Library Card Sign-up Month

September is Library Card Sign-up Month, a time when ALA and libraries nationwide join together to remind parents, caregivers, and students that signing up for a library card is the first step toward academic achievement and lifelong learning.

Banned Books Week

From September 22 through September 28, 2019, the Office for Intellectual Freedom (OIF) observed Banned Books Week, the annual event that celebrates the freedom to read and draws attention to the harms of censorship. This year OIF promoted and celebrated Banned Books Week under the banner theme of "Censorship Leaves Us in the Dark. Keep the Light On."

To kick off Banned Books Week at ALA in 2019, OIF partnered with City Lit Theater to host a "Books on the Chopping Block" performance at ALA headquarters. OIF also launched a new Celebrating Banned Books Week Facebook group. OIF's Dear Banned Author letter-writing campaign encouraged readers to reach out to banned and challenged authors during Banned Books Week, sharing what their words mean to them. OIF also partnered with the nonprofit organization Every Child a Reader to publish a list of 100 Frequently Challenged Children's Books, in celebration of the 100th anniversary of Children's Book Week. Titles include the Junie B. Jones series, *The Watsons Go to Birmingham—1963*; *Matilda*; and *Daddy's Roommate*. The list is available on the Every Child a Reader website.

New Fellowship

Lois Ann Gregory-Wood worked at ALA for 50 years, serving for 27 of those years as ALA Council secretariat. For thousands of ALA members, she was the face of ALA Council and governance. The Lois Ann Gregory-Wood Fellows Program celebrates her leadership and accomplishments, as well as seeking to encourage understanding and participation in ALA governance processes.

American Booksellers Association

333 Westchester Ave., Suite 202, White Plains, NY 10604
915-406-7500
World Wide Web http://www.bookweb.org

Founded in 1900, the American Booksellers Association (ABA) is a national not-for-profit trade organization headquartered in White Plains, New York, that works to help independently owned bookstores grow and succeed. Recognizing the key cultural and economic roles that independent bookstores play in their communities, ABA provides information, education, business tools, programs, and advocacy for local businesses across the country, working to strengthen and expand independent bookstores.

The association actively supports and defends free speech and the First Amendment rights of all Americans. A volunteer board of 11 booksellers governs the association.

At the end of 2019, for the tenth year in a row, ABA bookstore membership grew. There were 1,887 bookstore members operating in 2,524 locations nationwide. This is a 35 percent increase in the number of ABA member stores since 2009. During the year ABA welcomed 111 new indie bookstore members, an increase of approximately 12 stores over the previous year. The new stores included a romance bookstore, a veteran-owned bookstore, a youth-based bookstore, a bookmobile, and 20 branches of existing businesses. In addition, 25 established member stores were bought by new owners.

On Saturday, November 30, 2019, for the seventh year running, independent booksellers across the country took part in "Indies First" celebrations on Small Business Saturday. Stores held sales and presented an array of author events and other activities to kick off the holiday shopping season. Indie bookstore sales for the week that included Small Business Saturday were up 1.6 percent nationally, and Cyber Monday 2019 was the single highest online sales day recorded for ABA's IndieCommerce and IndieLite online platforms, with sales up 27 percent over Cyber Monday 2018.

Science fiction and fantasy author N. K. Jemison, who served as the 2019 spokesperson for Indies First, signed copies of her books at Greenlight Bookstore, WORD Bookstore, and Café con Libros in Brooklyn, New York, on Small Business Saturday. Jemison, *New York Times* bestselling author of *How Long 'Til Black Future Month?* and the Hugo Award–winning *The Obelisk Gate*, created a special Indies First promotional video and tweeted regularly leading up to the event.

On December 5, 2019, bestselling author James Patterson announced the names of a record 500 independent booksellers selected to receive $500 grants each, totaling $250,000, through his 2019 Holiday Bookstore Bonus Program. Two thousand five hundred forty-one booksellers were nominated to receive bonuses, and Patterson personally selected the 500 winners, which included 100 designated children's booksellers.

"I've said this many times before, but I can't say it enough: booksellers save lives," Patterson said. "Children's booksellers especially—they guide children to books they'll enjoy and, in turn, create a new generation of readers."

Now in its sixth year, the bonus program is a partnership between Patterson and ABA. For 2019, customers, booksellers, publishing industry colleagues, and others were invited to nominate a bookseller by answering the grant application's single question: "Why does this bookseller deserve a holiday bonus?" The chosen booksellers were lauded for their perseverance, enthusiasm, hand-selling expertise, and dedication to books and reading.

Also in 2019, the fifth Independent Bookstore Day (IBD)—held annually on the last Saturday in April—enjoyed the record participation of 580 indie bookstores nationwide. Participating stores featured author readings and signings, bookstore crawls, exclusive merchandise, unique events, and special pricing for book buyers.

In November ABA announced two recipients of the association's inaugural Entrepreneurial Excellence Award: Billie Bloebaum of Third Street Books in McMinnville, Oregon, who created Bookstore Romance Day, and Nicole Magistro of the Bookworm of Edwards in Edwards, Colorado, who created the Adopt-a-Reader program. The new annual award recognizes and celebrates the achievements of booksellers whose ideas, creativity, and execution have improved store operations, fostered community relationships, inspired new efficiencies, created a more inclusive environment, saved money, or increased sales. Bloebaum and Magistro each received a full scholarship to ABA's Winter Institute 2020 in Baltimore, Maryland, covering up to five nights in the host hotel, travel costs, and a stipend of $1,000.

Association and Governance

The results of balloting by the bookstore members of ABA to elect four directors to serve on the ABA board were announced in May 2019. Elected to three-year terms (2019–2022) as directors were Jenny Cohen of Waucoma Bookstore in Hood River, Oregon; Bradley Graham of Politics and Prose Bookstore in Washington, D.C.; Kris Kleindienst of Left Bank Books in St. Louis, Missouri; and Chris Morrow of Northshire Bookstore in Manchester Center, Vermont, and Saratoga Springs, New York.

Voting booksellers elected ABA vice president Jamie Fiocco of Flyleaf Books in Chapel Hill, North Carolina, for a two-year term as ABA president, with Bradley Graham elected ABA vice president / secretary.

Continuing on the 11-member board are Kenny Brechner of Devaney, Doak and Garrett Booksellers in Farmington, Maine; Pete Mulvihill of Green Apple Books in San Francisco, California; Christine Onorati of WORD Bookstores in Brooklyn, New York, and Jersey City, New Jersey; Kelly Estep of Carmichael's Bookstore in Louisville, Kentucky; and Angela Maria Spring of Duende District Bookstore in Washington, D.C., and Albuquerque, New Mexico. Tegan Tigani of Queen Anne Book Company in Seattle, Washington, was appointed to fill a vacancy on the board resulting from the election of Fiocco as incoming president.

Long-Serving ABA CEO Oren Teicher Retires

In March 2019 longtime ABA chief executive officer Oren J. Teicher announced his plans to retire at the end of the year. In October ABA announced that Allison Hill, CEO of Vroman's Bookstore in Pasadena, California, would replace Teicher, joining the organization as CEO effective March 1, 2020. In addition to the appointment of Hill, ABA announced that Joy Dallanegra-Sanger, ABA's senior program officer, would become the association's chief operating officer (COO), effective November 1.

Teicher, who became CEO of ABA in 2009, previously served the association as director of government affairs, founding president of the American Booksellers Foundation for Free Expression, chief operating officer, and associate executive director from 1990 to 2009.

Robert Sindelar, then-ABA board president, credited Teicher with helping to transform the retail landscape for indie booksellers. "His tireless efforts working on behalf of our member stores have helped make significant changes to the independent bookstore business model, and the growth and success so many of our stores are experiencing are due to his vision and leadership. It's hard to imagine the current indie bookstore landscape without Oren being a key part of it," Sindelar said.

On September 9 the National Book Foundation, presenter of the National Book Awards, announced that Teicher would receive its 2019 Literarian Award for Outstanding Service to the American Literary Community.

"I am deeply humbled and greatly honored to have been selected," said Teicher. "And while I will graciously accept the award on my behalf, I know that this recognition is appropriately shared by the thousands of indie booksellers who are a part of my extended family and have given me the opportunity to work on their behalf all these years."

During Teicher's tenure as ABA CEO, from 2009 to 2019, the number of independent bookstores in the United States grew from 1,651 to 2,534, with ABA membership and store sales increasing in lockstep.

Book Awards

In May 2019 booksellers at independent bookstores nationwide selected the winners of the 2019 Indies Choice Book Awards and the E. B. White Read-Aloud Awards in eight categories.

The 2019 **Indies Choice Book Award Winners**, reflecting the spirit of independent bookstores, are

- Adult Fiction: *Circe: A Novel*, by Madeline Miller (Lee Boudreaux Books)
- Adult Nonfiction: *Educated: A Memoir*, by Tara Westover (Random House)
- Adult Debut: *There There: A Novel*, by Tommy Orange (Knopf)
- Audiobook: *Circe: A Novel*, by Madeline Miller, read by Perdita Weeks (Hachette Audio)
- Young Adult: *The Poet X*, by Elizabeth Acevedo (HarperTeen)

The winners of the **E. B. White Read-Aloud Awards**, reflecting the playful, well-paced language, engaging themes, and universal appeal embodied by E. B. White's collection of beloved books, are

- Middle Reader: *Ghost Boys*, by Jewell Parker Rhodes (Little, Brown Books for Young Readers)

- Picture Book: *We Don't Eat Our Classmates*, by Ryan T. Higgins (Disney-Hyperion)

The **Indie Champion Award** is presented to the author or illustrator who booksellers feel understands the importance of independent bookstores to their communities at large and has a strong personal commitment to foster and support the mission and passion of independent booksellers. The 2019 winner is

- Jacqueline Woodson

Classic picture books chosen by indie booksellers for induction into the **Picture Book Hall of Fame** are

- *The Circus Ship*, by Chris Van Dusen (Candlewick)
- *Grandfather's Journey*, by Allen Say (HMH Books for Young Readers)
- *Why Mosquitoes Buzz in People's Ears*, by Verna Aardema and Leo and Diane Dillon (Illus.) (Dial Books)

In addition to the winners, five honorees were named in each category, with the exception of the Picture Book Hall of Fame. The 2019 **Honor Award** recipients are

- Adult Fiction: *An American Marriage: A Novel*, by Tayari Jones (Algonquin Books); *Convenience Store Woman: A Novel*, by Sayaka Murata, Ginny Tapley Takemori (Trans.) (Grove Press); *The Overstory: A Novel*, by Richard Powers (W. W. Norton & Company); *Tin Man: A Novel*, by Sarah Winman (G. P. Putnam's Sons); *Waiting for Eden: A Novel*, by Elliot Ackerman (Knopf)
- Adult Nonfiction: *All You Can Ever Know: A Memoir*, by Nicole Chung (Catapult); *Heartland: A Memoir of Working Hard and Being Broke in the Richest Country on Earth,* by Sarah Smarsh (Scribner); *Heavy: An American Memoir*, by Kiese Laymon (Scribner); *The Library Book*, by Susan Orlean (Simon & Schuster); *The Recovering: Intoxication and Its Aftermath*, by Leslie Jamison (Little, Brown Company)
- Adult Debut: *Friday Black: Stories*, by Nana Kwame Adjei-Brenyah (Mariner Books); *My Sister, the Serial Killer: A Novel*, by Oyinkan Braithwaite (Doubleday); *Only Killers and Thieves: A Novel*, by Paul Howarth (Harper); *The Line Becomes a River: Dispatches from the Border*, by Francisco Cantú (Riverhead); *The Tattooist of Auschwitz: A Novel*, by Heather Morris (Harper Paperbacks)
- Audiobook: *Educated: A Memoir*, by Tara Westover, read by Julia Whelan (Random House Audio); *Kill the Farm Boy: The Tales of Pell*, by Kevin Hearne, Delilah S. Dawson, read by Luke Daniels (Random House Audio); *Once Upon a River: A Novel*, by Diane Setterfield, read by Juliet Stevenson (Simon & Schuster Audio); *The Secrets Between Us: A Novel*, by Thrity Umrigar, read by Sneha Mathan (HarperAudio); *There There: A Novel*,

by Tommy Orange, read by Darrell Dennis, Shaun Taylor-Corbett, Alma Cuervo, and Kyla Garcia (Random House Audio)

- Young Adult: *Darius the Great Is Not Okay*, by Adib Khorram (Dial Books); *The Hazel Wood*, by Melissa Albert (Flatiron Books); *Hey, Kiddo*, by Jarrett J. Krosoczka (Graphix); *The Prince and the Dressmaker*, by Jen Wang (First Second); *Undead Girl Gang: A Novel*, by Lily Anderson (Razorbill)

E. B. White Read-Aloud Honor Books

- Middle Reader: *The Creature of the Pines (Unicorn Rescue Society)*, by Adam Gidwitz, Hatem Aly (Illus.) (Dutton Books for Young Readers); *Front Desk*, by Kelly Yang (Arthur A. Levine Books); *Love Sugar Magic: A Dash of Trouble*, by Anna Meriano, Mirelle Ortega (Illus.) (Walden Pond Press); *The Serpent's Secret (Kiranmala and the Kingdom Beyond #1)*, by Sayantani DasGupta (Scholastic Press); *Sweep: The Story of a Girl and Her Monster*, by Jonathan Auxier (Amulet Books)
- Picture Book: *The Day You Begin*, by Jacqueline Woodson, Rafael López (Illus.) (Nancy Paulsen Books); *Harriet Gets Carried Away*, by Jessie Sima (Simon & Schuster Books for Young Readers); *How to Be a Lion*, by Ed Vere (Doubleday Books for Young Readers); *The Rabbit Listened*, by Cori Doerrfeld (Dial Books); *Thank You Omu*, by Oge Mora (Little, Brown Books for Young Readers)

Indie Champion Honorees

- Hanif Abdurraqib
- Walter Isaacson
- Tayari Jones
- A. S. King
- Dav Pilkey

Award winners and honor books in all categories with the exceptions of Indie Champion and Picture Book Hall of Fame were chosen from titles appearing on the Indie Next Lists in 2018, with additional titles for the E. B. White Read-Aloud Awards nominated by bookseller members of the ABC Children's Group at ABA.

Membership Education and Events

ABA Winter Institute

The 14th annual ABA Winter Institute (Wi14), held in Albuquerque, New Mexico, January 22–25, 2019, drew a record number of booksellers, publishers, authors, and international guests from as far as Colombia, New Zealand, and Sweden. Approximately 700 booksellers from 387 stores joined more than 150 authors and 120 publisher partners for the event, which included an opening reception on Tuesday and continued with three full days of programming, including keynote presentations, educational sessions, the ABA Town Hall, and a popular author cocktail reception.

In his opening remarks on Tuesday, January 22, ABA CEO Oren Teicher noted that stores in all 50 states were represented at Wi14, with 200 booksellers attending for the first time. He thanked Shelf Awareness for sponsoring the opening reception, as it has done since the first gathering 13 years earlier in Long Beach, California, as well as lead sponsor Ingram Content Group and the growing roster of large and small publishers taking part.

Educational offerings lured many booksellers to the classroom for small business management seminars on staff management and human resources, strategic in-store merchandising, and used bookstore operations, as well as for the Paz "Introduction to Retail Bookselling" workshop and the IndieCommerce Institute.

Sessions on Wednesday addressed such topics as selling international and diverse books, hosting A+ educator nights, lowering the cost of goods, programs and partnerships to empower women, and maximizing and marketing preorders. Booksellers heard about new and upcoming titles during the Rep Picks lunch and attended one-on-one meetings with the IndieCommerce team.

Thursday's keynote featured author Margaret Atwood in conversation with Erin Morgenstern. Atwood reflected on her writing career, discussing the success of *The Handmaid's Tale* and offering insights on its forthcoming sequel, *The Testaments*.

The day continued with sessions on publisher event grids, developing leaders in your store, using ABACUS as a budgeting tool, building successful relationships with publishers, and the Open Discussion Project, which aims to promote civil conversation among left- and right-leaning individuals through book clubs held at independent bookstores across the United States.

At the Wi14 Town Hall meeting, booksellers had an opportunity to speak up about a number of issues, including ABA's actions on diversity since the last town hall, the challenge of a rising minimum wage, the importance of ABACUS, and issues with book supplies during the holidays.

On Friday, January 25, the final day of Wi14, booksellers began the morning by hearing about upcoming titles from some of the event's publisher-sponsors, then met with those and other publishers for further discussion. The day's education sessions included managing a multilocation business, mixing bookstores and bars, thriving as a new bookstore owner, planning for store longevity, and creating dazzling in-store displays.

Regional Spring Forums

All indie booksellers, ABA members and nonmembers alike, were invited to take part in ABA's 2019 Spring Forums. Held in conjunction with regional bookseller association meetings that take place annually each spring, the forums provide an opportunity for booksellers to discuss industry issues, share their ideas and concerns, and hear updates on ABA projects.

At each of the 10 regional forums, ABA presented an update on two initiatives critical to the success of any independent bookstore: an active preorders campaign and participation in the annual ABACUS financial survey. This new educational session focused on best practices for increasing preorders based on in-store experiences and feedback from ABA's Pre-Order Booksellers Task Force. Also provided was an overview of ABACUS data, including how participating stores can use their ABACUS reports to make sound financial decisions.

BookExpo

From May 29–31, 2019, more than 1,000 indie booksellers from across the country descended on New York City's Jacob K. Javits Center for the annual BookExpo trade show. In between educational sessions, author signings, and networking opportunities, ABA member booksellers and other publishing industry professionals roamed the floor to discover new books and catch up with colleagues.

The ABA Member Lounge, located among the nonbook offerings in the UnBound section of the trade show floor, was the place for booksellers to relax, have a snack, pick up galleys, and meet with ABA staff and fellow booksellers. This year, in addition to IndieCommerce one-on-ones, the lounge featured roundtable discussions led by ABA board members as well as discussions for users of various point-of-sale systems.

ABA's Town Hall and Annual Membership Meeting were held on Thursday afternoon, May 30, during BookExpo. The meeting included the formal announcement of ABA's May board election results, reports from outgoing ABA president Robert Sindelar and CEO Oren Teicher, a membership and financial update, and the opportunity for members to bring old and/or new business to the attention of the board of directors.

Sindelar's remarks were followed by the report of the vice president/secretary, Jamie Fiocco, owner of Flyleaf Books in Chapel Hill, North Carolina, and incoming ABA president. In her report, Fiocco announced the results of the ABA 2019 board election and provided an update on membership numbers, which she noted had risen again in 2018. On behalf of the board, Fiocco thanked retiring ABA CEO Oren Teicher for his "leadership and tireless dedication to independent bookselling and the book industry."

At Thursday's Town Hall, among the topics raised for discussion by booksellers were health insurance, electronic invoicing systems, rising minimum wages, publisher direct-to-consumer and B2B sales, getting involved in the ABACUS survey, publisher publicity and sales relationships, mentoring and programming for new booksellers, and the impact of Chinese tariffs on sales and profits. ABA board members and staff addressed many of the issues and noted areas for future study and action.

New Children's Town Hall Debuts during Ci7 in Pittsburgh

ABA held its inaugural Children's Institute Town Hall on Thursday, June 27, in Pittsburgh, Pennsylvania, in conjunction with the seventh annual Children's Institute (Ci7). Booksellers discussed the prospect of ABA developing more specific education for different types of stores, such as microstores, nonprofits, and hybrid stores; the Trump administration's proposed tariffs on Chinese goods; Baker and Taylor's recent decision to stop serving the retail book market; and the way children's books are perceived in the public eye as well as by publishers, among many other topics.

Popular Meetup Series Continues; ABACUS Provides Business Insight

Enthusiasm for ABA's online roundtable discussions, or meetups, continued to grow in 2019. ABA offers two such opportunities for live online interaction and education: a twice-monthly Marketing Meetup and a monthly Technology Meetup. All member booksellers are invited to participate.

In October 2019 ABA provided member bookstores participating in the 2018 ABACUS financial benchmarking survey with customized reports. Designed to provide easy-to-understand guidelines for identifying business performance improvement opportunities, the reports were generated based on financial data supplied by more than 300 independent bookstores from across the United States. The ABACUS report presents a company's own ratios alongside appropriate industry comparatives. In addition to the customized report, all survey participants have access to online reporting tools that sort by geographic region, number of employees, number of locations, square footage, and more. Via a secure online dashboard that offers sophisticated analytical tools, booksellers can run dynamic reports and explore trends across several criteria.

Advocacy

ABA's vigorous advocacy efforts on behalf of member bookstores continued throughout 2019. From underwriting studies that demonstrate the economic impact of independent retailers to spreading the powerful message of the IndieBound movement and networking with like-minded organizations, ABA is working to strengthen awareness about the crucial role independent retailers play in local economies and communities.

ABA's Advocacy Action Kit (AdvoKit) was created to help independent booksellers advocate on any number of issues, from minimum wage, access to capital, and e-fairness to overtime rules. The AdvoKit provides booksellers with crucial, state-specific tools to help them in their e-fairness and outreach efforts.

Among its key advocacy activities in 2019, ABA focused resources on the issue of states and communities giving away millions of dollars in tax subsidies to large retail corporations, growing concerns about antitrust issues, and Amazon's growing market power in many industries, as well as the ongoing sales tax fairness campaign. Although Amazon collects and remits sales tax on remote sales in all states on its direct sales, for the most part the company is not required to collect tax on behalf of its third-party sellers that conduct business on Amazon Marketplace.

ABA believes that Amazon is a modern-day monopoly. Its abuse of its dominance has had a negative impact on free expression and the health of America's book industry, including a chilling effect on the diversity of, and access to, books and information. ABA is bringing that argument to Congress and to state attorneys general and is asking booksellers to make the case. An Antitrust Action Kit that provides booksellers with crucial, state-specific tools to support the Amazon antitrust outreach is available on the ABA website.

In November 2019 the ABA board of directors sent letters to the attorneys general of each state calling for an investigation into Amazon's monopolistic and anticompetitive conduct. In the letters, which followed up on earlier letters sent by David Grogan, director of American Booksellers for Free Expression (ABFE), Advocacy and Public Policy at ABA, board members noted the attorneys generals' antitrust investigations into other Big Tech companies and urged them to commit to an investigation into Amazon, stating that "without regulatory action, Amazon is on its way to becoming a full-blown monopoly in the technology industry."

The letters also cited *Prime Numbers: Amazon and American Communities*, a study conducted by Civic Economics, to provide a contextual reference for Amazon's impact on the retail industry, stating the number of displaced storefronts and the net job loss in each state.

ABA board members also offered their time to state attorneys general interested in learning more about Amazon's effect on their businesses and the need for a timely investigation into the corporate giant.

ABFE is the bookseller's voice in the fight for free speech. Its mission is to promote and protect the free exchange of ideas, particularly those contained in books, by opposing restrictions on the freedom of speech; issuing statements on significant free expression controversies; participating in legal cases involving First Amendment rights; collaborating with other groups with an interest in free speech; and providing education about the importance of free expression to booksellers, other members of the book industry, politicians, the press, and the public.

In an effort to find new ways to bring its free expression message to a broader and younger audience, ABFE launched the *Counterspeak* podcast in 2018. Airing monthly, *Counterspeak* addresses issues pertaining to free speech and the First Amendment. The podcast is cohosted by ABFE, Advocacy and Public Policy director David Grogan and ABA content director Sydney Jarrard and features interviews with experts along with discussions of relevant current events. A new episode is available on the first Wednesday of each month on BookWeb, Spotify, iTunes, and YouTube.

Association of Research Libraries

Dupont Circle N.W., Washington, DC 20036
202-296-2296, e-mail webmgr@arl.org
World Wide Web http://www.arl.org

Kaylyn Groves
Senior Writer and Editor

The Association of Research Libraries (ARL) is a nonprofit organization of 124 research libraries in Canada and the United States whose mission is to advance research, learning, and scholarly communication. The association fosters the open exchange of ideas and expertise, promotes equity and diversity, and pursues advocacy and public policy efforts that reflect the values of the library, scholarly, and higher education communities. ARL forges partnerships and catalyzes the collective efforts of research libraries to enable knowledge creation and to achieve enduring and barrier-free access to information.

ARL's Action Plan 2019–2021 (https://www.arl.org/our-priorities/) lays out goals and actions in six priority areas: Advocacy and Public Policy; ARL Academy; Data and Analytics; Diversity, Equity, and Inclusion; Innovation; and Scholars and Scholarship.

Following are highlights of the association's achievements in 2019, many of which were undertaken in partnership with member libraries or other organizations.

Action Plan Highlights

In 2019 the association set priorities to advance the strategic role of research libraries as collaborative partners and as an integral part of the research and learning ecosystem. ARL's highly engaged membership and expert staff do so by focusing on the intersection of public policy, institutional policy, and practice, as they advance research and learning community strategic opportunities and related challenges. The association's focus is on

- Advocating for public policies in support of the mission and shared objective
- Catalyzing collective efforts to achieve enduring and barrier-free information
- Creating diverse, equitable, inclusive, and accessible services, collections, and work environments
- Providing data and analytics on research library practices, effectiveness, and impact
- Shaping and informing leadership

ARL's 2019–2021 priorities are carried out by the association's committees and staff in collaboration with strategic partners. Everything ARL does is possible through this combination of critical relationships. Highlights for 2019 are covered in the following pages.

ARL's overall progress is reflected in the percentage of members actively engaged in the work of the association (78 percent), access to ARL's expertise (20 publications, 10 statements on national and international topics, 21 presentations, and advice to members and others), participation by 138 fellows and scholars and numerous emerging leaders in ARL's educational programs, representation with key partners and stakeholders in public policy and research and learning, and successful association meetings, institutes, and forums.

At the start of a new year and new decade, ARL is excited about the opportunities presented by advancements in research and learning approaches; the potential for new forms of knowledge creation, sharing, and preservation; changing demographics and commensurate focus on diversity, equity, and inclusion; and the leadership role that research libraries will continue to play as a collaborative partner in a complex ecosystem.

2019 by the Numbers

Member Engagement

- One hundred twenty-four member institutions
- Ten new member representatives
- Seventy-eight percent of member representatives actively engaged in the work of the association

Expertise

- Thought leadership (20 publications and 21 presentations)
- Ten statements on enduring and equitable access to information, and diversity, equity, and inclusion
- Twenty-two visits to member institutions to discuss ARL Action Plan priorities

Educational Programs

- Eleven in-person institutes, 14 webinars, 4 virtual discussions, 1 foreign delegation
- Three hundred seventy-four institute participants, 88 fellows, 86 mentors, 50 scholars, 50 virtual discussion participants, 25 career coaches
- Over $730,000 invested in fellows and scholars programs, including sponsorships

Representation

- On three partner boards and steering committees (CNI, SCOSS, SPARC)
- At 54 professional meetings, including presenting and organizing
- With many U.S. public policy decision makers
- In 295 online media mentions

Other Events

- Two Association Meetings
- One ARL-CNI Fall Forum

Advocating for Public Policies in Support of Our Mission and Shared Objective

The association is the collective voice for research libraries and archives on public policy in the United States and internationally. In 2019 ARL advanced public policy on accessibility, copyright, free speech, higher education, and privacy. The association accomplished much of this work in partnership with the American Council on Education (ACE), American Library Association (ALA), Association of College & Research Libraries (ACRL), Canadian Association of Research Libraries (CARL), EDUCAUSE, U.S. National Archives and Records Administration (NARA), and U.S. National Library of Medicine (NLM).

Accessibility

The association hosted a two-day meeting led by the University of Virginia (UVA) Library to explore the legal framework and opportunities for shared accessible teaching materials. ARL and UVA released the joint white paper, *The Law and Accessible Texts: Reconciling Civil Rights and Copyrights*. The white paper analyzes how institutions of higher education can meet their mission of providing all students with equitable access to information within the current legal framework. Ensuring access to research and learning materials is critical in protecting the civil rights of people with disabilities.

Copyright

ARL met with several congressional offices and coordinated with other allies to slow down and/or reduce the possibility of increased litigation brought against libraries by the Copyright Alternative in Small-Claims Enforcement (CASE) Act on the creation of small-claims procedure for copyright cases. As part of the Library Copyright Alliance (LCA), ARL sent a letter to Speaker of the House Nancy Pelosi (D-CA) and House Minority Leader Kevin McCarthy (R-CA) urging them to vote against the CASE Act.

The association issued two amicus briefs at the U.S. Supreme Court as part of the Library Copyright Alliance: *Allen* v. *Cooper* and *Georgia* v. *Public.Resource.Org*. In *Allen* v. *Cooper*, LCA's brief supports Roy A. Cooper III, governor of North Carolina, arguing that abrogation of state sovereign immunity would have a negative impact on the digital preservation initiatives of state-run libraries and archives. In *Georgia* v. *Public.Resource.Org*, LCA supports Public.Resource.Org, arguing for the preservation of the comprehensive government edicts doctrine, which provides an essential safe harbor from potential copyright liability for libraries as they fulfill their role of preserving and providing access to the cultural record. The Library Copyright Alliance's mission is to foster global access to and fair use of information for creativity, research, and education.

ARL presented to the United States Patent and Trademark Office for intellectual property officials from other countries on the *Code of Best Practices in Fair Use for Software Preservation*, which provides clear guidance on the legality of archiving legacy software to ensure continued access to digital files of all kinds and to illuminate the history of technology.

The association also participated in three closed-door roundtables in the Senate regarding the modernization of the U.S. Copyright Office. In these ongoing roundtables ARL continues to defend against efforts to split the Copyright Office away from supervision and oversight by the Library of Congress, and continues to protect and advance equitable access to information in various proposals for changing the office's registration and record-keeping systems and processes.

Free Speech

ARL supports freedom of speech and condemns all hate speech and speech used to threaten and intimidate marginalized communities. For ARL members, the association wrote a review in March of U.S. Executive Order no. 13864, "Improving Free Inquiry, Transparency, and Accountability at Colleges and Universities." In November, ARL issued a statement condemning the acts of hate speech and violence that took place at Syracuse University.

Higher Education

The association convened a webinar for ARL members and select partners to discuss the risks of foreign government influence in the research enterprise, including presentations from representatives of the Federal Bureau of Investigation and ACE.

Privacy

ARL published *Research Library Issues* no. 297, which explored privacy from a legal, digital, and applied perspective, with a focus on the implications and opportunities for research libraries.

The association also completed a review of core interests and opportunities for research libraries in privacy and digital data policy. In 2020 this will be a focus of the ARL Digital Content Task Force and potentially a new working group set up through the Advocacy and Public Policy Committee on digital-information platform issues.

Catalyzing Collective Efforts to Achieve Enduring and Barrier-free Access to Information

ARL's priority in this area is to align library strategy, staffing, and spending to advance the principles and practices of open scholarship. Through collective action the association works to increase the amount of high-quality scholarship that is openly available, to position ARL members to lead on "open science by design" within their own institutions, and to provide leadership on high-impact collective collections initiatives. Much of this work is done in partnership—ranging from individual libraries, peer associations, and disciplinary communities.

Advancing the Principles and Practices of Open Scholarship

Open science by design is a strategy to remove barriers and move toward widespread open access to scientific data, research, and publications. It is based on the principle that research conducted openly and transparently leads to better science as well as more equitable access to knowledge. ARL hosted and participated in several events to promote barrier-free access to information and partnered nationally and internationally to inform open science practice. To shape the principles and inform the implementation of Plan S, ARL organized a meeting of member representatives with Plan S architect David Sweeney early in 2019. Plan S is an initiative to make full and immediate open access a reality. The initiative is supported by an international consortium of research funders. In the fall of 2019, with the International Alliance of Research Library Associations (IARLA), ARL endorsed the Plan S objectives and provided comments on its implementation, resulting in a visible role for the international research library community as a key stakeholder in Plan S. ARL presented at the Research Libraries UK (RLUK) international symposium on digital scholarship, resulting in ARL-RLUK collaboration in the Digital Scholarship Institute and the ARL Position Description Bank.

Increasing the Amount of High-Quality Scholarship That Is Openly Available

The association is committed to advancing open monographs as part of a movement to sustain the infrastructure of academy-based humanities and social sciences publishing. AAU, ARL, and the Association of University Presses (AUPresses) launched openmonographs.org to flip the funding model for university publishing. The new website for the joint initiative TOME (Toward an Open Monograph Ecosystem) will facilitate building a community of scholars, publishers, librarians, and university administrators that increases access to humanities and social sciences scholarship. In 2019 the number of TOME-funded books grew from 5 to 28, and there are more than 30 additional books in progress.

AAU, ARL, and AUPresses convened the third annual TOME meeting in Washington, D.C., in July. The group agreed to highlight TOME's connection to the larger conversation around sustainable scholarly infrastructure, including lowering the financial and time commitment for participating in TOME. For more information on the TOME meeting, please see the full report available on ARL.org.

ARL and AUPresses hosted the third meeting of press and library directors with reporting relationships (P2L3) in Detroit, Michigan, in June. The P2L3 theme was "a world not dependent on sales." Participants focused on the unique strength of the P2L community to sustain open access monograph publishing, given the organizational and operational alignment between the library and the press. P2L builds institutional capacity by sharing and combining staff for such activities as copyright consultations, outreach and advocacy, and implementation of open scholarship practices. The P2L community is well positioned to create standards and best practices around digital scholarship, including peer review, publication, and presentation. For more information on the P2L3 meeting, read the full report and view presentation slides available on ARL.org.

Statements and Publications to Advance Barrier-free Access to Information

ARL issued or endorsed several statements promoting barrier-free access to information: a statement supporting University of California's termination of its systemwide Elsevier journals contract, a statement supporting MIT's Open Access Framework for Publisher Contracts, an endorsement of the COAR/SPARC Good Practice Principles for Scholarly Communication Services, and an endorsement of Invest in Open Infrastructure.

ARL wrote a *Policy Notes* blog post on the UC–Elsevier negotiations and Plan S, focused on paying for publication as part of the cost of doing research. The association released *Research Library Issues* no. 298 on the critical role and participation of libraries and librarians in supporting the data science revolution at research universities. And ARL published a white paper from the IMLS-funded Supporting OA Collections in the Open project documenting a series of conversations with librarians with diverse backgrounds regarding their experiences and attitudes toward financially supporting open access content.

Creating Diverse, Equitable, Inclusive, and Accessible Services, Collections, and Work Environments

Research libraries work to advance access to economic and social prosperity, encourage full participation in society, and counter the historical lack of access to material resources about underrepresented human groups in collections that the association cultivates and stewards. In 2019 ARL collaborated with ACRL, ALA, DeEtta Jones & Associates (DJA), The Ohio State University (OSU), the Public Library Association (PLA), and the Society of American Archivists (SAA) to develop staff and interns.

Developing Current Staff and Student Recruits

More than 700 participants attended diversity, equity, and inclusion events offered or sponsored by ARL: the 2019 ARL Annual Leadership Symposium, the Leadership and Career Development Program (LCDP) and Fellowship for Digital and Inclusive Excellence webinars, the LCDP Capstone Institute, the ARL/SAA Mosaic Leadership Forum, and the IDEAL Conference and preconference for ARL directors at OSU. These programs promote diversity, equity, and inclusion in the library and archives workforce and prepare emerging and midcareer professionals from historically underrepresented groups to take on leadership roles.

ARL consulted on improving diversity, equity, and inclusion with the libraries at the University of Alberta, Emory University, Florida State University, University of Houston, the University of Iowa, University of Manitoba, Simon Fraser University, and Wayne State University, as well as with Duke University Press.

The association offered the Equity Toolkit to LCDP fellows, their career coaches, and select staff from fellows' institutions. The Equity Toolkit is an online course by DeEtta Jones and Associates that provides the knowledge, language, skills, and framework needed to become proficient working across cultures.

Twenty-five ARL library directors and staff participated in the ARL *On the Edge* webinar "From Safe Spaces to Brave Spaces" that explored how public space in libraries might embody the principles of safe and brave space. The program explored how libraries can create environments where users feel physically and psychologically safe to be fully engaged in research and learning, while at the same time in a physical space where productive and respectful debate can occur and where challenges to assumptions and ideologies can transpire.

ARL staff participated in the Archives Leadership Institute at Purdue University, exploring intercultural competency and diversity-skills development, among other issues, with 20 midcareer archivists. ARL's participation in the event supported Purdue's leadership in the three-year project funded by the National Historical Publications and Records Commission (NHPRC) and facilitated by NARA. Over the years, numerous archivists from ARL member institutions have participated in the Archives Leadership Institute, which helps bridge leadership development theories across communities of practice.

Developing Future Leaders

Looking to the future, the association launched the ACRL-ALA-ARL-PLA task force to develop a framework for proficiencies in racial equity in libraries and archives. ARL initiated work on creating a "path to inclusion" for ARL members, a comprehensive plan to ensure that the association and all of its events are welcoming and conducive to optimal participation and engagement by its diverse membership. The association hosted University of Maryland iSchool students—many of whom are likely to work in libraries in the future—to discuss accessibility of both resources and spaces and the implications of serving a growing population of researchers with differing needs.

Statements Promoting Diversity, Equity, and Inclusion

In 2019 ARL issued two statements asserting its commitment to diversity, equity, and inclusion as core values of the association. This commitment is deeply embedded in the mission of libraries and archives, and in the work ARL does as an institutional-member organization called upon to provide leadership in key issues and practices that define the profession. The specific statements are "ARL Affirms Commitment to Advancing Diversity, Equity, Inclusion" and "Association of Research Libraries Condemns Racist and Anti-Semitic Acts at Syracuse University," and are available on ARL.org.

Providing Data and Analytics on Research Library Practices, Effectiveness, and Impact

The Research and Analytics program pursues a research agenda for the association. ARL collects and analyzes data on all aspects of research libraries' roles in scholarly and scientific production, learning facilitation and learner success, and knowledge access and sustainability. In 2019 ARL members benefited from a data collection and analytics program focused on outcomes and impact in several ways. The program benefits from close collaboration between ACRL and CARL, and work with the broader assessment community.

Communicating the Impact and Relevance of Research Libraries and Archives

The association initiated the Research Library Impact Framework pilot projects with 17 teams composed of assessment practitioners from member libraries. These projects will help ARL members communicate the impact and relevance of research libraries' and archives' activities in ways that resonate with budget holders and stakeholders. The teams are working on answering five research questions: (1) How does the library help to increase research productivity and impact? (2) How do library spaces facilitate innovative research, creative thinking, and problem-solving? (3) How does the library contribute to equitable student outcomes and an inclusive learning environment? (4) How do the library's special collections specifically support and promote teaching, learning, and research? (5) How do the library's collections play a role in attracting and retaining top researchers and faculty to the institution?

To help members communicate the impact of research libraries, ARL publishes several annual reports. The *ARL Statistics 2017–2018*, *ARL Academic Law Library Statistics 2017–2018*, and *ARL Academic Health Sciences Library Statistics 2017–2018* describe the collections, staffing, expenditures, and service activities of the association's member libraries. Additionally, ARL published the *ARL Annual Salary Survey 2018–2019*, which analyzes salary data for professional staff working in member libraries. In 2019 the association established the ARL Salary Survey Task Force to review the current survey and recommend improvements to the collection of salary information for the fiscal year 2020–2021 cycle.

Providing Leading Research Library Assessment Instruments

ARL completed a market analysis of ClimateQUAL and LibQUAL+ in 2019, resulting in a plan to upgrade both instruments in 2020. ClimateQUAL is a tool for assessing organizational climate and diversity; LibQUAL+ is a tool for evaluating library service quality. The demographic questions on the ClimateQUAL survey will be refreshed. Details about the LibQUAL+ upgrade are pending.

ARL, ACRL, and ALA extended their Joint Advisory Task Force through August 31, 2022, to continue efforts to bring the Integrated Postsecondary Education Data System (IPEDS) Academic Libraries component up-to-date and in-line with current library practices. The ACRL/ARL Joint Advisory Task Force will develop recommendations regarding definitional issues and responses to questions raised by the academic library community in the area of shared print and electronic collections. IPEDS accepted the task force's previous recommendations and implemented them in the 2015, 2016, and 2019 survey cycles.

Shaping and Informing Leadership

The ARL Academy is a crucial resource for advancing professional development for library leaders as partners in the research enterprise. The unified suite of programs empowers ARL libraries and archives staff with the tools necessary to meet the current and future needs of users. Offerings focus on leadership and skills development; diversity, equity, and inclusion; and the challenges of organizational change.

Developing Leaders and Managers

Twenty-eight professionals from member and nonmember libraries completed the ARL Leadership Fellows program in 2019. The program facilitates the development of future senior-level leaders in large research libraries and archives. The 2018–2019 program sponsors were George Washington University, the University of Florida, and the University of Iowa. Six former Leadership Fellows became ARL member representatives this year.

Three hundred and forty-four library staff members participated in one of the nine Library Management Skills institutes that help develop their awareness, skills, and confidence as leaders and managers. The following member institutions hosted them: Indiana University–Bloomington, Texas Tech University, UC–Berkeley and UC–Davis together, the University of Miami, the University of Rochester, the University of Texas–Austin, USMAI Library Consortium (held two institutes), and Virginia Commonwealth University.

Attaining New Skills and Competencies

The University of Rochester hosted an ARL Digital Scholarship Institute (DSI) that trained 30 library professionals and graduate students in core methodologies and tools. The DSI is a five-day, cohort-based opportunity for individuals who are new to digital scholarship. The training provides both a knowledge base and the confidence to work with the cultural changes sweeping through research libraries and higher education today.

The ARL Academy hosted two *On the Edge* webinars for member representatives and staff. Twenty-five people participated in the "Matrix Organizations" webinar that covered how matrix management is being used to implement changes in programs and services and create a vibrant organization where people are excited to work. This session was offered in partnership with George Washington University. Twenty-five people participated in the "From Safe Spaces to Brave Spaces" webinar that explored how public space in libraries might embody the principles of safe and brave space. This session was offered in partnership with the University of Michigan.

Looking Ahead

ARL established the 2020 ARL Academy focused on leadership of Data Science, Digital Transformation, Analytics, and Innovation. The association also launched a research project on the changing roles of research library deans and directors in order to inform future programming.

Facilitating a Culture of Innovation within Research Libraries

In all it does, ARL seeks to foster a culture of innovation and to support its members in doing so. In 2019 the association launched the Venture Fund in order to build capacity and encourage innovation at scale. The purpose of the Venture Fund is to support prototypes or proofs of concept that scale so as to advance ARL priorities set by the members and the board. Cross-institutional proposals are given preference. The proposed venture must exist in some form already and have an identified community of users with the potential to scale. The first projects will be chosen in May 2020.

The Scholarly Publishing and Academic Resources Coalition

Heather Joseph
Executive Director

1201 Connecticut Ave. N.W., P.O. 607/608, Washington, DC 20036
202-630-5090, e-mail sparc@sparcopen.org
World Wide Web https://www.sparcopen.org

Background and Mission

The Scholarly Publishing and Academic Resources Coalition (SPARC) is a global coalition committed to making Open the default for research and education. SPARC promotes the faster and wider sharing of research outputs and educational materials to increase the impact of research, fuel the advancement of knowledge, and increase the return on research and education investments. SPARC staunchly supports efforts to promote diversity, inclusion, equity, and social justice in and through the library community.

SPARC is a catalyst for action. Supported by 240 members primarily in the U.S. and Canada, and with international affiliates active in Africa, Europe, and Japan, its pragmatic agenda focuses on collaborating with stakeholders in the global community to encourage new norms, practices, and policies that promote equitable access, sharing, and use of scholarship.

Strategy

To promote the changes in both infrastructure and culture needed to make Open the default in research and education, SPARC's strategy centers on

1. Advocating for policies that enable Open practices throughout research and education
2. Educating stakeholders on opportunities to change the scholarly communication system
3. Incubating projects that promote new models for sharing research outputs and developing educational materials that support the needs of scholars and society

SPARC works to identify shared values and opportunities for action between its library members and stakeholders in the global research and education environment, including faculty and administration, public and private research funders, and the public. SPARC places a premium on empowering students and early career professionals, and actively incorporates collaboration with them across all program areas.

Priorities

SPARC's work focuses on Open Access, Open Data, Open Education, Open Infrastructure, and Realigning Incentives. Additionally, to maximize progress, SPARC supports efforts that champion intellectual freedom, a free and open Internet, privacy, confidentiality, and equitable copyright and intellectual property policies.

The following were key priorities in 2019:

Conducting Policy Advocacy

SPARC's top priority continued to be to advance policies that promote Open Access to research outputs (including articles and data) and educational materials at the institutional, state, national, and international levels. SPARC has advanced this priority by

- Educating key policymakers (including Executive Branch/Administration, U.S. Congress, Canadian Administration, Canadian Parliament, and others) on SPARC's core policy priorities
- Developing proactive strategies to extend/expand policy progress in the United States and Canada, and globally, as well as defend against threats to existing policies
- Leveraging stakeholder communities to accelerate policy progress
- Working with the media to promote public awareness of the benefits of Open policies
- Working with public and private funders to create and implement Open policies in the United States and Canada, and globally

Advocating for Community-Controlled Infrastructure

SPARC concentrated its work on leveraging resources to sustain crucial infrastructure underpinning the scholarly communications ecosystem. That work included

- Producing a comprehensive landscape analysis of data infrastructure in the higher education sector that highlighted key areas of vulnerability and a companion "Solutions Roadmap," which outlines actions institutions can use to take control of their data infrastructure and which is designed to raise awareness and encourage proactive behavior
- Leading research and development efforts on new economic and organizational models for the collective provisioning of Open resources and infrastructure, including support for targeted new investment instruments, and actively collaborating with community efforts to accelerate progress, including Investing in Open Infrastructure (IOI)

Promoting Culture Change through Realigning Incentives

SPARC actively promoted the need for realignment of existing reward and incentive structures to advance Open as the default in research and education. SPARC's work to further this priority included

- Leveraging the leadership of research funders and higher education leaders at the university president/provost level to serve as champions and peer-influencers to promote incentive realignment
- Serving as organizers, in partnership with the National Academy of Sciences, of two roundtable meetings of leaders/stakeholders promoting peer-to-peer discussion and development of strategies to promote adoption of practices and policies rewarding open sharing of research outputs and educational resources
- Supporting the activities of six working groups that emerged from the initial roundtable convenings
- Encouraging inclusion of rewards/recognition for Open behaviors in all relevant funder and institutional documents including orientation materials, funding solicitations, and job postings in addition to evaluation and promotion guidelines
- Promoting exemplars that have made demonstrable progress toward re-aligning rewards
- Supporting research into current evaluation, reward, and incentive structures
- Leveraging the OpenCon community to promote culture change within the next generation

Providing Resources to Support Campus Action

SPARC produced and promoted resources that enable its members to take timely and informed actions. SPARC's work to advance this priority included

- Providing members up-to-the-moment updates and analyses of key policy and scholarly communications–related trends and developments
- Issuing action alerts and other opportunities for timely member library participation in advocacy, education, and partnership initiatives
- Delivering tools and resources to support member campus advocacy and education activities (for example, Connect OER, State Level Policy Trackers, and Big Deal Knowledge Database)
- Providing free member campus visits by the SPARC team to promote awareness, education, and advocacy for key program areas
- Convening International Open Access Week as a catalyst for action across the community

Continuing Priorities

Global Collaboration. SPARC continued to reflect and support the global nature of scholarly communications by

- Actively promoting the SPARC brand as a reflection of global presence and activity

- Co-sponsoring meetings outside the United States with partner organizations
- Identifying new opportunities and establishing partnerships with key stakeholders in other global regions

Supporting Students and Early Career Researchers. SPARC promoted the inclusion of students and early career academic professionals in all areas of Open Access by

- Supporting the OpenCon community for students and early career academic professionals
- Empowering local and issue-oriented community building for the next generation through OpenCon satellite events and community calls
- Strengthening joint advocacy efforts to leverage community presence on Open Access, Open Data, Open Education, and related issues
- Maintaining relationships with key national and international organizations representing students and early career academic professionals
- Undertaking a strategic review of SPARC's community building efforts to empower the next generation

Ensuring Organizational Stability and Strength. SPARC continued to place a premium on ensuring that its organizational structure is designed to achieve its mission by

- Deploying flexible employment arrangements to ensure high-level talent can be strategically deployed to meet changing resource needs
- Identifying and capitalizing on opportunities to build internal capacity through ongoing monitoring of dues structure, securing grant funding for program support, implementing visiting program officer opportunities, and expanded partnership arrangements
- Promoting and expanding member retention and recruitment efforts

Program Activities and Outcomes 2019

Policy and Advocacy

- SPARC is regularly invited to represent its community's views in policy forums and consultations in the United States as well as internationally. Its strong SPARC affiliates in Africa, Europe, and Japan provide it with a network of colleagues and collaborators that strengthens its advocacy presence and reach.
- SPARC led an effort to secure the continued funding for an Open Textbook pilot grant program at the U.S. Department of Education. In 2020, the program will receive $7 million, a $2 million increase over the previous year, to expand the use of open textbooks at colleges and universities, which are expected to save students multiple times the original investment.

- Supported by pro-bono legal counsel, SPARC led opposition to the proposed merger between textbook publishers Cengage and McGraw-Hill. It crafted a detailed brief for the Department of Justice and consulted with DOJ officials on follow-up actions. It also jump-started congressional and state legislative actions to review the merger, and is collaborating with higher education, consumer, and student organizations to continue to press for this merger to be reconsidered.
- Following SPARC's success incorporating language supporting OER in bipartisan career and technical education legislation passed by Congress, SPARC developed and disseminated a supporting implementation toolkit for state and local education leaders.
- SPARC released an updated State OER Policy Playbook and provided policy support to member libraries that resulted in the passage of state-level OER legislation in Connecticut, New Jersey, and Texas, as well as a statewide working group in Massachusetts.
- SPARC continues to convene the "Open Research Funders Group," whose members include the Gates, Sloan, Arnold, Arcadia, and Soros Foundations, among others, and provides the group with a forum for regular discussion and opportunities for collaboration in strengthening the Open research environment.
- Behind the scenes, SPARC has worked to promote a full overhaul of the 2013 White House Memorandum on Public Access to Publicly Funded Research Outputs.

Campus Education

- SPARC's annual International Open Access Week, a partnership with the international Open Access community, continues to grow in popularity and participation. This year's theme, "Open for Whom?", encouraged the community to focus on increasing equity and inclusion in their efforts to advance Open.
- SPARC supported members' local campus efforts by providing free visits by SPARC staff to member campuses, SPARC-sponsored speakers for events, practical guides, talking points, templates, and expert counsel on campus Open Access and Open Education issues.
- SPARC continued to expand online programs to cover hot topics of interest to members and conduct regular community calls to advance member institutions' efforts in a variety of different topic areas.
- SPARC expanded Connect OER, a comprehensive directory documenting library-centered OER activities across more than 100 member campuses.
- SPARC launched the third cohort of its Open Education Leadership Program, which prepares library professionals to continue to serve on the cutting edge of this emerging area.
- SPARC produced a monthly newsletter for members summarizing key happenings and hosted webcasts on important topics, including rapid reaction events to address breaking news.

Communication and Media

SPARC is regularly consulted and quoted as an expert source on topics relating to scholarly communications. Its programs have been featured in both the national and trade press by such outlets as Reuters, *Inside Higher Ed*, *Science*, MarketWatch, *Chicago Sun-Times*, and *The Chronicle of Higher Education*.

Through its website, SPARC highlighted the work of Open Access champions. SPARC honored the groundbreaking work of both Robert-Jan Smits and AmeliCA with its 2019 Innovator Awards.

SPARC-ACRL Forums

A major component of SPARC's community outreach occurs at meetings of the American Library Association (ALA), where SPARC works with the Association of College and Research Libraries (ACRL) and its scholarly communication committee to bring current issues to the attention of the community.

In January 2019 the SPARC-ACRL Midwinter Forum was held in Seattle, with many sessions focusing on empowerment of women and underrepresented communities and the importance of advocacy and social justice. Members of the SPARC staff hosted a workshop on the Open landscape at the annual ALA meeting, held in Washington, D.C., in June 2019.

Governance

SPARC is guided by a steering committee. The committee members are Beth Bernhardt (University of North Carolina–Greensboro), H. Austin Booth (New York University), Krista Cox (Association of Research Libraries), Rebecca Graham (University of Guelph), Jennifer Grayburn (Union College), Rachel Harding (University of Toronto), Joy Kirchner (York University), Vivian Lewis (McMaster University), Kevin Mulroy (Claremont Colleges), Shilpa Rele (Rowan University), Steven Escar Smith (University of Tennessee–Knoxville), Virginia Steel (University of California–Los Angeles), and Karen Williams (University of Arizona).

Council on Library and Information Resources

2221 S. Clark St., Arlington, VA 22202
World Wide Web http://www.clir.org
Twitter @CLIRNews

Kathlin Smith
Director of Communications

The Council on Library and Information Resources (CLIR) is an independent, nonprofit organization that forges strategies to enhance research, teaching, and learning environments in collaboration with academic and cultural institutions, scholars, specialists, and practitioners. CLIR President Charles Henry leads the 20-member staff and works in close liaison with eight CLIR Distinguished Presidential Fellows.

CLIR is supported by fees from sponsoring institutions, grants from public and private foundations, contracts with federal agencies, and donations from individuals. A list of current sponsors, members, and funders is available at https://www.clir.org/about/current-sponsors-and-funders/.

CLIR's board establishes policy, oversees the investment of funds, sets goals, and approves strategies for their achievement. A full listing of CLIR board members is available at https://www.clir.org/about/governance/.

CLIR's activities in 2019 are described in the following sections.

Initiatives and Partnerships

Digital Library Federation

A program of CLIR, the Digital Library Federation (DLF) is a community of practitioners who advance research, learning, social justice, and the public good through the creative design and wise application of digital library technologies. DLF connects CLIR's vision and research agenda to a network of practitioners working in digital libraries, archives, labs, museums, and elsewhere. Through in-person meetings and year-round working groups, DLF promotes work on standards and best practices; research and data management; practices that open new opportunities for research, teaching, and learning; professional development; the social contexts and impact of digital library work; and community-driven frameworks for policy advocacy.

DLF hosts or facilitates a wide range of activities, which are highlighted below. DLF also maintains resources, including a community calendar, jobs board, digitization cost calculator, and digitizing special formats wiki, all available through its website, https://www.diglib.org.

DLF Forum

DLF's annual signature event, the Forum, is open to digital library practitioners from member institutions and the broader community. The Forum provides an opportunity for DLF's advisory committee, working groups, and community members to conduct business and present their work; it also enables community members to share experiences and practices with one another and support a broader level of information sharing among professional staff. The Forum allows DLF to continually review and assess its progress with input from the community at large.

The 2019 DLF Forum, held in Tampa, Florida, drew attendees across three events: the second Learn@DLF workshop day, the Forum, and the National Digital Stewardship Alliance's (NDSA) Digital Preservation 2019. Each year, DLF offers Forum fellowships to encourage broad participation and diversity of attendees; in 2019 18 fellows received support. Many have posted about their experiences at https://www.diglib.org/category/forum.

The 2020 DLF Forum and affiliated events will be held in Baltimore, Maryland, November 8–12.

Working Groups

DLF hosts 12 working groups, which are typically informal, volunteer-led efforts. A full list is available at https://www.diglib.org/groups/. To assist in these and related efforts, DLF created the Organizer's Toolkit at https://wiki.diglib.org/About_DLF_and_the_Organizers%27_Toolkit, which serves as a resource for starting new initiatives or working groups, and for facilitating ongoing projects.

Authenticity Project Fellowship Program

In 2019 DLF and the HBCU Library Alliance launched the Authenticity Project, an IMLS-funded mentoring and professional development program for early- to mid-career library staff from HBCUs (historically black colleges and universities), along with conversational and project-based opportunities for building authentic connections and promoting genuine exchange among participants from HBCUs and predominantly white institutions.

In each of the project's three years, fifteen fellows will be matched with two experienced library professionals: an established mentor from an HBCU Library Alliance library or with a strong background in HBCUs, and a "conversation partner" working in an area of the fellow's interest from a predominantly white institution. In 2019 fellows worked with their mentors and conversation partners on topics ranging from grant writing and project management to self-care and inter-institutional collaboration.

Fellows receive full travel, lodging, and registration expenses to the annual DLF Forum and Learn@DLF workshops; access to online discussion spaces and in-person networking opportunities; and opportunities to apply for microgrant funding to undertake interinstitutional projects of strategic importance across institutions and communities. They also participate in quarterly facilitated, online networking and discussion sessions.

Additional information is available at https://www.diglib.org/opportunities/authenticity-project/.

National Digital Stewardship Alliance (NDSA)

DLF serves as the host institution for the NDSA, a consortium of more than 220 partnering organizations, including universities, professional associations, businesses, government agencies, and nonprofit organizations committed to the long-term preservation of digital information. NDSA activities are organized by three interest groups (Content, Standards and Practices, and Infrastructure), out of which smaller working groups often emerge. NDSA hosts the annual Digital Preservation conference, which, since 2016, has followed the DLF Forum. More information about NDSA is available at https://ndsa.org/.

Digital Library of the Middle East

CLIR is working with Stanford University Libraries, Qatar National Library, the Antiquities Coalition, and other institutions worldwide to implement a sustainable, extensible digital library platform and set of curatorial processes to federate records relating to the cultural heritage of the Middle East.

The Digital Library of the Middle East (DLME) is envisioned as an internationally shared digital inventory of cultural artifacts that provides detailed descriptions and images of artifacts along with information about the objects' history and provenance. It will ultimately encompass text, video, photographs, archives, manuscripts, 3-D data, and maps illuminating the region's history over 12 millennia, curated by scholars, specialists, and members of the cultures it represents. Records from the DLME will be made publicly available to encourage scholarly discoveries and greater appreciation of the region's rich heritage and living peoples, while helping safeguard fundamentally important expressions of our cultural commonwealth and shared humanity.

The DLME platform is expected to become public in early spring 2020. More information on the DLME is available at https://dlme.clir.org/.

Kurdish Heritage Institute Digitizing Initiative

In July 2019 CLIR received a grant from the U.S. Embassy in Baghdad for a project to digitize collections of the Kurdish Heritage Institute (KHI) in Sulaymaniyah, in Iraqi Kurdistan. The project, undertaken jointly by CLIR and KHI, will digitize KHI's extensive collection of books, culturally significant photos, and audio and video files. DLME project director Peter Herdrich and Amed Demirhan of Barzani National Memorial in Erbil, Kurdistan, are overseeing the 12-month project and working with the KHI staff to catalog, document, digitize, and store the KHI collection of Kurdish language books and cultural materials.

HBCU Library Alliance Partnership

In July 2019 CLIR and the HBCU Library Alliance announced a long-term partnership that aims to position historically black college and university (HBCU) libraries as centers of scholarly distinction with unparalleled digitized collections that provide insight into the influence and value of HBCUs in local, regional, national, and global communities; the African American community; and the global higher education community. Specific goals include assessing the research value of and risks to these collections; improving scholarly and public access through digitization, and establishing a leadership training program for HBCU library staff.

The partnership grew out of events and programming run jointly by the HBCU Library Alliance and CLIR's DLF, including the Authenticity Project Fellowship program (see item under DLF).

Leading Change Institute

CLIR and EDUCAUSE hosted the Leading Change Institute (LCI) June 2–7, 2019. Over six days, participants heard perspectives on the higher education landscape from an array of speakers and explored topics ranging from entrepreneurship to leading change through collaboration and creativity.

LCI aims to prepare and develop the next generation of leaders in libraries, information services, and higher education by engaging those who seek to further develop their skills for the benefit of higher education. Since the institute's inception in 2000 as the Frye Leadership Institute, 793 people have participated, representing a broad range of both domestic and international institutions of higher learning. A list of participants from 2019 and previous years is available at https://leadingchangeinstitute.org/alumni/.

Chief Information Officers Group

Since 2002 CLIR has facilitated a semiannual forum of directors of organizations that have merged their library and information technology units on the campuses of liberal arts colleges and small universities. At their meetings and through a listserv, members discuss library and computing issues as an integrated whole. They have explored such topics as organizational models for optimizing success; governance structures; fostering diversity, equity, and inclusion in merged organizations; data security and privacy; and digital scholarship. A list of current members is available at https://www.clir.org/initiatives-partnerships/cios/.

Affiliates

Affiliates are institutions or consortia with which CLIR has forged a supportive alliance in pursuit of common goals. In some cases, CLIR or DLF serve as a host institution or fiscal manager for an affiliate organization. Examples include NDSA, the International Image Interoperability Framework (IIIF), the International Internet Preservation Consortium (IIPC), and Open Repositories. In other cases, such as DLF's alliance with Taiga or Code4Lib, a major project is hosted for the group, such as communications infrastructure or a conference series. In still other cases, CLIR serves as an incubator for a new idea, such as the Digital Library of the Middle East, event partner (DLF + AMIA Hack Days), or collaborator on specific projects (as with Jisc and the HBCU Library Alliance Partnership).

These partnerships signal CLIR and DLF's commitment to a vision of interdependence, facilitating the integration of services, tools, platforms, and expertise in ways that will reduce costs and create greater efficiencies for the benefit of all.

Fellowships and Grants

Digitizing Hidden Special Collections and Archives

Digitizing Hidden Special Collections and Archives is a national grant competition administered by CLIR for digitizing rare and unique content in collecting institutions. Supported by The Andrew W. Mellon Foundation, the program is built on the model of CLIR's Cataloging Hidden Special Collections and Archives program, which ran from 2008 to 2014.

Since 2015 Digitizing Hidden Collections has awarded about $4 million annually to institutions holding collections of high value for research, teaching, and learning. A review panel, comprising experts from a range of scholarly and technical disciplines, evaluates proposals and recommends award recipients. Awards range from $50,000 to $250,000 for single-institution projects and $50,000 to $500,000 for collaborative projects. In 2019 CLIR awarded funds to 18 projects, involving 58 institutions in 17 U.S. states and Canada.

In 2019 CLIR published a five-part blog series, "Five Years of Listening," focusing on the evolution of the Digitizing Hidden Collections program. The series was written by CLIR's Director of Global Strategic Initiatives Nicole Ferraiolo. The final blog, "Still Listening," and links to previous blogs in the series are available at https://www.clir.org/2019/04/still-listening/.

More information about the Digitizing Hidden Collections program, including a list of funded projects, is available at https://www.clir.org/hiddencollections/.

Recordings at Risk

Launched in 2017 with funding from the Andrew W. Mellon Foundation, Recordings at Risk is a national regranting program to support the preservation of rare and unique audio and audiovisual content of high scholarly value through digital reformatting. It is intended to encourage professionals who may be constrained by limited resources or technical expertise to take action against the threats of media degradation and obsolescence. The program helps institutions identify priorities and develop practical strategies for digital reformatting, build relationships with partners, and raise awareness of best practices.

Grants from the open competitions range from $10,000 to $50,000 and cover costs of preservation reformatting for audio or audiovisual content by qualified external service providers. In 2019 CLIR awarded funds for 33 projects over two grant cycles (April and October) totaling $978,769. The seventh call for proposals opened in November 2019, with applications due in January 2020. To date the program has awarded $2.7 million.

More information about the program, including a list of funded projects, is available at https://www.clir.org/recordings-at-risk/.

Postdoctoral Fellowship Program

CLIR's Postdoctoral Fellowship Program, now in its 16th year, offers recent Ph.D. graduates an opportunity to work on projects that strengthen connections among library collections and services, promote the effective use of collections and technologies, and curate and preserve the products of current research. Launched in 2004, the program has supported 206 fellows at 87 host institutions across the United States, Canada, and overseas.

There were 16 fellows in the 2019 cohort, comprising individuals awarded the inaugural CLIR/DLF Postdoctoral Fellowships in Data Curation for African American and African Studies, supported by the Andrew W. Mellon Foundation; CLIR Postdoctoral Fellowships in Academic Libraries, supported by individual host institutions; CLIR/DLF Postdoctoral Fellowships in Data Curation for Latin American and Caribbean Studies, supported by Mellon; and CLIR/DLF Postdoctoral Fellowships in Data Curation for the Sciences and Social Sciences, supported by the Alfred P. Sloan Foundation.

All new 2019 fellows attended a summer seminar, hosted at Bryn Mawr College, addressing issues faced by 21st-century libraries, including data and software curation and management. The seminar provided an opportunity for fellows to participate in cohort-building activities. Fellows' supervisors joined the seminar for one day to discuss expectations and establish effective communication strategies.

In February 2019 CLIR published *3D/VR in the Academic Library: Emerging Practices and Trends*. Eight essays from experts in a variety of fields examine the use of three-dimensional and virtual reality technologies in research and teaching, and the library's vital role in supporting this work. The essays emerged from talks given at a colloquium in March 2018 that was organized by CLIR Postdoctoral Fellows. In April 2019 CLIR published a trio of papers documenting the experiences of the earliest CLIR/DLF Postdoctoral Fellows in Data Curation for the Sciences and Social Sciences, and the broader contexts in which they worked. Links to the report and papers are provided in the Publications section.

Additional information about the postdoctoral fellowship program, including a list of current and former fellows, is available at https://www.clir.org/fellowships/postdoc/.

Mellon Dissertation Fellowships

In 2019 CLIR announced 16 recipients of Mellon Fellowships for Dissertation Research in Original Sources, which are awarded to graduate students in the humanities and related social sciences who seek to conduct dissertation research with original sources over a nine- to twelve-month period. Since the program's inception, in 2001, CLIR has awarded 257 fellowships. A list of current and past fellowship recipients is available at https://www.clir.org/fellowships/mellon/fellowshiprecipients/.

Publications

Material Memory (podcast). In November 2019 CLIR launched its first-ever podcast. In theme-based seasons, *Material Memory* explores the effects of our changing environment—from digital technologies to the climate crisis—on our ability to access the record of our shared humanity, and the critical role that libraries, archives, museums, and other public institutions play in keeping cultural memory alive. A preview episode introduces the podcast in a conversation with CLIR president Charles Henry about the threats to our cultural record, what is at stake if it is lost, and what can be done to protect it. Season 1 celebrates the UN-designated Year of Indigenous Languages. In each of six episodes, host Joy Banks speaks with people involved in the work of restoring audio and audiovisual recordings of indigenous languages and their extraordinary efforts to make these recordings accessible to the communities they represent. Episodes are available through major podcast apps, as well as at https://material-memory.clir.org/.

3D/VR in the Academic Library: Emerging Practices and Trends. February 2019. Available at https://www.clir.org/pubs/reports/pub176/. Eight essays from experts in a variety of fields examine the use of three-dimensional and virtual reality technologies in research and teaching, and the library's vital role in supporting this work. The essays emerged from talks given at a miniconference in March 2018 that was organized by CLIR Postdoctoral Fellows in Data Curation for the Sciences and Social Sciences. Web only.

Postdoctoral Fellowships in Data Curation for the Sciences and Social Sciences: Early Experiences and Contexts. April 2019. Available at https://www.clir.org/postdoctoral-fellowships-dcsss-early-experiences-and-contexts/. A trio of papers document the experiences of the earliest CLIR Postdoctoral Fellows in Data Curation for the Sciences and Social Sciences, and the broader contexts in which they worked. The first, by Alice Bishop and Christa Williford, explains the major motivations for the creation of the data curation fellowships and identifies the range of disciplinary backgrounds represented among the first three cohorts of fellows made possible through Sloan Foundation support. The second, by Lori Jahnke and Andrew Asher, summarizes the findings of a two-year study of the experiences and impacts of these early fellowships while pointing to key factors in academic culture that affect researchers' investments of time and attention in making their data openly available and reusable. The third, by Jodi Reeves Eyre, is an analysis of 161 job postings in academic libraries between 2013 and 2017 intended to assess the importance of data-related skills to hiring institutions. Web only.

The Foundations of Discovery: A Report on the Assessment of the Impacts of the Cataloging Hidden Collections Program, 2008–2019, by Joy Banks. September 2019. Available at https://www.clir.org/pubs/reports/pub177/. This report presents a comprehensive analysis of final reports from all 128 projects funded through CLIR's Cataloging Hidden Special Collections and Archives program. The report describes the methods and findings of the analysis, including cataloging outputs, as well as impact on hiring, policies and procedures, communication tools, and research and outreach. Web only.

CLIR Issues 127–132. Available at https://www.clir.org/pubs/issues/.

Association for Library and Information Science Education

ALISE Headquarters, 4 Lan Drive, Suite 310 Westford, MA 01886
978-674-6190, e-mail office@alise.org
World Wide Web http://www.alise.org

Stephen Bajjaly
President 2019–2020

The Association for Library and Information Science Education (ALISE) is an independent, nonprofit professional association, founded in 1915 as the Association of American Library Schools (AALS). It changed to its current name in 1983 to reflect more accurately the mission, goals, and membership of the association. Its mission is to lead in innovative and high-quality research, teaching, and service for educators and scholars in library and information science and cognate disciplines internationally through engagement, advocacy, and knowledge creation and dissemination.

Membership

Membership is open to individuals and institutions. Personal members can include anyone interested in the objectives of the association, with categories including full-time (faculty member, administrator, librarian, researcher, or other interested individual); new professional (doctoral students as they transition to faculty member status, maximum of three years); part-time/retired (part-time or adjunct faculty, or retired professionals); and student (doctoral or other students, maximum of six years). Institutional members include schools with programs that offer a graduate degree in library and information science or a cognate field. International affiliate institutional membership is open to any school outside the United States or Canada that offers an educational program in library and information science at the professional level as defined or accepted by the country in which the school is located. Associate institutional membership status is accorded to libraries and organizations other than schools of library and information science.

Structure and Governance

ALISE is constituted of operational groups including the board of directors; committees; the council of deans, directors, and program chairs; school representatives; and special interest groups (SIGs). The association has been managed since October 2018 by McKenna Management, Inc. in Westford, Massachusetts, with Cambria Happ as executive director. The board of directors is composed of seven elected officers serving three-year terms. Officers for 2019–2020 were Stephen Bajjaly (Wayne State University), president; Sandra Hirsh (San Josė State University), vice-president/president-elect; Heidi Julien (University at Buffalo), past president; Heather Moulaison Sandy (University of Missouri), secretary/treasurer; Denice Adkins (University of Missouri), director for membership services; Rong

Tang (Simmons University), director for external relations; and Nicole Cooke (University of South Carolina), director for special interest groups. At the end of the Annual Conference in October 2020, Julien and Tang will conclude their terms of service and two newly elected officers will join the board: a new vice-president/president-elect and a new director for external relations.

The board establishes policy, sets goals and strategic directions, and provides oversight for the management of the association. Face-to-face meetings are held in conjunction with the Annual Conference to focus on policy, planning, programming, and other matters. For the remainder of the year, business is conducted through teleconferences, an online collaborative work platform, and e-mail.

Committees play a vital role in carrying out the work of the association. Since fall 2008, an open call for volunteers to serve on committees has been used to ensure broader participation in committee service, with members for the coming year appointed by the vice-president/president-elect for most committees. Principal areas of activity include awards, conference program planning, governance, nominations, research competitions, and tellers. (See https://www.alise.org/alise-committees for a full list.) Each committee is given an ongoing term of reference to guide its work as well as the specific charges for the year. Task forces can be charged to carry out tasks outside the scope of the existing standing committees.

The ALISE Council of Deans, Directors, and Program Chairs consists of the chief executive officers of each ALISE institutional member school. The group convenes at the Annual Conference and discusses issues via e-mail in the interim. Kathleen Burnett (Florida State University) serves as the 2019–2020 chair.

Within each institutional member school, a school representative is named to serve as a direct link between the membership and the ALISE board. These individuals communicate to the faculty of their school about ALISE and the association's events and initiatives and provide input on membership issues to the ALISE board.

Special interest groups (SIGs) enable members with shared interests to communicate and collaborate, with a particular emphasis on programs at the Annual Conference. New SIGs are established as areas of interest emerge. Ongoing SIGs, grouped by thematic clusters, are

- *Roles and Responsibilities:* Assistant/Associate Deans and Directors, Doctoral Students, Part-Time and Adjunct Faculty
- *Teaching and Learning:* Curriculum, Distance Education, Innovative Pedagogies
- *Topics and Courses:* Archival/Preservation Education; Gender Issues; Historical Perspectives; Information Ethics; Information Policy; International Library Education; Multicultural, Ethnic, and Humanistic Concerns; Research; School Library Media; Technical Services Education, Youth Services

Communication

Announcements, notifications, and membership updates are posted to the ALISE membership listserv. News and events are published on ALISE's official website (http://www.alise.org). The organization has been actively using its social media accounts, including Twitter (@alisehq) and Facebook (https://www.facebook.com/ALISEHQ/) to connect with its members and communities, as well as to post announcements and ALISE-related events in a timely manner.

Publications

The ALISE publications program has four components:

- The *Journal of Education for Library and Information Science* (*JELIS*) is a peer-reviewed quarterly journal edited by John Budd and Denice Adkins. The journal is a scholarly forum for discussion and presentation of research and issues within the field of library and information science (LIS) education. The University of Toronto Press began to serve as the publisher of JELIS in 2018. The journal is open access at a green level. It is indexed in Elsevier's Scopus, among other indexing sources.
- The *ALISE Library and Information Science Education Statistical Report* publishes data collected annually from its institutional members on their curriculum, faculty, students, income and expenditures, and continuing professional education. Members can gain free access to existing reports by logging in on the members-only area of the website.
- The ALISE Book Series published by Rowman & Littlefield addresses issues critical to Library and Information Science education and research through the publication of epistemologically grounded scholarly texts that are inclusive of regional and national contexts around the world. The series editors are Jaya Raju (University of Cape Town) and Dietmar Wolfram (University of Wisconsin–Milwaukee). Several book projects are underway in 2019–2020.
- The ALISE website is the public face of the association and provides information about the association and news of activities and opportunities of interest to members. It provides login access to the MemberClicks system, where members can access members-only benefits (reports, member directory, etc.), renew membership, register for the conference and webinars, and access other services.

Annual Conference

The 2020 annual conference will be held in Pittsburgh, Pennsylvania, on October 20–23, 2020. The conference theme is "Transforming LIS Education in an Interconnected World." Program co-chairs Suliman Hawamdeh (University of North Texas) and Keren Dali (University of Denver), with President Bajjaly, are planning the ALISE conference. The conference will offer presentations, poster sessions, and networking and placement opportunities, along with the unCommons—a gathering place to share, debate, brainstorm, and network. The ALISE Academy will close out the conference. Conference proceedings are housed by the IDEALS repository (https://www.ideals.illinois.edu/handle/2142/98928).

Professional Development

ALISE offers regular webinars free to members to facilitate virtual engagement with research and other membership interests during the year between conferences. Recent webinar offerings have included "Moving from Online Teaching to Connected Teaching," "How Do You Teach Soft Skills: Preparing Our Graduates for What Employers Want," and "Preparing Winning Grant Applications." Persons who are interested in offering a webinar may submit a proposal through the webinar submission web page (http://www.alise.org/webinar-proposals).

The ALISE Leadership Academy was offered for the second time January 30–21, 2020 in Palm Desert, CA. Based on feedback from LIS program leaders and past participants, the theme for this year's Leadership Academy was "Vision 2020: Leading in a Constantly Changing World." ALISE initiated the Leadership Academy to create communities within library and information science for the exploration of leadership roles as chairs, directors, and deans. We aim to build interest in leadership and to build the confidence of prospective leaders. The Academy also provides prior attendees a forum to reconvene, reflect on their learnings from the past year, and to gain new insights to deploy in the future.

Grants and Awards

ALISE supports research and recognizes accomplishments through its grants and awards programs. Research competitions include the ALISE Research Grant Competition, the ALISE / Bohdan S. Wynar Research Paper Competition, the ALISE/ProQuest Methodology Paper Competition, the ALISE / Eugene Garfield Doctoral Dissertation Competition, and the ALISE Community conn@CT Mini-Grants. Support for conference participation is provided by the University of Washington Information School Youth Services Graduate Student Travel Award, the Doctoral Student to ALISE Award, the ALISE/Jean Tague Sutcliffe Doctoral Student Research Poster Competition, and the ALISE Diversity Travel Award to the ALISE Annual Conference. This last award was created in collaboration with the ALA Office for Diversity Spectrum Scholarship Program, which created a parallel award, the ALA/ALISE Spectrum Travel Award to ALISE, partially funded by ALISE.

Awards recognizing outstanding accomplishments include the ALISE/ Norman Horrocks Leadership Award (for early-career leadership), the ALISE / Pratt-Severn Faculty Innovation Award, the ALISE Service Award, the ALISE Award for Professional Contribution, the ALISE/Connie Van Fleet Award for Research Excellence in Public Library Services to Adults, and the ALISE Excellence in Teaching Award. Winners are recognized at an awards luncheon at the Annual Conference. (For a list of award winners, see http://www.alise.org/awards-grants.)

Collaboration with Other Organizations

ALISE seeks to collaborate with other organizations on activities of mutual interest. ALISE members also serve on committees for various national organizations, including ALA committees and the FEDLINK Network.

ALISE continues to build its international connections, with members serving on the International Federation of Library Associations (IFLA) Standing Committees that address education and research, and support of initiatives to address access to information, including the Lyon Declaration that calls on the United Nations to incorporate information in advancing equity and sustainability in the development of the UN post-2015 millennium goals, which shape policies worldwide. ALISE has been expanding its collaborations with peer organizations including the Association for Information Science and Technology (ASIS&T) and the iSchools Organization.

Conclusion

ALISE is guided by its strategic plan for 2017–2020 (http://www.alise.org/alise-strategic-plan-2017-2020). The association looks forward to continuing its leading role in LIS education and research.

NASIG

PMB 305, 1902 Ridge Rd., West Seneca, NY 14224-3312
716-324-1859, e-mail info@nasig.org
World Wide Web http://www.nasig.org

Kristen Wilson
President 2019–2020

Background and Mission

NASIG is an independent organization working to advance and transform the management of information resources. The organization's goal is to facilitate and improve the distribution, acquisition, and long-term accessibility of information resources in all formats and business models.

There are three key components to NASIG's mission:

- NASIG supports a dynamic community of professionals including, but not limited to, librarians, publishers, and vendors engaging in understanding one another's perspectives and improving functionality throughout the information resources life cycle with an emphasis on scholarly communications, serials, and electronic resources.
- NASIG provides a rich variety of conference and continuing education programming to encourage knowledge sharing among its members and to support their professional and career development.
- NASIG promotes the development and implementation of best practices and standards for the distribution, acquisition, and long-term accessibility of information resources in all formats and business models throughout their life cycle. In addition to developing best practices, NASIG supports the development of standards by NISO, an affiliated organization.

Established in 1985, NASIG (formerly the North American Serials Interest Group, Inc.) is an independent organization that promotes communication, information, and continuing education about serials, electronic resources, and the broader issues of scholarly communication. NASIG welcomes anyone interested in the information chain. Inspired by the UKSG (formerly the United Kingdom Serials Group), NASIG held its first conference at Bryn Mawr College in June 1986. The annual conference, usually held in May or June, offers a premier opportunity to meet others representing the diverse interests of the information resources community and to hear speakers who are on the cutting edge of scholarly communication.

Members

Founded on strong professional friendships, NASIG constituents work diligently to maintain that personal spirit, exchange of ideas, and unity of purpose on a volunteer basis. Members include a dynamic group of librarians, publishers, vendors, educators, developers and many others involved in the creation, production, delivery, management, and access of serial information, the scholarly communication process, and emerging technologies.

Organization

NASIG has five administrative officers and six members-at-large who constitute the Executive Board. This team also has liaison responsibilities to standing committees and special working groups. The standing committees are Awards and Recognition, Bylaws, Communications, Conference Planning, Conference Proceedings Editors, Continuing Education, Digital Preservation, Equity & Inclusion, Evaluation and Assessment, Membership Services, Mentoring & Student Outreach, Newsletter, Nominations and Elections, Open Initiatives, Program Planning, Site Selection, and Standards.

In 2019 NASIG added two new standing committees, Digital Preservation and Open Initiatives. The charge of the digital preservation committee is to identify ways in which NASIG can raise awareness of and develop tools for reducing the risk of losing vulnerable digital scholarly content. The charge of the open initiatives committee is to ensure that NASIG is positioned to effectively support open access publishing, library-focused open source software communities, open educational resources, and other important open initiatives.

Opportunities

The annual conference provides a casual venue for preconferences, concurrent sessions, practical workshops, special events, and networking. An emphasis on thoughtful discourse and informality promotes an intensity of purpose not always possible at other conferences.

NASIG also has a strong commitment to continuing education. The organization seeks collaborative endeavors to educate individuals about changes, issues, and future possibilities on the information landscape.

An outstanding awards and grants program encourages students, librarians, and paraprofessionals to attend the annual conference and serve on committees. With awards such as the John Riddick Student Grants, the Marcia Tuttle International Award, the Serials Specialist Award, the Horizon Award, the Champion Award, the John Merriman Joint NASIG/UKSG Award, the Rose Robischon Scholarship, and the Fritz Schwartz Serials Education Scholarship, NASIG supports new and seasoned librarians in their continuing professional development.

Partnerships

NASIG has long recognized the value in collaborating with other associations in the information community and has developed several strategic partnerships to further the goals of both organizations. NASIG is a member of National Information Standards Organization (NISO) and Project COUNTER in recognition of the important role that standards play in the information industry and the valuable input that NASIG members can provide in developing and refining industry standards. NASIG is also a strategic affiliate of the Library Publishing Coalition (LPC). NASIG and LPC not only share a vision for a sustainable and open scholarship environment, but both organizations are actively using the development of best practices and shared expertise to make that vision a reality. NASIG is also a member of the International Federation of Library Associations and Institutions (IFLA) in the hopes that NASIG members can provide expertise to IFLA standing committees while also learning from the global IFLA community. NASIG's most long-lasting partnerships are with the library publishing and vendor community who are not only represented in the individual and organizational memberships, but also as conference and award sponsors. In addition to vendor sponsorship of awards, NASIG partners with its sister organization UKSG to provide the John Merriman Joint NASIG/UKSG Award to support a member exchange for each organization's conference every year.

NASIG has also collaborated with groups like Society for Scholarly Publishing and acted as sponsor and exhibitor at regional conferences such as the NC Serials Conference and the Ohio Valley Group of Technical Services Librarians (OVGTSL). NASIG looks forward to developing additional partners in the coming years.

Publications and Webinars

NASIG's main publication is its NASIG Newsletter, which provides regular updates from the NASIG board and NASIG committees five times a year. In addition, the newsletter provides sneak previews of the annual conference speakers and events and advice on navigating the conference's host city.

NASIG's commitment to the implementation of best practices can be seen in the development and continued revision of the core competencies series. Inspired by the American Library Association's Core Competencies for Librarianship, NASIG has formed task forces to produce the following three core competency documents:

- Core Competencies for Electronic Resources Librarians (approved and adopted by the NASIG Executive Board, July 22, 2013; revised January 26, 2016)
- Core Competencies for Print Serials Management (approved and adopted by the NASIG Executive Board, May 30, 2015; revised April 25, 2016)
- Core Competencies for Scholarly Communication Librarians (approved and adopted by the NASIG Executive Board, August 11, 2017; revised December 20, 2019)

The core competencies serve as professional development tools on campuses across the information community and have even found their way into the education and intern programs at major library and information science graduate programs. In 2019 NASIG's Continuing Education Committee also produced one NASIG webinar entitled Designing for Accessibility with Melissa Green, an IAAP Certified Professional in Accessibility Core Competencies (CPACC) and technology accessibility specialist at the University of Alabama's Center for Instructional

Technology. NASIG webinars have reduced rates for NASIG and NISO members, and recordings are made freely available six months after the event.

The proceedings of the 2018 NASIG conference were published in the *Serials Librarian*, volume 76, no. 1–4 (2019). Edited by Paul D. Moeller, Cindy Shirkey, Courtney McAllister, and Cecilia Genereux, the proceedings include reports on every session at the conference, including preconferences, and are freely available to NASIG members via the NASIG website after a six-month embargo.

Annual Conference

The 2019 NASIG conference was held June 4–8 in Pittsburgh, Pennsylvania, with the theme "Building Bridges." Vision sessions were presented by DeEtta Jones (founder and principal, DeEtta Jones Associates) and Philip Schreur (associate university librarian for technical and access services, Stanford University), and videos of these sessions were made freely available postconference via the NASIG YouTube channel. Preconference events included workshops on text mining, leadership, BIBFRAME, licensing, and scholarly communication.

In addition to hour-long concurrent sessions, members were also treated to lightning sessions highlighting vendor innovations and upcoming projects, student research, and the great ideas showcase. A variety of structured and unstructured events, including a first-timers' mentoring program, create an environment where the information community of practice can learn, network, and socialize to further the professional development of all involved.

The 2020 conference will be held in Spokane, Washington, June 8–12.

Awards and Grants

NASIG's commitment to the professional development of the information community is displayed in the awards and grants provided to professionals throughout their careers. The Horizon Award supports conference attendance for a promising new information professional, while the Birdie MacLennan Award supports conference attendance for a mid-career professional. The Rose Robischon Scholarship is focused on assisting those professionals who lack funds for conference travel, while the John Merriman Joint NASIG/UKSG Award and the Marcia Tuttle International Grant are both focused on increasing the international experience of NASIG members. The Capstone Award recognizes a professional who has made significant and distinguished contributions to the field of information resource management.

NASIG is committed to developing the next generation of information professionals with free membership for students, reduced registration rates for webinars and conferences, and three awards to support conference attendance. The John Riddick Student Grant, Fritz Schwartz Education Scholarship, and Mexican Student Grant bring multiple students to the NASIG conference each year. The student NASIG conference experience includes a mentor, an opportunity to present at the Student Showcase, and a number of events to make connections and learn from practitioners in the industry. NASIG also recognizes the talents and contributions of paraprofessionals with the First-Timer Award and the Paraprofessional Specialist Award which provide conference attendance support.

NASIG was honored to introduce the Diversity and Inclusion Award sponsored by Harrassowitz, in 2019. The purpose of this award is to further NASIG's mission to increase the diversity of its membership and provide financial support to attend the NASIG annual conference. Applicants must be a member of an underrepresented group in the NASIG community.

International Reports

International Federation of Library Associations and Institutions

Postal Address: P.O. Box 95312, 2509 CH Den Haag, Netherlands
Visiting Address: Prins Willem-Alexanderhof 5, 2595 BE The Hague, Netherlands
Tel. +31 70 3140884, fax +31 70 3834827, e-mail ifla@ifla.org
World Wide Web http://www.ifla.org

Beacher Wiggins

Director for Acquisitions and Bibliographic Access, Library of Congress
Secretary, IFLA Standing Committee on Acquisition and Collection Development, 2015–2019

Susan R. Morris

Special Assistant to the Director for Acquisitions and Bibliographic Access, Library of Congress
Member, IFLA Standing Committee on Cataloguing, 2015–2019

The International Federation of Library Associations and Institutions (IFLA) is the preeminent international organization representing librarians, other information professionals, and library users. Throughout 2019 IFLA promoted its four core values: freedom of access to information and expression, as stated in Article 19 of the Universal Declaration of Human Rights; the belief that such access must be universal and equitable to support human well-being; delivery of high-quality library and information services in support of that access; and the commitment to enabling all members of IFLA to participate without regard to citizenship, disability, ethnic origin, gender, geographical location, political philosophy, race, or religion.

World Library and Information Congress (WLIC): 85th IFLA General Conference and Council, Athens, Greece

The World Library and Information Congress / 85th IFLA General Conference and Council attracted more than 3,300 delegates from more than 130 countries to Athens, Greece, August 24–30, 2019. Conference attendance was nearly level with the 3,500 registrations at the 2018 WLIC in Kuala Lumpur, Malaysia, and significantly exceeded attendance at the WLIC in Columbus, Ohio, in August 2016, and Wrocław, Poland, in August 2017.

The conference theme, "Dialogue for Change," was especially appropriate as then-president of IFLA, Glòria Pérez-Salmerón, and Secretary General Gerald Leitner unveiled the new IFLA Strategy 2019–2024. The annual cultural evening at the Stavros Niarchos Foundation Cultural Centre featured traditional Greek food, dancing, and costumes while showing WLIC participants the spectacular Cultural Centre building, designed by the architect Renzo Piano with a solar "green canopy" to capture solar energy while affording a stunning view of the Acropolis.

Twenty-two satellite meetings, organized by IFLA sections, offered deeper discussions on specific topics, such as "Artificial Intelligence (AI) and Its Impact on Libraries and Librarianship," "Grey Literature: Scholarly Communication in a Digital World," and "RDA: Resource Description and Access 2019." The satellite meetings took place in several Greek cities and half a dozen countries—Austria, Croatia, Egypt, Germany, Italy including Vatican City, and Serbia.

The next World Library and Information Congress will take place in August 2020 in Dublin, Ireland. The 2021 WLIC is planned for Rotterdam, Netherlands, and the 2022 WLIC will be held in Auckland, New Zealand.

IFLA Global Vision and IFLA Strategy 2019–2024

The IFLA Strategy 2019–2024 developed from the IFLA Global Vision that President Pérez-Salmerón launched in March 2018. In keeping with IFLA's participatory, inclusive identity, the Federation had promoted development of the Global Vision through 185 workshops and meetings on five continents in 2018. Discussions focused on strengthening ties within the library world, identifying future challenges and opportunities, and prioritizing possible actions in response to social change. The IFLA officers and headquarters staff analyzed the outcomes of those discussions from September 2018 through March 2019 and drafted the new IFLA Strategy 2019–2024.

The energy and ideas that emerged from the Global Vision workshops are available indefinitely on the IFLA Global Vision Ideas Store (https://ideas.ifla.org/ideas/), where librarians can search for solutions to challenges and contribute their own successful ideas for use by the international library community. The Ideas Store was launched at the 2018 WLIC and continuously accepts new ideas from IFLA members.

The Global Vision informs the new IFLA Global Strategy with ten strategic opportunities in the areas of intellectual freedom, digital realm, better understanding of our communities' needs, ongoing technological change, better advocacy, communicating libraries' relevance and impact to stakeholders, the spirit of collaboration, need to challenge our current structures and behaviors, maximizing access to the world's documentary heritage, and encouraging younger library professionals.

The IFLA Strategy presents four strategic directions: strengthen the global voice of libraries; inspire and enhance professional practice; connect and empower the field; and optimize the organization. Each strategic direction is supported by four key initiatives. The first key initiative is "Show the power of libraries in achieving the Sustainable Development Goals" of the United Nations for the year 2030. Together, the four strategic directions and 16 key initiatives form a call to action for all libraries to inspire, engage, enable, and connect with their societies. To support decisions on such actions, IFLA continues to conduct its Trend Report, with the latest update published on December 23, 2019.

The IFLA Governing Board approved the Strategy on April 12, 2019. The IFLA Governing Board began a governance review to identify changes in governance structure that are necessary to support the new strategy. The review began with a Board workshop at IFLA Headquarters in The Hague, December 10–11, 2019. The aim was to issue a proposal for member comments by March 2020 and to ensure that a new governance structure is in place before the 2021 IFLA elections. The Board promised IFLA members that the revised governance structure would be participatory and inclusive.

Standards

In the current 2016–2021 Strategic Plan, key initiative 1.4, "Promoting IFLA Standards to support libraries in the provision of services to their communities," is tied to the strategic direction for "libraries in society," rather than the strategic direction for "information and knowledge." The definition of "IFLA standard" is quite broad and encompasses conceptual models, formatting codes, rules, guidelines, and best practices, ranging from the Statement of International Cataloguing Principles (ICP) to IFLA Guidelines for Library Services to People Experiencing Homelessness. The ICP and Library Reference Model are the foundation of many national and international cataloging codes, such as *RDA: Resource Description & Access* in the Anglo-heritage and Germanic library communities. At the close of the WLIC in Athens, the Professional Committee endorsed and issued two new sets of guidelines, on Public Internet Access in Libraries and on Setting Up a Digital Unification Project. IFLA has liaison relationships with several technical committees of the International Standardization Organization (ISO); representation on the European Committee for Standardization (CEN) Technical Committee—Conservation of Cultural Heritage; and an ex officio position on the International ISBN Agency Board.

Copyright and Libraries

IFLA advocates vigorously for open access to digital content and for the right of libraries to benefit from fair use and exemptions from copyright restrictions. Its Copyright and Other Legal Matters (CLM) strategic program is managed by an advisory committee working with IFLA Headquarters. Much of CLM's work requires close cooperation with other international organizations. The CLM Advisory Committee represents IFLA on the Standing Committee on Copyright and Related Rights (SCCR) of WIPO, the World Intellectual Property Organization. With other library organizations and several countries, CLM has persistently advocated that SCCR propose a treaty on Copyright Limitations and Exceptions for Libraries and Archives. In June 2018 SSCR approved an action plan for Limitations and Exceptions that began with a fact-finding and information-gathering phase. This phase culminated in the WIPO International Conference on Limitations and Exceptions for Libraries, Archives, Museums, and Educational and Research Institutions in October 2019, strongly supported by IFLA.

Through CLM, IFLA participated in UNESCO's work to promote access to educational resources under free and open licenses, particularly for resources that are publicly funded. At UNESCO's 40th General Conference in May 2019, members adopted a UNESCO Formal Recommendation and an action plan to promote such open access throughout the world. CLM also participates in workshops with WIPO and the International Publishers Association to promote mutual understanding.

From the time that the Marrakesh Treaty to Facilitate Access to Published Works for Persons Who Are Blind, Visually Impaired, or Otherwise Print Disabled (Marrakesh Treaty) was first agreed by a diplomatic conference in Marrakesh, Morocco, in June 2013, IFLA has worked tirelessly to promote the treaty. The treaty entered into force in June 2016, when it had been ratified by the requisite twenty countries. The treaty took effect in all countries of the European Union on January 1, 2019. The United States ratified the treaty on October 9, 2018, when the president signed Public Law No. 115-261, the Marrakesh Treaty Implementation Act. The United States formally deposited its instrument of ratification with WIPO on February 8, 2019, and the treaty took effect in the United States three months later. In view of the enormous publishing output of the United States, this implementation greatly advances libraries' ability to serve print-disabled users worldwide. IFLA issues an annual monitoring report on treaty compliance in countries that have joined the Marrakesh Treaty.

Cultural Heritage Disaster Reconstruction

IFLA's strategic direction recognizes culture as a basic human need and calls for sustained effort to preserve cultural heritage. Since 1996 IFLA has been a founding member of the International Committee of the Blue Shield and its successor, the Blue Shield, to protect cultural property in the event of natural and human disasters. Its current Blue Shield partners are the International Council on Archives, the International Council on Monuments and Sites, and the International Council of Museums. Since 2016, IFLA has maintained a Risk Register for Documentary Cultural Heritage, a repository of information about unique documentary heritage assets deemed to be at risk from natural or human-caused disasters throughout the world. The risk register is confidential, and an IFLA committee authenticates each submission. In 2019 IFLA expanded its interests to include preservation of indigenous languages and of digital cultural heritage resources.

Grants and Awards

The Federation continues to work with corporate partners and national libraries to maintain programs and opportunities that would otherwise not be possible, especially for librarians and libraries in developing countries. The Jay Jordan IFLA/OCLC Early Career Development Fellowships provided four weeks of intensive experience, based in OCLC headquarters in Dublin, Ohio, for library and information science professionals from countries with developing economies who were in the early stages of their careers. The Fellows for 2019 were from Bolivia, Jamaica, Lebanon, Mongolia, and Nigeria. In the course of twenty years, the program supported 95 librarians from 42 countries. In 2019 OCLC began evaluating new directions for the program and did not plan to name a cohort of Fellows for 2020.

Numerous awards and grants encourage travel to the annual IFLA conferences. The IFLA PressReader International Marketing Award was presented in 2019 to the University of British Columbia for its 2018 UBC Library Digital Colouring Books Campaign. The award includes a cash stipend and travel to the conference for three representatives of the winning organizations, who are selected by the IFLA Section on Management and Marketing in collaboration with the corporate sponsor.

The Standing Committee for the IFLA Academic and Research Libraries Section awards three travel grants, cosponsored by Sage and Ex Libris since 2015, for emerging library professionals or students to attend the WLIC. In addition, IFLA waived registration for 40 first-time conference attendees through its IFLA WLIC Participation Grants, with increased funding through a bequest by the late German librarian Angela Bersekowski. A second category, the IFLA New Professionals WLIC Attendance Grants, supported registration fees for 48 newer librarians.

Other IFLA awards recognize exemplary libraries or librarians. The IFLA Green Library Award recognizes a green or sustainable library project. Sponsored by DeGruyter, this relatively new award was designed by the IFLA Environment, Sustainability, and Libraries Special Interest Group. In 2019 the recipient was the Biblioteca Pública Municipal Daniel Guillard in Cali, Colombia, for its initiative "Gaia: En mi biblioteca la tierra también es de todos." This program involved all members of the local community in awareness of sustainability and green practice.

The IFLA/Systematic Award recognizes a library that best combines innovative architecture with information technology solutions, accounting for digital developments and local culture. The winning library must operate in a building that is newly built or newly repurposed as a library. With an award of $5,000 from Systematic, this is one of IFLA's most generous awards. In 2019 it was presented to the Oodi Helsinki Central Library, Finland.

The IFLA Dynamic Unit and Impact Award in 2019 was awarded to the Library Buildings and Equipment Section for its active programming, collaboration with other IFLA units, and effective communications strategy. The IFLA Metropolitan Libraries Short Film Award in 2019 went to the film "Why These Finnish Libraries Are the Best in the World—Espoo, Finland." The film was first screened at the Metropolitan Libraries Section's conference in Helsinki, May 8–10, 2019, and all conference participants voted on the award.

The IFLA Honorary Fellowships, IFLA Medal, and IFLA Scroll of Appreciation recognize service to IFLA by individuals. In 2019 two Americans, Deborah Jacobs and Donna Scheeder, president of IFLA from 2013 to 2015, were named IFLA Honorary Fellows, considered IFLA's highest award to individuals. Jacobs was honored for her work with the Global Libraries Foundation; Scheeder was recognized as a leading advocate for libraries within the United National Sustainable Development Goals for 2030. The IFLA Scroll of Appreciation was presented to the Greek National Committee for the Athens WLIC in 2019. In addition, two library leaders received the Scroll of Appreciation in recognition of their distinguished service to the international library community: Jeanne Drewes of the Library of Congress and Steven W. Witt, currently editor of the *IFLA Journal*. The IFLA Medal was awarded to Kai Eckholm in appreciation of his work as chair of FAIFE and other contributions to IFLA and to Barbara Schleihagen for her role on the IFLA Governing Board.

Membership and Finances

IFLA has more than 1,500 members in more than 150 countries, having added about 100 members in the past year. Initially established at a conference in Edinburgh, Scotland, in 1927, it has been registered in Netherlands since 1971 and has headquarters facilities at the Koninklijke Bibliotheek (Royal Library) in The Hague. Although IFLA did not hold a general conference outside Europe and North America until 1980, there has since been steadily increasing participation from Asia, Africa, South America, and Australia. The Federation maintains regional offices for Africa (in Pretoria, South Africa); Asia and Oceania (in Singapore); and Latin America and the Caribbean (in Buenos Aires, Argentina; formerly in Mexico City, Mexico, and Rio de Janeiro, Brazil).

IFLA offers a range of membership categories: international library associations, national library associations, other associations (generally regional or special library associations), institutions, institutional subunits, one-person libraries, school libraries, national association affiliates (limited to three consecutive years and open only to national associations with operating budgets of 10,000 Euros or less, to encourage membership in countries with developing economies), personal affiliates, student affiliates, new graduate members, and nonsalaried personal members.

UNESCO has given IFLA formal associate relations status, the highest level of relationship accorded to nongovernmental organizations by UNESCO. In addition, IFLA has observer status with the United Nations, WIPO, the International Organization for Standardization (ISO), and the World Trade Organization, and associate status with the International Council of Scientific Unions. IFLA participates in the Internet Governance Forum, under UN auspices.

Leading corporations in the information industry have formed working relationships with IFLA as Corporate Partners. The Corporate Partners provide financial and in-kind support and in turn gain the opportunity to convey information about their products and services to IFLA members and others who pay attention to IFLA's publications and activities. Several levels of corporate partnership are available. Most prominently, since 2014 OCLC has been IFLA's first and sole Platinum Partner, providing extraordinary support that continued in 2019. Other corporate partners choose to support IFLA at three exceptional levels—gold, silver, or bronze. Gold Corporate Partners in 2019 were Emerald and Sage Publications. Silver Partners were DeGruyter Saur, Elsevier, and Sabinet; Bronze Partners were Otto Harrassowitz GmbH and Zeutschel GmBh. The Federation's Associate Supporters were Annual Reviews and nbd/biblion.

The IFLA Foundation (Stichting IFLA) was established in 2007. The Foundation accepts private donations and bequests and also is funded by other IFLA income. It gives funding priority to proposals and projects that promise to have a long-term impact in developing and strengthening IFLA; are clearly related to at least one of IFLA's strategic priorities; and are not likely to be funded by other bodies. The Foundation also occasionally makes grants for attendance at the World Library and Information Conference; the grants are administered by the IFLA headquarters and governance structure rather than directly by the Foundation.

Personnel, Structure, and Governance

The secretary general of IFLA is Gerald Leitner. His e-mail address is iflasg@ifla.org. Helen Mandl is the deputy secretary general and the manager for member services. Her e-mail address is helen.mandl@ifla.org. In addition, IFLA Headquarters has a staff of twenty.

The editor of the quarterly *IFLA Journal* is Steven W. Witt. The journal has a ten-member editorial committee, chaired by Shali Zhang of the University of Montana and reporting to the IFLA Professional Committee, that arranges peer review for articles, monitors quality and consistency, and guides editorial direction. The journal is published by SAGE.

Christine Mackenzie of Melbourne, Australia, became IFLA's president for 2019–2021 at the close of the Athens WLIC. She is a past treasurer of IFLA and served as a hardworking president-elect in 2017–2019. She chose "Let's work together" as her presidential theme, highlighting the unity and inclusiveness that the IFLA Strategy 2019–2024 stresses.

The new president-elect is Barbara Lison, director of the Stadtbibliothek Bremen, Germany. The new treasurer is Antonia Arahova, director of the Presidential Library of Greece. The past president is Glòria Pérez-Salmerón, past president of FESABID (Federación Española de Sociedades de Archivística, Biblioteconomía, Documentación y Museística) and president of IFLA, 2017–2019. Her presidential theme was "Libraries: Motors for Change." She and Leitner promoted the theme as well as the Global Vision and IFLA Strategy around the globe in 2019, notably participating in the American Library Association Annual Conference in Washington, D.C., June 20–25, 2019.

Under the revised 2008 IFLA Statutes, the 19 members of IFLA's Governing Board (plus the secretary general, ex officio) are responsible for the Federation's general policies, management, and finance. Additionally, the Board represents the Federation in legal and other formal proceedings. The Board is comprised of the president, president-elect, secretary general (ex officio), up to ten directly elected members, the chair of the Professional Committee, the chairs of each IFLA division, and the chair of the Standing Committee of the Management of Library Associations Section. Currently the only American member of the Governing Board is Michael Dowling, director for chapter relations and international relations for the American Library Association. He is also one of two IFLA Governing Board members elected to the IFLA Executive Committee.

The Governing Board delegates responsibility for overseeing the direction of IFLA between Board meetings, within the policies established by the Board, to the IFLA Executive Committee, which includes the president, president-elect, treasurer, chair of the Professional Committee, and two members of the Governing Board, elected every two years by members of the Board from among its elected members. The secretary general of IFLA is a nonvoting member, ex officio, and acts as the Executive Committee's secretary.

The IFLA Professional Committee monitors the planning and programming of professional activities carried out by IFLA's professional groups—five divisions, forty-four sections, and special interest groups—and strategic programs.

The Professional Committee is composed of one elected officer from each division, plus a chair elected by the outgoing Committee; the president, the president-elect, and the professional support officer, who serves as secretary; and the chairs of the CLM (Copyright and Legal Matters) and FAIFE (Freedom of Access to Information and Freedom of Expression) committees, and two elected members of the Governing Board. Vicki McDonald, state librarian of Queensland, Australia, chairs the Professional Committee.

The five divisions of IFLA are I: Library Types; II: Library Collections; III: Library Services; IV: Support of the Profession; and V: Regions. Forty-four sections focus on topical interests, such as Statistics and Evaluation, Library Buildings and Equipment, and Rare Books and Special Collections, or on particular types of libraries or parts of the world.

The six IFLA strategic programs are the Library Development Programme (LDP); Preservation and Conservation (PAC); UNIMARC Strategic Programme, which maintains and develops the Universal MARC Format, UNIMARC; Committee on Standards; Freedom of Access to Information and Freedom of Expression (FAIFE); and Copyright and Other Legal Matters (CLM).

To ensure an arena within IFLA for discussion of new social, professional, or cultural issues, the Professional Committee approves the formation of special interest groups for a limited time. There currently are discussion groups for Access to Information Network/Africa (ATINA); Big Data; Digital Humanities/Digital Scholarship; Environment, Sustainability, and Libraries; Evidence for Global and Disaster Health; LGBTQ (Lesbian, Gay, Bisexual, Transgender, Queer/Questioning) Users; Library and Information Science Education in Developing Countries; Library History; Library Publishing; Linked Data; National Information and Library Policy; National Organizations and International Relations; New Professionals; Religions: Libraries and Dialogue; and Women, Information, and Libraries. Special interest groups operate for a maximum period of three years. If there is sufficient interest, a special interest group may then become a permanent IFLA section. The Indigenous Matters Section was established from a special interest group in 2015.

Two other long-standing IFLA projects are the IFLA website and the IFLA Voucher Scheme. The Voucher Scheme enables libraries to pay for international interlibrary loan requests using vouchers purchased from IFLA rather than actual currency or credit accounts. Beginning in 2019 IFLA charges a handling fee in addition to the voucher cost, but by eliminating bank charges and invoices for each transaction, the Voucher Scheme continues to reduce the administrative costs of international library loans and allows libraries to plan budgets with less regard to short-term fluctuations in the value of different national currencies. The Voucher Scheme has also encouraged participating libraries to voluntarily standardize their charges for loans.

The IFLA Governing Board in 2018 revised its Data Protection Policy to comply with the General Data Protection Regulation (GDPR) of the European Union. Under the revised policy, IFLA can publish contact details of its officers, staff, standing committee members, and special interest group conveners on its website and in section newsletters and the *IFLA Journal*. Consent from individuals is gathered on a data protection registration form. IFLA does not sell contact information for individuals.

Library and Archives Canada

Leslie Weir
Librarian and Archivist of Canada

Two thousand nineteen was a year of change for Library and Archives Canada (LAC), marked by the end of Dr. Guy Berthiaume's five-year mandate as Librarian and Archivist of Canada and the entry of librarian Leslie Weir into the role.

The past five years have been important and positive years in the shaping of the national institution in the 21st century. An emphasis was placed on collaboration, LAC's role in the community, and increasing access to the riches of its collection as well as putting it at the leading edge of new archival and library science technologies.

LAC and Its Partners

Without its partners, LAC cannot advance its work as efficiently or strategically. LAC seeks key partnerships with major players: universities; provinces and territories; nonprofit organizations; the private sector; and public sector institutions such as municipal libraries. These unique relationships benefit both the partnering organizations and, especially, their users. Thanks to its partners, LAC can share more information and expertise, host more conferences and exhibitions, offer more services, and provide more access.

LAC's agreements with the University of Ottawa, Dalhousie University, Université Laval, the Université de Sherbrooke, Western University, Carleton University, Memorial University, and the University of Toronto, among others, create knowledge hubs to share expertise, information, and technology, and to support research and outreach activities. In 2019 these partnerships enabled a number of joint academic conferences on women's rights, on what it means to be Métis, on raising future citizens, and on smart cities, for example.

The institution meets with its partners through its Stakeholders Forum and the National, Provincial, and Territorial Archivists Conference. LAC is also active in the International Council on Archives, the International Federation of Library Associations and Institutions (IFLA), and other global organizations with common objectives.

Community and Access

Libraries and archives have become a new kind of community resource: working with local organizations, promoting literacy, welcoming newcomers, and offering services both in communities and online.

Through the Documentary Heritage Communities Program (DHCP), LAC supports Canada's documentary heritage organizations by increasing their capacity to preserve and make their collections accessible. In 2019, for the fourth year running, LAC invested $1.5 million to support the development of Canada's archival, library, and museum communities, and the professional associations that represent them, by increasing their capacity to preserve, provide access to, and promote documentary heritage. Since 2015 LAC has contributed $7.5 million to support well over 170 projects.

One of LAC's key commitments to Canadians over the past five years has been to make the collection more accessible, and one of the best ways to do this is by hosting public events. LAC hosted more than 50 public events in 2019 including exhibitions, book launches, interviews, and conferences. Events have been well attended, a reflection of the collaborative work between LAC and the community in order to provide access to the work of the institution. LAC takes advantage of social media to extend its reach, engaging with users through Facebook, Twitter, Instagram, and YouTube.

Lastly, to effectively fulfill its mission LAC sought to implement new ways of reaching and serving its publics. With the objective of being closer to its clients, LAC moved its operations on Canada's east and west coasts to more popular sites: the Canadian Museum of Immigration at Pier 21 in Halifax, and the Vancouver Public Library.

At the Leading Edge of New Archival and Library Science Technologies

The scope and complexity of projects LAC has pursued over the past five years have helped to establish it as a leader among digitally enabled memory institutions worldwide. In particular, years of consultation and planning have led to the implementation of a new library system and the procurement of a system for managing born-digital acquisitions. At the same time, LAC continues to move forward with the planning of a second state-of-the-art analog preservation facility.

LAC has embarked on a large-scale, multistream initiative called the Digital Asset Management System (DAMS) to move its extensive collection of digital records to a new digital platform, making it easier for Canadians to access published and archival records of historical and modern-day significance. The new system, supported by Preservica, a global leader in active digital preservation software, addresses the multistream element of LAC's large-scale digital ingest and preservation initiative. It includes all processes, computer systems, software, and hardware that facilitate digital asset management, allowing bulk ingest of digital records, identification and migration of at-risk files, ingest and updating of metadata, and full text search of digital records.

The Way Forward

With the aforementioned projects as major focal points over the past five years, LAC is on a strong foundation as the second decade of the 21st century closes. The 2020s promise to be anything but static. Key drivers are LAC's two new buildings, which will see a significant transformation of the institution's services and an increasing need, and expectation, by the public for quicker and greater access to information. Service transformation and digital optimization will dictate the way forward.

To reach more users and provide them with the best possible experience, LAC is working to transform its services and virtual access to the collection. Users expect to find what they are looking for quickly, and to have a user-friendly, dynamic, and interactive online experience, and this is what LAC aims to deliver by making the most of what digital technology has to offer. It will continue to offer and feature more digital content through an expanded online presence and enhanced search tools that address the expectations and interests of all generations, including those who have grown up in the digital age and expect the collection to be easily accessible from anywhere in Canada.

As LAC begins transforming its services to better disseminate its collection's content, it must also prepare by optimizing its digital infrastructure and its ability to acquire, manage, and preserve the constantly growing digital content transferred to it by Canadian content producers (including federal government institutions, publishers, and other creators) and the content generated through digitization. In this context, the optimization of digital infrastructure and capability is essential to enable LAC to fulfill its mandate.

Further, LAC's role as custodian of enduring knowledge is expanding every year. In the digital age: technology is constantly evolving and new challenges are multiplying. With this in mind, LAC is committed to improving its services and continuing to offer a wide range of public activities and events to better meet the needs of Canadians.

As evidenced, the future is anything but boring and the institution is eager and readying for a new decade. LAC's immediate future looks exceptionally bright.

International Board on Books for Young People

Nonnenweg 12, Postfach, CH-4009 Basel, Switzerland
E-mail ibby@ibby.org
World Wide Web http://www.ibby.org

Mingzhou Zhang
President, 2018–2020

Liz Page
Executive Director

The founding of the International Board on Books for Young People (IBBY) was the result of the visionary commitment of Jella Lepman (1891–1970). Born in Stuttgart, Germany, she became a politically active journalist. In 1936 she emigrated with her son and daughter from Nazi Germany to London and became a British citizen, working for the British Foreign Office and the BBC during World War II and, beginning in 1941, for the American Broadcasting Station in Europe.

When the war ended, Lepman was engaged at the American headquarters in Germany as adviser for questions relating to children and young people. Despite a lack of funds, she organized an exhibition of children's illustrations and children's books from 20 countries in Munich in 1946. Three years later, with initial funding from the Rockefeller Foundation, she established the International Youth Library in Munich and was its director until 1957.

In the postwar years, individuals actively engaged in the field of children's literature in many countries became aware of the importance of children's books as a means for promoting international understanding and peace. They realized that children everywhere should have access to books with high literary and artistic standards and thus become enthusiastic and informed readers.

With this vision in mind, Lepman organized a meeting in Munich under the title "International Understanding through Children's Books" in November 1951. The goal of the meeting was the foundation of an international organization to promote children's books. The speeches and discussions at this conference were covered by news media worldwide. The meeting resulted in the establishment of a committee to form the International Board on Books for Young People—IBBY.

The committee met in Munich in 1952 and made a formal declaration of intent. The meeting was chaired by Swiss publisher Hans Sauerländer, and the effort was international in character from the beginning; the meeting included representatives from Austria, Germany, the Netherlands, Norway, Sweden, and Switzerland.

The success of this preparatory work resulted in the establishment of IBBY, which was registered as a nonprofit organization in Switzerland when the new organization's first General Assembly and Congress were held at the Swiss Federal Institute for Technology (ETHZ) in Zurich in October 1953. The congress brought together founding members including the authors Erich Kästner, Lisa Tetzner, Astrid Lindgren, Jo Tenfjord, Fritz Brunner, and Pamela Travers; the Swiss illustrators Alois Carigiet and Hans Fischer; the publishers Hans Sauerländer and Bettina Hürlimann; and specialists in reading research including Richard Bamberger.

The initial capital for the founding of IBBY was donated by the Swiss foundation Pro Juventute, and its secretary general, Otto Binder, was elected as IBBY's first president. In the early years IBBY also received support from the International Youth Library. However, the dues from the ten national sections that had joined IBBY by 1956 were not sufficient to establish a permanent office, and IBBY's activities were mainly carried out through donations and voluntary work. The organization of the administration was the task of the acting presidents who served for two-year terms during the first decade. Succeeding Otto Binder were Swedish publisher Hans Rabén (1956–1958), Italian professor of education Enzo Petrini (1958–1960), and Lepman (1960–1962).

A notable professionalization of IBBY and an extension of membership were achieved during the presidency of Bamberger (1962–1966). In addition, the publication of IBBY's quarterly journal, *Bookbird*, edited by Lepman, Bamberger, and Lucia Binder, became a permanent activity at this time. During the presidencies of Slovenian publisher Zorka Persic (1966–1970) and Finnish school principal Niilo Visapää (1970–1974), IBBY grew so large that it was no longer possible to rely entirely on voluntary work. In 1974 a permanent office, the IBBY Secretariat, was established in Basel. Leena Maissen was appointed its director and remained in that post until her retirement in 2003. Currently the post is held by Liz Page.

IBBY is a nonprofit organization that represents an international network of people who are committed to bringing books and children together. The annual dues from the national sections are IBBY's only source of regular income; projects are supported by sponsors. IBBY cooperates with many international organizations and children's book institutions around the world and exhibits at the International Children's Book Fair in Bologna and other international book fairs.

The biennial IBBY Congresses, which have taken place in 26 countries, have become increasingly important meeting points for the worldwide membership, now comprising 80 national sections, to share information and experiences.

Mission and Programs

IBBY's mission is

- To promote international understanding through children's books
- To give children everywhere the opportunity to have access to books with high literary and artistic standards
- To encourage the publication and distribution of quality children's books, especially in developing countries
- To provide support and training for those involved with children and children's literature
- To stimulate research and scholarly works in the field of children's literature
- To protect and uphold children's rights as outlined in the United Nations Convention on the Rights of the Child

As part of its mission, IBBY administers three major international awards: the Hans Christian Andersen Award, which is presented to an author and illustrator whose body of work has made lasting contributions to children's literature; the IBBY-Asahi Reading Promotion Award, which is given to a group or institution whose activities are judged to be making a lasting contribution to reading promotion programs for children and young people; and the IBBY-iRead Reading Promoter Award, which recognizes outstanding individuals who are working to promote the expansion and development of children's reading. All three awards are given biennially and presented at the IBBY congresses; the next awards will be presented at the 37th IBBY Congress in Moscow in 2020.

The IBBY Honour List is a biennial selection of outstanding recently published books, honoring writers, illustrators, and translators from IBBY member countries. An annotated catalog is published for each Honour List selection.

The IBBY Documentation Centre of Books for Young People with Disabilities offers information, consultation, and documentation services for organizations, research workers, teachers, students, librarians, publishers, authors, illustrators, policymakers, and the media who work with young people with special needs. A selective list, Outstanding Books for Young People with Disabilities, is prepared biennially and presented in an annotated catalog. The center is based at the North York Central Library Branch of the Toronto (Canada) Public Library.

Traveling exhibitions of the IBBY Honour List and the Outstanding Books for Young People with Disabilities selections are available from IBBY. Detailed information can be found on the IBBY website (http://www.ibby.org).

IBBY established International Children's Book Day in 1967 to inspire a love of reading and to call attention to children's books. Each year the day is sponsored by an IBBY national section and is celebrated on or around Hans Christian Andersen's birthday, April 2.

The IBBY Yamada workshop and project program relies on its international network to help produce and develop book cultures for children within regions that have special needs and lack support.

IBBY established its Children in Crisis program to provide support for children whose lives have been disrupted by war, civil disorder, or natural disaster. The two main activities supported are the therapeutic use of books and storytelling in the form of bibliotherapy, and the creation or replacement of collections of selected books that are appropriate to the situation. The Sharjah/IBBY Fund for Children in Crisis was active from 2012 to 2016. The fund supported projects in Afghanistan, Iran, Lebanon, Palestine, Pakistan, and Tunisia.

In response to the waves of refugees from Africa and the Middle East arriving on the Italian island Lampedusa, IBBY launched the project "Silent Books, from the world to Lampedusa and back" in 2012. The project involved creating the first library on Lampedusa to be used by local and immigrant children. The second part required creating a collection of silent books (wordless picture books) that could be understood and enjoyed by children regardless of language. These books were collected from IBBY National Sections. The books are deposited at the documentation and research archive in Rome (Palazzo della Esposizioni), while a second set is deposited at the library in Lampedusa and a third makes a traveling exhibition for the IBBY network.

Congresses

IBBY's biennial World Congresses, hosted by different national sections, bring together IBBY members and other people involved in children's books and reading development from all over the world. In addition to lectures, panel discussions, seminars, and book exhibitions, the IBBY Membership Assembly takes place. The presentation of the Hans Christian Andersen Awards, the IBBY-Asahi Reading Promotion Award, the IBBY-iRead Reading Promoter Award, and the IBBY Honour List are highlights of the biennial congresses. The 2020 congress is scheduled for September 5–7 in Moscow.

IBBY national sections also organize regional conferences to improve communication, networking, and professional exchange, and to strengthen ties of friendship and cooperation between the sections in the region.

Bookbird: A Journal of International Children's Literature is a refereed quarterly journal published by IBBY and is open to any topic in the field of international children's literature. *Bookbird* also has occasional themed issues. Calls for manuscripts are posted on the IBBY website. Regular features include coverage of children's literature studies, IBBY activities, and children's literature awards around the world. *Bookbird* also pays special attention to reading promotion projects worldwide. Its editor works in cooperation with an international editorial review board, guest reviewers, and correspondents who are nominated by IBBY national sections.

IBBY cooperates with several international organizations, including the International Federation of Library Associations and Institutions (IFLA), the International Publishers Association (IPA), and the International Literacy Association (ILA).

IBBY's U.S. National Section

The United States Board on Books for Young People, USBBY, is the U.S. national section of IBBY. It is a nonprofit organization devoted to building bridges of international understanding through children's and young adult books. The Friends of IBBY in the United States was founded in 1976 and became a national section of IBBY in 1984. Membership in USBBY is open to individuals and organizations interested in its mission.

A volunteer board includes USBBY's president, president-elect, past president, recording secretary, treasurer, and 12 directors, four elected and eight appointed, representing the membership as well as the patron organizations that support USBBY, such as ILA, the Children's Book Council (CBC), the American Library Association (ALA), and the National Council of Teachers of English (NCTE).

USBBY offers a forum for those interested in national and international activities relating to children's literature. It publishes a semiannual newsletter for its members, creates an annual list of the most outstanding international literature published or distributed in the United States for children and young adults, maintains an active website, sponsors a biennial regional conference that features speakers of international interest, and cosponsors sessions held at annual conferences of ALA, ILA, and NCTE.

USBBY sponsors the publication of a series of annotated bibliographies of outstanding international literature for young people, the Bridges to Understanding series, published by Scarecrow Press.

It also sponsors the creation of an annual USBBY Outstanding International Books (OIB) list, published yearly in School Library Journal, and a bookmark listing the selected titles is distributed via the USBBY website, http://www.usbby.org/list_oibl.html, and at meetings and conferences throughout the year.

The OIB committee selects international books that are deemed most outstanding of those published during the calendar year. Books selected for the list represent the best of children's literature from other countries; introduce American readers to outstanding authors and illustrators from other countries; help American children see the world from other points of view; provide a perspective or address a topic otherwise missing from children's literature in the United States; exhibit a distinct cultural flavor; and are accessible to American readers. Committee members judge the books based on artistic and literary merit, originality or creativity of approach, distinctiveness of topic, uniqueness of origin, and qualities that engage and appeal to children.

USBBY also submits nominations for the Hans Christian Andersen award and prepares a biennial selection of outstanding recently published books for the IBBY Honour List, the Silent Books project, and the IBBY list of Outstanding Books for Young People with Disabilities. In addition, it nominates programs for the IBBY-Asahi Reading Promotion Award and the IBBY-iRead Reading Promoter Award.

USBBY's Bridge to Understanding Award formally acknowledges the work of adults who use books to promote international understanding among children. The award was established in memory of Arlene Pillar, an educator who served USBBY as newsletter editor from 1984 until her death in 1990. Organizations eligible for this award include schools, libraries, Scout troops, clubs, and bookstores. The winning program may be a one-time event or an ongoing series that serves children ranging in age from kindergarten through tenth grade. The award carries a prize of $1,000 and a certificate. Recent winners included "Promoting Global Awareness in Second Graders," a project in the Madeira City School District in Cincinnati that involved four second-grade teachers as well as the elementary art, music, library, gym, and computer teachers. The project was described as helping students to "make personal connections to the characters of the books, develop empathy, and relate to other children of the world through literature."

Other USBBY activities include support of IBBY's Hands across the Sea Fund, which gives assistance to underfunded IBBY sections.

USBBY has an active twinning relationship with four other IBBY national sections, allowing USBBY members to know and work closely with specific countries and to internationalize USBBY perspectives. Specific initiatives within the twinning program may include payment of IBBY dues for underfunded national sections; provision of funding to purchase books or other needed resources for classrooms and libraries; providing funding or training for writers, illustrators, editors, librarians, and publishers; facilitating fellowships for writers, illustrators, editors, librarians, and publishers, or persons who want to study children's literature; supporting cultural exchange and visits between members of USBBY and twinning national sections; developing reciprocal website postings of newsletters, information about projects, lists of children's books published in each country, and relevant websites; and including news about twinning partners in "Global Partnerships," a regular column in the USBBY newsletter, Bridges. Current USBBY twinning partners are Haiti, Lebanon, Palestine, and El Salvador.

The USBBY Secretariat is at the Center for Teaching through Children's Books at National Louis University, 5202 Old Orchard Road, Suite 300, Skokie, IL 60077. It can be reached by telephone at 224-233-2798, and its e-mail is secretariat@usbby.org, website: http://www.usbby.org. USBBY's executive director is V. Ellis Vance, 5503 N. El Adobe Drive, Fresno, CA 93711-2363, e-mail executive.director@usbby.org.

Part 2
Legislation, Funding, and Grants

Legislation

Legislation and Regulations Affecting Libraries in 2019: A Report from ALA's Public Policy and Advocacy Office

Kathi Kromer
Associate Executive Director

Shawnda Hines
Assistant Director, Communications

American Library Association
Public Policy and Advocacy Office

In the first year of the 116th Congress, issues with key relevance to libraries included federal funding for libraries and library-eligible programs; equitable access to high-speed internet; copyright; and government information and services. In this context, the American Library Association (ALA) and its Public Policy and Advocacy Office (formerly known as the Washington Office) advocated for libraries on topics as diverse as net neutrality, E-rate, Copyright Office modernization, and digital lending. This report details these activities, related outcomes, and upcoming challenges for libraries on the national legislative and regulatory front.

Federal Funding

Appropriations Win for Libraries

Following a year of intense engagement by ALA members, Congress approved the largest increase in Library Services and Technology Act (LSTA) funding in 12 years. For fiscal year (FY) 2020 the Institute of Museum and Library Services (IMLS) received $252 million, a $10 million increase, with $6.2 million dedicated to LSTA. Highlights from the $195.4 million for LSTA include

- $166.8 million for LSTA Grants to States
- $5.3 million for LSTA Native American Library Services
- $10 million for LSTA Laura Bush 21st Century Librarian grants
- $13.4 million for LSTA National Leadership for Libraries

The Library of Congress and the National Library of Medicine received increases as well. Funding for several library-eligible programs in the Department of Education also received increases, including Striving Readers Comprehensive Literacy Grants, Title I Grants to Local Education Agencies, Title II Supporting Effective Instruction, Title IV (Part A) Well-Rounded Education, 21st Century Community Learning Centers, and the Carl D. Perkins Career and Technical Education Act. The Innovative Approaches to Literacy (IAL) program, another priority for ALA, escaped proposed elimination and received $27 million for FY 2020, the same level as for FY 2019.

The Strategic Road to Success

Despite ultimate funding increases, things did not look bright for library funding at the outset of 2019. The White House FY 2020 budget proposal, released more than a month late due to an unprecedented 35-day government shutdown, drastically cut funding for libraries for the third year in a row. IMLS had again been targeted for elimination in the administration's request to Congress, threatening more than $210 million in resources for libraries.

When ALA launched its nationwide engagement to fund libraries on the day the administration's budget was released, libraries were poised to act. Efforts to secure signatures for FY 2020 "Dear Appropriator" letters to gain support for LSTA and IAL, respectively, broke records overnight. Within the first 24 hours of the House letters' release, nearly every representative in Congress heard from library advocates in their district calling for representatives to sign the letters. Advocates continued to answer calls to action at key moments throughout the year-long appropriations process. The FY 2020 budget bill eventually passed the House and Senate—with increased funding for libraries in place—and was signed by the president in December 2019.

Level funding in the current fiscal environment is considered a win; increased funding is a major accomplishment. Library funding has steadily increased over the past three years. As advocates continue to demonstrate the impact libraries have on communities, ALA is in a stronger position than ever to start the FY 2021 budget cycle.

Net Neutrality, Telecom Policy, and Digital Inclusion

U.S. Court of Appeals Provides Mixed Decision on Net Neutrality

For more than a decade ALA has been on the front lines of the net neutrality battle, working together with other library and higher education organizations, as well as broader coalitions of net neutrality advocates. Most recently, libraries joined others to challenge the Federal Communication Commission (FCC)'s 2017 vote to roll back net neutrality rules. The battle over net neutrality continued in 2019 in Congress, in the courts, and at the state level.

In February 2019 the U.S. Court of Appeals for the D.C. Circuit heard oral arguments about whether the FCC was arbitrary and capricious in reversing its 2015 order. That order included protections against blocking, throttling, and paid prioritization of internet access and was intended to ensure that all traffic on the internet is treated equally. ALA filed amicus with the plaintiffs in the case, *Mozilla et al.*

v. *Federal Communications Commission*. Subsequently, several bills were introduced to the House on the topic. Of those, only the Democrats' Save the Internet Act (H.R. 1644) would reinstate the protections previously in place under the 2015 FCC Order. ALA joined other net neutrality advocates in encouraging people to tweet, send e-mail, and call members of Congress in support of the Act's passage. Likewise, ALA joined a coalition of more than 100 organizations to urge Senate Majority Leader Mitch McConnell to bring the Save the Internet Act (S.682) to a vote. The bill was approved in the House in 2019 but continues to face an uphill battle in the Senate.

Meanwhile, in October 2019 the U.S. Court of Appeals for the D.C. Circuit provided a mixed ruling. The court upheld the FCC's authority to issue its 2018 Order eliminating network neutrality protections. Yet, the ruling also vacated and remanded parts of the Order. Importantly, the court vacated the portion of the Order in which the FCC attempted to preempt state or local efforts to protect an open internet. As a result, advocates expect to see state-level action in 2020, when states such as California may move to implement net neutrality regulation. ALA will continue to work with open internet advocates to plan next steps for action.

FCC Releases Anticipated Category 2 Order for E-rate

In December 2019 the FCC released the long-awaited Category 2 (C2) Order, which determines the rules for how libraries and schools will apply for funding for wifi and associated costs starting in 2021 and into the foreseeable future. In September 2019 ALA filed two sets of comments with the FCC providing input on whether the current C2 budget system for internal connections (including wifi) funding should be made permanent after its five-year test period. ALA fully supports the C2 budget system as more libraries than ever before are now receiving funds, including rural remote libraries as well as those in urban centers. There were, however, improvements the FCC could make to ensure all libraries benefit from the availability of funding. ALA comments called for an increase in library budgets, a series of steps to simplify the process as it is made permanent, and the inclusion of filtering and security software and tools as eligible for funding. Several of ALA's recommendations were adopted in the final ruling. Most notably, beginning in FY 2021, the funding floor for small libraries was increased from the original $9,200 to $25,000. The per square foot formula for all libraries will be $4.50, which is also an effort to encourage an increase in rural library applications.

Also in 2019, ALA along with dozens of allies, including the Schools, Health and Libraries Broadband (SHLB) Coalition, submitted a joint statement to the FCC in opposition to an FCC proposal to place a cap on the federal Universal Service Fund, which supports E-rate and other programs intended to bridge the digital divide.

Rural Broadband and Spectrum Policies

In 2019 libraries continued to advocate for public interest spectrum policies and other measures to address the rural digital divide. Specifically, ALA issued a Notice of Ex Parte to the FCC concerning the licensing and use policies for the Educational Broadband Service spectrum, including support for the preservation of the current standards for educational and public interest use. In addition, ALA submitted a coalition letter to the Senate Committee on Commerce, Science and Transportation on the topic of addressing the rural digital divide, promoting competition, and making 5G more available and affordable for all Americans. The letter requested that the underutilized "C-band" of public airwaves between 3,700 and 4,200 MHz be reallocated through a public auction and supported authorizing shared access to unused midband spectrum for use by small and rural operators. ALA also endorsed the Rural Broadband Permitting Efficiency Act of 2019 (H.R. 292).

Support for Digital Inclusion Legislation

In addition, during the year ALA worked to support digital inclusion at the legislative level. For one, the Public Policy and Advocacy office (PPA) worked with Congresswoman Grace Meng (D-N.Y.-6) to draft legislation to address the homework gap. The congresswoman introduced the Closing the Homework Gap through Mobile Hotspots Act (H.R. 5243), which, among other things, would provide funding for libraries to loan hotspots to families with school-aged children who do not otherwise have access to home broadband. ALA also welcomed the introduction of the Digital Equity Act (S.1167) by Senator Patty Murray (D-Wash.), a bill that, if passed, would establish two grant programs: first, a capacity-building grant for states to increase digital inclusion efforts identified through a state-specific Digital Equity Plan, and, second, a national competitive grant program open to individual groups, coalitions, and communities. The bill also includes a focus on research and evaluation of the projects awarded by the programs. Libraries have long been committed to digital inclusion and lead the way on programs that meet the needs of learners at all stages, including those less likely to be online. ALA joined a new coalition of organizations in the early stages of strategy planning to secure nine additional cosponsors of the bill.

Copyright

Roundtables on U.S. Copyright Office Modernization

The push for Copyright Office modernization continued in 2019, following efforts in previous years to lessen (or remove) the authority of the Library of Congress over the Copyright Office. In fall 2019 Senate Judiciary Intellectual Property subcommittee staff held a series of roundtables on U.S. Copyright Office modernization. ALA requested and received an invitation to participate in the roundtables, as one of only three organizations representing the public interest. The purpose of the roundtables was to address rights holder concerns with copyright registration, the authority of the Register to manage the Office's modernization activities, and the robustness of Library of Congress information technology security, as well as legislative changes necessary for a modern and efficient Copyright Office system. Rights holders believe modernization efforts centralized under the Library of Congress hindered the Copyright Office, despite public testimony and reports to the contrary. While Senate Judiciary staff assured roundtable participants that Copyright Office independence was not a desired outcome, ALA commented on the effectiveness of the existing partnership between the Library of Congress and its units, including the Copyright Office.

Following the roundtables, staff made draft legislation to amend the copyright law available for comment. The draft legislation includes proposed centralization of information technology within the Library of Congress, increases the authority of the Register, provides liability waivers for rights holders who unknowingly complete registration in error, makes digital deposit the default for copyright examination purposes, separates the process of examination from best edition deposit, and introduces a Copyright Office Advisory Board. ALA and the Association of Research Libraries (ARL) submitted comments on the draft. The Senate Judiciary Intellectual Property subcommittee plans to introduce legislation in early 2020.

Meanwhile, Copyright Register Karyn Temple announced her resignation to accept a position with the Motion Picture Association. Under Temple's leadership, the Copyright Office made great strides in its modernization efforts. Associate Register of Copyrights and Director of Policy and International Affairs Maria Strong was named acting register.

Music Modernization Act "Mechanical" Blanket License

In 2019 the U.S. Copyright Office issued a notice of inquiry and call for comments on the implementation regulations of the Music Modernization Act's "mechanical" blanket license provisions. PPA, along with music librarians and academic copyright librarians, asked that provisions include a reasonably priced license for libraries, museums, archives, and nonprofit educational institutions that wish to use sound recordings from their collections. PPA suggested that the blanket license could be modeled after existing blanket licenses for college radio stations. Without a blanket license, nonprofit educational and cultural institutions would have no option for seeking permission to use musical recordings from the newly established collective for digital uses of musical works.

CASE Act Stalls in the Senate

The Copyright Alternative in Small-Claims Enforcement (CASE) Act (H.R. 2426) passed in the House in October 2019 but subsequently stalled in the Senate (S. 1273) despite support from most rights holders and strong bipartisan support within the Senate Judiciary Committee. The CASE Act intends to create a small claims tribunal in the U.S. Copyright Office for independent rights holders to bring claims of infringement to an alternative court, outside of the expensive federal court proceeding. Stakeholder groups, including ALA, have opposed CASE for various reasons, including the constitutionality of a judicial court within the legislative branch; the bill's potential to encourage copyright trolling; liability damages that far exceed damages assessed in state small claims courts; lack of due process for alleged infringers; and the ability of rights holders to bring lawsuits before filing for copyright registration. While Senate efforts to negotiate alternative legislation dwindled at the end of the year, the CASE Act is expected to be reintroduced in 2020.

#eBooksForAll Campaign Continues Fierce Push for Library Lending Rights

The biggest library story of 2019 was Macmillan Publishers' change in licensing terms for libraries, limiting purchases to only one e-book title for the first two months after a new release starting November 1, 2019. ALA led and coordinated policy and strategic advocacy efforts on library digital content lending. Activities included direct negotiations with publishers, mass mobilization of library advocates, and a report to the U.S. House of Representatives Subcommittee on Antitrust, Commercial and Administrative Law as part of its investigation into competition in digital markets. [See the special report by Shawnda Hines and Alan Inouye on p. 3 of this volume for in-depth coverage—*Ed.*]

Other Upcoming and Ongoing Copyright Issues

In 2020 PPA will continue to monitor and advocate for libraries when it comes to U.S. Copyright Office modernization efforts, the CASE Act, the Music Modernization Act, and digital content lending. An additional issue for the year to come is the planned series of hearings to consider changes to the Digital Millennium Copyright Act (DMCA) of 1998. In these hearings the primary concern is Section 512, the online service provider liability provision. Section 512 says that online service providers, including libraries who offer public computing, cannot be held liable for third-party infringing acts. In order to get the liability protection, online service providers agree to take down infringing content once notified by a rights holder. Rights holders have argued that online service providers should do more to prevent infringing content from being posted online. Online service providers argue that they are doing all that they can to limit infringing content from being posted on their platforms.

PPA has requested consideration of an additional provision of interest to libraries in the upcoming roundtables: the triennial rulemaking on anticircumvention of technological protection measures that prevent access to digital works. The rulemaking has created temporary exemptions for fair use, circumventing digital rights management to allow e-book text-to-speech conversions, the inclusion of audio captions in motion pictures and television programming, and film clip extracts from digital media for scholarship and classroom use.

Government Information

Preparation for the 2020 Census and Advocacy on Key Issues

During 2019 ALA continued efforts to ensure libraries are well prepared for potential activities and demands that may arise from the decennial census. In addition to the comprehensive *Libraries' Guide to the 2020 Census*, ALA produced tip sheets, webinars, and events designed to engage libraries to be proactive in ensuring a fair and accurate count of their communities. In addition to calling for library workers to participate in state and local Complete Count Committees, ALA launched *Library Census Champions*, a collaborative effort between United for Libraries and the Census Counts campaign to establish a new network of state, local, and tribal library Trustees helping their libraries and communities prepare for the 2020 Census.

February 2019 brought good news when Congress completed work on the Census Bureau's budget for 2019 and included provisions that ALA had sought, directing the Census Bureau to open local outreach sites in communities across the country, which could potentially be located in libraries. On April 1, Census Day, ALA President Loida Garcia-Febo raised the profile of libraries' role in the 2020 Census by participating in a press conference held by the U.S. Census Bureau at the National Press Club in Washington, D.C. Speaking alongside three top leaders of the Bureau, the president of the Annie E. Casey Foundation, and the governor of the Chickasaw Nation, Garcia-Febo focused her remarks on libraries' critical role in achieving an equitable count in the census, pointing out that 99 percent of hard-to-count areas are located within five miles of a public library.

Census Day 2019 also marked ALA's joint amicus brief to the U.S. Supreme Court opposing the last-minute addition of a citizenship question to the 2020 Census. ALA firmly opposed the addition, saying in a public statement that "adding a citizenship question to the 2020 Census would suppress Census response, distorting the statistics and making them less informative." Together with the American Statistical Association, the American Sociological Association, and the Population Association of America, ALA filed in support of the plaintiffs in *Department of Commerce* v. *New York*. The case was appealed directly to the Supreme Court after a federal court ruled for the plaintiffs and ordered the Commerce Department to remove the question. In June the Supreme Court ruled against the administration's proposed addition, removing a significant distraction from preparations for a complete count, though not ruling out the possibility of adding such a question in the future.

ALA continued working in coalition to support the full funding needed to enable a successful census. Among other efforts, this included a letter to U.S. Census Bureau Chief Steven Dillingham urging the Bureau to promptly devote funding to open local Questionnaire Assistance Centers in hard-to-count communities for the 2020 Census (February 2019); ALA testimony to the Senate Commerce Appropriations Subcommittee advocating for funding for the Census Bureau in order to properly conduct the census (May 2019); and a coalition letter with the Census Project targeting U.S. House of Representatives members to call for robust funding for the census and investment in key activities such as cybersecurity, outreach to hard-to-count populations, and collaboration with local partners (June 2019). ALA also secured funding for census-related activities in libraries and awarded more than $100,000 in $2,000 mini-grants to 59 libraries nationwide. As planned census activities proceed in 2020, ALA will continue to support a strong library contribution to the effort.

Data Modernization Initiatives Move Forward

Libraries advocated for several government data modernization initiatives in 2019. Alongside other library associations and additional coalition partners, ALA expressed support for the Grant Reporting Efficiency and Agreements Transparency (GREAT) Act of 2019 (H.R. 150, S. 1829). The Act, which aimed to modernize reporting by recipients of federal grants and improve access to grant data, including for IMLS and its grantees, was signed into law at the year's close.

On another front, ALA, together with the American Association of Law Libraries (AALL) and the Association of Research Libraries (ARL), expressed support for Hugh Halpern's nomination to become director of the Government Publishing Office (GPO). GPO administers the Federal Depository Library Program (FDLP) and related activities that provide public access to government information. The Senate approved Halpern's appointment in December 2019. Prior to the vote, GPO had not had a Senate-confirmed director for more than two years. Previously, Halpern worked for 30 years in the U.S. House of Representatives, where he was recognized for a lifetime of bipartisan service.

ALA also lent its support to a coalition letter addressed to the House of Representatives regarding the Access to Congressionally Mandated Reports Act (H.R. 736). The act would improve government transparency and create a central repository of agency reports submitted to Congress. It was subsequently passed in the House and has been introduced to the Senate (S.195).

Emerging Policy Issues

Many policy issues affect the broad range of services that libraries provide to their communities. Raising awareness among decision makers about the services that libraries provide in these areas and advocating for the recognition and inclusion of libraries in related legislation are together a key part of library advocacy.

As part of its focus on emerging policy issues, ALA continued its support for library initiatives related to STEM and coding, jobs and the workforce, and small business development. Building on the strong partnership between ALA and Google, developed through the Libraries Ready to Code initiative (which supported library capacity and engagement in promoting computational thinking skills), the pair began a new project in January 2019. The $1 million Libraries Lead with Digital Skills initiative launched with the 50-state Grow with Google tour, which continues to stop in libraries across the country to support digital skills-building for adults and highlight what libraries do to promote workforce development and economic opportunity in their communities. Following each state tour, ALA opened microfunding applications to local public libraries to cover their own digital literacy skills training for individuals and small businesses.

PPA will continue to support library initiatives related to workforce and small business development in 2020, as well advocate for library inclusion in related legislation and regulation such as the reauthorization of the Workforce Innovation and Opportunity Act (WIOA).

Looking Forward to 2020

In 2020 ALA's Public Policy and Advocacy office will continue to advocate on key library issues, including federal funding for libraries, digital lending, and improvements to government information practices. This advocacy will include ongoing work to support a growing cohort of library leaders trained through ALA Policy Corps program, who are prepared to drive library advocacy forward. ALA will maintain existing relationships with agencies such as the FCC and USAC to protect E-rate funding and improve the program. And, as the 2020 Census rolls out, ALA will devote a special effort to working with the Census Bureau and allies in the advocacy community to lend key library support to achieving a complete count. ALA will also continue its coalition work, joining with other advocates to support the reinstatement of net neutrality, favorable copyright legislation, and, in preparation for the 2020 general elections, civic engagement.

Funding Programs and Grant-Making Agencies

National Endowment for the Humanities

400 7th St. S.W., Washington, DC 20506
202-606-8400, 800-634-1121
TDD (hearing impaired) 202-606-8282 or 866-372-2930 (toll free)
E-mail info@neh.gov, World Wide Web http://neh.gov

The National Endowment for the Humanities (NEH) is an independent federal agency created in 1965. It is one of the largest funders of humanities programs in the United States.

Because democracy demands wisdom, NEH promotes excellence in the humanities and conveys the lessons of history to all Americans, seeking to develop educated and thoughtful citizens. It accomplishes this mission by providing grants for high-quality humanities projects in six funding areas: education, preservation and access, public programs, research, challenge grants, and digital humanities.

Grants from NEH enrich classroom learning, create and preserve knowledge, and bring ideas to life through public television, radio, new technologies, museum exhibitions, and programs in libraries and other community places. Recipients typically are cultural institutions, such as museums, archives, libraries, colleges and universities, and public television and radio stations, as well as individual scholars. The grants

- Strengthen teaching and learning in the humanities in schools and colleges
- Preserve and provide access to cultural and educational resources
- Provide opportunities for lifelong learning
- Facilitate research and original scholarship
- Strengthen the institutional base of the humanities

For more than a half century, NEH has reached millions of people with projects and programs that preserve and study the nation's culture and history while providing a foundation for the future.

The endowment's mission is to enrich cultural life by promoting the study of the humanities. According to the National Foundation on the Arts and the Humanities Act, "The term 'humanities' includes, but is not limited to, the study of the following: language, both modern and classical; linguistics; literature; history; jurisprudence; philosophy; archaeology; comparative religion; ethics; the history, criticism, and theory of the arts; those aspects of social sciences which have humanistic content and employ humanistic methods; and the study and application of the humanities to the human environment with particular attention to reflecting our diverse heritage, traditions, and history and to the relevance of the humanities to the current conditions of national life."

The act, adopted by Congress in 1965, provided for the establishment of the National Foundation on the Arts and the Humanities in order to promote progress and scholarship in the humanities and the arts in the United States. The act included the following findings:

- The arts and the humanities belong to all the people of the United States.
- The encouragement and support of national progress and scholarship in the humanities and the arts, while primarily matters for private and local initiative, are also appropriate matters of concern to the federal government.
- An advanced civilization must not limit its efforts to science and technology alone, but must give full value and support to the other great branches of scholarly and cultural activity in order to achieve a better understanding of the past, a better analysis of the present, and a better view of the future.
- Democracy demands wisdom and vision in its citizens. It must therefore foster and support a form of education, and access to the arts and the humanities, designed to make people of all backgrounds and wherever located masters of technology and not its unthinking servants.
- It is necessary and appropriate for the federal government to complement, assist, and add to programs for the advancement of the humanities and the arts by local, state, regional, and private agencies and their organizations. In doing so, the government must be sensitive to the nature of public sponsorship. Public funding of the arts and humanities is subject to the conditions that traditionally govern the use of public money. Such funding should contribute to public support and confidence in the use of taxpayer funds. Public funds provided by the federal government ultimately must serve public purposes the Congress defines.
- The arts and the humanities reflect the high place accorded by the American people to the nation's rich culture and history and to the fostering of mutual respect for the diverse beliefs and values of all persons and groups.

What NEH Grants Accomplish

Since its founding, NEH has awarded more than 70,000 competitive grants.

Interpretive Exhibitions

Interpretive exhibitions provide opportunities for lifelong learning in the humanities for millions of Americans. Since 1967 NEH has awarded approximately $310 million in grants for interpretive exhibitions, catalogs, and public programs, which are among the most highly visible activities supported by the endowment. NEH support finances exhibitions; reading, viewing, and discussion programs; web-based programs; and other public education programs at venues across the country.

Renewing Teaching

Over NEH's history, more than 100,000 high school and college teachers have deepened their knowledge of the humanities through intensive summer study supported by the endowment; tens of thousands of students benefit from these better-educated teachers every year.

Reading and Discussion Programs

Since 1982 NEH has supported reading and discussion programs in the nation's libraries, bringing people together to discuss works of literature and history. Scholars in the humanities provide thematic direction for the discussion programs. Using selected texts and such themes as "Work," "Family," "Diversity," and "Not for Children Only," these programs have attracted more than 2 million Americans to read and talk about what they've read. Funded programs have ranged from veterans reading groups focused on classic Greek and Roman texts about the experience of war, to community reading and discussion programs examining 200 years of Maine state history and humanities-focused reading and discussion programs for at-risk youth.

Chronicling America

NEH's National Digital Newspaper Program is supporting projects to convert microfilm of historically important U.S. newspapers into fully searchable digital files. Developed in partnership with the Library of Congress, this long-term project ultimately will make more than 30 million pages of newspapers accessible online. For more on this project, visit http://chroniclingamerica.loc.gov.

Stimulating Private Support

About $2 billion in humanities support has been generated by NEH's Challenge Grants program, which requires most grant recipients to raise $3 in nonfederal funds for every dollar they receive.

Presidential Papers

Ten presidential papers projects, from Washington to Eisenhower, have received support from NEH. Matching grants for the ten projects have leveraged millions of dollars in nonfederal contributions.

New Scholarship

NEH grants enable scholars to do in-depth study. Jack Rakove explored the making of the Constitution in his Original Meanings, and James McPherson chronicled the Civil War in his Battle Cry of Freedom. Projects supported by NEH grants have earned nearly 20 Pulitzer Prizes.

History on Screen

Since 1967 NEH has awarded approximately $310 million to support the production of films for broad public distribution, including the Emmy Award–winning series *The Civil War,* the Oscar-nominated films *Brooklyn Bridge, The Restless Conscience,* and *Freedom on My Mind,* and film biographies of John and Abigail Adams, Eugene O'Neill, and Ernest Hemingway. More than 8 million saw the April 2010 debut of *The Buddha,* a documentary made for PBS by filmmaker David Grubin, and it has been streamed into hundreds of classrooms nationwide. Over seven successive nights on PBS, more than 33 million people watched Ken Burns's *The Roosevelts* (2014), which chronicles the lives of Teddy, Eleanor, and Franklin. The NEH-funded series *The Vietnam War* (2018), by Ken Burns and Lynn Novick, was seen by 39 million viewers.

American Voices

NEH support for scholarly editions makes the writings of prominent and influential Americans accessible. Ten presidents are included, along with such key figures as Martin Luther King, Jr., George C. Marshall, and Eleanor Roosevelt. Papers of prominent writers—among them Emily Dickinson, Walt Whitman, Mark Twain, and Robert Frost—are also available.

Library of America

Millions of books have been sold as part of the Library of America series, a collection of the riches of the nation's literature. Begun with NEH seed money, the 303 volumes published to date include the works of such figures as Henry Adams, Edith Wharton, William James, Eudora Welty, and W. E. B. Du Bois.

The Library of America also received a $150,000 grant for the publication of *American Poetry: The Seventeenth and Eighteenth Centuries* (two volumes) and an expanded volume of selected works by Captain John Smith—a key figure in the establishment of the first permanent English settlement in North America, at Jamestown, Virginia—and other early exploration narratives.

Technical Innovation

NEH support for the digital humanities is fueling innovation and new tools for research in the humanities. Modern 3D technology allows students to visit sites ranging from ancient Egypt to the 1964–1965 New York World's Fair. Spectral imaging was used to create an online critical edition of explorer David Livingstone's previously unreadable field diary of 1871.

Science and the Humanities

The scientific past is being preserved with NEH-supported editions of the letters of Charles Darwin, the works of Albert Einstein, and the 14-volume papers of Thomas Edison. Additionally, NEH and the National Science Foundation have joined forces in Documenting Endangered Languages (DEL), a multiyear effort to preserve records of key languages that are in danger of becoming extinct.

EDSITEment

EDSITEment (http://edsitement.neh.gov) assembles the best humanities resources on the web, drawing more than 400,000 visitors each month. Incorporating these Internet resources, particularly primary documents, from more than 350 peer-reviewed websites, EDSITEment features more than 500 online lesson plans in all areas of the humanities. Teachers use EDSITEment's resources to enhance lessons and to engage students through interactive technology tools that hone critical-thinking skills.

Federal-State Partnership

The Office of Federal-State Partnership links NEH with the nationwide network of 56 humanities councils, which are located in each state, the District of Columbia, Puerto Rico, the U.S. Virgin Islands, the Northern Mariana Islands, American Samoa, and Guam. Each council funds humanities programs in its own jurisdiction.

Directory of State Humanities Councils

Alabama

Alabama Humanities Foundation
1100 Ireland Way, Suite 202
Birmingham, AL 35205-7001
205-558-3980, fax 205-558-3981
http://www.alabamahumanities.org

Alaska

Alaska Humanities Forum
421 W. 1st Ave., Suite 200
Anchorage, AK 99501
907-272-5341, fax 907-272-3979
http://www.akhf.org

Arizona

Arizona Humanities Council
Ellis-Shackelford House
1242 N. Central Ave.
Phoenix, AZ 85004-1887
602-257-0335, fax 602-257-0392
http://www.azhumanities.org

Arkansas

Arkansas Humanities Council
407 President Clinton Ave., Suite 201
Little Rock, AR 72201
501-320-5761, fax 501-537-4550
http://www.arkansashumanitiescouncil.org

California

Cal Humanities
538 9th St., # 210
Oakland, CA 94607
415-391-1474, fax 415-391-1312
http://www.calhum.org

Colorado

Colorado Humanities
7935 E. Prentice Ave., Suite 450
Greenwood Village, CO 80111
303-894-7951, fax 303-864-9361
http://www.coloradohumanities.org

Connecticut

Connecticut Humanities Council
100 Riverview Center, Suite 270
292 Main Street
Middletown, CT 06457
860-685-2260, fax 860-685-7597
http://cthumanities.org

Delaware

Delaware Humanities
100 W. Tenth St., Suite 509
Wilmington, DE 19801
302-657-0650, fax 302-657-0655
http://dehumanities.org

District of Columbia

Humanities D.C.
925 U St. N.W.
Washington, DC 20001
202-387-8393, fax 202-387-8149
http://wdchumanities.org

Florida

Florida Humanities Council
599 Second St. S.
St. Petersburg, FL 33701-5005
727-873-2000, fax 727-873-2014
http://www.floridahumanities.org

Georgia

Georgia Humanities Council
50 Hurt Plaza S.E., Suite 595
Atlanta, GA 30303-2915
404-523-6220, fax 404-523-5702
http://www.georgiahumanities.org

Hawaii

Hawai'i Council for the Humanities
First Hawaiian Bank Bldg.
3599 Waialae Ave., Room 25
Honolulu, HI 96816
808-732-5402, fax 808-732-5432
http://www.hihumanities.org

Idaho

Idaho Humanities Council
217 W. State St.
Boise, ID 83702
208-345-5346, fax 208-345-5347
http://www.idahohumanities.org

Illinois

Illinois Humanities Council
125 S. Church St., Suite 650
Chicago, IL 60603-5200
312-422-5580, fax 312-422-5588
http://www.ilhumanities.org

Indiana

Indiana Humanities
1500 N. Delaware St.
Indianapolis, IN 46202
317-638-1500, fax 317-634-9503
http://www.indianahumanities.org

Iowa

Humanities Iowa
100 Library, Room 4039
Iowa City, IA 52242-1420
319-335-4153, fax 319-335-4154
http://humanitiesiowa.org

Kansas

Kansas Humanities Council
112 S.W. 6th Ave., Suite 400
Topeka, KS 66603-3895
785-357-0359, fax 785-357-1723
https://www.humanitieskansas.org

Kentucky

Kentucky Humanities
206 E. Maxwell St.
Lexington, KY 40508
859-257-5932, fax 859-257-5933
http://www.kyhumanities.org

Louisiana

Louisiana Endowment for the Humanities
938 Lafayette St., Suite 300
New Orleans, LA 70113-1782
504-523-4352, fax 504-529-2358
http://www.leh.org

Maine

Maine Humanities Council
674 Brighton Ave.
Portland, ME 04102-1012
207-773-5051, fax 207-773-2416
http://www.mainehumanities.org

Maryland

Maryland Humanities Council
108 W. Centre St.
Baltimore, MD 21201-4565
410-685-0095, fax 410-685-0795
http://www.mdhumanities.org

Massachusetts

Mass Humanities
66 Bridge St.
Northampton, MA 01060
413-584-8440, fax 413-584-8454
http://www.masshumanities.org

Michigan

Michigan Humanities Council
119 Pere Marquette Drive, Suite 3B
Lansing, MI 48912-1270
517-372-7770, fax 517-372-0027
http://michiganhumanities.org

Minnesota

Minnesota Humanities Center
987 Ivy Ave. E.
St. Paul, MN 55106-2046
651-774-0105, fax 651-774-0205
http://www.mnhum.org

Mississippi

Mississippi Humanities Council
3825 Ridgewood Rd., Room 311
Jackson, MS 39211
601-432-6752, fax 601-432-6750
http://www.mshumanities.org

Missouri

Missouri Humanities Council
The Grand Central Building at Union Station
415 South 18th St., Suite 100
St. Louis, MO 63103
Toll free: 1-800-357-0909
314-781-9660, fax 314-781-9681
http://www.mohumanities.org

Montana

Humanities Montana
311 Brantly
Missoula, MT 59812-7848
406-243-6022, fax 406-243-4836
http://www.humanitiesmontana.org

Nebraska

Nebraska Humanities Council
215 Centennial Mall South, Suite 330
Lincoln, NE 68508
402-474-2131, fax 402-474-4852
http://www.humanitiesnebraska.org

Nevada

Nevada Humanities
1670-200 N. Virginia St.
P.O. Box 8029
Reno, NV 89507-8029
775-784-6587, fax 775-784-6527
http://www.nevadahumanities.org

New Hampshire

New Hampshire Humanities
117 Pleasant St.
Concord, NH 03301-3852
603-224-4071, fax 603-224-4072
http://www.nhhc.org

New Jersey

New Jersey Council for the Humanities
28 W. State St., Suite 6
Trenton, NJ 08608
609-695-4838, fax 609-695-4929
http://www.njhumanities.org

New Mexico

New Mexico Humanities Council
4115 Silver Ave. S.E.
Albuquerque, NM 87108
505-633-7370, fax 505-633-7377
http://www.nmhum.org

New York

Humanities New York
150 Broadway, Suite 1700
New York, NY 10038
212-233-1131, fax 212-233-4607
http://www.humanitiesny.org

North Carolina

North Carolina Humanities Council
320 East 9th St., Suite 414
Charlotte, NC 28202
704-687-1520, fax 704-687-1550
http://www.nchumanities.org

North Dakota

Humanities North Dakota
418 E. Broadway, Suite 8
Bismarck, ND 58501
701-255-3360, fax 701-223-8724
http://www. humanitiesnd.org

Ohio

Ohio Humanities Council
471 E. Broad St., Suite 1620
Columbus, OH 43215-3857
614-461-7802, fax 614-461-4651
http://www.ohiohumanities.org

Oklahoma

Oklahoma Humanities
424 Concord Dr., Suite E
Oklahoma City, OK 73102
405-235-0280, fax 405-235-0289
http://www.okhumanities.org

Oregon

Oregon Council for the Humanities
921 S.W. Washington St., #150
Portland, OR 97205
503-241-0543, fax 503-241-0024
http://www.oregonhumanities.org

Pennsylvania

Pennsylvania Humanities Council
325 Chestnut St., Suite 715
Philadelphia, PA 19106-2607
215-925-1005, fax 215-925-3054
http://www.pahumanities.org

Rhode Island

Rhode Island Council for the Humanities
131 Washington St., Suite 210
Providence, RI 02903
401-273-2250, fax 401-454-4872
http://www.rihumanities.org

South Carolina

South Carolina Humanities
2711 Middleburg Drive, Suite 203
P.O. Box 5287
Columbia, SC 29254
803-771-2477, fax 803-771-2487
http://www.schumanities.org

South Dakota

South Dakota Humanities Council
1215 Trail Ridge Rd., Suite A
Brookings, SD 57006
605-688-6113, fax 605-688-4531
http://sdhumanities.org

Tennessee

Humanities Tennessee
807 Main Street, Suite B
Nashville, TN 37201
615-770-0006, fax 615-770-0007
http://www.humanitiestennessee.org

Texas

Humanities Texas
1410 Rio Grande St.
Austin, TX 78701
512-440-1991, fax 512-440-0115
http://www.humanitiestexas.org

Utah

Utah Humanities
202 W. 300 North
Salt Lake City, UT 84103
801-359-9670, fax 801-531-7869
http://www.utahhumanities.org

Vermont

Vermont Humanities
11 Loomis St.
Montpelier, VT 05602
802-262-2626, fax 802-262-2620
http://www.vermonthumanities.org

Virginia

Virginia Foundation for the Humanities
145 Ednam Drive
Charlottesville, VA 22903-4629
434-924-3296, fax 434-296-4714
http://www.virginiahumanities.org

Washington

Humanities Washington
130 Nickerson St., Suite 304
Seattle, WA 98109
206-682-1770, fax 206-682-4158
http://www.humanities.org

West Virginia

West Virginia Humanities Council
1310 Kanawha Blvd. East
Charleston, WV 25301
304-346-8500, fax 304-346-8504
http://www.wvhumanities.org

Wisconsin

Wisconsin Humanities Council
3801 Regent St.
Madison, WI 53705
608-262-0706, fax 608-263-7970
http://www.wisconsinhumanities.org

Wyoming

Wyoming Humanities Council
1315 E. Lewis St.
Laramie, WY 82072-3459
307-721-9243, fax 307-742-4914
http://www.thinkwy.org

American Samoa

Amerika Samoa Humanities Council
P.O. Box 5800
Pago Pago, AS 96799
684-633-4870, fax 684-633-4873
http://ashcouncil.org

Guam

Humanities Guahan
222 Chalan Santo Papa
Reflection Center, Suite 106
Hagatna, Guam 96910
671-472-4460, fax 671-472-4465
http://www.humanitiesguahan.org

Northern Marianas Islands

Northern Marianas Humanities Council
P.O. Box 506437
Saipan, MP 96950
670-235-4785, fax 670-235-4786
http://northernmarianashumanities.org

Puerto Rico

Fundación Puertorriqueña de las Humanidades
109 San José St., 3rd floor
Box 9023920
San Juan, PR 00902-3920
787-721-2087, fax 787-721-2684
http://www.fphpr.org

NEH Overview

Division of Education Programs

Through grants to educational institutions and professional development programs for scholars and teachers, this division is designed to support study of the humanities at all levels of education.

Grants support the development of curricula and materials, faculty study programs, and conferences and networks of educational institutions.

Contact: 202-606-8500, e-mail education@neh.gov.

Seminars and Institutes

Grants support summer seminars and institutes in the humanities for college and school teachers. These faculty-development activities are conducted at colleges and universities in the United States and abroad. Those wishing to participate in seminars should submit their seminar applications to the seminar director.

Contact: 202-606-8471, e-mail sem-inst@neh.gov.

Landmarks of American History and Culture

Grants for Landmarks workshops provide support to teachers and community college faculty. These professional development workshops are conducted at or near sites important to American history and culture (such as presidential residences or libraries, colonial-era settlements, major battlefields, historic districts, and sites associated with major writers or artists) to address central themes and issues in American history, government, literature, art history, and related subjects in the humanities.

Contact: 202-606-8463, e-mail landmarks@neh.gov.

Division of Preservation and Access

Grants are made for projects that will create, preserve, and increase the availability of resources important for research, education, and public programming in the humanities.

Support may be sought to preserve the intellectual content and aid bibliographic control of collections; to compile bibliographies, descriptive catalogs, and guides to cultural holdings; and to create dictionaries, encyclopedias, databases, and electronic archives. Applications also may be submitted for education and training projects dealing with issues of preservation or access; for research and development leading to improved preservation and access standards, practices, and tools; and for projects to digitize historic U.S. newspapers and to document endangered languages. Grants are also made to help smaller cultural repositories preserve and care for their humanities collections. Proposals may combine preservation and access activities within a single project.

Contact: 202-606-8570, e-mail preservation@neh.gov.

Division of Public Programs

Public humanities programs promote lifelong learning in American and world history, literature, comparative religion, philosophy, and other fields of the humanities. They offer new insights into familiar subjects and invite conversation about important humanities ideas and questions.

The Division of Public Programs supports an array of public humanities programs that reach large and diverse public audiences through a variety of program formats, including interpretive exhibitions, radio and television broadcasts, lectures, symposia, interpretive multimedia projects, printed materials, and reading and discussion programs.

Grants support the development and production of television, radio, and digital media programs; the planning and implementation of museum exhibitions, the interpretation of historic sites, the production of related publications, multimedia components, and educational programs; and the planning and implementation of reading and discussion programs, lectures, symposia, and interpretive exhibitions of books, manuscripts, and other library resources.

Contact: 202-606-8269, e-mail publicpgms@neh.gov.

Division of Research Programs

Through fellowships to individual scholars and grants to support complex, frequently collaborative research, the Division of Research Programs contributes to the creation of knowledge in the humanities.

Fellowships and Stipends

Grants provide support for scholars to undertake full-time independent research and writing in the humanities. Grants are available for a maximum of one year and a minimum of two months of summer study.

Contact: 202-606-8200, e-mail (fellowships) fellowships@neh.gov (summer stipends) stipends@neh.gov.

Research

Grants provide up to three years of support for collaborative research in the preparation for publication of editions, translations, and other important works in the humanities, and in the conduct of large or complex interpretive studies, including archaeology projects and humanities studies of science and technology. Grants also support research opportunities offered through independent research centers and international research organizations.

Contact: 202-606-8200, e-mail research@neh.gov.

Office of Challenge Grants

Nonprofit institutions interested in developing new sources of long-term support for educational, scholarly, preservation, and public programs in the humanities can be assisted in these efforts by an NEH Challenge Grant. Grantees are required to raise $3 in nonfederal donations for every federal dollar offered. Both federal and nonfederal funds may be used to establish or increase institutional endowments and therefore guarantee long-term support for a variety of humanities needs. Funds also can be used for limited direct capital expenditures where such needs are compelling and clearly related to improvements in the humanities.

Contact: 202-606-8309, e-mail challenge@neh.gov.

Office of Digital Humanities

The Office of Digital Humanities encourages and supports projects that utilize or study the impact of digital technology on research, education, preservation, and public programming in the humanities. Launched as an initiative in 2006, Digital Humanities was made permanent as an office within NEH in 2008.

NEH is interested in fostering the growth of digital humanities and lending support to a wide variety of projects, including those that deploy digital technologies and methods to enhance understanding of a topic or issue; those that study the impact of digital technology on the humanities; and those that digitize important materials, thereby increasing the public's ability to search and access humanities information.

The office coordinates the endowment's efforts in the area of digital scholarship. Currently NEH has numerous programs throughout the agency that are actively funding digital scholarship, including Humanities Collections and Resources, Institutes for Advanced Topics in the Digital Humanities, Digital Humanities Challenge Grants, Digital Humanities Start-Up Grants, and many others. NEH is also actively working with other funding partners in the United States and abroad in order to better coordinate spending on digital infrastructure for the humanities.

Contact: 202-606-8401, e-mail odh@neh.gov.

A full list of NEH grants programs and deadlines is available on the endowment's website at http://www.neh.gov/grants.

Institute of Museum and Library Services

955 L'Enfant Plaza North, S.W., Suite 4000, Washington, DC 20024-2135
202-653-4657, fax 202-653-4600
World Wide Web http://www.imls.gov

Vision and Mission

The vision of the Institute of Museum and Library Services (IMLS) is a nation where museums and libraries work together to transform the lives of individuals and communities. The agency's mission is to advance, support, and empower America's museums, libraries, and related organizations' grant-making, research, and policy development.

Overview

IMLS is an independent grant-making agency and the primary source of federal support for the nation's approximately 120,000 libraries and 35,000 museums and related organizations. IMLS helps ensure that all Americans have access to museum, library, and information services. The agency supports innovation, lifelong learning, and cultural and civic engagement, enabling museums and libraries from geographically and economically diverse areas to deliver essential services that make it possible for individuals and communities to thrive. The agency strives to inspire libraries and museums to advance innovation, learning, and civic engagement and to provide leadership through research, policy development, and grant making.

IMLS was created with the passage of the Museum and Library Services Act (MLSA) in 1996, which, as amended, authorizes the agency to award financial assistance; collect data; form strategic partnerships; and advise the president, Congress, and other federal agencies on museum, library, and information services. Federal library programs began in 1956, and the agency has consolidated the federal museum programs dating to 1976. Today it is responsive to the needs and opportunities expressed by communities through their libraries and museums and brings cutting-edge approaches to curating essential information within cities, regions, and the nation.

The agency has an expansive reach across the country and into a large variety of institutions. Its discretionary grants are selected through a highly respected and competitive peer-review process, drawing on professionals located across the nation. IMLS builds capacity within the museum and library fields to enable better service to communities and to enhance community decision making by sharing trends and data.

IMLS is led by a director who is a presidential appointee confirmed by the Senate and advised by the National Museum and Library Services Board (NMLSB). The NMLSB is a 23-member advisory body that includes the IMLS director, the deputy director for libraries, the deputy director for museums, and 20 presidentially appointed individuals with expertise in, or commitment to, library or museum services. Based on its knowledge and experience, the NMLSB advises the IMLS director on general policy and practices and helps with the selections for the National Medal for Museum and Library Service.

In fiscal year (FY) 2019 IMLS's work was enhanced by an additional $2 million congressional appropriation. The agency allocated $189.3 million to the Library Services and Technology Act (LSTA) budget, which funds the Grants to States and discretionary grants programs. The agency was also allocated a $34.7 million budget for the Museums Services Act and $3 million for research, evaluation, and data collection. The FY 2020 budget includes an additional $10 million in congressional appropriations allocating an additional $6 million to the LSTA funds and $3 million to the Museum Services funds.

Passage of the Museum and Library Services Act of 2018 (PL 115-410) in December 2018 reauthorizes the existing programs and functions of IMLS and provides new authority, including to develop and support new museum, library, and information professionals.

Strategic Goals

As highlighted in *Transforming Communities*, the IMLS Strategic Plan for 2018–2022, the agency's goals are to

1 Promote Lifelong Learning. IMLS supports learning and literacy for people of all ages through museums and libraries.

2 Build Capacity. IMLS strengthens the capacity of museums and libraries to improve the well-being of their communities.

3 Increase Public Access. IMLS makes strategic investments that increase access to information, ideas, and networks through libraries and museums.

4 Achieve Excellence. IMLS strategically aligns its resources and relationships to support libraries and museums nationwide.

Transforming Communities is available for download on the IMLS website at https://www.imls.gov/about-us/strategic-plan.

Scope of Responsibilities

This section provides highlights of IMLS's role in supporting and sustaining America's libraries and museums and the services they provide to citizens, as authorized by the MLSA.

Library Services

IMLS library service programs support the following goals:

- To enhance coordination among federal programs that relate to library and information services
- To promote continuous improvement in library services in all types of libraries in order to better serve the people of the United States

- To facilitate access to resources in all types of libraries for the purpose of cultivating an educated and informed citizenry
- To encourage resource sharing among all types of libraries for the purpose of achieving economical and efficient delivery of library services to the public
- To promote literacy, education, and lifelong learning and to enhance and expand the services and resources provided by libraries, including those services and resources relating to workforce development, 21st-century skills, and digital literacy skills
- To enhance the skills of the current library workforce and to recruit future professionals to the field of library and information services
- To ensure the preservation of knowledge and library collections in all formats and to enable libraries to serve their communities during disasters
- To enhance the role of libraries within the information infrastructure of the United States in order to support research, education, and innovation
- To promote library services that provide users with access to information through national, state, local, regional, and international collaborations and networks

Museum Services

IMLS museum service programs support the following goals:

- To encourage and support museums in carrying out their public service role of connecting society to the cultural, artistic, historical, natural, and scientific understandings that constitute our heritage
- To encourage and support museums in carrying out their educational role
- To encourage leadership, innovation, and applications of the most current technologies and practices to enhance museum services through international, national, regional, state, and local networks and partnerships
- To assist, encourage, and support museums in carrying out their stewardship activities to achieve the highest standards in conservation and care of the cultural, historic, natural, and scientific heritage of the United States to benefit future generations
- To assist, encourage, and support museums in achieving the highest standards of management and service to the public, and to ease the financial burden borne by museums as a result of their increasing use by the public
- To support resource sharing and partnerships among museums, libraries, schools, and other community organizations
- To encourage and support museums as a part of economic development and revitalization in communities
- To ensure that museums of various types and sizes in diverse geographic regions of the United States are afforded attention and support

- To support efforts at the state level to maximize museum resources and services

Library Grants

The IMLS Grants to States program awards population-based formula grants to each State Library Administrative Agency (SLAA) in the 50 States, the District of Columbia, the Commonwealth of Puerto Rico, the U.S. Virgin Islands, American Samoa, Guam, and the Commonwealth of the Northern Mariana Islands. The formula consists of a minimum amount set by law plus a supplemental amount based on population (dependent on annual appropriations). Population data are based on the information available from the U.S. Census Bureau website.

The 2010 Act sets base allotments of $680,000 for states and $60,000 for Pacific Territories. The Act limits administrative costs at the state level to 4 percent and requires a 34 percent match from nonfederal state or local funds. Programs and services delivered by each SLAA support the purposes and priorities set forth in the Library Services and Technology Act (LSTA). SLAAs set goals and objectives for their states regarding the use of Grants to States funds within the statutorily required five-year plan approved by IMLS. These goals and objectives are determined through a planning process that includes statewide needs assessments. States take special precautions to ensure that federal funds do not supplant state investments.

Additional information about the IMLS Grants to States program, including application and submission information, is available at https://www.imls.gov/grants/grant-programs/grants-states.

Support for Pacific Territories and Freely Associated States

Grants to the Pacific Territories and the Freely Associated States (FAS) are sanctioned under a Special Rule, which authorizes a small competitive grants program in the Pacific region and the U.S. Virgin Islands. There are seven eligible entities: Guam (GU), American Samoa (AS), the Commonwealth of Northern Mariana Islands (CNMI), the Federated States of Micronesia (FSM), the Republic of the Marshall Islands (RMI), the Republic of Palau (PW), and the U.S. Virgin Islands (VI).

The funds for this grant program are taken from the allotment amounts for the FAS (FSM, RMI, and PW). The territories (GU, AS, CNMI, VI) receive allotments through the Grants to States program and, in addition, may apply for funds under the competitive program. Up to 5 percent of this program's funding is set aside for Mid-Continent Research for Education and Learning (McREL) to facilitate the grants review process. These projects support the LSTA purposes.

Library Discretionary Grants

Library Services Discretionary Grants Programs include National Leadership Grants, Native American Library Services Basic Grants, Native American Library Services Enhancement Grants, Native Hawaiian Library Services, and the Laura Bush 21st Century Librarian Program. In June 2019 IMLS announced 60 grants totaling $16,288,536 to support libraries across the country. The awards were made through the FY 2019 National Leadership Grants for Libraries Program and the Laura Bush 21st Century Librarian Program.

Use of Funds

SLAAs may use IMLS grant funding for

- Expanding services for individuals of all ages to support such individuals' needs for education, lifelong learning, workforce development, and digital literacy skills
- Establishing or enhancing electronic and other linkages and improved coordination among and between libraries and entities
- Providing training and professional development to enhance the skills of the current library workforce and leadership, and advance the delivery of library and information services; and recruiting future professionals to the field
- Developing public and private partnerships with other agencies and community-based organizations
- Targeting library services to individuals of diverse geographic, cultural, and socioeconomic backgrounds, to individuals with disabilities, and to individuals with limited functional literacy or information skills
- Targeting library and information services to persons having difficulty using a library and to underserved urban and rural communities, including low-income children
- Developing library services that provide access to information through local, state, regional, national, and international collaborations and networks
- Carrying out other activities as described in the State Library Administrative Agency's plan

Museum Grants

To be eligible for an IMLS grant, a museum must

- Be either a unit of state or local government or a private nonprofit organization that has tax-exempt status under the Internal Revenue Code
- Be located in one of the 50 states of the United States of America, the District of Columbia, the Commonwealth of Puerto Rico, Guam, American Samoa, the Virgin Islands, the Commonwealth of the Northern Mariana Islands, the Republic of the Marshall Islands, the Federated States of Micronesia, or the Republic of Palau
- Qualify as either a museum that, using a professional staff, is organized on a permanent basis for essentially educational or aesthetic purposes; owns or uses tangible objects, either animate or inanimate; cares for these objects; and exhibits these objects to the general public on a regular basis through facilities that it owns or operates *or* a public or private nonprofit

agency responsible for the operation of a museum applying on behalf of that museum

Museum Discretionary Grants

IMLS offered five major museum grant programs in FY 2019:

1. The Museums for America program supports projects that strengthen individual museums as active resources for lifelong learning, as vital components of livable communities, and as good stewards of the nation's collections.
2. National Leadership Grants for Museums support projects that address critical needs of the museum field and that have the potential to advance practice in the profession so that museums can improve services for the American public. Related organizations—such as museum associations, universities, foundations, and nonprofits—can apply for grants in this category.
3. The National Museum of African American History and Culture Act directs the IMLS director to consult with the council and director of the National Museum of African American History and Culture to establish grant opportunities to strengthen African American museums by improving care of collections, developing professional management, or providing internship and fellowship programs.
4. The Native American/Native Hawaiian Museum Services program supports the capacity of federally recognized Native American tribes and organizations that primarily serve and represent Native Hawaiians to enhance museum services to sustain heritage, culture, and knowledge through exhibitions, educational services and programming, professional development, and collections stewardship.
5. Museums Empowered, a special initiative of the Museums for America program, grants support activities for professional development and capacity-building in individual museums. The grant program focuses on four areas of relevant needs in the museum field: Digital Technology, Diversity and Inclusion, Evaluation, and Organizational Management.

Among other grants offered or cosponsored by IMLS in FY 2019 were the Community Catalyst Initiative, Inspire! Grants for Small Museums, and Save America's Treasures. Additionally, IMLS offered two technical assistance programs, two national awards programs, and the Collections Assessment for Preservation program, which works to help small and midsized museums better care for their collections.

Further information about IMLS grants is available at https://www.imls.gov/grants/grant-programs and https://www.imls.gov/grants/grant-programs/grants-states.

Museum and Library Cooperative Agreements

IMLS has numerous cooperative agreements to support and enhance agency priorities and services to the library and museum community. Highlights follow.

Measures That Matter

Measures That Matter is a partnership between Chief Officers of State Library Associations (COSLA) and IMLS that seeks to examine, evaluate, and map the landscape of public library data collection in the United States. The project will develop a Library Data and Outcomes Action Plan with key library stakeholder groups for a more coordinated approach to the collection of public library data nationally. The goal is to build a framework within which outcomes, outputs, and indicators can be drawn upon to consistently and effectively demonstrate the role, value, and impact of public libraries.

Inclusive Internship Initiative: Mentored Internships for Diversity

In FY 2019 the American Library Association's (ALA) Public Library Association (PLA) sponsored a paid, mentored public library internship program for high school juniors and seniors from diverse backgrounds. The Inclusive Internship Initiative (III), with support from IMLS, is a summer-long mentored learning project through which library mentors and interns engage with multiple facets of library life, from administration to programming to user services. Interns are given opportunities to connect with one another and learn from mentors across the country at a library "master class" in Washington, D.C., before returning to their host institutions to develop and execute their summer projects alongside their mentors.

Sustaining and Advancing Indigenous Cultures

The Association of Tribal Archives, Libraries, and Museums (ATALM) provides continuing education programs targeted to the needs of tribal archivists, librarians, and museum staff; and is conducting a survey of tribal archives, libraries, and museums, followed by a report documenting activities, challenges, and needs. Funded activities will contribute to improving the informational, educational, and cultural programs and services available to the nation's 5.2 million indigenous peoples. The ATALM conference in October 2018 reached 850 people, with over 225 tribes represented as well as 42 states, and 260 presenters. IMLS will continue to track the number of professional development and capacity-building training opportunities provided through this cooperative agreement, and the number of professionals trained.

Museums for All

The Association of Children's Museums (ACM) is working with IMLS on a nationwide museum access program for low-income families. Following a successful pilot with children's museums, the signature program is now being expanded to include all types of museums. Museums for All invites electronic benefit transfer cardholders to visit participating museums for free or at greatly reduced admission year-round. By promoting affordable museum experiences, ACM and IMLS are encouraging families of all backgrounds to visit museums regularly, building lifelong museum habits that bolster the role of museums as community anchors. At the close of FY 2019 there were more than 450 participating museums, serving over 2.2 million visitors and representing 48 states, the District of Columbia, and the Virgin Islands. This was a 46 percent increase in museums participating in Museums for All between FY 2018 and FY 2019 and a 70 percent increase in visitors served.

StoryCorps

For almost a decade, StoryCorps has worked to record and preserve the stories of IMLS National Medal Winners. With support from IMLS, StoryCorps travels to each medal-winning library and museum to capture the voices of their people and hear about their programs and communities. More about the National Medal for Museum and Library Service appears later in this report. To listen to StoryCorps / IMLS recordings, visit https://storycorps.org/participate/host/institute-for-museum-and-library-services/.

Interagency Collaboration

The Museum and Library Services Act (MLSA) authorizes the IMLS director to support interagency collaboration: initiatives, materials, or technology to support workforce development activities undertaken by libraries; resource and policy approaches to eliminate barriers to fully leveraging the roles of libraries and museums in supporting the early learning, literacy, lifelong learning, digital literacy, workforce development, and education needs of the people of the United States; and initiatives, materials, or technology to support educational, cultural, historical, scientific, environmental, and other activities undertaken by museums.

The MLSA also authorizes the director to coordinate the policies and activities of IMLS with the policies and activities of other agencies and offices of the federal government having interest in or responsibilities for the improvement of museums, libraries, and information services. The statute expressly requires the director to coordinate with other agencies to improve literacy through school libraries and through programs supported by the Head Start and Workforce Investment Acts. It also authorizes the director to ensure that IMLS policies and activities are coordinated with federal programs and activities that increase the capacity of libraries and museums to participate in economic and community development, education and research; in improving digital literacy skills; and in disseminating health information.

IMLS has a wide range of interagency partnerships, including advancing broadband adoption, coordinating early learning activities, supporting the effective delivery of workforce development services, and distributing federal information impacting the health and well-being of Americans. Examples follow.

U.S. Citizenship and Immigration Services

IMLS has a memorandum of understanding with U.S. Citizenship and Immigration Services to provide information and outreach to local libraries and museums to help newly arrived individuals understand the benefits of citizenship and learn how to undertake the citizenship process.

National Book Festival and National Student Poets Program

IMLS has served as a charter sponsor of the Library of Congress's National Book Festival since its inception in 2001. The National Student Poets Program is the nation's highest honor for youth poets, with an annual ceremony hosted in conjunction with the festival. In partnership with the Alliance for Young Artists and Writers, IMLS honored five outstanding youth poets chosen from among thousands of award-winning student writers. The National Student Poets ceremony was held July 17, 2019, at the Smithsonian National Museum of the American Indian. The young poets, representing five different regions of the country, read original works as part of a ceremony featuring U.S. Poet Laureate, Joy Harjo, and former IMLS director Kathryn K. Matthew.

Policy Research, Analysis, Data Collection, and Dissemination

The IMLS director is authorized to conduct policy research, analyses, and data collections annually with SLAAs; national, state, and regional library and museum organizations; and other relevant agencies and organizations. IMLS is further mandated to

- Identify national needs for and trends in museum, library, and information services
- Measure the impact and effectiveness of museum, library, and information services including the impact of federal programs authorized under this chapter
- Identify best practices
- Develop plans to improve museum, library, and information services and to strengthen national, state, local, regional, and international communications and cooperative networks

IMLS provides reliable and objective data and analysis to inform policy decisions. The primary data products maintained by IMLS are the Public Libraries Survey and the State Library Administrative Agency Survey. See the section on IMLS Library Surveys later in this report for further information.

National Medal for Museum and Library Service

The National Medal for Museum and Library Service is the nation's highest honor for institutions that make significant and exceptional contributions to their communities. Since 1994 IMLS has presented the award to institutions that demonstrate extraordinary and innovative approaches to public service, exceeding the expected levels of community outreach. The winners are honored at a National Medal award ceremony held in Washington, D.C.

To learn about the ten libraries and museums honored with the 2019 National Medal, visit https://www.imls.gov/issues/national-initiatives/national-medal-museum-and-library-service/2019-medals.

Strategic Priorities and Initiatives

IMLS initiatives and special programs are designed to help libraries and museums address critical needs, such as stimulating economic development through job training and skill development, facilitating family learning, and sustaining our heritage and community cohesion. Special emphasis is given to community engagement; literacy and early learning; reaching rural residents, veterans, underserved, and other special populations; STEM (Science, Technology, Engineering, and Math) programs; and access to collections, both physical and digital. Pending availability of funding, these efforts will continue in FY 2020.

Community Catalyst Initiative

Many museums and libraries carry out their missions in ways that extend beyond traditional formats and objectives, often serving their cities and towns as enablers of community vitality and co-creators of positive community change. IMLS is helping to identify and support conceptual frameworks and successful approaches that support this type of work through its Community Catalyst Initiative. The initiative calls upon libraries and museums to engage in collaborative arrangements that facilitate and support local community development and economic revitalization. Libraries and museums are encouraged to identify and leverage local assets, along with their own resources and competencies, to achieve greater reach and impact within their communities.

An evaluation of the agency's Community Catalyst Initiative (CCI) was launched this fiscal year. IMLS is assessing CCI's capacity-building effects within a cohort setting, where grantees come together to receive training, share progress on their projects, and discuss challenges and new insights in working with their local communities. The agency also offered five CCI listening session workshops across the country, reaching a broader range of museums and libraries, to further validate the applicability of the tools and resources that can be applied to help improve civic, health, digital, early, and STEM literacies. IMLS published 24 tools and resources from CCI grantees on the IMLS website.

Understanding the Social Wellbeing Impacts of the Nation's Libraries and Museums, a study launched in August 2018 and continued in FY 2019, is the first step in a long-term civic literacy initiative. The goal of the project is to gain a better understanding on a national level of the conditions under which museums and libraries contribute to quality of life and well-being in the communities they serve. IMLS awarded a cooperative agreement to the Reinvestment Fund, an evaluation firm, to conduct the analysis. Qualitative and quantitative data collection progressed during FY 2019. When the analysis is completed in FY 2020, IMLS will share the findings to help museums and libraries identify gaps and areas where further research is needed.

Veterans and Military Families

The Community Salute Initiative augments the capacity of libraries and museums to meet the unique and critical needs of the nation's more than 22 million veterans and their military families. Libraries and museums serve veterans by assisting them in building skills, by offering healing resources, and by providing access to employment or training opportunities.

The work to date has examined how libraries and museums are responding to the needs of veterans and their families and identified potential new approaches to provide better and more integrated community-based services for this important constituency. These approaches are grounded in community development/engagement practices as well as insights from policy experts, funders, and service providers for veterans and their families.

IMLS worked with a cooperator, FSG, to produce five resource documents tailored for libraries and museums that provide qualitative and quantitative approaches to help museums and libraries better serve veterans and their families/caregivers. The agency is taking these approaches to local communities for use when they informally convene with veterans' service providers, museums, libraries, and local government representatives.

Science, Technology, Engineering, and Math

Science, Technology, Engineering, and Math (STEM) and making-related programs offered through libraries and museums provide local communities with authentic and contextual learning experiences, tools, and spaces as well as training of formal and informal educators. IMLS continues to fund this area through its regular competitive grant making and Grants to States funding (through the Library Services and Technology Act). Libraries and museums offer people of all ages and backgrounds mentor-led learning opportunities that spark curiosity and build interest in STEM subjects and career pathways. These opportunities introduce learners who are underrepresented in the STEM workforce to important STEM concepts, skills, and experiences including engaging in authentic scientific practices using new technologies and state-of-the-art equipment.

In September, IMLS announced $1.9 million in new funding from the Department of Education expanding an initiative that introduces underserved youth to STEM and making-based activities. New York Hall of Science (NYSCI) will continue to lead this project through a cooperative agreement with IMLS. Originally initiated as a pilot in 2014, the project provides elementary and middle school students with engaging activities to inspire an interest in science, technology, engineering, and mathematics with the aim of improving retention in STEM disciplines. This national project, now expanded both in scope and scale, will equip children's museums and science centers with making activities, resources, tools, and training, enabling them to train up to forty 21st Century Community Learning Centers across eight states, with the goal of reaching up to 1,000 students. A new survey, part of the third-party evaluation, will assess the outcomes of the project, including changes in interest, skills, and behaviors related to STEM and making among youth participants.

As a key federal partner working with Congress, IMLS demonstrated the role of museums and libraries in teaching and modeling inquiry-based methods through making, which emphasizes learning-through-doing (active learning) in a social environment. In FY 2019 IMLS held a Congressional Maker Faire in partnership with the Congressional Maker Caucus and the Nation of Makers. IMLS also hosted three fully booked panels on making: "Making Amongst Veterans," "Everyone a Maker: The Impact of Diverse US Maker Communities," and "Small Business Makers—Made in the USA."

Rural/Small Towns

Through its various grant-making authorities, IMLS reaches across the United States and territories into smaller and rural communities with more dispersed populations. IMLS programs support services for tribal entities and build the capacity of museums of African American history and culture. The need for support in these varied communities is expansive: supporting smaller historic houses or general museums in conserving and cataloging collections; helping tribal archives to collect oral histories and preserve language; enhancing digital literacy skills by training staff at museums and libraries on how to work with their patrons to facilitate job searches and other needs; and launching Open e-Books, which distributes free children's content—millions of current e-books—through eligible libraries, working with publishers and nonprofit organizations.

IMLS sees the need to continue supporting and advancing rural museums and libraries as essential community assets that must be considered as part of community revitalization and cohesion-building efforts. The agency is building relationships with small and rural libraries and cultural institutions and those who work in rural and small communities (e.g., USDA, EPA, extension services) to raise awareness of the value of these institutions. IMLS will continue to explore how better to position these institutions within their local community networks and with local investors.

In addition, IMLS has invested in rural and small communities by supporting basic infrastructure, including access to library- and museum-provided broadband connectivity and helping residents gain digital access to employment information and critical job skills. The Museums for America (MFA), Museum Assessment Program (MAP), and Collections Assessment for Preservation (CAP) programs all offer valuable support to many small museums in rural areas and small towns. Rural public libraries often serve as their communities' sole resource for Internet access, particularly where there are economic barriers to home connections and challenges to accessing high-quality Wi-Fi connections. Public libraries, supported by the Grants to States program (LSTA funding), provide Internet access to Americans who use their public libraries to perform life-changing and life-enhancing tasks in the areas of education, health and wellness, and job training.

Accelerating Promising Practices for Small Libraries

In FY 2019 IMLS implemented the Accelerating Promising Practices (APP) program for libraries, offering a notice of funding opportunity and awarding $1.2 million for the first cohort. The first year of work established an initial grantee cohort of 30 institutions, as well as mentors and an evaluator. This funding opportunity is designed specifically to strengthen the ability of small and rural libraries, archives, and related organizations to serve their communities, with awards ranging from $10,000 to $50,000. APP is under the umbrella of National Leadership Grants for Libraries, which supports projects that enhance the quality of library and archives services nationwide by advancing theory and practice.

Capacity Building and Community Engagement

The Museum Assessment Program (MAP), offered to the museum community through a cooperative agreement with the American Alliance of Museums, has been a legacy program that helps museums assess strengths and weaknesses and plan for the future. A MAP assessment requires the museum staff and governing authority to complete a self-study. Following the study, a site visit is conducted by one or more museum professionals, who tour the museum and meet with staff, governing officials, and volunteers and produce a report evaluating the museum's operations, making recommendations, and suggesting resources. Three types of MAP assessments are offered: Organizational, Collections Stewardship, and Community Engagement.

The Collections Assessment for Preservation (CAP) program is a joint effort of IMLS and the Foundation for Advancement in Conservation to help small and midsized museums better care for their collections. The program provides small and midsized museums with partial funding toward a general conservation assessment of an institution's collections, buildings, and building systems, as well as its policies and procedures relating to collections care. Participants who complete the program receive an assessment report with recommendations and further guidance. In FY 2019 more than 140 museums in over 30 states participated in both assessment programs, and over 500 museums in 40 states participated between FY 2015 and FY 2018.

IMLS funded Museums for Digital Learning, work that builds capacity of the museum field to work with cross-disciplinary teacher teams and develop cross-disciplinary and inquiry-based digital education resources. The cooperative agreement was executed with Newfields in August 2019, along with the Field Museum and History Colorado, who will develop digital content and educator materials. Ten educators representing different disciplines, grade levels, and geographic areas were recruited as co-creators to work with the two museums. The platform and content development are on schedule, and the project team is planning to build approximately nine digital modules for elementary, middle, and high school levels. Teacher testing of products and platform is slated for the spring of 2020. Awareness was raised in the museum sector about the project at six IMLS regional workshops and the Museum Computer Network conference.

Broadband

IMLS cohosted the National Tribal Broadband Summit, September 23–24, 2019, with the Departments of the Interior and Education, the Federal Communications Commission (FCC), and the White House's Intergovernmental Affairs and Domestic Policy Council. The summit drew 250 participants from federal, state, and tribal governments; telecommunications companies; tribal chief information officers and librarians; and other cultural entities. At the summit, the FCC and other federal agencies, including the United States Department of Agriculture, announced significant new funding that is available to IMLS stakeholders.

IMLS also participated on the White House Broadband Interagency Working Group to amplify and leverage the role of libraries and museums in promoting digital inclusion and literacy, particularly in rural and tribal communities. The Administration's strategies recognize libraries and museums as critical community anchors that support digital inclusion and literacy. IMLS developed two reports that have been published by the White House American Broadband Initiative, in addition to contributing IMLS content to the government-wide website, broadband usa.ntia.doc.gov.

Professional Development

A major focal area for IMLS is empowering library and museum staff members to provide users with opportunities to develop the digital skills they need for better success in such areas as education, workforce development, and civic engagement. Funded projects offer open source curricula, training, tools, and credentials for a library audience to learn web literacy skills and develop digital competencies. Additionally, online courses with in-person group study sessions facilitated by librarians can cover a range of academic, professional, and personal development subjects. For example:

- The agency funded research from the University of Pittsburgh, University of California–Irvine, Queens College, and Pennsylvania State University exploring the experiences of underrepresented minority LIS graduate students participating in cohort-based recruitment programs. Case studies of three cohort-based programs will be conducted, and findings will inform an LIS recruitment and retention model that addresses gaps in support and isolation among underrepresented minority graduate students.
- Agency grant data from the FY 2019 Museums Empowered grant program and Museum Assessment Program indicate a significant increase in the number of museums applying for "organizational management," which is tied to training and strengthening the workforce at all stages of careers. In addition, IMLS has seen a significant increase since FY 2014 in the number of professional development awards (from 12 to 65) under Museums for America, Museums Empowered, and National Leadership Grants for Museums.

IMLS Library Surveys

IMLS manages a federal statistical program that identifies national trends and the public use and effectiveness of museum, library, and information services. The statistical survey programs provide reliable and objective data in a wide variety of formats used by policymakers and practitioners to inform policy decisions. For example, these data are used by policymakers at the state and local levels to compare conditions in libraries of comparable sizes; by researchers to analyze state-of-the-art public librarianship; and by private companies seeking reliable national, state, and local statistics for developing business plans and marketing strategies within the library sector of the economy. These statistical survey programs include

- The Public Libraries Survey, which provides information on key metrics of library health and services across the United States and outlying territories, and tracks trends in libraries. In addition to the long-standing library data collections efforts, IMLS uses other federal data to analyze how public libraries serve their communities and produces a report of overall findings, research briefs highlighting topics of general interest, and a public use data file.
- The State Library Administrative Agency Survey conducted every two years, which studies the current state and health of state library administrative agencies. IMLS produces a summary report of the overall survey findings and a public use data file that are used by the chief officers of state library agencies; federal policymakers; government and library administrators at federal, state, and local levels; researchers; and ALA.

For IMLS surveys and data, visit https://www.imls.gov/research-tools/data-collection and see "Highlights of IMLS Public Library Surveys" beginning on page 296 of this volume.

Safety and Disaster Preparedness

During natural disasters, museums and libraries often serve as community resources, gathering places, and providers of information. If their facilities are intact, they can play crucial roles in recovery efforts, including

- Serving as places of physical refuge and sources of Wi-Fi, Internet access, phone access, and electricity
- Providing help, advice, and information about recovery assistance such as registering with FEMA and hosting financial planning seminars
- Serving as safe gathering places during times of crisis, using arts and cultural assets to help with recovery, healing, and resilience building
- Serving as gathering places for FEMA workers, Red Cross workers, and others who require physical headquarters for their relief work
- Serving as sources of volunteer networks that are familiar with community needs
- Serving as partners in creating community plans for emergency preparedness and disaster response

IMLS has made significant investments in strengthening institutional capacity to prepare for and respond to disasters among the nation's museums and libraries. As holders of cultural and natural heritage, these institutions can experience catastrophic losses in times of floods, hurricanes, tornadoes, fires, and human-made disasters, but can also be integral to community efforts to recover and build resiliency. Grant-supported activities have ranged from developing emergency preparedness plans and recovery strategies at institutional or community levels to carrying out conservation surveys, treatment, and environmental improvements relating to affected natural and cultural collections.

IMLS Website and Publications

The IMLS website (www.imls.gov) provides a wealth of information on the agency's activities, including IMLS-sponsored conferences, webinars, publications, and grant programs. Through an electronic newsletter, *IMLS News*, and the blog, IMLS provides information on grant deadlines, success stories, and opportunities.

IMLS is on twitter @US_IMLS and Facebook at https://www.facebook.com/USIMLS.

EveryLibrary

P.O. Box 406, Riverside, IL 60546
312-574-0316, e-mail info@everylibrary.org
World Wide Web http://www.everylibrary.org | action.everylibrary.org | SaveSchoolLibrarians.org

John Chrastka
Executive Director

Founded in December 2012 to address a gap in existing voter outreach and public advocacy about library elections and budget negotiations with municipal funding partners of libraries, EveryLibrary has since expanded its focus to include direct engagement with the public as advocates and activists for library issues, activism about school library budgets and policy issues, and support for partner library organizations' legislative and funding agendas.

EveryLibrary is the first and only nationwide political action committee for libraries. It received its designation from the IRS as a 501(c)4 social welfare organization and is chartered as a nonprofit corporation in the state of Illinois. EveryLibrary's mission statement is "Building voter support for libraries." Its vision statement, and the inspiration for its name, is "Any library funding issue anywhere should matter to every library everywhere."

Board and Advisors

EveryLibrary is administered by a board of directors and is run by staff. It has no members. Its 2019 board of directors included John Chrastka, president and executive director; Erica Findley, treasurer; Patrick "PC" Sweeney, secretary and political director; and Brian D. Hart, Harmony V. Faust, and Peter Bromberg, directors. EveryLibrary was happy to celebrate that Patrick "PC" Sweeney was honored in 2019 with a "40 Under 40" award winner by the American Association of Political Consultants (AAPC) for his work building political support for libraries.

Organizational History—Campaign Focus

As a 501(c)4 organization, EveryLibrary works with library boards and staff on Informational Communications Campaigns and with local citizen ballot committees as they conduct "Get Out the Vote" and "Vote Yes" campaigns for their local library's ballot measure. These library ballot campaigns are either advisory or binding and can include bonds, levies, mill levies, warrant articles, parcel taxes, measures, or other referenda placed before voters by library boards or by municipal councils. EveryLibrary's support includes providing pro bono technical assistance and training to library leaders as well as early campaign financial support and consulting to campaign committees and citizen's groups. EveryLibrary has helped take 110 libraries to their Election Days, winning 80 percent and securing over $330 million (aggregated per annum) in stable funding for those libraries.

EveryLibrary is funded by individual donors, both monthly and annually, and corporate (vendor) donors. Being able to provide its services for free to libraries and committees allows EveryLibrary to focus on best practices for campaigns rather than revenue generation from direct consulting.

Libraries 2020 Campaign Launch

In December 2019 EveryLibrary and the EveryLibrary Institute, NFP. announced the kickoff of the Libraries 2020 campaign, a first-of-its-kind nationwide voter engagement campaign for libraries. Using advanced voter engagement strategies, the Libraries 2020 campaign is designed to build political power, lasting public engagement, and true voter support for library funding across the country. The campaign brings the skills, competencies, and successes of both EveryLibrary, the only national political action committee for libraries, and the EveryLibrary Institute, a nonprofit library think tank focused on the future of library funding.

EveryLibrary has a track record of building voter support for public libraries and for putting school libraries on the agenda. With a digital home at Libraries2020.org, the campaign will employ a range of tools and resources available to political action committees to create and field an advocacy campaign across social digital and social media, traditional media, and field campaigns. The EveryLibrary Institute will harness voter and public perception research and the capacities within the philanthropic community to help sustain a robust, smart, and targeted campaign. Together, EveryLibrary and the EveryLibrary Institute will utilize their networks across the library community, within the political field, and beyond the library sector in order to position the Libraries 2020 campaign for success.

Library Ballot Measures

In 2019 EveryLibrary supported 14 campaigns to establish, renew, or expand funding for operations, collections, programs, services, and staffing; to establish a library district; and to issue a bond for construction or remodeling of library facilities. Highlights from the year included helping to establish the Southwest LaPlata County, Colorado, library district. Funding had been cut by the county commission and without a new taxing district, two public libraries would have closed in this rural community.

Other highlights include Spokane County, Washington, where Proposition 1, a new operating levy to expand services and stabilize the library's future, passed with a 53 percent Yes vote. About 93 percent of the library's budget is funded by property taxes. Without this increase in funding from the levy, the library district would have cut services and staff, and, over the next few years, branches may have been forced to close. In Washington State's Pend Oreille County Library District, 63 percent voted to restore a property tax levy for operations; without this funding, two branch libraries in the rural county would have closed. In Palatine, Illinois, 64 percent of voters approved a tax increase that will allow the library to maintain services while keeping its infrastructure up to date. In DeSoto, Missouri, 62 percent of voters said Yes to restoring the levy rate to .35 cent, which will dramatically increase services for all. In Rockton, Illinois, 69 percent of voters approved a bond for the Talcott Free Library to finish its building expansion project and truly become an anchor for the village's main street.

On the loss side, voters in Lafayette Parish, Louisiana, approved a $10 million "rededication levy" that takes funding from library reserves to pay for a flood control project. While the measure passed, the net result is a significant loss of funding reserves for the library. The River Grove, Illinois, Public Library lost a bond measure 462 to 1,016 in the face of strong local antitax sentiments. One turnaround campaign was for the Pine River Library District in Bayfield, Colorado. In the 2018 midterm elections the district lost a levy campaign by just nine votes. EveryLibrary helped them reevaluate their approach and successfully reran the measure, passing with a 58 percent Yes vote.

Direct Political Actions

Throughout 2019 EveryLibrary helped dozens of libraries safeguard their funding from local political threats through direct political actions and lobbying activities and behind-the-scenes support for leaders and activists as they campaigned for their libraries. Many direct actions are operationalized through the action.everylibrary.org platform. This digital tool allows EveryLibrary to field petitions and e-mail campaigns targeted at elected officials and use social-influencing campaigns to affect positive change for libraries and library issues. EveryLibrary can set up a direct action for a library in crisis in only a few hours. Donor support allows EveryLibrary to employ a combination of grassroots and advertising very effectively.

Highlights include direct political actions for the Stillwater County, Montana, Library as it faced an 11 percent budget cut. In Baldwin County, Georgia, EveryLibrary worked closely with the Friends of the Mary Vinson Library to run an effective digital and on-the-ground campaign to prevent a loss of state grant money. In Menominee County, Michigan, it was organizing against a 25 percent cut. In Citrus County, Florida, the action was to contact the county commissioners to reverse their line-item cut of the digital subscription to the *New York Times*. It had been cut under the allegation that the *Times* was a "fake news" source.

SaveIMLS.org Campaign

President Trump's fiscal year 2020 budget again targeted federal library programs for complete elimination. This was the third year the president's budget called for the total shutdown of the Institute of Museum and Library Services (IMLS). In 2019 EveryLibrary continued to rally Americans from all walks of life and across the political spectrum against the proposed cuts to critical public funding of libraries, museums, and archives. Over the last three years, through its SaveIMLS.org campaign, EveryLibrary has empowered 20,000 Americans to send a message to Congress to reverse the cuts and expand support for IMLS. EveryLibrary endorses the "one dollar per capita" funding request for the Library Services and Technology Act (LSTA) put forward by the Chief Officers of State Library Agencies (COSLA).

SaveSchoolLibrarians.org

Through an ongoing partnership with Follett Learning, EveryLibrary supports school library budgets and school librarians through its SaveSchoolLibrarians.org digital action site. Over 42,000 people have signed up to take direct action on behalf of school libraries and their librarians. This opt-in list of dedicated, accessible library advocates is unique in the school library advocacy ecosystem.

In 2019 EveryLibrary continued to develop and expand its focus on education policy by joining and supporting national education coalitions as well as by engaging the policy discussion directly as conference presenters and thought leaders. In February, EveryLibrary presented a policy panel at the South by Southwest EDU (SXSW EDU) conference called "Why is the Largest Classroom in the School Empty?" and a session called "Libraries are Being Starved—Whose Fault Is It?" A key component of EveryLibrary's school library support strategy is to join and actively participate in education-facing coalitions. In 2019 these included new roles with the National Summer Learning Association Coalition and the Future Ready Librarians Coalition.

One mission-critical part of EveryLibrary's school library focus is its support for state school library organizations' legislative advocacy, engagement with policy and rules-making, coalition roles, and voter-facing outreach campaigns for statewide education initiatives. EveryLibrary worked closely with several state school or multitype library associations including the Florida Association for Media in Education, the Georgia Library Media Association, the Iowa Library Association, the Michigan Association for Media in Education, and the Pennsylvania School Librarians Association to help advance their legislative agendas and address impending problems head-on.

Speaking, Training, and Publishing

The EveryLibrary board voted to transfer ownership and responsibility for the *Political Librarian*, an open-access journal of public policy and tax policy, to the EveryLibrary Institute, NFP. The Institute has taken responsibility for prior issues and will continue to publish new issues under the same ISSN (2471-3155) on the Open Scholarship platform at Washington University of St. Louis.

The EveryLibrary leadership team was in high demand in 2019 as conference, webinar, and seminar speakers, presenters, workshop leaders, and keynoters. Their presentational approach is rooted in the data about voter and public perception of libraries and informed by successful advocacy campaigns and direct activism for public and school libraries across the country. Executive director John Chrastka and political director Patrick "PC" Sweeney marked the publication of their book *Before the Ballot: Building Political Support for Library Funding* (ALA/Neal Schuman), an up-to-date guide for library leaders and local citizen stakeholders to plan successful Informational Communications campaigns and Get Out the Vote campaigns respectively.

Organizational Agenda

EveryLibrary will continue to work in 2020 to fulfill its core mission of building voter support for libraries. Through its Libraries 2020 campaign the organization is working to close the gap between how the public appreciates libraries and the willingness of voters to approve new funding for libraries. Likewise, Libraries 2020 is focused on changing the funding landscape for school libraries through direct action. By helping librarians build partnerships and join coalitions based on its value system, EveryLibrary hopes to empower librarians in the political process.

EveryLibrary's six strategic priorities in 2020 are

- To deepen efforts to support local library communities that go on the ballot to renew or extend their basic taxpayer-approved funding and cultivate opportunities for libraries that want to enhance services and facilities through municipal budgets or voter-approved measures
- To join and support coalitions that align with the mission of libraries as institutions, that promote and extend the rights and prosperity of the people libraries serve, and that protect the rights, employment, and pensions of the people who work in all types of libraries
- To continue to build a unique and extensive network of Americans who believe in the power of libraries to change lives and build communities, and who are ready to become advocates and activists for libraries
- To support the role of library boards and commissions in governing libraries, making policy, and setting budgets that are responsive to diverse local priorities and create inclusive, prosperous, and vibrant communities
- To focus its support of School Library programs as effective solutions for some of the biggest problems facing schools and districts around the country
- To be a leader and a listener in a national discussion about the role that public, academic, and school libraries have in people's lives, and work within the profession and across civil society to find the best ways to preserve, protect, and extend everyone's right to use libraries

Budget, Donor Transparency, and Reporting

EveryLibrary puts its donor funding to work in three ways: directly on local library campaigns—for both public libraries and school libraries; on building its national reach as an advocacy organization for libraries; and on staff and projects that run the organization. As the only national 501(c)4 for libraries, it "bundles" small donations from around the country and sends them to local Vote Yes committees where needed.

EveryLibrary is entirely supported by individual donors and library vendor donors. It does not ask for or receive any funding from grant-making, philanthropic, or charitable organizations. As an independent 501(c)4, EveryLibrary is ineligible for government grants (federal or state). EveryLibrary's operating budget allocates one-third going to direct campaign expenditures, one-third to salaries and operations, and one-third to growing its organizational reach. To keep costs low, staff and interns collaborate in a paid coworkings space in Brooklyn, New York, and across the country in a virtual office environment that has few fixed expenses. Its office environment is supported by G-Suite; Nation Builder hosts its public-facing web pages; and it utilizes PayPal, Stripe, and Act Blue for third-party donation processors.

EveryLibrary provides a high level of transparency about its donations and is one of only a few national political action groups that encourage donors to self-disclose. EveryLibrary voluntarily provides annual financial disclosure information to GuideStar, a large national nonprofit clearinghouse and rating service, where it currently holds a "Gold Rate" certification.

President's Budget Proposals to Eliminate Key Agencies, 2017–2021

($ million)

Federally Funded Agency	FY 2017 Enacted Appropriations	FY 2018 President's Budget Proposal	FY 2018 Enacted Omnibus	FY 2019 President's Budget Proposal	FY 2019 Enacted Omnibus	FY 2020 President's Budget Proposal	FY 2020 Enacted Omnibus	FY 2021 President's Budget Proposal
Institute of Museum and Library Services	$231	Elimination*	$240	Elimination*	$242	Elimination*	$252	Elimination*
National Endowment for the Arts	$150	Elimination*	$152.8	Elimination*	$155	Elimination*	$167.5	Elimination*
National Endowment for the Humanities	$150	Elimination*	$152.8	Elimination*	$155	Elimination*	$167.5	Elimination*

*President's budget proposal includes minor funds to close the agency.

Part 3
Library/Information Science Education, Placement, and Salaries

Career Resources for Library and Information Professionals

Susanne Markgren

Finding a job—or more importantly—finding a job that you enjoy, finding a job that provides you with growth, finding a job that nurtures and supports your ambitions and goals, and finding a job that helps you cultivate a long and satisfying career, can be a challenge. It can, and probably will, take a long and winding road to get you to where you want to be. Just know that each role you fill, each skill you learn, and each colleague or mentor or supervisor you interact with, can (and will) help guide the way. The first job you get most likely won't be the dream job, but that job—and every one after it—will help to guide you on your individual career pathway, and hopefully steer you toward a successful and satisfying career.

There are many pathways to consider when seeking employment and/or advancement in your library career. And there are many different options and strategies that can assist you along the way. Keeping an open mind is always a good option, as is seeking out different and nontraditional opportunities that may be conducive to your specific circumstances at any specific time. Our profession is a draw for many because of its diversity and flexibility. This article provides readers with a variety of resources and tools that will help in the navigation of one's career path.

Coverage from the *Library Journal* survey "Placements and Salaries 2019" (excerpted immediately following this article) offers a positive outlook for recent graduates. With rising pay for the sixth year in a row, and narrowing gender disparities in salaries, we seem to be headed in the right direction. As for job satisfaction, 74 percent of 2018 graduates are satisfied with their placements (in LIS), while 83 percent of graduates working in non-library settings claimed the same level of satisfaction. Just another reason to keep one's options open and keep an open mind.

The graduates taking part in the *LJ* survey mentioned using generic job sites (Monster, Indeed, Glassdoor, LinkedIn, etc.), as well as association, professional, and government job sites, and others such as ALA's job list—always a favorite—as helpful in their job searches. Some of the sage advice that these graduates provided include developing presentation skills, a willingness to relocate, being able to demonstrate social skills in interviews, practicing mock interviewing, and looking at (or reading) job postings as soon as one begins a LIS program.

The resources presented in this article have been curated based on popularity, longevity, and influence in the library and information community. All are freely available online, and as with every online information source, users should employ

Susanne Markgren is coauthor of the career guidance books *How to Thrive as a Library Professional: Achieving Success and Satisfaction* (Libraries Unlimited, 2019), with Linda Miles, and *Career Q&A: A Librarian's Real-Life, Practical Guide to Managing a Successful Career* (Information Today, Inc., 2013) with Tiffany Eatman Allen.

critical analysis and judgment to determine currency, accuracy, and bias based on their individual needs.

The Directory of Organizations in Part 6 of this volume may also prove useful for job seekers. Many of these organizations, institutions, libraries, and associations maintain their own job sites and social media accounts where active job listings can be found.

Organization of the Resources

The resources that follow are organized in three principal sections. The first, "Career Advice Sites and Resources," lists informational websites, useful for those seeking more information and advice on specific areas of librarianship and archive work. Many of these are association sites, some of which have mentoring programs, Q&As, and materials offering guidance on résumé writing, preparing for interviews, and negotiating salaries.

The second section lists "Podcasts" geared for working librarians and information professionals. These podcasts provide listeners with news and real-world examples and advice from working professionals.

Following is a two-part section of "Job Listings" resources—the first specific to librarians, archivists, and information professionals; the second covering a broader range of resources. The selected sites primarily post jobs in the United States, but some also post international opportunities. It is good practice to search a variety of job sites, systematically, to get the best and most comprehensive snapshot of available positions. It's also a good idea to seek out specific libraries, companies, institutions, and associations on social media sites. Where available, Twitter handles (@ALA_JobLIST, for instance) have been included at the end of each listing.

Career Advice Sites and Resources

American Association of Law Libraries (AALL)—Career Center

https://www.aallnet.org/careers/career-center
Offers information on careers in law libraries, advice on how to find a job, and access to the *AALL Biennial Salary Survey & Organizational Characteristics* (*AALL Salary Survey*). @aallnet

American Association of School Librarians (AASL)—Education and Careers

http://www.ala.org/aasl/about/ed
Career and education resources for those seeking to enter or advance in the school library field. Job listing are found at ALA JobLIST. @aasl

American Library Association (ALA) JobLIST—Career Development Resources

http://www.ala.org/educationcareers/employment/career-resources
A wealth of resources from the American Library Association (ALA) to help one prepare for a productive and effective job search as well as enhance career

development efforts, including a printable Career Development Resource Guide, and information on the Placement Center and upcoming events and conferences. @ALA_JobLIST and @alaplacement

Association of College and Research Libraries (ACRL)

http://www.ala.org/acrl
Under the heading "Professional Tools" are useful descriptions of various positions and information on recruitment and retention. Job listings are found at ALA JobLIST. @ALA_ACRL

Bureau of Labor Statistics, U.S. Department of Labor, Occupational Outlook Handbook, Librarians

https://www.bls.gov/ooh/education-training-and-library/librarians.htm
Provides information on librarian jobs and salaries, and insight into the growth and outlook of the profession.

How to Thrive as a Library Professional: Achieving Satisfaction and Success

https://thriveasalibraryprofessional.wordpress.com
A companion to the book, which focuses on what professional practice means for working librarians, and "where the rubber hits the road" as theory and action come together in the workplace.

Library Career People

http://yourlibrarycareer.com
A Q&A forum and career development archive of professional guidance and advice for librarians, library staff, and those thinking of entering the profession. @LibCareerPeople

Library Worklife—HR E-News for Today's Leaders

http://ala-apa.org/newsletter
Offers sections, articles, and advice on salaries, career advancement, recruitment, and more. @alaapa

Public Library Association (PLA)—Careers in Public Librarianship

http://www.ala.org/pla/tools/careers
Information and career advice about public librarianship from a leading ALA division. Job listings are found at ALA JobLIST. @ALA_PLA

Medical Library Association (MLA) Career Center

http://www.mlanet.org/p/cm/ld/fid=352
Explore a career in the health sciences or medical profession. Includes information, resources, and connections for students and job seekers alike. @MedLibAssn

MLIS SKILLS AT WORK—A Snapshot of Job Postings for Spring 2019

https://ischool.sjsu.edu/sites/main/files/file-attachments/career_trends.pdf
Prepared annually by the Masters of Library and Information Science (MLIS) online degree program at the San José State University (SJSU) School of Information. @SJSUiSchool

RBMS—Careers and Scholarships

http://rbms.info/careers-faq
Advice and resources for those interested in careers in special collections. Maintained by the Rare Books and Manuscripts Section (RBMS) of the Association of College Research Libraries (ACRL), a division of ALA. @RBMSinfo

SAA(Society of American Archivists) Online Career Center

https://careers.archivists.org | @archivists_org

Podcasts

Circulating Ideas: The Librarian Interview Podcast

https://circulatingideas.com
Circulating Ideas facilitates conversations about the innovative people and ideas allowing libraries to thrive in the 21st century.

The Librarian's Guide to Teaching

https://librariansguidetoteaching.weebly.com
Hosted by two instruction librarians interested in sharing their experiences teaching information literacy, discussing current trends, and having meaningful conversations about librarianship.

Library Pros

https://www.thelibrarypros.com
A librarian and information technology pro talking libraries, library tech, and everything in between.

Linking our Libraries

https://linkingourlibraries.libsyn.com
The hosts share information with all types of libraries, archives, and other nonprofit staff and leaders, working to build their skills.

School Librarians United

https://schoollibrariansunited.libsyn.com
A podcast dedicated to the nuts and bolts of running a successful school library. Tune in to learn all about the issues and challenges school librarians face every day.

T is for Training

https://tisfortraining.wordpress.com
A podcast dedicated to improvement through learning. Also, it is about training, presenting, learning, teaching, understanding, and compassion.

Job Listings for Librarians, Archivists, and Information Professionals

ALA JobLIST

http://joblist.ala.org | @ALA_JobLIST

ALISE (Association for Library and Information Science Education) Job Placement

https://www.alise.org/alise-job-placement | @alisehq

American Association of Law Librarians (AALL) —Career Center

https://careers.aallnet.org/jobs | @aallnet

Archives Gig

https://archivesgig.wordpress.com | @archivesgig

ARLIS/NA JobList

https://www.arlisna.org/professional-resources/arlis-na-joblist | @ARLIS_NA

INALJ

http://inalj.com | @INALJ (different states have their own handles)

Library Technology Jobs

https://librarytechnology.org/jobs

Metropolitan New York Library Council (METRO) Jobs

https://metro.org/jobs | @mnylc

NASIG Jobs

http://nasigjobs.wordpress.com | @NASIG

Association for Information Science and Technology (ASIS&T) Careers

https://asist-jobs.careerwebsite.com | @asist_org

Association of Research Libraries (ARL)—Job/Residency/Internship Listings

http://www.arl.org/leadership-recruitment/job-listings | @ARLnews

Special Library Association (SLA) Jobs

https://careers.sla.org | @SLAhq

Job Listings Not Specific to Librarians, Archivists, and Information Professionals

Higher Education

Chronicle of Higher Education: Vitae

https://chroniclevitae.com | @chronicle

EDUCAUSE Job Posting Service

https://jobs.educause.edu | @educause

HigherEdJobs.com

http://www.higheredjobs.com | @insidehighered

Government

USAJobs.gov

https://www.usajobs.gov | @USAJOBS

Interdisciplinary (mega job sites)

Glassdoor

https://www.glassdoor.com/index.htm | @Glassdoor

Indeed

https://www.indeed.com | @indeed

LinkedIn Jobs

https://www.linkedin.com/jobs | @LinkedIn

Monster

https://www.monster.com | @Monster

SimplyHired

https://www.simplyhired.com | @SimplyHired

Zip Recruiter

https://www.ziprecruiter.com | @ZipRecruiter

Discussion Lists

Job listings are regularly posted and reposted on electronic discussion (e-mail) lists. Many library schools/iSchools and library associations maintain their own discussion lists. The following are lists of lists, maintained by large library organizations.

ALA Electronic Discussion Lists—Index of Lists

http://lists.ala.org/sympa/lists | @ALALibrary

International Federation of Library Associations and Institutions (IFLA)—Mailing Lists

https://www.ifla.org/mailing-lists | @IFLA

Placements and Salaries 2019: The Analytics Age

Suzie Allard

The most recent *Library Journal* (*LJ*) Placements & Salaries survey reveals that 2018 graduates from library and information science (LIS) programs have more and better employment options than their predecessors. Some highlights from the survey:

- Positive trends have occurred in employment, full-time employment, and average annual salary.
- Gender-based pay parity is improving.
- More graduates are working in LIS institutions as compared to other settings (a downside: the leading LIS employer for 2018 graduates, the public library, offers the lowest pay).
- Responding graduates named user experience/usability analysis among the top two primary job duties for the first time since the survey began.

Who Are the Surveyed Graduates?

Forty-one of the 52 U.S.-based American Library Association (ALA)–accredited schools participated in the annual survey for the 2018 calendar year, reported by *LJ* in fall 2019. Collectively, these 52 schools yielded 4,763 graduates—8.5 percent more than reported for 2017, despite the fact that one fewer school participated in the survey this year. Twenty-nine percent of the 2018 graduates submitted

Table 1 / Status of 2018 Graduates

School Region	Number of Schools Reporting	Number of Graduates Responding	Employed in LIS Field	Employed Outside of LIS	Currently Unemployed or Continuing Education	Total Answering	Percentage Employed Full Time
Midwest	12	445	280	25	14	319	88
Northeast	10	256	223	23	10	256	79
South Central	8	211	188	20	3	211	91
Southeast	7	263	159	24	7	190	92
West (Pacific/ Mountain)	4	207	176	18	13	207	80
Total	41	1,382	1,026	110	47	1,183	86

Suzie Allard (sallard@utk.edu) is professor of information sciences and associate dean of research, University of Tennessee College of Communication and Information, Knoxville, and winner of the 2013 *Library Journal* Teaching Award.

Adapted from *Library Journal*, November, 2019. For additional information and content, visit libraryjournal.com.

Table 2 / Placements and Full-Time Salaries of 2018 Graduates by Region

Placement Region	Number of Placements	No. Responding				Low Salary ($)			High Salary ($)			Average Salary ($)				Difference in Average M/F Salary†	Median Salary ($)			
		Women	Men	Non-binary*	All	Women	Men	Non-binary*	Women	Men	Non-binary*	Women	Men	Non-binary*	All		Women	Men	Non-binary*	All
Southeast	272	154	32	4	190	16,000	30,000	25,550	160,000	165,000	61,000	49,392	61,363	44,375	51,302	24.2%	46,826	53,000	45,475	47,000
Midwest	272	125	38	2	166	21,840	28,000	35,360	107,500	122,500	48,000	51,937	57,511	41,680	53,036	10.7	50,000	50,000	41,680	50,000
Northeast	250	119	35	6	160	34,800	30,000	30,000	125,000	117,500	61,000	55,743	61,808	50,185	56,862	10.9	52,500	57,500	52,750	53,000
South Central	186	111	29	1	141	20,000	26,000	52,500	107,500	102,500	52,500	46,707	45,892	52,500	46,581	-1.7	44,529	45,000	52,500	45,000
Pacific	176	74	20	4	98	23,000	40,000	47,300	140,000	147,500	80,000	78,508	81,550	61,825	78,448	3.9	69,247	69,500	60,000	68,547
Mountain	59	20	9	—	29	35,000	25,000	—	75,000	77,500	—	52,835	46,944	—	51,007	-11.1	50,752	49,000	—	50,000
Canada/Int'l.	23	7	4	2	13	22,000	32,000	26,000	82,500	144,000	46,000	50,829	73,775	36,000	55,608	45.1	49,000	59,550	36,000	46,000
Total	1,238	610	167	19	797											10.1	50,000	52,000	52,000	50,000

This table represents only salaries reported as full time. Some data were reported as aggregate without breakdown by gender or region. Comparison with other tables may show different number of placements.

* Includes nonbinary, other, and declined to answer gender.

†The nonbinary sample is too small to yield statistically significant results when compared to placements and salaries of other genders. Therefore, all gender comparisons shown are male-to-female only.

questionnaires sharing the outcomes and experiences of their job searches. This response rate was 2 percent lower than for 2017, but there were 400 more graduates participating.

Most respondents described themselves as female (78 percent). There was a small increase in the proportion of male graduates (20 percent). Those who described their gender as "Nonbinary," "Other," or "Prefer Not to Answer" collectively comprised 2.8 percent of responses. The sample size for this group was too small to yield statistically significant results.

Respondents were 76 percent white/non-Hispanic, 9 percent Asian/Pacific Islanders, 5 percent Hispanic/Latinx, 5 percent Black/African American, and 3 percent biracial/multiracial. Less than 1 percent identified as Native Alaskan/American/Canadian or another race. These results are similar to 2017.

More than half of responding graduates were between 26 and 35 years old (54 percent), which yielded an average age of 33. Consistent with previous surveys, most were 35 or under (68 percent) and only 12 percent were older than 45. Just over half of the graduates said they were pursuing their first career (54 percent), down slightly from 2017.

As in prior years, the 2018 graduates tend to be career-changers (46 percent). Just over half of respondents (51 percent) were not working in a library when they began an LIS master's program. The prevailing career pipeline to LIS for second-career graduates is education (37.9 percent, up slightly from 2017). Business-oriented fields, such as finance, accounting, banking, sales, and logistics, were the first professions for 9 percent of career-changers. Communications also tends to preface LIS studies; 8.3 percent of respondents had worked in marketing, communications, advertising and public relations, publishing, or journalism. Legal and criminal justice careers were the antecedent for 6.2 percent of the 2018 career-changers, while technology fields were the starting point for 5.8 percent, identifying as IT specialists, programmers, and data analysts. Another 5.8 percent worked first in entertainment and the arts, including film, theater, visual arts, graphic arts, photography, museums, and interior design.

Grads Find Work

Almost nine out of ten 2018 graduates (87 percent) are employed in the LIS field. About three-quarters of respondents said they are employed by an LIS organization, and 12 percent said they are working in an LIS capacity at another type of organization. Nine percent are working outside the LIS field in a non-LIS capacity.

More than half of employed respondents said they are working in a public library (33 percent) or an academic library (22 percent). Others work in K–12 schools (11 percent) and private industry in general (11 percent). Just 4 percent have jobs in archives/special collections, special libraries, and nonprofit nonlibrary institutions; 3 percent work in government libraries and 3 percent in other academic units.

Seventy-four percent of these employed 2018 graduates are satisfied with their placements. Interestingly, those doing library work in non-library settings have a higher satisfaction level (83 percent) than those working in LIS institutions (75 percent). Graduates working outside the LIS field in a non-LIS capacity were

(text continues on page 246)

Table 3 / 2018 Total Graduates and Placements by School*

	Graduates				Employed Full Time				Response	
Schools	**Women**	**Men**	**Non-binary****	**All**	**Women**	**Men**	**Non-binary****	**All**	**No. Rec'd.**	**Rate**
Alabama	83	19	—	102	17	7	—	24	30	29.4%
Albany	21	9	—	30	1	3	—	4	5	16.7
Arizona	38	9	—	47	3	3	1	7	9	19.1
Buffalo	57	20	—	77	12	4	—	16	18	23.4
Catholic*	18	4	—	22	3	1	—	4	6	27.3
Clarion	123	18	—	141	12	2	2	16	21	14.9
Emporia State	111	33	—	144	16	6	4	26	31	21.5
Florida State	67	19	—	86	10	5	2	17	18	20.9
Hawaii–Manoa	17	4	—	21	6	2	—	8	10	47.6
Illinois Urbana-Champaign	187	44	1	232	27	6	2	35	46	19.8
Indiana–Bloomington	68	17	—	85	10	3	—	13	15	17.6
Indiana–Purdue	52	14	—	66	14	4	—	18	21	31.8
Iowa	22	8	—	30	10	6	—	16	17	56.7
Kent State*	180	38	—	218	15	3	—	18	27	12.4
Kentucky	69	13	—	82	16	2	—	18	22	26.8
Long Island	101	19	—	120	4	3	—	7	13	10.8
Louisiana State	56	8	—	64	24	6	—	30	31	48.4
Maryland	52	17	—	69	17	2	2	21	24	34.8
Michigan*	103	57	—	160	77	39		116	125	78.1
Missouri	23	9	1	33	6	2	1	9	9	27.3
N.C.–Chapel Hill*	59	13	—	72		—	—	—	72	100.0
N.C.–Greensboro	100	19	5	124	50	8	2	60	71	57.3
North Texas	311	99	—	410	26	7	—	33	35	8.5
Oklahoma	49	9	—	58	9	2	—	11	17	29.3
Pratt	60	9	—	69	16	3	1	20	23	33.3
Queens	65	25	—	90	33	7	—	40	59	65.6
Rutgers	69	31	4	104	12	4	—	16	22	21.2
San Jose*	476	81	—	557	85	14	5	104	155	27.8
Simmons***	—	—	283	283	40	9	3	53	64	22.6
South Carolina	88	18	—	106	23	1	—	24	26	24.5
Southern Mississippi	50	6	—	56	20	4	—	24	24	42.9
St. Catherine	28	4	—	32	14	2	—	16	20	62.5
St. John's	21	1	—	22	10	1	—	11	16	72.7
Syracuse	127	29	—	156	6	4	—	10	15	9.6
Tennessee	48	11	—	59	16	6	1	23	26	44.1
Texas Women's	190	2	—	192	24	1		25	26	13.5
Valdosta State	88	14	—	102	36	3	2	41	44	43.1
Washington	99	32	1	132	16	8	1	25	33	25.0
Wayne State	127	27	—	154	42	10	2	54	75	48.7
Wisconsin–Madison*	46	13	—	59	26	7	1	34	39	66.1
Wisconsin–Milwaukee	73	24	—	97	10	7	—	17	20	20.6
Total	3,622	846	295	4,763	814	217	32	1,064	1,380	29.0%

Tables do not always add up, individually or collectively, due to omitted data from schools and/or individuals.

* Some schools conducted their own survey and provided raw data. Comparison with other tables may show different numbers of placements.

**Includes nonbinary, other, and declined to answer gender.

***Simmons did not provide a gender breakdown of 2018 graduates.

Table 4 / Placements by Full-Time Salary of Reporting 2018 Graduates

	Average Salary ($)				Median Salary ($)			Low Salary ($)			High Salary ($)			Placements			
Schools	Women	Men	Non-binary**	All	Women	Men	Non-binary**	Women	Men	Non-binary**	Women	Men	Non-binary**	Women	Men	Non-binary**	Total Placements
Alabama	45,053	41,560	—	44,354	43,000	43,680	—	25,000	30,000	—	75,000	51,000	—	12	3	—	15
Albany	40,000	65,000	—	52,500	40,000	65,000	—	40,000	65,000	—	40,000	65,000	—	1	1	—	2
Arizona	—	45,750	—	45,750	—	45,750	—	—	42,500	—	—	49,000	—	—	2	—	2
Buffalo	51,796	48,797	—	51,251	50,000	48,797	—	38,162	39,594	—	75,000	58,000	—	9	2	—	11
Catholic*	45,667	80,000	—	54,250	47,000	80,000	—	43,000	80,000	—	47,000	80,000	—	3	1	—	4
Clarion	47,965	45,300	30,000	46,173	46,173	45,300	30,000	36,000	41,800	30,000	59,000	48,800	30,000	10	2	1	13
Emporia State	49,207	64,667	52,150	52,473	49,900	53,000	52,150	35,400	46,000	47,300	70,000	95,000	57,000	11	3	2	16
Florida State	41,050	61,499	25,550	48,279	45,000	57,000	25,550	25,000	50,000	25,550	51,400	92,000	25,550	6	5	1	12
Hawaii–Manoa	52,519	49,000	—	51,932	55,000	49,000	—	33,000	49,000	—	69,094	49,000	—	5	1	—	6
Illinois Urbana-Champaign	51,973	51,583	43,930	51,291	52,000	50,000	43,930	25,000	31,000	35,360	86,000	80,000	52,500	19	6	2	27
Indiana–Bloomington	46,290	48,200	—	46,768	43,000	41,600	—	33,800	40,000	—	62,000	63,000	—	9	3	—	12
Indiana–Purdue	43,409	36,667	—	41,853	42,250	40,000	—	21,840	30,000	—	75,000	40,000	—	10	3	—	13
Iowa	45,103	36,328	—	41,593	47,500	40,000	—	30,075	25,000	—	63,000	47,500	—	9	6	—	15
Kent State*	44,679	37,000	—	43,719	40,750	37,000	—	32,000	28,000	—	72,000	46,000	—	14	2	—	16
Kentucky	42,319	47,500	—	42,966	40,250	47,500	—	31,400	43,000	—	69,000	52,000	—	14	2	—	16
Long Island	62,850	63,855	—	63,453	62,850	58,500	—	55,700	56,000	—	70,000	77,064	—	2	3	—	5
Louisiana State	41,122	37,431	—	40,480	40,000	37,861	—	22,000	27,000	—	65,000	47,000	—	19	4	—	23
Maryland	60,769	83,000	45,725	61,615	54,000	83,000	45,725	39,500	50,000	38,950	160,000	116,000	52,500	13	2	2	17
Michigan*	89,229	87,056	—	88,505	87,500	85,000	—	35,000	38,000	—	140,000	147,500	—	72	36	—	108

Missouri	57,300	40,000	48,000	51,029	55,900	40,000	48,000	50,000	38,000	48,000	67,400	42,000	48,000	4	2	1	7
N.C.–Greensboro	41,762	35,529	52,000	41,120	41,281	34,000	52,000	24,103	31,000	52,000	60,000	43,500	52,000	44	7	1	52
North Texas	50,622	49,270	—	50,321	50,000	51,500	—	29,000	30,618	—	67,000	60,000	—	21	6	—	27
Oklahoma	45,432	45,060	—	45,339	40,835	45,060	—	32,000	42,000	—	72,800	48,119	—	6	2	—	8
Pratt	62,308	71,500	61,000	63,375	55,000	71,500	61,000	45,000	53,000	61,000	110,000	90,000	61,000	13	2	1	16
Queens	56,171	61,306	—	56,764	52,473	65,817	—	36,000	47,000	—	125,000	71,100	—	23	3	—	26
Rutgers	52,356	54,333	—	52,895	53,424	58,000	—	47,000	30,000	—	57,000	75,000	—	8	3	—	11
San Jose*	57,720	54,300	56,333	57,172	54,000	52,500	63,000	23,000	40,000	26,000	106,000	73,000	80,000	57	10	3	70
Simmons	53,237	60,125	52,536	54,234	52,000	53,500	53,000	38,856	42,000	49,608	87,000	100,000	55,000	31	8	3	43
South Carolina	51,446	51,000	—	51,423	55,000	51,000	—	16,000	51,000	—	72,000	51,000	—	19	1	—	20
Southern Mississippi	41,820	43,500	—	42,030	45,015	43,500	—	20,000	42,000	—	56,000	45,000	—	14	2	—	16
St. Catherine	44,460	44,000	—	44,403	40,000	44,000	—	30,720	44,000	—	55,000	44,000	—	7	1	—	8
St. John's	54,963	58,500	—	55,356	54,351	58,500	—	45,500	58,500	—	72,000	58,500	—	8	1	—	9
Syracuse	38,167	64,250	—	53,071	45,000	53,000	—	22,000	51,000	—	47,500	100,000	—	3	4	—	7
Tennessee	49,045	45,417	—	47,956	50,002	43,738	—	29,972	26,000	—	68,000	73,000	—	14	6	—	20
Texas Women's	57,880	40,000	—	57,029	53,500	40,000	—	41,000	40,000	—	105,000	40,000	—	20	1	—	21
Valdosta State	42,349	43,000	—	42,390	42,250	43,000	—	25,000	30,000	—	60,000	56,000	—	30	2	—	32
Washington	51,588	75,500	61,000	59,174	51,264	55,000	61,000	32,000	45,500	61,000	70,000	165,000	61,000	11	5	1	17
Wayne State	49,895	46,906	54,500	49,671	47,840	46,217	54,500	23,000	36,500	46,000	86,000	59,000	63,000	31	6	2	39
Wisconsin–Madison*	49,194	66,872	—	54,497	48,238	54,250	—	38,900	45,000	—	64,000	144,000	—	14	6	—	20
Wisconsin–Milwaukee	50,616	55,600	—	52,881	49,167	57,000	—	45,000	35,000	—	60,000	75,000	—	6	5	—	11
Average / Total	54,358	59,734	49,838	55,357	50,000	52,000	52,250	16,000	25,000	25,550	160,000	165,000	80,000	622	170	20	813

This table represents placements and salaries reported as full time. Some individuals or schools omitted information, rendering information unusable.
* Some schools conducted their own survey and provided raw data.
**Includes nonbinary, unsure, and declined to answer gender.

(continued from page 242)

almost evenly split between being satisfied (53 percent) and dissatisfied (47 percent). The graduates who are happy at work say they are achieving their goals and putting their training to use in their preferred environment.

High levels of full-time employment (86 percent) and permanent positions (91 percent) trended into a fifth year. Among the 14 percent of grads who are employed part time, 54 percent have one position and 36 percent have two. Only 4 percent of respondents said they are unemployed, down from 6 percent in 2017.

Salaries Keep Going Up—Mostly

The survey showed rising pay for LIS graduates for the sixth year in a row. The reported average full-time starting salary among 2018 grads is $55,357—a healthy 6.2 percent increase over the previous year and an impressive 24 percent increase over 2011. The average hourly rate of $19.76, which is up almost 4 percent over the prior two years, translates into an annual full-time salary of more than $41,000.

Building on the narrowing gender disparities seen in last year's data, salaries of 2018 graduates closed the gap even further. The average salary for a male graduate employed full time is $59,734 versus $54,358 for female hires; the differential is 9.9 percent. While the figures are still far from equal pay for equal work, the overall gender differential is smaller than it was among graduates in 2017 (12.6 percent) and 2016 (about 18 percent).

Public libraries hired the largest proportion of 2018 graduates (33 percent) but on average offered the lowest pay of any library type. The average beginning salary in public libraries, which had inched up in recent years, was $44,743, down $318 from the previous year.

College/university libraries attracted 22 percent of the 2018 graduates, down slightly from the prior two years. The overall average academic library salary was $50,754, up 3.7 percent over 2017.

School library full-time salaries averaged $53,196, 3 percent more than for 2017 graduates. Eleven percent of 2018 grads accepted positions in K–12 schools, a slight uptick from 2017.

Private industry drew 11 percent of 2018 graduates, who have an average salary of $86,451, the highest compensation of all settings.

Government libraries hired 3 percent of the 2018 graduates, at an average salary of $52,682. The hiring level parallels 2017, but average salary is 4.7 percent lower.

Special libraries were the destination for 4 percent of the 2018 graduates, with an average salary of $53,072—an increase of 7.1 percent over the 2017 salary level. This work setting stands out in that gender-related wage disparity tilts strongly in favor of female graduates: Women working in special libraries earn an average salary of $56,141—16 percent more than men.

Archives / special collections were chosen by 4 percent of the 2018 graduates. The average salary in this setting increased by 9.8 percent this year, to $47,665.

Employment in nonprofit settings accounted for 4 percent of 2018 graduates, with the average salary up 7.4 percent over 2017, to $55,425.

A range of other organizations such as vendors, library cooperatives and networks, government agencies, and academic units, collectively hired 4 percent of the class of 2018. The average salary of $68,638 was a 35.4 percent improvement over 2017.

Salaries Vary by Region

Average full-time salaries are highest in the Pacific region ($78,448). For 2018 the lowest was the South Central region ($46,581). This regional differential of $31,867 is 59 percent greater than the contrast seen between the highest- and lowest-paying regions in 2017.

The other five regions cluster more closely, with average salaries ranging from the low to mid-$50,000s. The Southeast region claimed the highest individual salary earned in 2018 ($165,000) and the highest salary paid to a female graduate ($160,000), but was also responsible for the lowest reported salary ($16,000, paid to a woman). Of course, salary level is only part of the picture when comparing work opportunities in different regions, given substantial variations in the cost of living.

Job Settings, Duties, and Titles

Working 2018 graduates were asked to categorize their current position setting. More than two-thirds called themselves librarians working in a library (67 percent) versus 4 percent who said they are librarians not working in a library. Graduates who termed themselves "non-librarians" were almost equally likely to say they were working in a library (15 percent) or outside of one (14 percent).

Those respondents not working in libraries reported applying their LIS skills by managing data or digital assets, developing and managing collections, managing technology or web resources (including in the user experience realm), working in records management, or doing research. Non-librarians working in libraries tended to work as paraprofessionals while seeking a professional position, although employment in technology or management capacities was also cited. Non-librarians not working in libraries pointed to activities such as metadata and

Table 5 / Average Salary for Starting Library Positions, 2011–2018

Year	Library Schools Represented	Average Full-Time Starting Salary	Difference in Average Salary	Percentage Change
2011	41	$44,565	$2,009	4.72
2012	41	44,503	-62	-0.14
2013	40	45,650	1,147	2.58
2014	39	46,987	1,337	2.93
2015	39	48,371	1,384	2.95
2016	40	51,798	3,427	7.08
2017	41	52,152	354	0.68
2018	41	55,357	3,205	6.20

Table 6 / Full-Time Salaries of Reporting Professionals by Primary Job Assignment

Primary Job Assignment	No. Rec'd.	Percent of Total	Low Salary	High Salary	Average Salary	Median Salary
Reference/Information Services	83	10.4	$27,300	$80,000	$50,869	$50,000
User Experience/Usability Analysis	78	9.7	38,000	147,500	94,654	92,500
School Librarian/School Library Media Specialist	74	9.2	22,000	105,000	53,383	51,575
Children's Services	63	7.9	25,000	65,000	45,150	46,777
Administration	49	6.1	31,836	165,000	58,507	51,000
Archival and Preservation	42	5.2	26,000	67,500	47,116	47,500
Metadata, Cataloging, and Taxonomy	37	4.6	25,550	75,000	47,436	50,000
Training, Teaching, and Instruction	33	4.1	30,000	80,000	53,317	52,500
Data Analytics	30	3.7	40,000	160,000	79,720	72,500
YA/Teen Services	29	3.6	24,103	80,000	48,141	48,119
Teacher Librarian	26	3.2	26,000	105,000	53,494	48,750
Adult Services	24	3.0	35,000	56,000	44,998	45,000
Circulation	21	2.6	20,000	63,000	36,289	32,000
Digital Content Management	16	2.0	38,500	61,350	46,116	44,000
Public Services	16	2.0	16,000	73,000	41,471	38,782
Technical Services	14	1.7	25,000	81,000	45,913	43,500
Access Services	13	1.6	28,000	68,000	43,729	42,000
Information Technology	12	1.5	36,000	78,000	58,344	60,500
Data Curation and Management	11	1.4	32,000	87,000	52,871	50,000
Collection Development/Acquisitions	11	1.4	30,000	60,000	44,396	45,000
Records Management	10	1.2	33,722	92,000	54,972	51,000
Outreach	10	1.2	30,000	65,000	51,256	52,500
Solo Librarian	10	1.2	23,000	90,500	43,990	42,000
Emerging Technologies	7	0.9	37,461	73,000	54,689	53,000
Systems Technology	7	0.9	38,000	62,000	53,278	52,000
Market Intelligence/Business Research	6	0.7	28,000	110,000	61,500	57,500
Patron Programming	5	0.6	37,000	50,000	43,506	44,529
Knowledge Management	4	0.5	32,000	67,000	52,250	55,000
Website Design	3	0.4	45,500	57,000	52,500	55,000
Assessment	3	0.4	25,000	60,000	46,667	55,000
Government Documents	3	0.4	35,400	49,000	40,250	36,350
Communications, PR, and Social Media	2	0.2	45,000	48,000	46,500	46,500
Rights and Permissions	2	0.2	44,000	44,000	44,000	44,000
Grant Writing	1	0.1	51,400	51,400	51,400	51,400
Other	45	5.6	25,000	116,000	54,350	51,500
Total Answering	801	100.0	$16,000	$165,000	$55,435	$50,000

This table represents full-time placements reported by primary job assignment.
Some individuals omitted placement information; therefore comparison with other tables may show different numbers of placements and average and median salaries.

vocabulary design, digital curation, information systems building, knowledge management, and user behavior and training.

Asked to name their primary job duty, the graduates' responses mirrored the 2017 answers for four classic items while introducing one notable change: The appearance of user experience/usability analysis in second place (9 percent). The most popular answer to this question was, again, reference and information services (10 percent). Other responses in the top five positions were school librarian/school library media specialist (9 percent), children's services (8 percent), and administration (6 percent). Roles in archives and preservation stood at 5 percent.

The variety of job titles provided by respondents is testament to the broad applicability of an LIS degree. Uncommon, emerging, or unconventional titles included GIS and Data Visualization Librarian, UX and Assessment Librarian, User Engagement Librarian, Director of Data Analytics, Open Data Literacy Consultant, Electronic Health Records Manager, Moving Image and Sound Digital Archivist, Epic Programmer Analyst, Data Librarian Ontologist, STEM Librarian, Market Research Visual Storyteller, and Crisis Management and Information Fusion Lead.

Sixteen percent of 2018 graduates think their job is in an emerging field in LIS. Among these respondents, work activities include assessment, assisting patrons with arts software and virtual reality devices, training users in business analysis skills, data curation, embedded librarian in online courses to create electronic learning objects, human-centered system design, GIS and data visualization instruction, strategic projects for internal management, and ontology for modeling semantic data.

Working Grads Share Experiences, Skills, Resources, and Advice

When asked about experiences or skill sets that contributed to landing their first professional positions, 52 percent of surveyed 2018 graduates identified an internship, a practicum, or field experience. Forty-nine percent mentioned technology skills, such as database searching or coding, while subject specialization knowledge (including cataloging) was cited by 43 percent. Forty-one percent of the grads valued networking opportunities with professionals in their area of interest.

The graduates listed a range of job-seeking resources. Some used generalized employment sites like Indeed, Monster, LinkedIn, Glassdoor, ZipRecruiter, and Handshake. They used professional organizations, especially the American Library Association, whose online job list was a favorite. Other cited associations were the American Association of Law Libraries, the Association of Research Libraries, the Library Information Technology Association, the Society of American Archivists, and state library associations. Government job sites, university job sites and listservs, and HigherEdJobs.com were noted, along with targeted resources such as INALJ, LibJobs, Libtechjobs, LibGig, and ArchivesGig.

The class of 2018 had this advice for the next cohort of job seekers in the field: Gather multiple opinions about your application materials; develop your presentation skills; be willing to relocate and consider opportunities overseas; demonstrate your people/social skills in interviews; practice mock interviews; remember that you are interviewing the employer, too; and start reading job postings when you begin your LIS program.

Table 7 / Comparison of Full-Time Salaries by Type of Organization and Placement Region

	Total Placements	Low Salary	High Salary	Average Salary	Median Salary
Public Libraries					
Northeast	50	$30,000	$72,000	$49,085	$49,040
Southeast	52	16,000	64,000	40,592	41,408
South Central	34	20,000	72,800	39,653	39,797
Midwest	50	21,840	80,000	43,255	41,750
Mountain	9	25,000	75,000	47,911	49,000
Pacific	18	42,000	73,000	56,602	55,500
Canada/Int'l.	1	49,000	49,000	49,000	49,000
All Public	214	16,000	80,000	44,743	45,000
College/University					
Northeast	39	30,000	125,000	57,988	55,000
Southeast	44	25,000	165,000	49,030	47,750
South Central	41	25,000	68,750	44,345	47,000
Midwest	51	28,000	75,000	48,363	47,840
Mountain	7	42,000	53,000	47,429	48,000
Pacific	22	35,400	92,000	61,366	60,500
Canada/Int'l.	2	32,000	37,800	34,900	34,900
All Academic	206	25,000	165,000	50,754	50,000
School Libraries					
Northeast	20	36,000	80,000	56,228	56,850
Southeast	36	30,000	105,000	50,270	45,500
South Central	30	25,500	69,000	50,110	51,075
Midwest	9	38,500	70,000	54,897	53,000
Mountain	3	41,000	68,000	55,000	56,000
Pacific	11	23,000	105,000	69,099	69,094
Canada/Int'l.	2	22,000	26,000	24,000	24,000
All School	111	22,000	105,000	53,196	51,000
Government Libraries					
Northeast	1	71,100	71,100	71,100	71,100
Southeast	13	43,680	87,500	59,550	56,233
South Central	6	33,722	56,000	42,787	42,000
Midwest	5	38,900	72,500	49,880	43,000
Mountain	0				
Pacific	2	36,350	41,369	38,860	38,860
Canada/Int'l.	1	46,000	46,000	46,000	46,000
All Government	28	33,722	87,500	52,682	53,500

Table 7 / Comparison of Full-Time Salaries by Type of Organization and Placement Region *(cont.)*

	Total Placements	Low Salary	High Salary	Average Salary	Median Salary
Private Industry					
Northeast	16	$38,000	$117,500	$80,625	$87,500
Southeast	10	51,400	112,500	76,640	78,750
South Central	10	47,000	107,500	76,550	74,750
Midwest	24	40,000	107,500	72,479	77,750
Mountain	3	42,500	77,500	64,000	72,000
Pacific	34	77,500	147,500	111,324	112,500
Canada/Int'l.	6	32,000	82,500	61,017	66,250
All Private Industry	103	32,000	147,500	86,451	82,500
Special Libraries					
Northeast	5	34,800	75,000	51,160	45,500
Southeast	9	41,600	75,000	51,563	45,000
South Central	5	26,000	62,500	50,000	52,500
Midwest	5	33,800	65,000	48,360	50,000
Mountain	1	50,000	50,000	50,000	50,000
Pacific	5	42,000	117,500	66,100	60,000
Canada/Int'l.	0	—	—	—	—
All Special	30	26,000	117,500	53,072	50,000
Archives/Special Collections					
Northeast	9	40,000	55,000	47,167	45,000
Southeast	4	40,000	50,000	44,750	44,500
South Central	4	39,500	57,000	46,500	44,750
Midwest	3	37,620	48,500	44,818	48,333
Mountain	4	35,000	54,000	47,500	50,500
Pacific	3	55,000	61,000	57,667	57,000
Canada/Int'l.	0	—	—	—	—
All Archives/Special Collections	27	35,000	61,000	47,665	47,500
Nonprofit Organizations					
Northeast	10	43,000	87,000	53,161	49,804
Southeast	5	36,000	92,500	54,500	50,000
South Central	5	30,000	44,000	40,400	44,000
Midwest	9	38,000	86,000	58,556	56,000
Mountain	1	51,500	51,500	51,500	51,500
Pacific	1	45,000	45,000	45,000	45,000
Canada/Int'l.	1	144,000	144,000	144,000	144,000
All Nonprofit	32	30,000	144,000	55,425	50,000
Other Organizations					
Northeast	9	54,000	107,500	70,389	65,000
Southeast	17	32,000	160,000	71,382	65,000
South Central	6	27,300	56,000	39,667	39,400
Midwest	10	35,000	122,500	78,850	74,250
Mountain	1	67,500	67,500	67,500	67,500
Pacific	2	45,200	102,500	73,850	73,850
Canada/Int'l.	0	—	—	—	—
All Other	45	27,300	160,000	68,638	62,500

This table represents only full-time salaries and all placements reported by type. Some individuals omitted placement information, rendering some information unusable.

Table 8 / Full-Time Salaries by Type of Organization and Gender

	Total Placements				Low Salary ($)			High Salary ($)			Average Salary ($)				Median Salary ($)			
	Women	Men	Non-binary*	All	Women	Men	Non-binary*	Women	Men	Non-binary*	Women	Men	Non-binary*	All	Women	Men	Non-binary*	All
Public Libraries	183	31	4	218	16,000	25,000	30,000	75,000	80,000	63,000	44,327	47,060	45,340	44,734	45,000	47,000	44,180	45,000
College/University Libraries	141	61	7	210	25,000	27,000	25,550	125,000	165,000	61,000	50,553	51,752	48,764	50,806	50,000	50,000	52,000	50,000
School Libraries	98	12	3	113	22,000	32,000	26,000	105,000	77,064	80,000	53,803	48,597	48,317	53,105	52,000	42,750	38,950	51,000
Government Libraries	22	6	1	29	35,000	33,722	46,000	72,500	87,500	46,000	51,766	57,873	46,000	52,831	53,500	55,617	46,000	54,000
Private Industry	67	37	0	104	32,000	38,000	—	140,000	147,500	—	87,782	83,327	—	86,197	82,500	82,500	—	82,500
Special Libraries	26	5	1	32	33,800	26,000	52,500	117,500	65,000	52,500	56,141	48,400	52,500	54,818	50,000	53,000	52,500	50,500
Archives/Special Collections	23	5	1	29	35,000	39,500	57,000	61,000	57,000	57,000	47,889	46,700	57,000	47,998	48,333	42,000	57,000	48,333
Nonprofit Organizations	26	5	1	32	30,000	40,000	49,608	92,500	144,000	49,608	53,577	66,200	49,608	55,425	50,000	50,000	49,608	50,000
Other Organizations	37	8	2	47	27,300	50,000	61,000	160,000	122,500	63,000	63,560	89,874	62,000	67,972	60,000	96,000	62,000	62,500

This table represents only full-time salaries and all placements reported by type. Some individuals omitted placement information, rendering some information unusable.
*Includes nonbinary, other, and declined to answer gender.

Accredited Master's Programs in Library and Information Studies

This list of graduate programs accredited by the American Library Association is issued by the ALA Office for Accreditation. Regular updates and additional details appear on the Office for Accreditation's website at http://www.ala.org/CFApps/lisdir/index.cfm. A total of 139 U.S. and Canadian institutions offering both accredited and nonaccredited programs in librarianship are included in the 73rd edition (2020–2021) of *American Library Directory* (Information Today, Inc.).

Northeast: D.C., Md., Mass., N.J., N.Y., Pa., R.I.

Catholic University of America, School of Arts and Sciences, Dept. of Lib. and Info. Science, 620 Michigan Ave. N.E., Washington, DC 20064. Youngok Choi, chair. Tel. 202-319-5085, fax 319-5574, e-mail cua-slis@cua.edu, World Wide Web http://lis.cua.edu. Admissions contact: Louise Gray. Tel. 202-319-5085, fax 319-5574, e-mail grayl@cua.edu.

Clarion University of Pennsylvania, College of Business Admin. and Info. Sciences, Dept. of Info. and Lib. Science, 210 Carlson Lib. Bldg., Clarion, PA 16214. Linda L. Lillard, chair. Tel. 866-272-5612, fax 814-393-2150, e-mail libsci@clarion.edu, World Wide Web http://www.clarion.edu/libsci. Admissions contact: Michelle Ritzler. Tel. 866-393-2337, e-mail gradstudies@clarion.edu.

Drexel University, College of Computing and Informatics, Dept. of Info. Science, 3141 Chestnut St., Philadelphia, PA 19104-2875. Xia Lin, dept. head. Tel. 215-895-2474, fax 215-895-2494, e-mail istinfo@drexel.edu, World Wide Web http://drexel.edu/cci/academics/graduate-programs/ms-In-information. Admissions contact: Matthew Lechtenburg. Tel. 215-895-1951, e-mail ml333@drexel.edu.

Long Island University, College of Education, Info. and Technology, Palmer School of Lib. and Info. Science, 720 Northern Blvd., Brookville, NY 11548-1300. David A. Jank, dir. Tel. 516-299-2866, fax 516-299-4168, e-mail post-palmer@liu.edu, World Wide Web http://www.liu.edu/palmer. Admissions contact: Amy Ingrilli. Tel. 516-299-2857, e-mail amy.ingrilli@liu.edu.

Pratt Institute, School of Info. and Lib. Science, 144 W. 14 St., New York, NY 10011. Anthony Cocciolo, dean. Tel. 212-647-7682, fax 212-367-2492, e-mail infosils@pratt.edu, World Wide Web http://www.pratt.edu/academics/information/. Admissions contact: Quinn Lai. Tel. 212-647-7682, e-mail infosils@pratt.edu.

Queens College, Grad. School of Lib. and Info. Studies, Rm. 254, Rosenthal Lib., 65-30 Kissena Blvd., Flushing, NY 11367-1597. Kwong bor Ng, chair. Tel. 718-997-3790, fax 718-997-3797, e-mail qc_gslis@qc.cuny.edu, World Wide Web https://www.qc.cuny.edu/admissions/graduate/degree/pages/degreedetail.aspx?DegreeID=86. Admissions contact: Roberta Brody. Tel. 718-997-3790, e-mail roberta_brody@qc.edu.

Rutgers University, School of Communication and Info., Dept. of Lib. and Info. Science, New Brunswick, NJ 08901-1071. Marie Radford, chair. Tel. 848-932-7602, e-mail mlis@comminfo.rutgers.edu, World Wide Web http://comminfo.rutgers.edu. Admissions contact: Lilia Pavlovsky. Tel. 732-932-7576.

Saint John's University, College of Liberal Arts and Sciences, Div. of Lib. and Info. Science, 8000 Utopia Pkwy., Queens, NY 11439. James Vorbach, dir. Tel. 718-990-1834, fax 718-990-2071, e-mail vorbach@stjohns.edu, World Wide Web http://www.stjohns.edu/dlis. Admissions contact: Michael Crossfox. Tel. 718-990-6200, e-mail dlis@stjohns.edu.

Simmons College, School of Lib. and Info. Science, 300 The Fenway, Boston, MA 02115. Sanda Erdelez, dir. Tel. 617-521-2800, fax 617-521-3192, e-mail gslis@simmons.edu, World Wide Web http://slis.simmons.edu/.

Admissions contact: Kate Benson. Tel. 617-521-2868, e-mail slisadm@simmons.edu.

Syracuse University, School of Info. Studies, 343 Hinds Hall, Syracuse, NY 13244. Caroline Hawthornthwaite, dir. Tel. 315-443-2911, fax 315-443-6886, e-mail ischool@syr.edu, World Wide Web https://ischool.syr.edu/academics/graduate/masters-degrees/. Admissions contact: Blythe Bennett. Tel. 315-443-2911, e-mail mslis@syr.edu.

University at Albany, State Univ. of New York, College of Emergency Preparedness, Homeland Security and Cybersecurity, Draper 340, Albany, NY 12222. Philip B. Eppard, chair. Tel. 518-442-5258, fax 518-442-5632, e-mail cehc@albany.edu, World Wide Web http://www.albany.edu/cehc/graduate-programs-cehc.php. Admissions contact: Graduate Admissions. Tel. 518-442-3980, e-mail graduate@albany.edu.

University at Buffalo, State Univ. of New York, Graduate School of Educ., Dept. of Info. Sci, 534 Baldy Hall, Buffalo, NY 14260-1020. Heidi Julien, chair. Tel. 716-645-2412, fax 716-645-3775, e-mail ub-lis@buffalo.edu, World Wide Web http://ed.buffalo.edu/information/academics/masters/library-science.html. Admissions contact: Cory Meyers. Tel. 716-645-2110, e-mail gse-info@buffalo.edu.

University of Maryland, College of Info. Studies, 4105 Hornbake Bldg., College Park, MD 20742. Paul T. Jaeger, MLIS Program co-dir. Tel. 301-405-2033, fax 301-314-9145, e-mail ischooladmission@umd.edu, World Wide Web http://ischool.umd.edu/mlis. Admissions contact: Joanne Briscoe. Tel. 301-405-2038, e-mail ischooladmission@umd.edu.

University of Pittsburgh, School of Computing and Info., Info. Culture and Data Stewardship, 135 N. Bellefield Ave., Pittsburgh, PA 15260. Bruce R. Childers, chair. Tel. 412-624-5230, fax 412-648-7001, e-mail sciadmit@pitt.edu, World Wide Web http://www.sci.pitt.edu. Admissions contact: Shabana Reza. Tel. 412-624-3988, e-mail shabana.reza@pitt.edu.

University of Rhode Island, Grad. School of Lib. and Info. Studies, Rodman Hall, 94 W. Alumni Ave., Kingston, RI 02881. Valerie Karno, dir. Tel. 401-874-2878, fax 401-874-4964, e-mail vkarno@uri.edu, World Wide Web http://www.uri.edu/artsci/lsc.

Southeast: Ala., Fla., Ga., Ky., La., Miss., N.C., S.C., Tenn., P.R.

East Carolina University, College of Educ., Lib. Science Degree Program, Mailstop 172, ECU, Greenville, NC 27858. Lana Kaye Dotson, program coord. Tel. 252-328-4389, fax 252-328-4368, e-mail dotsonl@ecu.edu, World Wide Web http://bit.ly/ECUML. Admissions contact: Camilla King. Tel. 252-328-6012, e-mail gradschool@ecu.edu.

Florida State University, College of Communication and Info., School of Info., 142 Collegiate Loop, P.O. Box 3062100, Tallahassee, FL 32306-2100. Kathleen Burnett, dir. Tel. 850-644-5775, fax 850-644-9763, e-mail kathleen.burnett@cci.fsu.edu, World Wide Web http://ischool.cci.fsu.edu. Admissions tel. 850-645-3280, e-mail ischooladvising@admin.fsu.edu.

Louisiana State University, College of Human Sciences and Education, School of Lib. and Info. Science, 267 Coates Hall, Baton Rouge, LA 70803. Carol Barry, dir. Tel. 225-578-3158, fax 225-578-4581, e-mail slis@lsu.edu, World Wide Web http://slis.lsu.edu. Admissions contact: LaToya Coleman Joseph. Tel. 225-578-3150, e-mail lcjoseph@lsu.edu.

North Carolina Central University, School of Lib. and Info. Sciences, P.O. Box 19586, Durham, NC 27707. Jon P. Gant, dean. Tel. 919-530-6485, fax 919-530-6402, e-mail slisadmissions@nccu.edu, World Wide Web http://www.nccuslis.org. Admissions contact: Nina Clayton.

University of Alabama, College of Communication and Info. Sciences, School of Lib. and Info. Studies, Box 870252, Tuscaloosa, AL 35487-0252. James Elmborg, dir. Tel. 205-348-2719, fax 205-348-3746, e-mail info@slis.ua.edu, World Wide Web http://www.slis.ua.edu. Admissions contact: Lita Shive. Tel. 205-348-1527, e-mail lmshive@slis.ua.edu.

University of Kentucky, College of Communication and Info., School of Lib. and Info. Science, 320 Little Lib., Lexington,

KY 40506-0224. Jeffrey T. Huber, dir. Tel. 859-257-8876, fax 859-257-4205, e-mail ukslis@uky.edu, World Wide Web http://www.uky.edu/cis/slis. Admissions contact: Will Buntin. Tel. 859-257-3317, e-mail wjbunt0@uky.edu.

University of North Carolina at Chapel Hill, School of Info. and Lib. Science, CB 3360, 100 Manning Hall, Chapel Hill, NC 27599-3360. Gary Marchionini, dean. Tel. 919-962-8366, fax 919-962-8071, e-mail info@ils.unc.edu, World Wide Web http://www.sils.unc.edu. Admissions contact: Lara Bailey.

University of North Carolina at Greensboro, School of Educ., Dept. of Lib. and Info. Studies, 446 School of Educ. Bldg., P.O. Box 26170, Greensboro, NC 27402-6170. Lisa O'Connor, chair. Tel. 336-334-3477, fax 336-334-4120, e-mail lis@uncg.edu, World Wide Web http://soe.uncg.edu/academics/departments/lis. Admissions contact: Nora Bird. Tel. 336-256-1313, e-mail njbird@uncg.edu.

University of Puerto Rico, Info. Sciences and Technologies, P.O. Box 21906, San Juan, PR 00931-1906. José Sánchez-Lugo, dir. Tel. 787-763-6199, fax 787-764-2311, e-mail egcti@uprrp.edu, World Wide Web http://egcti.upr.edu. Admissions contact: Migdalia Dávila-Pérez. Tel. 787-764-0000 ext. 3530, e-mail migdalia.davila@upr.edu.

University of South Carolina, College of Info. and Communications, School of Lib. and Info. Science, 1501 Greene St., Columbia, SC 29208. R. David Lankes, dir. Tel. 803-777-3858, fax 803-777-7938, e-mail rdlankes@sc.edu, World Wide Web http://www.libsci.sc.edu. Admissions contact: Tel. 803-777-3887, e-mail slisss@mailbox.sc.edu.

University of South Florida, College of Arts and Sciences, School of Info., 4202 E. Fowler Ave., CIS 1040, Tampa, FL 33620. James Andrews, dir. Tel. 813-974-3520, fax 813-974-6840, e-mail si@usf.edu, World Wide Web http://www.usf.edu/si. Admissions contact: Daniel Kahl. Tel. 813-974-8022.

University of Southern Mississippi, College of Educ. and Health Sciences, School of Lib. and Info. Science, 118 College Dr., No. 5146, Hattiesburg, MS 39406-0001. Theresa Welsh, dir. Tel. 601-266-4228, fax 601-266-5774, e-mail slis@usm.edu, World Wide Web http://www.usm.edu/slis. Admissions tel. 601-266-5137, e-mail graduatestudies@usm.edu.

University of Tennessee, College of Communication and Info., School of Info. Sciences, 451 Communication Bldg., Knoxville, TN 37996. Diane Kelly, dir. Tel. 865-974-2148, fax 865-974-4967, e-mail sis@utk.edu, World Wide Web http://www.sis.utk.edu, Admissions tel. 865-974-2858, e-mail tnarnold@utk.edu.

Valdosta State Univ., Dept. of Lib. and Info. Studies, 1500 N. Patterson St., Odum 4600, Valdosta, GA 31698-0133. Linda R. Most, dept. head. Tel. 229-333-5966, fax 229-259-5055, e-mail mlis@valdosta.edu, World Wide Web http://www.valdosta.edu/mlis. Admissions contact: Sheila Peacock.

Midwest: Ill., Ind., Iowa, Kan., Mich., Minn., Mo., Ohio, Wis.

Chicago State University, College of Education, Department of Info. Studies, 9501 S. King Dr., Education Bldg., Room 208, Chicago, IL 60628-1598. Kimberly Black, chair. Tel. 773-995-2598, fax 773-821-2203, e-mail kblack21@csu.edu, World Wide Web https://www.csu.edu/collegeofeducation/Infomediastudies. Admissions contact: Gloria Adams. Tel. 773-995-2404, e-mail graduateprograms@csu.edu.

Dominican Univ., School of Info. Studies, 7900 W. Division St., River Forest, IL 60305. Kate Marek, dean. Tel. 708-524-6983, fax 708-524-6657, e-mail sois@dom.edu, World Wide Web http:/sois.dom.edu/. Admissions contact: Aracelis Sanchez. Tel. 708-524-6456, e-mail asanche2@dom.edu.

Emporia State University, School of Lib. and Info. Management, Campus Box 4025, 1 Kellogg Circle, Emporia, KS 66801-5415. Wooseob Jeong, dean. Tel. 620-341-5203, fax 620-341-5233, e-mail sliminfo@emporia.edu, World Wide Web http://emporia.edu/slim. Admissions contact: Kathie Buckman. Tel. 620-341-5065.

Indiana University, School of Informatics, Computing and Engineering, Info. and Lib. Science, Luddy Hall, Suite 2999C, 700 N. Woodlawn Ave., Bloomington, IN 47408. Raj Achayra, dean. Tel. 812-855-2018, fax 812-855-6166, e-mail ilsmain@indiana.edu,

World Wide Web http://www.ils.indiana.edu/about/accreditation.html. Admissions contact: Stephanie Smith.

Indiana University–Purdue University Indianapolis, School of Informatics and Computing, Dept. of Lib. and Info. Science, 535 W. Michigan St., IT475, Indianapolis, IN 46202. Andrea Copeland, chair. Tel. 317-278-4636, fax 317-278-7669, e-mail soicindy@iupui.edu, World Wide Web http://soic.iupui.edu/lis. Admissions e-mail soicapps@iupui.edu.

Kent State University, School of Info., P.O. Box 5190, Kent, OH 44242-0001. Kendra Albright, dir. Tel. 330-672-2782, fax 330-672-7965, e-mail ischool@kent.edu, World Wide Web http://catalog.kent.edu/colleges/ci/info/library-information-science-mlis/#text. Admissions contact: Cheryl Tennant.

Saint Catherine University, Graduate College, School of Business and Professional Studies, MLIS Program/Information Management Department, 2004 Randolph Ave. No. 4125, St. Paul, MN 55105. Joyce Yakawa, interim dean. Tel. 651-690-6802, fax 651-690-8724, e-mail imdept@stkate.edu, World Wide Web https://www.stkate.edu/academics/academic-programs/gc-library-and-information-science. Admissions contact: Ashley Wells. Tel. 612-214-0741, e-mail aewells@stkate.edu.

University of Illinois at Urbana-Champaign, School of Info. Science, 501 E. Daniel St., Champaign, IL 61820-6211. Kate McDowell, assoc. dean for acad. affairs. Tel. 217-333-3280, fax 217-244-3302, e-mail ischool@illinois.edu, World Wide Web http://ischool.illinois.edu. Admissions contact: Moises Orozco Villicana. Tel. 217-300-5007, e-mail orozco6@illinois.edu.

University of Iowa, Graduate College, School of Lib. and Info. Science, 3087 Main Lib., Iowa City, IA 52242-1420. David Eichmann, dir. Tel. 319-335-5707, fax 319-335-5374, e-mail slis@uiowa.edu, World Wide Web http://slis.grad.uiowa.edu. Admissions contact: Carol Ives. Tel. 319-335-5709, e-mail carol-ives@uiowa.edu.

University of Michigan, School of Info., 4322 North Quad, 105 S. State St., Ann Arbor, MI 48109-1285. Elizabeth Yakel, sr. assoc. dean. Tel. 734-763-2285, fax 734-764-2475, e-mail umsi.admissions@umich.edu, World Wide Web https://www.si.umich.edu/programs/master-science-information. Admissions contact: Laura Elgas.

University of Missouri, College of Educ., Info. Science and Learning Technologies, 303 Townsend Hall, Columbia, MO 65211. Jenny Bossaller, chair. Tel. 877-747-5868, fax 573-884-0122, e-mail sislt@missouri.edu, World Wide Web http://lis.missouri.edu. Admissions tel. 573-882-4546.

University of Wisconsin–Madison, College of Letters and Sciences, Info. School, 600 N. Park St., Madison, WI 53706. Kyung-Sun Kim, interim dir. Tel. 608-263-2900, fax 608-263-4849, e-mail info@ischool.wisc.edu, World Wide Web http://ischool.wisc.edu. Admissions contact: Tanya Hendricks Cobb. Tel. 608-263-2909, e-mail student-services@slis.wisc.edu.

University of Wisconsin–Milwaukee, School of Info. Studies, P.O. Box 413, Milwaukee, WI 53201. Tomas Lipinski, dean. Tel. 414-229-4707, fax 414-229-6699, e-mail soisinfo@uwm.edu, World Wide Web http://www4.uwm.edu/sois.

Wayne State University, School of Info. Science, 106 Kresge Lib., Detroit, MI 48202. Hermina Anghelesco, interim dir. Tel. 313-577-1825, fax 313-577-7563, e-mail asklis@wayne.edu, World Wide Web http://www.slis.wayne.edu. Admissions contact: Matthew Fredericks. Tel. 313-577-2446, e-mail mfredericks@wayne.edu.

Southwest: Ariz., Okla., Texas

Texas Woman's University, School of Lib. and Info. Studies, P.O. Box 425769, Denton, TX 76204-5438. Ling Hwey Jeng, dir. Tel. 940-898-2602, fax 940-898-2611, e-mail slis@twu.edu, World Wide Web http://www.twu.edu/slis. Admissions contact: Mary Honard. E-mail slis@twu.edu.

University of Arizona, College of Social and Behavioral Sciences, School of Info., 1103 E. Second St., Tucson, AZ 85721. P. Bryan Heidorn, dir. Tel. 520-621-3565, fax 520-621-3279, e-mail si-info@email.arizona.edu, World Wide Web https://ischool.arizona.edu/ma-library-information-science. Admissions contact: Barb Vandervelde. Tel.

520-621-3567, e-mail barbv@email.arizona.edu.

University of North Texas, College of Info., Dept. of Info. Science, 1155 Union Circle, No. 311068, Denton, TX 76203-5017. Jiangping Chen, chair. Tel. 940-565-2445, fax 940-369-7600, e-mail lis-chair@unt.edu, World Wide Web http://information science.unt.edu./master-science. Admissions contact: Toby Faber. Tel. 940-565-2445, e-mail ci-advising@unt.edu.

University of Oklahoma, School of Lib. and Info. Studies, College of Arts and Sciences, 401 W. Brooks, Norman, OK 73019-6032. Susan Burke, dir. Tel. 405-325-3921, fax 405-325-7648, e-mail slisinfo@ou.edu, World Wide Web http://www.ou.edu/cas/slis/programs/mlis. Admissions contact: Sarah Connelly.

University of Texas at Austin, School of Info., Suite 5.202, 1616 Guadalupe St., Austin, TX 78701-1213. Eric T. Meyer, dean. Tel. 512-471-3821, fax 512-471-3971, e-mail info@ischool.utexas.edu, World Wide Web http://www.ischool.utexas.edu. Admissions contact: Carla Criner. Tel. 512-471-5654, e-mail criner@ischool.utexas.edu.

West: Calif., Colo., Hawaii, Wash.

San José State University, School of Info., Applied Sciences and Arts, One Washington Sq., San Jose, CA 95192-0029. Sandy Hirsh, dir. Tel. 408-924-2490, fax 408-924-2476, e-mail sjsuischool@gmail.com, World Wide Web http://ischool.sjsu.edu. Admissions contact: Linda Main. Tel. 408-924-2494, e-mail linda.main@sjsu.edu.

University of California, Los Angeles, Graduate School of Educ. and Info. Studies, Dept. of Info. Studies, Box 951520, Los Angeles, CA 90095-1520. Jean-François Blanchette, chair. Tel. 310-825-8799, fax 310-206-3076, e-mail info@gseis.ucla.edu, World Wide Web http://is.gseis.ucla.edu. Admissions contact: Susan Abler. Tel. 310-825-5269, e-mail abler@gseis.ucla.edu.

University of Denver, Morgridge College of Educ., Research Methods and Info. Science, 1999 E. Evans Ave., Denver, CO 80208-1700. Nicholas Cutforth, chair. Tel. 303-871-3587, fax 303-871-4456, e-mail mce@du.edu, World Wide Web http://www.du.edu/education. Admissions contact: Rachel Riley. Tel. 303-871-2508, e-mail rachel.riley@du.edu.

University of Hawaii, College of Natural Sciences, Lib. and Info. Science Program, 2550 McCarthy Mall, Honolulu, HI 96822. Rich Gazan, chair. Tel. 808-956-7321, fax 808-956-5835, e-mail slis@hawaii.edu, World Wide Web http://www.hawaii.edu/lis.

University of Southern California, Marshall School of Business, 3550 Trousdale Parkway, DML 312, Los Angeles, CA 90089-0183. Gary Shaffer, dept. head. Tel. 213-640-4034, e-mail mmlis.program@marshall.usc.edu, World Wide Web http://librarysciencedegree.usc.edu. Admissions tel. 877-830-8647, e-mail info@librarysciencedegree.usc.edu.

University of Washington, The Information School, 370 Mary Gates Hall, Seattle, WA 98195-2840. Anind Dey, dean. Tel. 206-685-9937, fax 206-616-3152, e-mail ischool@uw.edu, World Wide Web http://ischool.uw.edu. Admissions contact: Tel. 206-543-1794, e-mail mlis@uw.edu.

Canada

Dalhousie University, School of Info. Management, Kenneth C. Rowe Management Bldg., Halifax, NS B3H 4R2. Sandra Toze, dir. Tel. 902-494-3656, fax 902-494-2451, e-mail sim@dal.ca, World Wide Web http://www.sim.management.dal.ca. Admissions contact: JoAnn Watson. Tel. 902-494-2471, e-mail joann.watson@dal.ca.

McGill University, School of Info. Studies, 3661 Peel St., Montreal, QC H3A 1X1. Kimiz Dalkir, dir. Tel. 514-398-4204, fax 514-398-7193, e-mail sis@mcgill.ca, World Wide Web http://www.mcgill.ca/sis. Admissions contact: Kathryn Hubbard. Tel. 514-398-4204 ext. 0742, e-mail sis@mcgill.ca.

University of Alberta, School of Library and Information Studies, Faculty of Education, 7-105 Education North, Edmonton, AB T6G 2G5. Toni Samek, chair. Tel. 780-492-4578, fax 780-492-2430, e-mail slis@ualberta.ca, World Wide Web http://www.slis.ualberta.

ca. Admissions contact: Joan White. Tel. 780-492-3679, e-mail slis@ualberta.ca.

University of British Columbia, School of Information, Irving K. Barber Learning Centre, Suite 470, 1961 East Mall, Vancouver, BC V6T 1Z1. Luanne Freund, dir. Tel. 604-822-2404, fax 604-822-6006, e-mail ischool.info@ubc.ca, World Wide Web http://www.slais.ubc.ca. Admissions contact: Sandra Abah. Tel. 604-822-3459, e-mail ischool.program@ubc.ca.

Université de Montréal, École de bibliothéconomie et des sciences de l'information, C.P. 6128, Succursale Centre-Ville, Montreal, QC H3C 3J7. Lyne Da Sylva, acting dir. Tel. 514-343-6044, fax 514-343-5753, e-mail ebsiinfo@ebsi.umontreal.ca, World Wide Web http://www.ebsi.umontreal.ca. Admissions contact: Alain Tremblay. Tel. 514-343-6044, e-mail alain.tremblay.1@umontreal.ca.

University of Ottawa, School of Info. Studies, Desmarais Bldg., Ottawa, ON K1N 6N5. Helene Carrier, interim dir. Tel. 613-562-5130, fax 613-562-5854, e-mail esis@uOttawa.ca, World Wide Web http://arts.uottawa.ca/sis/. Admissions contact: Catherine Bernard. Tel. 613-562-5800 ext. 1324, e-mail artsgrad@uottawa.ca.

University of Toronto, Faculty of Info., 140 George St., Toronto, ON M5S 3G6. Wendy Duff, dean. Tel. 416-978-3202, fax 416-978-5762, e-mail inquire.ischool@utoronto.ca, World Wide Web http://www.ischool.utoronto.ca. Admissions contact: Barbara Brown. Tel. 416-978-8589, e-mail barb.brown@utoronto.ca.

University of Western Ontario, Grad. Programs in Lib. and Info. Science, Faculty of Info. and Media Studies, Room 240, North Campus Bldg., London, ON N6A 5B7. Nick Dyer-Whitheford, acting dean; Pam McKenzie, assoc. dean. Tel. 519-661-4017, fax 519-661-3506, e-mail mlisinfo@uwo.ca, World Wide Web http://www.fims.uwo.ca. Admissions contact: Shelley Long.

Library Scholarship Sources

For a more complete list of scholarships, fellowships, and assistantships offered for library study, see *Financial Assistance for Library and Information Studies,* published annually by the American Library Association (ALA). The document is also available on the ALA website at http://www.ala.org/educationcareers/scholarships.

American Association of Law Libraries. (1) Degree Candidates Scholarships are available for individuals studying to become law librarians as either a library or law school student, or to library school graduates seeking an advanced degree in a related field. Preference is given to AALL members, but scholarships are not restricted to members. Applicants with law library experience are also given preference, but it is not required. Evidence of financial need must be submitted. (2) AALL Scholarship is awarded annually to individuals seeking a degree from an accredited library or law school, and who intend to have a career in legal information, or to a library school graduate seeking an advanced degree in a related field; (3) LexisNexis John R. Johnson Memorial Scholarship is awarded annually to individuals seeking a degree from an accredited library or law school, and who intend to have a career in legal information, or to a library school graduate seeking an advanced degree in a related field. (4) George A. Strait Minority Scholarship is awarded annually to college graduates, with library experience, and who are members of a minority group as defined by current U.S. guidelines, and are degree candidates in an accredited library or law school and intend to have a career in law librarianship. (5) Marcia J. Koslov Scholarship supports AALL members who work in a government law library by providing funding to attend continuing education programs. For information, write to AALL Scholarship Committee, 105 W. Adams St., Suite 3300, Chicago, IL 60603.

American Library Association. (1) ALA Century Scholarship of $2,500 that funds services or accommodation for a library school student(s) with disabilities admitted to an ALA-accredited library school. (2) David A. Clift Scholarship of $3,000 to a U.S./Canadian citizen or permanent resident who is pursuing an MLS in an ALA-accredited program. (3) Tom and Roberta Drewes Scholarship of $3,000 to a library support-staff member who is a U.S./Canadian citizen or permanent resident and is pursuing an MLS in an ALA-accredited program. (4) Mary V. Gaver Scholarship of $3,000 to a U.S./Canadian citizen or permanent resident who is pursuing an MLS specializing in youth services in an ALA-accredited program. (5) Miriam L. Hornback Scholarship of $3,000 to an ALA or library support staffer who is a U.S./Canadian citizen or permanent resident who is pursuing an MLS in an ALA-accredited program. (6) Christopher Hoy/ERT Scholarship of $5,000 to a U.S./Canadian citizen or permanent resident who is pursuing an MLS in an ALA-accredited program. (7) Tony B. Leisner Scholarship of $3,000 to a library support-staff member who is a U.S./Canadian citizen or permanent resident pursuing an MLS in an ALA-accredited program. (8) Peter Lyman Memorial/SAGE Scholarship in New Media to support a student in an ALA-accredited master's program in Library and Information Studies pursuing a specialty in new media. (9) Robert L. Oakley Memorial Scholarship of $1,000 to support research and advanced study for librarians in their early careers to midcareers who are interested and/or active in the fields of intellectual property, public policy, copyright and their impacts on libraries, and the ways libraries serve their communities. (10) W. David Rozkuszka Scholarship of $3,000 to an individual who is currently working with government documents in a library and is working toward a master's degree in library science. (11) Spectrum Scholarship Program is ALA's national diversity and recruitment effort designed to address the specific issue of underrepresentation of critically needed ethnic librarians within the profession while serving as a model for ways to bring attention to larger diversity issues in the future. For information, write to ALA Scholarship Clearinghouse, 50 E. Huron St., Chicago, IL 60611, or see http://www.ala.org/scholarships.

ALA/Association for Library Service to Children. (1) Bound to Stay Bound Books Scholarship provides financial assistance for the education of individuals who intend to pursue an MLS or advanced degree and who plan to work in the area of library service to children. (2) Frederic G. Melcher Scholarship provides financial assistance for individuals who intend to pursue an MLS degree and who plan to work in children's librarianship. For information, write to ALA Scholarship Clearinghouse, 50 E. Huron St., Chicago, IL 60611, or see http://www.ala.org/scholarships.

ALA/Association of College and Research Libraries. The WESS-SEES De Gruyter European Librarianship Study Grant supports research in European studies with an emphasis on librarianship, the book trade, resource documentation, and similar information-science-related topics. An award of €2,500 is given to cover travel to and from Europe and transportation, room, and board in Europe, for up to 30 consecutive days. Application is electronic only. For information, contact award co-chairs Kristen Totleben at ktotleben@library.rochester.edu or Lana Soglasnova at Svetlana.soglasnova@utoronto.edu or ACRL program officer Chase Ollis at collis@ala.org.

ALA International Relations Committee. Bogle Pratt International Library Travel Fund of $1,000 is given to an ALA personal member to attend their first international conference. Applications should be submitted via e-mail to the ALA International Relations Office, intl@ala.org.

ALA/Library and Information Technology Association. (1) LITA/Christian (Chris) Larew Memorial Scholarship of $3,000 for study in an ALA-Accredited Master of Library Science (MLS) program to encourage the entry of qualified persons into the library and information technology field. (2) LITA/OCLC Spectrum Scholarship of $5,000 to a U.S. or Canadian citizen who is a qualified member of a principal minority group (American Indian or Alaskan native, Asian or Pacific Islander, African American, or Hispanic) for study in an ALA-Accredited Master of Library Science (MLS) program who has a strong commitment to the use of automated systems in libraries and plans to follow a career in the library and automation field; (3) LITA/LSSI Minority Scholarship of $2,500 to a U.S. or Canadian citizen who is a qualified member of a principal minority group (American Indian or Alaskan native, Asian or Pacific Islander, African American, or Hispanic) for study in an ALA-Accredited Master of Library Science (MLS) program who has a strong commitment to the use of automated systems in libraries and plans to follow a career in the library and automation field. For information, write to ALA Scholarship Clearinghouse, 50 E. Huron St., Chicago, IL 60611, or see http://www.ala.org/scholarships.

ALA/Public Library Association. Demco New Leaders Travel Grant of up to $1,500 for a varying number of PLA Members to enhance their professional development by making possible their attendance at major professional development activities. For information, write to PLA Awards Program, ALA/PLA, 50 E. Huron St., Chicago, IL 60611, or see http://www.ala.org/pla/awards.

American-Scandinavian Foundation. Fellowships (up to $23,000) and grants (up to $5,000) to pursue research, study, or creative arts projects in Denmark, Finland, Iceland, Norway, or Sweden. For information, write to Fellowships and Grants, American-Scandinavian Foundation, 58 Park Ave., New York, NY 10026, or see http://www.amscan.org/fellowships-and-grants/.

Association for Library and Information Science Education (ALISE). (1) ALISE Community conn@CT mini-grants of $750 for ALISE members to address a library and information need of a social justice organization through community engagement (in a collaborative manner). (2) A varying number of research grants totaling $5,000 for members of ALISE. For information, write to ALISE, 4 Lan Drive, Suite 310, Westford, MA 01886.

Association of Bookmobile and Outreach Services (ABOS). (1) The Bernard Vavrek Scholarship of $1,000 to a student who is currently enrolled and has completed at least one semester in a library and/or information science graduate degree program, and who is interested in becoming an outreach/bookmobile librarian. (2) The John Philip Award of $300 to recognize outstanding contributions and leadership by an individual in bookmobile and outreach services. (3) The Carol Hole Conference Attendance Award of three $500 awards to cover conference registration and a stipend for the winners' travel expenses and/or accommodations for a conference. For information, write to Cathy Zimmerman, ABPS Awards Chair, Scott County Library System, 200 N. 6th Ave., Eldridge, IA 52748.

Association of Jewish Libraries. (1) One or two academic scholarships of $1,000 to a student enrolled or accepted in a graduate school of library and information science. Additionally, free full conference registration is included and encouraged. (2) an academic scholarship of $750 CDN to a student enrolled or accepted in a graduate school of library and information science. Additionally, free full conference registration is included and encouraged. (3) A conference subvention award for attending the Association of Jewish Libraries annual conference. Free full conference registration, travel, and (shared) room are included. For information, see http://jewishlibraries.org/student_scholarship.

Association of Seventh-Day Adventist Librarians. The D. Glenn Hilts Scholarship for a member of the Seventh-Day Adventist Church in an ALA-accredited graduate library program or, if attending outside the United States or Canada, a program recognized by the International Federation of Library Associations (IFLA). Recipient must be enrolled as a full-time student and use the scholarship only for tuition and books. For information, write to Lori Curtis, ASDAL Scholarship and Awards Committee, Del Webb Memorial Library, Loma Linda University, 11072 Anderson St., Loma Linda, CA 92350.

Beta Phi Mu. (1) The Sarah Rebecca Reed Scholarship consisting of two $2,250 awards for individuals beginning LIS studies at an ALA-accredited school. (2) The Frank B. Sessa Scholarship of ten $150 awards for Beta Phi Mu members' continuing education. (3) The Harold Lancour Scholarship of $1,750 for a librarian conducting foreign research. (4) The Blanche E. Woolls Scholarship for School Library Media Service of $2,250 for an individual beginning LIS studies with a concentration in School Library Media. (5) The Eugene Garfield Doctoral Dissertation Scholarship of up to six $3,000 awards for doctoral students who are working on their dissertations in LIS and related fields. For information, write to Beta Phi Mu Honor Society, P.O. Box 42139, Philadelphia, PA 19101, or see https://www.betaphimu.org/scholarships_overview.html.

Canadian Association of Law Libraries. (1) The Diana M. Priestly Scholarship of $2,500 for a student enrolled in an approved Canadian law school or accredited Canadian library school. (2) CALL/ACBD Research Grant of up to $3,000 for research in areas of interest to members and to the association. (3) CALL/ACBD Education Reserve Fund Grants for CALL members to further their education in pursuits that do not fit the guidelines of already established scholarships. (4) The James D. Lang Memorial Scholarship to support attendance at a continuing education program. (5) The Eunice Beeson Memorial Travel Fund to assist members of the Association who wish to attend the annual meeting but, for financial reasons, are unable to do so. (6) Janine Miller Fellowship of $2,500 for one CALL member to attend the Law via the Internet Conference. For information, see https://www.callacbd.ca/Awards.

Canadian Federation of University Women. (1) The Aboriginal Women's Award of $10,000 for studies in specific programs of Law, Medicine, or Nurse Practitioner or a Master of Aboriginal Studies. (2) The Ruth Binnie Fellowship of $6,000 for a student in master's studies that focus on one or more aspect(s) of the field of human ecology/home economics/family and consumer sciences. (3) The Canadian Home Economics Association Fellowship of $6,000 for a student enrolled in a postgraduate program in the field of human ecology/home economics/family and consumer sciences in Canada. (4) the CFUW Memorial Fellowship of $8,000 for a student who is currently enrolled in a master's program in science, mathematics, or engineering in Canada or abroad. (5) The Bourse Georgette LeMoyne award of $5,000 for graduate study in any field at a Canadian university (the candidate must be studying in French). (6) The Elizabeth and Rachel Massey Award of $5,000 for postgraduate studies in the visual arts or in music. (7) The Margaret McWilliams Pre-Doctoral Fellowship of $13,000 for a female student who has completed at least one full year as a full-time student in doctoral-level studies. (8) The 1989 Ecole Polytechnique Commemorative Award of $7,000 (two awards) for graduate studies in any field at the doctoral level and one award of $5,000 for master's study. The applicant must justify the relevance of her work to women. (9) The Linda Souter Humanities Award of $6,000 for a master's or doctoral student studying in the area of the humanities. (10) The Alice E. Wilson Award of $6,000 for four mature students returning to graduate studies in any field after at least three years. For information, write to Fellowships Program Manager, Canadian Federation of University Women, 331 Cooper Street, Suite 502, Ottawa, ON K2P 0G5, Canada, or see http://www.fcfdu.org/fellowshipsawards/listoffellowshipsandawards.aspx.

Chinese American Librarians Association. (1) The Sheila Suen Lai Scholarship of $500 to a Chinese descendant who has been accepted in an ALA-accredited program. (2) The CALA Scholarship of Library and Information Science of $1,000 to a Chinese descendant who has been accepted in an ALA-accredited program. (3) Lisa Zhao Scholarship to engage in professional conferences and development activities and to support and contribute to CALA. Two awards include a $500 Current Students Award open to full-time students enrolled in an ALA-accredited library school, and a $500 New Librarians Award for a current CALA member who graduated from an ALA-accredited library school within the past five years and has been a member of CALA for at least three years. For information, write to Meng Xiong Liu, Clark Library, San José State University, 1 Washington Sq., San Jose, CA 95192-0028.

Council on Library and Information Resources. Mellon Fellowships for Dissertation Research in Original Sources offers up to 15 awards of $2,000 per month for periods ranging from 9 to 12 months and an additional $1,000 upon participating in a symposium on research in original sources and submitting a report acceptable to CLIR on the research experience. For information, write to the Council on Library and Information Resources, 2221 South Clark Street, Arlington, VA 22202.

Massachusetts Black Librarians' Network. $500 for students of African descent entering an ALA-accredited master's program in library science. For information, write to Massachusetts Black Librarians' Network, P.O. Box 400504, Cambridge, MA 02140.

Medical Library Association. (1) The Cunningham Memorial International Fellowship for health sciences librarians from countries other than the United States and Canada. (2) A scholarship of up to $5,000 for a person entering an ALA-accredited library program, with no more than one-half of the program yet to be completed. (3) A scholarship of up to $5,000 for a minority student studying health sciences librarianship. (4) A varying number of Research, Development, and Demonstration Project Grants of $100 to $1,000 for U.S. or Canadian citizens, preferably MLA members. (5) The Clarivate Analytics/MLA Doctoral Fellowship of $2,000 for doctoral work in medical librarianship or information science. (6) The Librarians without Borders Ursula Poland International Scholarship of $1,000 to fund an international project by a U.S. or Canadian health sciences librarian. For information, write to MLA Grants and Scholarships Coordinator, awards@mlahq.org, or see http://www.mlanet.org/page/awards.

Mountain Plains Library Association. A varying number of grants of up to $600 for applicants who are members of the association and have been for the preceding two years. For information, write to Judy Zelenski, Executive Secretary, MPLA, 14293 W. Center Drive, Lakewood, SD 80228.

Society of American Archivists. (1) The F. Gerald Ham Scholarship of $10,000 for up to two graduate students in archival education at a U.S. university that meets the society's criteria for graduate education. (2) The Mosaic Scholarship of $5,000 for up to two U.S. or Canadian minority students enrolled in a graduate program in archival administration. (3) The Josephine Foreman Scholarship of $10,000 for a U.S. citizen or permanent resident who is a minority graduate student enrolled in a program in archival administration. (4) The Oliver Wendell Holmes Travel Award of $1,000 to enable foreign students involved in archival training in the United States or Canada to attend the SAA Annual Meeting. (5) The Donald Peterson Student Travel Award of up to $1,500 to enable graduate students or recent graduates to attend the meeting. (6) The Harold T. Pinkett Minority Student Awards to enable minority students or graduate students to attend the meeting. (7) The Brenda S. Banks Travel Award to recognize and acknowledge individuals of color who have demonstrated professional archival experience and who manifest an interest in becoming active members of the Society of American Archivists. For details, write to Teresa Brinati, Society of American Archivists, 17 N. State St., Suite 1425, Chicago, IL 60607, or see http://www2.archivists.org/governance/handbook/section12.

Special Libraries Association. Leadership Symposium Scholarship of $1,000 for travel expenses and registration at symposium (value $395) for members who demonstrate a desire and commitment to advance their leadership skills and abilities within SLA units. For information, write to Special Libraries Association, 7918 Jones Branch Dr., Suite 300, McLean, Virginia 22102.

Library Scholarship and Award Recipients, 2019

Compiled by the staff of *Library and Book Trade Almanac*

Scholarships and awards are listed by organization.

American Association of Law Libraries (AALL)

AALL and Thomson Reuters/George A. Strait Minority Scholarship. *Winners:* Oheneba Amponsa, Daniel Warren Cardwell, Melissa Eng, Nadia Montenegro.

AALL Educational Scholarships. To assist individuals studying to become law librarians with their educational expenses. *Winners:* (college graduate seeking library degree) Nadia Montenegro, Pearl McCrea; (law school graduate seeking library degree) Jennifer Chapman; (law school graduate seeking nonlaw degree/continuing education) Casandra Laskowski.

AALL Grants. To enable law librarians to participate in professional educational opportunities at the AALL Annual Meeting or to engage in original research on topics important to law librarianship. *Winners:* Tina Ching, Andre Lamar Davison, Janet Kearney, Sarah Lin, Emily Moog, James Gerald Murphy, Michelle Jean Penn, Laura Ray, Aaron Retteen, Eileen L. Santos, Olivia Smith, Ashley Evans Stewart, Ashley Sundin, Sharalyn Williams, Jennifer Wondracek.

AALL Hall of Fame Award. Recognizes significant, substantial, and long-standing contributions to the profession and service to the Association. *Winners:* Paul George, Jolande Goldberg, Robert Oaks.

AALL Marcia J. Koslov Scholarship. To an AALL member to finance conference or seminar attendance. *Winner:* Not awarded in 2019.

AALL Spectrum Article of the Year Award. *Winner:* Rachel P. Licona and Taryn Marks for "Enhancing the Online Learning Environment" (March/April 2018).

Joseph L. Andrews Legal Literature Award. *Winners:* Harris County (Texas) Law Library for *Pro Se Litigant Handbook/Manual para Litigantes Pro Se*; Shamika D. Dalton, et al., for *Celebrating Diversity: A Legacy of Minority Leadership in the American Association of Law Libraries* (second edition).

Emerging Leader Award. To recognize newer members who have made significant contributions to AALL and/or to the profession and have demonstrated the potential for leadership and continuing service. *Winners:* Kristina J. Alayan, Michelle Hook Dewey, Anna C.B. Russell.

Excellence in Community Engagement Award. For outstanding achievement in public relations activities. *Winners:* Harris County (Texas) Law Library for "Harvey Recovery Resources" (web page); King County (Washington) Law Library for Self-Represented Litigant (SRL) workshops.

Excellence in Marketing Award. Recognizes outstanding achievement in marketing activities by an individual, group of individuals, library, chapter, special interest section, consortium, caucus, or any other group affiliated with the Association. *Winners:* Award discontinued.

Marian Gould Gallagher Distinguished Service Award. To recognize extended and sustained service to law librarianship. *Winners:* James S. Heller, Kenneth J. Hirsh, Jacquelyn J. Jurkins, Darcy Kirk.

Innovations in Technology Award. To recognize an AALL member, special interest section, chapter, or library for innovative use of technology in the development and creation of an application or resource for law librarians or legal professionals. *Winners:* Theresa K. Tarves, Penn State Law, for "Legal-Tech Virtual Lab"; Legal Educational Technology Department, University of North Texas Dallas College of Law, for "The Virtual Crime Scene."

Law Library Advocate Award. To an AALL member who has been a strong advocate of private law librarianship through service to the SIS, their organization, or the larger legal community and demonstrates outstanding potential for continued service and leadership within the profession. *Winner:* Diana Koppang.

Law Library Journal Article of the Year. *Winner:* Peter W. Martin for "District Court Opinions That Remain Hidden Despite a Longstanding Congressional Mandate of Transparency—The Result of Judicial Autonomy and Systemic Indifference."

Law Library Publications Award. *Winners:* Award discontinued.

LexisNexis / John R. Johnson Memorial Scholarships. *Winners:* (college graduate seeking library degree) Marissa Rydzewski; (law school graduate seeking library degree) Annalee Hickman, Geraldine Kalim; (library school graduate seeking law degree) Kristopher Turner.

LexisNexis Research Fund Grants. *Winners:* Joan Bellistri and Sara Galligan for "Law Library Services for Self-Represented Litigants: A Survey."

Minority Leadership Development Award. *Winner:* Marcelo Rodriguez, research and training librarian, U.S. Court of Appeals, Second Circuit, New York, New York.

Robert L. Oakley Advocacy Award. To recognize an AALL member who has been an outstanding advocate and has contributed significantly to the AALL policy agenda at the federal, state, local, or international level. *Winner:* Keith Ann Stiverson, director of the library and senior lecturer (retired), Chicago-Kent College of Law, Chicago, Illinois.

Bethany J. Ochal Award for Distinguished Service to the Profession. To honor members who have made significant contributions to law librarianship and are nearing the end of their library careers or have recently retired. *Winners:* Coral Henning, Sacramento (California) County Pubic Law Library; Carol Ebbinghouse, Second District Court of Appeals for California Law Library, Pasadena, California; Terry Long, Virginia State Law Library; Mariann Sears, Harris County (Texas) Law Library.

Volunteer Service Award. Honors volunteers who have made significant contributions to the work of AALL. *Winner:* Julie Pabarja.

American Library Association (ALA)

ALA Excellence in Library Programming Award ($5,000). For a cultural/thematic library program or program series that engages the community in planning, sponsorship, and/or active participation, addresses an identified community need, and has a measurable impact. *Donor:* ALA Cultural Communities Fund. *Winner:* Loudon County (Virginia) Public Library for "Science on Tap," to better engage adults in the community.

ALA Honorary Membership. To recognize outstanding contributions of lasting importance to libraries and librarianship. *Honoree:* Not awarded in 2019.

ALA / Information Today, Inc. Library of the Future Award ($1,500). For a library, consortium, group of librarians, or support organization for innovative planning for, applications of, or development of patron training programs about information technology in a library setting. *Donors:* Information Today, Inc., and IIDA. *Winner:* Tulsa (Oklahoma) City-County Library for the Digital Literacy Lab.

Hugh C. Atkinson Memorial Award. For outstanding achievement (including risk taking) by academic librarians that has contributed significantly to improvements in library automation, management, and/or development or research. *Offered by:* ACRL, ALCTS, LITA, and LLAMA. *Winner:* John Price Wilkin, dean of libraries and university librarian, University of Illinois at Urbana-Champaign.

Carroll Preston Baber Research Grant (up to $3,000). For innovative research that could lead to an improvement in library services to any specified group(s) of people. *Donor:* Eric R. Baber. *Winner:* Not awarded in 2019.

Beta Phi Mu Award ($1,000). For distinguished service in library education. *Donor:* Beta Phi Mu International Library and Information Science Honorary Society. *Winner:* Dr. Mirah J. Dow, director of the Ph.D. program at Emporia State University School of Library and Information Management.

Bogle-Pratt International Library Travel Fund Award ($1,000). To ALA members to attend their first international conference. *Donors:* Bogle Memorial Fund and Pratt Institute School of Information and Library Science. *Winner:* Ayaba Logan.

W. Y. Boyd Literary Award. See "Literary Prizes, 2019" in Part 5.

David H. Clift Scholarship ($3,000). To worthy U.S. or Canadian citizens enrolled in an ALA-accredited program toward an MLS degree. *Winner:* Brynne Campbell.

Melvil Dewey Medal. To an individual or group for recent creative professional achievement in library management, training, cataloging and classification, and the tools and techniques of librarianship. *Donor:* OCLC. *Winner:* June Garcia.

Tom and Roberta Drewes Scholarship ($3,000). To a library support staff member pursuing a master's degree in an ALA-accredited program. *Donor:* Quality Books. *Winner:* Sheryl Orman.

EBSCO/ALA Conference Sponsorship Award ($1,000). To enable librarians to attend the ALA Annual Conference. *Donor:* EBSCO. *Winners:* Rebecca J. Campbell, Tracy S. Drake, Alice Erickson, Aubrey Iglesias, Ji Hye Lee, Ayaba Logan, Brianna N. Thurman.

Equality Award ($1,000). To an individual or group for an outstanding contribution that promotes equality in the library profession. *Donor:* Rowman & Littlefield. *Winner:* Julius C. Jefferson, Jr., Library of Congress; Lorelle R. Swader, ALA Offices and Member Relations.

Elizabeth Futas Catalyst for Change Award ($1,000). A biennial award to recognize a librarian who invests time and talent to make positive change in the profession of librarianship. *Donor:* Elizabeth Futas Memorial Fund. *Winner (2018):* Linda Crowe.

Loleta D. Fyan Public Library Research Grant (up to $5,000). For projects in public library development. *Donor:* Fyan Estate. *Winner:* Not awarded in 2019.

Gale, a Cengage Company, Learning Financial Development Award ($2,500). To a library organization for a financial development project to secure new funding resources for a public or academic library. *Donor:* Gale, a Cengage Company. *Winner:* Not awarded in 2019.

Mary V. Gaver Scholarship ($3,000). To a student pursuing an MLS degree and specializing in youth services. *Winner:* Bean Yogi.

Ken Haycock Award for Promoting Librarianship ($1,000). For significant contribution to public recognition and appreciation of librarianship through professional performance, teaching, or writing. *Winner:* Patricia Helm Smith, Texas Library Association.

Miriam L. Hornback Scholarship ($3,000). To an ALA or library support staff person pursuing a master's degree in library science. *Winner:* Colleen A. Kingsbury.

Paul Howard Award for Courage ($1,000). To a librarian, library board, library group, or an individual for exhibiting unusual courage for the benefit of library programs or services. *Donor:* Paul Howard Memorial Fund. Awarded biennially. *Winner (2019):* Tyler Magill, Alderman Library, University of Virginia.

John Ames Humphry/OCLC/Forest Press Award ($1,000). To one or more individuals for significant contributions to international librarianship. *Donor:* OCLC/Forest Press. *Winner:* Deborah Jacobs.

Tony B. Leisner Scholarship ($3,000). To a library support staff member pursuing a master's degree. *Donor:* Tony B. Leisner. *Winner:* Julia Stone.

Joseph W. Lippincott Award ($1,500). For distinguished service to the library profession. *Donor:* Joseph W. Lippincott III. *Winner:* Kathleen de la Pena McCook.

Peter Lyman Memorial/Sage Scholarship in New Media. To support a student seeking an MLS degree in an ALA-accredited program and pursing a specialty in new media. *Donor:* Sage Publications. *Winner:* Kelli Hayes.

James Madison Award. To recognize efforts to promote government openness. *Winner:* Not awarded in 2019.

Schneider Family Book Awards. See "Literary Prizes, 2019" in Part 5.

Scholastic Library Publishing Award ($1,000). To a librarian whose "unusual contributions to the stimulation and guidance of reading by children and young people exemplifies achievement in the profession." *Sponsor:*

Scholastic Library Publishing. *Winner:* Judi Moreillon.

Lemony Snicket Prize for Noble Librarians Faced with Adversity ($3,000 plus a $1,000 travel stipend to enable attendance at the ALA Annual Conference). To honor a librarian who has faced adversity with integrity and dignity intact. *Sponsor:* Lemony Snicket (author Daniel Handler). *Winner:* Not awarded in 2019.

Spectrum Doctoral Fellowships. To provide full tuition support and stipends to minority U.S. and Canadian LIS doctoral students. *Donor:* Institute of Museum and Library Services. *Winner:* Not awarded in 2019.

Spectrum Initiative Scholarships ($5,000). To minority students admitted to ALA-accredited library schools. *Donors:* ALA and Institute of Museum and Library Services. *Winners:* Spectrum Initiative Scholarships ($5,000). To minority students admitted to ALA-accredited library schools. *Donors:* ALA and Institute of Museum and Library Services. *Winners:* Nada Abdelrahim, Elizabeth Ajunwa, Amy Bartko, Nicholas Berrios, Taylor Brooks, Iliana Burgos, Nicholas Caldwell, Lauren Camarillo, Danielle Castro, Joanne Chern, Frances Chung, Cynthia Cortes, Alexandra Dade, Reza Davallow Ghajar, Catherine de la Cruz, Doreen Dixon, Eiman Elnoshokaty, Hebah Emara, Rayheem Eskridge, Michael Fast Buffalo Horse, Jossel Kay Franco, Bridgette Garcia, Gladys Garcia, Rebecca Garcia, Joan Hua, Gabi Huesca, Neah Ingram-Monteiro, Brianna Limas, Miguel Loeza, Jennifer Loubriel, Amanie Mahmood, Sarah McCall, Nix Mendy, Liana Nand, Yik Wan Karen Ng, Carol Ng-He, Minh Phuong Trinh Nguyen, Courtney Nomiyama, Veronica Ramirez, Priscilla Resendiz, Tania Maria Rios, Diana Rocha, Cristina Ruiz, Conrrado Saldivar, Magali Sanchez, Allan Jason Sarmiento, Constanza Serna, Tomoko Shida, Raivynn Smith, Karina Anne Soni, Zakir Suleman, Meneka Thiru, Jose Vila, Karen Wang, Kevin Whiteneir, Rita de Cassia Wilkenfeld, Alisa Williams, Winnie Wong, Sarah Yasuda

Sullivan Award for Public Library Administrators Supporting Services to Children. To a library supervisor/administrator who has shown exceptional understanding and support of public library services to children. *Donor:* Peggy Sullivan. *Winner:* Sue Ann Pekel, children's librarian, Bentonville (Arkansas) Public Library.

H. W. Wilson Library Staff Development Grant ($3,500). To a library organization for a program to further its staff development goals and objectives. *Donor:* H. W. Wilson Company. *Winner:* North Bergen (New Jersey) Free Public Library.

American Association of School Librarians (AASL)

AASL/ABC-CLIO Leadership Grant (up to $1,750). To AASL affiliates for planning and implementing leadership programs at state, regional, or local levels. *Donor:* ABC-CLIO. *Winner:* South Carolina Association of School Librarians.

AASL Collaborative School Library Award ($2,500). For expanding the role of the library in elementary and/or secondary school education. *Donor:* Scholastic Book Fairs. *Winners:* Carolyn Foote and Melinda Darrow, Westlake High School, Austin, Texas.

AASL Distinguished School Administrator Award ($2,000). For expanding the role of the library in elementary and/or secondary school education. *Donor:* ProQuest. *Winner:* Shirley Simmons, Norman (Oklahoma) Public Schools.

AASL/Frances Henne Award ($1,250). To a school library media specialist with five or fewer years in the profession to attend an AASL regional conference or ALA Annual Conference for the first time. *Donor:* Libraries Unlimited. *Winner:* Holly Schwarzmann.

AASL Innovative Reading Grant ($2,500). To support the planning and implementation of an innovative program for children that motivates and encourages reading, especially for struggling readers. *Sponsor:* Capstone. *Winner:* Susan Gauthier, East Baton Rouge Parish (Louisiana) Schools.

AASL President's Crystal Apple Award. To an individual, individuals, or group for a significant impact on school libraries and students. *Winner:* Marina "Marney" Welmers.

Distinguished Service Award ($3,000). For outstanding contributions to librarianship and school library development. *Donor:* Rosen Publishing Group. *Winner:* Joyce Valenza.

Intellectual Freedom Award ($2,000 plus $1,000 to the media center of the recipient's choice). To a school library media specialist and AASL member who has upheld the principles of intellectual freedom. *Donor:* ProQuest. *Winner:* Not awarded in 2019.

National School Library of the Year Award ($10,000). Honors school libraries exemplifying implementation of AASL's National School Library Standards for Learners, School Librarians, and School Libraries. *Donor:* Follett Library Resources. *Winner:* High School District 214, Arlington Heights, Illinois.

Association for Library Collections and Technical Services (ALCTS)

ALCTS Presidential Citations for Outstanding Service. *Winners:* Julie Mosbo, Miranda Bennett.

Hugh C. Atkinson Memorial Award. *See under:* American Library Association.

Ross Atkinson Lifetime Achievement Award ($3,000). To recognize the contribution of an ALCTS member and library leader who has demonstrated exceptional service to ALCTS and its areas of interest. *Donor:* EBSCO. *Winner:* Stephen Bosch.

Paul Banks and Carolyn Harris Preservation Award ($1,500). To recognize the contribution of a professional preservation specialist who has been active in the field of preservation and/or conservation for library and/or archival materials. *Donor:* Preservation Technologies. *Winner:* Paula De Stefano.

Blackwell's Scholarship Award. *See under:* Outstanding Publication Award.

ProQuest Coutts Award for Innovation in Electronic Resources Management ($2,000). To recognize significant and innovative contributions to electronic collections management and development practice. *Donor:* Coutts Information Services. *Winner:* Maria Savova.

George Cunha and Susan Swartzburg Preservation Award ($1,250). To recognize cooperative preservation projects and/or individuals or groups that foster collaboration for preservation goals. *Sponsor:* Hollinger Metal Edge. *Winner:* Eastern Academics Scholars Trust (EAST) Project Team.

First Step Award (Wiley Professional Development Grant) ($1,500). To enable librarians new to the serials field to attend the ALA Annual Conference. *Donor:* John Wiley & Sons. *Winner:* Ilda Cardenas.

Harrassowitz Award for Leadership in Library Acquisitions ($1,500). For significant contributions by an outstanding leader in the field of library acquisitions. *Donor:* Harrassowitz. *Winner:* Sion Romaine.

Margaret Mann Citation (includes $2,000 scholarship award to the U.S. or Canadian library school of the winner's choice). To a cataloger or classifier for achievement in the areas of cataloging or classification. *Donor:* Online Computer Library Center (OCLC). *Winner:* Terry Reese, Jr..

Outstanding Collaboration Citation. For outstanding collaborative problem-solving efforts in the areas of acquisition, access, management, preservation, or archiving of library materials. *Winner:* Collaboration Across Borders: Opening Access to Holdings of the National Library of Cuba.

Outstanding Publication Award ($250). To honor the year's outstanding monograph, article, or original paper in the field of acquisitions, collection development, and related areas of resource development in libraries. *Winner:* Trevor Owens for the monograph *The Theory and Craft of Digital Preservation* (Baltimore: Johns Hopkins University Press, 2018).

Esther J. Piercy Award ($1,500). To a librarian with no more than ten years' experience for contributions and leadership in the field of library collections and technical services. *Donor:* YBP Library Services. *Winner:* Casey Mullin.

Edward Swanson Memorial Best of *LRTS* Award ($250). To the author(s) of the year's best paper published in the division's official journal. *Winners:* Amy Jankowski, Anne Schultz, and Laura Soito for "Motley Crew: Collaboration across an Academic Library to Revive and Orphaned Collection."

Ulrich's Serials Librarianship Award ($1,500). For distinguished contributions to serials librarianship. *Sponsor:* ProQuest. *Winner:* Ed Jones.

Association for Library Service to Children (ALSC)

ALSC/Baker & Taylor Summer Reading Program Grant ($3,000). For implementation of an outstanding public library summer reading program for children. *Donor:* Baker & Taylor. *Winner:* Lewiston (New York) Public Library.

ALSC/Booklist/YALSA Odyssey Award. To the producer of the best audiobook for children and/or young adults available in English in the United States. See Odyssey Award in "Literary Prizes, 2019" in Part 5.

ALSC/Candlewick Press "Light the Way" Grant ($3,000). To a library conducting exemplary outreach to underserved populations. *Donor:* Candlewick Press. *Winner:* Suffolk (Virginia) Public Library (Morgan Memorial Library).

May Hill Arbuthnot Honor Lectureship. To an author, critic, librarian, historian, or teacher of children's literature who prepares a paper considered to be a significant contribution to the field of children's literature. *Winner:* Debbie Reese, "An Indigenous Critique of Whiteness in Children's Literature."

Mildred L. Batchelder Award. See "Literary Prizes, 2019" in Part 5.

Louise Seaman Bechtel Fellowship ($4,000). For librarians with 12 or more years of professional-level work in children's library collections, to read and study at Baldwin Library, University of Florida. *Donor:* Bechtel Fund. *Winners:* Beth McIntyre and Caroline Ward.

Pura Belpré Award. See "Literary Prizes, 2019" in Part 5.

Bound to Stay Bound Books Scholarships ($7,000). For men and women who intend to pursue an MLS or other advanced degree and who plan to work in the area of library service to children. *Donor:* Bound to Stay Bound Books. *Winners:* Henry Christopher, Anna Elizabeth Mitchell, Marcella Ovalle, Gina Samaniego.

Randolph Caldecott Medal. See "Literary Prizes, 2019" in Part 5.

Carnegie-Whitney Awards (up to $5,000). For the preparation of print or electronic reading lists, indexes, or other guides to library resources that promote reading or the use of library resources at any type of library. *Donors:* James Lyman Whitney and Andrew Carnegie Funds. *Winners:* Gil Ben-Herut and Jon Kuene for "Bhakti Virtual Archive (BHAVA)"; Rachel Ivy Clarke for "List of Lists: An Index of Diversity Book Lists for Adults"; Louis Jones for "Michigan Black History Bibliography"; Karen Gavigan for "Social Justice in Young Adult Graphic Novels: A Global Perspective"; Megan McCaffrey for "Children in Trauma Bibliography"; Naomi Magola for "BeTWEEN the Lines: An Annotated Bibliography of Mental Health Books for Tweens"; Lindsay Schriftman for "Let's Be Changemakers: A Resource Guide for Social Innovation Education"; Dana Thompson for "Recommended Reads for Visual Literacy"; Clarissa West-White for "Research Guide & Resources for Homeless College & High School Students."

Century Scholarship ($2,500). For a library school student or students with disabilities admitted to an ALA-accredited library school. *Winner:* Sarah McKinsey.

Children's Literature Legacy Award. See "Literary Prizes, 2019," in Part 5.

Distinguished Service Award ($1,000). To recognize significant contributions to, and an impact on, library services to children and/or ALSC. *Winner:* Maria B. Salvadore.

Theodor Seuss Geisel Award. See "Literary Prizes, 2019" in Part 5.

Maureen Hayes Author/Illustrator Visit Award (up to $4,000). For an honorarium and travel expenses to make possible a library talk to children by a nationally known author/illustrator. *Sponsor:* Simon & Schuster Children's Publishing. *Winner:* Hocutt-Ellington Memorial Library, Clayton, North Carolina.

Frederic G. Melcher Scholarships ($6,000). To two students entering the field of library service to children for graduate work in an ALA-accredited program. *Winner:* Rosa Flores, Alondra Gaddis.

John Newbery Medal. See "Literary Prizes, 2019" in Part 5.

Penguin Random House Young Readers Group Awards ($600). To children's librarians in school or public libraries with ten or fewer years of experience to attend the ALA Annual Conference. *Donor:* Penguin Young Readers Group and Random House Children's Books. *Winners:* Alexandra Bell, Bloomington (Illinois) Public Library,

Bloomington; Jeanmarie Gielty, Cleveland (Ohio) Public Library; Hadeal Salamah, District of Columbia Public Library; Dawn Wilbert, Decatur (Texas) Public Library.

Robert F. Sibert Medal. See "Literary Prizes, 2019" in Part 5.

Laura Ingalls Wilder Medal. See Children's Literature Legacy Award in "Literary Prizes, 2019," in Part 5.

Association of College and Research Libraries (ACRL)

ACRL Academic or Research Librarian of the Year Award ($5,000). For outstanding contribution to academic and research librarianship and library development. *Donor:* YBP Library Services. *Winner:* Kaetrena Davis Kendrick, University of South Carolina Lancaster–Medford Library.

ACRL/CLS Innovation in College Librarianship Award ($3,000). To academic librarians who show a capacity for innovation in the areas of programs, services, and operations; or creating innovations for library colleagues that facilitate their ability to better serve the library's community. *Winners:* Bill Jones and Ben Rawlins, State University of New York (SUNY)–Geneseo Milne Library.

ACRL/DLS Routledge Distance Learning Librarian Conference Sponsorship Award ($1,200). To an ACRL member working in distance-learning librarianship in higher education. *Sponsor:* Routledge/Taylor & Francis. *Winner:* Victoria (Torrie) Raish, Pennsylvania State University.

ACRL/EBSS Distinguished Education and Behavioral Sciences Librarian Award. To an academic librarian who has made an outstanding contribution as an education and/or behavioral sciences librarian through accomplishments and service to the profession. *Donor:* John Wiley & Sons. *Winner:* Joyce Garczynski, Towson (Maryland) University.

ACRL/STS Oberly Award for Bibliography in the Agricultural or Natural Sciences. Awarded biennially for the best English-language bibliography in the field of agriculture or a related science in the preceding two-year period. *Donor:* Eunice Rockwood Oberly. *Winners (2019):* Douglas Karlen and Lorraine Pellack for "Iowa Crop Variety Yield Testing: A History and Annotated Bibliography."

ACRL/WGSS Award for Career Achievement in Women and Gender Studies Librarianship. *Winner:* Carrie Kruse, College Library, University of Wisconsin–Madison.

ACRL/WGSS Award for Significant Achievement in Women and Gender Studies Librarianship. *Winners:* Rose L. Chou, American University, Washington, D.C.; Annie Pho, University of San Francisco.

Hugh C. Atkinson Memorial Award. *See under:* American Library Association.

CJCLS/EBSCO Community College Learning Resources Program Award ($750). *Winner:* Laura Luiz, Bakersfield (California) College.

Miriam Dudley Instruction Librarian Award. For a contribution to the advancement of bibliographic instruction in a college or research institution. *Winner:* Megan Oakleaf, Syracuse University.

ESS De Gruyter European Librarianship Study Grant (€2,500). Supports research pertaining to European studies, librarianship, or the book trade. *Sponsor:* Walter de Gruyter Foundation for Scholarship and Research. *Winner:* Jennifer K. Nelson, University of California–Berkeley School of Law.

Excellence in Academic Libraries Awards ($3,000). To recognize outstanding college and university libraries. *Donor:* YBP Library Services. *Winners:* (university) Case Western Reserve University; (college) Swarthmore College; (community college) College of Western Idaho.

Instruction Section Innovation Award ($3,000). To librarians or project teams in recognition of a project that demonstrates creative, innovative, or unique approaches to information literacy instruction or programming. *Donor:* ProQuest. *Winners:* Oregon State University (OSU) Libraries and Press for Its Undergrad Research and Writing Studio.

Marta Lange/Sage-CQ Press Award. To recognize an academic or law librarian for contributions to bibliography and information service in law or political science. *Donor:* Sage-CQ Press. *Winner:* Lynda Kellam, University of North Carolina–Greensboro.

Katharine Kyes Leab and Daniel J. Leab American Book Prices Current Exhibition Catalog Awards (citations). For the best catalogs published by American or Canadian institutions in conjunction with exhibitions of books and/or manuscripts. *Sponsor:* Leab Endowment. *Winners:* (electronic exhibitions) University of Victoria Libraries; (expensive) University of Alberta's Bruce Peel Special Collections Library; (moderately expensive) University of Miami Lowe Art Museum and University of Miami Libraries; (inexpensive) Penn State Libraries Eberly Family Special Collections; (brochures) Austin History Center, Austin (Texas) Public Library; University of Pennsylvania Libraries Kislak Center for Special Collections, Rare Books and Manuscripts.

Ilene F. Rockman Instruction Publication of the Year Award ($3,000). To recognize an outstanding publication relating to instruction in a library environment. *Sponsor:* Emerald Group. *Winner:* Stefanie R. Bluemle, for "Post-Facts: Information Literacy and Authority after the 2016 Election."

Association of Specialized Government and Cooperative Library Agencies (ASGCLA)

ASGCLA Cathleen Bourdon Service Award. To recognize an ASGCLA personal member for outstanding service and leadership to the division. *Winner:* Liz Bishoff.

ASGCLA Exceptional Service Award. To recognize exceptional service to patients, the homebound, and inmates, and to medical, nursing, and other professional staff in hospitals. *Winner:* Heather Pelham, Georgetown County (South Carolina) Library System.

ASGCLA Leadership and Professional Achievement Award. To recognize leadership and achievement in the areas of consulting, multitype library cooperation, statewide service and programs, and state library development. *Winner:* Mary L. Chute, State Librarian, New Jersey State Library.

Francis Joseph Campbell Award. For a contribution of recognized importance to library service for the blind and physically handicapped. *Winner:* Kim Charlson, Perkins Braille and Talking Book Library, Watertown, Massachusetts.

Federal Achievement Award. For achievement in the promotion of library and information service and the information profession in the Federal community. *Winner:* Richard Huffine, Chief of the Library and Public Information Center, Federal Deposit Insurance Corporation.

Federal Rising Stars Initiative. To an ASGCLA member new to the profession in a federal or armed forces library or government information management setting. *Winner:* Not awarded in 2019.

KLAS/National Organization on Disability Award for Library Service to People with Disabilities ($1,000). To a library organization to recognize an innovative project to benefit people with disabilities. *Donor:* Keystone Systems. *Winner:* South Carolina State Library, Talking Book Services, for "Assistive Technology Petting Zoo" project.

Black Caucus of the American Library Association (BCALA)

Baker & Taylor Support Staff Award. For dedicated and outstanding performance by a library support staff member. *Winners:* Gail Littleton, Virginia Commonwealth University; Renee Robertson Tecco, Pubic Library of Cincinnati/Hamilton County.

BCALA Book Literary Award. *Winners:* (first novelist) Malcolm Hansen for *They Come in All Colors* (Atria Books); (poetry) Neal Hall for *Door of No Return*; (fiction) Tayari Jones for *An American Marriage* (Algonquin Books); (nonfiction) Jeffrey C. Stewart for *The New Negro: The Life of Alain Locke* (Oxford University Press).

BCALA Trailblazer's Award. Presented once every five years in recognition of outstanding and unique contributions to librarianship. *Winners (2015):* Thomas Alford, Mary Biblo.

DEMCO/BCALA Excellence in Librarianship Award. To a librarian who has made significant contributions to promoting the status of African Americans in the library profession. *Winner:* Rudolph Clay.

E. J. Josey Scholarship Award. *Winners:* Not awarded in 2019.

Ethnic and Multicultural Information and Exchange Round Table (EMIERT)

David Cohen Multicultural Award ($300). To recognize articles of significant research and publication that increase understanding and promote multiculturalism in North

American libraries. *Donor:* Routledge. *Winners:* Not awarded in 2019.

EMIERT Distinguished Librarian Award. Given biennially to recognize significant accomplishments in library services that are national or international in scope and that include improving, spreading, and promoting multicultural librarianship. *Winner:* Clara Chu, Mortenson Center for International Library Programs.

Coretta Scott King Awards. See "Literary Prizes, 2019" in Part 5.

Exhibits Round Table (ERT)

Christopher J. Hoy/ERT Scholarship ($5,000). To an individual or individuals who will work toward an MLS degree in an ALA-accredited program. *Donor:* Family of Christopher Hoy. *Winner:* Mackenzie Schley.

Freedom to Read Foundation

Freedom to Read Foundation Gordon M. Conable Conference Scholarship. To enable a library school student or new professional to attend the ALA Annual Conference. *Winner:* Amanda Vazquez.

Freedom to Read Foundation Roll of Honor (citation): To recognize individuals who have contributed substantially to the foundation. *Winners:* Pamela R. Klipsch.

Judith Krug Fund Banned Books Week Event Grants ($1,000 to $2,500). To support activities that raise awareness of intellectual freedom and censorship issues during the annual Banned Books Week celebration. *Winners:* Academy of the Sacred Heart, New Orleans, Louisiana; Belen (New Mexico) Public Library; Oceanside (California) Public Library; Park University Library, Parkville, Missouri; Worcester County (Maryland) Public Schools.

Gay, Lesbian, Bisexual, and Transgender Round Table (GLBTRT)

Larry Romans Mentorship Award ($1,000). To recognize librarians who, through their sustained mentoring efforts, have made a difference in our profession. *Winner:* July Siebecker.

Stonewall Book Awards. See "Literary Prizes, 2019" in Part 5.

Government Documents Round Table (GODORT)

James Bennett Childs Award. To a librarian or other individual for distinguished lifetime contributions to documents librarianship. *Winner:* Not awarded in 2019.

GODORT-Sponsored ALA Emerging Leader Award. A leadership development program that enables newer library workers from across the country to participate in problem-solving work groups, network with peers, gain an inside look into ALA structure, and have an opportunity to serve the profession in a leadership capacity. *Winner:* Azalea Janel Ebbay, San Diego Central Public Library.

Bernadine Abbott Hoduski Founders Award. To recognize documents librarians who may not be known at the national level but who have made significant contributions to the field of local, state, federal, or international documents. *Winner:* Kris Kasianovitz.

Margaret T. Lane/Virginia F. Saunders Memorial Research Award. *Winner:* Susanne Caro (ed.), et al., *Government Information Essentials* (American Library Association).

NewsBank/Readex/GODORT/ALA Catharine J. Reynolds Research Grant. To documents librarians for travel and/or study in the field of documents librarianship or an area of study benefiting their performance. *Donor:* NewsBank and Readex Corporation. *Winners:* Hayley Johnson.

ProQuest/GODORT/ALA Documents to the People Award. To an individual, library, organization, or noncommercial group that most effectively encourages or enhances the use of government documents in library services. *Winner:* Laura Harper.

Larry Romans Mentorship Award ($1,000). To recognize librarians who, through their sustained mentoring efforts, have made a difference in our profession. *Winner:* July Siebecker.

W. David Rozkuszka Scholarship ($3,000). To provide financial assistance to individuals currently working with government documents in a library while completing a master's program in library science. *Winner:* Ben Chiewphasa and Lauren Hall.

Intellectual Freedom Round Table (IFRT)

Gerald Hodges Intellectual Freedom Chapter Relations Award. *Winner:* Utah Library Association.

John Phillip Immroth Memorial Award for Intellectual Freedom ($500). For notable contribution to intellectual freedom fueled by personal courage. *Winner:* Jim Duncan.

Eli M. Oboler Memorial Award. See "Literary Prizes, 2019" in Part 5.

Library and Information Technology Association (LITA)

Hugh C. Atkinson Memorial Award. *See under:* American Library Association.

Ex Libris Student Writing Award ($1,000 and publication in *Information Technology and Libraries*). For the best unpublished manuscript on a topic in the area of libraries and information technology written by a student or students enrolled in an ALA-accredited library and information studies graduate program. *Donor:* Ex Libris. *Winner:* Sharon Han for "Weathering the Twitter Storm: Early Uses of Social Media as a Disaster Response Tool for Public Libraries During Hurricane Sandy."

LITA/Christian Larew Memorial Scholarship in Library and Information Technology ($3,000). To encourage the entry of qualified persons into the library and information technology field. *Sponsor:* Informata.com. *Winner:* Not awarded in 2019.

LITA/Library Hi Tech Award for Outstanding Communication for Continuing Education in Library and Information Science. To an individual or institution for outstanding communication in library and information technology. *Donor:* Emerald Group. *Winner:* North Carolina State University Libraries.

LITA/OCLC Frederick G. Kilgour Award for Research in Library and Information Technology ($2,000 and expense-paid attendance at the ALA Annual Conference). To bring attention to research relevant to the development of information technologies. *Donor:* OCLC. *Winner:* Charles McClure, School of Information, Florida State University.

Library History Round Table (LHRT)

Phyllis Dain Library History Dissertation Award. Given irregularly in odd-numbered years to the author of a dissertation treating the history of books, libraries, librarianship, or information science. *Winner (2017):* Margaret Yu-Yin Hung for "English Public Libraries, 1919–1975: Vocation and Popularisation." Next awarded in 2023.

Donald G. Davis Article Award (certificate). Awarded biennially for the best article written in English in the field of U.S. and Canadian library history. *Winner (2018):* Jennifer Burek Pierce, "The Reign of Children: The Role of Games and Toys in American Public Libraries, 1877–1925" (*Information and Culture*).

Eliza Atkins Gleason Book Award. Presented every third year to the author of a book in English in the field of library history. *Winner* (2019): Wayne Wiegand and Shirley Wiegand for *The Desegregation of Public Libraries in the Jim Crow South: Civil Rights and Local Activism* (Louisiana State University Press).

Justin Winsor Library History Essay Award ($500). To the author of an outstanding essay embodying original historical research on a significant subject of library history. *Winner:* Not awarded in 2019.

Library Leadership and Management Association (LLAMA)

Hugh C. Atkinson Memorial Award. *See under:* American Library Association.

John Cotton Dana Library Public Relations Awards ($10,000). To libraries or library organizations of all types for public relations programs or special projects ended during the preceding year. *Donors:* H. W. Wilson Foundation and EBSCO. *Winners:* Ypsilanti (Michigan) District Libraries for "TALK: Text and Learn for Kindergarten"; Enoch Pratt Free Library, Baltimore, Maryland, for its effort to go fine-free after finding library fines disproportionately impacted some of the city's most vulnerable communities; Vancouver (British Columbia) Public Library for "Get Lost in the Rooftop Garden"; Spokane (Washington) Public Libraries for "Imagine the Library of the Future"; Greater Victoria (British Columbia) Public

Library for "Change Your Mind"; Los Angeles (California) Public Libraries for "The New Americans Initiative"; Saline County (Arkansas) Library for "Power of the Card"; Delaware County (Ohio) District Library for "Your Library."

Library Research Round Table (LRRT)

Jesse H. Shera Award for Excellence in Published Research. For a research article on library and information studies published in English during the calendar year. *Winners:* Alexander Poole for "Be Damn Pushy at Times: The Committee on the Status for Women and Feminism in the Archival Profession, 1972–1998," published in *American Archivist*.

Jesse H. Shera Award for Support of Dissertation Research. To recognize and support dissertation research employing exemplary research design and methods. *Winner:* Rene Burress for "School Libraries and Every Student Succeeds Act: A Qualitative Analysis."

Map and Geospatial Information Round Table (MAGIRT)

MAGIRT Honors Award. To recognize outstanding achievement and major contributions to map and geospatial librarianship. *Winner:* Louise Ratliff.

New Members Round Table (NMRT)

NMRT ALA Student Chapter of the Year Award. To an ALA student chapter for outstanding contributions to the association. *Winner:* University of South Carolina.

NMRT Annual Conference Professional Development Attendance Award (formerly the Marshall Cavendish Award) (tickets to the ALA Annual Conference event of the winners' choice). *Winners:* Amy Manns, DeSales University, and Carmen Redding, North Dakota State Library.

NMRT Professional Development Grant. To new NMRT members to encourage professional development and participation in national ALA and NMRT activities. *Winner:* Maddie Hines.

Shirley Olofson Memorial Award ($1,000). To an individual to help defray costs of attending the ALA Annual Conference. *Winner:* Megan Donnelly, Francine G. McNairy Library and Learning Forum, Millersville University.

Office for Diversity

Achievement in Library Diversity Research Honor. To an ALA member who has made significant contributions to diversity research in the profession. *Winner:* Not awarded in 2019.

Diversity Research Grants ($2,500). To the authors of research proposals that address critical gaps in the knowledge of diversity issues within library and information science. *Winners:* Dr. Reysa Alenzuela, University of the South Pacific, Emalus Campus School of Law (Republic of Vanuatu), for "Cultural Competency Awareness of Ni-Vanuatu Librarians and Vanuatu Libraries Contribution to Vibrant Cultural Identity"; Holly Yu, California State University, Los Angeles, for "Integration of Library Use Data with Campus Learning Analytics for Student Success"; research team at the University of Kentucky for "Library Staff and Drag Queen Perspectives and Decision-Making about Drag Queen Storytimes."

Office for Information Technology Policy

L. Ray Patterson Copyright Award. To recognize an individual who supports the constitutional purpose of U.S. copyright law, fair use, and the public domain. *Sponsor:* Freedom to Read Foundation. *Winner:* Not awarded in 2019.

Office for Literacy and Outreach Services (OLOS)

Jean E. Coleman Library Outreach Lecture. *Sponsor:* OLOS Advisory Committee. *Lecturer:* Satia Marshall Orange.

Public Library Association (PLA)

Baker & Taylor Entertainment Audio Music/Video Product Grant ($2,500 worth of audio music or video products). To help a public library to build or expand a collection of either or both formats. *Donor:* Baker & Taylor. *Winner:* Liberty (Maine) Library.

Gordon M. Conable Award ($1,500). To a public library staff member, library trustee, or public library for demonstrating a commitment to intellectual freedom and the Library Bill of Rights. *Sponsor:* LSSI. *Winner:* Fairfax County (Virginia) Public Library.

Demco New Leaders Travel Grants (up to $1,500). To PLA members who have not attended a major PLA continuing education event in the past five years. *Winners:* Not awarded in 2019.

EBSCO Excellence in Rural Library Service Award ($1,000). Honors a library serving a population of 10,000 or fewer that demonstrates excellence of service to its community as exemplified by an overall service program or a special program of significant accomplishment. *Donor:* EBSCO. *Winner:* Copper Queen Library, Bisbee, Arizona.

Helping Communities Come Together Award recognizes a public library's ability to identify community needs specifically in times of crisis and division, and respond in creative and exemplary ways. *Donor:* The Singer Group. *Winner:* Sonoma County (California) Library.

John Iliff Award ($1,000). To a library worker, librarian, or library for the use of technology and innovative thinking as a tool to improve services to public library users. *Sponsor:* Innovative. *Winner:* Mark Williams, Milton (Ontario) Public Library.

Allie Beth Martin Award ($3,000). To honor a public librarian who has demonstrated extraordinary range and depth of knowledge about books or other library materials and has distinguished ability to share that knowledge. *Donor:* Baker & Taylor. *Winner:* Sondra Eklund, City of Fairfax (Virginia) Regional Library.

Charlie Robinson Award ($1,000). To honor a public library director who, over a period of seven years, has been a risk taker, an innovator, and/or a change agent in a public library. *Donor:* Baker & Taylor. *Winner:* Clyde Scoles, Toledo Lucas County (Ohio) Public Library.

Romance Writers of America Library Grant ($4,500). To a library to build or expand a fiction collection and/or host romance fiction programming. *Donor:* Romance Writers of America. *Winner:* Suffolk (Virginia) Public Library.

Upstart Innovation Award ($2,000). To recognize a public library's innovative achievement in planning and implementing a creative community service program. *Donor:* Upstart/Demco. *Winner:* Southern Adirondack Library System, Saratoga Springs, New York.

Public Programs Office

Sara Jaffarian School Library Program Award for Exemplary Humanities Programming ($4,000). To honor a K–8 school library that has conducted an outstanding humanities program or series. *Donors:* Sara Jaffarian and ALA Cultural Communities Fund. *Winner:* Wyoming (Ohio) Middle School.

Reference and User Services Association (RUSA)

Award for Excellence in Reference and Adult Library Services ($1,500). To recognize a library or library system for developing an imaginative and unique library resource to meet patrons' reference needs. *Donor:* Reference USA. *Winner:* Heather Holtzman, Paula Knipp, and Kassie Sherman, St. Petersburg College for the "Speed Dating" project, an interactive series of instructional and supplementary materials to educate students and faculty on the different types of databases offered by the college.

BRASS Academic Business Librarianship Travel Award ($1,250). To recognize a librarian new to the field of academic business librarianship and support his or her attendance at the ALA Annual Conference. *Donor:* Business Expert Press. *Winner:* Abigail Morgan, Miami University, Ohio.

BRASS Excellence in Business Librarianship Award ($4,000). For distinguished activities in the field of business librarianship *Donor:* Mergent. *Winner:* Todd Hines, Stanford University GSB Library.

BRASS Public Librarian Support Award ($1,250). To support attendance at the ALA Annual Conference of a public librarian who has performed outstanding business reference service. *Donor:* Morningstar. *Winner:* Not awarded in 2019.

BRASS Research Grant Award ($2,500). To an ALA member seeking support to conduct research in business librarianship. *Donor:* Emerald Publishing. *Winner:* Amanda B. Click, New York University, Abu Dhabi.

BRASS Student Travel Award ($1,250). To enable a student enrolled in an ALA-accredited master's program to attend the ALA Annual Conference. *Donor:* Simply Analytics. *Winner:* Zoeanna Mayhook, University of Washington.

Sophie Brody Medal. See "Literary Prizes, 2019" in Part 5.

CODES Zora Neale Hurston Award. To recognize the efforts of RUSA members in promoting African American literature. *Donor:* Harper Collins. *Winner:* Not awarded in 2019.

CODES Louis Shores Award (citation). To an individual, team, or organization in recognition of excellence in reviewing of books and other materials for libraries. *Winner:* Donna Seaman, adult books editor, *Booklist.*

ETS Achievement Award. To recognize excellence in service to RUSA's Emerging Technologies Section (ETS). *Winner:* Not awarded in 2019.

HS Genealogy/History Achievement Award ($1,500). To encourage and commend professional achievement in historical reference and research librarianship. *Donor:* ProQuest. *Winner:* Mary Lovell Swetnam, special collections librarian, Virginia Beach (Virginia) Public Library.

HS Learning History Research and Innovation Award ($2,500). To an MLS-degreed librarian from an ALA-accredited school to facilitate and further research relating to history and history librarianship. *Donor:* Gale Cengage. *Winner:* Jennifer Brannock, University of Southern Mississippi Libraries.

Margaret E. Monroe Library Adult Services Award ($1,250). To a librarian for his or her impact on library service to adults. *Donor:* NoveList. *Winner:* Nicolette Warisse Sosulski, business librarian, Portage (Michigan) District Library.

Isadore Gilbert Mudge Award ($5,000). For distinguished contributions to reference librarianship. *Donor:* Credo Reference. *Winners:* Kay Ann Cassell, School of Communication and Information, Rutgers University.

RSS Service Achievement Award. To an RSS member who has made either a sustained contribution toward attaining the goals of the Reference Services Section or a single significant contribution that has resulted in a positive impact upon the work of the section. *Winner:* Not awarded in 2019.

John Sessions Memorial Award (plaque). To a library or library system in recognition of work with the labor community. *Donor:* Department for Professional Employees, AFL/CIO. *Winner:* Not awarded in 2019.

STARS Mentoring Award ($1,250). To a library practitioner new to the field of interlibrary loan, resource sharing, or electronic reserves, to attend the ALA Annual Conference. *Donor:* Atlas Systems. *Winner:* Kim Ammons, Mount Holyoke College Library, and Virginia Taylor, Virginia Commonwealth University.

STARS Virginia Boucher Distinguished ILL Librarian Award ($2,000). To a librarian for outstanding professional achievement, leadership, and contributions to interlibrary loan and document delivery. *Winner:* Zack Lane, Butler Library, Columbia University Libraries.

United for Libraries

Trustee Citation. To recognize public library trustees for individual service to library development on the local, state, regional, or national level. *Winner:* Alfred E. Martin.

United for Libraries/Baker & Taylor Awards. To recognize library friends groups for outstanding efforts to support their libraries. *Donor:* Baker & Taylor. *Winner:* Not awarded in 2019.

United for Libraries Major Benefactors Citation. To individuals, families, or corporate bodies that have made major benefactions to public libraries. *Winner:* Not awarded in 2019.

United for Libraries Public Service Award. To a legislator who has been especially supportive of libraries. *Winner:* Not awarded in 2019.

United for Libraries/Thrift Books Friends Grant ($850 plus free conference registration). Enables one member of a Friends of the Library group at a public library to attend the ALA Annual Conference. *Donor:*

Thrift Books. *Winner:* Marlene White, Friends of the Daviess County (Kentucky) Public Library.

Young Adult Library Services Association (YALSA)

Baker & Taylor/YALSA Collection Development Grants ($1,000). To YALSA members who represent a public library and work directly with young adults, for collection development materials for young adults. *Donor:* Book Wholesalers, Inc. *Winners:* Elise Martinez, Zion-Benton (Illinois) Public Library, and Meghan Salsbury, Belgrade (Montana) Community Library.

Baker & Taylor/YALSA Conference Scholarship Grants ($1,000). To young adult librarians in public or school libraries to attend the ALA Annual Conference for the first time. *Donor:* Baker & Taylor. *Winners:* Shira Pilarski, Farmington (Michigan) Community Library, and Jill Slay, Putnam City West High School Library, Oklahoma City.

Dorothy Broderick Student Scholarship ($1,000). To enable a graduate student to attend the ALA Conference for the first time. *Sponsor:* YALSA Leadership Endowment. *Winner:* Meagan Kellerman, Dominican University.

Margaret A. Edwards Award. See "Literary Prizes, 2019" in Part 5.

Great Books Giveaway (books, videos, CDs, and audiocassettes valued at a total of $40,000). *Winners:* Tilden Campus Library, Brooklyn, New York, and Joeten-Kiyu Public Library, Susupe, Saipan, Japan.

Frances Henne/YALSA/VOYA Research Grant ($1,000). To provide seed money to an individual, institution, or group for a project to encourage research on library service to young adults. *Donor:* Greenwood Publishing Group. *Winner:* David Wang, Elmhurst Branch, Queens (New York) Library.

William C. Morris YA Debut Award. See "Literary Prizes, 2019" in Part 5.

Michael L. Printz Award. See "Literary Prizes, 2019" in Part 5.

YALSA/MAE Award ($500 for the recipient plus $500 for his or her library). For an exemplary young adult reading or literature program. *Sponsor:* Margaret A. Edwards Trust. *Winner:* Cicely Lewis, Meadowcreek High School, Lawrenceville, Georgia.

YALSA Service to Young Adults Outstanding Achievement Award ($2,000). Biennial award to a YALSA member who has demonstrated unique and sustained devotion to young adult services. *Winner (2018):* Mary K. Chelton, Graduate School of Library and Information Studies, Queens College, City University of New York.

Art Libraries Society of North America (ARLIS/NA)

ARLIS/NA Distinguished Service Award. To honor an individual whose exemplary service in art librarianship, visual resources curatorship, or a related field, has made an outstanding national or international contribution to art information. *Winner:* Janice Ekdahl.

ARLIS/NA Wolfgang M. Freitag Internship Award ($3,000). To provide financial support for students preparing for a career in art librarianship or visual resource librarianship. *Winner:* Jennifer Follen.

Melva J. Dwyer Award. To the creators of exceptional reference or research tools relating to Canadian art and architecture. *Winner:* Lindsey Sharman (editor) for *The Writing on the Wall: The Work of Joane Cardinal-Schubert* (University of Calgary Press).

Gerd Muehsam Award. To one or more graduate students in library science programs to recognize excellence in a graduate paper or project. *Winner:* Megan Sallabedra for "Finding the Material: Collecting and Protecting Intellectual Property in Ephemeral Works of Art."

Sotheby's Institute of Art Research Awards ($3,000, and an additional $2,000 to the winner's sponsor institution). *Winners:* Not awarded in 2019.

George Wittenborn Memorial Book Awards. See "Literary Prizes, 2019" in Part 5.

Asian/Pacific Americans Libraries Association (APALA)

APALA Scholarship ($1,000). For a student of Asian or Pacific background who is enrolled in, or has been accepted into, a master's or doctoral degree program in library and/or information science at an ALA-accredited school. *Winner:* Bean Yogi.

APALA Travel Grant ($500). To a U.S. or Canadian citizen or permanent resident enrolled in a master's or doctoral degree program in library and/or information science at an ALA-accredited school, or a professional possessing a master's degree or doctoral degree in library and/or information science, to enable attendance at the ALA Annual Conference. *Winner:* Lisa Zhu.

Emerging Leaders Sponsorship. To enable newer library workers to participate in problem-solving work groups, network with peers, gain an inside look into ALA structure, and have an opportunity to serve the profession. *Winner:* Michelle Lee.

Association for Information Science and Technology (ASIS&T)

ASIS&T Award of Merit. For an outstanding contribution to the field of information science. *Winner:* Christine Borgman.

ASIS&T Best Information Science Book. *Winner:* Colin Burke for *America's Information Wars: The Untold Story of Information Systems in America's Conflicts and Politics from World War II to the Internet Age.*

ASIS&T New Leaders Award. To recruit, engage, and retain new ASIS&T members and to identify potential for new leadership in the society. *Winners:* Not awarded in 2019.

ASIS&T ProQuest Doctoral Dissertation Award ($1,000 plus expense-paid attendance at ASIS&T Annual Meeting). *Winner:* Tim Gorichanaz for "Understanding Self-Documentation."

ASIS&T Research in Information Science Award. For a systematic program of research in a single area at a level beyond the single study, recognizing contributions in the field of information science. *Winner:* Kevin Crowston.

Clarivate Doctoral Dissertation Proposal Scholarship ($2,000). *Winner:* Adele Paul-Hus for "Beyond Funding: What Can Acknowledgments Reveal about Credit Attribution in Science?"

Clarivate Outstanding Information Science Teacher Award ($1,500). To recognize the unique teaching contribution of an individual as a teacher of information science. *Winner:* Hazel Hall, Edinburgh Napier University (Scotland).

James M. Cretsos Leadership Award. To recognize new ASIS&T members who have demonstrated outstanding leadership qualities in professional ASIS&T activities. *Winner:* Kenwal Ameen and Rebekkah Willson.

Watson Davis Award for Service. For outstanding continuous contributions and dedicated service to the society. *Winner:* Lynn Silipigni Connaway.

Pratt Severn Best Student Research Paper Award. To encourage student research and writing in the field of information science. *Winner:* Matthew Weirick Johnson for "Dating Apps, Categorical Fields, and Health Information Sharing: Exploring the Utility of Dating Application Features Related to HIV, STIs, and PrEP for Promoting Regular Testing and PrEP Usage."

John Wiley Best *JASIST* Paper Award. *Winners:* Ian Ruthven, Steven Buchanan, and Cara Jardine for "Isolated, Overwhelmed, and Worried: Young, First-Time Mothers Asking for Information and Support Online."

Bob Williams History Fund Research Grant Award. *Winner:* Not awarded in 2019.

Bob Williams History Fund Best Research Paper Award. *Winner:* Not awarded in 2019.

Association for Library and Information Science Education (ALISE)

ALISE Award for Professional Contribution. *Winner:* Melissa Gross and Kathy Burnett, Florida State University.

ALISE Diversity Travel Award ($750 for travel expenses, complimentary registration to the ALISE annual conference, and one-year student membership). To increase diversity in LIS education/research for an individual who wishes to address issues of diversity through doctoral study or teaching. *Winner:* Raymond Pun, California State University.

ALISE/Eugene Garfield Doctoral Dissertation Competition. *Winner:* Timothy Gorichanaz,

Drexel University, for "Understanding Self-Documentation."

ALISE/Norman Horrocks Leadership Award. To recognize a new ALISE member who has demonstrated outstanding leadership qualities in professional ALISE activities. *Winner:* Keren Dali, University of Denver.

ALISE/Pratt-Severn Faculty Innovation Award. To recognize innovation by full-time faculty members in incorporating evolving information technologies in the curricula of accredited master's degree programs in library and information studies. *Winner:* Nadia Ciadi, University of Toronto.

ALISE/ProQuest Methodology Paper Competition. *Winner:* Lynn Silipigni Connaway, Chris Cyr, Brittany Brannon, Peggy Gallagher, and Erin Hood, OCLC, for "Speaking on the Record: Combining Interviews with Search Log Analysis in User Research."

ALISE Research Grant Competition (one or more grants totaling $5,000). *Winner:* Anthony Bernier, San José State University, for "Recasting First Generation Student Experience for LIS Success."

ALISE Service Award. *Winner:* Denice Adkins, University of Missouri.

ALISE/Jean Tague Sutcliffe Doctoral Student Research Poster Competition. *Winners:* (first place) Megan Threats, University of North Carolina–Chapel Hill; (second place) Laura Ridenour, University of Wisconsin–Milwaukee; (third place) Brian Dobreski, University of Tennessee, Knoxville.

ALISE/University of Washington Information School Youth Services Graduate Student Travel Award. To support the costs associated with travel to and participation in the ALISE Annual Conference. *Winner:* Kristie Escobar, Florida State University.

ALISE/Connie Van Fleet Award for Research Excellence in Public Library Services to Adults. To recognize LIS research concerning services to adults in public libraries. *Winner:* Not awarded in 2019.

ALISE/Bohdan S. Wynar Research Paper Competition. *Winner:* Margaret Zimmerman, University of Iowa, for "Mapping Literacies: Comparing Information Horizons Mapping to Measures of Information and Health Literacy."

Doctoral Students to ALISE Grant. To support the attendance of one or more promising LIS doctoral students at the ALISE Annual Conference. *Sponsor:* Libraries Unlimited/Linworth. *Winner:* Cynthia Orozco, University of California, Los Angeles.

Library Journal/ALISE Excellence in Teaching Award (formerly the ALISE Award for Teaching Excellence in the Field of Library and Information Science Education). *Winner:* Nicole Cooke, University of South Carolina.

OCLC/ALISE Library and Information Science Research Grant Competition. To promote independent research that helps librarians integrate new technologies into areas of traditional competence and contributes to a better understanding of the library environment. *Winner:* Not awarded in 2019.

Association of Jewish Libraries (AJL)

AJL Scholarships ($1,000). For students enrolled in accredited library schools who plan to work as Judaica librarians. *Winner:* Not awarded in 2019.

Fanny Goldstein Merit Award. To honor loyal and ongoing contributions to the association and to the profession of Jewish librarianship. *Winners:* Elliot H. Gertel.

Life Membership Award. To recognize outstanding leadership and professional contributions to the association and to the profession of Jewish librarianship. *Winner:* Not awarded in 2019.

Association of Research Libraries

ARL Diversity Scholarships (stipend of up to $10,000). To a varying number of MLS students from underrepresented groups who are interested in careers in research libraries. *Sponsors:* ARL member libraries and the Institute of Museum and Library Services. *Winners:* Lauren A. Camarillo, University of Illinois at Urbana-Champaign; Bran Eveland Cron, University of Illinois at Urbana-Champaign; Adaliz N. Cruz, Simmons University; Marilu Duque, University of Michigan; Eiman Elnoshokaty, University of British Columbia; Lese Fandel, Indiana

University–Purdue University Indianapolis (IUPUI); Carlos A. Grooms, North Carolina Central University; Neah Ingram-Monteiro, University of British Columbia; Hiva Kadivar, North Carolina Central University; Cani S. McMillian, University of Michigan; Emily Ping O'Brien, Texas Woman's University; Tashiana Monique Scott-Cochran, North Carolina Central University; Jeremy E. Thompson Jr., University of Arizona; Renée A. Torres, San José State University; Erik Valenzuela, University of Southern California; Doris Watts, Emporia State University.

Association of Seventh-Day Adventist Librarians

D. Glenn Hilts Scholarship ($1,500) for a member or members of the Seventh-Day Adventist Church who are enrolled in a graduate library program. *Winners:* Adaliz Cruz, Simmons University; Bliss Kuntz, University of Colorado–Denver.

Beta Phi Mu

Beta Phi Mu Award. *See under:* American Library Association.

Eugene Garfield Doctoral Dissertation Fellowships ($3,000). *Winners:* Jessica Lapp, University of Toronto, for "The Provenance of Protest: An Exploration of Feminist Activist Archiving"; Emily Maemura, University of Toronto, for "Logics of Order and Aggregation in Web Archiving Systems"; J. Elizabeth Mills, University of Washington, for "Never the Same Storytime Twice: An Exploration of the Nature and Role of Reflection in Public Library Storytime Assessment"; Adèle Paul-Hus, Université de Montréal, for "Acknowledgements and Their Functions within the Reward System of Science"; Laura Ridenour, University of Wisconsin–Milwaukee, for "Examining the Notion of the Boundary Object in Information Systems: The Transdisciplinary Oeuvre of Cognitive Science"; Megan Threats, University of North Carolina at Chapel Hill, for "The Influence of Information Behaviors and Technologies on the Adoption of HIV Protective and Risk Reduction Behaviors among Young, Black Men Who Have Sex with Men."

Harold Lancour Scholarship for Foreign Study ($1,750). For graduate study in a country related to the applicant's work or schooling. *Winner:* Christopher Hollister, Lockwood Library, University of Buffalo.

Sarah Rebecca Reed Scholarship ($2,250). For study at an ALA-accredited library school. *Winner:* Ruth Mahaffey, Emporia State University.

Frank B. Sessa Scholarship for Continuing Professional Education ($1,500). For continuing education for a Beta Phi Mu member. *Winners:* Joy Banks, At-Large, Clarion University; Anne Mlod, Pi Lambda Sigma Chapter, Syracuse University; Megan De Armond, Theta Chapter, Pratt Institute; Cristina Ramirez, Iota Chapter, Catholic University; Laura Litwer, Beta Omega Chapter, University of South Carolina.

Blanche E. Woolls Scholarship ($2,250). For a beginning student in school library media services. *Winner:* Rachel Hatcher, San José State University.

Bibliographical Society of America (BSA)

BSA Fellowships ($1,500–$6,000). For scholars involved in bibliographical inquiry and research in the history of the book trades and in publishing history. *Winners:* (BSA-ASECS Fellowship for Bibliographical Studies in the Eighteenth Century) Megan Peiser and Emily Spunaugle, Oakland University, for "Gender, Disability, and Finding Women in the Archives: Establishing the Provenance of the Marguerite Hicks Collection, 1660–1820"; (BSA-Mercantile Library Fellowship in North American Bibliography) Caroline Wigginton, University of Mississippi, for "Indigenuity: Native Craftwork and the Material of Early American Books"; (BSA-Rare Book School Fellowship) Matthew da Mota, University of Toronto; (BSA Short Term Fellowships) Ainoa Castro Correa, Universidad de Salamanca, for "The Book Before the Book"; Hwisang Cho, Emory University, for "Writing in Squares: The Eurasian Nexus in Korean Buddhist Textuality"; Stephanie Frampton, Massachusetts

Institute of Technology, for "Cicero's Library: The Roman Book and the Making of the Classics"; Carson Koepke, Yale University, for "The Role of Tironian Notes in Early Medieval Educational Culture"; Jane Raisch, University of York, for "Unmasking the First Facsimiles (1500–1800)"; Andrea Van Leerdam, Utrecht University, for "Woodcuts as Reading Aids: Illustrations and Knowledge Transfer in Netherlandish Medical-Astrological Books, 1500–1550"; Matthew Wills, University of California San Diego, for "Mediating the Message: Book Culture and Propaganda in Mao's China"; (Katharine F. Pantzer Junior Fellowship in Bibliography and the British Book Trades) Janet Tyson for "A Curious Undertaking: The Collaborative Making of a Herbal in Georgian Britain"; (Katharine F. Pantzer Senior Fellowship in Bibliography and the British Book Trades) Anna Reynolds, University of Oxford and University of York: "Binding Waste in Early Modern England"; (Pine Tree Fellowship in Culinary Bibliography) Caroline Barta, University of Texas at Austin, for "Kitchen Literature: A Biography of the Cookbook"; (Pine Tree Fellowship in Hispanic Bibliography) Lorenzo di Tommaso, Concordia University, for "Apocalypse of Pseudo-Methodius in Mediaeval Spain"; (Reese Fellowship for American Bibliography and the History of the Book in America) Eric Lamore, University of Puerto Rico at Mayagüez, for "Abigail Field Mott's 1829 Abridged Edition of Olaudah Equiano's Interesting Narrative: A Critical Edition"; (Charles J. Tannenbaum Fellowship in Cartographical Bibliography) Rodney Kite-Powell, Tampa History Center, for "Collectors' Bias in Assembling a Map Collection"; (Charles J. Tannenbaum Fellowship in Cartographical Bibliography and the Reese Fellowship for American Bibliography and the History of the Book in America) Jill Falcon Mackin, Edna Manitowabi, and Tasha Beeds, Montana State University, for "Anishinaabe Movement through a Sacred Landscape: Red Sky's Birchbark Scrolls."

William L. Mitchell Prize for Research on Early British Serials ($1,000). Awarded triennially for the best single work published in the previous three years. *Winner (2018)*: Dr. Paul Tankard, *Facts and Inventions: Selections from the Journalism of James Boswell* (Yale University Press).

New Scholars Program. To promote the work of scholars who are new to the field of bibliography. *Winners:* Lucas Dietrich, Lesley University, for "A Sensational Job: Maria Amparo Ruiz de Burton, J.B. Lippincott Co., and Commission Printing"; Megan Piorko, Georgia State University, for "Seventeenth-Century Chymical Collections: A Study of Unique Copies of 'Fasciculus Chemicus'"; Lindsay Van Tine, Americas Center at the University of Virginia, for "Bibliography, Bookdealing, and the Bibliotheca Americana."

St. Louis Mercantile Library Prize in American Bibliography ($2,000). Awarded triennially for outstanding scholarship in the bibliography of American history and literature. *Sponsor:* St. Louis Mercantile Library, University of Missouri, St. Louis. *Winner (2020):* To be announced.

Justin G. Schiller Prize for Bibliographical Work on Pre–20th Century Children's Books ($2,000). A triennial award to encourage scholarship in the bibliography of historical children's books. *Winner (2019): The Book and Periodical Illustrations of Arthur Hughes: A Spark of Genius 1832–1914,* by Maroussia Oakley (Oak Knoll Press & Private Libraries Association).

Catholic Library Association

Regina Medal. For continued, distinguished contribution to the field of children's literature. *Winner:* Kate DiCamillo.

Chinese American Librarians Association (CALA)

CALA Conference Travel Grant. *Winners:* Andrew Lee, Crystal Chen, Huifen Chang, Jia He, Katherina Lee, Kuei Chiu, and Yan Liu.

CALA Distinguished Service Award. To a librarian who has been a mentor, role model, and leader in the fields of library and information science. *Winner:* Lian Ruan.

CALA Outstanding Library Leadership Award in Memory of Dr. Margaret Chang Fung.

Winner: Qi Chen, Calumet College of St. Joseph, Whiting, Indiana.

CALA President's Recognition Award. *Winners:* (individuals) Qi Chen, Guoying Liu, Yongming Wang, Yuan Li, Icy Smith, Sai Deng, Michael Bailou Huang; (teams) Assessment & Evaluation Committee, Awards Committee, Scholarship Committee, Constitution & Bylaws Committee, Web Committee.

CALA Scholarship of Library and Information Science ($1,000). *Winner:* Jodi Tam, San José State University.

Sheila Suen Lai Scholarship ($500). *Winner:* Yuqiao Cao, University of North Carolina at Chapel Hill.

Lisa Zhao Scholarship ($500). *Winners:* Biyang Yu, Florida State University; and Minhao Jiang, Wayne State University.

Coalition for Networked Information (CNI)

Paul Evan Peters Award. Awarded biennially to recognize notable and lasting international achievements relating to high-performance networks and the creation and use of information resources and services that advance scholarship and intellectual productivity. *Sponsors:* Association of Research Libraries, CNI, EDUCAUSE. *Winner (2020):* Francine Berman, Rensselaer Polytechnic University and Radcliffe Institute, Harvard University.

Paul Evan Peters Fellowship ($5,000 a year for two years). Awarded biennially to a student or students pursuing a graduate degree in librarianship or the information sciences. *Sponsors:* Association of Research Libraries, CNI, EDUCAUSE. *Winners (2018):* Bergis Jules and Laima Augustaitis.

Council on Library and Information Resources (CLIR)

CLIR Postdoctoral Fellowships in Scholarly Information Resources. *Current fellows:* Rebecca Y. Bayeck, Mary Borgo Ton, Andrew Brown, Maia Call, Guillaume Candela, Christian Casey, Alicia Cowart, Faithe Day, Zachary Furste, Amani Morrison, Aditya Ranganath, Brian A. Robinson, Azure Stewart, Sean Tennant, Kimber Thomas, Kevin Winstead.

Digitizing Hidden Special Collections and Archives Awards. *Sponsor:* Andrew W. Mellon Foundation. *Winners:* Asheville Art Museum Association, Inc. for "Digital Black Mountain College Collection and Interconnective Timeline"; Ball State University for "Unearthing a Half-Century of Archaeological Research in Indiana: Digitizing the Report of Investigations and Archaeological Report Series, and Associated Diagnostic Artifacts"; CUNY Television for "Uncovering the City University of New York's Audiovisual Heritage"; Law Library Microform Consortium for "The Early State Records for 26 U.S. States and Territories West of the Appalachians: a Digital Record from European Contact to Early Statehood Based on the Library of Congress' Microfilm Collection"; Michigan Technological University for "Michigan Miners at Home and Work: Digitizing, Mapping, and Sharing Employee Records"; Moravian Archives, Memorial University of Newfoundland, Nunatsiavut Government, and Moravian Church in Newfoundland and Labrador for "Uncommon Bonds: Labrador Inuit and Moravian Missionaries"; National Native American Boarding School Healing Coalition, Saginaw Chippewa Indian Tribe of Michigan, Museum of Indian Arts and Culture, and Indigenous Digital Archive project for "Digitizing the Records of U.S. Indian Boarding Schools"; San Francisco Art Institute for "Thinking Out Loud: Digitizing 80 Years of Lectures and Public Programs at the San Francisco Art Institute"; Mattress Factory, Ltd. for "The Greer Lankton Collection: Documenting the Life and Work of Transgender Artist Greer Lankton (1958–1996)"; Regents of the University of California (University of California, Berkeley) for "Land, Wealth and Power: Private Land Claims in California, ca. 1852 –1892"; Regents of the University of Michigan for "Digitizing Natural History Materials from University of Michigan's Special Collections"; Regents of the University of New Mexico dba KNME-TV, New Mexico PBS, KRWG, KENW, KUNM, KANW, WGBH Educational Foundation, and Library of Congress for "New Mexico Public Media Digitization Project"; Indiana University, Saint Mary's College, Loyola University Chicago, Berea College, College of Wooster, DePauw University, Illinois Wesleyan University, Earlham College, Northern Illinois University, University of Saint Mary of the Lake, Southern Baptist Theological Seminary, Saint Olaf College, Knox College, Saint Meinrad Archabbey, Seminary, and School of Theology, Goshen College, Marquette University, Bowling Green State University, Ohio Wesleyan University, University of Dayton, Xavier University, Truman State University, and Muskegon Museum of Art for "Peripheral Manuscripts: Digitizing Medieval Manuscript Collections in the Midwest"; University of La Verne for "Cataloging and Digitizing the Esther Funk Collection in University of La Verne's Cultural & Natural History Collections"; University of South Carolina for "New Insights on South Carolina and the American Civil Rights Movement: National Interracial Activism in the South Carolina Council on Human Relations Papers"; Virginia Polytechnic Institute and State University for "Entomo-3D: Digitizing Virginia Tech's Insect Collection"; Wichita State University, KMUW Public Radio, WGBH, Library of Congress, Kansas Public Broadcasting Council of Stations, Vietnamese Public Radio, KHCC Radio, High Plains Public Radio, KPR Radio, KRPS Radio, KPTS TV for "The Kansas Public Media Preservation Project"; Woodson Research Center, Fondren Library, Rice University for "Digitizing Hidden Selections of Houston's African American and Jewish Heritage."

Mellon Fellowships for Dissertation Research in Original Sources. *Sponsor:* Andrew W. Mellon Foundation. *Winners:* Hilary Barker, Colin Bos, Olivia Cacchione, Henry Clements, Marlena Cravens, Matthew Foreman, Anne Grasberger, Jasmin Howard, Clarissa Ibarra, Carl Kubler, Dana Landress, Xiuyuan Mi, Sauda Nabukenya, Catalina Ospina, Paloma Rodrigo Gonzales, Anna Weerasinghe.

EDUCAUSE

EDUCAUSE Community Leadership Award. *Winner:* Mark Askren, senior advisor to the president, University of Nebraska–Lincoln.

EDUCAUSE DEI Leadership Award. To acknowledge and celebrate exemplary leadership in advancing equity, diversity, and inclusion. *Winner:* Melissa Woo, senior vice president for information technology and enterprise chief information officer, Stony Brook University.

EDUCAUSE Leadership Award. To acknowledge leadership in higher education information technology. *Winners:* Linda Jorn, associate vice provost for learning technologies and DoIT director of academic technology, University of Wisconsin–Madison.

EDUCAUSE Rising Star Award. To recognize early-career information technology professionals who demonstrate exceptional achievement in the area of information technology in higher education. *Winner:* Tina Pappas, associate director of innovation and technology, Rutgers, the State University of New Jersey.

Friends of the National Library of Medicine

Michael E. DeBakey Library Services Outreach Award. To recognize outstanding service and contributions to rural and underserved communities by a practicing health sciences librarian. *Winner:* Rachel Fenske, Biomedical Library, University of South Alabama.

Institute of Museum and Library Services

National Medal for Museum and Library Service. For extraordinary civic, educational, economic, environmental, and social contributions ($5,000). *Winners:* Jamestown S'Klallam Tribal Library, Sequim, Washington; Inter-university Consortium for Political and Social Research, Ann Arbor, Michigan; New Haven (Connecticut) Free Public Library; Gulfport (Florida) Public Library; Meridian (Idaho) Library District;

Barona Band of Mission Indians—Barona Cultural Center and Museum, Lakeside, California; New Children's Museum, San Diego, California; Orange County Regional History Center, Orlando, Florida; National Civil Rights Museum at the Lorraine Motel, Memphis, Tennessee; South Carolina Aquarium, Charleston, South Carolina.

International Association of School Librarians (IASL)

Ken Haycock Leadership Development Grant ($1,000). To enable applicants from any nation to attend their first IASL Annual Conference. *Winner:* Victoria Calarco, Owasco Elementary School, Auburn, New York.

Jean Lowrie Leadership Development Grant ($1,000). To enable applicants from developing nations to attend their first IASL Annual Conference. *Winner:* Kolawole Akinjide Aramide, University of Ibadan, Nigeria.

Takeshi Murofushi Research Award ($500). For funding a research project, preferably of international interest. *Winner:* Not awarded in 2019.

Diljit Singh Leadership Development Grant ($1,000). To enable applicants from developing nations to attend their first IASL conference. *Winner:* Geraldine Nanjala, Ndege Primary School, Kenya.

International Board on Books for Young People (IBBY)

IBBY-Asahi Reading Promotion Award ($10,000). Awarded biennially to projects that are making a lasting contribution to reading promotion for young people. *Offered by:* International Board on Books for Young People. *Sponsor:* Asahi Shimbun. *Winner (2018):* Les Doigts Qui Rêvent (Reading Fingers), to fill the lack of access to tactile illustrated books for visually impaired children in France, Europe, and the world.

International Federation of Library Associations and Institutions (IFLA)

International Federation of Library Associations and Institutions (IFLA) Honorary Fellowship. For distinguished service to IFLA. *Winners:* Deborah Jacobs and Donna Scheeder.

IFLA Medal. To a person or organization for a distinguished contribution either to IFLA or to international librarianship. *Winners:* Kai Ekholm and Barbara Schleihagen.

Jay Jordan IFLA/OCLC Early Career Development Fellowships. To library and information science professionals from countries with developing economies who are in the early stages of their careers. *Winners:* John Oluwaseye Adebayo, Nigeria; Ramiro Jose Rico Carranza, Bolivia; Samar Jammoul, Lebanon; Davaasuren Myagmar, Mongolia; Tracey-Ann Ricketts, Jamaica.

Dr. Shawky Salem Conference Grant (up to $1,900). To enable an expert in library and information science who is a national of an Arab country to attend the IFLA Conference for the first time. *Winner:* Not awarded in 2019.

Library Journal

DEMCO/*Library Journal* Paralibrarian of the Year Award. *Winner:* Not awarded in 2019.

Gale/*Library Journal* Library of the Year. *Sponsor:* Gale Cengage Learning. *Winner:* Los Angeles County Library.

Library Journal/ALISE Excellence in Teaching Award (formerly the ALISE Award for Teaching Excellence in the Field of Library and Information Science Education). *See under:* Association for Library and Information Science Education (ALISE).

Library Journal Best Small Library in America ($20,000). To honor a public library that profoundly demonstrates outstanding service to populations of 25,000 or less. *Cosponsors: Library Journal* and the Bill and Melinda Gates Foundation. *Winner:* Copper Queen Library, Bisbee, Arizona.

Library Journal Librarian of the Year. *Winner:* Skye Patrick, Los Angeles County Library.

Library of Congress

Kluge Fellowships in Digital Studies. To promote examination of the impact of the digital revolution on society, culture, and international relations using the library's collections and resources. *Fellow:* Not awarded in 2019.

Library of Congress Literacy Awards. *Sponsor:* David M. Rubenstein. *Winners:* (David M. Rubenstein Prize, $150,000, for a groundbreaking or sustained record of advancement of literacy by any individual or entity) ProLiteracy Worldwide, Syracuse, New York; (American Prize, $50,000, for a project developed and implemented successfully during the past decade for combating illiteracy and/or aliteracy) American Action Fund for Blind Children and Adults, Baltimore, Maryland; (International Prize, $50,000, for the work of an individual, nation, or nongovernmental organization working in a specific country or region) ConTextos, Chicago, Illinois, and San Tecla, La Libertad, El Salvador.

Library of Congress Prize for American Fiction. See "Literary Prizes, 2019" in Part 5.

Medical Library Association (MLA)

Virginia L. and William K. Beatty MLA Volunteer Service Award. To recognize a medical librarian who has demonstrated outstanding, sustained service to the Medical Library Association and the health sciences library profession. *Winner:* Amy Gische Lyons.

Estelle Brodman Award for the Academic Medical Librarian of the Year. To honor significant achievement, potential for leadership, and continuing excellence at midcareer in the area of academic health sciences librarianship. *Winner:* Mark MacEachern.

Clarivate Analytics/Frank Bradway Rogers Information Advancement Award. To recognize outstanding contributions to the application of technology to the delivery of health science information, to the science of information, or to the facilitation of the delivery of health science information. *Sponsor:* Thomson Reuters. *Winner:* Not awarded in 2019.

Lois Ann Colaianni Award for Excellence and Achievement in Hospital Librarianship. To a member of MLA who has made significant contributions to the profession in the area of overall distinction or leadership in hospital librarianship. *Winner:* Heather J. Martin.

Cunningham Memorial International Fellowships. For health sciences librarians from countries outside the United States and Canada, to provide for attendance at the MLA Annual Meeting and observation and supervised work in one or more medical libraries. *Winner:* Deepali Kuberkar.

Louise Darling Medal. For distinguished achievement in collection development in the health sciences. *Winner:* Susan K. Kendall.

Janet Doe Lectureship. *Winner:* Gerald J. Perry, AHIP, FMLA, "The Activist Health Sciences Librarian."

EBSCO/MLA Annual Meeting Grants (up to $1,000). To enable four health sciences librarians to attend the MLA Annual Meeting. *Winners:* Daina Dickman, AHIP; Shanda Hunt; Liz Kellermeyer; and Tariq Rahaman.

Ida and George Eliot Prize. To recognize a work published in the preceding calendar year that has been judged most effective in furthering medical librarianship. *Winners:* Blake W. Hawkins; Martin Morris; Tony Nguyen, AHIP; John Siegel, AHIP; and Emily Vardell for "Advancing the Conversation: Next Steps for Lesbian, Gay, Bisexual, Trans, and Queer (LGBTQ) Health Sciences Librarianship."

Carla J. Funk Governmental Relations Award ($500). To recognize a medical librarian who has demonstrated outstanding leadership in the area of governmental relations at the federal, state, or local level, and who has furthered the goal of providing quality information for improved health. *Sponsor:* Kent A. Smith. *Winner:* Not awarded in 2019.

Murray Gottlieb Prize. *See under:* Erich Meyerhoff Prize below.

T. Mark Hodges International Service Award. To honor outstanding achievement in promoting, enabling, or delivering improved health information internationally. *Winner:* Not awarded in 2019.

David A. Kronick Traveling Fellowship ($2,000). *Sponsor:* Bowden-Massey Foundation. *Winner:* Not awarded in 2019.

Joseph Leiter NLM/MLA Lectureship. *Winner:* Nadya Okamoto.

Donald A. B. Lindberg Research Fellowship ($10,000). To fund research aimed at expanding the research knowledge base, linking the information services provided by librarians to improved health care and advances in biomedical research. *Winners:* Mary Grace Flaherty for "Using an Emerging Condition to Understand Health Information Use, Diagnostic Delay and Health Services Utilization."

Lucretia W. McClure Excellence in Education Award. To an outstanding educator in the field of health sciences librarianship and informatics. *Winner:* Whitney A. Townsend.

John P. McGovern Award Lectureship. *Winner:* Katherine (Katie) L. Watson.

Medical Informatics Section Career Development Grant ($1,500). To support a career development activity that will contribute to advancement in the field of medical informatics. *Winner:* Lori Winterfeldt.

Erich Meyerhoff Prize (formerly the Murray Gottlieb Prize). For the best unpublished essay on the history of medicine and allied sciences written by a health sciences librarian. *Sponsor:* MLA History of the Health Sciences Section. *Winner:* Aaron Jackson for "Reforming the Veteran: Propaganda and Agency in WWI Reconstruction Hospitals."

MLA Chapter Project of the Year Award. *Winner:* North Atlantic Health Sciences Libraries–NAHSL.

MLA Continuing Education Grant ($100–$500). *Winners:* Heather Edmonds and Alexandria Quesenberry.

MLA Scholarship (up to $5,000). For graduate study at an ALA-accredited library school. *Winner:* Jordan Wrigley.

MLA Scholarship for Under-Represented Students (up to $5,000). For graduate study at an ALA-accredited library school. *Winner:* Bradrick McClam.

Marcia C. Noyes Award. For an outstanding contribution to medical librarianship. *Winner:* M.J. Tooey, AHIP, FMLA.

President's Award. To an MLA member for a notable or important contribution made during the past association year. *Winners:* Education Steering Committee: Elizabeth Laera, AHIP; Merinda McLure, AHIP; Beth Hill, AHIP; Kristin Hitchcock, AHIP; Carrie L. Iwema, AHIP; Keith C. Mages, AHIP; Peace Ossom Williamson, AHIP; Stephanie M. Swanberg, AHIP; Stephanie Fulton, AHIP; Latrina Keith; Elizabeth G. Hinton, AHIP; Erika L. Sevetson; Melissa De Santis, AHIP; Donna Berryman, AHIP; and Julia Esparza, AHIP.

Rittenhouse Award. For the best unpublished paper on medical librarianship submitted by a student enrolled in, or having been enrolled in, a course for credit in an ALA-accredited library school or a trainee in an internship program in medical librarianship. *Donor:* Rittenhouse Book Distributors. *Winner:* Kearin Reid, AHIP, for "Learning Objects in the Flipped Classroom: A Review of the Literature with Implications for Practice."

Music Library Association

Vincent H. Duckles Award. For the best book-length bibliography or other tool in music. *Winner:* Inger Sørensen for *J.P.E. Hartmann, Thematic-Bibliographic Catalogue of His Works*, edited by Birthe Skou; Danish Humanist Texts and Studies, Volume 56 (Copenhagen: Dansk Center for Musikudgivelse, Det Kongelige Bibliotek, 2017).

Dena Epstein Award for Archival and Library Research in American Music. To support research in archives or libraries internationally on any aspect of American music. *Winner:* Not awarded in 2019.

Kevin Freeman Travel Grants. To colleagues who are new to the profession to enable them to attend the MLA Annual Meeting. *Winners:* Jeannie Chen, Andrea Copland, Yuri Shimoda, Zachary Tumlin, and Sarah Ward; *Diversity Scholarship awardee:* Ellen Ogihara.

Walter Gerboth Award. To members of the association who are in the first five years of their professional library careers, to assist research-in-progress in music or music librarianship. *Winner:* Joy M. Doan for "Constructing a Fuller Narrative of William Grant Still and Classic Hollywood"; and Matthew Vest for a critical edition of the extant works of Ernst Bachrich (1892–1942).

Richard S. Hill Award. For the best article on music librarianship or article of a music-bibliographic nature. *Winners:* Beth Iseminger, Nancy Lorimer, Casey Mullin, and Hermine Vermeij for "Faceted Vocabularies for Music: A New Era in Resource Discovery" in *Notes* 73.3 (2017): 409–431.

MLA Citation. Awarded in recognition of contributions to the profession over a career. *Winner:* Jay Weitz.

Eva Judd O'Meara Award. For the best review published in *Notes. Winner:* Derek Stauff for his review of Volumes 1 and 8 of Andreas Hammerschmidt's *Gesamtausgabe*, edited by Michael Heinemann, Sven Rössel, and Konstanze Kremtz (Altenburg: Verlag Klaus-Jürgen Kamprad, 2015) in *Notes* 74.1 (2017): 125–130.

A. Ralph Papakhian Special Achievement Award. To recognize extraordinary service to the profession of music librarianship over a relatively short period of time. *Winners:* Not awarded in 2019.

National Library Service for the Blind and Physically Handicapped, Library of Congress

Library of the Year Awards ($1,000). *Winner:* (Regional Library of the Year) Carnegie Library of Pittsburgh (Pennsylvania), Library for the Blind and Physically Handicapped; (Subregional Library/Advisory and Outreach Center of the Year) Staunton (Virginia) Talking Book Center.

REFORMA (National Association to Promote Library and Information Services to Latinos and the Spanish-Speaking)

Elizabeth A. Martinez Lifetime Achievement Award. To recognize those who have achieved excellence in librarianship over an extended period of service and who have made significant and lasting contributions to REFORMA and the Latino community. *Winner:* Orlando "Lando" Archibeque.

REFORMA scholarships (up to $1,500). To students who qualify for graduate study in library science and who are citizens or permanent residents of the United States. *Winners:* (Rose Trevino Memorial Scholarship) *Winner:* Luisa Leija. (REFORMA Scholarship) *Winners:* Cynthia Cortes and Renee Torres.

Arnulfo D. Trejo Librarian of the Year Award. To recognize a librarian who has promoted and advocated services to the Spanish-speaking and Latino communities and made outstanding contributions to REFORMA. *Winner:* Maria Cotto, Pawtucket (Rhode Island) Public Library.

Society of American Archivists (SAA)

C. F. W. Coker Award for Description. To recognize creators of tools that enable archivists to produce more effective finding aids. *Winner:* Lou Reed papers processed by the Archives Unit on behalf of the Music Division in the Library for the Performing Arts of the New York Public Library.

Distinguished Service Award. To recognize an archival institution, education program, nonprofit organization, or governmental organization that has given outstanding service to its public and has made an exemplary contribution to the archives profession. *Winner:* New England Archivists Mentoring Program.

Diversity Award. To an individual, group, or institution for outstanding contributions to advancing diversity within the archives profession, SAA, or the archival record. *Winner:* Puerto Rico Citizenship Archives Project.

Fellows' Ernst Posner Award. For an outstanding essay dealing with a facet of archival administration, history, theory, or methodology, published in *American Archivist. Winner:* Jeremy Evans and Melissa Hernández Durán for "Rights Review for Sound Recordings: Strategies Using Risk and Fair Use Assessments (Fall/Winter 2018, Vol. 81.2).

Josephine Forman Scholarship ($10,000). *Sponsor:* General Commission on Archives and History of the United Methodist Church. *Winner:* Ashley Flores, University of California, Los Angeles.

Mark A. Greene Emerging Leader Award. To recognize early-career archivists who have completed archival work of broad merit, demonstrated significant promise of leadership, performed commendable service to the archives profession, or accomplished a combination of these requirements. *Winner:* Wendy Hagenmaier, Georgia Institute of Technology.

F. Gerald Ham and Elsie Ham Scholarship ($7,500). To recognize an individual's past performance in a graduate archival studies program and his or her potential in the field. *Winner:* Erin Voisin, Louisiana State University.

Philip M. Hamer and Elizabeth Hamer Kegan Award. For individuals and/or institutions that have increased public awareness of a specific body of documents. *Winner:* Dickinson College Archives and Special Collections for Carlisle Indian School Digital Resource Center.

Oliver Wendell Holmes Travel Award. To enable overseas archivists already in the United States or Canada for training to attend the SAA Annual Meeting. *Winner:* Not awarded in 2019.

J. Franklin Jameson Archival Advocacy Award. For individuals and/or organizations that promote greater public awareness of archival activities and programs. *Winners:* Tempestt Hazel; The Kitchen Sisters (Davia Nelson and Nikki Silva).

Sister M. Claude Lane, O.P., Memorial Award. For a significant contribution to the field of religious archives. *Winner:* Jillian Ewalt, Marian Library, University of Dayton.

Waldo Gifford Leland Award. To encourage and reward writing of superior excellence and usefulness in the field of archival history, theory, or practice. *Winner:* Trevor Owens for *The Theory and Craft of Digital Preservation* (Johns Hopkins University Press, 2018).

Theodore Calvin Pease Award. For the best student paper ($100 and publication in *American Archivist*). *Winner:* Emily Larsen, University of British Columbia, for "Big Brother, Big Data: Digital Preservation of Big Data in Government" (Spring/Summer 2019, Vol. 83, No. 1).

Donald Peterson Student Travel Award (up to $1,000). To enable a student or recent graduate to attend the SAA Annual Meeting. *Winner:* Alexis Recto, University of California, Los Angeles.

Harold T. Pinkett Student of Color Award. To encourage minority students to consider careers in the archival profession, and to promote minority participation in SAA. *Winners:* Angela Osbourne, San José State University, and Antonia Charlemagne-Marshall, University of West Indies.

Preservation Publication Award. To recognize an outstanding work published in North America that advances the theory or the practice of preservation in archival institutions. *Winners:* Heather Bowden and Walker Sampson for *The No-Nonsense Guide to Born-Digital Content* (Facet, 2018).

SAA Fellows. To a limited number of members for their outstanding contribution to the archival profession. *Honored*: Jeannette Bastian, Terry Baxter, Louis Jones, and Cheryl Stadel-Bevans.

SAA Mosaic Scholarship ($5,000). To minority students pursuing graduate education in archival science. *Winners:* Lisle Pino, San José State University.

SAA Spotlight Award. To recognize the contributions of individuals who work for the good of the profession and of archival collections, and whose work would not typically receive public recognition. *Winners:* Kelli Luchs, Las Vegas News Bureau archivist, Las Vegas Convention and Visitors Authority; Ilana Short, former manager of photography collections, Nevada State Museum.

Special Libraries Association (SLA)

SLA James M. Matarazzo Rising Star Award. To SLA members in the first five years of membership who demonstrate exceptional promise of leadership. *Winners:* Natasha Chowdory, Angela Pagliaro, Kristin Petersheim, Mea Warren.

SLA John Cotton Dana Award. For exceptional support and encouragement of special librarianship. *Winner:* Guy St. Clair.

SLA Fellows. *Honored*: Geraldine Clement-Stoneham, Nick Collison, Ulla de Stricker, Heather Kotula, Kendra K. Levine.

SLA Hall of Fame Award. For outstanding performance and distinguished service to SLA. *Winners:* Bill Fisher and Marilyn Bromley.

Rose L. Vormelker Award. To SLA members for exceptional service through the education and mentoring of students and working professionals. *Winner:* Eve Wider.

Theatre Library Association

Brooks McNamara Performing Arts Librarian Scholarship. *Winner:* Not awarded in 2019.

Louis Rachow Distinguished Service in Performing Arts Librarianship Award. For extraordinary contributions to performing arts. *Winner:* Norton Owen, Jacob's Pillow, Becket, Massachusetts.

George Freedley Memorial Award. *Winner:* Debra Caplan, *Yiddish Empire: The Vilna Troupe, Yiddish Theater, and the Art of Itinerancy* (University of Michigan Press).

Richard Wall Award. See "Literary Prizes, 2019" in Part 5.

Other Awards of Distinction

Robert B. Downs Intellectual Freedom Award. To recognize individuals or groups who have furthered the cause of intellectual freedom, particularly as it affects libraries and information centers and the dissemination of ideas. *Offered by:* Graduate School of Library and Information Science, University of Illinois at Urbana-Champaign. *Sponsor:* Libraries Unlimited/ABC-CLIO. *Winner:* Education Justice Project, Champaign, Illinois.

I Love My Librarian Awards ($5,000, a plaque, and a $500 travel stipend to attend the awards ceremony). To recognize librarians for service to their communities, schools, and campuses. Winners are nominated by library patrons. *Sponsors:* Carnegie Corporation of New York and the *New York Times*. *Winners:* Jesús Alonso-Regalado, University at Albany, State University of New York; Stephanie Lynn Dannehl, Bertrand (Nebraska) Community School; Cathy Gulley Evans, James Frederick Smith Library, St. Mary's Episcopal School, Memphis, Tennessee; Melissa Glanden, Powhatan (Virginia) High School; MaryAnne Hansen, Renne Library, Montana State University, Bozeman, Montana; Homa Naficy, The American Place, Hartford (Connecticut) Public Library; Maria Papanastassiou, Arlington Heights (Illinois) Memorial Library; Leah Plocharcyzk, John D. MacArthur Campus Library, Florida Atlantic University; Janet Tom, San Francisco Public Library, Tracie Walker-Reed, H. Grady Spruce High School, Dallas, Texas.

RWA Cathie Linz Librarian of the Year. To a librarian who demonstrates outstanding support of romance authors and the romance genre. *Offered by:* Romance Writers of America. *Winner:* Stephen Ammidown, Bowling Green State University.

USBBY Bridge to Understanding Award ($1,000). To acknowledge the work of adults who use books to promote international understanding among children. *Offered by:* United States Board on Books for Young People. *Winner:* To be announced.

Women's National Book Association Award. Awarded biennially to a living American woman who derives part or all of her income from books and allied arts and who has done meritorious work in the world of books. *Offered by:* Women's National Book Association (WNBA). *Winners (2019):* Lisa Lucas, executive director, National Book Foundation.

Part 4
Research and Statistics

Library Research and Statistics

Number of Libraries in the United States and Canada

Statistics are from the *American Library Directory (ALD)* 2020–2021 (Information Today, Inc., 2020). Data are exclusive of elementary and secondary school libraries.

Libraries in the United States

Public Libraries	16,912*
Public libraries, excluding branches	9,617
Main public libraries that have branches	1,437
Public library branches	7,295
Academic Libraries	3,575*
Community college	1,077
Departmental	231
Medical	5
Religious	6
University and college	2,432
Departmental	1,155
Law	194
Medical	229
Religious	246
Armed Forces Libraries	227*
Air Force	62
Medical	3
Army	104
Medical	21
Marine Corps	12
Navy	49
Law	1
Medical	9
Government Libraries	813*
Law	351
Medical	110

Special Libraries (excluding public, academic, armed forces, and government)	4,621*
Law	653
Medical	839
Religious	371
Total Special Libraries (including public, academic, armed forces, and government)	5,795
Total law	1,199
Total medical	1,216
Total religious	795
Total Libraries Counted (*)	26,148

Libraries in Regions Administered by the United States

Public Libraries	18*
Public libraries, excluding branches	9
Main public libraries that have branches	3
Public library branches	9
Academic Libraries	38*
Community college	3
Departmental	1
University and college	35
Departmental	18
Law	3
Medical	3
Religious	1
Armed Forces Libraries	2*
Air Force	1
Army	1
Government Libraries	3*
Law	1
Medical	1
Special Libraries (excluding public, academic, armed forces, and government)	5*
Law	3
Religious	1
Total Special Libraries (including public, academic, armed forces, and government)	14
Total law	7
Total medical	4
Total religious	2
Total Libraries Counted (*)	66

Libraries in Canada

Public Libraries	2,210*
Public libraries, excluding branches	800
Main public libraries that have branches	158
Public library branches	1,409
Academic Libraries	324*
Community college	78
Departmental	15
Religious	1
University and college	242
Departmental	165
Law	16
Medical	12
Religious	32
Government Libraries	161*
Law	25
Medical	4
Special Libraries (excluding public, academic, armed forces, and government)	542*
Law	86
Medical	128
Religious	20
Total Special Libraries (including public, academic, armed forces, and government)	632
Total law	127
Total medical	144
Total religious	69
Total Libraries Counted (*)	3,237

Summary

Total U.S. Libraries	26,148
Total Libraries Administered by the United States	66
Total Canadian Libraries	3,237
Grand Total of Libraries Listed	29,451

Note: Numbers followed by an asterisk are added to find "Total libraries counted" for each of the three geographic areas (United States, U.S.-administered regions, and Canada). The sum of the three totals is the "Grand total of libraries listed" in *ALD*. For details on the count of libraries, see the preface to the 73rd edition of *ALD—Ed.*

Highlights of IMLS Public Library Surveys

The Institute of Museum and Library Services (IMLS) collects and disseminates statistical information about public libraries in the United States and its outlying areas. This article presents highlights from two recent IMLS surveys of public libraries and state library administrative agencies. For more information, see "Institute of Museum and Library Services" in Part 2 of this volume and visit https://www.imls.gov/research-tools/data-collection for the most current and comprehensive IMLS survey data and reports.

Public Libraries Survey

The following are highlights from the IMLS report *Public Libraries in the United States, Fiscal Year 2016*, released in June 2019. Based on an annual public library survey (PLS), the report collected data from 98 percent of public libraries in all 50 U.S. states, the District of Columbia, and outlying territories.

Library Visits and Use

- In fiscal year (FY) 2016 there were 9,057 active public libraries in the United States providing access to information and services through 16,568 central and branch libraries and 659 bookmobiles.
- In FY 2016 there were 1.35 billion visits to public libraries, or 4.36 visits per person, with just over 7 items checked out per person.
- Between FY 2009 and FY 2016 visits per person decreased by 18.66 percent while reference transactions per person decreased by 24.04 percent.
- The public accessed reference services at public libraries more than 245 million times in FY 2016.
- In FY 2016 reference transactions per person were substantially higher in libraries in cities and suburbs than in towns and rural areas. Across population size groupings, there were more visits and reference transactions per person in libraries serving small service areas than in those serving larger populations.

Collections and Circulation

- In FY 2016 patrons had access to 1.46 billion items and over a quarter million public access Internet computers in public libraries.
- Public libraries continued to adapt their collections to modern demands by adding more e-books and audio and video materials—both physical units and downloadable items.
- In FY 2016 e-books constituted 26.87 percent of all collection materials, up from 1.44 percent in FY 2007.

- The 1.46 billion collection materials available to the public in FY 2016 represented 4.69 materials per person, an increase from 3.14 per person in FY 2007.
- Between FY 2007 and FY 2016 total circulation per person decreased overall, with annual declines noted after FY 2010; children's circulation varied little over the same ten-year period.

Programs and Attendance

- The 5.18 million programs offered by public libraries in FY 2016 represent a 58 percent increase over the 3.28 million programs offered in FY 2007.
- Total programs offered and young adults' programs offered per 1,000 people in FY 2019 represent increases of 10 percent and nearly 10 percent, respectively, over FY 2015.
- In FY 2016 libraries offered 2.85 million children's programs and 503,334 young adults' programs, accounting for approximately two-thirds of the total programs offered.
- Between FY 2012 and FY 2016 total programs offered and program attendance per 1,000 people increased by 25.83 percent and 18.93 percent respectively. During the same period, children's programs offered per 1,000 people increased by 16.62 percent, and attendance at children's programs per 1,000 people increased by 15.37 percent.
- Library programs in FY 2016 were attended by 113.08 million patrons, continuing the trends of annual increases in library programming (a 9.53 percent increase over FY 2015) and attendance (a 6.66 percent increase over FY 2015).

Public Access Computers and User Sessions

- In FY 2016 public libraries reported 294,216 public access Internet computers, or 4.74 computers per 5,000 people, and 276.44 million user sessions, or nearly one session per person.
- In FY 2016 there were 939.58 user sessions per public access Internet computer and 17.76 public access Internet computers per stationary outlet.
- The number of public access Internet computers per 5,000 people varied across the states in FY 2016, ranging from 9.28 in Vermont to 1.96 in Hawaii.
- Public access Internet computer user sessions per person showed little variation across locales in FY 2016. The number of public access Internet computers per stationary outlet (i.e., central and branch libraries) varied by locale and with libraries in cities having 30.63 computers per stationary outlet, more than in all other locales.
- In FY 2016 libraries with small population service areas both offered more Public access Internet computers and logged more user sessions per person than libraries with larger population service areas.

Revenue and Expenditures

- Operating revenue and expenditures, both of which decreased following the 2008 recession, have increased over the last three fiscal years. In FY 2016 revenue and expenditures continued to move closer to pre-recession values.
- In FY 2016 total operating revenue per person ranged from as high as $83.91 in the District of Columbia to as low as $18.75 in Georgia.
- In FY 2016 total operating expenditures per person varied across the states, ranging from as high as $82.91 in the District of Columbia to as low as $16.86 per person in Mississippi.
- Across all locale types and population sizes, in FY 2016 public library staff expenditures represented about two-thirds (67 percent) of all operating expenditures.

Public Library Staff

- In FY 2016 there were 140,054 paid full-time equivalent (FTE) staff at public libraries compared to 139,213 in FY 2015.
- In FY 2016 library staff assisted library patrons via 245.70 million reference transactions, or 0.79 transaction per person.
- There were no marked differences in staffing levels between FY 2016 and FY 2015, though the last decade has seen an overall decline of approximately one staff FTE per 25,000 people.
- Overall, just over two-thirds of full-time equivalent librarians held an American Library Association–accredited master's degree in library or information science. Over one-third (35 percent) of all paid staff hold the title of librarian, and approximately 68 percent of those holding the title of librarian have an ALA-MLS.

State Library Administrative Agencies Survey

Following are highlights from the IMLS report *State Library Administrative Agencies Survey, Fiscal Year 2016,* released in October 2017. Based on a biennial survey, the report collected data from State Library Administrative Agencies throughout the 50 states and the District of Columbia.

Introduction

A State Library Administrative Agency (SLAA) is the official state agency charged with the extension and development of public library services throughout the state. It has the authority to administer state plans in accordance with the provisions of the federal Library Services and Technology Act (LSTA).

Across the 50 states and the District of Columbia, SLAAs are located in various state government agencies and report to different authorities. They coordinate and distribute federal funds from the IMLS Grants to States program in addressing statewide and local needs.

Although all SLAAs coordinate and distribute federal funds authorized by the administration of the LSTA, not all share the same function and role within their respective states. Most SLAAs provide important reference and information services to the state government, administer the state library or serve as the state archives, operate libraries for people who are blind or physically handicapped, and support the State Center for the Book. In some states, the SLAA also may function as the public library at large, providing library services to the general public.

Revenue and Expenditures

- Total reported revenues for the 51 SLAAs across all sources were just over $1 billion in FY 2016.
- Revenues from the federal government for all SLAAs totaled $154.3 million (15 percent), while state revenues totaled $856.2 million (82 percent), and revenues from other sources totaled $33.4 million (3.0 percent).
- Total expenditures for FY 2016 across all SLAAs were $1.03 billion. Most expenditures were in financial assistance to libraries ($663.9 million) and operating expenditures including staffing, collections, and other expenses ($344.2 million), with smaller expenditures allocated to other services ($21.4 million) and capital outlay ($1.4 million).
- A closer review of SLAAs' operating expenditures reveals that 53 percent of all operating expenditures were used to support staffing (salaries and wages and employee benefits), whereas 10 percent were used for collections and 37 percent for other expenses.
- From FY 2012 to FY 2014, just after the recession, SLAA revenues and expenditures both increased modestly (5.0 percent and 2.0 percent, respectively), but both financial indicators subsequently decreased by about 5.0 percent from FY 2014 to FY 2016. In FY 2016 revenues and expenditures were roughly at FY 2012 levels—less than 1.0 percent and 2.0 percent below FY 2012, respectively.

Workforce and Staff Development

- The 51 SLAAs reported nearly 2,633 total full-time staff positions for FY 2016, which was a 6.4 percent decrease from FY 2012.
- A total of 367.5 staff—14 percent of all budgeted full-time equivalent (FTE) staff—was reported within the service of administration, 536.7 budgeted FTEs (20 percent) were reported within library development, and 1,276.3 budgeted FTEs (48 percent) were reported within library services. The remaining 452.3 FTE positions (17 percent) were allocated to other services.

Services

- According to FY 2016 survey data, primary services SLAAs provide to libraries and library cooperatives include consulting, administrative library system support, LSTA statewide grant programs, and LSTA statewide services. Most SLAAs provided each of these services.

- During FY 2016, 49 SLAAs (96 percent) provided some form of consulting services to libraries and library cooperatives, with the most common forms identified as library management or organizational development (96 percent), continuing education (94 percent), youth services (96 percent), technology and connectivity (92 percent), and E-Rate consulting (90 percent).
- Fifty SLAAs provided assistance for continuing education programs to at least one type of library in FY 2016. In addition, 44 SLAAs (86 percent) reported having statewide reading programs. The most common target audiences for SLAA reading programs were the middle childhood and early childhood groups.
- Thirty-five SLAAs (69 percent) provided some type of literacy program in FY 2016. The most commonly offered literacy program was on digital literacy, offered by 33 SLAAs (65 percent), followed by information literacy and language literacy, both offered by 29 SLAAs (57 percent).
- Operational assistance describes services provided by SLAAs to assist and support the development of libraries or to link libraries to external networks. Although the majority of SLAAs provided assistance in the form of interlibrary loan referral and reference referral services (84 and 82 percent, respectively) in FY 2016, only about half provided cooperative purchasing of materials.
- Coordination and integration of library services include working with the materials, services, and programs designed to meet users' needs. By far, SLAAs provided statewide resource-sharing services more than other coordination and integration services in FY 2016. Statewide resource sharing describes organized efforts to support the sharing of services and materials. Only a small share of SLAAs provided support for coordination on acquisitions using other federal program funds (29 percent).

Library Acquisition Expenditures, 2019–2020: U.S. Public, Academic, Special, and Government Libraries

The information in these tables is taken from the 2020–2021 edition of *American Library Directory* (*ALD*) (Information Today, Inc.). The tables report acquisition expenditures by public, academic, special, and government libraries.

Understanding the Tables

Number of libraries includes only those U.S. libraries in *ALD* that reported annual acquisition expenditures. Libraries that reported annual income but not expenditures are not included in the count. Academic libraries include university, college, and junior college libraries. Special academic libraries, such as law and medical libraries, that reported acquisition expenditures separately from the institution's main library are counted as independent libraries.

The amount in the *total acquisition expenditures* column for a given state is generally greater than the sum of the categories of expenditures. This is because the total acquisition expenditures amount also includes the expenditures of libraries that did not itemize by category.

Figures in *categories of expenditure* columns represent only those libraries that itemized expenditures. Libraries that reported a total acquisition expenditure amount but did not itemize are only represented in the total acquisition expenditures column.

Table 1 / Public Library Acquisition Expenditures

State	Number of Libraries	Total Acquisition Expenditures	Category of Expenditures (in U.S. dollars)								
			Books	Other Print Materials	Periodicals/ Serials	Manuscripts & Archives	AV Equipment	AV Materials	Microforms	Electronic Reference	Preservation
Alabama	9	2,310,248	500,369	11,091	6,087	0	4,700	30,750	0	87,055	20,200
Alaska	9	1,854,186	893,275	17,876	85,635	43,021	0	292,211	500	228,457	6,871
Arizona	16	16,989,050	2,522,963	88,424	93,630	575	0	1,090,769	0	377,384	0
Arkansas	6	705,549	263,433	250	21,274	500	0	39,307	0	42,186	0
California	44	69,505,933	23,951,920	131,195	1,440,837	6,500	43,417	8,247,886	39,578	10,321,386	68,161
Colorado	12	13,267,558	3,925,626	434,162	363,509	0	15,000	1,951,007	0	2,343,522	0
Connecticut	33	17,999,884	1,997,552	8,138	579,670	4,705	0	479,626	1,080	848,988	39,362
Delaware	2	71,429	40,000	0	5,000	0	0	0	0	0	0
District of Columbia	0	0	0	0	0	0	0	0	0	0	0
Florida	25	22,955,846	10,341,879	844,731	878,789	0	52,514	3,682,273	39,305	5,229,386	0
Georgia	10	2,046,769	838,643	42,253	72,331	0	2,026	252,210	1,850	231,928	198
Hawaii	1	4,667,509	2,792,035	58,456	136,482	0	0	0	36,042	1,644,494	0
Idaho	6	536,487	116,220	1,736	82	0	0	6,261	0	11,360	0
Illinois	68	87,242,565	10,355,629	9,718	459,112	3,000	38,594	3,054,653	8,250	4,420,914	4,000
Indiana	41	24,411,411	8,917,891	800	1,005,413	0	127,840	4,024,747	15,854	5,211,123	0
Iowa	41	4,620,144	1,737,192	55,884	124,847	4,000	9,840	569,540	5,690	467,861	0
Kansas	24	4,819,187	1,068,809	0	113,883	0	4,300	356,881	5,000	98,664	3,600
Kentucky	18	11,638,251	2,288,848	109,345	292,249	0	30,224	917,954	0	1,800,921	40,776
Louisiana	8	11,311,550	4,099,234	58,554	432,787	0	175,561	1,523,634	5,582	3,455,769	0
Maine	19	1,017,062	309,874	1,000	72,005	2,000	5,000	69,103	800	237,102	1,000
Maryland	2	7,791,058	0	0	0	0	0	0	0	0	0
Massachusetts	44	10,988,418	2,489,900	49,954	296,509	0	2,717	832,708	10,734	545,156	700
Michigan	47	25,843,002	3,517,978	176,532	307,788	0	30,000	1,157,614	10,038	1,024,493	500
Minnesota	17	78,051,055	1,738,299	64,813	20,830	0	83	323,916	3,898	415,231	516
Mississippi	5	819,046	471,781	0	80,664	0	0	28,981	26,000	149,093	2,162

Missouri	23	17,483,046	4,323,905	183,329	309,935	0	10,045	2,074,545	32,651	2,839,069	150
Montana	14	1,016,913	427,571	98,472	65,874	200	4,373	139,490	0	100,382	7,302
Nebraska	18	11,364,475	232,114	119,000	17,966	0	47	43,968	440	1,406,775	0
Nevada	3	378,269	123,010	0	12,878	0	0	34,565	0	23,084	894
New Hampshire	25	685,031	393,396	1,031	17,578	0	0	97,000	600	68,309	400
New Jersey	40	14,947,906	9,319,047	106,614	790,970	500	21,500	1,732,134	71,000	1,275,043	6,956
New Mexico	11	2,837,265	1,507,625	214,272	48,238	0	6,000	313,914	9,013	470,450	0
New York	75	37,662,487	12,747,519	49,236	805,305	0	219,754	2,229,600	40,210	2,062,128	3,950
North Carolina	8	5,454,751	764,686	33,103	57,754	0	7,000	177,157	1,040	34,682	0
North Dakota	9	1,498,975	510,503	300	45,579	0	0	97,880	2,000	300,005	1,000
Ohio	39	57,888,625	14,851,544	323,775	2,371,106	1,031	44,457	7,501,455	244,600	9,401,494	197,013
Oklahoma	13	13,024,342	4,866,187	4,546	859,468	0	0	2,177,435	4,485	1,900,882	0
Oregon	16	3,804,502	1,675,175	0	149,257	0	3,500	760,371	7,065	210,894	0
Pennsylvania	39	19,123,340	3,366,301	846,770	666,131	156,260	2,226	2,096,672	164,604	1,197,308	234,155
Rhode Island	7	9,796,968	573,670	71,214	45,579	0	0	144,170	70	861,204	650
South Carolina	9	9,828,680	2,646,583	31,426	114,500	0	0	4,858,473	0	647,398	0
South Dakota	8	2,186,629	817,391	15,756	61,425	0	16,846	326,127	2,558	294,882	0
Tennessee	12	4,976,175	23,731,900	276,606	720,857	1,000	2,438,770	8,658,606	0	18,428,323	12,107
Texas	70	45,912,789	4,809,871	2,535	300,330	0	14,827	964,255	11,520	1,292,067	34,700
Utah	7	3,042,543	1,211,389	0	7,000	0	0	666,678	0	326,538	0
Vermont	16	488,359	264,721	90	17,517	215	0	82,445	0	33,651	500
Virginia	21	9,977,219	3,871,469	150,148	300,027	41,810	22,043	1,283,140	23,844	1,440,675	1,336,701
Washington	13	4,638,456	896,665	65,834	70,062	0	1,975	249,160	622	318,082	400
West Virginia	7	1,234,244	515,558	3,000	47,100	0	0	152,366	13,500	239,356	1,500
Wisconsin	41	5,198,309	2,021,138	75,260	109,167	0	15,952	674,772	2,746	278,325	0
Wyoming	6	734,217	97,878	0	4,710	0	0	15,727	0	0	0
Puerto Rico	0	0	0	0	0	0	0	0	0	0	0
Total	1,057	706,647,712	181,746,166	4,837,229	14,905,726	265,317	3,371,131	66,484,136	842,769	84,643,479	2,026,424
Estimated % of Acquisition Expenditures			25.72	0.68	2.11	0.04	0.48	9.41	0.12	11.98	0.29

Table 2 / Academic Library Acquisition Expenditures

State	Number of Libraries	Total Acquisition Expenditures	Category of Expenditures (in U.S. dollars)								
			Books	Other Print Materials	Periodicals/ Serials	Manuscripts & Archives	AV Equipment	AV Materials	Microforms	Electronic Reference	Preservation
Alabama	7	4,414,197	325,768	6,031	2,095,794	0	0	38,322	0	876,910	29,807
Alaska	2	1,900,000	200,000	20,000	1,600,000	0	0	17,500	2,500	50,000	0
Arizona	3	2,625,186	20,330	0	42,850	0	0	750	0	241,924	0
Arkansas	6	9,920,924	979,276	419,834	5,626,174	34,264	2,000	28,472	426,218	511,257	6,187
California	36	70,648,519	2,991,358	548,107	5,588,989	102,199	37,081	157,711	26,433	10,439,597	110,659
Colorado	9	17,524,669	1,136,926	24,832	477,205	0	0	119,339	0	5,056,113	27,747
Connecticut	7	10,331,989	956,684	32,628	2,933,898	0	80,000	25,127	0	617,150	13,276
Delaware	2	12,839,012	0	0	0	0	0	0	0	0	0
District of Columbia	2	6,803,069	439,600	110,000	1,803,000	0	0	3,267	34,380	1,409,960	47,000
Florida	12	32,001,261	3,396,763	252,370	14,084,355	0	0	269,124	88,340	8,503,416	106,106
Georgia	10	19,574,433	495,652	0	79,273	0	98	26,150	0	1,745,558	300
Hawaii	0	0	0	0	0	0	0	0	0	0	0
Idaho	1	4,318,101	0	0	0	0	0	0	0	0	0
Illinois	23	51,305,737	1,387,334	7,648	2,970,242	0	0	73,767	20,779	2,260,088	69,337
Indiana	12	15,821,376	1,233,491	20,385	4,379,176	0	18	45,190	4,496	2,666,832	23,506
Iowa	13	22,481,257	2,069,601	391,576	5,745,004	0	6,000	53,816	33,353	2,017,613	79,027
Kansas	10	7,404,440	431,607	300	6,044,560	3,000	0	18,181	1,000	625,912	26,800
Kentucky	6	13,282,878	128,841	17,945	1,300,620	0	2,886	1,062	14,722	272,628	4,969
Louisiana	7	4,439,751	238,280	2,935	1,704,474	500	0	4,935	36,508	1,839,629	23,182
Maine	3	10,402,740	1,264,860	177,656	7,564,612	0	0	0	53,849	475,000	32,730
Maryland	12	11,463,723	1,514,628	34,648	8,361,219	12,434	0	39,469	6,642	1,368,821	49,919
Massachusetts	10	23,434,382	953,866	0	2,453,607	36,000	19,011	63,560	1,550	7,327,776	132,781
Michigan	20	22,113,274	1,952,014	65,821	9,025,889	5,203	0	146,324	1,358,172	6,339,714	43,611
Minnesota	9	5,583,056	655,240	10,000	1,694,494	8,200	53,955	79,268	18,459	1,047,655	41,311
Mississippi	1	96,040	10,000	0	2,700	0	0	0	0	83,340	0

Missouri	16	11,633,600	473,143	0	1,784,172	8,767	4,120	101,474	115,045	884,929	31,576
Montana	1	172,720	69,825	0	74,192	0	0	0	0	0	0
Nebraska	6	15,219,553	396,613	89,831	2,112,046	15,000	0	62,021	66,665	1,674,700	16,480
Nevada	0	0	0	0	0	0	0	0	0	0	0
New Hampshire	0	0	0	0	0	0	0	0	0	0	0
New Jersey	9	60,243,579	983,438	0	2,553,516	1,000	0	21,329	0	1,966,247	4,732
New Mexico	3	3,315,114	133,311	0	2,684,913	11,802	0	15,878	16,450	107,334	27,574
New York	32	39,582,781	6,670,347	251,509	10,118,948	29,596	66,463	265,080	48,644	9,373,193	242,392
North Carolina	18	71,297,049	1,023,737	82,542	3,699,115	0	1,106,546	136,814	157,167	1,026,945	13,000
North Dakota	2	2,965,537	365,806	0	2,011,935	0	0	30,752	684	539,766	16,594
Ohio	19	32,153,117	2,199,883	0	3,619,047	3,682	9,998	123,472	18,913	983,139	49,204
Oklahoma	5	4,570,905	197,109	575	2,518,918	1,000	0	2,433	0	970,780	9,717
Oregon	6	21,683,521	742,555	0	2,418,862	0	32,779	70,337	0	625,837	18,704
Pennsylvania	18	11,870,621	1,397,440	8,603	2,616,624	1,688	0	77,600	23,791	2,447,291	29,233
Rhode Island	3	1,855,603	439,983	0	925,966	5,840	0	23,270	3,000	450,870	6,674
South Carolina	6	6,381,487	1,021,816	289,130	769,178	20,000	137,300	87,153	60,264	2,450,960	47,510
South Dakota	2	2,587,077	240,113	0	1,735,145	0	718	18,515	2,816	106,460	24,476
Tennessee	8	6,345,282	266,242	0	753,668	0	0	38,858	8,900	808,346	1,613
Texas	26	53,594,567	4,458,397	20,000	15,642,577	5,050	89,327	150,651	67,935	4,855,369	111,716
Utah	3	7,930,967	449,582	0	445,188	0	5,000	35,458	0	206,205	21,249
Vermont	2	1,307,596	219,613	4,240	934,697	0	0	27,815	0	116,359	4,872
Virginia	10	26,546,240	3,269,091	0	6,680,183	0	0	215,634	11,903	4,570,793	57,528
Washington	7	9,821,770	1,053,338	0	5,985,979	2,000	27,400	46,173	6,000	669,491	5,000
West Virginia	7	2,611,839	140,867	57	69,386	6,750	14,300	11,792	11,017	411,206	7,500
Wisconsin	7	9,684,844	312,534	1,720	650,480	1,879	0	75,861	982	1,544,877	1,755
Wyoming	0	0	0	0	0	0	0	0	0	0	0
Puerto Rico	5	549,862	136,347	5,000	175,702	5,000	3,263	8,802	0	212,948	2,300
Total	444	784,655,245	49,443,249	2,895,923	156,558,572	320,854	1,698,263	2,858,506	2,747,577	92,780,938	1,619,654
Estimated % of Acquisition Expenditures			6.30	0.37	19.95	0.04	0.22	0.36	0.35	11.82	0.21

Table 3 / Special Library Acquisition Expenditures

State	Number of Libraries	Total Acquisition Expenditures	Category of Expenditures (in U.S. dollars)								
			Books	Other Print Materials	Periodicals/ Serials	Manuscripts & Archives	AV Equipment	AV Materials	Microforms	Electronic Reference	Preservation
Alabama	0	0	0	0	0	0	0	0	0	0	0
Alaska	0	0	0	0	0	0	0	0	0	0	0
Arizona	2	5,324	3,500	0	324	0	0	0	0	0	1,000
Arkansas	0	0	0	0	0	0	0	0	0	0	0
California	7	304,464	114,834	0	49,122	600	0	24,090	0	85,088	730
Colorado	0	0	0	0	0	0	0	0	0	0	0
Connecticut	1	1,000	0	0	0	0	0	0	0	0	0
Delaware	0	0	0	0	0	0	0	0	0	0	0
District of Columbia	2	71,000	48,000	0	20,000	0	0	0	2,000	0	1,000
Florida	0	0	0	0	0	0	0	0	0	0	0
Georgia	0	0	0	0	0	0	0	0	0	0	0
Hawaii	0	0	0	0	0	0	0	0	0	0	0
Idaho	0	0	0	0	0	0	0	0	0	0	0
Illinois	5	4,241,500	53,300	30,000	58,500	4,000	0	2,200	0	51,500	5,000
Indiana	1	86,000	0	0	0	0	0	0	0	0	0
Iowa	1	10,000	0	0	0	0	0	0	0	0	0
Kansas	1	6,000	3,000	0	3,000	0	0	0	0	0	0
Kentucky	0	0	0	0	0	0	0	0	0	0	0
Louisiana	1	18,000	5,000	0	13,000	0	0	0	0	0	0
Maine	0	0	0	0	0	0	0	0	0	0	0
Maryland	1	1,000	500	0	300	100	0	0	0	0	100
Massachusetts	0	0	0	0	0	0	0	0	0	0	0
Michigan	0	0	0	0	0	0	0	0	0	0	0
Minnesota	1	50,000	20,000	5,000	9,000	0	0	0	0	16,000	0
Mississippi	0	0	0	0	0	0	0	0	0	0	0

Missouri	0	0	0	0	0	0	0	0	0	0	0
Montana	0	0	0	0	0	0	0	0	0	0	0
Nebraska	0	0	0	0	0	0	0	0	0	0	0
Nevada	0	0	0	0	0	0	0	0	0	0	0
New Hampshire	2	92,000	16,000	10,000	5,000	20,000	0	0	0	32,000	9,000
New Jersey	3	24,700	12,500	0	2,500	2,000	0	0	0	2,000	2,700
New Mexico	1	2,500	1,000	0	1,000	0	0	0	0	0	500
New York	8	500,716	257,665	0	47,178	0	4,000	0	0	38,475	152,500
North Carolina	0	0	0	0	0	0	0	0	0	0	0
North Dakota	1	8,098	2,660	0	3,975	0	0	0	0	0	1,463
Ohio	2	518,259	10,300	0	225	1,536	0	100	0	6,085	0
Oklahoma	1	160,000	8,000	0	45,000	0	0	0	0	0	0
Oregon	0	0	0	0	0	0	0	0	0	0	0
Pennsylvania	0	0	0	0	0	0	0	0	0	0	0
Rhode Island	0	0	0	0	0	0	0	0	0	0	0
South Carolina	0	0	0	0	0	0	0	0	0	0	0
South Dakota	1	105,000	0	0	0	0	0	0	0	0	0
Tennessee	0	0	0	0	0	0	0	0	0	0	0
Texas	3	1,582,030	3,030	12,000	2,000	0	0	0	0	805,000	0
Utah	1	75,000	5,000	5,000	10,000	0	5,000	0	0	50,000	0
Vermont	0	0	0	0	0	0	0	0	0	0	0
Virginia	4	183,337	86,409	82	47,060	4,026	0	0	0	44,000	1,740
Washington	1	19,800	7,000	0	10,200	0	0	0	0	0	2,600
West Virginia	0	0	0	0	0	0	0	0	0	0	0
Wisconsin	2	85,500	4,000	0	20,000	0	0	0	0	60,000	0
Wyoming	0	0	0	0	0	0	0	0	0	0	0
Puerto Rico	0	0	0	0	0	0	0	0	0	0	0
Total	53	8,151,228	661,698	62,082	347,384	32,262	9,000	26,390	2,000	1,190,148	178,333
Estimated % of Acquisition Expenditures			8.12	0.76	4.26	0.40	0.11	0.32	0.02	14.60	2.19

Table 4 / Government Library Acquisition Expenditures

State	Number of Libraries	Total Acquisition Expenditures	Category of Expenditures (in U.S. dollars)								
			Books	Other Print Materials	Periodicals/ Serials	Manuscripts & Archives	AV Equipment	AV Materials	Microforms	Electronic Reference	Preservation
Alabama	1	275,000	75,000	0	0	0	0	0	0	200,000	0
Alaska	0	0	0	0	0	0	0	0	0	0	0
Arizona	1	2,012	2,000	0	12	0	0	0	0	0	0
Arkansas	0	0	0	0	0	0	0	0	0	0	0
California	4	539,005	234,264	0	1,442	0	0	0	0	145,582	0
Colorado	0	0	0	0	0	0	0	0	0	0	0
Connecticut	0	0	0	0	0	0	0	0	0	0	0
Delaware	0	0	0	0	0	0	0	0	0	0	0
District of Columbia	0	0	0	0	0	0	0	0	0	0	0
Florida	0	0	0	0	0	0	0	0	0	0	0
Georgia	0	0	0	0	0	0	0	0	0	0	0
Hawaii	0	0	0	0	0	0	0	0	0	0	0
Idaho	0	0	0	0	0	0	0	0	0	0	0
Illinois	0	0	0	0	0	0	0	0	0	0	0
Indiana	0	0	0	0	0	0	0	0	0	0	0
Iowa	0	0	0	0	0	0	0	0	0	0	0
Kansas	1	515,260	26,852	0	396,491	0	0	0	0	85,690	6,227
Kentucky	0	0	0	0	0	0	0	0	0	0	0
Louisiana	2	1,803,887	615,201	0	54,114	0	0	1,000	887	263,521	8,034
Maine	1	380,116	0	0	0	0	0	0	0	0	0
Maryland	1	37,000	5,000	0	32,000	0	0	0	0	0	0
Massachusetts	0	0	0	0	0	0	0	0	0	0	0
Michigan	0	0	0	0	0	0	0	0	0	0	0
Minnesota	1	74,500	10,000	0	45,500	0	0	0	0	19,000	0
Mississippi	0	0	0	0	0	0	0	0	0	0	0

Missouri	0	0	0	0	0	0	0	0	0	0	0
Montana	0	0	0	0	0	0	0	0	0	0	0
Nebraska	0	0	0	0	0	0	0	0	0	0	0
Nevada	0	0	0	0	0	0	0	0	0	0	0
New Hampshire	0	0	0	0	0	0	0	0	0	0	0
New Jersey	0	0	0	0	0	0	0	0	0	0	0
New Mexico	0	0	0	0	0	0	0	0	0	0	0
New York	0	0	0	0	0	0	0	0	0	0	0
North Carolina	0	0	0	0	0	0	0	0	0	0	0
North Dakota	0	0	0	0	0	0	0	0	0	0	0
Ohio	0	0	0	0	0	0	0	0	0	0	0
Oklahoma	0	0	0	0	0	0	0	0	0	0	0
Oregon	0	0	0	0	0	0	0	0	0	0	0
Pennsylvania	1	125,000	0	0	0	0	0	0	0	0	0
Rhode Island	0	0	0	0	0	0	0	0	0	0	0
South Carolina	0	0	0	0	0	0	0	0	0	0	0
South Dakota	0	0	0	0	0	0	0	0	0	0	0
Tennessee	0	0	0	0	0	0	0	0	0	0	0
Texas	0	0	0	0	0	0	0	0	0	0	0
Utah	0	0	0	0	0	0	0	0	0	0	0
Vermont	0	0	0	0	0	0	0	0	0	0	0
Virginia	0	0	0	0	0	0	0	0	0	0	0
Washington	0	0	0	0	0	0	0	0	0	0	0
West Virginia	1	650,000	50,000	0	400,000	0	0	0	0	200,000	0
Wisconsin	1	10,000	0	0	0	0	0	0	0	0	0
Wyoming	0	0	0	0	0	0	0	0	0	0	0
Puerto Rico	0	0	0	0	0	0	0	0	0	0	0
Total	15	4,411,780	1,018,317	0	929,559	0	0	1,000	887	913,793	14,261
Estimated % of Acquisition Expenditures			23.08	0.00	21.07	0.00	0.00	0.02	0.02	20.71	0.32

Year in Architecture 2019: Where Function Meets Fabulous

Library Journal Staff

If you're looking for drama, you'll find it in some of the stunning design on display in *Library Journal's* 2019 Year in Architecture roundup. Among these projects, the unique roof on the Anna C. Mott branch at Ohio's Toledo Lucas County Public Library gives a grand hat tip to its abolitionist namesake, while the Norman Public Library in Oklahoma offers a contemplative prospect. Across the country, the shapes of new and remodeled libraries alike are functional, flexible, and fabulous, making their mark through smart design choices large and small.

Among the trends we saw, the continuing emphasis on outdoor space and room for relaxation collide and produce reading porches. Nooks created through modular furniture, fixturing, and built-ins help create cozy separate places for adults and kids within the larger open spaces that are inherently flexible. Raw roofs that let the systems hang out in plain sight reflect an industrial trend, warmed up by wood finishes and sometimes literal fireplaces. And stair seating continues its upward climb.

College kids never had it so good. New academic building projects prioritize warm study spaces and connection to nature; several have extensive green roofs to introduce new outdoor access. Public libraries continue to take shape around the people who use them, offering a full range of approaches to matching convening space with access to materials and building in experiences along the way. These new buildings and additions and renovations will give anyone hankering to build plenty of inspiration.

Taking the Long View

The new Norman Public Library East branch of the Pioneer Library System, Oklahoma, which features flexible spaces inside and an outdoor programming area, is oriented to take full advantage of its site. Clerestory windows bring in an abundance of natural light and accentuate the unbroken prairie views; passive sustainable design strategies include stormwater management and a thermally treated exterior.

Heart of Glass

Temple University's new 220,000-square-foot Charles Library in Philadelphia, Pennsylvania, offers contrasts of lines and materials inside and out, starting with a granite slab–clad exterior wrapped around sidewalk-to-roof windows. Large wooden arches, which double as entryways, add drama to the light-filled interior. Cedar and steel finishes add warmth and sleek lines to the three-story domed

Adapted from *Library Journal*, November 14, 2019. For the Year in Architecture 2019, *Library Journal* solicited information from academic and public libraries nationwide that had undergone new builds and renovation/addition projects completed between July 1, 2018, and June 30, 2019.

central atrium, visually connected to upper levels by a central oculus. A 70 percent green roof and perennial reading garden bring nature—and sustainable design—to the campus.

Stepping Up

Through the children's portal to the main Westport Library, Connecticut, users can see the grandstand structure featuring carpeted stepped seating. Talk about a perch with prospect.

Stairs as seating continue to trend. A grand example with colorful cushion accents at Brambleton Library, Loudon County, Virginia, connects the two levels with an expansive open feeling. A glass side wall preserves sightlines and provides safety while helping to block noise.

Updates Bring the Outside In

The Jack R. Hunt Library occupies the third and fourth floors of the new student athenaeum at Embry-Riddle Aeronautical University, Daytona Beach, Florida. The bird-in-flight–inspired steel and glass building serves as a campus beacon; a central interior spine supports a dynamic 200-foot arching ribbed skylight and surrounding windows to flood the interior with light. Cool modern blue and white finishes, echoing the abundance of sky, set off a variety of seating and work options throughout the 42,000-square-foot library.

Princeton University's Firestone Library renovation seamlessly blends the original Gothic exterior with fresh, contemporary updates. Housing for special collections, museum-quality exhibition spaces, and specialized research support services have been given updated, harmonious finishes throughout the 430,000-square-foot library, with glass walls maximizing natural light in open study and work spaces. Lighting sensors, thermally insulated windows with UV control glazing, chilled beam technology for energy-efficient heating and cooling, a green roof, and LED light fixtures significantly reduce energy use.

The Cheryl and Philip Milstein Center for Teaching and Learning at Barnard College spans multiple levels inside and out. Walkways and outdoor terraces connect the Manhattan campus with the 128,000-square-foot library's many spaces and services, accessed via a series of interior staircases that serve as a visual signature throughout. On the exterior, patinated zinc shingles complement the surrounding buildings, and green roofs help reduce trapped heat, cut energy use and storm water runoff, and offer inviting study spaces.

Taking It Outside

Upgrades to Florida's Sanibel Public Library extend from infrastructure to finishes. A new business center, makerspace, and children's and teen spaces are enhanced by interior and exterior palettes reflecting the natural surroundings. Warm woods and white beach stones enhance custom cabinetry, seashore patterns and colors add cheer to flooring and furnishings, and an expanded outdoor porch offers readers a view.

The new Borrego Springs Library of San Diego County Library, California, celebrates the surrounding desert and sky with long horizontal planes that float above the desert floor, thanks to pilings that offset flash flood risk, and a large open patio. The building was designed for Zero Net Energy, and is co-located with a county park and sheriff's office.

The challenge of modernizing the Gutekunst Public Library in State Center, Iowa, while protecting the character of the 1924 historic building was achieved with a connected addition. The new, "respectful" extension provides flexible spaces for community and library use, new staff workroom, clear sight lines, and a wraparound reading porch with a view of the town's Main Street, all accessible via a central elevator connecting all floors.

Renovations to the Mission Branch Library of the City of Santa Clara Library System, California, offer improved interior spaces, tech upgrades, an expansive patio with natural plantings, and upgraded energy efficiency in a modern, vibrant space that reflects its Bay Area community. Sunshine-hued accents, a natural wood ceiling, and floor-to-ceiling windows bring the outdoors in.

The new Dublin Branch of the Columbus Metropolitan Library, Ohio, features a rain garden that not only adds beauty and natural connection to the 41,000-square-foot, three-story new building, but also contributes to its sustainability, along with 83.66 tons of demolition debris that was diverted from landfills and used or recycled.

Opposites Attract

Quiet and loud: The quiet zone, enclosed by a glass wall, encourages concentration at Galaxie Library, Dakota County Library, Apple Valley, Minnesota, while the deep blue walls subtly continue the galaxy theme. For those who need even more tranquility, a small calming space allows overstimulated patrons to take a break.

Old and new: Joining an 1869 Victorian mansion to a former Masonic hall to create Keene Public Library, the largest library in New Hampshire (70,000 square feet), an elegant two-story glass connector manages to marry a modern entry and community hub with its historic surroundings.

Public and private: Chicago Public Library's new Northtown Branch is the third co-located housing and library combo built through a partnership with the Chicago Housing Authority. The ground floor will house the library's community space, children's area with early-learning play zone, YOUmedia for teens, and adult reading and computer sections, while the housing above will provide 44 senior housing units, 14 affordable.

Land and sea: Designed in collaboration with the community that has concerns about development, the Half Moon Bay Library, California, is made to fit into its residential neighborhood while subtly reflecting its coastal location and the area's agricultural roots, through warm, stained Douglas Fir wood and translucent white panels intended to evoke ocean fog.

Inside and out: A multipurpose room on the top floor of the three-story, glass and stucco addition to the Missouri City Branch Library, Fort Bend County Libraries,

(text continues on page 316)

Table 1 / New Academic Buildings, 2019

Institution	Project Cost	Gross Area (Sq. Ft.)	Sq. Ft. Cost	Constr. Cost	Furniture/ Equip. Cost	Seating Capacity	Architect
Charles Library, Temple University, Philadelphia, Pa.	$175,000,000	220,000	$618	$135,854,000	$15,195,000	1,800	Snøhetta
Cheryl and Philip Milstein Center for Teaching and Learning, Barnard College, New York, N.Y.	137,000,000	128,000	n.a.	n.a.	n.a.	n.a.	Skidmore, Owings & Merrill LLP
Jack R. Hunt Library, Embry-Riddle Aeronautical University, Daytona Beach, Fla.	70,000,000	222,000	284	63,000,000	1,000,000	400	ikon.5 architects

Table 2 / Academic Library Buildings, Additions and Renovations, 2019

Institution	Project Cost	Gross Area (Sq. Ft.)	Sq. Ft. Cost	Constr. Cost	Furniture/ Equip. Cost	Seating Capacity	Architect
Harvey S. Firestone Memorial Library, Princeton University, Princeton, N.J.	$140,000,000	430,000	n.a.	n.a.	n.a.	n.a.	Shepley Bulfinch; Frederick Fisher and Partners of Los Angeles
John M. Olin Library, Washington University, St. Louis, Mo.	20,000,000	45,800	n.a.	n.a.	n.a.	570	Ann Beha Architects; V Three Studios LLC
Wisconsin School of Business Learning Commons, University of Wisconsin, Madison, Wisc.	11,000,000	35,000	192	6,727,900	1,806,300	645	Potter Lawson; MSR Design
Boston University Alumni Medical Library, Boston University Medical Campus, Boston	4,055,000	13,000	269	3,500,000	555,000	231	Finegold Alexander Architects
Connelly Library, La Salle University, Philadelphia, Pa.	1,847,000	19,000	79	1,500,000	347,000	200	Kimmel Bogrette Architecture + Site
Learning Lab—Bizzell Memorial Library, University of Oklahoma, Norman, Okla.	850,000	6,000	100	600,000	250,000	177	REES Associates Inc.

Table 3 / New Public Library Buildings, 2019

Community	Pop. ('000)	Code	Project Cost	Constr. Cost	Gross Area (Sq. Ft.)	Sq. Ft. Cost	Equip. Cost	Architect
California								
Borrego Springs	5	B	$13,410,000	$10,500,000	14,100	$744.68	$750,000	Roesling Nakamura Terada Architects
Half Moon Bay	28	B	25,000,000	19,000,000	22,000	863.64	1,000,000	Noll & Tam Architects
Los Angeles	827	B	8,323,000	6,485,000	7,797	831.73	617,000	Withee Malcolm Architects
Colorado								
Edgewater	6	B	2,423,728	1,546,497	10,000	154.65	654,568	RATIO | HPA
District of Columbia								
Cleveland Park	63	B	19,100,000	n.a.	28,850	n.a.	260,000	Perkins Eastman DC
Florida								
Tampa	45	M	7,072,161	5,681,000	24,000	236.71	800,000	FleischmanGarcia Architecture
Georgia								
Valdosta	115	MS	6,393,165	3,449,168	36,128	95.47	651,818	BFB Gladwin Architects
Illinois								
Chicago	48	O	10,994,355	9,036,304	16,300	554.37	75,000	Perkins + Will
Chicago	93	O	9,349,026	7,301,952	12,800	570.47	117,930	John Ronan Architects
Chicago	43	O	7,216,018	5,619,983	15,700	357.96	242,995	Skidmore, Owings and Merrill
Indiana								
Indianapolis	61	B	7,235,981	5,683,570	20,050	283.47	377,898	krM Architecture
New Palestine	59	B	5,700,000	4,000,000	15,000	266.67	300,000	krM Architecture
Kansas								
Lenexa	44	B	21,150,000	16,950,000	39,000	434.62	1,750,000	Holzman Moss Bottino Architecture; Hollis + Miller Architects
Kentucky								
Hebron	130	B	13,612,356	8,127,000	26,000	312.58	1,345,045	Brandstetter Carroll, Inc.

Symbol Code: B—Branch Library; BS—Branch & System Headquarters; M—Main Library; MS—Main & System Headquarters; S—System Headquarters; O—Combined Use Space; n.a.—not available

Louisiana								
New Orleans	11	B	4,512,812	3,756,157	7,800	481.56	756,655	Manning Architects
Missouri								
St. Louis	26	B	11,325,748	6,500,000	21,000	309.52	290,000	Bond Architects; Mackey Mitchell Associates
St. Louis	50	B	6,412,785	5,500,000	21,685	257.43	310,000	Bond Architects; Mackey Mitchell Associates
Nebraska								
Ravenna	1	M	1,400,000	1,281,700	7,000	183.10	29,700	Miller & Associates
North Carolina								
Wilmington	110	B	6,667,000	5,705,755	19,500	292.60	420,055	Vines Architecture
Ohio								
Columbus	18	B	9,323,433	6,574,401	18,000	365.24	347,700	Moody Nolan
Dayton	30	B	8,022,386	6,079,496	21,031	289.07	641,369	Ruetchle Architects
Dublin	66	B	21,100,000	14,949,731	41,000	364.63	784,269	NBBJ
Toledo	13	B	10,802,711	8,946,266	18,953	472.02	389,760	Bostwick Design Partnership; Buehrer Group Architecture and Engineering, Inc.
Oklahoma								
Norman	53	B	6,032,204	4,457,171	12,000	371.43	920,910	MSR Design: The McKinney Partnership Architects
Tennessee								
Murfreesboro	289	B	2,200,000	1,768,236	5,950	297.18	412,296	Johnson + Bailey
Texas								
Houston	39	BS	8,303,675	5,962,790	23,779	250.76	902,998	AUTOARCH Architects
Virginia								
Brambleton	400	B	9,300,000	4,200,000	40,629	103.37	4,000,000	HGA
Canada								
Calgary	1,200	M	176,250,000	n.a.	240,000	n.a.	n.a.	Snøhetta; DIALOG
Winnipeg	44	M	6,515,000	5,218,133	13,500	386.53	277,480	Cibinel Architecture

Symbol Code: B—Branch Library; BS—Branch & System Headquarters; M—Main Library; MS—Main & System Headquarters; S—System Headquarters; O—Combined Use Space; n.a.—not available

(continued from page 312)

Texas, opens onto a balcony with views of the community, used for public special events as well as library-hosted ones.

Raising the Roof

In Ohio, Toledo Lucas County Public Library's new Mott branch, named for social activist Anna C. Mott, is topped by a dynamic roof inspired by geometries used in Underground Railroad quilts. The overhang is calibrated to shade high summer light but let in low winter light.

The children's area at the Thornhill Branch, St. Louis County Library, Missouri, features reading nooks and playful passages to make the space itself echo the experiences of comfort, discovery, and reflection that reading represents.

Kids can keep moving at the Michigan Road Branch of the Indianapolis Public Library, Indiana, which integrates toddler-height pass-throughs right into its shelving so active play actively connects to the collection.

The library drive-through in the parking garage adjacent to the main building of Lenexa City Center Library, Kansas, allows patrons to pick up holds without being exposed to weather and drop off book returns right into the automated conveyance system.

Defining Spaces

The demonstration kitchen at the expanded and remodeled Centennial Branch of the Anoka County Library, Minnesota, features a close-up camera that shows (and records) exactly what's cooking. The room doubles as a makerspace and can open to the main library through sliding glass doors for larger events.

In restoring the South Branch of Cleveland Public Library, Ohio, an original Carnegie building, designers were tasked with carrying out unrealized 1911 plans for an addition and updating for modern library service. Modern accents patterned on the historic building's geometry pair with original dark woodwork and shelving.

An innovative facing and shelving arrangement of the media collection at Ohio's Auglaize County Library's Wapakoneta Branch creates a room within a room feel while preserving the option of flexible rearrangement as circulation shifts to digital and the footprint contracts.

By clustering its collection into a concentrated island of shelving rather than traditional stacks, Pittsburgh's Baldwin Borough Public Library frees up flexible space for seating that can be used for tutoring, as a summer teen hangout, and as a community meeting place.

Table 4 / Public Library Buildings, Additions and Renovations, 2019

Community	Pop. ('000)	Code	Project Cost	Constr. Cost	Gross Area (Sq. Ft.)	Sq. Ft. Cost	Equip. Cost	Architect
Alabama								
Pinson	7	M	$1,831,230	$1,380,000	8,686	$158.88	$185,000	Hendon Huckestein Architects
Arizona								
Tucson	30	B	3,400,000	2,550,000	8,000	318.75	200,000	Line and Space
California								
Santa Clara	28	B	4,998,608	4,259,000	8,400	507.02	190,608	Noll & Tam Architects
Connecticut								
Westport	28	M	21,000,000	16,500,000	50,000	330.00	1,500,000	HMA2 Architects
Florida								
Sanibel	7	M	5,980,492	4,489,718	30,000	149.66	520,000	HBM Architects
Georgia								
Bogart	1	B	2,283,722	1,684,949	9,600	175.52	310,162	CAS Architecture
Milledgeville	49	O	1,458,608	1,350,601	7,328	184.31	32,000	Architectural Collaborative
Moultrie	49	M	2,033,000	1,172,962	22,000	53.32	512,667	McMillan Pazdan Smith
Illinois								
Dolton	23	M	2,195,071	1,421,188	25,000	56.85	508,883	StudioGC architecture + interiors
Northbrook	33	M	410,787	321,092	4,100	78.32	57,435	Product Architecture + Design
Chicago	43	B	7,358,712	1,895,137	16,500	114.86	200,028	Skidmore, Owings and Merrill
Chicago	64	B	11,545,413	4,695,039	14,382	326.45	306,530	bKL Architects
Indiana								
Ellettsville	138	B	2,458,582	1,956,488	13,678	143.04	344,345	Matheu Architects
Iowa								
State Center	2	M	1,434,763	1,314,697	4,207	312.50	14,719	Studio MELEE
Sioux City	83	B	1,554,352	1,1,52,952	12,150	94.89	239,269	FEH Design

Symbol Code: B—Branch Library; BS—Branch & System Headquarters; M—Main Library; MS—Main & System Headquarters; S—System Headquarters; O—Combined Use Space; n.a.—not available

Table 4 / Public Library Buildings, Additions and Renovations, 2019 *(cont.)*

Community	Pop. ('000)	Code	Project Cost	Constr. Cost	Gross Area (Sq. Ft.)	Sq. Ft. Cost	Equip. Cost	Architect
Kentucky								
Lebanon	19	M	3,299,573	2,597,000	18,800	138.14	360,000	Nomi Design
Maine								
Portland	80	B	940,000	722,000	1,250	577.60	136,500	Reed & Co. Architects
Massachusetts								
Stoughton	28	M	14,000,000	11,843,603	31,000	382.05	323,170	Finegold Alexander Architects
Michigan								
Marquette	36	M	4,079,596	3,194,740	63,000	50.71	588,550	Integrated Designs, Inc.
South Lyon	17	M	1,253,000	961,000	6,055	158.71	137,000	Merritt Cieslak Design
Minnesota								
Circle Pines	42	B	5,497,122	4,446,993	14,600	304.59	320,129	Leo A Daly
Apple Valley	52	B	4,600,000	3,245,000	29,745	109.09	912,000	BTR
Hastings	27	B	4,030,000	3,159,000	17,918	176.30	406,000	Kodet Architectural Group
Fergus Falls	19	M	9,400,000	6,800,000	26,300	258.56	850,000	Bentz Thompson Rietow
Minnetonka	100	BS	7,600,000	3,500,000	56,000	62.50	889,000	Gensler
Missouri								
Blue Springs	42	B	2,223,425	1,687,921	17,896	94.32	300,059	Sapp Design Architects; Helix Architecture + Design
Manchester	61	B	5,500,576	4,600,000	26,560	173.19	350,000	Bond Architects
Nebraska								
Grand Island	51	M	1,614,230	1,180,844	17,150	68.85	324,476	The Clark Enersen Partners
New Hampshire								
Keene	23	M	10,500,000	8,800,000	69,947	125.81	250,000	Tappé Architects
Manchester	110	M	288,605	160,295	2,850	56.24	97,186	Stibler Associates

Symbol Code: B—Branch Library; BS—Branch & System Headquarters; M—Main Library; MS—Main & System Headquarters; S—System Headquarters; O—Combined Use Space; n.a.—not available

New Jersey								
Hoboken	53	M	5,034,897	3,596,591	21,550	166.90	253,919	Dennis Kowal Architects
Verona	16	M	4,200,000	2,968,720	15,500	191.53	751,080	Solutions Architecture
New York								
Ovid	7	M	3,038,286	2,530,764	3,576	707.71	93,990	SWBR
Ohio								
Wapakoneta	10	M	1,035,000	800,000	20,000	40.00	135,000	Fanning Howey
Cleveland	6	B	4,500,000	3,807,000	13,450	283.05	95,500	HBM Architects
Sylvania	19	B	5,089,520	4,187,192	21,246	197.08	314,858	HBM Architects
Pennsylvania								
Pittsburgh	20	M	2,032,600	1,699,867	5	329.43	71,531	GBBN Architects
Bala Cynwyd	6	B	2,959,336	2,206	13,450	283.05	95,500	Vitetta
Carbondale	20	M	37,445	25,000	3,600	6.94	3,445	J.P. Jay Associates
Erie	246	MS	238,070	172,732	3,600	47.98	37,367	Bostwick Design Partnership
Tennessee								
Madison	38	B	2,380,000	1,820,707	20,000	91.04	380,000	Gold - Turner Group
Texas								
Missouri City	75	B	7,100,641	6,027,478	29,467	204.55	380,000	Gold - Turner Group
Sherman	42	M	2,689,620	2,195,112	15,934	137.76	288,868	Hidell And Associates Architects, Inc
Washington								
Kent	75	B	7,100,641	6,027,478	29,467	204.55	380,000	Gold - Turner Group
Point Roberts	1	B	1,182,000	846,000	2,900	291.72	119	King Architecture
West Virginia								
Bridgeport	8	M	432,236	393,508	15,000	26.23	10,828	Omni Associates
Wisconsin								
Superior	44	B	2,070,000	1,542,600	33,000	46.20	380,000	MSR Design; LHB Engineers & Architects

Symbol Code: B—Branch Library; BS—Branch & System Headquarters; M—Main Library; MS—Main & System Headquarters; S—System Headquarters; O—Combined Use Space; n.a.—not available

Table 5 / Six-Year Cost Summary

	Fiscal 2014	Fiscal 2015	Fiscal 2016	Fiscal 2017	Fiscal 2018	Fiscal 2019
Number of new buildings	29	38	33	26	20	29
Number of ARRs	55	54	59	44	37	49
Sq. ft. new buildings	717,973	896,195	831,110	616,436	775,395	799,232
Sq. ft. ARRs	1,164,535	1,222,795	1,297,229	1,090,370	936,894	908,624
New Buildings						
Construction cost	$212,257,074	$274,900,907	$257,213,872	$207,532,385	$250,938,025	$184,280,310
Equipment cost	34,002,671	26,895,130	37,522,113	21,316,125	28,190,468	19,425,446
Site cost	18,929,131	12,031,896	19,242,482	6,968,634	12,993,856	12,608,571
Other cost	49,676,815	68,193,630	73,601,931	41,281,588	53,008,395	33,743,217
Total—Project cost	314,866,191	360,746,279	397,152,182	309,498,732	360,630,814	445,147,544
ARRs—Project cost	260,983,928	311,990,635	237,347,021	299,877,478	193,355,042	199,979,075
New and ARR Project Cost	$575,850,119	$672,736,914	$634,499,203	$609,376,210	$553,985,856	$645,126,619

Symbol Code: ARR—Additions, Renovations, and Remodels

Table 6 / Funding Sources

	Fiscal 2014	Fiscal 2015	Fiscal 2016	Fiscal 2017	Fiscal 2018	Fiscal 2019
Federal, new buildings	$25,617,538	$475,000	$350,000	$25,260,000	$500,000	$7,462,157
Federal, ARRs	6,239,463	1,500,000	2,423,000	0	179,000	3,659,656
Federal, total	$31,857,001	$1,975,000	$2,773,000	$25,260,000	$679,000	$11,121,813
State, new buildings	$64,563,247	$15,169,766	$15,025,234	$3,994,000	$31,590,106	$3,414,869
State, ARRs	19,563,872	5,251,244	2,787,038	18,570,711	5,818,200	10,625,887
State, total	$84,127,119	$20,421,010	$17,812,272	$22,564,711	$37,408,306	$14,040,756
Local, new buildings	$215,147,978	$331,311,400	$371,719,254	$271,148,486	$314,825,218	$154,816,713
Local, ARRs	188,446,449	244,614,937	199,559,402	237,888,791	182,254,371	107,203,069
Local, total	$403,594,427	$575,926,337	$571,278,656	$509,037,277	$497,079,589	$262,019,782
Gift, new buildings	$13,312,404	$24,430,676	$14,388,312	$10,626,623	$21,435,733	$13,611,075
Gift, ARRs	50,361,901	63,353,240	32,636,393	43,448,173	5,549,824	30,870,546
Gift, total	$63,674,305	$87,783,916	$47,024,705	$54,074,796	$26,985,557	$44,481,621
Total—Funds Used	$583,252,852	$686,106,263	$638,888,633	$610,936,784	$562,152,452	$331,663,972

Symbol Code: ARR—Additions, Renovations, and Remodels

Public Library State Rankings, 2017

State	Library visits per capita[1]	Registered users per capita[1]	Total circulation[2] per capita[1]	Reference transactions per capita[1]
Alabama	43	23	46	10
Alaska	18	27	26	35
Arizona	38	42	28	20
Arkansas	35	9	37	6
California	36	21	38	46
Colorado	5	5	5	26
Connecticut	4	45	21	9
Delaware	29	49	35	46
District of Columbia	19	10	32	4
Florida	41	23	42	5
Georgia	51	49	50	23
Hawaii	47	8	48	50
Idaho	10	10	7	12
Illinois	9	45	12	11
Indiana	17	34	4	28
Iowa	11	7	14	35
Kansas	12	5	8	18
Kentucky	34	14	27	7
Louisiana	37	34	45	7
Maine	6	23	25	27
Maryland	28	14	10	2
Massachusetts	3	38	15	22
Michigan	27	39	19	12
Minnesota	31	3	13	28
Mississippi	47	16	51	46
Missouri	24	18	11	38
Montana	30	43	33	38
Nebraska	22	4	18	38
Nevada	40	43	30	45
New Hampshire	15	16	20	31
New Jersey	23	39	34	19
New Mexico	26	1	31	28
New York	20	32	29	3
North Carolina	42	27	43	24
North Dakota	43	51	39	20
Ohio	1	2	2	1
Oklahoma	32	10	24	33
Oregon	8	18	1	38
Pennsylvania	39	45	41	32
Rhode Island	13	48	36	34
South Carolina	45	31	40	35
South Dakota	25	41	22	49
Tennessee	46	37	47	38
Texas	50	27	44	38
Utah	21	21	6	14
Vermont	2	32	23	15

State	Library visits per capita[1]	Registered users per capita[1]	Total circulation[2] per capita[1]	Reference transactions per capita[1]
Virginia	33	18	17	16
Washington	15	27	3	38
West Virginia	49	36	49	51
Wisconsin	14	23	9	24
Wyoming	7	10	16	16

State	Public access Internet computers per 5,000 population[3]	Public access Internet computers per stationary outlet	Print materials[4] per capita[1]	E-books per capita[1]
Alabama	25	25	36	24
Alaska	9	40	16	16
Arizona	29	2	51	31
Arkansas	28	38	29	35
California	49	12	43	44
Colorado	19	8	41	37
Connecticut	15	23	5	33
Delaware	24	3	46	37
District of Columbia	7	1	46	51
Florida	44	4	49	46
Georgia	38	9	44	49
Hawaii	51	42	31	50
Idaho	11	35	20	43
Illinois	13	14	14	14
Indiana	12	18	10	20
Iowa	3	46	7	4
Kansas	6	44	10	1
Kentucky	22	7	32	7
Louisiana	18	26	26	30
Maine	4	49	1	15
Maryland	40	5	39	45
Massachusetts	32	31	3	9
Michigan	17	22	22	26
Minnesota	30	28	28	25
Mississippi	35	39	38	48
Missouri	39	34	21	28
Montana	14	43	25	19
Nebraska	2	41	12	8
Nevada	50	27	50	47
New Hampshire	21	50	4	5
New Jersey	34	20	19	29
New Mexico	20	29	23	39
New York	27	19	8	18
North Carolina	45	21	45	31
North Dakota	23	45	17	21
Ohio	16	16	13	3

State	Public access Internet computers per 5,000 population[3]	Public access Internet computers per stationary outlet	Print materials[4] per capita[1]	E-books per capita[1]
Oklahoma	31	30	33	23
Oregon	43	32	26	13
Pennsylvania	48	36	35	11
Rhode Island	10	13	15	10
South Carolina	37	10	37	42
South Dakota	8	48	8	17
Tennessee	41	17	42	6
Texas	42	6	48	40
Utah	46	24	30	34
Vermont	1	51	2	41
Virginia	36	11	34	22
Washington	32	15	40	36
West Virginia	46	47	24	12
Wisconsin	25	33	18	2
Wyoming	5	37	6	27

State	Audio physical materials per capita[1]	Audio downloadable materials per capita[1]	Video physical materials per capita[1]	Video downloadable materials per capita[1]
Alabama	40	31	42	26
Alaska	15	10	2	26
Arizona	44	19	42	12
Arkansas	37	23	30	21
California	44	29	44	26
Colorado	23	30	19	12
Connecticut	6	34	11	39
Delaware	31	46	14	26
District of Columbia	51	50	46	47
Florida	40	15	38	26
Georgia	50	48	50	39
Hawaii	44	50	46	47
Idaho	21	40	21	47
Illinois	4	18	12	12
Indiana	4	27	7	12
Iowa	9	7	7	39
Kansas	12	4	3	26
Kentucky	31	19	28	8
Louisiana	37	31	19	12
Maine	9	13	7	8
Maryland	23	43	36	26
Massachusetts	6	17	12	7
Michigan	12	25	14	10
Minnesota	23	45	30	47
Mississippi	48	48	44	39
Missouri	19	38	25	21

State	Audio physical materials per capita[1]	Audio downloadable materials per capita[1]	Video physical materials per capita[1]	Video downloadable materials per capita[1]
Montana	31	14	26	39
Nebraska	23	8	23	39
Nevada	37	37	30	26
New Hampshire	9	5	5	12
New Jersey	15	25	14	3
New Mexico	28	36	23	12
New York	15	35	14	39
North Carolina	48	47	51	26
North Dakota	30	12	34	10
Ohio	1	5	1	1
Oklahoma	34	38	36	26
Oregon	15	11	14	21
Pennsylvania	19	2	39	2
Rhode Island	28	16	21	21
South Carolina	40	33	39	26
South Dakota	21	19	30	39
Tennessee	40	9	46	5
Texas	44	41	46	26
Utah	12	24	26	12
Vermont	8	42	7	47
Virginia	34	22	39	12
Washington	23	43	28	26
West Virginia	34	1	34	3
Wisconsin	3	3	5	5
Wyoming	2	28	4	21

State	Total paid FTE staff[5] per 25,000 population[6]	Paid FTE librarians per 25,000 population[6]	Percentage of total FTE librarians with ALA-MLS degrees[7]
Alabama	39	29	36
Alaska	29	29	28
Arizona	44	49	15
Arkansas	34	40	34
California	45	47	5
Colorado	12	27	18
Connecticut	8	4	20
Delaware	41	42	29
District of Columbia	3	22	1
Florida	43	45	10
Georgia	51	51	1
Hawaii	36	41	3
Idaho	15	32	33
Illinois	2	10	22
Indiana	4	14	24
Iowa	17	3	46
Kansas	6	6	38

State	Total paid FTE staff[5] per 25,000 population[6]	Paid FTE librarians per 25,000 population[6]	Percentage of total FTE librarians with ALA-MLS degrees[7]
Kentucky	23	8	47
Louisiana	14	12	40
Maine	13	5	37
Maryland	18	19	30
Massachusetts	19	9	21
Michigan	28	25	19
Minnesota	35	33	25
Mississippi	48	20	51
Missouri	16	35	39
Montana	38	28	43
Nebraska	26	13	45
Nevada	49	50	12
New Hampshire	9	2	31
New Jersey	25	31	4
New Mexico	30	26	35
New York	7	17	13
North Carolina	47	48	6
North Dakota	40	23	41
Ohio	1	16	17
Oklahoma	21	7	48
Oregon	22	34	11
Pennsylvania	37	42	16
Rhode Island	11	15	8
South Carolina	33	38	14
South Dakota	31	18	49
Tennessee	46	46	32
Texas	50	44	23
Utah	32	36	27
Vermont	10	1	44
Virginia	27	37	9
Washington	20	39	7
West Virginia	42	24	50
Wisconsin	24	21	26
Wyoming	5	11	42

State	Total operating revenue per capita[1]	State operating revenue per capita[1]	Local operating revenue per capita[1]	Other operating revenue per capita[1]
Alabama	46	29	45	28
Alaska	9	25	8	40
Arizona	43	42	40	49
Arkansas	36	16	38	22
California	29	36	21	31
Colorado	7	39	7	10
Connecticut	10	41	12	3
Delaware	42	8	42	37
District of Columbia	1	47	1	32

State	Total operating revenue per capita[1]	State operating revenue per capita[1]	Local operating revenue per capita[1]	Other operating revenue per capita[1]
Florida	40	27	36	46
Georgia	50	11	49	47
Hawaii	44	2	51	36
Idaho	26	24	23	20
Illinois	4	13	2	16
Indiana	11	9	11	25
Iowa	22	30	20	18
Kansas	14	19	13	9
Kentucky	23	23	18	33
Louisiana	13	28	10	38
Maine	27	40	34	1
Maryland	15	3	28	8
Massachusetts	19	18	17	11
Michigan	20	21	16	23
Minnesota	25	22	24	13
Mississippi	51	12	50	34
Missouri	17	36	15	19
Montana	41	33	37	42
Nebraska	30	38	22	29
Nevada	35	5	41	43
New Hampshire	18	46	14	17
New Jersey	12	35	9	26
New Mexico	33	26	33	30
New York	2	10	5	2
North Carolina	45	20	44	48
North Dakota	38	14	39	27
Ohio	3	1	31	4
Oklahoma	28	32	25	24
Oregon	5	43	4	14
Pennsylvania	39	7	46	7
Rhode Island	16	4	29	5
South Carolina	37	15	35	50
South Dakota	34	47	30	44
Tennessee	49	45	47	45
Texas	48	47	43	51
Utah	31	34	27	38
Vermont	24	47	26	6
Virginia	32	17	32	41
Washington	8	44	6	21
West Virginia	47	6	48	34
Wisconsin	21	31	19	12
Wyoming	6	47	3	15

State	Total operating expenditures[8] per capita[1]	Salaries and benefits	Total collection expenditures[9]	Other operating expenditures[10]
Alabama	46	15	48	45
Alaska	8	33	35	4
Arizona	44	48	31	40
Arkansas	36	44	36	30
California	28	41	39	16
Colorado	9	43	2	8
Connecticut	5	4	13	13
Delaware	40	18	47	39
District of Columbia	1	3	9	2
Florida	42	50	40	25
Georgia	50	9	50	51
Hawaii	43	29	44	36
Idaho	26	37	25	21
Illinois	3	34	5	3
Indiana	12	45	4	9
Iowa	24	14	17	33
Kansas	11	51	10	1
Kentucky	32	38	20	27
Louisiana	18	47	14	10
Maine	23	15	37	23
Maryland	15	6	8	32
Massachusetts	16	10	11	28
Michigan	25	46	21	14
Minnesota	22	40	24	15
Mississippi	51	27	51	47
Missouri	20	49	6	12
Montana	41	12	41	42
Nebraska	29	28	18	31
Nevada	35	13	32	44
New Hampshire	17	2	23	29
New Jersey	13	7	22	20
New Mexico	34	31	16	41
New York	2	8	12	7
North Carolina	45	17	46	46
North Dakota	39	35	33	38
Ohio	4	39	1	6
Oklahoma	27	42	15	24
Oregon	6	32	7	5
Pennsylvania	38	26	43	34
Rhode Island	14	5	38	19
South Carolina	37	24	30	43
South Dakota	33	19	28	37
Tennessee	49	23	49	50
Texas	47	19	45	48
Utah	30	36	18	26
Vermont	19	19	26	17
Virginia	31	11	34	35
Washington	7	22	3	11

State	Total operating expenditures[8] per capita[1]	Salaries and benefits	Total collection expenditures[9]	Other operating expenditures[10]
West Virginia	48	30	42	49
Wisconsin	21	25	27	22
Wyoming	10	1	29	18

1 Per capita is based on the total unduplicated population of legal service areas. The determination of the unduplicated figure is the responsibility of the state library agency and should be based on the most recent state population figures for jurisdictions in the state.

2 The data element definition for total circulation (TOTCIR) changed in FY 2016. Missing data for changed data elements are not imputed until data have been collected systematically for at least three years; therefore, missing data were not imputed in FY 2017.

3 Per 5,000 population is based on the total unduplicated population of legal service areas. The determination of the unduplicated figure is the responsibility of the state library agency and should be based on the most recent state population figures for jurisdictions in the state.

4 These materials include books in print. The data element definition for print materials (BKVOL) changed in FY 2016. Missing data for changed data elements are not imputed until data have been collected systematically for at least three years; therefore, missing data were not imputed in FY 2017. Print materials per capita excludes records with missing data.

5 Paid staff were reported in full-time-equivalents (FTEs). To ensure comparable data, 40 hours was set as the measure of full-time employment (for example, 60 hours per week of part-time work by employees in a staff category divided by the 40-hour measure equals 1.50 FTEs). FTE data were reported to two decimal places but rounded to one decimal place in the table.

6 Per 25,000 population is based on the total unduplicated population of legal service areas. The determination of the unduplicated figure is the responsibility of the state library agency and should be based on the most recent state population figures for jurisdictions in the state.

7 ALA-MLS—A master's degree from a graduate library education program accredited by the American Library Association (ALA). Librarians with an ALA-MLS are also included in total librarians.

8 Total operating expenditures includes total staff expenditures, collection expenditures, and other operating expenditures.

9 Total collection expenditures includes expenditures for print, electronic, and other materials.

10 Other operating expenditures not included in staff or collections.

Note: The District of Columbia, although not a state, is included in the state rankings. Special care should be used in comparing its data to state data. Caution should be used in making comparisons with the state of Hawaii, as Hawaii reports only one public library for the entire state. Although the data in this table come from a census of all public libraries and are not subject to sampling error, the census results may contain nonsampling error. Additional information on nonsampling error, response rates, and definitions may be found in *Data File Documentation Public Libraries Survey: Fiscal Year 2017*.

Source: IMLS, Public Libraries Survey, FY 2017. Data users who create their own estimates using data from these tables should cite the Institute of Museum and Library Services as the source of the original data only.

Book Trade Research and Statistics

Prices of U.S. and Foreign Published Materials

George Aulisio
Editor, ALA ALCTS Library Materials Price Index Editorial Board

The Library Materials Price Index (LMPI) Editorial Board of the American Library Association's Association for Library Collections and Technical Services' (ALCTS) Publications Committee continues to monitor prices for a range of library materials from sources within North America and other key publishing centers around the world.

The U.S. Consumer Price Index (CPI) increased by 2.3 percent in 2019. The 2019 CPI increase is the highest increase recorded in the previous five years. CPI figures are obtained from the Bureau of Labor Statistics at http://www.bls.gov/.

In 2017, all tables that utilized a base index price increase had their base year reset to 2010. All indexes continue to utilize the 2010 base year. Percent changes in average prices from 2015–2019 are conveniently noted in Chart 1.

	Average Price Percent Change				
Index	**2015**	**2016**	**2017**	**2018**	**2019**
U.S. Consumer Price Index	0.7	2.1	2.1	1.9	2.3
U.S. Periodicals (Table 1)	6.0	7.1	5.6	5.7	6.7
U.S. Legal Serials Services (Table 2)	13.9	9.5	11.7	14.1	23.6
U.S. Hardcover Books (Table 3)	3.1	0.4*	4.9*	-11.8	0.9
N.A. Academic Books (Table 4)	1.3	-11.6	16.6	0.0	-0.9
N.A. Academic E-Books (Table 4A)	-4.3	-5.2	0.6	5.3	0.3
N.A. Academic Textbooks (Table 4B)	10.5	-3.1	0.3	-3.2	2.0
U.S. College books (Table 5)	-0.6	3.4	-2.8	-0.6	1.3
U.S. Mass market paperbacks (Table 6)	0.1	2.3*	0.8	0.5	2.5
U.S. Paperbacks (Table 7)	1.1	20.3*	-23.8*	14.9	-15.6
U.S. Audiobooks (Table 7A)	-14.7	-16.7*	29.3	14.1	1.6
U.S. E-Books (Table 7B)	-12.8	36.3*	-20.3*	0.7	0.4
+Serials (Table 8)	5.8	6.0	6.5	5.8	6.0
+Online Serials (Table 8A)	6.4	6.2	5.6	5.8	6.2
British academic books (Table 9)	7.1	9.9	-0.5	7.0	-1.8

* = figures revised from previous editions based on new data
+Dataset changes each year.

U.S. Published Materials

Tables 1 through 7B indicate average prices and price indexes for library materials published primarily in the United States. These indexes are U.S. Periodicals (Table 1), U.S. Legal Serials Services (Table 2), U.S. Hardcover Books (Table 3), North American (N.A.) Academic Books (Table 4), N.A. Academic E-Books (Table 4A), N.A. Academic Textbooks (Table 4B), U.S. College Books (Table 5), U.S. Mass Market Paperback Books (Table 6), U.S. Paperbacks (excluding mass market) (Table 7), U.S. Audiobooks (Table 7A), and U.S. E-Books (Table 7B).

Periodical and Serials Prices

The U.S. Periodical Price Index (USPPI) (Table 1) was reestablished by Stephen Bosch, University of Arizona, in 2014. The table is updated for 2020 using data supplied by EBSCO Information Services. This report includes 2016–2020 data indexed to the base year of 2010. Table 1 is derived from a selected set of titles that, as much as possible, will remain as the sample base for future comparisons. The data in Table 1 are from a print-preferred list, but over half of the titles in the index (55%) are based on online pricing so that the data provide a strong mix of both print and online pricing. Including both print and online pricing makes the data in Table 1 more characteristic of a current academic library's serials collection. The subscription prices used are publishers' list prices, excluding publisher discount or vendor service charges. The pricing data for 2010–2014, the base years for the new USPPI, published in 2014, were created from one single report that pulled pricing information for a static set of titles for the five-year period. The pricing data for 2016–2020 are based on that same sampling of titles but are not an exact match due to changes that occur with serial titles. Between the 2010–2014 and 2016–2020 lists, some titles fell off the list due to pricing not being available, while other titles on the list for which pricing had not been available in 2014 now have pricing available.

The new USPPI treats a little more than 6,000 titles in comparison with the original title list, which covered only about 3,700 titles. The previous versions of the USPPI treated Russian translations as a separate category. Russian translations are no longer a focus of this index and are not tracked as a category. These were once seen as a major cost factor, but this is no longer the case, and therefore their inclusion in or exclusion from the index no longer makes sense. There are Russian translation titles in the index, but they are not reported separately.

The main barrier to creating this index is the difficulty of maintaining the title list and obtaining standard retail pricing for titles on the list. Changes in serials titles due to ceased publication, movement to open access, mergers, combining titles in packages, moving to direct orders, and publication delays are a few of the situations that can affect obtaining current pricing information. The new index retains viable titles from the previous index's title lists and includes new title data. The new titles are the most frequently ordered serials in EBSCO's system. From that list of serials, titles were selected for the new index to ensure that the distribution by subject was similar to the distribution in the original index. There are more titles in the selected title set than the number of titles that produced prices over the past six years. This should allow the current index to be sustainable into the future as titles fall off the list and pricing becomes available for titles that may have been delayed or are no longer in memberships.

The first five years of data, published in 2014, showed consistent price changes across subject areas because price data represented a historical look at the prices of the same set of journals. The data for 2016, 2017, 2018, 2019, and 2020 are based on the same sample list but do not reflect an identical list of titles as the data for 2010–2014 due to the issues mentioned above. Across subject areas, the changes in price were less volatile in 2020, with the overall 6.7 percent increase mirroring price changes seen in other pricing studies, nearly all of which show a 6 percent increase. Also, at the subject level, the sample sizes are smaller, so a few changes can cause a large swing in the overall price for that area. In 2020, price increases were consistent across subjects. There was only a variation of 5.9 percent—from 9.0 percent to 3.1 percent. In 2019, the variation was lower, at 4.6 percent—from 7.9 percent to 3.3 percent.

Direct comparisons between Table 1 and Table 8 should be avoided, especially at the subject level. Both tables show the overall rate of increase in serial prices to be around 6 percent; however, beyond that point, there is little that makes a statistically valid comparison. Table 1 represents journals that reflect the collections of an average library, whereas Table 8 is based on a larger set of data coming from a broad mix of sources. Also, Table 1 contains more trade and popular titles, whereas Table 8 contains more foreign titles, prices for which can be impacted by the strength of the U.S. dollar.

The most important trend seen in the data from Table 1 is that increases in prices have remained constant since the economic recovery began in 2010. Price increases have hovered around 6 percent annually during that time. This year, titles in areas of scientific, technical, engineering, and medical (STEM) and social science subjects dominate the list of areas with the largest price increases. Technology, food science, political science, math and computer science, psychology, health sciences, and engineering all showed increases of over 7.5 percent. Average prices for journals in the science and technology area are still far higher than in other areas, and that trend continues, with the average cost of chemistry journals being $5,821.98 and of physics journals being $4,908.89.

In this price index, as with similar indexes, the accuracy of the average price percent change is closely tied to the number of titles in the sample size. Average price changes are far more volatile when utilizing small datasets. For that reason, drawing conclusions about price changes in subject areas with a limited number of titles is less accurate than for subject areas with greater numbers of titles or with the broader index. For example, technology periodicals went up 9 percent this year, but to conclude that all journals in the technology area will increase a similar amount is likely incorrect. If a specific inflation figure for a small subject area were needed, it would be better to look at an average over a period of time or the overall number for the price study (6.7 percent) than to use the actual numbers year-by-year. The variation in pricing is too volatile in smaller sample sizes to be comparable on a year-to-year basis. In a small sample size, the change in just one or two titles could easily have a large impact on the overall price for an area.

(text continues on page 336)

Table 1 / U.S. Periodicals: Average Prices and Price Indexes, 2016–2020

Index Base 2010 = 100

Subject	LC Class	Titles	2010 Average Price	2016 Average Price	2017 Average Price	2018 Average Price	2019 Average Price	2020 Average Price	Percent Change 2018–2019	Index
Agriculture	S	236	$579.48	$949.98	$999.86	$1,051.46	$1,126.69	$1,193.42	5.9%	205.9
Anthropology	GN	54	373.64	508.32	534.23	567.65	604.61	632.59	4.6	169.3
Arts and architecture	N	107	112.39	210.16	221.69	240.09	248.88	263.15	5.7	234.1
Astronomy	QB	29	1,793.08	2,357.62	2,535.77	2,694.19	2,825.88	3,016.56	6.7	168.2
Biology	QH	363	2,053.06	3,005.63	3,175.68	3,349.06	3,545.21	3,724.27	5.1	181.4
Botany	QK	59	1,361.09	1,832.23	1,943.26	2,023.14	2,111.87	2,210.81	4.7	162.4
Business and economics	HA-HJ	468	351.29	565.40	594.64	629.22	672.60	715.44	6.4	203.7
Chemistry	QD	148	3,396.26	4,563.48	4,795.48	5,079.87	5,436.71	5,821.98	7.1	171.4
Education	L	232	354.92	586.71	623.66	664.01	715.72	764.75	6.9	215.5
Engineering	T	549	1,244.39	1,914.45	2,032.26	2,156.78	2,312.29	2,487.11	7.6	199.9
Food science	TX	45	356.17	696.11	757.01	846.02	874.98	950.90	8.7	267.0
General works	A	120	85.84	118.19	122.15	125.44	133.87	141.36	5.6	164.7
Geography	G-GF	80	670.60	1,113.96	1,197.68	1,269.36	1,365.38	1,465.69	7.3	218.6
Geology	QE	68	1,368.79	1,882.01	1,963.12	2,016.45	2,189.39	2,334.76	6.6	170.6
Health sciences	R	820	1,009.55	1,612.55	1,706.93	1,802.25	1,925.13	2,072.46	7.7	205.3

History	C,D,E,F	309	202.39	307.40	326.78	344.31	368.20	388.16	5.4	191.8
Language and literature	P	297	168.12	239.28	251.04	263.33	278.60	296.39	6.4	176.3
Law	K	222	214.01	345.17	360.59	383.39	399.64	426.02	6.6	199.1
Library science	Z	90	290.02	402.03	429.11	451.90	483.57	518.17	7.2	178.7
Math and computer science	QA	351	1,242.13	1,730.80	1,821.26	1,943.05	2,062.37	2,231.34	8.2	179.6
Military and naval science	U,V	27	239.90	395.39	415.56	436.84	459.58	479.95	4.4	200.1
Music	M	52	82.18	160.12	167.19	174.46	183.22	193.65	5.7	235.6
Philosophy and religion	B-BD, BH-BX	213	232.37	333.18	356.24	366.92	386.11	407.26	5.5	175.3
Physics	QC	157	2,845.54	3,922.45	4,109.00	4,318.84	4,609.20	4,908.89	6.5	172.5
Political science	J	97	312.76	711.02	753.49	802.48	858.56	930.48	8.4	297.5
Psychology	BF	121	648.21	1,037.82	1,096.60	1,171.26	1,251.74	1,349.53	7.8	208.2
Recreation	GV	68	69.79	156.75	164.37	175.75	186.81	196.00	4.9	280.8
Science (general)	Q	93	998.51	1,679.52	1,769.79	1,885.58	2,019.79	2,150.36	6.5	215.4
Social sciences	H	43	351.40	745.61	786.17	822.27	870.00	916.41	5.3	260.8
Sociology	HM-HX	237	482.59	839.19	887.91	945.26	1,014.77	1,087.04	7.1	225.2
Technology	TA-TT	122	535.73	874.46	935.51	990.00	1,064.76	1,160.29	9.0	216.6
Zoology	QL	126	1,454.26	2,046.39	2,144.29	2,253.37	2,386.17	2,460.12	3.1	169.2
Totals and Averages		6,003	$843.46	$1,299.81	$1,372.66	$1,451.31	$1,547.55	$1,651.94	6.7%	195.9

Compiled by Stephen Bosch, University of Arizona, based on subscription information supplied by EBSCO Information Services.

(continued from page 333)

The Legal Serials Services Index (Table 2) is compiled by Ajaye Bloomstone, Louisiana State University Law Center Library, using data collected from various legal serials vendors. The base year for this index is 2010. This index presents price data covering the years 2010 through 2020.

As in past years, vendors were asked to provide cost data on particular titles with the assumption that the title or set has been held as an active subscription

Table 2 / U.S. Legal Serials Services: Average Prices and Price Indexes, 2010–2020

Index Base: 2010 = 100

Year	Titles	Average Price	Percent Change	Index
2010	217	$1,724.23	3.5%	100.0
2011	217	1,913.95	11.0	111.0
2012	219	2,058.66	7.6	119.4
2013	218	2,241.42	8.9	130.0
2014	219	2,473.44	10.4	143.5
2015	218	2,818.02	13.9	163.4
2016	217	3,085.34	9.5	178.9
2017	218	3,446.12	11.7	199.9
2018	217	3,932.85	14.1	229.3
2019	191	4,653.97	18.3	270.0
2020	186	$5,754.39	23.6%	333.7

Compiled by Ajaye Bloomstone, Louisiana State University.

over a period of time by a large academic research law library. The cost recorded in the index is intended to be based on the upkeep of titles, not necessarily the cost incurred in purchasing a new set, though sometimes the cost is the same, and sometimes the cost of updates can be more expensive than purchasing a new set. A nuance of legal publishing is that for some of the larger legal publishers, hard prices for a calendar year are not set at the beginning of the calendar year but halfway through, so only gross price estimates may be available in time for publication of this article. In addition to titles issued regularly (e.g., journals and law reviews), legal serials may also be updated throughout the year with both regular and irregular updates or releases, new editions, and new or revised volumes. If a title is updated irregularly, the price for its renewal may increase or decrease from one year to the next, depending on the publisher's plans for keeping the title current. It is noteworthy that although legal serials in print format are still produced, titles seem to be migrating, albeit slowly, to an electronic-only format.

Some prices were provided to the compiler with the caveat "no longer available for new sales." There is also a trend for titles purchased in print to come with an electronic component. For such titles, the purchasing library may have no choice but to accept both formats even if the print is preferred. If one were able to purchase the print format without the electronic component, the cost might conceivably change. This leads one to believe that some titles may cease publication entirely. For instance, if the publication is not to be phased out immediately, then the title might, at some point soon, no longer be available in print. In fact, more than 20 titles used to compile Table 2 ceased publication in 2019. To compensate, new titles were added with the intent to match the previous year's cost of the ceased publications plus the average percentage of an increase for the remainder of the titles from 2018 to 2019. Further decreases have occurred between 2019 and 2020 due to titles discontinuing print, ceasing altogether, or migrating to electronic format, but 186 titles continue to be active. For 2020, titles ceasing in print have not been replaced by new titles, and calculations have only been made on the basis of the active titles contained in the current 2020 list.

Book Prices

U.S. Hardcover Books (Table 3), U.S. Mass Market Paperback Books (Table 6), U.S. Paperbacks (excluding mass market) (Table 7), U.S. Audiobooks (Table 7A), and U.S. E-Books (Table 7B) are prepared by Narda Tafuri, University of Scranton, and are derived from data provided by book wholesaler Baker & Taylor. Figures for 2017 should be considered preliminary and may be revised in next year's tables to reflect additional late updates to the Baker & Taylor database. The figures for this edition of *Library and Book Trade Almanac* were provided by Baker & Taylor and are based on the Book Industry Study Group's BISAC categories. The BISAC juvenile category (fiction and nonfiction) is divided into children's and young adult. For more information on the BISAC categories, visit http://www.bisg.org.

Overall, average book prices saw slight increases in 2019 with the exception of U.S. paperback books. List prices for U.S. paperback books showed a steep decline overall (Table 7) of -15.6 percent. Hardcover book prices (Table 3) and e-book prices showed insignificant increases of 0.9 percent and 0.4 percent. The price of audiobooks (Table 7A) exhibited an increase of 1.6 percent, with mass market paperbacks (Table 6) having the largest increase, of 2.5 percent.

North American Academic Books (Table 4), North American Academic E-Books (Table 4A), and North American Academic Textbooks (Table 4B) are prepared by Stephen Bosch. The data used for this index are derived from all titles treated by ProQuest Books and GOBI Library Solutions from EBSCO in their approval plans during the calendar years listed.

The current version of North American Academic Books: Average Prices and Price Indexes 2017–2019 (Table 4) has been stable for the past several years, so it is a good summary of changes in the academic book market since 2010. The index includes e-books as well as paperback editions as supplied by these vendors, and this inclusion of paperbacks and e-books as distributed as part of the approval plans has influenced the prices reflected in the index figures. The index is inclusive of the broadest categories of materials as that is the marketplace in which academic libraries operate, and the index attempts to chart price changes that impact that market. Direct comparisons with earlier published versions show variations since the number of titles treated, and their average prices, have changed. This is especially true for those versions published before 2009. Data for the current indexes are supplied by ProQuest Books (formerly Ingram Content Group–Coutts Information Services) and by GOBI Library Solutions from EBSCO (formerly

(text continues on page 346)

Table 3 / U.S. Hardcover Books: Average Prices and Price Indexes, 2016–2019

Index Base: 2010 = 100

	2010	2016 Final			2017 Final			2018 Preliminary			2019 Preliminary		
BISAC Category	Average Price	Volumes	Average Price	Index	Volumes	Average Price	Index	Volumes	Average Price	Index	Volumes	Average Price	Index
Antiques and collectibles	$51.44	147	$82.21	159.8	133	$72.28	140.5	102	$72.86	141.6	99	$65.75	127.8
Architecture	85.52	951	108.58	127.0	1,045	114.32	133.7	908	95.05	111.1	916	93.03	108.8
Art	71.53	2,156	78.01	109.1	2,171	83.05	116.1	2,043	74.88	104.7	2,230	72.97	102.0
Bibles	37.50	201	41.49	110.6	254	40.99	109.3	246	43.09	114.9	184	54.36	145.0
Biography and autobiography	53.41	1,886	50.11	93.8	1,830	50.20	94.0	1,715	46.08	86.3	1,517	41.15	77.1
Body, mind, and spirit	36.91	172	29.11	78.9	196	27.36	74.1	211	25.47	69.0	277	26.27	71.2
Business and economics	134.61	4,991	162.97	121.1	5,912	173.56	128.9	4,589	161.17	119.7	4,317	142.10	105.6
Children	24.63	15,195	25.44	103.3	15,062	24.36	98.9	16,611	26.33	106.9	16,096	24.89	101.1
Comics and graphic novels	31.51	637	39.87	126.5	669	42.17	133.8	662	43.56	138.2	680	48.57	154.1
Computers	138.53	1,105	163.90	118.3	1,282	176.40	127.3	1,156	175.65	126.8	1,134	163.01	117.7
Cooking	30.91	1,205	29.69	96.1	1,221	29.77	96.3	1,149	29.80	96.4	1,092	29.99	97.0
Crafts and hobbies	33.28	155	31.62	95.0	172	32.07	96.4	187	30.26	90.9	157	32.11	96.5
Design	76.59	438	71.09	92.8	369	70.43	92.0	354	67.06	87.6	364	65.98	86.2
Drama	42.91	111	96.50	224.9	80	111.54	259.9	67	84.70	197.4	84	109.89	256.1
Education	117.59	2,957	137.59	117.0	3,672	155.59	132.3	2,619	142.26	121.0	2,434	132.08	112.3
Family and relationships	32.24	200	52.04	161.4	193	48.24	149.6	222	46.27	143.5	205	47.53	147.4
Fiction	32.20	4,912	29.82	92.6	5,329	29.55	91.8	4,930	29.46	91.5	4,947	29.70	92.2
Foreign language study	132.47	237	126.86	95.8	242	130.05	98.2	274	124.47	94.0	213	123.13	93.0
Games and activities	52.07	169	35.37	67.9	138	49.25	94.6	183	44.37	85.2	143	38.24	73.4
Gardening	36.42	103	33.71	92.5	133	45.85	125.9	124	37.93	104.1	117	39.88	109.5
Health and fitness	48.51	366	77.90	160.6	418	85.49	176.2	337	65.87	135.8	382	74.49	153.6
History	82.65	6,477	104.21	126.1	6,260	102.13	123.6	5,863	93.94	113.7	6,176	102.34	123.8
House and home	44.61	90	36.84	82.6	122	42.32	94.9	123	38.83	87.1	130	41.13	92.2

Humor	21.94	291	21.74	99.1	303	22.53	102.7	349	22.89	104.3	291	19.25	87.7
Language arts and disciplines	117.67	1,614	147.61	125.4	1,566	156.55	133.0	1,377	144.37	122.7	1,472	136.28	115.8
Law	174.48	2,449	188.88	108.3	2,565	186.22	106.7	2,387	180.52	103.5	2,292	175.48	100.6
Literary collections	83.49	241	94.74	113.5	296	102.43	122.7	252	86.52	103.6	268	138.88	166.3
Literary criticism	117.63	2,945	128.30	109.1	2,594	131.89	112.1	2,396	126.78	107.8	2,609	121.11	103.0
Mathematics	133.23	1,092	144.11	108.2	1,400	177.63	133.3	1,037	154.02	115.6	1,023	140.37	105.4
Medical	171.13	3,176	183.36	107.1	3,848	199.26	116.4	3,050	183.53	107.2	3,592	172.63	100.9
Music	87.84	667	100.92	114.9	695	102.10	116.2	602	89.60	102.0	669	93.91	106.9
Nature	74.89	474	98.99	132.2	538	103.88	138.7	420	85.53	114.2	455	94.17	125.7
Performing arts	76.27	869	104.34	136.8	946	124.11	162.7	814	101.82	133.5	777	117.12	153.6
Pets	24.66	111	22.79	92.4	103	27.74	112.5	69	20.83	84.5	55	27.37	111.0
Philosophy	108.93	1,680	123.58	113.5	1,687	122.75	112.7	1,603	110.73	101.7	1,839	113.48	104.2
Photography	107.99	873	68.09	63.1	930	75.58	70.0	832	71.25	66.0	806	70.15	65.0
Poetry	40.76	472	54.15	132.8	320	39.58	97.1	291	36.35	89.2	280	37.60	92.2
Political science	110.32	3,491	118.28	107.2	3,928	124.68	113.0	3,471	112.88	102.3	5,482	126.42	114.6
Psychology	109.85	1,383	155.18	141.3	1,842	163.93	149.2	1,450	148.61	135.3	2,734	142.66	129.9
Reference	302.69	366	262.84	86.8	357	382.04	126.2	338	384.96	127.2	306	291.30	96.2
Religion	80.88	2,907	81.06	100.2	3,020	83.86	103.7	3,003	79.70	98.5	2,587	88.07	108.9
Science	192.20	4,057	208.87	108.7	4,623	206.46	107.4	3,910	178.97	93.1	4,144	184.23	95.9
Self-help	27.11	311	25.17	92.8	361	29.37	108.3	414	25.74	94.9	421	23.90	88.1
Social science	100.47	4,188	134.49	133.9	5,765	141.00	140.3	4,695	127.06	126.5	5,347	125.52	124.9
Sports and recreation	41.23	636	56.52	137.1	646	66.08	160.3	602	55.60	134.9	536	51.31	124.4
Study aids	101.54	20	88.66	87.3	21	112.76	111.0	15	102.43	100.9	9	172.10	169.5
Technology and engineering	164.66	3,735	182.84	111.0	4,061	205.86	125.0	3,164	203.45	123.6	3,016	184.04	111.8
Transportation	84.28	297	68.62	81.4	278	74.42	88.3	288	62.28	73.9	281	74.32	88.2
Travel	41.32	221	39.67	96.0	283	39.83	96.4	476	40.19	97.3	207	40.55	98.1
True crime	34.83	89	35.05	100.6	66	29.63	85.1	84	33.77	96.9	89	30.43	87.4
Young adult	35.99	2,290	38.07	105.8	2,404	40.14	111.5	2,116	35.81	99.5	1,995	37.24	103.5
Totals and Averages	$89.54	85,806	$102.04	114.0	92,349	$110.77	123.7	84,180	$96.88	108.2	87,476	$97.76	109.2

Compiled by Narda Tafuri, University of Scranton, from data supplied by Baker & Taylor.

Table 4 / North American Academic Books: Average Prices and Price Indexes, 2017–2019

Index Base: 2010 = 100

		2010		2017		2018		2019			
Subject Area	**LC Class**	**Titles**	**Average Price**	**Titles**	**Average Price**	**Titles**	**Average Price**	**Titles**	**Average Price**	**Percent Change 2018–2019**	**Index**
Agriculture	S	1,139	$107.44	1,822	$118.71	1,586	$114.09	1,915	$115.92	1.6%	107.9
Anthropology	GN	609	91.96	788	93.04	790	98.31	857	94.56	-3.8	102.8
Botany	QK	260	125.84	437	148.27	337	149.82	456	136.82	-8.7	108.7
Business and economics	H	10,916	97.31	14,796	106.04	13,354	107.07	14,431	107.54	0.4	110.5
Chemistry	QD	667	223.03	871	208.69	791	200.68	918	191.15	-4.7	85.7
Education	L	4,688	86.47	7,305	88.06	6,256	92.00	7,122	93.01	1.1	107.6
Engineering and technology	T	6,913	133.45	11,603	145.33	9,392	148.15	11,202	153.75	3.8	115.2
Fine and applied arts	M-N	5,535	57.17	8,119	72.22	6,869	77.19	7,694	74.66	-3.3	130.6
General works	A	80	75.60	270	91.78	251	109.68	290	98.42	-10.3	130.2
Geography	G	1,144	104.98	1,850	129.12	1,612	113.22	1,900	123.05	8.7	117.2
Geology	QE	276	114.34	392	117.02	351	123.12	429	133.49	8.4	116.8
History	C-D-E-F	10,079	65.29	14,380	74.42	13,470	78.64	15,105	73.36	-6.7	112.4
Home economics	TX	812	44.35	805	75.90	859	60.45	1,170	63.04	4.3	142.1
Industrial arts	TT	265	52.60	231	61.02	229	62.68	297	57.59	-8.1	109.5
Language and literature	P	19,364	57.31	28,485	62.65	27,174	62.36	30,452	58.25	-6.6	101.6

Law	K	4,596	125.35	6,809	125.90	6,812	127.59	6,728	128.39	0.6	102.4
Library and information science	Z	636	90.18	952	114.52	926	110.28	921	99.72	-9.6	110.6
Mathematics and computer science	QA	3,965	103.85	5,503	109.25	5,010	113.69	5,318	116.20	2.2	111.9
Medicine	R	8,679	112.66	12,602	133.70	11,147	126.05	12,452	137.62	9.2	122.1
Military and naval science	U-V	773	79.99	1,213	71.03	1,162	79.21	1,391	78.80	-0.5	98.5
Philosophy and religion	B	7,386	81.75	11,985	81.17	11,369	83.89	12,153	80.10	-4.5	98.0
Physical education and recreation	GV	1,788	56.03	2,772	68.82	2,559	69.03	2,983	71.12	3.0	127.0
Physics and astronomy	QB	1,627	128.36	2,310	129.35	2,107	143.00	2,342	127.36	-10.9	99.2
Political science	J	3,549	99.70	5,486	99.65	5,310	102.70	5,991	96.67	-5.9	97.0
Psychology	BF	1,730	76.65	2,946	88.73	2,717	83.32	2,944	82.11	-1.5	107.1
Science (general)	Q	631	108.4	1,034	112.56	954	107.42	1,175	112.86	5.1	104.1
Sociology	HM	6,666	88.75	11,218	92.68	10,276	93.29	11,518	89.35	-4.2	100.7
Zoology	QH, QL-QR	3,029	140.26	4,036	137.44	3,438	133.32	3,916	133.28	0.0	95.0
Totals and Averages		107,802	$89.15	161,020	$96.76	147,108	$96.73	164,070	$95.87	-0.9%	107.5

Compiled by Stephen Bosch, University of Arizona, from electronic data provided by ProQuest (formerly Ingrams Content Group–Coutts Information Services), and GOBI Library Solutions from EBSCO (formerly YBP Library Services). The data represent all titles (includes e-books, hardcover, trade and paperback books, as well as annuals) treated for all approval plan customers serviced by the vendors. This table covers titles published or distributed in the United States and Canada during the calendar years listed. This index does include paperback editions and electronic books. The inclusion of these items does impact pricing in the index.

Table 4A / North American Academic E-Books: Average Prices and Price Indexes, 2017–2019

Index Base: 2010 = 100

		2010		2017		2018		2019			
Subject Area	**LC Class**	**Titles**	**Average Price**	**Titles**	**Average Price**	**Titles**	**Average Price**	**Titles**	**Average Price**	**Percent Change 2018–2019**	**Index**
Agriculture	S	697	$168.73	811	$134.35	706	$133.99	874	$132.96	-0.8%	78.8
Anthropology	GN	385	109.96	348	101.50	364	104.30	393	103.92	-0.4	94.5
Botany	QK	190	175.23	192	163.95	146	174.31	193	159.51	-8.5	91.0
Business and economics	H	8,481	102.87	7,207	107.35	6,519	117.21	6,797	118.09	0.8	114.8
Chemistry	QD	521	232.57	416	206.61	388	209.77	446	186.38	-11.1	80.1
Education	L	2,852	99.96	3,386	89.64	2,839	104.20	3,231	101.52	-2.6	101.6
Engineering and technology	T	4,976	152.33	5,281	158.34	4,424	163.46	5,281	165.33	1.1	108.5
Fine and applied arts	M-N	1,493	83.35	2,345	92.74	2,213	101.64	2,338	96.52	-5.0	115.8
General works	A	53	89.13	122	104.47	98	101.13	132	97.67	-3.4	109.6
Geography	G	829	117.83	880	131.75	755	125.77	828	141.23	12.3	119.9
Geology	QE	178	146.85	158	128.30	148	141.93	186	152.31	7.3	103.7
History	C-D-E-F	5,189	89.42	6,406	83.45	5,936	92.25	6,233	87.41	-5.3	97.7
Home economics	TX	211	78.08	306	101.68	293	86.37	435	81.29	-5.9	104.1
Industrial arts	TT	23	46.11	46	82.77	53	93.52	77	66.08	-29.3	143.3
Language and literature	P	7,664	103.12	10,146	86.05	9,657	90.07	10,276	81.88	-9.1	79.4

Law	K	2,433	147.66	2,665	133.25	2,786	139.62	2,650	147.22	5.4	99.7
Library and information science	Z	387	89.43	371	122.97	376	119.59	378	111.23	-7.0	124.4
Mathematics and computer science	QA	3,000	112.65	2,255	114.32	2,092	127.44	2,231	128.80	1.1	114.3
Medicine	R	6,404	134.60	5,699	145.71	5,190	142.45	5,741	164.83	15.7	122.5
Military and naval science	U-V	487	105.07	535	78.44	518	89.70	598	93.88	4.7	89.3
Philosophy and religion	B	4,262	110.31	5,371	90.54	5,163	96.99	5,189	94.03	-3.1	85.2
Physical education and recreation	GV	791	76.57	1,226	76.90	1,161	84.05	1,257	89.00	5.9	116.2
Physics and astronomy	QB	1,288	147.50	1,058	145.19	985	166.71	1,078	145.53	-12.7	98.7
Political science	J	2,638	110.10	2,705	103.19	2,690	112.97	2,738	110.76	-2.0	100.6
Psychology	BF	1,062	91.35	1,427	92.16	1,343	96.84	1,342	95.97	-0.9	105.1
Science (general)	Q	462	122.51	446	116.94	403	119.28	495	125.52	5.2	102.5
Sociology	HM	4,520	103.73	5,366	97.02	4,910	105.57	5,140	103.29	-2.2	99.6
Zoology	QH, QL-QR	2,336	164.82	1,739	152.03	1,514	149.98	1,655	152.48	1.7	92.5
Totals and Averages		63,812	$116.25	68,913	$108.79	63,670	$114.61	68,212	$114.95	0.3%	98.9

Compiled by Stephen Bosch, University of Arizona, from electronic data provided by ProQuest (formerly Ingrams Content Group–Coutts Information Services), and GOBI Library Solutions from EBSCO (formerly YBP Library Services). The data represent all e-book titles treated for all approval plan customers serviced by the vendors. This table covers titles published or distributed in the United States and Canada during the calendar years listed. It is important to note that e-books that were released in a given year may have been published in print much earlier.

Table 4B / North American Academic Textbooks: Average Prices and Price Indexes, 2017–2019

(Index Base: 2010 = 100)

		2010		2017		2018		2019			
Subject Area	**LC Class**	**Titles**	**Average Price**	**Titles**	**Average Price**	**Titles**	**Average Price**	**Titles**	**Average Price**	**Percent Change 2018–2019**	**Index**
Agriculture	S	49	$115.80	78	$127.73	64	$136.09	65	$133.22	-2.1%	104.3
Anthropology	GN	35	90.65	75	111.91	56	91.22	54	103.15	13.1	113.8
Botany	QK	11	109.52	11	135.13	7	77.83	8	119.10	53.0	108.7
Business and economics	H	694	121.36	1,315	127.15	1,070	117.33	1,058	121.32	3.4	100.0
Chemistry	QD	94	134.59	117	185.26	115	151.54	109	130.15	-14.1	96.7
Education	L	271	87.75	497	82.91	418	86.98	525	83.92	-3.5	95.6
Engineering and technology	T	744	116.38	1,266	140.86	1,039	132.04	1,142	141.11	6.9	121.2
Fine and applied arts	M-N	73	93.33	179	93.58	119	95.92	171	104.39	8.8	111.9
General works	A	0	0.00	12	93.92	9	77.86	6	114.52	47.1	n.a.
Geography	G	78	105.21	130	118.51	106	108.43	127	121.51	12.1	115.5
Geology	QE	36	117.97	29	123.08	28	141.86	46	165.25	16.5	140.1
History	C-D-E-F	81	81.49	225	76.44	219	95.69	158	91.78	-4.1	112.6
Home economics	TX	39	89.52	50	170.20	38	116.56	39	145.85	25.1	162.9
Industrial arts	TT	14	84.72	19	94.65	14	116.57	6	99.87	-14.3	117.9
Language and literature	P	309	77.71	694	86.98	563	81.68	559	89.22	9.2	114.8

Law	K	242	102.09	456	112.18	484	107.95	464	120.14	11.3	117.7
Library and information science	Z	19	70.30	37	74.34	45	84.37	33	70.01	-17.0	99.6
Mathematics and computer science	QA	683	96.11	1,045	115.91	1,072	114.87	997	117.72	2.5	122.5
Medicine	R	1512	126.75	2,336	148.14	1,840	141.32	2,153	138.65	-1.9	109.4
Military and naval science	U-V	3	122.65	14	104.26	29	106.12	27	138.42	30.4	112.9
Philosophy and religion	B	101	72.13	192	70.29	158	70.07	179	70.29	0.3	97.4
Physical education and recreation	GV	51	79.39	133	96.52	106	106.38	129	96.87	-8.9	122.0
Physics and astronomy	QB	243	107.38	423	129.33	397	140.64	402	131.64	-6.4	122.6
Political science	J	110	80.09	255	92.14	232	96.94	267	92.27	-4.8	115.2
Psychology	BF	138	95.95	251	113.32	170	119.55	210	120.23	0.6	125.3
Science (general)	Q	33	97.14	78	89.84	66	101.15	79	95.33	-5.8	98.1
Sociology	HM	353	86.97	797	101.46	596	102.94	674	102.18	-0.7	117.5
Zoology	QH, QL-QR	227	109.82	354	144.31	313	131.79	354	139.56	5.9	127.1
Totals and Averages		6,243	$107.94	11,068	$121.74	9,373	$117.79	10,041	$120.16	2.0%	111.3

Compiled by Stephen Bosch, University of Arizona, from electronic data provided by ProQuest (formerly Ingrams Content Group–Coutts Information Services), and GOBI Library Solutions from EBSCO (formerly YBP Library Services). The data represent all textbook titles treated for all approval plan customers serviced by the vendors. This table covers titles published or distributed in the United States and Canada during the calendar years listed.

(continued from page 337)

YBP Library Services). Prior to ProQuest/Coutts supplying data, the book pricing data were obtained from Blackwell Book Services.

Over time, the data and the data suppliers have changed due to changes in the industry. When compared with earlier versions, The North American Academic Books Price Index (NAABPI) now contains many more titles in the source data, which has affected the index considerably. ProQuest Books treats far more titles in their approval programs than the former Blackwell Book Services. For indexes published before 2009, Blackwell was a supplier of data for the index. Blackwell was purchased in 2009 by YBP, and the vendor data used to create the index changed at that time. After 2009 the data came from Ingram (Coutts) and YBP, while prior to 2009 the data came from Blackwell and YBP. With recent changes at both ProQuest and GOBI, there have been changes to how the annual price data are pulled for books. Starting in 2016, each vendor supplied data in separate files for print, e-books, and textbooks. Prior to 2016, this was not the case, and this change caused large variations in the numbers of titles in the tables as well the average prices. The data for 2014 were normalized in 2016 to conform to the current sets of data, so the numbers of titles and prices have changed from those published in 2015 and previous years. In the future, this approach to gathering the data, with separate data files for print, electronic, and texts, will improve the consistency of the data, especially for e-books. In 2017 the base index year was moved to 2010 to provide consistency across the indexes published by the Library Materials Price Index Editorial Board.

The overall average price in the North American Academic Books Price Index (Table 4) was nearly flat, as it decreased -0.9 percent in 2019. Previous years showed variability, with a large increase in 2017 of 16.6 percent and a decrease in 2016 of -6.9 percent. Currently, prices have been relatively flat since 2017 and are hovering around $96 per title. The number of titles has been more volatile going from 167,100 in 2016 to 147,108 in 2018 and jumping up again to 164,070 in 2019. The overall growth in available titles, as well as increasing prices, are pressure points for library budgets. The slight decrease in price in 2019 was primarily due to a large increase in the number of titles available in the lower price ranges ($0–$30, and $30–$60 price bands). There were approximately 6,500 more titles treated in the lowest price ranges this year. Also, many of these books were print books, which tend to be less expensive than e-books. Overall, the ratio of print to electronic remains constant, with e-books being 43 percent of the titles in 2018, dropping slightly to 42 percent in 2019. Nearly all price bands showed only modest growth in the number of titles between 2018 and 2019 except for the price bands below $60. This led to the slight decrease in pricing in 2019. See Figure 1.

One thing that stands out when looking at the data by price band is that the highest end of the price bands ($120 and up) continues to have a huge impact on the average cost of books. The impact on pricing from the titles in the $120 and up price band is confirmed when looking at the actual dollar values in groups (i.e., the sum of all prices for titles in the group). The increase in the top end of the index was the main factor in the overall changes in the index for 2016–2017 as well as the minimal growth leading to no increase in 2019. The growth in the highest range could not offset the greater growth in the lower ranges. Although the $0–$30

Figure 1 / Number of Titles in Sample Grouped by Price 2016–2019

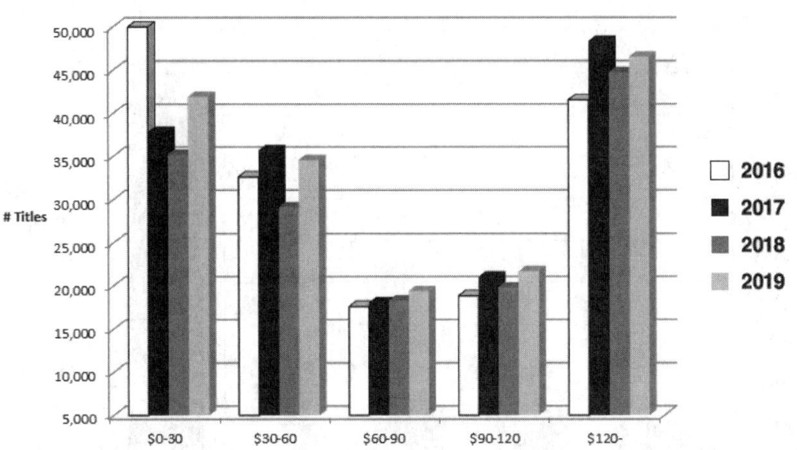

price band has the second largest number of titles, the total cost of the books in this price band amounts to the smallest portion of the total cost of all books in Table 4. Again, changes in the number of titles available is a significant driver in increase and decrease, as within the price bands the average price remains constant except for the area with prices over $120, which showed a slight decrease in the overall average price over the past four years. Unlike serials, where inflation in price drives higher costs, these data show that changes in the number of titles, not inflationary increases in price, were the primary driver in escalating costs. See Figures 2 and 3.

Table 4A treats e-books as a separate index in order to observe the differences between Table 4 and Table 4A. Currently, many titles are not yet published simultaneously in both print and e-book format, so the number of titles in the e-book index should remain smaller than the broader index. It is safe to say that in the future, the number of titles in the broader index will decline as publishers produce increasing numbers of print-on-demand e-books. Many e-book pricing models add extra charges of as much as 50 to 100 percent to the retail price for multiuser licenses. However, most e-books from aggregators will have multiple pricing models; the fact that criteria for the supplied data worked with the lowest cost license model available is a probable factor in keeping the overall prices for e-books lower than expected. The overall price for e-books did show a slight increase of 0.3 percent in 2019. This is due to changes in the number of titles available in the lower ends of the price bands. Fewer titles in the low end of the price index contributed to an increase in the overall price. The index does show that for the library market, e-books are more expensive than print. Many publishers and e-book aggregators are still adding e-book versions of print books from backlists, and these are showing up in the index. This fact also accounts for the wide swings in numbers of titles in the index from year to year.

Figure 2 / Comparison of Total Costs in Sample Grouped by Price

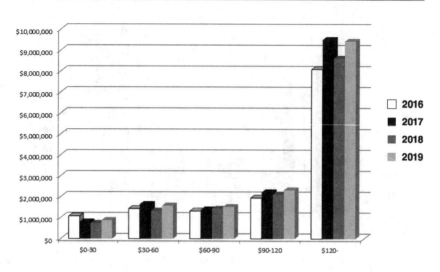

Figure 3 / Comparison of Average Price Grouped by Price Band

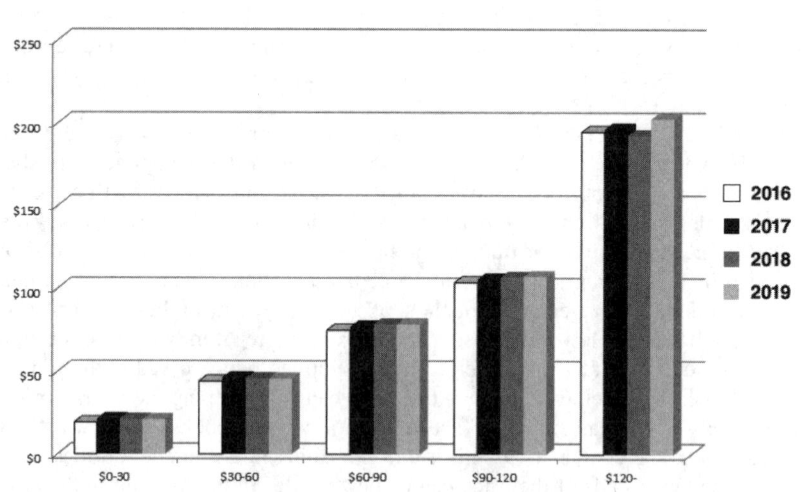

In the academic market, the assumption is that e-books are more expensive than their print counterparts. The cheaper versions of e-books available to consumers through such channels as Amazon and Google Books are not available to libraries at similar prices, if they are available at all. At best, the academic pricing will match the print price for single-user license models, with multiuser models being far more expensive than the print price. The e-book index points out the difference in price: the average price of an e-book in 2019 was $114.95, while the average price for all books was $95.87. The average price of a print book drops to $82.30 when removing e-books from the overall index. The high price for e-books is not surprising, since most pricing models for academic e-books generally charge a higher price than the list print price for access to the e-books. However, over the past few years, it is becoming common practice for single-user licenses to be priced at close to the same price as print, but multiuser licenses are still significantly more expensive than print. Responding to customer demands, publishers and vendors offer e-books on multiple platforms with multiple pricing models; consequently, there can be multiple prices for the same title. In these instances, only the first license level, which is normally single user, is included in the data. Where multiple prices are available for different use models, the lowest price is included in the index. Because electronic access is a major market trend, it is appropriate to have e-books as a separate index. It is also important to note that the e-book market is rapidly changing. The availability of additional pricing models could be a factor in the downward shift in e-book prices. Furthermore, by using the lowest price available for e-books, this approach may be artificially keeping the average price of e-books low for libraries that generally buy multiuser licenses.

The cost of textbooks has been a hot topic on many college campuses. The index for textbooks (Table 4B) documents price changes in this area. The data show that textbooks tend to be more expensive than other types of books, with an average price of $120.16 for textbooks and $95.87 for regular academic books in 2019. This represents a 2 percent increase since 2018; however, over the past four years, the price has held mostly flat at around $121.00 per title. Based on the available data published in Table 4B, the average price of textbooks seems to have plateaued over the past few years. This is good news for students, though textbooks remain more expensive than regular print or e-books. On the one hand, it is a positive development as it seems textbook publishers are responding to market pressure and scaling back large price increases. On the other hand, prices are not yet dropping significantly, and textbooks remain expensive. Pressure on the textbook market from alternative sources, such as rental services for either print or electronic versions and resales of used copies, may have slowed price increases but have not resulted in an overall significant price drop. E-book versions of textbooks are included in the textbook index, so migration to e-book format does not seem to be lowering costs. This is not much consolation for students. This price index does not include package prices for inclusive access programs.

Overall, price changes vary among subject areas. In 2019, there were several double-digit increases in subject areas, and many areas showed price decreases. This is a normal occurrence. The 2019 data indicate that those areas with the largest increases were not concentrated in specific subject areas but were widely distributed. Overall, prices for STEM books are still higher than those in the humanities. STEM publishers have tended to be early adopters of e-books and have been publishing e-books for a while. The high average prices in science and the social sciences reflect the availability and higher pricing of e-books in these areas.

It is good to remember that price indexes become less accurate at describing price changes the smaller the sample becomes. For example, across Tables 4, 4A, and 4B, "general works" is a small sample and showed a very large price change in 2019, but it would be incorrect to conclude that all book prices in those areas increased or decreased at like amounts. In small samples, the inclusion or exclusion of a few expensive items can have a major impact on prices for the category. Because the sample is very small, these titles caused the overall price to jump dramatically.

The U.S. College Books Price Index (Table 5), prepared by Narda Tafuri, contains average price and index number data for the years 2017 through 2019, and the percentage change in price between 2018 and 2019. In 2017, the index base year was reset to 2010. Previous instances of this table have an index base year of 1989.

Data for the index were compiled from 4,553 reviews of books published in *Choice* in 2019. An additional 18 print titles reviewed in *Choice* were omitted from the analysis due to price ($500 or more). These books were removed from the analysis so that the average prices were not skewed. The total number of books reviewed for this analysis has declined by -3.5 percent from the previous year's total of 4,718 titles. This index includes some paperback prices; as a result, the average price of books is less than if only hardcover books were included.

For 2019 the overall average price for books in the humanities, sciences, and social and behavioral sciences (including reference books) was $73.11, a slight increase of 1.3 percent from the average 2018 price of $72.20. The average price of reference books was $128.78, a large -12.3 percent decrease from the previous year's average price of $146.75. When excluding reference books, the average 2019 book price was $70.36, a 2.5 percent increase from the average 2018 price of $68.68.

The average 2019 price for humanities titles increased by 4.6 percent over the previous year. The average price for science and technology titles decreased by -0.8 percent. Since 2010, there has been an overall book price increase of 10.3 percent when reference books are included.

When isolated, the average 2019 price of reference books decreased substantially by -12.3 percent from the previous year. The overall price of reference books has seen fluctuations in pricing over the past several years. New for 2019 is the subcategory of library and information sciences, which appears in the category of reference.

Questions regarding this index may be addressed to the author at narda.tafuri@scranton.edu.

Serials Prices

Average Price of Serials (Table 8) and Average Price of Online Serials (Table 8A), compiled by Stephen Bosch, provide average prices and percent increases for serials based on titles in select abstracting and indexing products. The serials in this price survey are published in the United States as well as overseas and are indexed in the Clarivate Analytics' (formerly ISI) Arts and Humanities Citation Index,

(text continues on page 362)

Table 5 / U.S. College Books: Average Prices and Price Indexes, 2017–2019

Index Base: 2010 = 100

	2010		2017				2018				2019				Percent Change
Subject	Titles	Average Price	Titles	Average Price	Indexed to 2010	Indexed to 2016	Titles	Average Price	Indexed to 2010	Indexed to 2017	Titles	Average Price	Indexed to 2010	Indexed to 2018	2018–2019
HUMANITIES	91	$58.99	60	$68.91	116.8	95.0	49	$71.55	121.3	103.8	47	$81.60	138.3	114.0	14.0%
Art and architecture	149	61.69	146	66.65	108.0	97.1	118	66.01	107.0	99.0	117	70.57	114.4	106.9	6.9
Fine Arts	92	67.13	81	58.17	86.7	78.2	54	60.75	90.5	104.4	54	61.24	91.2	100.8	0.8
Architecture	48	61.53	44	77.72	126.3	91.5	37	65.50	106.5	84.3	39	75.49	122.7	115.3	15.3
Photography	28	53.02	17	58.04	109.5	102.7	10	61.89	116.7	106.6	6	73.33	138.3	118.5	18.5
Communication	112	59.97	101	65.40	109.1	84.2	83	69.52	115.9	106.3	52	72.94	121.6	104.9	4.9
Language and literature	94	68.66	86	77.10	112.3	95.3	61	87.98	128.1	114.1	82	82.60	120.3	93.9	-6.1
African and Middle Eastern	24	62.28	10	51.69	83.0	103.8	12	77.33	124.2	149.6	6	64.17	103.0	83.0	-17.0
Asian and Oceanian	24	71.99	13	89.30	124.0	127.7	13	76.84	106.7	86.0	17	78.53	109.1	102.2	2.2
Classical	24	78.76	17	69.69	88.5	80.3	23	93.69	119.0	134.4	28	89.41	113.5	95.4	-4.6
English and American	394	61.96	206	69.06	111.5	94.2	201	78.96	127.4	114.3	227	80.68	130.2	102.2	2.2
Germanic	22	70.36	6	75.00	106.6	95.0	21	81.13	115.3	108.2	21	87.55	124.4	107.9	7.9
Romance	70	59.00	42	72.30	122.5	111.8	35	80.88	137.1	111.9	32	79.94	135.5	98.8	-1.2
Slavic	32	35.95	10	60.69	168.8	80.7	11	80.00	222.5	131.8	17	81.60	227.0	102.0	2.0
Performing arts	30	61.97	15	75.93	122.5	120.3	9	76.88	124.1	101.3	14	84.45	136.3	109.8	9.8
Film	130	64.13	92	89.34	139.3	109.5	85	82.03	127.9	91.8	114	89.53	139.6	109.1	9.1
Music	123	61.01	99	71.30	116.9	95.7	85	68.22	111.8	95.7	93	76.14	124.8	111.6	11.6
Theater and dance	45	62.38	36	88.53	141.9	106.0	23	75.73	121.4	85.5	44	80.01	128.3	105.7	5.7
Philosophy	198	63.45	162	77.58	122.3	110.0	186	75.81	119.5	97.7	232	74.13	116.8	97.8	-2.2
Religion	272	57.18	192	65.64	114.8	106.0	196	66.42	116.2	101.2	196	69.99	122.4	105.4	5.4
TOTAL HUMANITIES	2,002	$61.60	1,435	$71.20	115.6	98.2	1,312	$73.51	119.3	103.2	1,438	$76.90	124.8	104.6	4.6
SCIENCE AND TECHNOLOGY	110	$58.09	77	$58.83	101.3	84.9	82	$58.81	101.2	100.0	95	$60.44	104.0	102.8	2.8
History of science and technology	78	54.10	51	68.63	126.9	129.1	51	58.41	108.0	85.1	59	57.41	106.1	98.3	-1.7
Astronautics and astronomy	63	55.58	72	57.90	104.2	119.0	50	51.92	93.4	89.7	41	54.00	97.2	104.0	4.0

Table 5 / U.S. College Books: Average Prices and Price Indexes, 2017–2019 *(cont.)*

Index Base: 2010 = 100

	2010		2017				2018				2019				Percent Change
Subject	**Titles**	**Average Price**	**Titles**	**Average Price**	**Indexed to 2010**	**Indexed to 2016**	**Titles**	**Average Price**	**Indexed to 2010**	**Indexed to 2017**	**Titles**	**Average Price**	**Indexed to 2010**	**Indexed to 2018**	**2018–2019**
Biology	151	72.74	141	63.15	86.8	77.8	76	59.55	81.9	94.3	95	72.01	99.0	120.9	20.9
Botany	85	85.09	77	69.93	82.2	71.3	63	59.98	70.5	85.8	70	56.79	66.7	94.7	-5.3
Zoology	121	64.33	89	63.05	98.0	92.9	74	60.81	94.5	96.4	96	62.41	97.0	102.6	2.6
Chemistry	42	115.42	29	121.51	105.3	115.4	21	101.78	88.2	83.8	13	102.74	89.0	100.9	0.9
Earth science	102	63.33	112	71.36	112.7	89.2	79	66.39	104.8	93.0	68	74.46	117.6	112.2	12.2
Engineering	103	88.38	86	106.40	120.4	93.6	47	93.51	105.8	87.9	43	80.28	90.8	85.9	-14.1
Health sciences	146	56.14	142	66.61	118.6	92.3	102	66.77	118.9	100.2	195	69.78	124.3	104.5	4.5
Information and computer science	83	73.50	93	63.83	86.8	101.7	59	59.41	80.8	93.1	66	77.36	105.3	130.2	30.2
Mathematics	108	61.97	107	77.02	124.3	113.9	81	77.71	125.4	100.9	74	81.00	130.7	104.2	4.2
Physics	50	54.74	52	81.59	149.1	102.3	39	69.52	127.0	85.2	39	63.49	116.0	91.3	-8.7
Sports and physical education	67	54.06	78	69.44	128.4	82.8	63	55.41	102.5	79.8	87	62.40	115.4	112.6	12.6
TOTAL SCIENCE	1,309	$67.13	1,206	$71.36	106.3	94.0	887	$65.15	97.1	91.3	1,041	$67.83	101.0	104.1	4.1
SOCIAL AND BEHAVIORAL SCIENCES	129	$66.32	70	$80.47	121.3	101.6	64	$77.53	116.9	96.3	43	$70.20	105.9	90.5	-9.5
Anthropology	139	63.60	115	84.95	133.6	104.3	85	79.38	124.8	93.4	95	89.67	141.0	113.0	13.0
Business management and labor	150	58.00	122	52.56	90.6	96.0	95	51.53	88.8	98.0	69	53.52	92.3	103.9	3.9
Economics	270	61.16	125	63.79	104.3	113.4	114	56.48	92.3	88.5	105	60.99	99.7	108.0	8.0
Education	158	62.56	24	72.30	115.6	96.7	26	74.18	118.6	102.6	43	72.74	116.3	98.1	-1.9
History, geography, and area studies	154	58.16	90	72.33	124.4	94.1	95	66.02	113.5	91.3	63	58.55	100.7	88.7	-11.3
Africa	38	69.05	24	70.34	101.9	105.0	31	68.20	98.8	97.0	17	72.77	105.4	106.7	6.7
Ancient history	49	57.90	40	74.73	129.1	84.8	51	86.00	148.5	115.1	39	86.19	148.9	100.2	0.2
Asia and Oceania	72	60.88	63	70.69	116.1	110.3	65	73.55	120.8	104.0	71	64.47	105.9	87.7	-12.3

Central and Eastern Europe	56	66.53	50	71.05	106.8	102.3	65	76.17	114.5	107.2	31	67.21	101.0	88.2	-11.8
Latin America and Caribbean	54	59.31	60	77.51	130.7	113.9	59	75.24	126.9	97.1	49	76.56	129.1	101.8	1.8
Middle East and North Africa	43	65.57	51	60.38	92.1	80.1	36	69.60	106.1	115.3	28	66.12	100.8	95.0	-5.0
North America	444	45.50	335	50.33	110.6	98.4	343	54.62	120.0	108.5	245	48.96	107.6	89.6	-10.4
United Kingdom	80	69.56	66	74.36	106.9	89.5	78	70.68	101.6	95.1	39	56.44	81.1	79.9	-20.1
Western Europe	138	59.14	106	75.01	126.8	110.4	110	85.13	143.9	113.5	74	61.88	104.6	72.7	-27.3
Political science	4	84.36	68	58.55	69.4	87.4	60	62.46	74.0	106.7	58	74.12	87.9	118.7	18.7
Comparative politics	183	66.34	186	64.47	97.2	88.0	201	67.63	101.9	104.9	115	71.06	107.1	105.1	5.1
International relations	213	65.64	147	61.87	94.3	88.8	141	61.58	93.8	99.5	91	57.20	87.1	92.9	-7.1
Political theory	73	56.74	118	71.12	125.3	98.0	127	73.98	130.4	104.0	104	72.32	127.5	97.8	-2.2
U.S. politics	253	53.03	150	61.03	115.1	93.6	178	63.46	119.7	104.0	125	60.62	114.3	95.5	-4.5
Psychology	126	60.55	121	72.33	119.5	82.7	137	71.95	118.8	99.5	189	81.34	134.3	113.1	13.1
Sociology	226	60.71	182	79.50	131.0	100.8	145	72.71	119.8	91.5	167	71.12	117.1	97.8	-2.2
TOTAL BEHAVIORAL SCIENCES	3,052	$59.09	2,313	$66.58	112.7	97.7	2,306	$67.28	113.9	101.1	1,860	$66.73	112.9	99.2	-0.8
TOTAL GENERAL, HUMANITIES, SCIENCE AND SOCIAL SCIENCE (without Reference)	6,363	$61.53	4,954	$69.08	112.3	97.4	4,505	$68.68	111.6	99.4	4,339	$70.36	114.4	102.4	2.4
REFERENCE															
General	29	$61.17	20	$101.90	166.6	99.4	19	$154.73	253.0	151.8	17	$118.52	193.8	76.6	-23.4
Humanities	128	117.12	83	136.80	116.8	114.4	70	132.66	113.3	97.0	45	104.93	89.6	79.1	-20.9
Library and information sciences	n.a.	n.a.	n.a.	n.a.	n.a.	n.a.	n.a.	n.a.	n.a.	n.a.	32	80.48	n.a.	n.a.	n.a.
Science and technology	76	133.19	42	110.55	83.0	74.7	34	164.90	123.8	149.2	34	140.05	105.2	84.9	-15.1
Social and behavioral sciences	216	152.91	146	142.88	93.4	94.7	90	149.17	97.6	104.4	86	156.80	102.5	105.1	5.1
TOTAL REFERENCE	449	$133.44	291	$133.66	100.2	97.3	213	$146.75	110.0	109.8	214	$128.78	96.5	87.8	-12.2
GRAND TOTAL	6,812	$66.27	5,245	$72.67	109.7	97.2	4,718	$72.20	108.9	99.4	4,553	$73.11	110.3	101.3	1.3%

Compiled by Narda Tafuri, University of Scranton.
n.a. = not available

Table 6 / U.S. Mass Market Paperback Books: Average Prices and Price Indexes, 2016–2019

Index Base: 2010 = 100

	2010	2016 Final			2017 Final			2018 Preliminary			2019 Preliminary		
BISAC Category	**Average Price**	**Volumes**	**Average Price**	**Index**	**Volumes**	**Average Price**	**Index**	**Volumes**	**Average Price**	**Index**	**Volumes**	**Average Price**	**Index**
Antiques and collectibles	$8.77	n.a.	n.a.	n.a.	n.a.	n.a.	n.a.	n.a.	n.a.	n.a.	n.a.	n.a.	n.a.
Architecture	n.a.	n.a.	n.a.	n.a.	n.a.	n.a.	n.a.	n.a.	n.a.	n.a.	n.a.	n.a.	n.a.
Art	n.a.	n.a.	n.a.	n.a.	n.a.	n.a.	n.a.	n.a.	n.a.	n.a.	n.a.	n.a.	n.a.
Bibles	n.a.	n.a.	n.a.	n.a.	n.a.	n.a.	n.a.	n.a.	n.a.	n.a.	n.a.	n.a.	n.a.
Biography and autobiography	7.51	7	$10.71	142.6	5	$9.28	123.6	7	$9.85	131.2	3	$9.99	133.0
Body, mind, and spirit	7.99	2	8.99	112.5	n.a.	n.a.	n.a.	n.a.	n.a.	n.a.	n.a.	n.a.	n.a.
Business and economics	9.32	n.a.	n.a.	n.a.	1	8.99	96.5	3	8.99	96.5	n.a.	n.a.	n.a.
Children	6.22	224	6.98	112.2	177	6.97	112.1	225	7.01	112.7	181	7.56	121.5
Comics and graphic novels	n.a.	n.a.	n.a.	n.a.	n.a.	n.a.	n.a.	n.a.	n.a.	n.a.	n.a.	n.a.	n.a.
Computers	n.a.	n.a.	n.a.	n.a.	n.a.	n.a.	n.a.	n.a.	n.a.	n.a.	n.a.	n.a.	n.a.
Cooking	n.a.	n.a.	n.a.	n.a.	n.a.	n.a.	n.a.	n.a.	n.a.	n.a.	n.a.	n.a.	n.a.
Crafts and hobbies	n.a.	n.a.	n.a.	n.a.	n.a.	n.a.	n.a.	n.a.	n.a.	n.a.	n.a.	n.a.	n.a.
Design	n.a.	n.a.	n.a.	n.a.	n.a.	n.a.	n.a.	n.a.	n.a.	n.a.	n.a.	n.a.	n.a.
Drama	6.30	n.a.	n.a.	n.a.	n.a.	n.a.	n.a.	n.a.	n.a.	n.a.	n.a.	n.a.	n.a.
Education	n.a.	n.a.	n.a.	n.a.	n.a.	n.a.	n.a.	n.a.	n.a.	n.a.	n.a.	n.a.	n.a.
Family and relationships	7.99	n.a.	n.a.	n.a.	n.a.	n.a.	n.a.	n.a.	n.a.	n.a.	n.a.	n.a.	n.a.
Fiction	6.80	2,998	7.23	106.3	2,753	7.31	107.5	2,713	7.24	106.5	2,436	7.41	109.0
Foreign language study	7.08	n.a.	n.a.	n.a.	n.a.	n.a.	n.a.	n.a.	n.a.	n.a.	n.a.	n.a.	n.a.
Games and activities	n.a.	2	8.99	n.a.	n.a.	n.a.	n.a.	1	8.50	n.a.	n.a.	n.a.	n.a.
Gardening	n.a.	n.a.	n.a.	n.a.	n.a.	n.a.	n.a.	n.a.	n.a.	n.a.	n.a.	n.a.	n.a.
Health and fitness	7.92	n.a.	n.a.	n.a.	1	9.99	126.1	3	8.66	109.3	2	10.99	138.8
History	9.95	4	9.49	95.4	5	9.99	100.4	3	9.99	100.4	4	8.99	90.4
House and home	n.a.	n.a.	n.a.	n.a.	n.a.	n.a.	n.a.	n.a.	n.a.	n.a.	n.a.	n.a.	n.a.
Humor	n.a.	1	7.99	n.a.	1	9.99	n.a.	2	12.49	n.a.	n.a.	n.a.	n.a.

Language arts and disciplines	13.25	n.a.	n.a.	n.a.	n.a.	n.a.	n.a.	n.a.	n.a.	n.a.	1	7.99	60.3
Law	n.a.	n.a.	n.a.	n.a.	n.a.	n.a.	n.a.	n.a.	n.a.	n.a.	n.a.	n.a.	n.a.
Literary collections	5.95	n.a.	n.a.	n.a.	n.a.	n.a.	n.a.	n.a.	n.a.	n.a.	n.a.	n.a.	n.a.
Literary criticism	7.99	n.a.	n.a.	n.a.	n.a.	n.a.	n.a.	n.a.	n.a.	n.a.	n.a.	n.a.	n.a.
Mathematics	n.a.	n.a.	n.a.	n.a.	n.a.	n.a.	n.a.	n.a.	n.a.	n.a.	n.a.	n.a.	n.a.
Medical	8.99	n.a.	n.a.	n.a.	n.a.	n.a.	n.a.	n.a.	n.a.	n.a.	n.a.	n.a.	n.a.
Music	n.a.	n.a.	n.a.	n.a.	n.a.	n.a.	n.a.	n.a.	n.a.	n.a.	n.a.	n.a.	n.a.
Nature	n.a.	n.a.	n.a.	n.a.	n.a.	n.a.	n.a.	n.a.	n.a.	n.a.	n.a.	n.a.	n.a.
Performing arts	9.99	n.a.	n.a.	n.a.	n.a.	n.a.	n.a.	n.a.	n.a.	n.a.	1	8.99	90.0
Pets	7.99	n.a.	n.a.	n.a.	n.a.	n.a.	n.a.	n.a.	n.a.	n.a.	n.a.	n.a.	n.a.
Philosophy	6.47	n.a.	n.a.	n.a.	n.a.	n.a.	n.a.	n.a.	n.a.	n.a.	n.a.	n.a.	n.a.
Photography	n.a.	n.a.	n.a.	n.a.	n.a.	n.a.	n.a.	n.a.	n.a.	n.a.	n.a.	n.a.	n.a.
Poetry	7.95	1	3.99	50.2	n.a.	n.a.	n.a.	n.a.	n.a.	n.a.	n.a.	n.a.	n.a.
Political science	7.97	n.a.	n.a.	n.a.	1	8.99	112.8	1	9.99	125.3	1	9.99	125.3
Psychology	n.a.	n.a.	n.a.	n.a.	n.a.	n.a.	n.a.	1	13.99	n.a.	1	4.99	n.a.
Reference	7.99	5	15.70	196.5	n.a.	n.a.	n.a.	n.a.	n.a.	n.a.	n.a.	n.a.	n.a.
Religion	7.99	n.a.	n.a.	n.a.	n.a.	n.a.	n.a.	n.a.	n.a.	n.a.	n.a.	n.a.	n.a.
Science	n.a.	1	13.99	n.a.	n.a.	n.a.	n.a.	n.a.	n.a.	n.a.	n.a.	n.a.	n.a.
Self-help	7.99	n.a.	n.a.	n.a.	n.a.	n.a.	n.a.	6	13.99	175.1	4	12.74	159.4
Social science	n.a.	n.a.	n.a.	n.a.	n.a.	n.a.	n.a.	n.a.	n.a.	n.a.	n.a.	n.a.	n.a.
Sports and recreation	7.99	1	9.99	125.0	n.a.	n.a.	n.a.	n.a.	n.a.	n.a.	n.a.	n.a.	n.a.
Study aids	n.a.	n.a.	n.a.	n.a.	n.a.	n.a.	n.a.	n.a.	n.a.	n.a.	n.a.	n.a.	n.a.
Technology and engineering	n.a.	n.a.	n.a.	n.a.	n.a.	n.a.	n.a.	n.a.	n.a.	n.a.	n.a.	n.a.	n.a.
Transportation	n.a.	n.a.	n.a.	n.a.	n.a.	n.a.	n.a.	n.a.	n.a.	n.a.	n.a.	n.a.	n.a.
Travel	n.a.	n.a.	n.a.	n.a.	n.a.	n.a.	n.a.	n.a.	n.a.	n.a.	n.a.	n.a.	n.a.
True crime	7.64	13	8.45	110.6	12	8.41	110.1	7	8.28	108.4	6	8.82	115.4
Young adult	8.13	6	7.99	98.3	5	8.39	103.2	25	10.67	131.2	34	9.64	118.6
Totals and Averages	$6.83	3,265	$7.25	106.1	2,961	$7.31	107.0	2,997	$7.29	106.7	2,674	$7.47	109.4

Compiled by Narda Tafuri, University of Scranton, from data supplied by Baker & Taylor.
n.a. = not available

Table 7 / U.S. Paperback Books (Excluding Mass Market): Average Prices and Price Indexes, 2016–2019

Index Base: 2010 = 100

	2010	2016 Final			2017 Final			2018 Preliminary			2019 Preliminary		
BISAC Category	**Average Price**	**Volumes**	**Average Price**	**Index**	**Volumes**	**Average Price**	**Index**	**Volumes**	**Average Price**	**Index**	**Volumes**	**Average Price**	**Index**
Antiques and collectibles	$25.53	148	$35.35	138.5	114	$40.67	159.3	88	$41.90	164.1	86	$40.10	157.1
Architecture	45.31	785	50.25	110.9	762	49.39	109.0	741	49.53	109.3	897	50.32	111.1
Art	38.25	1,830	50.28	131.4	1,720	41.04	107.3	1,725	40.16	105.0	1,720	39.15	102.4
Bibles	38.66	618	44.05	113.9	714	40.54	104.9	713	45.73	118.3	629	47.75	123.5
Biography and autobiography	20.35	2,575	20.25	99.5	2,393	20.56	101.0	2,561	20.61	101.3	2,246	20.60	101.2
Body, mind, and spirit	18.03	728	18.20	101.0	689	18.24	101.2	750	18.11	100.4	786	18.92	105.0
Business and economics	69.30	7,065	93.01	134.2	5,956	88.76	128.1	7,017	85.43	123.3	6,439	73.19	105.6
Children	10.42	12,264	14.96	143.6	11,825	16.10	154.6	11,517	12.81	122.9	11,523	12.32	118.3
Comics and graphic novels	16.11	2,153	18.60	115.5	2,057	18.49	114.8	2,310	19.12	118.7	2,183	20.60	127.9
Computers	70.42	4,291	128.17	182.0	2,602	96.95	137.7	3,397	106.98	151.9	3,294	101.29	143.8
Cooking	19.95	1,030	20.82	104.4	934	21.35	107.0	928	21.13	105.9	818	21.55	108.0
Crafts and hobbies	19.34	929	19.90	102.9	816	20.46	105.8	688	21.48	111.0	566	22.53	116.5
Design	63.98	254	38.29	59.9	242	40.56	63.4	234	41.06	64.2	254	44.81	70.0
Drama	18.95	522	19.68	103.9	652	22.54	118.9	557	20.31	107.2	465	22.60	119.3
Education	42.98	4,589	66.40	154.5	4,479	58.30	135.6	4,349	64.64	150.4	3,865	55.28	128.6
Family and relationships	18.72	614	22.98	122.7	523	21.44	114.5	585	22.28	119.0	613	21.52	114.9
Fiction	17.99	10,791	17.01	94.6	10,455	16.77	93.2	10,313	17.53	97.4	9,491	17.46	97.1
Foreign language study	31.33	856	49.40	157.7	1,013	41.69	133.1	796	44.35	141.6	893	41.93	133.8
Games and activities	16.57	1,831	14.27	86.1	1,258	15.57	94.0	695	17.40	105.0	625	17.98	108.5
Gardening	23.45	124	22.51	96.0	129	23.12	98.6	120	21.42	91.3	123	22.26	94.9
Health and fitness	26.95	1,034	36.39	135.0	1,039	30.93	114.8	1,053	31.36	116.4	955	31.70	117.6
History	35.79	6,431	39.15	109.4	6,348	38.73	108.2	6,335	40.31	112.6	6,542	40.27	112.5
House and home	21.19	89	20.15	95.1	104	26.21	123.7	86	22.43	105.8	108	23.99	113.2
Humor	14.37	301	15.42	107.3	302	15.80	110.0	260	15.48	107.7	253	15.57	108.4

Language arts and disciplines	64.46	2,313	77.03	119.5	1,696	72.90	113.1	1,589	60.76	94.3	1,641	56.78	88.1
Law	72.07	3,860	87.35	121.2	3,120	83.10	115.3	3,388	90.99	126.2	2,979	83.58	116.0
Literary collections	36.42	400	33.46	91.9	406	27.41	75.3	437	28.66	78.7	451	24.47	67.2
Literary criticism	36.57	2,061	43.32	118.4	1,935	43.30	118.4	2,152	50.81	138.9	2,320	44.31	121.2
Mathematics	86.13	1,565	97.31	113.0	953	78.54	91.2	1,533	106.69	123.9	1,356	76.99	89.4
Medical	90.22	6,442	132.71	147.1	3,696	86.85	96.3	5,254	118.82	131.7	4,470	89.56	99.3
Music	22.83	2,662	30.42	133.3	1,975	29.32	128.4	1,808	27.54	120.6	1,968	29.77	130.4
Nature	37.28	606	49.37	132.4	565	34.67	93.0	584	46.76	125.4	652	42.85	114.9
Performing arts	33.53	832	38.71	115.5	858	38.23	114.0	947	42.83	127.7	965	38.10	113.6
Pets	17.34	159	20.31	117.1	110	18.29	105.5	112	18.72	108.0	121	20.17	116.3
Philosophy	52.66	1,787	55.64	105.7	1,532	42.46	80.6	1,870	53.25	101.1	1,897	41.70	79.2
Photography	31.30	404	33.86	108.2	416	35.12	112.2	289	33.96	108.5	308	40.07	128.0
Poetry	16.73	2,064	17.23	103.0	2,033	17.24	103.1	2,142	17.22	102.9	1,976	17.28	103.3
Political science	41.00	3,952	49.95	121.8	3,881	47.27	115.3	4,394	59.06	144.0	4,289	50.66	123.6
Psychology	47.98	2,240	61.13	127.4	1,949	53.42	111.3	2,052	61.69	128.6	2,129	51.85	108.1
Reference	84.85	573	156.03	183.9	488	189.53	223.4	421	186.25	219.5	331	148.88	175.5
Religion	22.08	6,765	26.32	119.2	6,776	25.74	116.6	6,619	27.02	122.4	6,258	27.19	123.2
Science	116.37	5,449	131.20	112.7	2,443	89.79	77.2	4,847	133.87	115.0	4,115	99.20	85.2
Self-help	17.84	991	17.92	100.4	948	17.72	99.3	1,119	17.18	96.3	1,250	17.90	100.3
Social science	45.05	5,580	56.91	126.3	4,554	48.54	107.8	5,579	60.94	135.3	5,575	49.61	110.1
Sports and recreation	22.30	1,107	24.91	111.7	1,013	26.04	116.8	910	26.53	119.0	975	27.38	122.8
Study aids	49.24	708	38.60	78.4	748	34.23	69.5	691	42.95	87.2	2,462	44.00	89.4
Technology and engineering	111.20	4,112	139.22	125.2	2,279	98.34	88.4	3,983	147.69	132.8	3,004	121.53	109.3
Transportation	36.26	531	36.39	100.3	523	38.89	107.3	500	34.42	94.9	395	43.50	120.0
Travel	20.93	1,679	21.01	100.4	1,499	21.74	103.9	1,619	21.17	101.1	1,529	21.43	102.4
True crime	20.94	142	19.53	93.2	168	20.16	96.3	213	20.07	95.9	211	19.80	94.6
Young adult	14.86	2,717	25.49	171.5	2,724	18.40	123.8	2,934	18.02	121.3	2,865	18.40	123.8
Totals and Averages	$42.06	123,553	$55.97	133.1	106,414	$42.92	102.0	115,804	$53.71	127.7	111,866	$45.31	107.7

Compiled by Narda Tafuri, University of Scranton, from data supplied by Baker & Taylor.
* = figures revised from previous editions based on new data from Baker & Taylor.

Table 7A / U.S. Audiobooks: Average Prices and Price Indexes, 2016–2019

Index Base: 2010 = 100

	2010	2016 Final			2017 Final			2018 Preliminary			2019 Preliminary		
BISAC Category	**Average Price**	**Volumes**	**Average Price**	**Index**	**Volumes**	**Average Price**	**Index**	**Volumes**	**Average Price**	**Index**	**Volumes**	**Average Price**	**Index**
Antiques and collectibles	$36.66	3	$26.66	72.7	3	$33.32	90.9	n.a.	n.a.	n.a.	n.a.	n.a.	n.a.
Architecture	41.24	7	25.42	61.6	10	31.49	76.4	2	$22.99	55.7	8	$33.12	80.3
Art	58.21	22	16.95	29.1	24	28.36	48.7	16	31.54	54.2	8	31.05	53.3
Bibles	43.28	7	122.85	283.9	6	49.98	115.5	2	49.99	115.5	3	76.31	176.3
Biography and autobiography	50.79	1,688	31.87	62.7	1,445	37.46	73.7	1,241	42.80	84.3	1,378	43.63	85.9
Body, mind, and spirit	32.98	148	28.99	87.9	158	29.41	89.2	147	35.86	108.7	180	35.14	106.5
Business and economics	49.70	1,316	27.82	56.0	883	32.32	65.0	799	35.66	71.7	656	36.87	74.2
Children	37.80	1,295	34.83	92.2	1,701	31.14	82.4	1,333	36.52	96.6	1,553	37.25	98.5
Comics and graphic novels	n.a.	1	9.99	n.a.	3	8.99	n.a.	n.a.	n.a.	n.a.	68	37.49	n.a.
Computers	45.00	30	27.05	60.1	42	29.30	65.1	27	42.32	94.0	33	38.05	84.6
Cooking	44.97	45	32.23	71.7	63	35.24	78.4	58	39.69	88.3	16	37.30	82.9
Crafts and hobbies	24.98	2	27.47	110.0	2	12.99	52.0	3	22.32	89.4	5	39.79	159.3
Design	n.a.	1	9.99	n.a.	n.a.	n.a.	n.a.	6	51.31	n.a.	1	39.99	n.a.
Drama	33.21	152	14.36	43.2	60	20.23	60.9	163	18.48	55.6	97	22.24	67.0
Education	45.71	51	40.11	87.7	39	33.89	74.1	41	33.58	73.5	39	38.20	83.6
Family and relationships	41.17	246	29.57	71.8	204	32.02	77.8	183	34.16	83.0	185	37.01	89.9
Fiction	50.38	19,260	24.32	48.3	11,019	34.04	67.6	9,917	39.33	78.1	11,450	40.15	79.7
Foreign language study	45.11	45	110.24	244.4	96	79.65	176.6	100	206.97	458.8	152	85.46	189.5
Games and activities	n.a.	5	27.99	n.a.	10	40.79	n.a.	5	39.99	n.a.	2	22.49	n.a.
Gardening	47.82	2	31.49	65.9	5	26.98	56.4	n.a.	n.a.	n.a.	1	14.99	31.3
Health and fitness	43.09	289	32.62	75.7	289	39.77	92.3	264	38.61	89.6	242	40.17	93.2
History	58.07	1,210	33.47	57.6	904	44.42	76.5	809	47.40	81.6	811	46.40	79.9
House and home	n.a.	33	38.79	n.a.	39	41.41	n.a.	20	35.48	n.a.	13	34.45	n.a.
Humor	36.62	103	27.07	73.9	62	29.53	80.6	93	41.75	114.0	75	35.67	97.4

Language arts and disciplines	38.34	41	30.47	79.5	39	37.71	98.3	29	34.50	90.0	47	38.01	99.1
Law	64.49	41	28.46	44.1	31	42.50	65.9	34	34.16	53.0	25	31.15	48.3
Literary collections	52.07	72	34.98	67.2	45	33.45	64.2	69	43.17	82.9	67	41.97	80.6
Literary criticism	42.53	54	29.32	68.9	32	31.68	74.5	34	41.10	96.6	27	32.61	76.7
Mathematics	n.a.	8	26.24	n.a.	10	21.49	n.a.	4	26.99	n.a.	7	46.70	n.a.
Medical	40.13	24	22.07	55.0	49	36.06	89.9	36	41.82	104.2	31	32.70	81.5
Music	35.67	94	27.55	77.2	142	28.20	79.1	61	30.91	86.6	64	41.50	116.4
Nature	41.20	87	21.69	52.6	63	31.88	77.4	53	35.10	85.2	91	41.98	101.9
Performing arts	40.60	185	37.84	93.2	72	35.41	87.2	99	40.51	99.8	116	40.91	100.8
Pets	38.33	61	39.42	102.9	46	37.77	98.5	29	38.02	99.2	18	42.77	111.6
Philosophy	53.05	135	27.26	51.4	103	23.53	44.4	54	37.87	71.4	74	34.24	64.5
Photography	n.a.	2	34.99	n.a.	n.a.	n.a.	n.a.	n.a.	n.a.	n.a.	n.a.	n.a.	n.a.
Poetry	33.59	24	15.07	44.9	46	22.24	66.2	56	27.17	80.9	106	28.89	86.0
Political science	48.04	404	29.37	61.1	324	37.68	78.4	377	39.25	81.7	369	43.08	89.7
Psychology	45.42	191	28.38	62.5	157	37.66	82.9	162	37.25	82.0	99	35.16	77.4
Reference	59.99	11	23.17	38.6	15	35.79	59.7	8	46.62	77.7	7	32.14	53.6
Religion	33.94	1,243	25.78	76.0	1,249	26.94	79.4	1,152	30.51	89.9	930	35.13	103.5
Science	51.89	193	28.64	55.2	158	33.96	65.4	212	38.97	75.1	168	41.25	79.5
Self-help	39.43	534	32.81	83.2	382	33.75	85.6	427	36.21	91.8	516	35.42	89.8
Social science	48.07	312	25.33	52.7	298	35.10	73.0	322	35.98	74.9	265	41.89	87.1
Sports and recreation	48.48	223	25.98	53.6	145	36.42	75.1	111	38.35	79.1	144	42.01	86.7
Study aids	19.41	2	52.98	272.9	n.a.	n.a.	n.a.	3	41.63	214.5	2	63.00	324.5
Technology and engineering	53.33	82	93.02	174.4	103	101.94	191.2	31	45.18	84.7	13	39.29	73.7
Transportation	46.28	17	32.10	69.4	9	30.21	65.3	10	47.49	102.6	2	49.99	108.0
Travel	50.96	145	17.03	33.4	39	30.91	60.7	32	43.67	85.7	49	42.32	83.0
True crime	52.58	173	33.89	64.5	182	38.99	74.2	189	36.65	69.7	193	43.11	82.0
Young adult	44.81	1,742	29.40	65.6	1,463	39.21	87.5	1,118	44.63	99.6	1,222	43.82	97.8
Totals and Averages	$48.00	32,061	$26.89	56.0	22,269	$34.87	72.6	19,941	$39.69	82.7	21,628	$40.33	84.0

Compiled by Narda Tafuri, University of Scranton, from data supplied by Baker & Taylor.

Table 7B / U.S. E-Books: Average Prices and Price Indexes, 2016–2019

Index Base: 2010 = 100

	2010	2016 Final			2017 Final			2018 Preliminary			2019 Preliminary		
BISAC Category	Average Price	Volumes	Average Price	Index	Volumes	Average Price	Index	Volumes	Average Price	Index	Volumes	Average Price	Index
Antiques and collectibles	$30.24	100	$19.20	63.5	118	$16.64	55.0	171	$9.88	32.7	153	$10.84	35.9
Architecture	66.57	438	39.92	60.0	818	21.98	33.0	381	47.84	71.9	420	40.99	61.6
Art	41.56	2,663	15.81	38.0	2,356	18.16	43.7	1,397	34.93	84.0	1,530	25.99	62.5
Bibles	6.11	280	12.26	200.7	2,148	11.88	194.4	418	9.74	159.4	267	12.30	201.3
Biography and autobiography	15.47	6,567	20.37	131.7	7,908	17.24	111.5	7,111	20.05	129.6	6,859	21.60	139.6
Body, mind, and spirit	13.95	2,114	11.88	85.2	2,580	11.26	80.7	2,898	11.32	81.2	3,407	12.15	87.1
Business and economics	44.82	8,432	47.83	106.7	9,248	41.29	92.1	27,580	51.52	115.0	23,692	66.78	149.0
Children	13.82	16,469	20.79	150.4	26,145	17.92	129.7	26,960	15.39	111.4	25,264	18.57	134.4
Comics and graphic novels	11.39	1,099	9.05	79.5	876	8.97	78.7	980	8.25	72.5	810	9.36	82.2
Computers	62.09	4,164	72.58	116.9	3,177	82.11	132.2	3,653	78.42	126.3	2,159	63.06	101.6
Cooking	16.79	2,054	15.17	90.4	2,691	12.13	72.2	2,690	13.22	78.8	2,747	11.89	70.8
Crafts and hobbies	17.63	1,103	12.84	72.8	1,176	11.34	64.3	608	13.95	79.1	545	14.24	80.8
Design	37.03	125	24.28	65.6	170	20.84	56.3	112	24.39	65.9	122	29.64	80.0
Drama	4.86	1,710	10.32	212.3	1,546	12.03	247.4	1,085	11.01	226.5	1,317	9.44	194.2
Education	45.95	4,505	40.96	89.1	7,660	40.50	88.1	4,145	44.77	97.4	3,989	41.62	90.6
Family and relationships	14.79	1,837	16.37	110.7	1,762	13.05	88.2	2,310	12.69	85.8	2,321	14.51	98.1
Fiction	7.06	62,343	12.71	180.0	75,766	9.84	139.3	82,846	11.39	161.3	81,312	13.56	192.1
Foreign language study	46.68	906	34.71	74.4	1,678	23.12	49.5	2,282	21.91	46.9	1,527	25.42	54.5
Games and activities	12.85	700	9.49	73.9	930	8.67	67.5	1,481	6.77	52.7	342	15.81	123.1
Gardening	17.41	247	13.31	76.5	555	12.43	71.4	301	15.59	89.6	280	15.97	91.7
Health and fitness	18.78	2,394	14.83	79.0	3,002	13.58	72.3	3,059	13.63	72.6	2,884	15.75	83.9
History	48.20	9,425	38.50	79.9	13,019	29.92	62.1	9,416	42.16	87.5	8,451	44.90	93.2
House and home	21.57	246	12.60	58.4	392	14.00	64.9	244	16.45	76.3	211	16.67	77.3
Humor	11.15	1,231	10.15	91.1	848	10.58	94.9	1,110	13.43	120.4	805	14.36	128.8

Language arts and disciplines	75.61	1,986	78.29	103.5	2,844	82.27	108.8	2,930	68.08	90.0	2,537	104.42	138.1
Law	112.19	2,168	95.77	85.4	2,657	86.63	77.2	3,020	114.22	101.8	2,521	117.58	104.8
Literary collections	20.27	1,088	18.92	93.3	2,159	15.68	77.4	1,512	15.49	76.4	6,212	4.62	22.8
Literary criticism	87.17	2,672	69.07	79.2	3,136	70.67	81.1	3,629	83.02	95.2	2,920	77.52	88.9
Mathematics	112.32	1,463	85.19	75.8	1,506	56.58	50.4	993	81.86	72.9	731	89.79	79.9
Medical	135.71	3,477	110.50	81.4	3,574	96.30	71.0	3,289	106.14	78.2	2,213	94.18	69.4
Music	32.65	1,506	22.35	68.5	2,538	20.88	64.0	3,031	16.39	50.2	1,698	23.96	73.4
Nature	59.48	780	45.70	76.8	806	39.73	66.8	850	27.08	45.5	719	26.59	44.7
Performing arts	32.17	1,763	32.06	99.7	1,879	24.11	75.0	2,073	25.17	78.2	1,934	23.36	72.6
Pets	14.50	402	12.79	88.2	805	10.50	72.4	443	10.42	71.9	413	12.78	88.1
Philosophy	71.43	2,530	45.86	64.2	3,608	34.82	48.7	2,747	51.04	71.5	2,491	43.93	61.5
Photography	27.23	442	20.52	75.4	514	17.08	62.7	313	19.22	70.6	260	22.94	84.2
Poetry	9.54	3,088	8.24	86.3	5,189	8.77	91.9	5,010	8.07	84.6	4,623	8.75	91.7
Political science	59.74	4,153	51.50	86.2	5,231	42.57	71.3	4,714	54.33	90.9	3,509	46.14	77.2
Psychology	56.42	1,951	44.26	78.5	2,720	43.12	76.4	2,073	44.40	78.7	1,751	39.41	69.9
Reference	22.92	4,373	16.72	72.9	2,999	18.62	81.2	1,268	39.13	170.7	872	60.50	263.9
Religion	27.81	8,220	23.05	82.9	13,497	20.67	74.3	11,560	26.30	94.6	10,170	26.29	94.5
Science	155.80	3,978	99.79	64.0	5,749	65.79	42.2	3,554	95.76	61.5	2,828	89.54	57.5
Self-help	14.06	3,728	14.21	101.1	5,351	12.17	86.5	5,275	13.18	93.8	6,575	12.24	87.1
Social science	56.83	5,067	49.58	87.2	6,985	40.93	72.0	4,750	49.46	87.0	3,813	51.22	90.1
Sports and recreation	19.22	1,776	17.59	91.5	1,920	17.26	89.8	1,453	20.33	105.8	1,320	20.46	106.4
Study aids	13.94	18,528	30.11	216.0	2,388	32.76	235.0	1,332	13.90	99.7	3,537	27.63	198.2
Technology and engineering	158.44	2,987	128.19	80.9	3,996	86.25	54.4	2,531	121.43	76.6	1,626	115.59	73.0
Transportation	33.12	309	23.76	71.7	271	24.87	75.1	322	27.52	83.1	313	28.14	85.0
Travel	15.84	2,134	12.86	81.2	2,521	14.67	92.6	1,937	17.56	110.8	2,877	12.15	76.7
True crime	10.37	474	21.85	210.7	411	20.53	197.9	515	21.36	206.0	584	24.10	232.4
Young adult	11.96	5,167	23.82	199.2	5,501	20.04	167.6	6,052	18.40	153.8	5,990	20.19	168.8
Totals and Averages	$41.61	217,362	$30.24	72.7	257,324	$25.29	60.8	260,414	$29.19	70.2	246,451	$29.30	70.4

Compiled by Narda Tafuri, University of Scranton, from data supplied by Baker & Taylor.

(continued from page 350)

Science Citation Index, and Social Sciences Citation Index, as well as in EBSCO's Academic Search Premier/Ultimate and Masterfile Premier and Elsevier's Scopus. This is the fifth year where titles indexed in Scopus are included in the data. Adding Scopus expands this price survey from about 11,000 titles in 2015 to the current 18,626. The increase in the sample size makes the results more likely to reflect pricing trends accurately.

Tables 8 and 8A cover prices for periodicals and serials for five years, 2016 through 2020. The 2020 pricing is the actual renewal pricing for serial titles indexed in the selected products. These tables were derived from pricing data supplied by EBSCO Information Services and reflect broad pricing changes aggregated from serials indexed in the six major products mentioned above. U.S. Periodicals: Average Prices and Price Indexes (Table 1) is based on price changes seen in a static set of approximately 6,000 serial titles. Average Price of Serials (Table 8) is based on a much broader set of titles, approximately 18,626; however, the titles are not static, so although the table is useful in showing price changes for periodicals it does not rise to the level of a price index. The indexes selected for this price survey were deemed to be representative of serials frequently purchased by academic and public libraries. There are some foreign titles in the indexes, so the scope is broader, and this may give a better picture of the overall price pressures experienced in libraries. Table 8 contains both print and online serials pricing. Table 8A is a subset of the titles treated in Table 8 and contains only online serials pricing.

The most important trend seen in the data in Table 8 is that increases in prices have remained constant since the economic recovery began. Price increases have hovered around 6 percent annually since 2010. For titles with online availability (Table 8A), the rates of increase are very similar, also averaging around 6 percent over the past five years and is 6.2 percent for 2020. There is a difference between the average prices for print serials and online serials, so, at least for this set of data, print formats do cost less than their online counterparts. Several large publishers have made online pricing available only through custom quotes, so there is not a standard retail price, and the pricing data are not available for this survey. Consequently, the number of titles covered in the online survey (Table 8A) is less than the number of titles in Table 8, but online titles are now 55 percent of the overall dataset.

Another interesting trend is that science subject areas do not dominate the list of subjects with the largest price increases. The subject areas that displayed large increases were quite varied. Arts and architecture, psychology, education, health sciences, math and computer science, geography, sociology, and political science saw higher increases than most. Some of these same areas showed the highest increases in the online table (Table 8A), as well. Average prices of journals in the science and technology areas have been far higher than in other areas, and this trend continues, with the average cost of chemistry and physics journals (Table 8) being $4,797.13 and $3,851.42, respectively. Although these STEM titles are not inflating at high rates, the impact of a 5 percent increase in a $4,000 title is much higher than a 9 percent increase on a $300 title. Online journals (Table 8A) showed similar average prices for chemistry ($5,098.01) and physics ($4,359.52).

In this price study, as in similar price studies, the data become less accurate at describing price changes as the sample size becomes smaller. For that reason, drawing conclusions about price changes in subject areas with a limited number of titles will be less accurate than for large areas or the broader price survey. Price changes are far more volatile where smaller datasets are used. For example, in Table 8, library science, with 195 titles, showed price changes of 30.7, 3.4, 5.0, and 4.7 percent between 2016 and 2020. Librarians are encouraged to look at an average price change over the period or the overall number for the price study (6.0 percent) to calculate inflation. Year-to-year price changes in small subject areas are too unstable to be reliable for this purpose.

Foreign Prices

As shown in the chart below, in 2019 the U.S. dollar decreased in strength against the Canadian dollar (-4.4 percent), British pound sterling (-2.6 percent), and the Japanese Yen (-1.2 percent), but increased against the Euro (2.3 percent).

	12/31/2015	12/31/2016	12/31/2017	12/31/2018	12/31/2019
Canada	1.39	1.35	1.26	1.36	1.3
Euro	0.92	0.95	0.83	0.87	0.89
U.K.	0.68	0.81	0.74	0.78	0.76
Japan	120.42	117.03	112.55	109.85	108.53

Data from Bureau of Fiscal Services. U.S. Treasury Department (http://www.fiscal.treasury.gov/fsreports/rpt/treasRptRateExch/treasRptRateExch_home.htm).

Foreign Book Prices

British Academic Books (Table 9), compiled by George Aulisio, University of Scranton, indicates the average prices and price indexes from 2016 through 2019. The percent of change in titles and average price is calculated for 2018 to 2019, and the index price shows the percent of change between 2019 and the base year of 2010. This index is compiled using data from GOBI Library Solutions and utilizes prices from cloth editions except when not available. The data also draw from select titles from continental Europe and Africa. The index does not separate more expensive reference titles. Small numbers of titles that include higher-priced reference sets may not be reliable indicators of price changes. This table does not include e-book prices.

Data in the "Totals and Averages" row include the total of the LC Classes profiled in this table, not the total of all books profiled by GOBI Library Solutions. In 2019, total British academic books profiled by GOBI increased to 19,350 titles. This is the second year the table has recorded an increase in titles.

In 2019 British academic books experienced an overall price decrease of -1.8 percent, bringing the average price for all books profiled to £72.61. The 2019 price increase comes at a time when the United Kingdom's Consumer Price Index saw a relatively moderate 1.4 percent inflation as of December 2019 (http://www.ons.gov.uk).

(text continues on page 370)

Table 8 / Average Price of Serials, Based on Titles in Select Serial Indexes, 2016–2020

Subject	LC Class	Titles	2016 Average Price	2017 Average Price	Percent Change 2016–2017	2018 Average Price	Percent Change 2017–2018	2019 Average Price	Percent Change 2018–2019	2020 Average Price	Percent Change 2019–2020
Agriculture	S	552	$929.77	$988.43	6.3%	$1,045.97	5.8%	$1,113.72	6.5%	$1,183.56	6.3%
Anthropology	GN	160	461.18	489.64	6.2	536.11	9.5	562.41	4.9	590.26	5.0
Arts and architecture	N	266	299.52	322.75	7.8	344.49	6.7	360.04	4.5	389.81	8.3
Astronomy	QB	73	1,762.59	1,854.06	5.2	1,935.86	4.4	2,037.22	5.2	2,163.49	6.2
Biology	QH	1,164	2,239.83	2,366.06	5.6	2,504.41	5.8	2,653.66	6.0	2,789.38	5.1
Botany	QK	181	1,398.94	1,479.45	5.8	1,541.71	4.2	1,630.43	5.8	1,701.46	4.4
Business and economics	HA-HJ	1,475	1,003.36	1,165.54	16.2	1,221.55	4.8	1,286.65	5.3	1,353.24	5.2
Chemistry	QD	383	3,939.03	4,127.26	4.8	4,313.78	4.5	4,562.93	5.8	4,797.13	5.1
Education	L	488	620.75	664.22	7.0	709.85	6.9	763.38	7.5	815.22	6.8
Engineering	T	1,682	1,643.09	1,750.42	6.5	1,953.25	11.6	2,077.98	6.4	2,211.96	6.4
Food Science	TX	97	988.40	1,197.67	21.2	1,272.23	6.2	1,328.30	4.4	1,406.57	5.9
General works	A	233	262.57	273.48	4.2	295.57	8.1	310.24	5.0	324.56	4.6
Geography	G-GF	309	908.33	979.06	7.8	1,054.43	7.7	1,124.84	6.7	1,197.93	6.5
Geology	QE	241	1,563.25	1,665.30	6.5	1,767.07	6.1	1,900.27	7.5	2,018.97	6.2
Health sciences	R	3,715	1,165.55	1,241.40	6.5	1,328.88	7.0	1,410.08	6.1	1,505.79	6.8
History	C,D,E,F	986	308.47	332.44	7.8	353.92	6.5	376.98	6.5	399.18	5.9
Language and literature	P	1,134	318.02	337.01	6.0	361.12	7.2	382.08	5.8	403.49	5.6

Law	K	439	443.55	467.55	5.4	495.66	6.0	521.72	5.3	549.55	5.3
Library science	Z	195	650.99	850.73	30.7	879.95	3.4	924.18	5.0	967.71	4.7
Math and computer science	QA	872	1,326.80	1,394.36	5.1	1,481.87	6.3	1,566.86	5.7	1,671.71	6.7
Military and naval science	U,V	101	488.93	509.97	4.3	532.93	4.5	580.82	9.0	615.51	6.0
Music	M	157	229.78	243.38	5.9	259.07	6.4	273.39	5.5	288.14	5.4
Philosophy and religion	B-BD, BH-BX	628	338.79	360.10	6.3	379.33	5.3	395.93	4.4	414.14	4.6
Physics	QC	452	3,109.83	3,265.84	5.0	3,429.68	5.0	3,637.83	6.1	3,851.42	5.9
Political science	J	288	570.59	603.55	5.8	647.13	7.2	691.63	6.9	736.30	6.5
Psychology	BF	348	787.05	832.28	5.7	889.42	6.9	967.88	8.8	1,036.37	7.1
Recreation	GV	151	421.08	455.40	8.2	489.60	7.5	523.77	7.0	556.57	6.3
Science (general)	Q	223	1,174.95	1,255.35	6.8	1,305.93	4.0	1,376.91	5.4	1,464.45	6.4
Social sciences	H	145	706.94	755.77	6.9	799.28	5.8	843.80	5.6	892.65	5.8
Sociology	HM-HX	791	720.13	766.55	6.4	818.14	6.7	873.85	6.8	930.42	6.5
Technology	TA-TT	366	1,077.49	1,219.69	13.2	1,288.20	5.6	1,378.40	7.0	1,463.57	6.2
Zoology	QL	331	1,277.37	1,336.70	4.6	1,410.32	5.5	1,476.51	4.7	1,553.83	5.2
Totals and Averages		18,626	$1,125.09	$1,204.60	7.1%	$1,285.40	6.7%	$1,363.44	6.1%	$1,445.54	6.0%

Compiled by Stephen Bosch, University of Arizona. Data on serial pricing are supplied by EBSCO and based on titles indexed in EBSCO Academic Search Ultimate, EBSCO Masterfile Complete, Clarivate Analytics (formerly ISI) Arts and Humanities Citation Index, Clarivate Analytics Science Citation Index, Clarivate Analytics Social Sciences Citation Index, and Elsevier's Scopus.

Table 8A / Changes in the Average Price of Online Serials 2016–2020, Based on Titles in Select Serial Indexes

			2016	2017		2018		2019		2020	
Subject	**LC Class**	**Titles**	**Average Price**	**Average Price**	**Percent Change 2016–2017**	**Average Price**	**Percent Change 2017–2018**	**Average Price**	**Percent Change 2018–2019**	**Average Price**	**Percent Change 2019–2020**
Agriculture	S	245	$1,194.36	$1,258.77	5.4%	$1,323.68	5.2%	$1,422.01	7.4%	$1,513.63	6.4%
Anthropology	GN	107	578.31	613.67	6.1	655.90	6.9	696.89	6.3	733.09	5.2
Arts and Architecture	N	126	447.20	486.74	8.8	517.15	6.2	545.49	5.5	585.91	7.4
Astronomy	QB	46	2,304.56	2,435.71	5.7	2,547.50	4.6	2,683.05	5.3	2,862.83	6.7
Biology	QH	676	2,177.21	2,300.79	5.7	2,431.36	5.7	2,591.72	6.6	2,716.98	4.8
Botany	QK	111	1,584.62	1,670.39	5.4	1,723.09	3.2	1,814.10	5.3	1,879.97	3.6
Business and Economics	HA-HJ	825	1,313.09	1,572.33	19.7	1,637.99	4.2	1,722.99	5.2	1,810.42	5.1
Chemistry	QD	220	4,051.25	4,294.63	6.0	4,525.32	5.4	4,829.14	6.7	5,098.01	5.6
Education	L	353	751.55	805.28	7.1	858.97	6.7	927.01	7.9	990.36	6.8
Engineering	T	850	1,790.60	1,918.23	7.1	2,227.75	16.1	2,373.02	6.5	2,528.72	6.6
Food Science	TX	49	1,332.07	1,684.48	26.5	1,783.95	5.9	1,861.32	4.3	1,967.82	5.7
General Works	A	66	471.97	509.08	7.9	531.09	4.3	572.55	7.8	613.59	7.2
Geography	G-GF	195	856.60	921.52	7.6	990.90	7.5	1,067.04	7.7	1,142.48	7.1
Geology	QE	134	1,559.32	1,661.07	6.5	1,744.59	5.0	1,877.03	7.6	1,997.84	6.4
Health Sciences	R	1,736	1,307.86	1,392.28	6.5	1,487.17	6.8	1,575.61	5.9	1,686.88	7.1
History	C,D,E,F	536	404.16	438.51	8.5	466.43	6.4	502.43	7.7	534.34	6.4
Language and Literature	P	623	412.18	439.73	6.7	473.71	7.7	505.86	6.8	535.96	6.0

Law	K	185	613.06	650.98	6.2	693.78	6.6	728.74	5.0	764.61	4.9
Library Science	Z	121	815.02	1,121.03	37.5	1,150.48	2.6	1,208.72	5.1	1,264.12	4.6
Math and Computer Science	QA	582	1,352.69	1,430.59	5.8	1,535.37	7.3	1,636.30	6.6	1,764.56	7.8
Military and Naval Science	U,V	63	603.27	633.59	5.0	662.48	4.6	724.70	9.4	770.41	6.3
Music	M	88	307.78	326.10	6.0	347.64	6.6	367.35	5.7	386.29	5.2
Philosophy and Religion	B-BD, BH-BX	333	462.46	495.77	7.2	523.17	5.5	549.86	5.1	577.60	5.0
Physics	QC	296	3,435.38	3,634.24	5.8	3,836.62	5.6	4,097.26	6.8	4,359.52	6.4
Political Science	J	200	678.76	718.67	5.9	773.67	7.7	831.37	7.5	883.87	6.3
Psychology	BF	209	875.53	924.32	5.6	984.81	6.5	1,072.24	8.9	1,157.95	8.0
Recreation	GV	74	663.67	721.12	8.7	775.85	7.6	832.24	7.3	882.55	6.0
Science (general)	Q	128	1,506.18	1,612.45	7.1	1,665.97	3.3	1,756.31	5.4	1,866.45	6.3
Social Sciences	H	86	879.52	943.19	7.2	999.16	5.9	1,056.01	5.7	1,121.22	6.2
Sociology	HM-HX	552	833.53	885.97	6.3	943.56	6.5	1,011.83	7.2	1,079.72	6.7
Technology	TA-TT	166	1,551.35	1,825.65	17.7	1,928.32	5.6	2,075.63	7.6	2,207.11	6.3
Zoology	QL	181	1,472.14	1,537.94	4.5	1,616.40	5.1	1,708.78	5.7	1,814.56	6.2
Totals and Averages		10,162	$1,279.11	$1,381.20	8.0%	$1,478.62	7.1%	$1,573.72	6.4%	$1,671.66	6.2%

Compiled by Stephen Bosch, University of Arizona. Data on serial pricing are supplied by EBSCO and based on titles indexed in EBSCO Academic Search Ultimate, EBSCO Masterfile Complete, Clarivate Analytics (formerly ISI) Arts and Humanities Citation Index, Clarivate Analytics Science Citation Index, Clarivate Analytics Social Sciences Citation Index, and Elsevier's Scopus.

Table 9 / British Academic Books: Average Prices and Price Indexes, 2016–2019

Index Base: 2010 = 100

		2010		2016		2017		2018		2019			
Subject	**LC Class**	**Titles**	**Average Price (£)**	**Titles**	**Average Price (£)**	**Titles**	**Average Price (£)**	**Titles**	**Average Price (£)**	**Titles**	**Average Price (£)**	**Percent Change 2018–2019**	**Index**
Agriculture	S	154	£63.97	142	£77.66	125	£79.66	142	£85.45	154	£84.11	-1.6%	131.5
Anthropology	GN	154	50.85	148	53.08	121	60.79	150	65.47	173	74.65	14.0	146.8
Botany	QK	45	66.08	19	84.68	27	80.32	30	77.10	36	89.13	15.6	134.9
Business and economics	H-HJ	1,913	60.54	1,897	73.35	1,767	77.80	2,185	84.35	2,185	80.42	-4.7	132.8
Chemistry	QD	96	105.68	57	113.66	47	104.58	58	127.93	61	121.99	-4.6	115.4
Education	L	558	52.21	577	179.48	575	78.43	723	77.96	731	78.83	1.1	151.0
Engineering and technology	T-TS	742	61.84	681	78.93	692	82.39	654	86.12	693	90.24	4.8	145.9
Fine and applied arts	M, N	1,037	35.95	908	51.19	917	53.71	974	59.66	989	60.88	2.0	169.3
General works	A	30	60.03	27	106.91	33	92.37	33	108.43	37	85.11	-21.5	141.8
Geography	G-GF, GR-GT	276	65.69	447	75.21	315	87.06	317	86.29	342	81.01	-6.1	123.3
Geology	QE	33	52.28	28	69.53	30	57.36	30	74.38	51	58.66	-21.1	112.2
History	C,D,E,F	1,822	42.55	1,914	55.21	1,790	54.96	2,051	60.70	2,215	57.95	-4.5	136.2
Home economics	TX	46	30.48	32	67.49	48	83.35	36	78.58	37	91.70	16.7	300.9
Industrial arts	TT	41	28.47	27	51.62	25	61.26	36	53.10	23	51.59	-2.8	181.2
Language and literature	P	3,987	31.58	3,070	46.86	2,902	50.52	3,112	55.95	3,219	55.93	0.0	177.1

Law	K	1,153	83.10	1,117	101.35	1,207	100.34	1,276	101.89	1,313	99.48	-2.4	119.7
Library and information science	Z	100	53.58	106	69.09	98	62.98	93	68.03	85	79.97	17.6	149.3
Mathematics and computer science	QA	207	48.29	188	61.90	186	71.56	195	71.84	222	78.73	9.6	163.0
Medicine	R	1,182	55.12	905	69.56	859	70.12	931	73.90	1,081	76.98	4.2	139.7
Military and naval sciences	U, V	184	40.95	171	59.75	127	59.93	181	65.54	165	57.91	-11.6	141.4
Philosophy and religion	B-BD, BH-BX	1,336	48.17	1,098	61.29	1,075	68.74	1,364	73.64	1,505	69.70	-5.4	144.7
Physics and astronomy	QB, QC	214	64.83	179	66.85	167	69.30	206	73.19	200	75.70	3.4	116.8
Political Science	J	737	71.88	827	73.83	802	77.93	787	87.59	1,107	77.96	-11.0	108.5
Psychology	BF	265	39.69	304	73.32	337	72.28	378	76.47	414	80.74	5.6	203.4
Science (general)	Q	60	40.70	62	80.73	71	75.80	82	67.59	99	71.83	6.3	176.5
Sociology	HM-HX	1,169	58.24	1,361	71.40	1,358	73.25	1,649	78.65	1,685	73.91	-6.0	126.9
Sports and Recreation	GV	192	36.76	180	71.38	204	81.24	207	84.02	216	80.04	-4.7	217.8
Zoology	QH, QL-QR	382	65.79	254	67.99	271	73.11	262	80.40	321	85.51	6.4	130.0
Totals and Averages		18,115	£50.50	16,726	£69.46	16,176	£69.11	18,142	£73.94	19,350	£72.61	-1.8%	143.8

Compiled by George Aulisio, University of Scranton, based on information provided by GOBI Library Solutions.

(continued from page 363)

Table 9 shows how average prices have increased or decreased in comparison with the 2010 base year. For 2019, the overall index price for all LC subjects profiled in this table is at 143.8 percent. All LC classes listed are currently above their 2010 base prices. The highest increases in comparison with the 2010 base prices are home economics (300.9 percent), sports and recreation (217.8 percent), and psychology (203.4 percent). There are currently no known reliable indicators for a 2019 industry forecast.

Using the Price Indexes

Librarians are encouraged to monitor publishing industry trends and changes in economic conditions when preparing budget forecasts and projections. The ALA ALCTS Library Materials Price Index (LMPI) Editorial Board endeavors to make information on publishing trends readily available by sponsoring the annual compilation and publication of price data contained in our published tables. The indexes cover newly published library materials and document prices and rates of percent changes at the national and international level. They are useful benchmarks to compare against local costs, but because they reflect retail prices in the aggregate, they are not a substitute for cost data that reflect the collecting patterns of individual libraries, and they are not a substitute for specific cost studies.

Differences between local prices and those found in national indexes arise partially because these indexes exclude discounts, service charges, shipping and handling fees, and other discounts or costs that a library might see. Discrepancies may also relate to a library's subject coverage, its mix of titles purchased—including both current and backfiles—and the proportion of the library's budget expended on domestic or foreign materials. These variables can affect the average price paid by an individual library, although the individual library's rate of increase may not differ greatly from the national indexes.

Closing Note

The LMPI Editorial Board is interested in pursuing studies that would correlate a particular library's costs with the national prices. The group welcomes interested parties to its meeting at ALA Annual. The Library Materials Price Index Editorial Board consists of compilers George Aulisio, Ajaye Bloomstone, Stephen Bosch, and Narda Tafuri. George Aulisio currently serves as editor, and Rachel Fleming, University of Tennessee at Chattanooga, serves as assistant editor.

Book Title Output and Average Prices: 2017–2019

Constance Harbison
Baker & Taylor

The figures appearing in this report were provided for publication in *Library and Book Trade Almanac* by book wholesaler Baker & Taylor and are based on the Book Industry Study Group's BISAC Subject Headings. Figures for 2017 and 2018 have been revised since the previous edition was published, reflecting updates to the Baker & Taylor database. Figures for 2019 are considered preliminary at the time of this report.

Annual book title output in the United States has been generally on the upswing since the Great Recession, with a 5.2 percent decrease noted after 2016, followed by three years of relatively stable output (see Table 1). After reaching a post-recession high of 216,040 volumes in 2016 (up from 2009's 178,841), revised total production figures for 2017 and 2018 were 204,621 and 204,768, respectively, with preliminary 2019 results standing at 203,757. Typically, preliminary figures are revised upward as late-arriving materials are added to the database, suggesting that the final "total" 2019 output shown in Table 1 will be consistent with, if not higher than, the 2018 number.

Output and Prices by Format and Category

Output and pricing of hardcover titles have held relatively steady over the past three years (Tables 2 and 3), while preliminary 2019 figures show mass market output falling slightly, with average prices for the format remaining stable (Table 4). Although the picture for trade paperbacks is less clear (Table 5), the most recent figures suggest that output may have hit bottom in 2017 and that prices are relatively stable. Physically packaged audiobook output reached a high water mark in 2016, when more than 32,000 volumes were produced; since then, total annual output for the format has remained in the 20,000 range and prices appear to be going up (Table 6).

Average e-book pricing can be seen to fluctuate from 2017 to 2019 (Table 7), but a clear pattern of higher prices appears only in the audiobook format, as mentioned above. For the longer view required to reliably identify pricing trends over time, readers are encouraged to refer to this report in previous annual editions of *Library and Book Trade Almanac*, which was known as *The Bowker Annual* until 2009.

Children's books are the dominant category represented in Table 1 and, commensurately, this category ranks highly in most of the individual publication formats. The numbers appear solid from 2017 to 2019, with little change in annual output or average price—a possible exception again being the audiobook format, where prices are on the rise. The young adult category appears stable in both output and pricing for most publication formats, though it's worth noting that a limited number of audiobooks target the YA market.

(text continues on page 384)

Table 1 / American Book Production, 2017–2019

BISAC Category	2017	2018	2019
Antiques and Collectibles	247	190	185
Architecture	1,809	1,648	1,814
Art	3,917	3,777	3,958
Bibles	968	959	812
Biography and Autobiography	4,227	4,283	3,766
Body, Mind, and Spirit	886	961	1,061
Business and Economics	12,595	12,030	11,080
Children	27,099	28,404	27,831
Comics and Graphic Novels	2,727	2,972	2,869
Computers	4,136	4,582	4,645
Cooking	2,156	2,080	1,913
Crafts and Hobbies	991	884	736
Design	611	591	618
Drama	751	626	555
Education	8,544	7,188	6,407
Family and Relationships	716	808	819
Fiction	18,534	17,954	16,873
Foreign Language Study	1,290	1,100	1,163
Games and Activities	1,397	880	771
Gardening	262	244	240
Health and Fitness	1,486	1,422	1,353
History	12,722	12,280	12,796
House and Home	226	209	238
Humor	606	611	544
Language Arts and Disciplines	3,392	3,028	3,179
Law	5,811	5,900	5,401
Literary Collections	702	689	717
Literary Criticism	4,531	4,550	4,928
Mathematics	2,696	2,830	2,600
Medical	7,585	8,334	8,095
Music	2,685	2,424	2,645
Nature	1,107	1,005	1,106
Performing Arts	1,812	1,766	1,753
Pets	213	181	175
Philosophy	3,223	3,488	3,741
Photography	1,347	1,123	1,115
Poetry	2,353	2,433	2,254
Political Science	7,850	7,876	9,797
Psychology	3,924	3,594	4,935
Reference	846	759	639
Religion	9,802	9,626	8,864
Science	7,332	8,902	8,451
Self-Help	1,311	1,540	1,674
Social Science	10,388	10,377	10,979
Sports and Recreation	1,659	1,513	1,518
Study Aids	772	708	2,469
Technology and Engineering	6,416	7,177	6,062
Transportation	802	790	676
Travel	1,782	2,095	1,736
True Crime	246	304	306
Young Adult	5,131	5,073	4,895
Total	204,621	204,768	203,757

Table 2 / Hardcover Output and Average Per-Volume Prices, 2017–2019

	2017			2018			2019		
BISAC Category	**Vols.**	**$ Total**	**Avg.**	**Vols.**	**$ Total**	**Avg.**	**Vols.**	**$ Total**	**Avg.**
Antiques and Collectibles	133	$9,613.24	$72.28	102	$7,431.30	$72.86	99	$6,508.84	$65.75
Architecture	1,045	119,460.77	114.32	908	86,306.50	95.05	916	85,215.50	93.03
Art	2,171	180,303.83	83.05	2,043	152,985.29	74.88	2,230	162,731.22	72.97
Bibles	254	10,410.22	40.99	246	10,599.41	43.09	184	10,003.13	54.36
Biography and Autobiography	1,830	91,859.85	50.20	1,715	79,022.59	46.08	1,517	62,428.40	41.15
Body, Mind, and Spirit	196	5,361.92	27.36	211	5,374.02	25.47	277	7,275.48	26.27
Business and Economics	5,912	1,026,090.28	173.56	4,589	739,623.12	161.17	4,317	613,446.61	142.10
Children	15,062	366,923.33	24.36	16,611	437,397.45	26.33	16,096	400,639.79	24.89
Comics and Graphic Novels	669	28,212.88	42.17	662	28,836.00	43.56	680	33,027.23	48.57
Computers	1,282	226,146.98	176.40	1,156	203,053.02	175.65	1,134	184,856.23	163.01
Cooking	1,221	36,343.70	29.77	1,149	34,241.63	29.80	1,092	32,749.19	29.99
Crafts and Hobbies	172	5,516.40	32.07	187	5,658.27	30.26	157	5,041.31	32.11
Design	369	25,989.16	70.43	354	23,740.26	67.06	364	24,017.88	65.98
Drama	80	8,922.94	111.54	67	5,675.23	84.70	84	9,231.02	109.89
Education	3,672	571,329.71	155.59	2,619	372,577.61	142.26	2,434	321,483.89	132.08
Family and Relationships	193	9,310.14	48.24	222	10,272.80	46.27	205	9,744.11	47.53
Fiction	5,329	157,461.55	29.55	4,930	145,245.95	29.46	4,947	146,936.37	29.70
Foreign Language Study	242	31,473.27	130.05	274	34,105.93	124.47	213	26,227.23	123.13
Games and Activities	138	6,796.79	49.25	183	8,119.94	44.37	143	5,468.92	38.24
Gardening	133	6,097.55	45.85	124	4,702.84	37.93	117	4,665.41	39.88
Health and Fitness	418	35,735.56	85.49	337	22,199.11	65.87	382	28,454.90	74.49
History	6,260	639,354.01	102.13	5,863	550,794.75	93.94	6,176	632,059.66	102.34
House and Home	122	5,163.04	42.32	123	4,776.53	38.83	130	5,347.02	41.13
Humor	303	6,826.80	22.53	349	7,989.15	22.89	291	5,600.64	19.25
Language Arts and Disciplines	1,566	245,154.54	156.55	1,377	198,792.51	144.37	1,472	200,606.78	136.28
Law	2,565	477,666.56	186.22	2,387	430,903.69	180.52	2,292	402,194.30	175.48
Literary Collections	296	30,319.29	102.43	252	21,804.23	86.52	268	37,219.14	138.88

Table 2 / Hardcover Output and Average Per-Volume Prices, 2017–2019 *(cont.)*

	2017			2018			2019		
BISAC Category	**Vols.**	**$ Total**	**Avg.**	**Vols.**	**$ Total**	**Avg.**	**Vols.**	**$ Total**	**Avg.**
Literary Criticism	2,594	342,128.76	131.89	2,396	303,759.39	126.78	2,609	315,965.14	121.11
Mathematics	1,400	248,688.09	177.63	1,037	159,714.86	154.02	1,023	143,602.55	140.37
Medical	3,848	766,755.67	199.26	3,050	559,765.02	183.53	3,592	620,103.25	172.63
Music	695	70,956.42	102.10	602	53,937.25	89.60	669	62,823.62	93.91
Nature	538	55,885.20	103.88	420	35,922.44	85.53	455	42,848.02	94.17
Performing Arts	946	117,411.57	124.11	814	82,882.63	101.82	777	91,002.59	117.12
Pets	103	2,856.78	27.74	69	1,437.26	20.83	55	1,505.13	27.37
Philosophy	1,687	207,073.09	122.75	1,603	177,505.65	110.73	1,839	208,688.15	113.48
Photography	930	70,285.77	75.58	832	59,283.19	71.25	806	56,537.44	70.15
Poetry	320	12,666.71	39.58	291	10,578.77	36.35	280	10,527.87	37.60
Political Science	3,928	489,745.60	124.68	3,471	391,822.55	112.88	5,482	693,033.76	126.42
Psychology	1,842	301,961.16	163.93	1,450	215,479.24	148.61	2,734	390,029.21	142.66
Reference	357	136,388.77	382.04	338	130,115.32	384.96	306	89,137.61	291.30
Religion	3,020	253,261.63	83.86	3,003	239,325.82	79.70	2,587	227,845.52	88.07
Science	4,623	954,473.43	206.46	3,910	699,757.03	178.97	4,144	763,438.19	184.23
Self-Help	361	10,601.86	29.37	414	10,655.64	25.74	421	10,059.99	23.90
Social Science	5,765	812,885.96	141.00	4,695	596,564.49	127.06	5,347	671,164.81	125.52
Sports and Recreation	646	42,687.78	66.08	602	33,471.85	55.60	536	27,499.53	51.31
Study Aids	21	2,367.90	112.76	15	1,536.44	102.43	9	1,548.87	172.10
Technology and Engineering	4,061	835,995.47	205.86	3,164	643,700.62	203.45	3,016	555,072.86	184.04
Transportation	278	20,688.51	74.42	288	17,936.73	62.28	281	20,884.20	74.32
Travel	283	11,271.00	39.83	476	19,128.63	40.19	207	8,394.35	40.55
True Crime	66	1,955.90	29.63	84	2,836.30	33.77	89	2,708.22	30.43
Young Adult	2,404	96,485.51	40.14	2,116	75,766.69	35.81	1,995	74,297.14	37.24
Total	92,349	$10,229,322.85	$110.77	84,180	$8,155,112.94	$96.88	87,476	$8,551,898.22	$97.76

Table 3 / Hardcover Output and Average Per-Volume Prices, Less than $81, 2017–2019

	2017			2018			2019		
BISAC Category	**Vols.**	**$ Total**	**Avg.**	**Vols.**	**$ Total**	**Avg.**	**Vols.**	**$ Total**	**Avg.**
Antiques and Collectibles	102	$4,613.30	$45.23	71	$2,935.46	$41.34	77	$3,587.91	$46.60
Architecture	531	26,382.91	49.69	557	28,670.19	51.47	499	24,624.23	49.35
Art	1,577	71,805.99	45.53	1,500	70,067.70	46.71	1,622	74,438.06	45.89
Bibles	242	8,950.36	36.98	233	8,553.49	36.71	164	6,519.27	39.75
Biography and Autobiography	1,647	50,432.84	30.62	1,570	47,713.81	30.39	1,402	43,203.25	30.82
Body, Mind, and Spirit	189	4,165.92	22.04	206	4,803.04	23.32	265	5,188.13	19.58
Business and Economics	1,442	61,092.20	42.37	1,434	59,703.67	41.63	1,400	59,198.50	42.28
Children	14,668	297,211.31	20.26	16,006	331,883.24	20.73	15,654	325,779.34	20.81
Comics and Graphic Novels	595	19,173.08	32.22	582	19,157.30	32.92	584	19,237.66	32.94
Computers	180	10,479.83	58.22	207	12,327.02	59.55	186	10,611.31	57.05
Cooking	1,203	33,385.46	27.75	1,130	31,541.79	27.91	1,079	29,553.24	27.39
Crafts and Hobbies	167	4,833.43	28.94	183	5,208.27	28.46	153	4,594.81	30.03
Design	271	12,445.71	45.93	255	11,896.81	46.65	270	12,138.10	44.96
Drama	29	1,509.60	52.06	31	1,438.45	46.40	28	1,455.32	51.98
Education	615	30,992.11	50.39	532	27,877.03	52.40	508	27,384.24	53.91
Family and Relationships	160	3,944.04	24.65	177	3,934.95	22.23	163	3,873.67	23.76
Fiction	5,297	153,693.44	29.02	4,906	141,885.18	28.92	4,918	143,456.61	29.17
Foreign Language Study	92	5,009.60	54.45	100	5,577.17	55.77	72	4,274.13	59.36
Games and Activities	117	3,837.81	32.80	164	5,427.02	33.09	132	4,096.03	31.03
Gardening	119	3,921.10	32.95	120	4,098.84	34.16	109	3,779.41	34.67
Health and Fitness	282	8,740.79	31.00	252	7,353.91	29.18	258	7,470.74	28.96
History	2,935	127,750.64	43.53	2,933	126,545.84	43.15	2,891	127,818.99	44.21
House and Home	118	4,648.04	39.39	119	4,426.53	37.20	125	4,897.02	39.18
Humor	296	5,918.86	20.00	346	7,004.15	20.24	290	5,450.64	18.80
Language Arts and Disciplines	222	11,622.56	52.35	246	13,545.25	55.06	274	15,438.32	56.34
Law	265	15,234.91	57.49	337	18,871.90	56.00	307	17,319.89	56.42

Table 3 / Hardcover Output and Average Per-Volume Prices, Less than $81, 2017–2019 *(cont.)*

	2017			2018			2019		
BISAC Category	**Vols.**	**$ Total**	**Avg.**	**Vols.**	**$ Total**	**Avg.**	**Vols.**	**$ Total**	**Avg.**
Literary Collections	162	6,390.36	39.45	160	6,337.18	39.61	129	4,532.14	35.13
Literary Criticism	693	38,512.25	55.57	716	39,836.75	55.64	705	40,569.84	57.55
Mathematics	127	7,138.21	56.21	162	9,085.83	56.09	137	8,132.15	59.36
Medical	335	18,214.92	54.37	283	15,644.32	55.28	363	20,722.18	57.09
Music	313	13,729.86	43.87	297	12,500.28	42.09	304	12,939.61	42.56
Nature	265	9,327.03	35.20	267	9,272.70	34.73	250	8,412.14	33.65
Performing Arts	246	11,026.42	44.82	253	10,758.42	42.52	286	12,556.91	43.91
Pets	97	2,280.04	23.51	69	1,437.26	20.83	52	1,210.13	23.27
Philosophy	454	22,801.92	50.22	528	28,808.41	54.56	474	24,966.42	52.67
Photography	764	34,720.81	45.45	703	31,511.40	44.82	702	32,415.87	46.18
Poetry	286	8,241.16	28.82	271	8,289.02	30.59	254	6,998.05	27.55
Political Science	943	44,995.08	47.71	1,075	50,564.50	47.04	1,169	56,747.39	48.54
Psychology	282	13,376.76	47.44	308	14,411.43	46.79	268	13,198.11	49.25
Reference	113	3,331.73	29.48	117	4,010.28	34.28	112	3,269.70	29.19
Religion	1,773	66,194.22	37.33	1,853	69,755.98	37.64	1,429	50,420.92	35.28
Science	591	27,015.67	45.71	608	28,710.24	47.22	636	30,054.53	47.26
Self-Help	349	8,266.98	23.69	408	9,770.69	23.95	419	9,590.04	22.89
Social Science	1,021	52,455.51	51.38	1,025	51,878.13	50.61	1,098	55,511.69	50.56
Sports and Recreation	475	14,440.63	30.40	480	15,577.61	32.45	440	13,912.22	31.62
Study Aids	10	536.90	53.69	9	552.75	61.42	4	196.94	49.24
Technology and Engineering	195	10,759.52	55.18	226	12,291.20	54.39	237	13,071.15	55.15
Transportation	217	10,044.15	46.29	243	10,827.29	44.56	216	8,985.77	41.60
Travel	259	7,537.12	29.10	451	14,944.69	33.14	194	6,033.40	31.10
True Crime	65	1,862.95	28.66	81	2,389.30	29.50	87	2,523.28	29.00
Young Adult	2,254	62,224.94	27.61	2,023	54,172.56	26.78	1,908	53,392.84	27.98
Total	45,650	$1,477,220	$32.36	46,813	$1,515,786	$32.38	45,303	$1,475,752	$32.58

Table 4 / Mass Market Paperbacks Output and Average Per-Volume Prices, 2017–2019

	2017			2018			2019		
BISAC Category	**Vols.**	**$ Total**	**Avg.**	**Vols.**	**$ Total**	**Avg.**	**Vols.**	**$ Total**	**Avg.**
Biography and Autobiography	5	$46.42	$9.28	7	68.93	$9.85	3	$29.97	$9.99
Business and Economics	1	8.99	8.99	3	26.97	8.99	n.a.	n.a.	n.a.
Children	177	1,233.23	6.97	225	1,577.69	7.01	181	1,368.16	7.56
Fiction	2,753	20,127.38	7.31	2,713	19,648.04	7.24	2,436	18,050.28	7.41
Games and Activities	n.a.	n.a.	n.a.	1	8.50	8.50	n.a.	n.a.	n.a.
Health and Fitness	1	9.99	9.99	3	25.97	8.66	2	21.98	10.99
History	5	49.95	9.99	3	29.97	9.99	4	35.96	8.99
Humor	1	9.99	9.99	2	24.98	12.49	n.a.	n.a.	n.a.
Language Arts and Disciplines	n.a.	n.a.	n.a.	n.a.	n.a.	n.a.	1	7.99	7.99
Performing Arts	n.a.	n.a.	n.a.	n.a.	n.a.	n.a.	1	8.99	8.99
Political Science	1	8.99	8.99	1	9.99	9.99	1	9.99	9.99
Psychology	n.a.	n.a.	n.a.	1	13.99	13.99	1	4.99	4.99
Self-Help	n.a.	n.a.	n.a.	6	83.94	13.99	4	50.96	12.74
True Crime	12	100.88	8.41	7	57.93	8.28	6	52.94	8.82
Young Adult	5	41.95	8.39	25	266.73	10.67	34	327.66	9.64
Total	2,961	$21,637.77	$7.31	2,997	$21,843.63	$7.29	2,674	$19,969.87	$7.47

n.a. = not available

Table 5 / Trade Paperbacks Output and Average Per-Volume Prices, 2017–2019

	2017			2018			2019		
BISAC Category	**Vols.**	**$ Total**	**Avg.**	**Vols.**	**$ Total**	**Avg.**	**Vols.**	**$ Total**	**Avg.**
Antiques and Collectibles	114	$4,636.08	$40.67	88	$3,687.55	$41.90	86	$3,448.51	$40.10
Architecture	762	37,632.02	49.39	741	36,703.19	49.53	897	45,134.66	50.32
Art	1,720	70,592.48	41.04	1,725	69,279.69	40.16	1,720	67,340.40	39.15
Bibles	714	28,944.85	40.54	713	32,605.69	45.73	629	30,034.19	47.75
Biography and Autobiography	2,393	49,192.26	20.56	2,561	52,770.65	20.61	2,246	46,257.74	20.60
Body, Mind, and Spirit	689	12,568.69	18.24	750	13,581.57	18.11	786	14,873.37	18.92
Business and Economics	5,956	528,631.62	88.76	7,017	599,481.01	85.43	6,439	471,301.12	73.19
Children	11,825	190,435.55	16.10	11,517	147,502.84	12.81	11,523	141,983.66	12.32
Comics and Graphic Novels	2,057	38,038.00	18.49	2,310	44,169.05	19.12	2,183	44,979.88	20.60
Computers	2,602	252,256.35	96.95	3,397	363,397.84	106.98	3,294	333,638.93	101.29
Cooking	934	19,945.08	21.35	928	19,610.15	21.13	818	17,629.08	21.55
Crafts and Hobbies	816	16,691.92	20.46	688	14,775.69	21.48	566	12,754.44	22.53
Design	242	9,814.60	40.56	234	9,607.76	41.06	254	11,381.45	44.81
Drama	652	14,694.16	22.54	557	11,310.43	20.31	465	10,510.32	22.60
Education	4,479	261,104.07	58.30	4,349	281,131.83	64.64	3,865	213,672.56	55.28
Family and Relationships	523	11,212.89	21.44	585	13,033.81	22.28	613	13,189.78	21.52
Fiction	10,455	175,360.64	16.77	10,313	180,798.91	17.53	9,491	165,722.37	17.46
Foreign Language Study	1,013	42,228.01	41.69	796	35,301.11	44.35	893	37,440.26	41.93
Games and Activities	1,258	19,592.79	15.57	695	12,095.60	17.40	625	11,234.74	17.98
Gardening	129	2,982.24	23.12	120	2,570.31	21.42	123	2,737.74	22.26
Health and Fitness	1,039	32,139.13	30.93	1,053	33,020.19	31.36	955	30,271.54	31.70
History	6,348	245,860.14	38.73	6,335	255,340.71	40.31	6,542	263,466.00	40.27
House and Home	104	2,725.93	26.21	86	1,928.76	22.43	108	2,590.53	23.99
Humor	302	4,771.65	15.80	260	4,025.25	15.48	253	3,940.10	15.57
Language Arts and Disciplines	1,696	123,639.84	72.90	1,589	96,539.99	60.76	1,641	93,178.38	56.78

Law	3,120	259,259.96	83.10	3,388	308,261.23	90.99	2,979	248,982.62	83.58
Literary Collections	406	11,130.41	27.41	437	12,523.50	28.66	451	11,035.04	24.47
Literary Criticism	1,935	83,792.32	43.30	2,152	109,333.23	50.81	2,320	102,799.91	44.31
Mathematics	953	74,853.18	78.54	1,533	163,553.11	106.69	1,356	104,399.72	76.99
Medical	3,696	320,999.49	86.85	5,254	624,259.49	118.82	4,470	400,350.78	89.56
Music	1,975	57,908.08	29.32	1,808	49,794.57	27.54	1,968	58,578.86	29.77
Nature	565	19,590.03	34.67	584	27,306.85	46.76	652	27,936.29	42.85
Performing Arts	858	32,805.37	38.23	947	40,556.71	42.83	965	36,770.26	38.10
Pets	110	2,011.83	18.29	112	2,097.05	18.72	121	2,440.36	20.17
Philosophy	1,532	65,050.92	42.46	1,870	99,579.70	53.25	1,897	79,099.61	41.70
Photography	416	14,609.54	35.12	289	9,813.71	33.96	308	12,341.45	40.07
Poetry	2,033	35,056.11	17.24	2,142	36,880.69	17.22	1,976	34,136.38	17.28
Political Science	3,881	183,461.92	47.27	4,394	259,507.02	59.06	4,289	217,282.48	50.66
Psychology	1,949	104,118.74	53.42	2,052	126,581.28	61.69	2,129	110,378.17	51.85
Reference	488	92,490.13	189.53	421	78,413.18	186.25	331	49,277.86	148.88
Religion	6,776	174,430.62	25.74	6,619	178,842.04	27.02	6,258	170,173.57	27.19
Science	2,443	219,353.53	89.79	4,847	648,880.21	133.87	4,115	408,220.35	99.20
Self-Help	948	16,799.86	17.72	1,119	19,224.99	17.18	1,250	22,371.86	17.90
Social Science	4,554	221,064.89	48.54	5,579	339,976.12	60.94	5,575	276,584.13	49.61
Sports and Recreation	1,013	26,382.03	26.04	910	24,140.46	26.53	975	26,699.94	27.38
Study Aids	748	25,605.79	34.23	691	29,676.55	42.95	2,462	108,319.90	44.00
Technology and Engineering	2,279	224,115.72	98.34	3,983	588,245.46	147.69	3,004	365,065.69	121.53
Transportation	523	20,340.41	38.89	500	17,212.26	34.42	395	17,181.73	43.50
Travel	1,499	32,587.29	21.74	1,619	34,274.08	21.17	1,529	32,760.41	21.43
True Crime	168	3,386.25	20.16	213	4,275.42	20.07	211	4,177.79	19.80
Young Adult	2,724	50,129.33	18.40	2,934	52,872.11	18.02	2,865	52,715.89	18.40
Total	106,414	$4,567,024.74	$42.92	115,804	$6,220,350.60	$53.71	111,866	$5,068,792.80	$45.31

Table 6 / Audiobook Output and Average Per-Volume Prices, 2017–2019

	2017			2018			2019		
BISAC Category	**Vols.**	**$ Total**	**Avg.**	**Vols.**	**$ Total**	**Avg.**	**Vols.**	**$ Total**	**Avg.**
Antiques and Collectibles	3	$99.97	$33.32	n.a.	n.a.	n.a.	n.a.	n.a.	n.a.
Architecture	10	314.90	31.49	2	$45.98	$22.99	8	$264.92	$33.12
Art	24	680.61	28.36	16	504.70	31.54	8	248.43	31.05
Bibles	6	299.86	49.98	2	99.98	49.99	3	228.94	76.31
Biography and Autobiography	1,445	54,122.95	37.46	1,241	53,113.04	42.80	1,378	60,120.56	43.63
Body, Mind, and Spirit	158	4,647.26	29.41	147	5,271.09	35.86	180	6,324.91	35.14
Business and Economics	883	28,540.33	32.32	799	28,488.36	35.66	656	24,186.05	36.87
Children	1,701	52,976.64	31.14	1,333	48,683.41	36.52	1,553	57,847.82	37.25
Comics and Graphic Novels	3	26.97	8.99	n.a.	n.a.	n.a.	68	2,549.32	37.49
Computers	42	1,230.61	29.30	27	1,142.60	42.32	33	1,255.59	38.05
Cooking	63	2,220.00	35.24	58	2,302.06	39.69	16	596.84	37.30
Crafts and Hobbies	2	25.97	12.99	3	66.97	22.32	5	198.96	39.79
Design	n.a.	n.a.	n.a.	6	307.87	51.31	1	39.99	39.99
Drama	60	1,213.81	20.23	163	3,011.81	18.48	97	2,157.65	22.24
Education	39	1,321.65	33.89	41	1,376.81	33.58	39	1,489.67	38.20
Family and Relationships	204	6,531.36	32.02	183	6,251.14	34.16	185	6,846.41	37.01
Fiction	11,019	375,113.20	34.04	9,917	390,059.33	39.33	11,450	459,765.95	40.15
Foreign Language Study	96	7,646.07	79.65	100	20,697.22	206.97	152	12,990.12	85.46
Games and Activities	10	407.90	40.79	5	199.95	39.99	2	44.98	22.49
Gardening	5	134.88	26.98	n.a.	n.a.	n.a.	1	14.99	14.99
Health and Fitness	289	11,493.03	39.77	264	10,193.90	38.61	242	9,720.66	40.17
History	904	40,157.80	44.42	809	38,345.88	47.40	811	37,633.71	46.40
House and Home	39	1,615.11	41.41	20	709.54	35.48	13	447.85	34.45
Humor	62	1,831.04	29.53	93	3,882.78	41.75	75	2,675.01	35.67
Language Arts and Disciplines	39	1,470.52	37.71	29	1,000.56	34.50	47	1,786.29	38.01

Law	31	1,317.62	42.50	34	1,161.54	34.16	25	778.68	31.15
Literary Collections	45	1,505.22	33.45	69	2,978.76	43.17	67	2,811.89	41.97
Literary Criticism	32	1,013.65	31.68	34	1,397.44	41.10	27	880.59	32.61
Mathematics	10	214.90	21.49	4	107.96	26.99	7	326.87	46.70
Medical	49	1,766.95	36.06	36	1,505.54	41.82	31	1,013.62	32.70
Music	142	4,004.27	28.20	61	1,885.27	30.91	64	2,656.28	41.50
Nature	63	2,008.33	31.88	53	1,860.18	35.10	91	3,819.77	41.98
Performing Arts	72	2,549.18	35.41	99	4,010.92	40.51	116	4,745.81	40.91
Pets	46	1,737.43	37.77	29	1,102.51	38.02	18	769.77	42.77
Philosophy	103	2,423.51	23.53	54	2,044.98	37.87	74	2,533.89	34.24
Poetry	46	1,023.03	22.24	56	1,521.58	27.17	106	3,062.75	28.89
Political Science	324	12,208.44	37.68	377	14,797.56	39.25	369	15,895.82	43.08
Psychology	157	5,913.25	37.66	162	6,033.85	37.25	99	3,480.81	35.16
Reference	15	536.89	35.79	8	372.93	46.62	7	224.95	32.14
Religion	1,249	33,647.50	26.94	1,152	35,147.47	30.51	930	32,673.51	35.13
Science	158	5,364.98	33.96	212	8,261.87	38.97	168	6,930.04	41.25
Self-Help	382	12,891.87	33.75	427	15,463.58	36.21	516	18,276.16	35.42
Social Science	298	10,459.96	35.10	322	11,586.12	35.98	265	11,101.54	41.89
Sports and Recreation	145	5,280.66	36.42	111	4,256.85	38.35	144	6,049.56	42.01
Study Aids	n.a.	n.a.	n.a.	3	124.90	41.63	2	125.99	63.00
Technology and Engineering	103	10,500.30	101.94	31	1,400.49	45.18	13	510.80	39.29
Transportation	9	271.87	30.21	10	474.91	47.49	2	99.98	49.99
Travel	39	1,205.54	30.91	32	1,397.54	43.67	49	2,073.45	42.32
True Crime	182	7,096.43	38.99	189	6,926.53	36.65	193	8,321.18	43.11
Young Adult	1,463	57,358.62	39.21	1,118	49,891.37	44.63	1,222	53,552.75	43.82
Total	22,269	$776,422.84	$34.87	19,941	$791,467.63	$39.69	21,628	$872,152.08	$40.33

n.a. = not available

Table 7 / E-Book Output and Average Per-Volume Prices, 2017–2019

	2017			2018			2019		
BISAC Category	**Vols.**	**$ Total**	**Avg.**	**Vols.**	**$ Total**	**Avg.**	**Vols.**	**$ Total**	**Avg.**
Antiques and Collectibles	118	$1,963.29	$16.64	171	$1,690.12	$9.88	153	$1,659.28	$10.84
Architecture	818	17,979.79	21.98	381	18,226.52	47.84	420	17,214.06	40.99
Art	2,356	42,786.22	18.16	1,397	48,795.22	34.93	1,530	39,765.27	25.99
Bibles	2,148	25,511.20	11.88	418	4,069.91	9.74	267	3,283.29	12.30
Biography and Autobiography	7,908	136,362.71	17.24	7,111	142,604.36	20.05	6,859	148,132.49	21.60
Body, Mind, and Spirit	2,580	29,050.01	11.26	2,898	32,813.43	11.32	3,407	41,404.91	12.15
Business and Economics	9,248	381,868.77	41.29	27,580	1,421,012.12	51.52	23,692	1,582,057.20	66.78
Children	26,145	468,630.18	17.92	26,960	414,892.30	15.39	25,264	469,144.73	18.57
Comics and Graphic Novels	876	7,856.93	8.97	980	8,089.59	8.25	810	7,579.20	9.36
Computers	3,177	260,853.64	82.11	3,653	286,473.08	78.42	2,159	136,139.71	63.06
Cooking	2,691	32,628.71	12.13	2,690	35,569.37	13.22	2,747	32,669.38	11.89
Crafts and Hobbies	1,176	13,336.89	11.34	608	8,482.73	13.95	545	7,758.83	14.24
Design	170	3,542.30	20.84	112	2,732.08	24.39	122	3,615.94	29.64
Drama	1,546	18,590.91	12.03	1,085	11,944.30	11.01	1,317	12,430.86	9.44
Education	7,660	310,210.77	40.50	4,145	185,563.54	44.77	3,989	166,021.78	41.62
Family and Relationships	1,762	22,993.87	13.05	2,310	29,313.83	12.69	2,321	33,670.98	14.51
Fiction	75,766	745,274.62	9.84	82,846	943,325.97	11.39	81,312	1,102,622.58	13.56
Foreign Language Study	1,678	38,792.25	23.12	2,282	49,990.64	21.91	1,527	38,813.96	25.42
Games and Activities	930	8,065.99	8.67	1,481	10,022.25	6.77	342	5,408.09	15.81
Gardening	555	6,896.14	12.43	301	4,693.60	15.59	280	4,471.21	15.97
Health and Fitness	3,002	40,771.47	13.58	3,059	41,692.81	13.63	2,884	45,417.48	15.75
History	13,019	389,512.95	29.92	9,416	396,944.87	42.16	8,451	379,478.23	44.90
House and Home	392	5,489.56	14.00	244	4,014.95	16.45	211	3,517.56	16.67
Humor	848	8,973.54	10.58	1,110	14,902.13	13.43	805	11,562.22	14.36
Language Arts and Disciplines	2,844	233,971.88	82.27	2,930	199,473.84	68.08	2,537	264,903.45	104.42

Law	2,657	230,166.81	86.63	3,020	344,939.93	114.22	2,521	296,413.81	117.58
Literary Collections	2,159	33,855.08	15.68	1,512	23,426.52	15.49	6,212	28,681.99	4.62
Literary Criticism	3,136	221,621.38	70.67	3,629	301,269.79	83.02	2,920	226,370.99	77.52
Mathematics	1,506	85,203.32	56.58	993	81,285.98	81.86	731	65,636.45	89.79
Medical	3,574	344,186.69	96.30	3,289	349,086.25	106.14	2,213	208,420.36	94.18
Music	2,538	52,997.85	20.88	3,031	49,679.09	16.39	1,698	40,692.42	23.96
Nature	806	32,022.75	39.73	850	23,019.70	27.08	719	19,117.69	26.59
Performing Arts	1,879	45,311.28	24.11	2,073	52,171.78	25.17	1,934	45,186.27	23.36
Pets	805	8,453.10	10.50	443	4,617.94	10.42	413	5,278.37	12.78
Philosophy	3,608	125,637.29	34.82	2,747	140,203.06	51.04	2,491	109,418.46	43.93
Photography	514	8,781.46	17.08	313	6,014.95	19.22	260	5,964.42	22.94
Poetry	5,189	45,490.75	8.77	5,010	40,414.33	8.07	4,623	40,446.93	8.75
Political Science	5,231	222,698.78	42.57	4,714	256,096.08	54.33	3,509	161,891.63	46.14
Psychology	2,720	117,277.66	43.12	2,073	92,040.96	44.40	1,751	69,006.83	39.41
Reference	2,999	55,840.30	18.62	1,268	49,622.51	39.13	872	52,752.54	60.50
Religion	13,497	279,006.60	20.67	11,560	304,050.57	26.30	10,170	267,390.14	26.29
Science	5,749	378,246.53	65.79	3,554	340,328.03	95.76	2,828	253,230.90	89.54
Self-Help	5,351	65,115.58	12.17	5,275	69,545.68	13.18	6,575	80,498.39	12.24
Social Science	6,985	285,905.17	40.93	4,750	234,942.32	49.46	3,813	195,319.39	51.22
Sports and Recreation	1,920	33,138.73	17.26	1,453	29,534.62	20.33	1,320	27,001.96	20.46
Study Aids	2,388	78,237.04	32.76	1,332	18,513.57	13.90	3,537	97,729.39	27.63
Technology and Engineering	3,996	344,646.33	86.25	2,531	307,345.26	121.43	1,626	187,956.22	115.59
Transportation	271	6,739.87	24.87	322	8,859.91	27.52	313	8,808.61	28.14
Travel	2,521	36,985.05	14.67	1,937	34,008.14	17.56	2,877	34,947.23	12.15
True Crime	411	8,436.17	20.53	515	11,001.47	21.36	584	14,076.77	24.10
Young Adult	5,501	110,238.12	20.04	6,052	111,372.04	18.40	5,990	120,956.29	20.19
Total	257,324	$6,508,154.28	$25.29	260,414	$7,600,724.05	$29.19	246,451	$7,221,937.14	$29.30

(continued from page 371)

Fiction, a major category across all publication formats, on the whole has experienced reduced output in recent years; however, preliminary 2019 hardcover figures reveal no statistically significant change from the 2017 or 2018 numbers, either in total output or pricing. Mass market fiction output has continued to erode year to year, as prices remain stable. In the trade paperback format, fiction shows signs of a slight decline in output since 2017 but with no marked change in prices. Audiobook fiction is tending to price higher at the same time as output remains relatively level. In the e-book category, fiction output continues to be robust; pricing will need to be monitored to see if increases from 2017 to 2019 reflect a true trend, which the recent numbers may indicate.

Multiple categories combine to make nonfiction overall the largest part of the U.S. publication mix, year after year. Those that stand out as print heavyweights include, in hardcover, art, biography and autobiography, business and economics, history, law, technology and engineering, and social sciences, and, in trade paperback, business and economics, education, history, law, medical, political science, religion, and social science. In terms of output, these categories can be seen to have held their own from 2017 to 2019, with—perhaps unsurprisingly—a notable increase in the number of hardcover political science books in 2019.

Number of Book Outlets in the United States and Canada

The *American Book Trade Directory* (Information Today, Inc.) has been published since 1915. Revised annually, it features lists of booksellers, wholesalers, periodicals, reference tools, and other information about the U.S. and Canadian book markets. The data shown in Table 1, the most current available, are from the 2020–2021 edition of the directory.

The 11,301 stores of various types shown are located throughout the United States, Canada, and regions administered by the United States. "General" bookstores stock trade books and children's books in a general variety of subjects. "College" stores (both general and specified) carry college-level textbooks. "Educational" outlets handle school textbooks up to and including the high school level. "Mail order" outlets (both general and specified) sell general trade books by mail and are not book clubs; all others operating by mail are classified according to the kinds of books carried.

"Antiquarian" dealers sell old and rare books. Stores handling secondhand books are classified as "used." "Paperback" stores have more than 80 percent of their stock in paperbound books. Stores with paperback departments are listed under the appropriate major classification ("general," "department store," "stationer," and so forth). Bookstores with at least 50 percent of their stock on a particular subject are classified by subject.

Table 1 / Bookstores in the United States and Canada, 2019

Category	United States	Canada
Antiquarian General	412	38
Antiquarian Mail Order	127	5
Antiquarian Specialized	80	1
Art Supply Store	12	1
College General	2,364	128
College Specialized	94	5
Comics	179	23
Computer Software	2	0
Cooking	217	8
Department Store	328	17
Educational	126	24
Federal Sites	297	1
Foreign Language	11	2
General	2,107	429
Gift Shop	78	5
Juvenile	50	11
Mail Order General	40	4
Mail Order Specialized	153	8
Metaphysics, New Age and Occult	97	13
Museum Store and Art Gallery	381	27
Nature and Natural History	30	5

Table 1 / Bookstores in the United States and Canada, 2019
(cont.)

Category	United States	Canada
Newsdealer	9	1
Office Supply	6	1
Other	1,622	289
Paperback	21	1
Religious	833	80
Self Help/Development	12	4
Stationer	3	2
Toy Store	27	67
Used	337	46
Totals	10,055	1,246

Part 5
Reference Information

Ready Reference

How to Obtain an ISBN

Beat Barblan
United States ISBN/SAN Agency

The International Standard Book Numbering (ISBN) system was introduced into the United Kingdom by J. Whitaker & Sons Ltd. in 1967 and into the United States in 1968 by R. R. Bowker. The Technical Committee on Documentation of the International Organization for Standardization (ISO TC 46) is responsible for the international standard.

The purpose of this standard is to "establish the specifications for the International Standard Book Number (ISBN) as a unique international identification system for each product form or edition of a monographic publication published or produced by a specific publisher." The standard specifies the construction of an ISBN, the rules for assignment and use of an ISBN, and all metadata associated with the allocation of an ISBN.

Types of monographic publications to which an ISBN may be assigned include printed books and pamphlets (in various product formats); electronic publications (either on the Internet or on physical carriers such as CD-ROMs or diskettes); educational/instructional films, videos, and transparencies; educational/instructional software; audiobooks on cassette or CD or DVD; braille publications; and microform publications.

Serial publications, printed music, and musical sound recordings are excluded from the ISBN standard as they are covered by other identification systems.

The ISBN is used by publishers, distributors, wholesalers, bookstores, and libraries, among others, in more than 200 countries and territories as an ordering and inventory system. It expedites the collection of data on new and forthcoming editions of monographic publications for print and electronic directories used by the book trade. Its use also facilitates rights management and the monitoring of sales data for the publishing industry.

As of January 1, 2007, a revision to the ISBN standard substantially increased the numbering capacity of the system. The 10-digit ISBN identifier (ISBN-10) was replaced by the ISBN 13-digit identifier (ISBN-13). All facets of book publishing are now expected to use the ISBN-13, and the ISBN agencies throughout the world are now issuing only ISBN-13s to publishers. Publishers with existing ISBN-10s need to convert their ISBNs to ISBN-13s by the addition of the EAN prefix 978 and recalculation of the new check digit:

ISBN-10: 0-8352-8235-X
ISBN-13: 978-0-8352-8235-2

As the inventory of 978 prefixes has started to exhaust, ISBN agencies have begun assigning ISBN-13s with the "979" prefix. There is no 10-digit equivalent for 979 ISBNs.

Construction of an ISBN

An ISBN currently consists of 13 digits separated into the following parts:

1. A prefix of "978" for an ISBN-10 converted to an ISBN-13 and a prefix of "979" for ISBN-13s without a 10-digit equivalent
2. Group or country identifier, which identifies a national or geographic grouping of publishers
3. Publisher identifier, which identifies a particular publisher within a group
4. Title identifier, which identifies a particular title or edition of a title
5. Check digit, the single digit at the end of the ISBN that validates the ISBN-13

For more information regarding ISBN-13 conversion services provided by the U.S. ISBN Agency at R. R. Bowker, LLC, visit the ISBN Agency website at http://www.isbn.org, or contact the U.S. ISBN Agency at isbn-san@bowker.com.

Publishers requiring their ISBNs to be converted from the ISBN-10 to ISBN-13 format can use the U.S. ISBN Agency's free ISBN-13 online converter at http://isbn.org/converterpub.asp. Publishers can also view their ISBNs online by accessing their personal account at http://www.myidentifiers.com.

Displaying the ISBN on a Product or Publication

When an ISBN is written or printed, it should be preceded by the letters ISBN, and each part should be separated by a space or hyphen. In the United States, the hyphen is used for separation, as in the following example: ISBN 978-0-8352-8235-2. In this example, 978 is the prefix that precedes the ISBN-13, 0 is the group identifier, 8352 is the publisher identifier, 8235 is the title identifier, and 2 is the check digit. The group of English-speaking countries, which includes the United States, Australia, Canada, New Zealand, and the United Kingdom, uses the group identifiers 0 and 1. The 979 assignments by the United States ISBN Agency will start with 979-8. The 8 will be unique to the United States. Of course, as with the 978-0 and 978-1, an ISBN starting with 979-8 will allow U.S. publishers and self-publishers to market their books anywhere in the world.

The ISBN Organization

The administration of the ISBN system is carried out at three levels—through the International ISBN Agency in the United Kingdom, through the national agencies, and through the publishing houses themselves. The International ISBN Agency, which is responsible for assigning country prefixes and for coordinating the worldwide implementation of the system, has an advisory panel that represents the

International Organization for Standardization (ISO), publishers, and libraries. The International ISBN Agency publishes the *Publishers International ISBN Directory,* which is a listing of all national agencies' publishers with their assigned ISBN publisher prefixes. R. R. Bowker, as the publisher of *Books in Print,* with its extensive and varied database of publishers' addresses, was the obvious place to initiate the ISBN system and to provide the service to the U.S. publishing industry. To date, the U.S. ISBN Agency has entered more than 450,000 publishers into the system.

ISBN Assignment Procedure

Assignment of ISBNs is a shared endeavor between the U.S. ISBN Agency and the publisher. Publishers can apply online through the ISBN Agency's website www.myidentifiers.com. Once the order is processed, an e-mail confirmation will be sent with instructions for managing the account. The publisher then has the responsibility of assigning an ISBN to each title, keeping an accurate record of each number assigned, and registering each title in the *Books in Print* database at www.myidentifiers.com. It is the responsibility of the ISBN Agency to validate assigned ISBNs and keep a record of all ISBN publisher prefixes in circulation.

ISBN implementation is very much market-driven. Major distributors, wholesalers, retailers, and so forth recognize the necessity of the ISBN system and request that publishers register with the ISBN Agency. Also, the ISBN is a mandatory bibliographic element in the International Standard Bibliographical Description (ISBD). The Library of Congress Cataloging in Publication (CIP) Division directs publishers to the agency to obtain their ISBN prefixes.

Location and Display of the ISBN

On books, pamphlets, and other printed material, the ISBN shall be printed on the verso of the title leaf or, if this is not possible, at the foot of the title leaf itself. It should also appear on the outside back cover or on the back of the jacket if the book has one (the lower right-hand corner is recommended). The ISBN shall also appear on any accompanying promotional materials following the provisions for location according to the format of the material.

On other monographic publications, the ISBN shall appear on the title or credit frames and any labels permanently affixed to the publication. If the publication is issued in a container that is an integral part of the publication, the ISBN shall be displayed on the label. If it is not possible to place the ISBN on the item or its label, then the number should be displayed on the bottom or the back of the container, box, sleeve, or frame. It should also appear on any accompanying material, including each component of a multitype publication.

Printing of ISBN in Machine-Readable Coding

All books should carry ISBNs in the EAN-13 bar code machine-readable format. All ISBN EAN-13 bar codes start with the EAN prefixes 978 and 979 for books. As of January 1, 2007, all EAN bar codes should have the ISBN-13 appearing immediately above the bar code in eye-readable format, preceded by the acronym

"ISBN." The recommended location of the EAN-13 bar code for books is in the lower right-hand corner of the back cover (see Figure 1).

Figure 1 / Printing the ISBN in Bookland/EAN Symbology

Five-Digit Add-On Code

In the United States, a five-digit add-on code is used for additional information. In the publishing industry, this code is used for price information. The lead digit of the five-digit add-on has been designated a currency identifier, when the add-on is used for price. Number 5 is the code for the U.S. dollar, while 6 denotes the Canadian dollar. Publishers that do not want to indicate price in the add-on should print the code 90000 (see Figure 2).

Figure 2 / Printing the ISBN Bookland/EAN Number in Bar Code with the Five-Digit Add-On Code

978 = ISBN Bookland/EAN prefix
5 = Code for U.S. $ in the add-on code
2499 = $24.99

90000 means no information

Reporting the Title and the ISBN

After the publisher reports a title to the ISBN Agency, the number is validated and the title is listed in the many R. R. Bowker hard-copy and electronic publications, including *Books in Print*; *Forthcoming Books*; *Paperbound Books in Print*; *Books in Print Supplement*; *Books Out of Print*; *Books in Print Online*; *Books in Print Plus-CD ROM*; *Children's Books in Print*; *Subject Guide to Children's Books in*

Print; *Books Out Loud: Bowker's Guide to AudioBooks*; *Bowker's Complete Video Directory*; *Software Encyclopedia*; *Software for Schools*; and other specialized publications.

For an ISBN application and information, visit the ISBN Agency website at www.myidentifiers.com, call the toll-free number 877-310-7333, fax 908-795-3518, or write to the United States ISBN Agency, 630 Central Ave., New Providence, NJ 07974.

The ISSN, and How to Obtain One

U.S. ISSN Center
Library of Congress

In the early 1970s the rapid increase in the production and dissemination of information and an intensified desire to exchange information about serials in computerized form among different systems and organizations made it increasingly clear that a means to identify serial publications at an international level was needed. The International Standard Serial Number (ISSN) was developed and became the internationally accepted code for identifying serial publications.

The ISSN is an international standard. ISO 3297:2020, the 6th edition of the standard, will be published in 2020. The sixth edition expands on the role of ISSN for digital resources and includes additional detailed technical information about how to implement the ISSN standard in various technical environments.

The scope of the ISSN is "continuing resources," a concept that was introduced with the 2007 edition. Continuing resources include not only serials such as journals, magazines, open-ended series, and blogs but also open-ended publications such as updating databases, updating loose-leaf services, and certain types of updating websites.

The number itself has no significance other than as a brief, unique, and unambiguous identifier. The ISSN consists of eight digits in the Arabic numerals 0 to 9, except for the last ("check") digit, which is calculated using Modulus 11 and uses an "X" in place of the numeral 10 to maintain the ISSN at 8 digits. The numbers appear as two groups of four digits separated by a hyphen and preceded by the letters ISSN—for example, ISSN 1234-5679.

The ISSN is not self-assigned by publishers. Administration of the ISSN is coordinated through the ISSN Network, an intergovernmental organization within the UNESCO/UNISIST program. The ISSN Network consists of national ISSN centers, coordinated by the ISSN International Centre, located in Paris. National ISSN Centers are responsible for registering serials published in their respective countries. Responsibility for the assignment of ISSN to titles from multinational publishers is allocated among the ISSN Centers in which the publisher has offices. A list of these publishers and the corresponding ISSN centers is located on the ISSN International Centre's website, http://www.issn.org.

The ISSN International Centre handles ISSN assignments for international organizations and for countries that do not have a national center. It also maintains and distributes the ISSN Register and makes it available in a variety of products, most commonly via the ISSN Portal, an online subscription database containing full metadata records for each ISSN as well as other features and functionality. In January 2018, a new ISSN Portal was released that includes free look-up and access to a subset of ISSN metadata. The ISSN Register is also available via Z39.50 access, and as a data file. Selected ISSN data can also be obtained in customized files or database extracts that can be used, for example, to check the accuracy or completeness of a requestor's list of titles and ISSN. Another available ISSN service is OAI-PMH, a customizable "harvesting" protocol through which external applications can automatically and regularly gather new and updated metadata on a defined schedule. The ISSN Register contains bibliographic records corresponding to each ISSN assignment as reported by national ISSN centers. The database contains records for more than 2 million ISSNs.

The ISSN is used all over the world by serials publishers to identify their serials and to distinguish their titles from others that are the same or similar. It is used by subscription services and libraries to manage files for orders, claims, and back issues. It is used in automated check-in systems by libraries that wish to process receipts more quickly. Copyright centers use the ISSN as a means to collect and disseminate royalties. It is also used as an identification code by postal services and legal deposit services. The ISSN is included as a verification element in interlibrary lending activities and for union catalogs as a collocating device. The ISSN is also incorporated into bar codes for optical recognition of serial publication identification and metadata and into the standards for the identification of issues and articles in serial publications. A key use of the ISSN is as an identifier in online systems, where it can serve to connect catalog records or citations in abstracting and indexing databases with full-text journal content via OpenURL resolvers or reference linking services, and as an identifier and link in archives of electronic and print serials.

Because serials are generally known and cited by title, assignment of the ISSN is inseparably linked to the key title, a standardized form of the title derived from information in the serial issue. Only one ISSN can be assigned to a title in a particular medium. For titles issued in multiple media—e.g., print, online, CD-ROM—a separate ISSN is assigned to each medium version. If a major title change occurs or the medium changes, a new ISSN must be assigned. Centers responsible for assigning ISSNs also construct the key title and create an associated bibliographic record.

A significant new feature of the 2007 ISSN standard was the Linking ISSN (ISSN-L), a mechanism that enables collocation or linking among different media versions of a continuing resource. The Linking ISSN allows a unique designation (one of the existing ISSNs) to be applied to all media versions of a continuing resource while retaining the separate ISSN that pertains to each version. When an ISSN is functioning as a Linking ISSN, the eight digits of the base ISSN are prefixed with the designation "ISSN-L." The Linking ISSN facilitates search, retrieval, and delivery across all medium versions of a serial or other continuing resource for improved ISSN functionality in OpenURL linking, search engines, library catalogs, and knowledge bases. The ISSN standard also supports interoperability by specifying the use of ISSN and ISSN-L with other systems such as DOI, OpenURL, URN, and EAN bar codes. ISSN-L was implemented in the ISSN Register in 2008. To help ISSN users implement the ISSN-L in their databases, two free tables are available from the ISSN International Centre's home page: one lists each ISSN and its corresponding ISSN-L; the other lists each ISSN-L and its corresponding ISSNs.

In the United States, the U.S. ISSN Center at the Library of Congress is responsible for assigning and maintaining the ISSNs for all U.S. serial and other continuing resource publications. Publishers wishing to have an ISSN assigned should follow the instructions on the U.S. ISSN Center's website to complete an application form and submit required materials to the Center. Although some of the 91 ISSN centers worldwide charge for ISSNs, ISSN assignment by the U.S. ISSN Center is free.

To obtain an ISSN for a U.S. publication, or for more information about ISSNs in the United States, libraries, publishers, and other ISSN users should visit the U.S. ISSN Center's website, http://www.loc.gov/issn, or contact the U.S. ISSN Center, U.S. Programs, Law, and Literature, Library of Congress, 101 Independence Ave. S.E., Washington, DC 20540-4284 (telephone 202-707-6452, e-mail issn@loc.gov).

For information about ISSN products and services, and for application procedures that non-U.S. parties should use to apply for an ISSN, visit the ISSN International Centre's website, http://www.issn.org, or contact the International Centre at 45 rue de Turbigo, 75003 Paris, France (telephone 33-1-44-88-22-20, e-mail issnic@issn.org).

How to Obtain an SAN

Beat Barblan
United States ISBN/SAN Agency

SAN stands for Standard Address Number. The SAN system, an American National Standards Institute (ANSI) standard, assigns a unique identification number that is used to positively identify specific addresses of organizations in order to facilitate buying and selling transactions within the industry. It is recognized as the identification code for electronic communication within the industry.

For purposes of this standard, the book industry includes book publishers, book wholesalers, book distributors, book retailers, college bookstores, libraries, library binders, and serial vendors. Schools, school systems, technical institutes, and colleges and universities are not members of this industry, but are served by it and therefore included in the SAN system.

The purpose of the SAN is to ease communications among these organizations, of which there are several hundreds of thousands that engage in a large volume of separate transactions with one another. These transactions include purchases of books by book dealers, wholesalers, schools, colleges, and libraries from publishers and wholesalers; payments for all such purchases; and other communications between participants. The objective of this standard is to establish an identification code system by assigning each address within the industry a unique code to be used for positive identification for all book and serial buying and selling transactions.

Many organizations have similar names and multiple addresses, making identification of the correct contact point difficult and subject to error. In many cases, the physical movement of materials takes place between addresses that differ from the addresses to be used for the financial transactions. In such instances, there is ample opportunity for confusion and errors. Without identification by SAN, a complex record-keeping system would have to be instituted to avoid introducing errors. In addition, problems with the current numbering system—such as errors in billing, shipping, payments, and returns—are significantly reduced by using the SAN system. The SAN also eliminates one step in the order fulfillment process: the "look-up procedure" used to assign account numbers. Previously a store or library dealing with 50 different publishers was assigned a different account number by each of the suppliers. The SAN solved this problem. If a publisher prints its SAN on its stationery and ordering documents, vendors to whom it sends transactions do not have to look up the account number, but can proceed immediately to process orders by SAN.

Libraries are involved in many of the same transactions as book dealers, such as ordering and paying for books and charging and paying for various services to other libraries. Keeping records of transactions—whether these involve buying, selling, lending, or donations—entails operations suited to SAN use. SAN stationery speeds up order fulfillment and eliminate errors in shipping, billing, and crediting; this, in turn, means savings in both time and money.

History

Development of the Standard Address Number began in 1968, when Russell Reynolds, general manager of the National Association of College Stores (NACS), approached R. R. Bowker and suggested that a "Standard Account Number" system be implemented in the book industry. The first draft of a standard was prepared by an American National Standards Institute (ANSI) Committee Z39 subcommittee, which was co-chaired by Reynolds and Emery Koltay of Bowker. After Z39 members proposed changes, the current version of the standard was approved by NACS on December 17, 1979.

Format

The SAN consists of six digits plus a seventh *Modulus 11* check digit; a hyphen follows the third digit (XXX-XXXX) to facilitate transcription. The hyphen is to be used in print form, but need not be entered or retained in computer systems. Printed on documents, the Standard Address Number should be preceded by the identifier "SAN" to avoid confusion with other numerical codes (SAN XXXXXXX).

Check Digit Calculation

The check digit is based on *Modulus 11,* and can be derived as follows:

1.	Write the digits of the basic number.	2 3 4 5 6 7
2.	Write the constant weighting factors associated with each position by the basic number.	7 6 5 4 3 2
3.	Multiply each digit by its associated weighting factor.	14 18 20 20 18 14
4.	Add the products of the multiplications.	14 + 18 + 20 + 20 + 18 + 14 = 104
5.	Divide the sum by Modulus 11 to find the remainder.	104 ÷ 11 = 9 plus a remainder of 5
6.	Subtract the remainder from the Modulus 11 to generate the required check digit. If there is no remainder, generate a check digit of zero. If the check digit is 10, generate a check digit of X to represent 10, since the use of 10 would require an extra digit.	11 – 5 = 6
7.	Append the check digit to create the standard seven-digit Standard Address Number.	SAN 234-5676

SAN Assignment

R. R. Bowker accepted responsibility for being the central administrative agency for SAN, and in that capacity assigns SANs to identify uniquely the addresses of organizations. No SANs can be reassigned; in the event that an organization should cease to exist, for example, its SAN would cease to be in circulation entirely. If an organization using an SAN should move or change its name with no change in ownership, its SAN would remain the same, and only the name or address would be updated to reflect the change.

The SAN should be used in all transactions; it is recommended that the SAN be imprinted on stationery, letterheads, order and invoice forms, checks, and all other documents used in executing various book transactions. The SAN should always be printed on a separate line above the name and address of the organization, preferably in the upper left-hand corner of the stationery to avoid confusion with other numerical codes pertaining to the organization, such as telephone number, zip code, and the like.

SAN Functions

The SAN is strictly a Standard Address Number, becoming functional only in applications determined by the user; these may include activities such as purchasing, billing, shipping, receiving, paying, crediting, and refunding. It is the method used by Pubnet and PubEasy systems and is required in all electronic data interchange communications using the Book Industry Systems Advisory Committee (BISAC) EDI formats. Every department that has an independent function within an organization could have an SAN for its own identification.

For additional information or to make suggestions, write to ISBN/SAN Agency, R. R. Bowker, LLC, 630 Central Ave., New Providence, NJ 07974, call 877-310-7333, or fax 908-795-3518. The e-mail address is san@bowker.com. An SAN can be ordered online through the website www.myidentifiers.com, or an application can be requested by e-mail through san@bowker.com.

Distinguished Books

The Year's Notable Books

The Notable Books Council of the Reference and User Services Association, a division of the American Library Association, released its annual list of notable books on January 26, 2020. These titles were selected for their significant contribution to the expansion of knowledge or for the pleasure they can provide to adult readers.

Fiction

Trust Exercise by Susan Choi (Henry Holt and Company).

The Water Dancer by Ta-Nehisi Coates (One World, an imprint of Random House, a division of Penguin Random House).

The Innocents by Michael Crummey (Doubleday, a division of Penguin Random House).

Dominicana by Angie Cruz (Flatiron Books).

Everything Inside by Edwidge Danticat (Alfred A. Knopf, a division of Penguin Random House).

Girl, Woman, Other by Bernardine Evaristo (Black Cat, an imprint of Grove Atlantic).

Sabrina & Corina by Kali Fajardo-Anstine (One World, an imprint of Random House, a division of Penguin Random House).

The Topeka School by Ben Lerner (Farrar, Straus, and Giroux).

Lost Children Archive by Valeria Luiselli (Alfred A. Knopf, a division of Penguin Random House).

Lanny by Max Porter (Graywolf Press).

Normal People by Sally Rooney (Hogarth, an imprint of the Crown Publishing Group, a division of Penguin Random House).

On Earth We're Briefly Gorgeous by Ocean Vuong (Penguin Press, an imprint of Penguin Random House).

The Nickel Boys by Colson Whitehead (Doubleday a division of Penguin Random House).

Nonfiction

Elderhood: Redefining Aging, Transforming Medicine, Reimagining Life by Louise Aronson (Bloomsbury Publishing Inc.).

Yellow House by Sarah M. Broom (Grove Press, an imprint of Grove Atlantic).

Thick: And Other Essays by Tressie McMillan Cottom (The New Press).

A Good Provider Is One Who Leaves: One Family and Migration in the 21st Century by Jason DeParle (Viking, an imprint of Penguin Random House).

Mama's Last Hug: Animal Emotions and What They Tell Us About Themselves by Frans De Waal (W. W. Norton & Company).

Midnight in Chernobyl: The Untold Story of the World's Greatest Nuclear Disaster by Adam Higginbotham (Simon & Schuster).

Say Nothing: A True Story of Murder and Memory in Northern Ireland by Patrick Radden Keefe (Doubleday, a division of Penguin Random House).

Underland: A Deep Time Journey by Robert Macfarlane (W. W. Norton & Company).

Late Migrations: A Natural History of Love and Loss by Margaret Renkl (Milkweed Editions).

The Uninhabitable Earth: Life After Warming by David Wallace-Wells (Tim Duggan Books, an imprint of the Crown Publishing Group, a division of Penguin Random House).

The Impeachers: The Trial of Andrew Johnson and the Dream of a Just Nation by Brenda Wineapple (Random House, an imprint and division of Penguin Random House).

Poetry

The Tradition by Jericho Brown (Copper Canyon Press).

Deaf Republic by Ilya Kaminsky (Graywolf Press).

The Reading List

Established in 2007 by the Reference and User Services Association (RUSA), a division of the American Library Association, this list highlights outstanding genre fiction that merits special attention by general adult readers and the librarians who work with them.

RUSA's Reading List Council, which consists of 12 librarians who are experts in readers' advisory and collection development, selects books in eight categories: Adrenaline (suspense, thrillers, and action adventure), Fantasy, Historical Fiction, Horror, Mystery, Relationship (replacing Women's Fiction this year), Romance, and Science Fiction.

The RUSA website provides additional detail on each of the winning titles along with shortlists of "Readalikes" and runners up.

Adrenaline

The Passengers by John Marrs (Berkley, an imprint of Penguin Random House).

Fantasy

Gods of Jade and Shadow by Silvia Moreno-Garcia (Del Rey, an imprint of Random House, a division of Penguin Random House).

Historical Fiction

The Secrets We Kept by Lara Prescott (Borzoi Books, an imprint of Alfred A. Knopf).

Horror

The Twisted Ones by T. Kingfisher (Saga Press, an imprint of Simon & Schuster).

Mystery

The Right Sort of Man by Allison Montclair (Minotaur Books).

Relationship

When You Read This by Mary Adkins (Harper, a division of HarperCollins).

Romance

The Flatshare by Beth O'Leary (Flatiron Books).

Science Fiction

A Memory Called Empire by Arkady Martine (Tor, an imprint of Tom Doherty Associates).

The Listen List

Established in 2010 by the Reference and User Services Association (RUSA), the annual Listen List highlights outstanding audiobooks that merit special attention by general adult listeners and the librarians who work with them. Titles are chosen by RUSA's Listen List Council, which annually selects about a dozen audiobooks that may include fiction, nonfiction, poetry, and plays. To be eligible, titles must be available for purchase and circulation by libraries. This year's list recognizes 13 outstanding recordings.

An annotated version of the list on the RUSA website includes more information on each choice and lists additional audiobooks of interest.

Becoming by Michelle Obama, narrated by Michelle Obama (Books on Tape).

The Bride Test by Helen Hoang, narrated by Emily Woo Zeller (Dreamscape Media).

The Chain by Adrian McKinty, narrated by January LaVoy (Hachette Audio).

Daisy Jones & the Six by Taylor Jenkins Reid, narrated by Jennifer Beals, Pablo Schreiber, Benjamin Bratt, Judy Greer, Fred Berman, Ari Fliakos, January LaVoy, Robinne Lee, Julia Whelan, Jonathan Davis, Henry Leyva, Oliver Wyman, Nancy Wu, P. J. Ochlan, Arthur Bishop, Holter Graham, Brendan Wayne, Pete Larkin, Alex Jenkins Reid, Robert Petkoff, and Sara Arrington (Books on Tape).

Full Throttle by Joe Hill, narrated by Zachary Quinto, Wil Wheaton, Kate Mulgrew, Neil Gaiman, Ashleigh Cummings, Joe Hill, Laysla De Oliveira, Nate Corddry, Connor Jessup, Stephen Lang, and George Guidall (HarperAudio).

Ghost Wall by Sarah Moss, narrated by Christine Hewitt (Macmillan Audio).

Good Talk: A Memoir in Conversations. Jby Mira Jacob, narrated by Mira Jacob, Vikas Adam, Shiromi Arserio, McCartney Birdwell, Donte Bonner, Bill Cheng, Nicole Counts, Margaret Dunham, Chris Edmund, Alison Fraser, Cecila Flores, Kaitlyn Greenridge, Alison Hart, Chris Jackson, Victory Matsui, Kivlighan de Montebello, Meera Nair, Soneela Nankani, Lorna Raver, Rajiv Surendra, Oliver Wyman, and an ensemble cast (Books on Tape).

Notes from a Young Black Chef by Kwame Onwuachi and Joshua David Stein, narrated by Kwame Onwuachi (Books on Tape).

The Poison Thread by Laura Purcell, narrated by Jayne Entwistle and Elizabeth Knowelden (Books on Tape).

Queenie by Candice Carty-Williams, narrated by Shvorne Marka (Simon & Schuster Audio).

Red at the Bone by Jacqueline Woodson, narrated by Jacqueline Woodson, Quincy Tyler Bernstine, Peter Francis James, Shayna Small, and Bahni Turpin (Books on Tape).

Talking to Strangers: What We Should Know about the People We Don't Know by Malcolm Gladwell, narrated by Malcolm Gladwell (Hachette Audio).

We Cast a Shadow by Maurice Carlos Ruffin, narrated by Dion Graham (Books on Tape).

Best Fiction for Young Adults

Each year a committee of the Young Adult Library Services Association (YALSA), a division of the American Library Association, compiles a list of the best fiction appropriate for young adults ages 12 to 18. Selected on the basis of each book's proven or potential appeal and value to young adults, the titles span a variety of subjects as well as a broad range of reading levels. An asterisk denotes the title was selected as a top ten.

All Eyes on Us by Kit Frick (Simon & Schuster/Margaret K. McElderry). 978-1534404403.

All the Bad Apples by Moïra Fowley-Doyle (Penguin/Kathy Dawson). 978-0525552741.

The Art of Breaking Things by Laura Sibson (Viking). 978-0451481115.

Aurora Rising by Amie Kaufman and Jay Kristoff (Knopf). 978-1524720964.

Birthday by Meredith Russo (Flatiron). 978-1250129833.

The Bone Houses by Emily Lloyd-Jones (Little, Brown). 978-0316418416.

Butterfly Yellow by Thanhhà Lai (Harper). 978-0062229212.

Call It What You Want by Brigid Kemmerer (Bloomsbury). 978-1681198095.

Color Me In by Natasha Diaz (Delacorte). 978-0525578239.

A Curse So Dark and Lonely by Brigid Kemmerer (Bloomsbury). 978-1681195087.

Dig by A. S. King (Dutton). 978-1101994917.

The Disasters by M. K. England (HarperTeen). 978-0062657671.

The Downstairs Girl by Stacey Lee (Putnam). 978-1524740955.

Echo North by Joanna Ruth Meyer (Page Street). 978-1624147159.

*_The Field Guide to the North American Teenager_ by Ben Philippe (HarperCollins/Balzer+Bray). 978-0062824110.

Forward Me Back to You by Mitali Perkins (Farrar). 978-0374304928.

The Fountains of Silence by Ruta Sepetys (Philomel). 978-0399160318.

Full Disclosure by Camryn Garrett (Knopf). 978-1984829955.

Genesis Begins Again by Alicia D. Williams (Atheneum/Caitlyn Dlouhy). 978-1481465809.

*_Girls on the Verge_ by Sharon Biggs Waller (Holt). 978-1250151698.

The Good Luck Girls by Charlotte Nicole Davis (Tor Teen). 978-1250299703.

*_Heroine_ by Mindy McGinnis (HarperCollins/Katherine Tegen). 978-0062847195.

Her Royal Highness by Rachel Hawkins (Putnam). 978-1524738266.

How Not to Ask a Boy to Prom by S. J. Goslee (Brook). 978-1626724013.

How to be Remy Cameron by Julian Winters (Interlude). 978-1945053801.

How to Make Friends with the Dark by Kathleen Glasgow (Delacorte). 978-1101934753.

I Love You So Mochi by Sarah Kuhn (Scholastic). 978-1338302882.

The Infinite Noise by Lauren Shippen (Tor Teen). 978-1250297518.

Internment by Samira Ahmed (Brown). 978-0316522694.

It's a Whole Spiel: Love, Latkes, and Other Jewish Stories edited by Katherine Locke and Laura Silverman (Knopf). 978-0525646167.

I Wish You All the Best by Mason Deaver (Scholastic/Push). 978-1338306125.

The Kingdom by Jess Rothenberg (Holt). 978-1250293855.

Last Bus to Everland by Sophie Cameron (Roaring Brook). 978-1250149930.

The Light at the Bottom of the World by London Shah (Disney/Hyperion). 978-1368036887.

*_Like a Love Story_ by Abdi Nazemian (HarperCollins/Balzer+Bray). 978-0062839367.

Love from A to Z by S. K. Ali (Simon & Schuster/Salaam Reads). 978-1534442726.

*_Lovely War_ by Julie Berry (Viking). 978-0451469939.

The Lying Woods by Ashley Elston (Disney/Hyperion). 978-1368014786.

The Merciful Crow by Margaret Owen (Holt). 978-1250191922.

Michigan vs. the Boys by Carrie S. Allen (Can/KCP Loft). 978-1525301483.

The Music of What Happens by Bill Konigsberg (Scholastic/Arthur A. Levine). 978-1338215502.

The Never Tilting World by Rin Chupeco (HarperTeen). 978-0062821799.

**On the Come Up* by Angie Thomas (HarperCollins/Balzer+Bray). 978-0062498564.

**Patron Saints of Nothing* by Randy Ribay (Penguin/Kokila). 978-0525554912.

**Pet* by Akwaeke Emezi (Random/Make Me a World). 978-0525647072.

Rayne & Delilah's Midnite Matinee by Jeff Zentner (Crown). 978-1524720209.

The Revolution of Birdie Randolph by Brandy Colbert (Little, Brown). 978-0316448567.

Sick Kids in Love by Hannah Moskowitz (Entangled). 978-1640637320.

Ship of Smoke and Steel by Django Wexler (Tor Teen). 978-0765397249.

SLAY by Brittney Morris (Simon & Schuster/Simon Pulse). 978-1534445420.

Someday We Will Fly by Rachel DeWoskin (Viking). 978-0670014965.

Sorcery of Thorns by Margaret Rogerson (Simon & Schuster/Margaret K. McElderry). 978-1481497619.

Sorry for Your Loss by Jessie Ann Foley (HarperTeen). 978-0062571915.

Spin by Lamar Giles (Scholastic). 978-1338219210.

**The Stars and the Blackness between Them* by Junauda Petrus (Dutton). 978-0525555483.

Start Here by Trish Doller (Simon & Schuster/Simon Pulse). 978-1481479912.

Stepsister by Jennifer Donnelly (Scholastic). 978-1338268461.

Stronger, Faster, and More Beautiful by Arwen Elys Dayton (Delacorte). 978-0525580959.

There Will Come A Darkness by Katy Rose Pool (Holt). 978-1250211750.

Thirteen Doorways, Wolves behind Them All by Laura Ruby (HarperCollins/Balzer+Bray). 978-0062317643.

This Time Will Be Different by Misa Sugiura (HarperTeen). 978-0062473448.

Voices: The Final Hours of Joan of Arc by David Elliott (HMH). 978-1328987594.

War Girls by Tochi Onyebuchi (Razorbill). 978-0451481672.

We Are Lost and Found by Helene Dunbar (Sourcebooks/Fire). 978-1492681045.

The Weight of Our Sky by Hanna Alkaf (Simon & Schuster/Salaam Reads). 978-1534426085.

We Set the Dark on Fire by Tehlor Kay Mejia (HarperCollins/Katherine Tegen). 978-0062691316.

When the Ground Is Hard by Malla Nunn (Putnam). 978-0525515579.

Where I End and You Begin by Preston Norton (Disney/Hyperion). 978-1484798355.

Within These Lines by Stephanie Morrill (Blink). 978-0310765233.

**With the Fire on High* by Elizabeth Acevedo (HarperTeen). 978-0062662835.

You Asked for Perfect by Laura Silverman (Sourcebooks/Fire). 978-1492658276.

Quick Picks for Reluctant Young Adult Readers

The Young Adult Library Services Association (YALSA), a division of the American Library Association, annually chooses a list of outstanding titles that will stimulate the interest of reluctant teen readers. This list is intended to attract teens who, for whatever reason, may choose not to read.

The list includes fiction and nonfiction titles published from late 2018 through 2019. An asterisk denotes the title was selected as a top ten.

Nonfiction

Dreamland (YA Edition): The True Tale of America's Opiate Epidemic by Sam Quinones. Bloomsbury YA. 2019. $18.99. ISBN: 978-1547601318. This YA adaptation depicts the opiate epidemic that is roiling the United States.

Grand Theft Horse by Greg Neri. Tu Books. 2018. $18.99. ISBN: 978-1620148556. Gail Raffu became an outlaw when she stole Urgent Envoy, a horse she was part owner of, because her partners wanted to race him too early and use drugs to help him win. She battled the corrupt racing system for years to protect the horse.

Monstrous: The Lore, Gore, and Science Behind Your Favorite Monsters by Carlyn Beccia. Carolrhoda Books. 2019. $19.99. ISBN: 978-1512449167. Explore the real-world origins of eight popular monsters, including Dracula, werewolves, and Godzilla. Readers investigate detailed drawings of monster anatomy, learn how to separate monster fact from fiction, and discover fun tips for everything from keeping a sea monster in your bathtub to recognizing blood-sucking animals.

Shout by Laurie Halse Anderson. Penguin Random House. 2019. $17.99. ISBN: 978-0670012107. Laurie Halse Anderson's collection of poems about her turbulent childhood and teenage years, including her sexual assault by a trusted friend. Her battles and her bravery are revealed through emotionally charged verse. Other topics addressed include drug experimentation, finding one's way, and forgiveness of self and others.

Spooked! How a Radio Broadcast and The War of the Worlds Sparked the 1938 Invasion of America by Gail Jarrow. Calkins Creek. 2018. $18.95. ISBN: 978-1629797762. The 1938 radio broadcast of War of the Worlds sent people into a panic, causing some to flee their homes to save themselves from the perceived Martian invasion. When it was discovered that the broadcast was fiction, it called into question fake news and propaganda.

The Stonewall Riots: Coming Out in the Streets by Gayle E. Pitman. Harry N. Abrams. 2019. $17.99 ISBN: 978-1419737206. Explore the history of Stonewall through 50 "objects," including protest signs, artifacts from the riots, photographs of participants, and newspaper articles describing the events of June 1969. An overview of LGBTQ+ activism prior to Stonewall culminates in a detailed account of the riots and their aftermath.

**We Are Displaced: My Journey and Stories from Refugee Girls Around the World* by Malala Yousafzai. Hachette Book Group. 2018. $18.99. ISBN: 978-0316523646. This title features Malala's and others' experiences as young people displaced by war and violence. Their tales remind readers that many people around the world have been uprooted from the lives they knew and are struggling to be heard.

Will My Cat Eat My Eyeballs?: Big Questions from Tiny Mortals about Death by Caitlin Doughty. W. W. Norton Company. 2019. $25.95. ISBN: 978-0393652703. Written by a mortician in question-and-answer chapters, this book explores some of the more icky and intriguing questions about human corpses. With a perfect amount of snark and lighthearted illustrations, it's a fun (if morbid) read for anyone.

Fiction

**10 Blind Dates* by Ashley Elston. Disney Hyperion. 2019. $17.99. ISBN: 978-1368027496. After Sophie's boyfriend breaks up with her, she goes to spend the holidays with her loving grandparents and huge extended family. They set her up on ten blind dates. Some of these dates are hilarious failures, some promising, while her ideal future boyfriend may be nearby the whole time.

500 Words or Less by Juleah Del Rosario. Simon Pulse. 2018. $17.99. ISBN: 978-1534410442. Seventeen-year-old Nic tries to salvage her tarnished reputation by writing her classmates' college application essays for a fee. In doing so, she discovers a lot about the kids she goes to school with, and even more about who she is.

An Absolutely Remarkable Thing by Hank Green. Penguin: Dutton. 2018. $26.00. ISBN: 978-1524743444. April May makes first contact with what might be an art installation, or perhaps an alien being. Her viral video of the encounter gathers "likes" across the Internet. As more of the alien mystery reveals itself, April tries to manage her online persona without destroying her relationships or losing her life.

**Belly Up* by Eva Darrows. HarperCollins Inkyard Press. 2019. $18.99. ISBN: 978-1335012357. Serendipity spends one night with a boy and gets pregnant. At 17, deciding what to do is difficult, and changes this will bring to her life are overwhelming. With the support of her family and best friend, as well as a new boyfriend, she makes her way through.

Black Enough: Stories of Being Young and Black in America edited by Ibi Zoboi. Balzer+Bray. 2019. $17.99. ISBN: 978-0062698728. Short stories written by popular black YA authors. The young protagonists confront the typical teenage life experiences along with some unexpected ones, both tragic and romantic.

Creep by Eireann Corrigan. Scholastic. 2019. $17.99. ISBN: 978-1338095081. Olivia is excited to bond with her new neighbor, Janie Donahue, not to mention Janie's sweet older brother Ben. When threatening letters signed by "the Sentry" appear in the Donahue's home, the three immerse themselves in local history in order to outsmart the perpetrator and keep the Donahue family together.

A Curse So Dark and Lonely by Brigid Kemmerer. Bloomsbury YA. 2019. $18.99. ISBN: 978-1681195087. Here is a "Beauty and the Beast" remake in which the Beast and the Beauty are from two separate worlds. Having lost hope after 326 autumn seasons trying to break his life's curse, Rhen (Beast) doesn't see an end to his misfortune until Harper (Beauty) arrives.

A Danger to Herself and Others by Alyssa Sheinmel. Sourcebooks/Fire. 2019. $17.99. ISBN: 978-1492667247. Hannah is institutionalized and knows it's a mistake. She slowly shares pieces of the mysterious tragedy that happened before she was committed. A new friend comes along and helps her discover what really happened, with an end twist to keep the reader guessing.

Darius the Great Is Not Okay by Adib Khorram. Penguin Dial Books. 2018. $17.99 ISBN: 978-0525552963. Darius Kellner is a Persian American who has always felt out of place. He travels to Iran for the first time to visit family he formerly only knew through his computer screen. As he deals with clinical depression and his family, Darius meets Sohrab, a neighbor who turns best friend, and learns how to be himself.

Dry by Neal Shusterman. Simon & Schuster Books for Young Readers. 2018. $18.99. ISBN: 978-1481481960. Imagine what would happen if water become scarce. Would you turn into a water zombie and kill all your neighbors for their water, or try to find a savior?

Fifteen and Change by Max Howard. West 44 Books. 2018. $19.95. ISBN: 978-1538382608. Zeke is desperate to help his mom escape their impoverished life with her loser boyfriend. Taking a job at a pizza shop, he meets labor activists who encourage him to fight for better working conditions. Will he raise his voice in protest, even if it means postponing his own dreams?

Five Feet Apart by Rachael Lippincott. Simon & Schuster Books for Young Readers. 2018. $18.99. ISBN: 978-1534437333. Stella Grant's cystic fibrosis has kept her from living life as a "typical" kid. When she finally has a shot at a life-saving lung transplant, her resolve to stay six feet apart from everyone else is tested by fellow inpatient, Will Newman, when they must decide if love is worth breaking the rule for.

Girls with Sharp Sticks by Suzanne Young. Simon Pulse. 2019. $18.99. ISBN: 978-1534426139. The girls at Innovations Academy resemble beautiful, pleasing, and polished young women. But they are not quite what they seem.

The Giver by Lois Lowry. Art by Russell P. Craig. Houghton Mifflin Harcourt. 2019. $22.99. ISBN: 978-0544157880. This graphic novel adaptation of the Newbery Award–winning book by Lois Lowry beautifully depicts the dystopian tale of Jonas, who is given the lifelong assignment of Receiver of Memory. As he learns about his people's history, his colorless world expands and he begins to question everything he has been told.

Goodbye, Perfect by Sara Barnard. Simon Pulse–Simon & Schuster Children's. 2019. $19.99. ISBN: 978-1534402447. Eden McKinley thought she had problems in school and with her parents until her high-achieving best friend Bonnie runs off with their music teacher on the eve of final exams. As the police search for her friend, Eden's loyalty to her friends and family is tested.

Harley Quinn: Breaking Glass by Mariko Tamaki. Art by Steve Pugh. DC Ink. 2019. $16.99 ISBN: 978-1401283292. Harleen Quinzel finds herself in Gotham City, parentless, and is taken in by a fabulous group of drag queens. As the gentrification of their neighborhood threatens them, Harleen, now Harley Quinn, wants to do what she can, with the help of her friend Ivy—and maybe the Joker . . .?

**The Haunted* by Danielle Vega. Razorbill. 2019. $17.99. ISBN: 978-0451481467. Hendricks and her family have relocated to a small town looking for a clean slate from a previous traumatic experience, but their newly purchased home has a long, dark history.

Here to Stay by Sara Farizan. Algonquin for Young Readers. 2018. $17.95. ISBN: 978-1616207007. Bijan was just called up from JV to play varsity basketball. He's hoping his new star athlete status will give him a step up socially and help him talk to girls. But racism and bullying rear their heads on campus and his new visibility is turning into more of a problem than a solution.

**Heroine* by Mindy McGinnis. Katherine Tegen Books. 2019. $17.99. ISBN: 978-0062847195. When softball standout Mickey suffers a devastating injury, she turns to oxycodone to relieve her pain, and eventually her social anxiety. As her addiction spirals out of control, her family and her teammates struggle to keep Mickey from losing herself, and all she's worked for, to the drug.

Hot Dog Girl by Jennifer Dugan. G. P. Putnam Son's Books for Young Readers. 2019. $17.99. ISBN: 978-0525516255. Lou loves her small town, especially the amusement park where she and her best friend Seeley meet. She also loves Nick, a lifeguard at the park. When a fake-dating plan with Seeley to make Nick jealous goes awry, Lou has to figure out who it is she really has feelings for.

I'm Not Dying with You Tonight by Kimberly Jones and Gilly Segal. Sourcebooks/Fire. 2019. $17.99. ISBN: 978-1492678892. Lena, the neighborhood black girl, doesn't know Campbell, the out-of-state white girl, but when a violent outburst at their high school football game throws them together, they become a team focused on their own well-being and survival, as a series of nightmares block their way home.

In the Key of Nira Ghani by Natasha Deen. Running Press Kids. 2019. $17.99. ISBN: 978-0762465477. Nira Ghani challenges her Guyanese parents' dream of her becoming a doctor by following her love for the trumpet instead. A coming-of-age tale with a twist.

It's the End of the World as I Know It by Matthew Landis. Penguin Random House. 2019. $16.99. ISBN: 978-0735228016. Since Derrick's mother's death, he lives in fear of doomsday. Derrick's friends, father, and sister care for him deeply, but it is Derrick's unusual friendship with his quirky neighbor, Misty, that helps him live in the present rather than feel weighed down by the past and worried for the future.

Jackpot by Nic Stone. Crown Books for Young Readers. 2019. $17.99. ISBN: 978-1984829627. Seventeen-year-old Rico works long hours at the Gas 'n' Go to help support her mother and younger brother. When no one comes forward to claim a multi-million-dollar lottery prize, she teams up with Zan, whose wealthy family seems the opposite of hers in every way, in order to find the winning ticket.

The Justice Project by Michael Betcherman. Orca Book Publishers. 2019. $14.95. ISBN: 978-1459822504. When a serious injury derails Matt Barnes's promising football career he finds a new passion interning with the Justice Project to defend the wrongly convicted. While working on the case of alleged killer Ray Richardson, Matt and his fellow intern Sonya find new evidence that plunges them into a murder mystery.

Killing November by Adriana Mather. Knopf Books for Young Readers. 2019. $17.99. ISBN: 978-0525579083. Academy Absconditi is not your traditional boarding school. Everyone wields a weapon and deals in secrets. New student November is out of her league. With threats at every turn, she doesn't know who can be trusted. Then a dead body is discovered, and November has to find out who did it before she becomes the next victim.

Kiss Number 8 by Colleen AF Venable; illustrated by Ellen T. Crenshaw. Macmillan Roaring Brook Press/First Second. 2019. $17.99 ISBN: 978-1596437098. Amanda "Mads" does not understand kissing. Kisses 1–7 were nothing exciting at best, and hardly tolerable at worst. Kiss number 8, with a girl, threw her for a loop. As her own experience runs parallel to a family history she knew nothing about, Mads discovers much about kissing, and about herself.

Laura Dean Keeps Breaking Up With Me by Mariko Tamaki. Art by Rosemary Valero-O'Connell. Roaring Books/First Second. 2019. $21.00 ISBN: 978-250312846. 17-year-old Freddy finds herself in an on-again, off-again relationship with charismatic Laura Dean. She knows she needs to break things off so she can get on with her life, but can she?

The Liar's Daughter by Megan Cooley Peterson. Holiday House. 2019. $17.99. ISBN: 978-0823444182. Piper is dedicated to Father and his commands. She never complains, just does what she is told. Then one day, mean people show up, separate her from her family, and turn her world upside down.

Life Is Short and Then You Die edited by Kelley Armstrong. Imprint/Macmillan Children's Publishing Group. 2019. $17.99. ISBN: 978-1250196392. Growing up means experiencing lots of things for the first time. The teens in this collection of short stories by well-known YA authors are having their first experiences with death and murder.

Look Both Ways by Jason Reynolds. Atheneum/Caitlyn Dlouhy Books. 2019. $17.99. ISBN: 978-1481438285. Ten short stories of young teens as they travel home from school. The stories are woven together as the kids head in different directions on their ways home. Each story is poignant and heartfelt with pictures of realistic lives of the neighborhood kids.

The Love & Lies of Rukhsana Ali by Sabina Khan. Scholastic Press. 2019. $17.99. ISBN: 978-1338227017. Rukhsana cannot escape her family's conservative Muslim traditions when they learn she is gay. She risks losing everything when her parents hold her hostage in their native Bangladesh in order to "convert" her and marry her to a Bangladeshi man.

Love from A to Z by S. K. Ali. Salaam Reads. 2019. ISBN: 978-1534442726. $18.99. Adam and Zayneb, two Muslim teens, meet on a flight to Qatar. The fact that they meet at all is both a marvel and an oddity. The fact that they keep meeting again? It might just be love.

Michigan vs. The Boys by Carrie Allen. Kids Can Press. 2019. $17.99. ISBN: 978-1525301483. Michigan Manning is thrilled when she earns a spot on the boys' varsity hockey team. Despite becoming the team's leading scorer, she finds that her teammates don't welcome her. Even when "harmless" pranks cross the line into assault, Michigan fears that speaking up will cost her everything she loves.

Mike by Andrew Noriss. Scholastic. 2019. $17.99. ISBN: 978-1338285369. Floyd, a 15-year-old rising tennis star, starts seeing an imaginary boy named Mike during his tennis games. Floyd soon realizes that playing tennis isn't fun anymore and wants to take control of his life.

New Kid by Jerry Craft. HarperAlley. 2019. $12.99. ISBN: 978-0062691194. Budding cartoonist Jordan Banks is sent to an academic private school where the stakes of middle school are elevated by him being one of only a few black kids in a sea of white faces.

The Okay Witch by Emma Steinkellner. Aladdin. 2019. $12.99 ISBN: 978-1534431454. Moth accidentally finds out she's a witch in this graphic novel. She's part of a long line of witches. Her mom isn't thrilled about witches and her previously unknown grandmother isn't so crazy about humans, which leaves Moth stuck in the middle. They must work together when witch hunters move into town.

The Past and Other Things That Should Stay Buried by Shaun David Hutchinson. Simon Pulse. 2019. $18.99. ISBN: 978-1481498579. Dino's family runs a funeral home where, up until now, the bodies have stayed dead. July, Dino's ex-best friend, however, dies and then gets up and walks away. In her not-dead state, she and Dino must figure out why and how to fix it, while avoiding detection and grappling with current and past relationships.

Past Perfect Life by Elizabeth Eulberg. Bloomsbury. 2019. $18.99. ISBN: 978-1547600922. Allison Smith loves the life that she and her father have built in small-town Wisconsin, at least until the day the F.B.I. arrives at her door. Caught in the web of a devastating secret, Allison is suddenly forced to leave behind everything she knows to live with a family she didn't know existed.

Patron Saints of Nothing by Randy Ribay. Penguin Kokila. 2019. $17.99. ISBN: 978-0525554912. Jay is coasting out his senior year, about to enjoy Spring Break, and plans to start college in the fall. Learning of his cousin's death in the Philippines, his priorities are shaken. He heads to the Philippines to find answers about his cousin and President Duterte's war on drugs.

Pretty in Punxsutawney by Laurie Boyle Crompton. Blink. 2019. $17.99. ISBN: 978-0310762164. A new school year; a new school. Andie hopes her first day will go smoothly, especially since the boy she likes has promised to be her guide. But the day doesn't go exactly as planned and when Andie is doomed to repeat it, she wonders how to break the loop.

**Pumpkinheads* by Rainbow Rowell. Art by Faith Erin Hicks. Roaring Books/First Second. 2019. $21.99. ISBN: 978-1250312853. Deja and Josiah (Josi) have worked at the seasonal pumpkin patch all through high school. On their last day, Deja helps Josi finally talk to "Fudge Girl." After adventuring throughout the park, tasting all the snacks along the way, Josi finally finds the girl of his dreams.

The Revolution of Birdie Randolph by Brandy Colbert. Little, Brown Books for Young Readers. 2019. $17.99. ISBN: 978-0316448567. Chicago teenager Birdie Randolph studies hard and follows her parents' rules, at least until she meets Booker. Now she's sneaking out of the house and lying to her parents. With a secret boyfriend, and the arrival of a mysterious aunt bearing devastating family secrets, Birdie's summer promises to be revolutionary.

Run, Hide, Fight Back by April Henry. Henry Holt and Company. 2019. $17.99. ISBN: 978-1627795890. A random group of teens try to survive after a mall is overtaken by a group of men with guns. After watching people around them die, they realize they have to work together to get out alive.

Salt by Hannah Moskowitz. Chronicle Books. 2018. $17.99. ISBN: 978-1452131511. An orphaned family of children are monster hunters in the sea, using all the skills they learned from their parents.

Since We Last Spoke by Brenda Rufener. HarperTeen. 2019. $17.99. ISBN: 978-0062571083. Aggi and Max grew up together and finally admit their love for one another. Then the unthinkable happens: her sister and his brother are both dead after a car crash. Their families ban Aggi and Max from any contact. One wrenching year later, they reflect on their lost love.

Sleeping in My Jeans by Connie King Leonard. Ooligan Press. 2018. $16.00. ISBN:

978-1947845008. Sixteen-year-old Mattie is homeless, living with her mom and her little sister in the family's old station wagon. When their mother disappears, leaving them stranded on the streets overnight, it's up to Mattie to keep their family together. Can she trust the police, or her new friend, Jack, to help her?

Smooth Criminals, Vol. 1 by Kiwi Smith and Kurt Lustgarten. Art by Leisha Riddel. Boom! Box. 2019. $14.99. ISBN: 978-1684153859. When a computer hacker accidentally brings back a cat burglar from the 1960s, suddenly computer hacking is cool.

Swing by Kwame Alexander and Mary Rand Hess. HarperCollins Blink. 2018. $18.99. ISBN: 978-0310761914. Noah, Sam, and Walt have been best friends forever. Walt wants to get Noah to tell Sam he loves her, but Sam already has a boyfriend. Walt meets a girl who shares his fascination with jazz. Touching on topics including police violence and PTSD, *Swing* is a sweet romance from a boy's POV.

Teen Titans: Raven by Kami Garcia. Art by Gabriel Picolo. DC Ink. 2019. $16.99. ISBN: 978-1401286231. This graphic novel origin story opens on a scene between Raven and her mother discussing a recent shocking revelation when their car is hit. The mother dies, and Raven is left with amnesia. Taken in by her mother's estranged sister, Raven has to relearn who she is while navigating high school.

This Book Is Not Yet Rated by Peter Bognanni. Penguin Dial Books. 2019. $17.99. ISBN: 978-0735228078. Ethan has a passion for movies and a nostalgic love of the theater he and his late Dad spent so much time in. Now the university that owns the decrepit theater has plans to shut it down. Can Ethan and his "lost boys" band of employees save the art house?

**Two Can Keep a Secret* by Karen McManus. Delacorte Press. 2019. $19.99. ISBN: 978-1524714727. When Ellery and Ezra are forced to travel to their mother's remote Vermont hometown, they don't expect that their classmates will start going missing. When Ellery tries to solve the mystery, she's drawn into the secrets of the town.

**The Unfortunates* by Kim Liggett. Tor Teen. 2018. $17.99 ISBN: 978-0765381002. Grant Franklin Tavish IV, son of a wealthy senator, caused an accident that killed four teenagers. Racked with guilt, he is sent on the family traditional solo caving trip with the plan to kill himself. Instead, he and a group of stranded cavers need to work together to escape the cave alive.

**UNpregnant* by Jenni Hendriks and Ted Caplan. HarperCollins. 2019. $17.99. ISBN: 978-0062876249. Veronica discovers she's pregnant after her boyfriend poked holes in a condom. She decides to have an abortion but must travel 1,000 miles for the procedure. With her besties away, and her boyfriend now an unreliable option, Veronica asks former friend Bailey to drive her and nothing goes as planned.

Warrior of the Wild by Tricia Levenseller. Feiwel and Friends. 2019. $17.99. ISBN: 978-1250189943. Rasmira, daughter of the village leader, was betrayed and exiled during her warrior trial. She has to complete an undoable task to be able to go back to her village and family. If she completes her task, will her people respect her?

With the Fire on High by Elizabeth Acevedo. HarperTeen. 2019. $17.99. ISBN: 978-0062662835. Emani is a teen parent who loves to cook and wants to graduate high school so she can continue to provide for her growing daughter. When a new culinary program starts at her school, Emani may find opportunities that she never thought possible.

The Alex Awards

The Alex Awards are given to ten books written for adults that have special appeal to young adults ages 12 through 18. The winning titles are selected by a committee of the Young Adult Library Services Association (YALSA), a division of the American Library Association, from among the previous year's publishing. The award is sponsored by the Margaret A. Edwards Trust.

A Boy and His Dog at the End of the World by C. A. Fletcher (Orbit, a division of Hachette Group).

Do You Dream of Terra-Two? by Temi Oh (Saga Press/Gallery Books, an imprint of Simon & Schuster).

Dominicana by Angie Cruz (Flatiron Books, an imprint of Macmillan).

Gender Queer: A Memoir by Maia Kobabe (Lion Forge, an imprint of Oni Press).

High School by Sara Quin and Tegan Quin (MCD, a division of Farrar, Straus and Giroux/Macmillan).

In Waves by AJ Dungo (Nobrow).

Middlegame by Seanan McGuire (Tor.com, an imprint of Tom Doherty Associates/Macmillan).

The Nickel Boys by Colson Whitehead (Doubleday, a division of Penguin Random House).

Red, White & Royal Blue by Casey McQuiston (St. Martin's Griffin, a division of St. Martin's Publishing Group/Macmillan).

The Swallows by Lisa Lutz (Ballantine Books, an imprint of Penguin Random House).

Amazing Audiobooks for Young Adults

Each year, the Amazing Audiobooks Blogging Team of the Young Adult Library Services Association (YALSA), a division of the American Library Association, selects and annotates a list of notable audio recordings significant to young adults from those released in the past two years.

While the list as a whole addresses the interests and needs of young adults, individual titles need not appeal to this entire age range but rather to parts of it. An asterisk denotes the title was selected as a top ten.

Akata Warrior by Nnedi Okorafor, read by Yetide Badaki (Tantor Audio).

The Beast Player by Nahoko Uehashi, translation by Cathy Hirano, read by Caitlin Kelly (Macmillan Audio).

**Becoming* by Michelle Obama, read by Michelle Obama (Random House Audio).

Black Enough: Stories of Being Young & Black in America by Ibi Zoboi, Tracey Baptiste, Coe Booth, Dhonielle Clayton, Brandy Colbert, Jay Coles, Lamar Giles, and Leah Henderson, read by Bahni Turpin and Ron Butler (HarperAudio).

Brave Face: A Memoir by Shaun David Hutchinson, read by Shaun David Hutchinson (Simon & Schuster Audio).

Cheshire Crossing by Andy Weir, read by Sophie Amoss, Brittany Pressley, Kristen DiMercurio, Rebecca Soler, Lisa Flanagan, James Monroe, Neil Hellegers, Sean Patrick Hopkins, Peter Coleman, and Peter Bradbury (Random House Audio).

Daisy Jones & the Six by Taylor Jenkins Reid, read by Jennifer Beals, Benjamin Bratt, Judy Greer, and Pablo Schreiber (Random House Audio).

**Dig* by A. S. King, read by A. S. King, Mike Chamberlain, Tonya Cornelisse, and Kirby Heyborne (Listening Library).

Fantastic Beasts: The Crimes of Grindelwald—Makers, Mysteries and Magic by Mark Salisbury and Hana Walker-Brown, read by

Jennifer Beals, Benjamin Bratt, Judy Greer, and Pablo Schreiber (Pottermore Publishing).

**The Fountains of Silence* by Ruta Sepetys, read by Maite Jáuregui with Richard Ferrone, Neil Hellegers, Joshua Kane, Liza Kaplan, and Oliver Wyman (Listening Library).

Frankly in Love by David Yoon, read by Raymond J. Lee (Listening Library).

**Heroine* by Mindy McGinnis, read by Brittany Pressley (HarperCollins Audio).

**Hey Kiddo* by Jarrett J. Krosoczka, read by Jarrett J. Krosoczka, Jeanne Birdsall, Richard Ferrone, and Jenna Lamia (Scholastic Audio).

Hollow Kingdom by Kira Jane Buxton, read by Robert Petkoff (Blackstone Audio).

How Long 'Til Black Future Month by N. K. Jemisin, read by Shayna Small, Gail Nelson-Holgate, Robin Ray Eller, and Ron Butler (Hachette Audio).

**Internment* by Samira Ahmed, read by Soneela Nankani (Hachette Audio).

**Let Me Hear a Rhyme* by Tiffany D. Jackson, read by Adenrele Ojo, Korey Jackson, Adam Lazarre-White, and Nile Bullock (HarperCollins Audio).

Lovely War by Julie Berry, read by Jayne Entwistle, John Lee, Dion Graham, Nathaniel Parker, Steve West, Fiona Hardingham, and Allan Corduner (Listening Library).

**On the Come Up* by Angie Thomas, read by Bahni Turpin (HarperCollins Audio).

Notes from a Young Black Chef by Kwame Onwuachi and Joshua David Stein, read by Kwame Onwuachi (Random House Audio).

The Opposite of Always by Justin A. Reynolds, read by Nile Bullock (HarperAudio).

Pan's Labyrinth by Guillermo del Toro and Cornelia Funke, read by Thom Rivera (HarperCollins Audio).

Patron Saints of Nothing by Randy Ribay, read by Ramón de Ocampo (Listening Library).

Roller Girl by Victoria Jamieson, read by Almarie Guerra, Jesse Bernstein, Ron Butler, Abigail Caro, Robbie Daymond, Giordan Diaz, Em Eldridge, Christopher Gebauer, Kim Mai Guest, Kirby Heyborne, Hillary Huber, Rachel Jacobs, Jorjeana Marie, Kathleen McInerney, Alex McKenna, Cassandra Morris, P. J. Ochlan, Adenrele Ojo, Georgette Perna, Kate Reinders, Tara Sands, Monika Felice Smith, and Bahni Turpin (Listening Library).

**Shout* by Laurie Halse Anderson, read by Laurie Halse Anderson (Listening Library).

Spin by Lamar Giles, read by Bahni Turpin, Shawana Carter, and Sisi Aisha Johnson (Scholastic Audio).

Stain by A. G. Howard, read by Tim Bruce (Blackstone Audio).

Stronger, Faster, and More Beautiful by Arwen Elys Dayton, read by Michael Crouch, Karissa Vacker, Brittany Pressley, Christopher Gebauer, Ari Fliakos, and Rebecca Lowman (Listening Library).

The Things She's Seen by Ambelin Kwaymullina and Ezekiel Kwaymullina, read by Miranda Tapsell (Listening Library).

Thirteen Doorways, Wolves Behind Them by Laura Ruby, read by Lisa Flanagan (HarperAudio).

Two Can Keep a Secret by Karen M. McManus, read by Erin Spencer and Kirby Heyborne (Listening Library).

We Set the Dark on Fire by Tehlor Kay Mejia, read by Kyla Garcia (HarperCollins Audio).

White Bird by R. J. Palacio, read by Hillary Huber, Emily Ellet, Robbie Daymond, Graham Halstead, Lauren Ezzo, Sean Patrick Hopkins, Robert Fass, Michael Crouch, Tristan Morris, Adam Alexi-Malle, P. J. Ochlan, Karissa Vacker, Elizabeth Knowelden, and Lisa Flanagan (Listening Library).

Wicked Fox by Kat Cho, read by Emily Woo Zeller (Listening Library).

**With the Fire on High* by Elizabeth Acevedo, read by Elizabeth Acevedo (HarperAudio).

Outstanding International Books for Young Readers

The United States Board on Books for Young People (USBBY), the U.S. national section of the International Board on Books for Young People (IBBY), compiles an annual list of books that represent the best in international children's literature. The 42 titles on the 2020 Outstanding International Books List (OIB) are significant for both their exceptional quality and globe-spanning origins.

Preschool to Grade 2

Abadia, Ximo. *The Farmer*. Trans. from French by Grace Maccarone and Kelly Loughman. Illus. by the author. Holiday House. Switzerland.

Avingaq, Susan & Maren Vsetula. *The Pencil*. Illus. by Charlene Chua. Inhabit Media. Canada.

Basil, Krystia. *A Sky Without Lines*. Illus. by Laura Borràs. minedition. Hong Kong / set along the U.S./Mexico border.

Chernysheva, Natalia. *The Return*. Illus. by the author. Groundwood. Portugal.

Dekko, Espen. *Paws+Edward*. Trans. from Norwegian. Illus. by Mari Kanstad Johnsen. Kids Can. Norway.

Flett, Julie. *Birdsong*. Illus. by the author. Greystone. Canada.

Iglesias, Juan Pablo. *Daniel and Ismail*. Trans. From Spanish by Ilan Stavans (English), Eliezer Nowodworski and Frieda Press-Danieli (Hebrew), and Randa Sayegh (Arabic). Illus. by Alex Peris. Restless Books/Yonder. Chile.

Lee, Hyeon-Ju. *The Happiest Tree: A Story of Growing Up*. Trans. from Korean. Illus. by the author. Feiwel and Friends. Korea.

Meddour, Wendy. *Lubna and Pebble*. Illus. by Daniel Egnéus. Dial. UK.

Ram, Praba, and Sheela Preuitt. *Thukpa for All*. Illus. by Shilpa Ranade. Karadi Tales. India.

Read, Kate. *One Fox: A Counting Book Thriller*. Illus. by the author. Peachtree. UK.

Tanco, Miguel. *Count on Me*. Illus. by the author. Tundra. Canada.

Vermette, Katherena. *The Girl and the Wolf*. Illus. by Julie Flett. Theytus. Canada.

Vilela, Fernando. *Along the Tapajós*. Trans. from Portuguese by Daniel Hahn. Illus. by the author. Amazon Crossing. Brazil.

Yoshitake, Shinsuke. *The Boring Book*. Illus. by the author. Chronicle. Japan.

Grades 3 to 5

Abela, Deborah. *The Most Marvelous International Spelling Bee*. Sourcebooks Jabberwocky. Australia.

Alvarez, Lorena. *Hicotea: A Nightlights Story*. Illus. by the author. Nobrow. UK.

Blackcrane, Gerelchimeg. *The Moose of Ewenki*. Trans. from Chinese by Helen Mixter. Illus. by Jiu Er. Greystone. China.

Dahle, Gro. *Angryman*. Trans. from Norwegian by Tara Chace. Illus. by Svein Nyhus. North-South. Norway.

Huson, Brett D. *The Grizzly Mother*. Illus. by Natasha Donovan. HighWater Press. Canada.

Hutchinson, Michael. *The Case of Windy Lake*. Second Story. Canada.

Ørbeck-Nilssen, Constance. *Vanishing Colors*. Trans. from Norwegian by Kari Dickson. Illus. by Akin Duzakin. Eerdmans. Norway.

Rundell, Katherine. The Good Thieves. Simon & Schuster. UK / set in the U.S.

Smith, Heather. *The Phone Booth in Mr. Hirota's Garden*. Illus. by Rachel Wada. Orca. Canada / set in Japan.

Taylor, Sean and the Khayaal Theatre. *Riding a Donkey Backwards: Wise and Foolish Tales of Mulla Nasruddin*. Illus. by Shirin Adl. Candlewick. UK.

Vafaeian, Marjan. *The Parrot and the Merchant: A Tale by Rumi*. Trans. from Persian by Azita Rassi. Illus. by the author. Tiny Owl. Iran.

Vecchini, Silvia. *The Red Zone: An Earthquake Story*. Trans. from Italian by Anna Barton. Illus. by Sualzo. Abrams/Amulet. Italy.

Grades 6 to 8

Argueta, Jorge. *Caravan to the North: Misael's Long Walk*. Trans. from Spanish by Elizabeth Bell. Illus. by Manuel Monroy. Groundwood. Canada / set in Central America.

Gourlay, Candy. *Bone Talk*. David Fickling Books. UK / set in the Philippines.

Kadarusman, Michelle. *Girl of the Southern Sea*. Pajama Press. Canada / set in Indonesia.

Livina, Alexandra. *The Apartment: A Century of Russian History*. Trans. from Russian by Antonina W. Bouis. Illus. by Anna Desnitskaya. Abrams. Russia.

Mello, Roger. *Charcoal Boys*. Trans. from Portuguese by Daniel Hahn. Illus. by the author. Archipelago / Elsewhere Editions. Brazil.

Polak, Monique. *The Taste of Rain*. Orca. Canada / set in China.

Ross, Ailsa. *The Girl Who Rode a Shark and Other Stories of Daring Women*. Illus. by Amy Blackwell. Pajama Press. Canada.

Strange, Lucy. *Our Castle by the Sea*. Scholastic / Chicken House. UK.

Grades 9 to 12

Adams, K. C. *Perception: A Photo Series*. Illus. by the author. HighWater Press. Canada.

Akiwenzie-Damm, Kateri and others. *This Place: 150 Years Retold*. Illus. by various. HighWater Press. Canada.

Fried, Hédi. *Questions I Am Asked About the Holocaust*. Trans. from Swedish by Alice E. Olsson. Scribe. Sweden.

Kwaymullina, Ambelin & Ezekiel Kwaymullina. *The Things She's Seen*. Knopf. Australia.

Magnason, Andri Snær. *The Casket of Time*. Trans. from Icelandic by Björg Árnadóttir and Andrew Cauthery. Restless/Yonder. Iceland.

Petreca, Guilherme. *Ye*. Trans. from Portuguese by Andrea Rosenberg. Illus. by the author. IDW / Top Shelf. Brazil.

Sedgwick, Marcus, and Julian Sedgwick. *Voyages in the Underworld of Orpheus Black*. Illus. by Alexis Deacon. Candlewick/Walker. UK.

Notable Children's Books

Each year a committee of the Association for Library Service to Children (ALSC) identifies the best of the best in children's books. The criteria define "notable" as worthy of note or notice, important, distinguished, outstanding. As applied to children's books, notable should be thought to include books of especially commendable quality, books that exhibit venturesome creativity, and books of fiction, information, poetry, and pictures for all age levels (birth through age 14) that reflect and encourage children's interests in exemplary ways. [See "Literary Prizes, 2019" later in Part 5 for Caldecott, Newbery, and other award winners—*Ed.*]

Younger Readers

Across the Bay by Carlos Aponte. Illus. by the author. Penguin Workshop.

Art This Way by Tamara Shopsin. Illus. by Jason Fulford. Phaidon.

At the Mountain's Base by Traci Sorell. Illus. by Weshoyot Alvitre. Penguin/Kokila.

B Is for Baby by Atinuke. Illus. by Angela Brooksbank, Candlewick.

The Balcony by Melissa Castrillón. Illus. by the author. Simon & Schuster / Paula Wiseman.

Bear Came Along by Richard T. Morris. Illus. by LeUyen Pham. Little, Brown.

The Bell Rang by James E. Ransome. Illus. by the author. Atheneum/Caitlyn Dlouhy.

Between Us and Abuela: A Family Story from the Border by Mitali Perkins. Illus. by Sara Palacios. Farrar.

A Big Bed for Little Snow by Grace Lin. Illus. by the author. Little, Brown.

The Bluest of Blues: Anna Atkins and the First Book of Photographs by Fiona Robinson. Illus. by the author. Abrams.

Brown: My Alter Ego Is a Superhero by Håkon Øvreås. Illus. by Øyvind Torseter. Trans. by Kari Dickson. Enchanted Lion.

The Book Hog by Greg Pizzoli. Illus. by the author. Disney/Hyperion.

The Book Rescuer: How a Mensch from Massachusetts Saved Yiddish Literature for Generations to Come by Sue Macy. Illus. by Stacy Innerst. Simon & Schuster/Paula Wiseman.

Carter Reads the Newspaper by Deborah Hopkinson. Illus. by Don Tate. Peachtree.

Chick and Brain: Smell My Foot! by Cece Bell. Illus. by the author. Candlewick.

Dancing Hands: How Teresa Carreño Played the Piano for President Lincoln by Margarita Engle. Illus. by Rafael López. Atheneum.

Dinosaur Feathers by Dennis Nolan. Illus. by the author. Holiday/Neal Porter.

Do Fish Sleep? by Jens Raschke. Illus. by Jens Rassmus. Trans. by Belinda Cooper. Enchanted Lion.

Double Bass Blues by Andrea J. Loney. Illus. by Rudy Gutierrez. Knopf.

Field Trip to the Moon by John Hare. Illus. by the author. Holiday/Margaret Ferguson.

Firefighters' Handbook by Meghan McCarthy. Illus. by the author. Simon & Schuster/Paula Wiseman.

Flubby Is Not a Good Pet! by J. E. Morris. Illus. by the author. Penguin Workshop.

Fry Bread: A Native American Family Story by Kevin Noble Maillard. Illus. by Juana Martinez-Neal. Roaring Brook.

Going Down Home with Daddy by Kelly Starling Lyons. Illus. by Daniel Minter. Peachtree.

Grandpa's Top Threes by Wendy Meddour. Illus. by Daniel Egnéus. Candlewick.

Hey, Water! by Antoinette Portis. Illus. by the author. Holiday/Neal Porter.

How to Read a Book by Kwame Alexander. Illus. by Melissa Sweet. Harper.

It Began with a Page: How Gyo Fujikawa Drew the Way by Kyo Maclear. Illus. by Julie Morstad. Harper.

Just Right: Searching for the Goldilocks Planet by Curtis Manley. Illus. by Jessica Lanan. Roaring Brook.

The Last Peach by Gus Gordon. Illus. by the author. Roaring Brook.

Let's Scare Bear by Yuko Katakawa. Illus. by the author. Holiday.

Lion of the Sky: Haiku for All Seasons by Laura Purdie Salas. Illus. by Mercè López. Lerner/Millbrook.

Luca's Bridge/El Puente de Luca by Mariana Llanos. Illus. by Anna López Real. Penny Candy.

The Many Colors of Harpreet Singh by Supriya Kelkar. Illus. by Alea Marley. Sterling.

A Map into the World by Kao Kalia Yang. Illus. by Seo Kim. Carolrhoda/Lerner.

Moth by Isabel Thomas. Illus. by Daniel Egnéus. Bloomsbury.

My Footprints by Bao Phi. Illus. by Basia Tran. Capstone.

My Grandma and Me by Mina Javaherbin. Illus. by Lindsey Yankey. Candlewick.

My Papi Has a Motorcycle by Isabel Quintero. Illus. by Zeke Peña. Penguin/Kokila.

A New Home by Tania de Regil. Illus. by the author. Candlewick.

Nya's Long Walk: A Step at a Time by Linda Sue Park. Illus. by Brian Pinkney. Clarion.

One Fox: A Counting Book Thriller by Kate Read. Illus. by the author. Peachtree.

Paper Son: The Inspiring Story of Tyrus Wong, Immigrant and Artist by Julie Leung. Illus. by Chris Sasaki. Random/Schwartz & Wade.

Planting Stories: The Life of Librarian and Storyteller Pura Belpré by Anika Aldamuy Denise. Illus. by Paola Escobar. Harper.

Pokko and the Drum by Matthew Forsythe. Illus by the author. Simon & Schuster/Paula Wiseman.

The Proudest Blue: A Story of Hijab and Family by Ibtihaj Muhammad with S. K. Ali. Illus. by Hatem Aly. Little, Brown.

Queen of Physics: How Wu Chien Shiung Helped Unlock the Secrets of the Atom by Teresa Robeson. Illus. by Rebecca Huang. Sterling.

Saturday by Oge Mora. Illus. by the author. Little, Brown.

Sing a Song: How "Lift Every Voice and Sing" Inspired Generations by Kelly Starling Lyons. Illus. by Keith Mallett. Penguin / Nancy Paulsen.

Small in the City by Sydney Smith. Illus. by the author. Holiday / Neal Porter.

A Stone Sat Still by Brendan Wenzel. Illus. by the author. Chronicle.

Stop! Bot! by James Yang. Illus. by the author. Viking.

Stormy: A Story about Finding a Forever Home by Guojing. Illus. by the author. Random / Schwartz & Wade.

Thinker: My Puppy Poet and Me by Eloise Greenfield. Illus. by Ehsan Abdollahi. Sourcebooks/Jabberwocky.

Todos Iguales/All Equal: Un Corrido De Lemon Grove/A Ballad of Lemon Grove by Christy Hale. Illus. by the author. Lee & Low.

¡Vamos! Let's Go to the Market by Raúl González. Illus. by the author. HMH/Versify.

What Is Given from the Heart by Patricia C. McKissack. Illus. by April Harrison. Random / Schwartz & Wade.

When Aidan Became a Brother by Kyle Lukoff. Illus. by Kaylani Juanita. Lee & Low.

When Spring Comes to the DMZ by Uk-Bae Lee. Illus. by the author. Translated by Chungyon Won and Aileen Won. Plough.

Why? by Laura Vaccaro Seeger. Illus. by the author. Holiday / Neal Porter.

Middle Readers

All in a Drop: How Antony van Leeuwenhoek Discovered an Invisible World by Lori Alexander. Illus. by Vivien Mildenberger. HMH.

The Beast Player by Nahoko Uehashi. Illus. by Yuta Onoda. Trans. by Cathy Hirano. Holt/ Godwin.

Because of the Rabbit by Cynthia Lord. Scholastic.

The Bridge Home by Padma Venkatraman. Penguin / Nancy Paulsen.

The Distance Between Me and the Cherry Tree by Paola Peretti. Illus. by Carolina Rabei. Trans. by Denise Muir. Atheneum.

Each Tiny Spark by Pablo Cartaya. Penguin/ Kokila.

For Black Girls Like Me by Mariama J. Lockington. Farrar.

The Forgotten Girl by India Hill Brown. Scholastic.

Hector: A Boy, a Protest, and the Photograph That Changed Apartheid by Adrienne Wright. Illus. by the author. Page Street.

Indian No More by Charlene Willing McManis and Traci Sorrell. Lee & Low / Tu.

It Rained Warm Bread: Moishe Moskowitz's Story of Hope by Gloria Moskowitz-Sweet and Hope Anita Smith. Illus. by Lea Lyon. Holt / Christy Ottaviano.

Lalani of the Distant Sea by Erin Entrada Kelly. Illus. by Lian Cho. Greenwillow.

Let 'er Buck!: George Fletcher, the People's Champion by Vaunda Micheaux Nelson. Illus. by Gordon C. James. Carolrhoda/Lerner.

Lety Out Loud by Angela Cervantes. Scholastic.

Pie in the Sky by Remy Lai. Illus. by the author. Holt.

Scary Stories for Young Foxes by Christian McKay Heidicker. Illus. by Junyi Wu. Holt.

Some Places More than Others by Renée Watson. Bloomsbury.

Stargazing by Jen Wang. Illus. by the author. First Second.

Older Readers

Accused! The Trials of the Scottsboro Boys: Lies, Prejudice, and the Fourteenth Amendment by Larry Dane Brimner. Boyds Mills / Calkins Creek.

All the Greys on Greene Street by Laura Tucker. Illus. by Kelly Murphy. Viking.

Beverly, Right Here by Kate DiCamillo. Candlewick.

Born to Fly: The First Women's Air Race across America by Steve Sheinkin. Illus. by Bijou Karman. Roaring Brook.

Games of Deception: The True Story of the First U.S. Olympic Basketball Team at the 1936 Olympics in Hitler's Germany by Andrew Maraniss. Philomel.

Genesis Begins Again by Alicia D. Williams. Atheneum / Caitlyn Dlouhy.

I Can Make This Promise by Christine Day. Harper.

An Indigenous Peoples' History of the United States for Young People by Roxanne Dunbar-Ortiz. Adapted by Jean Mendoza and Debbie Reese. Beacon.

Infinite Hope: A Black Artist's Journey from World War II to Peace by Ashley Bryan. Illus. by the author. Atheneum / Caitlyn Dlouhy.

Look Both Ways: A Tale Told in Ten Blocks by Jason Reynolds. Atheneum / Caitlyn Dlouhy.

Maybe He Just Likes You by Barbara Dee. Aladdin.

New Kid by Jerry Craft. Illus. by the author. Harper.

Ordinary Hazards: A Memoir by Nikki Grimes. WordSong.

The Other Half of Happy by Rebecca Balcárcel. Chronicle.

Other Words for Home by Jasmine Warga. HarperCollins/Balzer+Bray.

A Place to Belong by Cynthia Kadohata. Illus. by Julia Kuo. Atheneum / Caitlyn Dlouhy.

The Poison Eaters: Fighting Danger and Fraud in Our Food and Drugs by Gail Jarrow. Boyds Mills / Calkins Creek.

Sal & Gabi Break the Universe by Carlos Hernandez. Disney/Hyperion.

A Story about Cancer (with a Happy Ending) by India Desjardins. Illus. by Marianne Ferrer. Quarto / Frances Lincoln.

Strange Birds: A Field Guide to Ruffling Feathers by Celia C. Pérez. Penguin/Kokila.

Survivors of the Holocaust: True Stories of Six Extraordinary Children edited by Kath Shackleton. Illus. by Zane Whittingham. Sourcebooks/Jabberwocky.

They Called Us Enemy by George Takei, Justin Eisinger, and Steven Scott. Illus. by Harmony Becker. Top Shelf.

This Promise of Change: One Girl's Story in the Fight for School Equality by Jo Ann Allen Boyce and Debbie Levy. Bloomsbury.

Torpedoed: The True Story of the World War II Sinking of "The Children's Ship" by Deborah Heiligman. Holt.

Tristan Strong Punches a Hole in the Sky by Kwame Mbalia. Disney/Hyperion.

Wait, What? A Comic Book Guide to Relationships, Bodies, and Growing Up by Heather Corinna. Illus. by Isabella Rotman. Limerence.

We Are Displaced: My Journey and Stories from Refugee Girls around the World by Malala Yousafzai. Little, Brown.

Where the Heart Is by Jo Knowles. Candlewick.

Words on Fire by Jennifer Nielsen. Scholastic.

The Year We Fell from Space by Amy Sarig King. Scholastic / Arthur A. Levine.

All Ages

I Remember: Poems and Pictures of Heritage edited by Lee Bennett Hopkins. Lee & Low.

Liberty Arrives!: How America's Grandest Statue Found Her Home by Robert Byrd. Illus. by the author. Dial.

A Place to Land: Martin Luther King Jr. and the Speech That Inspired a Nation by Barry Wittenstein. Illus. by Jerry Pinkney. Holiday / Neal Porter.

Soldier for Equality: José de la Luz Sáenz and the Great War by Duncan Tonatiuh. Illus. by the author. Abrams.

Thanku: Poems of Gratitude edited by Miranda Paul. Illus. by Marlena Myles. Lerner/Millbrook.

The Undefeated by Kwame Alexander. Illus. by Kadir Nelson. HMH/Versify.

You Are Home: An Ode to the National Parks by Evan Turk. Illus. by the author. Atheneum.

Notable Recordings for Children

This annual listing of notable compact disc (CD) and digital download (DD) recordings for children 14 years and younger is produced by the Association for Library Service to Children (ALSC), a division of the American Library Association. Chosen by children's librarians and educators, the list includes recordings deemed to be of especially commendable quality that demonstrate respect for young people's intelligence and imagination; exhibit venturesome creativity; and reflect and encourage the interests of children and young adolescents in exemplary ways.

5 O'Clock Band by Troy "Trombone Shorty" Andrews and Bill Taylor. Read by Dion Graham. Live Oak Media, CD, CD and book. Gr. K–3. Trombone Shorty's stellar musical score and Dion Graham's warm voicing embody the New Orleans soundscape of the musican's childhood.

Backstroke Raptor by Story Pirates. Gimlet Media, CD. Gr. K–4. Based on short stories written by elementary school students, this creative and unique mix of songs features guest artists such as Lin-Manuel Miranda.

Bernard Pepperlin by Cara Hoffman. Read by Gary Furlong. HarperAudio, DD. Gr. 2–5. Furlong's dynamic performance captures myriad memorable characters in this Alice in Wonderland spin-off.

The Bridge Home by Padma Venkatraman. Read by the author. Listening Library, DD. Gr. 4–8. With heartbreaking feeling and distinct voices, Venkatraman narrates her story of four children finding love and support on the streets of contemporary India.

Buenos Diaz by The Lucky Band. Rainy Day Dimes LLC, CD, DD. Gr. PreS. Easily switching between English and Spanish, the musicians perform catchy songs featuring great harmonies.

Charlotte's Web by E. B. White. Read by full cast. Listening Library, CD. Gr. K–4. Meryl Streep's soft narration frames this classic tale, headlined by Kirby Heyborne's naive Wilbur and January LaVoy's brilliant Charlotte.

Klawde: Evil Alien Warlord Cat: The Spacedog Cometh #3 by Johnny Marciano and Emily Chenoweth. Read by full cast. Listening Library, DD. Gr. 1–4. Through believable voicing of a displeased evil warlord alien cat, an amenable golden retriever spy, and naive humans, this installment of Klawde's adventures rockets to life.

Look Both Ways: A Tale Told in Ten Blocks by Jason Reynolds. Read by full cast. Simon & Schuster, CD, DD. Gr. 5+. An all-star cast of narrators brings humor to ten stories depicting the detours taken on the way home from school.

The LOVE by Alphabet Rockers. School Time Music, CD. Gr. 1–8. The Alphabet Rockers collaborative hip-hop album masterfully celebrates love, acceptance, and community while speaking to current cultural issues.

The Magic of Letters by Tony Johnston. Read by Marc Thompson. Live Oak Media, CD, CD and book, DD. Gr. PreS–K. Thompson pulls the listener into the magical world of language, emphasizing the energy and feeling of blending sounds together.

Mango, Abuela, and Me by Meg Medina. Read by full cast. Live Oak Media, CD, CD and book, DD. Gr. PreS–3. This family-led narration enhances the tale of a Spanish-speaking abuela moving in with her young English-speaking granddaughter and their journey to learn each other's languages.

Max and the Midknights by Lincoln Peirce. Read by full cast. Listening Library, CD. Gr. 2–6. Kristen DiMercurio leads an amazing full cast production filled with standout characters, pointed jokes, medieval music, and humorous sound effects.

New Kid. By Jerry Craft. Read by full cast. HarperAudio, DD. Gr. 4–8 Adapted from a powerful graphic novel about a boy who finds himself one of only a few students of color in his private school, this full-cast audio creates a vivid auditory landscape.

On the Come Up by Angie Thomas. Read by Bahni Turpin. HarperAudio, DD. Gr. 8+ Bahni Turpin skillfully captures Bri's struggle to balance her family's hardships with her aspiration to be a rapper.

Potato Pants! by Laurie Keller. Read by full cast. Weston Woods, CD, CD and book. Gr. PreS+. A full cast uses hilarious voicing and sound effects to take listeners on a rollicking good time during this epic attempt by a potato to purchase a pair of pants.

Redwood and Ponytail by K. A. Holt. Read by Tess Netting and Cassandra Morris. Hachette Audio, DD. Gr. 5+. Two voices, two girls, and two perspectives combine to powerful effect in this novel in verse about middle school, first love, and self-discovery.

Roller Girl by Victoria Jamieson. Read by full cast. Listening Library, CD. Gr. 4–8. The acclaimed graphic novel about Astrid's adventure into the world of roller derby is brought to life with a full cast, exemplary sound effects, and well-curated music.

Song for a Whale by Lynne Kelly. Read by Abigail Revasch with the author. Listening Library, DD, CD. Gr. 4–6. Revasch's narration honors the linguistic beauty of American sign language in this poignant story of Iris, a deaf girl who records a song for a whale unable to communicate with other whales.

To Night Owl from Dogfish by Holly Goldberg Sloan and Meg Wolitzer. Read by full cast. Listening Library, CD. Gr. 4–7. Told through e-mails and other correspondence, Cassandra Morris and Imani Parks lead a full cast in a funny and relatable tale of two girls determined to keep their fathers from dating.

Tristan Strong Punches a Hole in the Sky by Kwame Mbalia. Read by Amir Abdullah. Listening Library. Gr. 4+. Abdullah excels at performing a large cast of mythical characters, embodying everyone from the powerful John Henry to the hysterical Gum Baby, as young Tristan has to figure out how to save the world.

The Wall in the Middle of the Book by Jon Agee. Read by Everest de Montebello and Marc Thompson. Live Oak Media, CD, CD and book, DD. Gr. PreS. Sound effects, music, and dynamic narration enhance this story of a young knight who believes his side of the wall is safer than the other.

The Way You Make Me Feel by Maurene Goo. Read by Emily Woo Zeller. Tantor Audio, DD. Gr. 8+. Zeller's attitude-filled narration draws listeners into Clara's world as she is stuck working on a food truck all summer with her mortal enemy.

We Are Grateful: Otsaliheliga by Traci Sorell. Read by full cast. Live Oak Media, CD, CD and book. Gr. 1–3. This dynamic production utilizes music and sound effects to create an audio landscape that delivers a rich family-focused introduction to contemporary Cherokee language, culture, and customs.

We're Not from Here by Geoff Rodkey. Read by Dani Martineck. Listening Library, CD, DD. Gr. 5–8. Martineck captures the Mifunes' precarious situation with well-timed comic relief as the family, seeking asylum on Planet Choom, tries to change the minds of its hostile hosts.

When the Ground Is Hard by Malla Nunn. Read by Bahni Turpin. Listening Library, DD. Gr. 6+. Turpin beautifully voices the emotional ups and downs of a teen girl at a 1960s Swaziland boarding school as she learns about her past and finds her true self.

The Wizards of Once: Twice Magic by Cressida Cowell. Read by David Tennant. Hachette Audio, CD, DD. Gr. 3–6. Tennant's spellbinding performance brings to life a witch boy, a warrior girl, and an assortment of magical creatures on a quest to stop a terrible evil.

The Word Collector by Peter H. Reynolds. Read by Guy Lockard. Weston Woods, CD, CD and book. Gr. K–2. A wonder-filled performance by Lockard set against a musical score captures a young boy's discovery of the magic and transformative power of words.

Notable Children's Digital Media

The Association for Library Service to Children (ALSC), a division of the American Library Association, produces this annual list covering a diverse array of digital media for children 14 and younger. The Notable Children's Digital Media list recognizes real-time, dynamic, and interactive media content that enables and encourages active engagement and social interaction while informing, educating, and entertaining in exemplary ways.

Apart of Me. iOS/Android. Elementary, Middle School. A small but open-world role-playing game (RPG), in which players connect with real stories of love and loss while working through their own grief. Includes journaling and real-life "assignments," mindfulness exercises, and resources for further support.

Aquation: The Freshwater Access Game. iOS/Android. Elementary, Middle School. Produced by the Smithsonian, this simulation game educates children on water equity and challenges players to distribute resources and humanitarian aid around the globe.

Arithmagic—MathWizardGame. iOS/Android/Amazon. Elementary. Use addition, subtraction, multiplication, division, and other math skills to help a wizard cast math spells to defeat enemies.

Bandimal. iOS. PreK. This open-ended music composition app lets kids create drum loops, compose melodies, and add effects onto songs. Compositions can be saved to the collection.

Career Girls. Web. Elementary, Middle School. A diverse array of women professionals from around the world share their experiences for girls to explore careers. Content includes quizzes, extension activities, and resources for parents and teachers. Available in multiple languages.

The Cat in the Hat Builds That. iOS/Android/Amazon. PreK. This companion to the PBS KIDS series *The Cat in the Hat Knows a Lot about That* explores a variety of engaging STEM mini-games and activities. Includes supplemental materials and suggestions for caregiver/child interaction. Available in English and Spanish.

Drops. iOS/Android. Elementary, Middle School. Using simple navigation rather than relying on native language, this app and website teaches over 30 languages through audio/visual cues and mini-games. Available in multiple languages.

Funexpected Math. iOS. PreK, Elementary. This app leads kids through a beautifully animated world using a wide variety of mathematical games and activities. Challenges increase noticeably in difficulty, and replay value is moderately high as users continue to build skills.

GoNoodle—Kids Videos. iOS/Android/Amazon. PreK, Elementary. This app and website are full of short videos that provide music, movement, dance, stretching, yoga and mindfulness. A simple way to get kids moving in a safe and fun environment.

Hopster Coding Safari. iOS. PreK, Elementary. This drag-and-drop coding logic game teaches basic computational thinking. The controls are easy to use, and the puzzles increase in difficulty to build skills.

Jet's Bot Builder. iOS/Android/Amazon. PreK, Elementary. Children build and personalize their own robot as they travel through outer space with Jet and his friends in this adaptive STEM app from PBS KIDS. Closed captions available.

Little Chickies/Los Pollitos. iOS/Android. PreK. Listen to the traditional Spanish lullaby accompanied by cute animated chicks from the Canticos board book. Other interactive activities include chick-related art projects that can be saved in a digital scrapbook. Available in multiple languages.

Little Mouse's Encyclopedia. iOS/Android/Amazon. Elementary. Explore beautifully illustrated European habitats while learning details about various animal and plant species. Detailed biomes include forest, underground, and underwater. Available in multiple languages.

Me: A Kid's Diary. iOS. Elementary, Middle School. This digital journal app provides a guided introduction to multimedia storytelling and encourages self-expression. Users of different ages can create pages about themselves with prompts for silly drawings, self-portraits, gifs, photos, and sound recordings. Available in multiple languages.

My Child Lebensborn. iOS/Android. Middle School. Set in post–WWII Norway, this engrossing life-simulation game puts the player in the shoes of a foster parent. Players must make tough choices to guide their child through painful experiences like poverty, bullying, and shame. Available in multiple languages.

NAMOO—Wonders of Plant Life. iOS/Android. Elementary, Middle School. Through engaging and interactive 3D animation with enriching encyclopedic content, children can explore and discover the life cycle of a plant. Available in multiple languages.

Novel Effect. iOS/Android. Parent/Caregiver. Enhance storytime through voice-activated special effects. Choose from a comprehensive list of stories to read aloud, and the app will do the rest. Available in English and Spanish.

OurStory Kids. Android. Elementary, Middle School, Parent/Caregiver. Created by We Need Diverse Books, this website and app recommend diverse titles to readers based on an extensive number of customizable preferences. The site may be used to purchase titles from a variety of vendors.

PEEP Family Science: Colors. iOS/Android. PreK. Featuring characters from the television show *PEEP and the Big Wide World,* this app uses an array of short videos and tutorials to introduce the science of colors. Users explore colors through hands-on activities that use the scientific method in a fun, challenging way.

Pokémon Playhouse. iOS/Android/Amazon. PreK. Children meet and interact with a variety of Pokémon characters as they explore the Pokémon Playhouse, listen to stories, solve simple puzzles, search the stars, and much more.

Puku: Learn New Words. iOS/Android. Elementary. Kids learn new words through digital flashcards with matching and fill-in-the-blank activities. As they master new words, a worm-like creature grows. Word lists are customizable.

Sago Mini Village. iOS/Android/Amazon. PreK. Children build a gnome village by moving around various block pieces and accessories. No rules, instructions, or time limits are provided, so users can create their own parameters for play.

Storyline Online. iOS/Android. PreK, Elementary. Developed with the SAG-AFTRA Foundation, this website and app contain a diverse and growing selection of picture books read by celebrity readers. Each book includes supplemental curriculum material developed by educators.

Tami's Tower. iOS/Android/Amazon. PreK, Elementary. Produced by the Smithsonian, this game asks users to use basic engineering design principles to help Tami the golden lion tamarin solve the problem of how to reach the best fruit.

Think & Learn Code-a-pillar. iOS/Android/Amazon. PreK, Elementary. This companion app to the Code-a-Pillar toy teaches kids the basics of coding using simple commands to direct the Code-a-Pillar through start-to-finish puzzles. Toy not required for use. Available in multiple languages.

Thinkrolls: Space. iOS/Android/Amazon. Elementary. This app inspires children to use creative thinking and problem-solving strategies as they guide their alien character through a series of logic puzzles. Available in multiple languages.

Who Was? Adventure. iOS. Elementary. Kids test their knowledge of famous historical figures from the popular Who HQ series by answering trivia questions in increasingly difficult arcade style games.

Bestseller Lists of 2019

Sources included in this "Top Ten" roundup are *Publishers Weekly*, *USA Today*, Barnes and Noble, Amazon, and Goodreads for print books; and Amazon and Apple for Kindle and Apple Books digital titles, respectively. Library-centric lists include the top ten adult print book checkouts reported by two major U.S. public library systems—the New York Public Library and San Diego County Library—and the top five most popular library e-books and audiobooks as reported by OverDrive. [Due to varying selection criteria among the sources, apples-to-apples comparisons are not practicable—*Ed.*]

Print Bestsellers

Publishers Weekly

1. *Where the Crawdads Sing*. Delia Owens.
2. *Becoming*. Michelle Obama.
3. *Dog Man: For Whom the Ball Rolls*. Dav Pilkey.
4. *Educated*. Tara Westover.
5. *Wrecking Ball*. Jeff Kinney.
6. *Dog Man: Brawl of the Wild*. Dav Pilkey.
7. *Diary of an Awesome Friendly Kid*. Jeff Kinney.
8. *Girl, Wash Your Face*. Rachel Hollis.
9. *Girl, Stop Apologizing*. Rachel Hollis.
10. *The Tattooist of Auschwitz*. Heather Morris.

USA Today

1. *Where the Crawdads Sing*. Delia Owens.
2. *Becoming*. Michelle Obama.
3. *Educated*. Tara Westover.
4. *Dog Man: For Whom the Ball Rolls*. Dav Pilkey.
5. *Diary of a Wimpy Kid: Wrecking Ball*. Jeff Kinney
6. *The Tattooist of Auschwitz*. Heather Morris.
7. *Girl, Wash Your Face*. Rachel Hollis.
8. *Dog Man: Brawl of the Wild*. Dav Pilkey.
9. *The Guardians*. John Grisham.
10. *Dog Man: Fetch-22*. Dav Pilkey.

Barnes and Noble

1. *Where the Crawdads Sing*. Delia Owens.
2. *Becoming*. Michelle Obama.
3. *Educated*. Tara Westover.
4. *The Boy, the Mole, the Fox and the Horse*. Charlie Mackesy.
5. *The Subtle Art of Not Giving a F*ck*. Mark Manson.
6. *The Tattooist of Auschwitz*. Heather Morris.
7. *The Pioneers*. David McCullough.
8. *The Guardians*. John Grisham.
9. *The Institute*. Stephen King.
10. *Girl, Wash Your Face*. Rachel Hollis.

Amazon

1. *Where the Crawdads Sing*. Delia Owens.
2. *Becoming*. Michelle Obama.
3. *Educated*. Tara Westover.
4. *Dog Man: For Whom the Ball Rolls*. Dav Pilkey.
5. *Girl, Wash Your Face*. Rachel Hollis.
6. *Dog Man: Fetch-22*. Dav Pilkey.
7. *Diary of a Wimpy Kid: Wrecking Ball*. Jeff Kinney.
8. *The Wonderful Things You Will Be*. Emily Winfield Martin.
9. *School Zone Big Preschool Workbook, Ages 3–5*. Joan Hoffman.
10. *The 5 Love Languages*. Gary Chapman.

Goodreads Most Popular Books Added by Readers

1. *The Silent Patient*. Alex Michaelides.
2. *Daisy Jones & The Six*. Taylor Jenkins Reid.
3. *The Testaments*. Margaret Atwood.
4. *Ninth House*. Leigh Bardugo.
5. *Ask Again, Yes*. Mary Beth Keane.
6. *Talking to Strangers*. Malcolm Gladwell.
7. *The Institute*. Stephen King.
8. *The Dutch House*. Ann Patchett.
9. *The Giver of Stars*. Jojo Moyes.
10. *The Starless Sea*. Erin Morgenstern.

Digital Bestsellers

Amazon Kindle

1. *Where the Crawdads Sing*. Delia Owens.
2. *The Killer Collective*. Barry Eisler.
3. *Thin Air*. Lisa Gray.
4. *The Incredibles*. Disney Books.
5. *What You Did*. Claire McGowan.
6. *The Handmaid's Tale*. Margaret Atwood.
7. *Harry Potter and the Sorcerer's Stone*. J. K. Rowling.
8. *The Dressmaker's Gift*. Fiona Valpy.
9. *The Overdue Life of Amy Byler*. Kelly Harms.
10. *The 7 Habits of Highly Effective People*. Stephen R. Covey.

Apple Books*

Fiction

1. *Where the Crawdads Sing*. Delia Owens.
2. *The Silent Patient*. Alex Michaelides.
3. *Redemption*. David Baldacci.
4. *The New Girl*. Daniel Silva.
5. *After*. Anna Todd.
6. *Backlash*. Brad Thor.
7. *Summer of '69*. Elin Hilderbrand.
8. *One Good Deed*. David Baldacci.
9. *After We Collided*. Anna Todd.
10. *The Guardians*. John Grisham.

Nonfiction

1. *Educated*. Tara Westover.
2. *Becoming*. Michelle Obama.
3. *The Subtle Art of Not Giving a F*ck*. Mark Manson.
4. *Girl, Wash Your Face*. Rachel Hollis.
5. *World History*. Roger B. Beck and others.
6. *Bad Blood*. John Carreyrou.
7. *Howard Stern Comes Again*. Howard Stern.
8. *Biology*. Kenneth R. Miller and Joseph S. Levine.
9. *Can't Hurt Me*. David Goggins.
10. *The Americans*. Gerald A. Danzer and others.

* Apple does not release a unified list of best-selling adult fiction and nonfiction in the Apple Books format.

Top Print, Digital, and Audiobook Titles from the Library

New York Public Library Top Ten Print Checkouts System-wide†

1. *Becoming*. Michelle Obama.
2. *Educated*. Tara Westover.
3. *Little Fires Everywhere*. Celeste Ng.
4. *A Spark of Light*. Jodi Picoult.
5. *Where the Crawdads Sing*. Delia Owens.
6. *Pachinko*. Min Jin Lee.
7. *Circe*. Madeline Miller.
8. *Nine Perfect Strangers*. Liane Moriarty.
9. *Bad Blood*. John Carreyrou.
10. *Milkman*. Anna Burns.

San Diego County Library Top Ten Print Checkouts System-wide†

1. *Where the Crawdads Sing*. Delia Owens.
2. *Dark Sacred Night*. Michael Connelly.
3. *Becoming*. Michelle Obama.
4. *The Great Alone*. Kristin Hannah.
5. *The Reckoning*. John Grisham.
6. *Nine Perfect Strangers*. Liane Moriarty.
7. *Long Road to Mercy*. David Baldacci.
8. *Past Tense*. Lee Child.
9. *Crazy Rich Asians*. Kevin Kwan.
10. *The President Is Missing*. Bill Clinton and James Patterson.

† Lists include adult fiction and nonfiction checkouts only.

OverDrive's Top Five Most Popular Library Ebooks and Audiobooks

Ebooks

1. *Where the Crawdads Sing*. Delia Owens.
2. *Becoming*. Michelle Obama.
3. *Educated*. Tara Westover.
4. *Nine Perfect Strangers*. Liane Moriarty.
5. *Little Fires Everywhere*. Celeste Ng.

Audiobooks

1. *Becoming*. Michelle Obama.
2. *Where the Crawdads Sing*. Delia Owens.
3. *Educated*. Tara Westover.
4. *Girl, Wash Your Face*. Rachel Hollis.
5. *Harry Potter and the Sorcerer's Stone*. J. K. Rowling.

Literary Prizes, 2019

Compiled by the staff of *Library and Book Trade Almanac*

Academy of American Poets Fellowship ($25,000). For outstanding poetic achievement. *Offered by:* Academy of American Poets. *Winner:* Ilya Kaminsky.

Academy of American Poets Laureate Fellowships ($1,050,000). Grace Cavalieri, Poet Laureate of Maryland; Molly Fisk, Poet Laureate of Nevada County, California; Jaki Shelton Green, Poet Laureate of North Carolina; Fred L. Joiner, Poet Laureate of Carrboro, North Carolina; Robin Coste Lewis, Poet Laureate of Los Angeles, California; Claudia Castro Luna, Poet Laureate of Washington State; Ed Madden, Poet Laureate of Columbia, South Carolina; Adrian Matejka, Poet Laureate of Indiana; Jeanetta Calhoun Mish, Poet Laureate of Oklahoma; Paisley Rekdal, Poet Laureate of Utah; Raquel Salas Rivera, Poet Laureate of Philadelphia, Pennsylvania; Kim Shuck, Poet Laureate of San Francisco, California; TC Tolbert, Poet Laureate of Tucson, Arizona.

Jane Addams Children's Book Awards. For children's books that effectively promote the cause of peace, social justice, world community, and equality. *Offered by:* Jane Addams Peace Association. *Winners:* (younger children) Jacqueline Woodson for *The Day You Begin,* illustrated by Rafael Lopez (Nancy Paulsen Books); (older children) Jewell Parker Rhodes for *Ghost Boys* (Little, Brown Books for Young Readers).

Aesop Prize. For outstanding illustrated children's publications utilizing folkloric themes. *Offered by:* American Folklore Society. *Winners: Peg Bearskin,* as told by Mrs. Elizabeth Brewer, adapted by Philip Dinn and Andy Jones, illustrated by Denise Gallagher (Running the Goat Books & Broadsides); and Susan Tarcov for *Raisins and Almonds: A Yiddish Lullaby,* illustrated by Sonia Sánchez (Kar-Ben Publishing).

Agatha Awards. For mystery writing in the method exemplified by author Agatha Christie. *Offered by:* Malice Domestic Ltd. *Winners:* (contemporary novel) Ellen Byron for *Mardi Gras Murder* (Crooked Lane Books); (first novel) Dianne Freeman for *A Ladies Guide to Etiquette and Murder* (Kensington) and Shari Randall for *Curses Boiled Again* (St. Martin's); (historical) Sujata Massey for *The Widows of Malabar Hill* (Soho Crime); (young adult) Cindy Callaghan for *Potion Problems (Just Add Magic)* (Aladdin); (nonfiction) Jane Cleland for *Mastering Plot Twists* (Writer's Digest Books); (short story) Leslie Budewitz for "All God's Sparrows" (*Alfred Hitchcock Mystery Magazine*) and Tara Laskowski for "The Case of the Vanishing Professor" (*Alfred Hitchcock Mystery Magazine*).

Ambroggio Prize ($1,000 and publication by Bilingual Press/Editorial Bilingue). *Offered by:* Academy of American Poets. For a book-length poetry manuscript originally written in Spanish and with an English translation. *Winner:* Gloria Munoz for *Danzsirley/Dawn's Early.*

American Academy of Arts and Letters Award of Merit ($25,000). Given annually, in rotation, for the short story, sculpture, novel, poetry, drama, and painting. *Offered by:* American Academy of Arts and Letters. *Winner:* Lydia Millet (short story).

American Academy of Arts and Letters Awards in Literature ($10,000 each). To honor eight writers for exceptional accomplishment in any genre. *Offered by:* American Academy of Arts and Letters. *Winners:* Robert Alter, Marilyn Chin, Chris Hedges, Siri Hustvedt, Matthew Lopez, John McManus, Eileen Myles, Lauren Yee.

American Academy of Arts and Letters Blake-Dodd Prize ($25,000). Triennial prize to a nonfiction writer. *Offered by:* American Academy of Arts and Letters. *Winner (2017):* Elizabeth Kolbert.

American Academy of Arts and Letters Benjamin H. Danks Award ($20,000). Given annually, in rotation, to a composer of ensemble works, a playwright, and a writer. *Offered by:* American Academy of Arts and Letters. *Winner:* Heide Schreck (drama).

American Academy of Arts and Letters E. M. Forster Award ($20,000). To a young writer from the United Kingdom or Ireland for a stay in the United States. *Offered by:* American Academy of Arts and Letters. *Winner:* Sally Rooney.

American Academy of Arts and Letters Gold Medal in Fiction. For distinguished achievement. *Offered by:* American Academy of Arts and Letters. *Winner:* Toni Morrison.

American Academy of Arts and Letters Sue Kaufman Prize for First Fiction ($5,000). For a work of first fiction (novel or short stories). *Offered by:* American Academy of Arts and Letters. *Winner:* Jane Delury for *The Balcony* (Little, Brown and Company).

American Academy of Arts and Letters Addison M. Metcalf Award ($10,000). Given biennially to a young writer of fiction, nonfiction, drama, or poetry. *Offered by:* American Academy of Arts and Letters. *Winner (2019):* Aracelis Girmay.

American Academy of Arts and Letters Arthur Rense Poetry Prize ($20,000). Triennial prize to an exceptional poet. *Offered by:* American Academy of Arts and Letters. *Winner (2017):* August Kleinzahler.

American Academy of Arts and Letters Rosenthal Family Foundation Award ($10,000). To a young writer of considerable literary talent for a work of fiction. *Offered by:* American Academy of Arts and Letters. *Winner:* Tommy Orange for *There There* (Knopf).

American Academy of Arts and Letters John Updike Award ($10,000). Biennial prize to a writer in midcareer whose work has demonstrated consistent excellence. *Offered by:* American Academy of Arts and Letters. *Winner (2019):* D. A. Powell.

American Academy of Arts and Letters Harold D. Vursell Memorial Award ($20,000). To a writer whose work merits recognition for the quality of its prose style. *Offered by:* American Academy of Arts and Letters. *Winner:* John Keene.

American Academy of Arts and Letters E. B. White Award ($10,000). Biennial award to a writer for achievement in children's literature. *Offered by:* American Academy of Arts and Letters. *Winner (2019):* Katherine Patterson.

American Book Awards. For literary achievement by people of various ethnic backgrounds. *Offered by:* Before Columbus Foundation. *Winners:* Frank Abe, Greg Robinson, and Floyd Cheung (eds.), *John Okada: The Life & Rediscovered Work of the Author of* No-No Boy (University of Washington Press); May-lee Chai, *Useful Phrases for Immigrants: Stories* (Blair); Louise DeSalvo, *The House of Early Sorrows: A Memoir in Essays* (Fordham University Press); Heid E. Erdrich (ed.), *New Poets of Native Nations* (Graywolf Press); Ángel García, *Teeth Never Sleep: Poems* (University of Arkansas Press); Tommy Orange, *There There: A Novel* (Knopf); Halifu Osumare, *Dancing in Blackness: A Memoir* (University Press of Florida); Christopher Patton, *Unlikeness Is Us: Fourteen from the Exeter Book* (Gaspereau Press); Mark Sarvas, *Memento Park: A Novel* (Farrar, Straus and Giroux); Jeffrey C. Stewart, *The New Negro: The Life of Alain Locke* (Oxford University Press); William T. Vollmann, *Carbon Ideologies: Volume I, No Immediate Danger, Volume II, No Good Alternative* (Viking); G. Willow Wilson (author) and Nico Leon (illustrator), *Ms. Marvel Vol. 9: Teenage Wasteland* (Marvel); (editor/publisher award) UCLA Chicano Studies Research Center; (lifetime achievement award) Nathan Hare; (oral literature award) Moor Mother (Camae Ayewa).

American Indian Youth Literature Awards. Offered biennially to recognize excellence in books by and about American Indians. *Offered by:* American Indian Library Association. *Winners (2018):* (picture book) Michaela Goade, illustrator, Johnny Marks, Hans Chester, David Katzeek, Nora Dauenhauer, and Richard Dauenhauer (editors) for *Shanyaak'utlaax: Salmon Boy* (Sealaska Heritage Institute); (middle school) Arigon Starr (editor) featuring the work of Theo Tso, Jonathan Nelson, Kristina Bad Hand, Roy Boney, Jr., Lee Francis IV, Johnnie Diacon, Weshoyot Alvitre, Renee Nejo, and Michael Sheyahshe for *Tales of the Mighty Code Talkers, Volume 1* (Native Realities); (young adult) Lisa Charleyboy and Mary Beth Leatherdale (editors) for *#Not Your Princess: Voices of Native American Women* (Annick Press).

American Poetry Review / Honickman First Book Prize in Poetry ($3,000 and publication of the book). To encourage excellence in poetry and to provide a wide readership for a deserving first book of poems. *Winner:* Taneum Bambrick for *Vantage* (Copper Canyon Press).

Américas Book Award for Children's and Young Adult Literature. To recognize U.S. works of fiction, poetry, folklore, or selected nonfiction that authentically and engagingly portray Latin America, the Caribbean, or Latinos in the United States. *Sponsor:* Consortium of Latin American Studies Programs (CLASP). *Winners:* Junot Diaz for *Islandborn, illustrated by Leo Espinosa* (Dial Press); Duncan Tonatiuh for *Undocumented: A Worker's Fight* (Abrams Books).

Rudolfo and Patricia Anaya Lecture on the Literature of the Southwest. To honor a Chicano or Chicana fiction writer. *Offered by:* National Hispanic Cultural Center, University of New Mexico. *Winner:* Not awarded in 2019.

Hans Christian Andersen Literature Award (500,000 Danish kroner, about $90,000). Biennial prize to a writer whose work can be compared with that of Andersen. *Offered by:* Hans Christian Andersen Literary Committee. *Winner (2018):* A. S. Bayatt.

Anthony Awards. For superior mystery writing. *Offered by:* Boucheron World Mystery Convention. *Winners:* (novel) Lou Berney for *November Road* (William Morrow); (first novel) Oyinkan Braithwaite for *My Sister, the Serial Killer* (Doubleday); (paperback original) Lori Rader-Day for *Under a Dark Sky* (William Morrow Paperbacks); (short story) S.A. Cosby for "The Grass Beneath My Feet" (Tough blogazine); (critical/biographical) Michelle McNamara for *I'll Be Gone in the Dark: One Woman's Obsessive Search for the Golden State Killer* (HarperCollins).

Asian/Pacific American Awards for Literature. For books that promote Asian/Pacific American culture and heritage. *Sponsor:* Asian/Pacific American Librarians Association (APALA). *Winners:* (adult fiction) Thirii Myo Kyaw Myint for *The End of Peril, The End of Enmity, The End of Strife, A Haven* (Noemi Press); (adult nonfiction) Sharmila Sen for *Not Quite Not White: Losing and Finding Race in America* (Penguin Books); (young adult) Adib Khorram for *Darius the Great Is Not Okay* (Dial Books); (children's) Kelly Yang for *Front Desk* (Arthur A. Levine Books); (picture book) Minh Le for *Drawn Together, illustrated by Dan Santat* (Disney Hyperion).

Audio Publishers Association Awards (Audies). To recognize excellence in audiobooks. *Winners:* (audiobook of the year) *Children of Blood and Bone* by George Saunders, read by Bahni Turpin (Macmillan Audio); (drama) *The Martian Invasion of Earth* by H. G. Wells, dramatized by Nicholas Briggs, read by Richard Armitage and Lucy Briggs-Owen (Big Finish Productions); (autobiography/memoir) *Educated by Tara Westover*, Julia Whelan (Penguin Random House Audio); (best female narrator) *Educated by Tara Westover*, Julia Whelan (Penguin Random House Audio); (best male narrator) *Watchers by Dean Koontz,* read by Edoardo Ballerini (Brilliance Publishing); (business / personal development) *How to Be Heard* written and read by Julian Treasure (Blackstone Publishing); (faith-based fiction and nonfiction) The Man on the Mountaintop by Susan Trott, adapted by Libby Spurrier, read by Stanley Tucci, Toby Jones, Clare Corbett, Rachel Adkins, Jeff Hardy, and David Thorpe (Audible Studios); (fantasy) *Spinning Silver* by Naomi Novik, read by Lisa Flanagan (Penguin Random House Audio); (fiction) *The Tattoo Artist of Auschwitz* by Heather Morris, read by Richard Armitage (HarperAudio); (history/biography) *Darkest Hour* by Anthony McCarten, read by John Lee (HarperAudio); (humor) *The Greatest Love Story Ever Told,* written and read by Nick Offerman and Megan Mullally; (literary fiction and classics) *Bleak House* by Charles Dickens, read by Miriam Margolyes (Audible Studios); (middle grade) *Sunny* by Jason Reynolds, read by Guy Lockard (Simon & Schuster Audio); (multivoiced performance) *Dreamland Burning* by Jennifer Latham, read by Pyeng Threadgill and Luke Slattery (Hachette Audio); (mystery) *The Punishment She Deserves* by Elizabeth George, read by Simon Vance (Penguin Random House Audio); (narration by the author) *The Secret of Nightingale Wood*, written and read by Lucy Strange (Scholastic Audio); (nonfiction) *The Perfectionists* written and read by Simon

Winchester (HarperAudio); (original work) *Spin* by Harvey Edelman and Neil Fishman, adapted by David B. Coe, read by Jim Dale, Barrett Leddy, Lisa Livesay, Nicola Barber, Khristine Hyam, Nick Sullivan, John Brady, and Johnny Heller (HaperAudio); (romance) *His Viking Bride* by Olivia Norem, read by Greg Patmore (Olivia Norem); (science fiction) *The Hitchhiker's Guide to the Galaxy: Hexagonal Phase* by Eoin Colfer and Douglas Adams, read by John Lloyd, Simon Jones, Geoff McGivern, Mark Wing-Davey, Sandra Dickinson, Susan Sheridan, Samantha Beart, Toby Longworth, Andy Secombe, Mitch Benn, Jane Horrocks, Ed Byrne, Jon Culshaw, Jim Broadbent, Professor Stephen Hawking, Lenny Henry, Tom Alexander, Philip Pope, Theo Maggs, Phillipe Bosher, and John Marsh (Penguin Random House UK Audio); (short stories / collections) *Heads of the Colored People* by Nafissa Thompson-Spires, read by Adenrele Ojo (HighBridge Audio); (thriller/suspense) *Crimson Lake* by Candice Fox, read by Euan Morton (Macmillan Audio); (young adult) *Sadie* by Courtney Summers, read by Dan Bittner, Rebecca Soler, Gabra Zackman, and Fred Berman (Macmillan Audio); (young listeners up to age eight) *Before She Was Harriet* by Lesa Cline-Ransome, illustrated by James E. Ransome, read by SiSi Aisha Johnson, January LaVoy, Lisa Renee Pitts, and Bahni Turpin (Live Oak Media).

Bad Sex in Fiction Award (United Kingdom). To "draw attention to the crude, badly written, often perfunctory use of redundant passages of sexual description in the modern novel, and to discourage it." *Sponsor: Literary Review. Winners:* Didier DeCoin for *The Office of Gardens and Ponds* (MacLehose Press) and John Harvey for *Pax* (Holland House Books).

Women's Prize for Fiction (United Kingdom) (formerly the Bailey's Women's Prize for Fiction) (£30,000). For the best novel written by a woman and published in the United Kingdom. *Winner:* Tayari Jones for *An American Marriage* (Algonquin Books).

Bancroft Prizes ($10,000). For books of exceptional merit and distinction in American history, American diplomacy, and the international relations of the United States. *Offered by:* Columbia University. *Winners:* David W. Blight for *Frederick Douglass, Prophet of Freedom* (Simon & Schuster); Lisa Brooks for *Our Beloved Kin: A New History of King Philip's War* (Yale University Press.

Barnes & Noble Discover Great New Writers Awards. To honor a first novel and a first work of nonfiction by American authors. *Offered by:* Barnes & Noble. *Winners:* (fiction) Claire Adam for *Golden Child* (SJP for Hogarth); (nonfiction) Damon Young for *What Doesn't Kill You Makes You Blacker* (Ecco).

Mildred L. Batchelder Award. To the American publisher of a children's book originally published in a language other than English and subsequently published in English in the United States. *Offered by:* American Library Association, Association for Library Service to Children. *Winner:* Thames & Hudson for *The Fox on the Swing*, written by Evelina Daciute, illustrated by Ausra Kiudulaite, and translated by the Translation Bureau.

BBC National Short Story Award (United Kingdom) (£15,000). *Winner:* Jo Lloyd for "The Invisible."

Pura Belpré Awards. To a Latino/Latina writer and illustrator whose work portrays, affirms, and celebrates the Latino cultural experience in an outstanding work of literature for children and youth. *Offered by:* American Library Association, Association for Library Service to Children. *Winners:* (narrative) Elizabeth Acevedo for *The Poet X* (HarperTeen/HarperCollins); (illustration) Yuyi Morales for *Dreamers* (Neal Porter Books / Holiday House).

Helen B. Bernstein Book Award for Excellence in Journalism ($15,000). To a journalist who has written at book length about an issue of contemporary concern. *Offered by:* New York Public Library. *Winner:* Shane Bauer for *American Prison: A Reporter's Undercover Journey into the Business of Punishment* (Penguin Publishing Group).

Black Caucus of the American Library Association (BCALA) Literary Awards. *Winners:* (first novelist) Malcolm Hansen for *They Come in All Colors* (Atria Books); (poetry) Neal Hall for *Door of No Return*; (fiction) Tayari Jones for *An American Marriage* (Algonquin Books); (nonfiction) Jeffrey C. Stewart for *The New Negro: The Life of Alain Locke* (Oxford University Press).

Irma Simonton Black and James H. Black Award for Excellence in Children's Literature. To a book for young children in which the text and illustrations work together to create an outstanding whole. *Offered by:* Bank Street College of Education. *Winner:* Ryan T. Higgis for *We Don't Eat Our Classmates* (Disney Hyperion).

James Tait Black Memorial Prize (United Kingdom) (£10,000). To recognize literary excellence in fiction and biography. *Offered by:* University of Edinburgh. *Winners:* (fiction) Olivia Laing for *Crudo* (Picador); (biography) Lindsey Hilsum for *In Extremis* (Chatto and Windus).

James Tait Black Prize for Drama (United Kingdom) (£10,000). *Offered by:* University of Edinburgh in partnership with the National Theatre of Scotland and in association with the Traverse Theatre. *Winner:* Not awarded in 2019.

Blue Peter Book of the Year (United Kingdom). To recognize excellence in children's books. Winners are chosen by a jury of viewers, ages 8–12, of the BBC television children's program *Blue Peter. Winners:* (best story) Onjali Q. Rauf for *The Boy at the Back of the Class* (Orion Children's Books); (best book with facts) Clive Gifford for *The Colours of History*, illustrated by Marc-Etienne Peintre (QED Publishing).

Bookseller/Diagram Prize for Oddest Title of the Year. *Sponsor: The Bookseller* magazine. *Winner:* Charles L. Dobbins for *The Dirt Hole and Its Variations* (self-published).

Boston Globe/Horn Book Awards. For excellence in children's literature. *Winners:* (fiction and poetry) Kekla Magoon for *The Season of Styx Malone* (Lamb/Random House); (nonfiction) Jo Ann Allen Boyce and Debbie Levy for *The Promise of Change: One Girl's Story in the Fight for School Equality* (Bloomsbury); (picture book) Maxine Beneba Clarke for *The Patchwork Bicycle* (Candlewick Press).

W. Y. Boyd Literary Award for Excellence in Military Fiction ($5,000). For a military novel that honors the service of American veterans during a time of war. *Offered by:* American Library Association. *Donor:* W. Y. Boyd II. *Winner:* Ray McPadden for *And the Whole Mountain Burned* (Center Street).

Branford Boase Award (United Kingdom). To the author and editor of an outstanding novel for young readers by a first-time writer. *Winners:* Muhammad Khan (author) and Lucy Pearse (editor) for *I Am Thunder* (Macmillan Children's Books).

Bridport International Creative Writing Prizes (United Kingdom). For poetry and short stories. *Offered by:* Bridport Arts Centre. *Winners:* (poetry, £5,000) Fathima Zahara for "Things I Wish I Could Trade My Headscarf For"; (short story, £5,000) Ross Foster for "Henry"; (flash fiction, 250-word maximum, £1,000) Maria Donovan for "Aftermath"; (Peggy Chapman-Andrews Award for a First Novel) Sandra Jensen for *Seagull Pie*.

British Book Awards (aka the Nibbies) (United Kingdom). *Offered by: The Bookseller. Winners:* (book of the year) Sally Rooney for *Normal People* (Faber & Faber); (fiction) Sally Rooney for *Normal People* (Faber & Faber); (debut) Leila Slimani for *Lullaby, translated by Sam Taylor* (Simon & Schuster); (crime/thriller) Louise Candlish for *Our House* (Simon & Schuster); (children's illustrated and nonfiction) Matthew Syad (author) and Toby Triumph (illustrator) *You Are Awesome* (Wren & Rook); (children's fiction) David Walliams for *The Ice Monster*, illustrated by Tony Ross (HarperCollins Children's Books); (nonfiction) Michelle Obama for *Becoming* (Viking); (lifestyle) Henry Firth and Ian Theasby for *Bosh!* (HQ); (audio) Penguin Random House UK Audio for *Becoming* by Michelle Obama, narrated by the author; (illustrator of the year) Judith Kerr; (author of the year) Lee Child.

British Fantasy Awards. *Offered by:* British Fantasy Society. *Winners:* (Karl Edward Wagner Award) Ian Whates; (Sydney J Bounds Award for a newcomer) Tasha Suri for *Empire of Sand* (Orbit); (magazine/periodical) *Uncanny*; (nonfiction) Ruth EJ Booth for *Noise and Sparks* (*Shoreline of Infinity*); (comic/graphic novel) Kate Ashwin for *Widdershins, Volume 7: Curtain Call* (self-published); (independent press) Unsung Stories; (artist) Vince Haig; (anthology) Robert Shearman and Michael Kelly (eds.) for *Year's Best Weird Fiction, Volume 5* (Undertow); (collection) Priya Sharma for

All the Fabulous Beasts (Undertow); (film/television production) *Spider-Man: Into the Spider-Verse*, screenplay by Phil Lord and Rodney Rothman, directed by Bob Persichetti, Peter Ramsey, and Rodney Rothman (Sony Pictures); (audio) *Breaking the Glass Slipper* (podcast); (novella) Aliette de Bodard for *The Tea Master and the Detective* (Subterranean); (short story) G. V. Anderson for "Down Where the Sound Becomes Blunt" in *F&SF* 3-4/18; (August Derleth Award for horror novel) Catriona Ward for *Little Eve* (W&N); (Robert Holdstock Award for fantasy novel) Jen Williams for *The Bitter Twins* (Headline).

Sophie Brody Medal. For the U.S. author of the most distinguished contribution to Jewish literature for adults, published in the preceding year. *Donors:* Sophie and Arthur Brody Foundation. *Offered by:* American Library Association, Reference and User Services Association. *Winner:* Michael Lukas for *The Last Watchman of Old Cairo* (Spiegel & Grau).

Witter Bynner Poetry Fellowships ($10,000). To encourage poets and poetry. *Sponsor:* Witter Bynner Foundation for Poetry. *Winner:* Not awarded in 2019.

Caine Prize for African Writing (£10,000). For a short story by an African writer, published in English. *Winner:* Lesley Nneka Arimah for "Skinned" in *McSweeney's Quarterly Concern (Issue 53).*

Randolph Caldecott Medal. For the artist of the most distinguished picture book. *Offered by:* American Library Association, Association for Library Service to Children. *Winner:* Sophie Blackall for *Hello Lighthouse* (Little, Brown).

California Book Awards. To California residents to honor books of fiction, nonfiction, and poetry published in the previous year. *Offered by:* Commonwealth Club of California. *Winners:* (fiction) Rachel Kushner for *The Mars Room* (Scribner); (first fiction) Tommy Orange for *There There* (Knopf); (nonfiction) Susan Orlean for *The Library Book* (Simon & Schuster); (poetry) Samantha Giles for *Total Recall* (Krupskaya); (juvenile) Garret Weyr for *The Language of Spells* (Chronicle Books); (young adult) Kelly Loy Gilbert for *Picture Us in the Light* (Little, Brown Books for Young Readers); (contribution to publishing) Tyler Green for *Carleton Watkins: Making the West American* (University of California Press); (Californiana) Miriam Pawel for *The Browns of California* (Bloomsbury).

John W. Campbell Award. For the best new science fiction or fantasy writer whose first work of science fiction or fantasy was published in a professional publication in the previous two years. *Offered by:* Dell Magazines. *Winner:* Jeannette Ng for *Under the Pendulum Sun* (Angry Robot).

John W. Campbell Memorial Award. For science fiction writing. *Offered by:* Gunn Center for the Study of Science Fiction. *Winner:* Sam J. Miller for *Blackfish City* (Ecco Press).

Andrew Carnegie Medal for Excellence in Fiction and Nonfiction. For adult books published during the previous year in the United States. *Sponsors:* Carnegie Corporation of New York, ALA/RUSA, and *Booklist*. *Winners:* (fiction) Rebecca Makkai for *The Great Believers* (Viking); (nonfiction) Kiese Laymon for *Heavy: An American Memoir* (Scribner).

Carnegie Medal (United Kingdom). See CILIP Carnegie Medal.

Center for Fiction First Novel Prize ($10,000). *Offered by:* Center for Fiction, Mercantile Library of New York. *Winner:* De'Shawn Charles Winslow for *In West Mills* (Bloomsbury).

Chicago Folklore Prize. For the year's best folklore book. *Offered by:* American Folklore Society. *Winner:* Todd Lawrence and Elaine Lawless for *When They Blew the Levee: Race, Politics, and Community in Pinhook, Missouri* (University Press of Mississippi).

Chicago Tribune Nelson Algren Short Story Award ($3,500). For unpublished short fiction. *Offered by: Chicago Tribune. Winner:* Barry Pearce for "Chez Whatever."

Chicago Tribune Heartland Prize for Fiction ($7,500). *Offered by: Chicago Tribune. Winner:* Rebecca Makkai for *The Great Believers* (Viking).

Chicago Tribune Heartland Prize for Nonfiction ($7,500). *Offered by: Chicago Tribune. Winner:* Sarah Smarsh for *Heartland: A Memoir of Working Hard and Being Broke in the Richest Country on Earth* (Scribner).

Chicago Tribune Literary Award. To recognize lifetime achievement of a prominent writer, usually someone with strong connections to the Midwest. *Winner:* Henry Louis Gates.

Chicago Tribune Young Adult Literary Prize. To recognize a distinguished literary career. *Winner:* Not awarded in 2019.

Children's Africana Book Awards. To recognize and encourage excellence in children's books about Africa. *Offered by:* Africa Access, African Studies Association. *Winners:* (young readers) *Sing to the Moon* by Nansubuga Nagadya Isdahl, illustrated by Sandra van Doorn (Lerner); (older readers) Tomi Adeyemi for *Children of Blood and Bone* (Henry Holt); (new adult) Trevor Noah for *Born a Crime: Stories from a South African Childhood* (Spiegel & Grau).

Children's Literature Legacy Award (formerly the Laura Ingalls Wilder Award). Awarded to an author or illustrator whose books have made a substantial and lasting contribution to children's literature. *Offered by:* American Library Association, Association for Library Service to Children. *Winner:* Walter Dean Myers.

Cholmondeley Awards for Poets (United Kingdom) (£1,500). For a poet's body of work and contribution to poetry. *Winners:* Malika Booker, Fred D'Aguiar, Allen Fisher, and Jamie McKendrick.

CILIP Carnegie Medal (United Kingdom). For the outstanding children's book of the year. *Offered by:* CILIP: The Chartered Institute of Library and Information Professionals. *Winner:* Elizabeth Acevedo for *The Poet X* (Electric Monkey).

CILIP Kate Greenaway Medal and Colin Mears Award (United Kingdom) (£5,000 plus £500 worth of books donated to a library of the winner's choice). For children's book illustration. *Offered by:* CILIP: The Chartered Institute of Library and Information Professionals. *Winner:* Jackie Morris for *The Lost Words by Robert Macfarlane* (IndiBooks).

Arthur C. Clarke Award. For the best science fiction novel published in the United Kingdom. *Offered by:* British Science Fiction Association. *Winner:* Tade Thompson for *Rosewater* (Orbit).

David Cohen Prize for Literature (United Kingdom) (£40,000). Awarded biennially to a living British writer, novelist, poet, essayist, or dramatist in recognition of an entire body of work written in the English language. *Offered by:* David Cohen Family Charitable Trust. *Winner (2019):* Edna O'Brien.

Matt Cohen Award: In Celebration of a Writing Life (C$20,000). To a Canadian author whose life has been dedicated to writing as a primary pursuit, for a body of work. *Offered by:* Writers' Trust of Canada. *Sponsors:* Marla and David Lehberg. *Winner:* Olive Senior.

Commonwealth Short Story Prize (United Kingdom) (£5,000). To reward and encourage new short fiction by Commonwealth writers. *Offered by:* Commonwealth Institute. *Winners:* (regional winner, Africa) Mbozi Haimbe (Zambia) for "Madam's Sister"; (regional winner, Asia) Saras Manickam (Malaysia) for "My Mother Pattu"; (regional winner, Canada and Europe, and overall winner) Constantia Soteriou (Cyprus) for "Death Customs"; (regional winner, Caribbean) Alexia Tolas (Bahamas) for "Granma's Porch"; (regional winner, Pacific) Harley Hern (New Zealand) for "Screaming."

Costa Book Awards (United Kingdom) (£5,000 plus an additional £25,000 for Book of the Year). For literature of merit that is readable on a wide scale. *Offered by:* Booksellers Association of Great Britain and Costa Coffee. *Winners:* (biography) Jack Fairweather for *The Volunteer* (W. H. Allen); (novel) Jonathan Coe for *Middle England* (Knopf); (first novel) Sara Collins for *The Confessions of Frannie Langton* (Penguin); (children's) Jasbinder Bilan for *Asha & the Spirit Bird* (Chicken House); (poetry) Mary Jean Chan for *Fleche* (Faber & Faber).

Costa Short Story Award (United Kingdom). *Winners:* (first place, £3,500) Anna Dempsey for "The Dedicated Dancers of the Greater Oaks Retirement Community."

Crime Writers' Association (CWA) Dagger Awards (United Kingdom). *Winners:* (diamond dagger, for significant contribution to crime writing) Robert Goddard; (gold dagger, for best novel) M. W. Craven for *The Puppet Show* (Constable/Little, Brown); (gold dagger, for nonfiction) Ben Macintyre for *The Spy and the Traitor* (Viking); (Ian Fleming steel dagger, for best thriller) Holly Watt for *To the Lions* (Raven Books); (John

Creasey dagger, for best debut crime novel) Chris Hammer for *Scrublands* (Wildfire); (CWA historical dagger, for the best historical crime novel) S. G. MacLean for *Destroying Angel* (Quercus Fiction); (CWA short story dagger) Danuta Kot writing as Danuta Reah for "The Dummies' Guide to Serial Killing" in *The Dummies' Guide to Serial Killing and Other Fantastic Female Fables* (Fantastic Books); (international dagger, for a work translated into English) Dov Alfon for *A Long Night in Paris, translated by Daniella Zamir* (MacLehose Press); (CWA Dagger in the Library, for a body of work) Kate Ellis; (debut dagger, for a previously unpublished crime writer) Shelley Burr for *Wake*.

Benjamin H. Danks Award ($20,000). Given annually, in rotation, to a composer of ensemble works, a playwright, and a writer. *Offered by:* American Academy of Arts and Letters. *Winner:* Heide Schreck (drama).

Dartmouth Medal. For creating current reference works of outstanding quality and significance. *Donor:* Dartmouth College. *Offered by:* American Library Association, Reference and User Services Division. *Winner:* Brian W. Coad and James D. Reist for *Marine Fishes of Arctic Canada* (University of Toronto Press).

Derringer Awards. To recognize excellence in short crime and mystery fiction. *Sponsor:* Short Mystery Fiction Society. *Winners:* (flash story, up to 1,000 words) James Blakey for "The Bicycle Thief" in *The Norwegian American*; (short story, 1,001–4,000 words) Alan Orloff for "Dying in Dokesville" in *Malice Domestic 13: Mystery Most Geographical*; (long story, 4,001–8,000 words) Leslie Budewitz for "With My Eyes" in *Suspense Magazine* (January/February 2018); (novelette, 8,001–20,000 words) Gigi Pandian for *The Cambodian Curse and Other Stories by Gigi Pandian* (Henery Press).

Diagram Prize for Oddest Title of the Year. See Bookseller/Diagram Prize for Oddest Title of the Year.

Philip K. Dick Award. For a distinguished science fiction paperback published in the United States. *Sponsor:* Philadelphia Science Fiction Society and the Philip K. Dick Trust. *Winner:* Audrey Schulman for *Theory of Bastards* (Europa Editions).

Digital Book Awards. To recognize high-quality digital content available to readers as e-books and enhanced digital books. *Sponsor:* Digital Book World. *Winners:* (publisher of the year) Simon & Schuster; (publishing executive of the year) James Daunt, CEO, Waterstones; (DBW Medal for Leadership in Diversity) Crystal Swain-Bates; (DAISY Consortium Award for Accessibility in Publishing) VitalSource; (DBW Outstanding Achievement Awards) Margot Atwell, Kickstarter; Mary Ghikas, American Library Association; and DAISY Consortium; (best publishing technology) Bookchain, Scenarex; and Skill Flow Builder, Amazon; (best use of emerging technology) *Black Mirror*: "Bandersnatch," Netflix; (best use of podcasting in publishing) Laura Zats and Erik Hane for *Print Run*; (best publishing commentator of the year) Jane Friedman for *The Hot Sheet* and JaneFriedman.com; (best fiction) Ocean Vuong for *On Earth We're Briefly Gorgeous* (Penguin Press); (best nonfiction) *The Mueller Report* (The Internet Archive/Digital Public Library of America); (best business book) Peter Fader and Sarah Toms for *The Customer Centricity Playbook* (Wharton School Press); (best children's book) Jordan Reeves for *Born Just Right* (Jeter Publishing); (best suspense/horror book) Ann Davila Cardinal for *Five Midnights* (Tor Teen); (best poetry book) Eve L. Ewing for *1919* (Haymarket Books); (best religious/inspirational book) Amy Collier Artman for *Miracle Lady: Kathryn Kuhlman and the Transformation of Charismatic Christianity* (Eerdmans); (best book published by a university press) University of California Press for *Blind Injustice: A Former Prosecutor Exposes the Psychology and Politics of Wrongful Convictions* by Mark Godsey.

DSC Prize for South Asian Literature ($50,000). To recognize outstanding literature from or about the South Asian region and raise awareness of South Asian culture around the world. *Sponsor:* DSC Limited. *Winner:* Amitabha Bagchi for *Half the Night Is Gone* (Juggernaut Books).

Dublin Literary Award (Ireland) (€100,000). For a book of high literary merit, written in English or translated into English; if translated, the author receives €75,000 and the translator €25,000. *Offered by:* City of Dublin. *Winner:* Emily Ruskovich for *Idaho* (Chatto & Windus).

Dundee Picture Book Award (Scotland) (£1,000). To recognize excellence in storytelling for children. The winner is chosen by the schoolchildren of Dundee. *Winner:* Jim Whalley (writer) and Stephen Collins (illustrator) for *Baby's First Bank Heist* (Bloomsbury Children's Books).

Educational Writers' Award (United Kingdom) (£2,000). For noteworthy educational nonfiction for children. *Offered by:* Authors' Licensing and Collecting Society and Society of Authors. *Winners:* Alastair Humpreys (author) and Kevin Ward (illustrator) for *Alastair Humphreys' Great Adventurers: The Incredible Expeditions of 20 Explorers* (Big Picture Press).

Margaret A. Edwards Award ($2,000). To an author whose book or books have provided young adults with a window through which they can view their world and which will help them to grow and to understand themselves and their role in society. *Donor: School Library Journal. Winner:* M. T. Anderson for *Feed*; *The Astonishing Life of Octavian Nothing, Traitor to the Nation, Volume I: The Pox Party*; and *The Astonishing Life of Octavian Nothing, Traitor to the Nation, Volume II: The Kingdom on the Waves* (all published by Candlewick Press).

T. S. Eliot Prize for Poetry (United Kingdom) (£20,000). *Offered by:* Poetry Book Society. *Winner:* Roger Robinson for *A Portable Paradise*.

Encore Award (United Kingdom) (£10,000). Awarded for the best second novel. *Offered by:* Royal Society of Literature. *Winner:* Sally Rooney for *Normal People* (Faber & Faber).

European Union Prize for Literature (€5,000). To recognize outstanding European writing. *Sponsors:* European Commission, European Booksellers Federation, European Writers' Council, Federation of European Publishers. *Winners:* Laura Fredenthaler (Austria), Piia Leino (Finland), Sophie Daull (France), Réka Mán-Várhegyi (Hungary), Beqa Adamashvili (Georgia), Nikos Chryssos (Greece), Jan Carson (Ireland), Giovanni Dozzini (Italy), Daina Opolskaite (Lithuania), Marta Dzido (Poland), Tatiana Ţîbuleac (Romania), Ivana Dobrakovová (Slovakia), Halya Shyyan (Ukraine), and Melissa Harrison (United Kingdom).

FIL Literary Award in Romance Languages (formerly the Juan Rulfo International Latin American and Caribbean Prize) (Mexico) ($150,000). For lifetime achievement in any literary genre. *Offered by:* Juan Rulfo International Latin American and Caribbean Prize Committee. *Winner:* David Huerta.

Financial Times and McKinsey Business Book of the Year Award (£30,000). To recognize books that provide compelling and enjoyable insight into modern business issues. *Winner:* Caroline Criado-Perez for *Invisible Women: Exposing Data Bias in a World Designed for Men* (Chatto & Windus).

Flaherty-Dunnan First Novel Prize. See Center for Fiction Flaherty-Dunnan First Novel Prize.

Sid Fleischman Award for Humor. See Golden Kite Awards.

ForeWord Reviews Book of the Year Awards ($1,500). For independently published books. *Offered by: ForeWord Reviews* magazine. *Winners:* (editor's choice prize, fiction) Christine Higdon for *The Very Marrow of Our Bones* (ECW Press); (editor's choice prize, nonfiction) Rebecca Solnit for *Call Them By Their True Names* (Haymarket Books).

E. M. Forster Award ($20,000). To a young writer from the United Kingdom or Ireland for a stay in the United States. *Offered by:* American Academy of Arts and Letters. *Winner:* Sally Rooney.

Forward Prizes (United Kingdom). For poetry. *Offered by: The Forward. Winners:* (best collection, £10,000) Fiona Benson for *Vertigo and Ghost* (Cape Poetry); (Felix Dennis Prize for best first collection, £5,000) Steven Sexton for *If All the World and Love Were Young* (Penguin Books); (best single poem, £1,000) Parwana Fayyaz for "Forty Names" (PN Review).

Josette Frank Award. For a work of fiction in which children or young people deal in a positive and realistic way with difficulties in their world and grow emotionally and morally. *Offered by:* Bank Street College of Education and the Florence M. Miller Memorial Fund. *Winner:* Deb Caletti for *A Heart in a Body in the World* (Simon Pulse).

George Freedley Memorial Award. For the best English-language work about live theater published in the United States. *Offered by:* Theatre Library Association. *Winner:* Debra Caplan, *Yiddish Empire: The Vilna Troupe, Yiddish Theater, and the Art of Itinerancy* (University of Michigan Press).

French-American Foundation Translation Prize ($10,000). For a translation or translations from French into English of works of fiction and nonfiction. *Offered by:* French-American Foundation. *Donor:* Florence Gould Foundation. *Winners:* (fiction) Linda Coverdale for her translation of *Slave Old Man* by Patrick Chamoiseau (New Press) and Chris Clarke for his translation of *Imaginary Lives* by Marcel Schwob (Wakefield Press); (nonfiction) Malcolm Debevoise for his translation of *Good Government: Democracy beyond Elections* by Pierre Rosanvallon (Harvard University Press).

Frost Medal. To recognize achievement in poetry over a lifetime. *Offered by:* Poetry Society of America. *Winner:* Eleanor Wilner.

Lewis Galantière Award. Awarded biennially for a literary translation into English from any language other than German. *Offered by:* American Translators Association. *Winner (2018):* Sam Taylor for his translation of *The Heart* by Maylis de Kerangal (Farrar, Straus and Giroux).

Theodor Seuss Geisel Award. For the best book for beginning readers. *Offered by:* American Library Association, Association for Library Service to Children. *Winner:* Corey R. Tabor for *Fox the Tiger* (Balzer+Bray).

David Gemmell Legend Awards for Fantasy. For novels published for the first time in English during the year of nomination. *Discontinued in 2019.*

Giller Prize (Canada). See Scotiabank Giller Prize.

Gival Press Novel Award ($3,000 and publication by Gival Press). Given biennially. *Winner (2018):* William Orem for *Miss Lucy.*

Gival Press Oscar Wilde Award ($500 and publication by Gival Press). Given annually to an original, unpublished poem that relates LGBTQ life by a poet who is 18 or older. *Winner:* Michael Rodman for *Document (Undocumented).*

Gival Press Poetry Award ($1,000 and publication by Gival Press). Given biennially. *Winner (2019):* Matthew Pennock for *The Miracle Machine.*

Gival Press Short Story Award ($1,000 and publication by Gival Press). Given annually. *Winner:* A. J. Rodriguez for *Efimera.*

Giverny Award. For an outstanding children's science picture book. *Offered by:* 15 Degree Laboratory. *Winner:* Helaine Becker (author) and Dow Phumiruk (illustrator) for *Counting on Katherine: How Katherine Johnson Saved Apollo 13* (Christy Ottaviano Books/Henry Holt Books for Children).

Alexander Gode Medal. To an individual or institution for outstanding service to the translation and interpreting professions. *Offered by:* American Translators Association. *Winner:* Kent State University Translation Programs.

Golden Duck Awards for Excellence in Children's Science Fiction Literature. See LITA Excellence in Children's and Young Adult Science Fiction.

Golden Kite Awards. For children's books. *Offered by:* Society of Children's Book Writers and Illustrators. *Winners:* (middle grade fiction) Susan Hood for *Lifeboat 12* (Simon & Schuster); (nonfiction for younger readers) Barb Rosenstock for *Otis and Will Discover the Deep* (Little, Brown); (nonfiction for older readers) Elizabeth Partridge for *Boots on the Ground: America's War in Vietnam* (Viking); (picture book nonfiction) Carole Boston Weatherford for *Schomburg: The Man Who Built a Library* (Candlewick Press); (picture book illustration) Becca Stadtlander for *Made by Hand: A Crafts Sampler* (Candlewick Press); (picture book text) Jessie Oliveros for *The Remember Balloons* (Simon & Schuster); (young adult fiction) Jane Yolen for *Mapping the Bones* (Philomel); (Sid Fleischman Award) Angela Dominguez for *Stella Diaz Has Something to Say* (Roaring Brook Press).

Governor General's Literary Awards (Canada) (C$25,000, plus C$3,000 to the publisher). For works, in English and French, of fiction, nonfiction, poetry, and for translation. *Offered by:* Canada Council for the Arts. *Winners:* (fiction, English) Joan Thomas for *Five Wives* (Harper Avenue/HarperCollins); (poetry, English) Gwen Benaway for *Holy Wild* (Book*hug); (drama, English) Amanda Parris for *Other Side of the*

Game (Playwrights Canada Press); (nonfiction, English) Don Gillmor for *To the River: Losing My Brother* (Random House Canada/Penguin Random House Canada); (young people's literature—text, English) Erin Bow for *Stand on the Sky* (Scholastic Canada); (young people's literature—illustrated, English) Sydney Smith for *Small in the City* (Groundwood Books); (translation from French to English) Linda Gaboriau for *Birds of a Kind* (Playwrights Canada Press); (fiction, French) Céline Huyghebaert for *Le drap blanc* (Le Quartanier); (poetry, French) Anne-Marie Desmeules for *Le tendon et l'os* (L'Hexagone, Groupe Ville-Marie Littérature); (drama, French) Mishka Lavigne for *Havre* (Les Éditions L'Interligne); (nonfiction, French) Anne-Marie Voisard for *Le droit du plus fort : nos dommages, leurs intérêts* (Les Éditions Écosociété); (young people's literature—text, French) Dominique Demers for *L'albatros et la mésange* (Éditions Québec Amérique); (young people's literature—illustrated, French) Delphie Côté-Lacroix and Stéphanie Lapointe for *Jack et le temps perdu* (Quai no 5, Les Éditions XYZ); (translation from English to French) Catherine Leroux for *Nous qui n'étions rien* (Éditions Alto).

Dolly Gray Children's Literature Awards. Presented biennially for fiction or biographical children's books with positive portrayals of individuals with developmental disabilities. *Offered by:* Council for Exceptional Children, Division on Autism and Developmental Disabilities. *Winners (2018):* (intermediate book) Sally J. Pla for *The Someday Birds* (HarperCollins); (picture book) Julia Finley Mosca (author) and Daniel Rieley (illustrator) for *The Girl Who Thought in Pictures: The Story of Dr. Temple Grandin* (Innovation Press).

Kate Greenaway Medal and Colin Mears Award. See CILIP Kate Greenaway Medal.

Eric Gregory Awards (United Kingdom) (£4,000). For a published or unpublished collection by poets under the age of 30. *Winners:* James Conor Patterson, Sophie Collins, Mary Jean Chan, Dominic Leonard, Seán Hewitt, and Phoebe Stuckes.

Griffin Poetry Prizes (Canada) (C$65,000). To a living Canadian poet or translator and a living poet or translator from any country, which may include Canada. *Offered by:* Griffin Trust. *Winners:* (international) Don Mee Choi for her translation from Korean of *Autobiography of Death* by Kim Hyesoon (New Directions); (Canadian) Eve Joseph for *Quarrels* (Anvil Press).

Gryphon Award ($1,000). To recognize a noteworthy work of fiction or nonfiction for younger children. *Offered by:* the Center for Children's Books. *Winners:* Brian Selznick and David Serlin for *Baby Monkey, Private Eye* (Scholastic).

Dashiell Hammett Prize. For a work of literary excellence in the field of crime writing by a U.S. or Canadian writer. *Offered by:* North American Branch, International Association of Crime Writers. *Winner (2019):* To be announced. *Winner (2018)*: Lou Berney for *November Road* (William Morrow).

R. R. Hawkins Award. For the outstanding professional/scholarly work of the year. *Offered by:* Association of American Publishers. *Winner:* Oxford University Press for *Cyberwar: How Russian Hackers and Trolls Helped Elect a President* by Kathleen Hall Jamieson.

Anthony Hecht Poetry Prize ($3,000 and publication by Waywiser Press). For an unpublished first or second book-length poetry collection. *Winner:* James Davis for *Club Q.*

Drue Heinz Literature Prize ($15,000 and publication by University of Pittsburgh Press). For short fiction. *Winner:* Kate Wisel for *Driving in Cars with Homeless Men.*

O. Henry Awards. See PEN/O. Henry Prize.

William Dean Howells Medal. Given every five years in recognition of the most distinguished novel published during that period. *Offered by:* American Academy of Arts and Letters. *Winner (2015):* William H. Gass for *Middle C* (Vintage).

Hugo Awards. For outstanding science fiction writing. *Offered by:* World Science Fiction Convention. *Winners:* (novel) Mary Robinette Kowal for *The Calculating Stars* (Tor); (novella) Martha Wells for *Artificial Condition* (Tor.com); (novelette) Zen Cho for "If at First You Don't Succeed, Try, Try Again" (B&N Sci-Fi and Fantasy Blog, November 29, 2018); (short story) Alix E. Harrow for "A Witch's Guide to Escape: A Practical Compendium of Portal Fantasies" (*Apex Magazine*, February 2018); (series)

Becky Chambers for Wayfarers (Hodder & Stoughton/Harper Voyager); (related work) Archive of Our Own, a project of the Organization for Transformative Works; (graphic story) Marjorie Liu (author) and Sana Takeda (illustrator) for *Monstress, Volume 3: Haven* (Image Comics); (dramatic presentation, long form) Phil Lord and Rodney Rothman (screenplay) and Bob Persichetti, Peter Ramsey and Rodney Rothman (directors) for *Spider-Man: Into the Spider-Verse* (Sony); (dramatic presentation, short form) Josh Siegal and Dylan Morgan (writers) and Morgan Sackett (director) for *The Good Place*: "Janet" (NBC); (art book) Ursula K. Le Guin (author) and Charles Vess (illustrator) for *The Books of Earthsea: The Complete Illustrated Edition* (Saga Press/Gollancz); (Lodestar Award for Best Young Adult Book) Tomi Adeyemi for *Children of Blood and Bone* (Henry Holt).

ILA Children's and Young Adults' Book Awards. For first or second books in any language published for children or young adults. *Offered by:* International Literacy Association. *Winners:* (primary fiction) Jessica Love for *Julián Is a Mermaid* (Candlewick Press); (primary nonfiction) Monica Clark-Robinson for *Let the Children March* (Houghton Mifflin Harcourt); (intermediate fiction) Lisa Lewis Tyre for *Hope in the Holler* (Nancy Paulsen Books); (intermediate nonfiction) Erica Fyvie for *Trash Revolution: Breaking the Waste Cycle* (Kids Can Press); (young adult fiction) Adrienne Kisner for *Dear Rachel Maddow: A Novel* (Feiwel & Friends); (young adult nonfiction) Chessy Prout with Jenn Abelson for *I Have the Right To: A High School Survivor's Story of Sexual Assault, Justice, and Hope* (Margaret K. McElderry Books).

Independent Publisher Book Awards (IPPY). Created to recognize exemplary independent, university, and self-published titles across a wide spectrum of genres. *Sponsor:* Jenkins Group/Independent Publisher Online. *Winners:* (photography) Oliver Klink (photography) and Anne Wilkes Tucker, Peter Finke, and Geir Jordahl (essays) for *Cultures in Transition: Spirit—Heart—Soul* (True North Editions); (popular fiction) John Slayton for *Running to Graceland* (Wise Ink Creative Publishing); (literary fiction) Leesa Cross-Smith for *Whiskey & Ribbons* (Hub City Press); (short story fiction) (tie) Dorene O'Brien for *What It Might Feel Like to Hope* (Baobab Press) and Virginia Pye for *Shelf Life of Happiness* (Press 53); (poetry) Andrea Gibson for *Lord of the Butterflies* (Button Poetry); (juvenile fiction) Andrew Zimmern and H. E. McElhatton (writers) and Lisa Troutman (illustrator) for *AZ and the Lost City of Ophir* (Beaver's Pond Press); (young adult fiction) Miriam McNamara for *The Unbinding of Mary Reade* (Sky Pony Press); (historical fiction) (tie) John Thorndike for *A Hundred Fires in Cuba* (Beck & Branch) and Rosanna Micelotta Battigelli for *La Brigantessa* (Inanna Publications).

Indies Choice Book Awards. Chosen by owners and staff of American Booksellers Association member bookstores. *Winners:* (adult fiction) Madeline Miller for *Circe: A Novel* (Lee Boudreaux Books); (adult nonfiction) Tara Westover for *Educated: A Memoir* (Random House); (adult debut) Tommy Orange for *There There* (Knopf); (young adult) Elizabeth Acevedo for *The Poet X* (HarperTeen); (audiobook) *Circe: A Novel* by Madeline Miller, read by Perdita Weeks (Hachette Audio).

International Prize for Arabic Fiction ($50,000 and publication in English). To reward excellence in contemporary Arabic creative writing. *Sponsors:* Booker Prize Foundation, Emirates Foundation for Philanthropy. *Winner:* Hoda Barakat (Lebanon) for *The Night Mail* (Dar al-Adab).

Rona Jaffe Foundation Writers' Awards ($30,000 each). To identify and support women writers of exceptional talent in the early stages of their careers. *Offered by:* Rona Jaffe Foundation. *Winners:* Selena Anderson, Magogodi oaMphela Makhene, Sarah Passino, Nicolette Polek, Elizabeth Schambelan, and Debbie Urbanski.

Jerusalem Prize (Israel). Awarded biennially to a writer whose works best express the theme of freedom of the individual in society. *Offered by:* Jerusalem International Book Fair. *Winner (2019):* Joyce Carol Oates.

Jewish Book Council Awards. *Winners:* (Jewish Book of the Year) Pamela S. Nadell for *America's Jewish Women: A History from Colonial Times to Today* (W. W. Norton &

Company); (Lifetime Achievement Award) Robert Alter for *The Hebrew Bible: A Translation with Commentary* (W. W. Norton & Company); (American Jewish studies) Kenneth D. Wald for *The Foundations of American Jewish Liberalism* (Cambridge University Press); (anthologies and collections) Naomi B. Sokoloff and Nancy E. Berg (eds.) for *What We Talk about When We Talk about Hebrew (and What It Means to Americans)* (University of Washington Press); Dani Shapiro for *Inheritance: A Memoir of Genealogy, Paternity, and Love* (Alfred A. Knopf); (biography) David E. Lowe for *Touched with Fire: Morris B. Abram and the Battle against Racial and Religious Discrimination* (Potomac Books); (book club award) Alice Hoffman for *The World That We Knew* (Simon & Schuster); (children's literature) Lesléa Newman (author) and Amy June Bates (illustrator) for *Gittel's Journey: An Ellis Island Story* (Abrams Books for Young Readers); (contemporary Jewish life and practice) Bari Weiss for *How to Fight Anti-Semitism* (Crown); (debut fiction) Sarah Blake for *Naamah* (Riverhead Books); (education and Jewish identity) Deborah Lipstadt for *Antisemitism: Here and Now* (Schocken); (fiction) Etgar Keret *for Fly Already: Stories* (Riverhead Books); (food writing and cookbooks) András Koerner for *Jewish Cuisine in Hungary: A Cultural History with 83 Authentic Recipes* (Central European University Press); (history) Daniel Okrent for *The Guarded Gate: Bigotry, Eugenics and the Law That Kept Two Generations of Jews, Italians, and Other European Immigrants Out of America* (Scribner); (Holocaust) Michael Dobbs for *The Unwanted: America, Auschwitz, and a Village Caught In Between* (Alfred A.Knopf in association with the United States Holocaust Memorial Museum); (modern Jewish thought and experience) Elissa Bemporad for *Legacy of Blood: Jews, Pogroms, and Ritual Murder in the Lands of the Soviets* (Oxford University Press); (poetry) Ilya Kaminsky for *Deaf Republic* (Graywolf Press); (scholarship) Eric Lawee for *Rashi's Commentary on the Torah: Canonization and Resistance in the Reception of a Jewish Classic* (Oxford University Press); (Sephardic culture) Joshua Cole for *Lethal Provocation: The Constantine Murders and the Politics of French Algeria* (Cornell University Press); (visual arts) Rebecca Shaykin for *Edith Halpert, the Downtown Gallery, and the Rise of American Art* (Jewish Museum and Yale University Press); (women's studies) Naomi Seidman for *Sarah Schenirer and the Bais Yaakov Movement* (Littman Library of Jewish Civilization); (writing based on archival material) Elisabeth Gallas for *A Mortuary of Books: The Rescue of Jewish Culture after the Holocaust, translated by* Alex Skinner (New York University Press); (young adult literature) Rachel DeWoskin for *Someday We Will Fly* (Viking).

Sue Kaufman Prize for First Fiction ($5,000). For a work of first fiction (novel or short stories). *Offered by:* American Academy of Arts and Letters. *Winner:* Jane Delury for *The Balcony* (Little, Brown and Company).

Ezra Jack Keats Awards. For children's picture books. *Offered by:* New York Public Library and the Ezra Jack Keats Foundation. *Winners:* (new writer award) John Sullivan for *Kitten and the Night Watchman,* illustrated by Taeeun Yoo (Paula Weisman Books/Simon & Schuster); (new illustrator award) Oge Mora for *Thank You, Omu* (Little, Brown Books for Young Readers).

Kerlan Award. To recognize singular attainments in the creation of children's literature and in appreciation for generous donation of unique resources to the Kerlan Collection for the study of children's literature. *Offered by:* Kerlan Children's Literature Research Collections, University of Minnesota. *Winner:* Lois Ehlert and Claudia Mills.

Coretta Scott King Book Awards ($1,000). To an African American author and illustrator of outstanding books for children and young adults. *Offered by:* American Library Association, Ethnic and Multicultural Exchange Round Table (EMIERT). *Winners:* (author) Claire Hartfield for *A Few Red Drops* (Clarion Books); (illustrator) Ekua Holmes for *The Stuff of Stars,* written by Marion Dane Bauer (Candlewick Press).

Coretta Scott King/Virginia Hamilton Award for Lifetime Achievement. Given in even-numbered years to an African American author, illustrator, or author/illustrator for a body of books for children or young adults. In odd-numbered years, the award honors substantial contributions through active engagement with youth, using award-winning African American literature for children or young adults. *Winner:* Dr. Pauletta Bracy.

Coretta Scott King/John Steptoe Award for New Talent. To offer visibility to a writer and illustrator at the beginning of their careers. *Sponsor:* Coretta Scott King Book Award Committee. *Winners:* (author) Tiffany D. Jackson for *Monday's Not Coming* (Katherine Tegen Books); (illustrator) Oge Mora (also author) for *Thank You, Omu* (Little, Brown Books for Young Readers).

Kirkus Prize ($50,000). For outstanding fiction, nonfiction, and young readers literature. *Offered by: Kirkus Reviews. Winners:* (fiction) Colson Whiehead for *The Nickel Boys* (Doubleday); (nonfiction) Saeed Jones for *How We Fight for Our Lives: A Memoir* (Simon & Schuster); (young readers) Jerry Craft for *New Kid,* color by Jim Callahan (HarperCollins).

Lambda Literary Awards. To honor outstanding lesbian, gay, bisexual, and transgender (LGBT) literature. *Offered by:* Lambda Literary Foundation. *Winners:* (lesbian fiction) Larissa Lai for *The Tiger Flu* (Arsenal Pulp Press); (gay fiction) Joshua Whitehead for *Jonny Appleseed* (Arsenal Pulp Press); (bisexual fiction) Négar Djavadi for *Disoriental,* translated by Tina Kover (Europa Editions); (transgender fiction) Casey Plett for *Little Fish* (Arsenal Pulp Press); (nonfiction) Imani Perry for *Looking for Lorraine: The Radiant and Radical Life of Lorraine Hansberry* (Beacon Press); (bisexual nonfiction) Anthony Moll for *Out of Step: A Memoir* (Mad Creek Books/The Ohio State University Press); (transgender nonfiction) Julian Gill-Peterson for *Histories of the Transgender Child* (University of Minnesota Press; (lesbian poetry) Ru Puro for *Each Tree Could Hold a Noose or a House* (New Issues Poetry & Prose); (gay poetry) Justin Phillip Reed for *Indecency* (Coffee House Press); (bisexual poetry) Duy Doan for *We Play a Game* (Yale University Press); (transgender poetry) Raquel Salas Rivera for *lo terciario/the tertiary* (Timeless, Infinite Light); (lesbian mystery) Claire O'Dell for *A Study in Honor: A Novel* (HarperCollins/HarperVoyager); (gay mystery) Marshall Thornton for *Late Fees: A Pinx Video Mystery* (Kenmore Books); (lesbian memoir/biography) Zahra Patterson for *Chronology* (Ugly Duckling Presse); (gay memoir/biography) Darnell L. Moore for *No Ashes in the Fire: Coming of Age Black and Free in America* (Bold Type Books); (lesbian romance) Ann McMan for *Beowulf for Cretins: A Love Story* (Bywater Books); (gay romance) S. C. Wynne for *Crashing Upwards* (self-published); (anthology) The Other Foundation for *As You Like It: The Gerald Kraak Anthology Volume II* (Jacana Media); (children's/young adult) Kacen Callender for *Hurricane Child* (Scholastic/Scholastic Press); (drama) Mashuq Mushtaq Deen for *Draw the Circle* (Dramatists Play Service); (erotica) Blue Delliquanti & Kazimir Lee for *Miles & Honesty in SCFSX!* (self-published); (graphic novel) Tommi Parrish for *The Lie and How We Told It* (Fantagraphics Books); (science fiction/fantasy/horror) Isaac R. Fellman for *The Breath of the Sun* (Aqueduct); (studies) William T. Hoston for *Toxic Silence: Race, Black Gender Identity, and Addressing the Violence against Black Transgender Women in Houston* (Peter Lang International Academic Publishers).

Harold Morton Landon Translation Award ($1,000). For a book of verse translated into English. *Offered by:* Academy of American Poets. *Winner:* Clare Cavanagh for *Asymmetry* by Adam Zagajewski (Farrar, Straus and Giroux).

David J. Langum, Sr. Prize in American Historical Fiction ($1,000). To honor a book of historical fiction published in the previous year. *Offered by:* Langum Foundation. *Winner:* Mark Barr for *Watershed* (Hub City Press).

David J. Langum, Sr. Prize in American Legal History or Biography ($1,000). For a university press book that is accessible to the educated general public, rooted in sound scholarship, with themes that touch upon matters of general concern. *Offered by:* Langum Foundation. *Winner:* Kimberly M. Welch for *Black Litigants in the Antebellum South* (North Carolina).

Latner Writers' Trust Poetry Prize (C$25,000) (Canada). To a writer with an exceptional body of work in the field of poetry. *Offered by:* Writers' Trust of Canada. *Sponsor:* Latner Family Foundation. *Winner:* Stephen Collis.

James Laughlin Award ($5,000). To commend and support a second book of poetry. *Offered by:* Academy of American Poets. *Winner:* Aditi Machado for *Emporium* (Nightboat Books).

Ruth Lilly and Dorothy Sargent Rosenberg Poetry Fellowships ($25,800). To emerging poets to support their continued study and writing of poetry. *Offered by:* The Poetry Foundation. *Winners:* Justin Phillip Reed, Franny Choi, José Olivarez, Jane Huffman, and Michael Wasson.

Ruth Lilly Poetry Prize ($100,000). To a U.S. poet in recognition of lifetime achievement. *Offered by:* The Poetry Foundation. *Winner:* Marilyn Nelson.

Astrid Lindgren Memorial Award (Sweden) (5 million kroner, more than $575,000). In memory of children's author Astrid Lindgren, to honor outstanding children's literature and efforts to promote it. *Offered by:* Government of Sweden and the Swedish Arts Council. *Winner:* Bart Moeyaert.

LITA Excellence in Children's and Young Adult Science Fiction. *Sponsor:* Library and Information Technology Association. *Winners:* (Golden Duck List for picture books) Tim McCanna (author) and Tad Carpenter (illustrator) for *Bitty Bot's Big Beach Getaway* (Paula Wiseman/Simon & Schuster); David Biedrzycki for *Breaking News: Alien Alert* (Charlesbridge); Shanda McCloskey for *Doll-E 1.0* (Little Brown Books for Young Readers); Lisl H. Detlefsen (author) and Linzie Hunter (illustrator) for *If You Had a Jetpack* (Knopf); Patricia MacLachlan and Emily MacLachlan Charest (authors) and Matt Phelan (illustrator) for *Little Robot Alone* (Houghton Mifflin Harcourt); Stef Wade (author) and Melanie Demmer (illustrator) for *A Place for Pluto* (Capstone Editions). (Eleanor Cameron List for middle grade books) Drew Brockington for *CatStronauts: Robot Rescue* (Little, Brown); Christopher Edge for *Jamie Drake Equation* (Delacorte); Darcy Miller for *Margot and Mateo Save the World* (HarperCollins); Neill Cameron for *Mega Robo Bros* (Scholastic); Eliot Sappingfield for *A Problematic Paradox* (G. P. Putnam's Sons Books for Young Readers); Jeff Weigel for *Quantum Mechanics* (Lion Forge); Molly Brooks for *Sanity & Tallulah* (Disney/Hyperion); Mike Lawrence for *Star Scouts: The League of Lasers (Volume 2)* (First Second Publishing); Geoff Rodkey for *The Story Pirates Present: Stuck in the Stone Age* (Rodale Kids); Jonathan Roth for *Too Much Space! (Beep and Bob)* (Simon & Schuster); Greg Van Eekhout for *Voyage of the Dogs* (HarperCollins); Stuart Gibbs for *Waste of Space* (Simon & Schuster Books for Young Readers); Peter Brown for *The Wild Robot Escapes* (Little, Brown); (Hal Clement List for young adult books) Olivia A. Cole for *A Conspiracy of Stars* (Katherine Tegen Books); Fonda Lee for *Cross Fire* (Scholastic); Amie Kaufman and Meagan Spooner for *Unearthed* (Disney/Hyperion); Will McIntosh for *The Future Will Be B.S.-Free* (Delacorte Press); Rachel Caine and Ann Aguirre for *Honor among Thieves* (Katherine Tegen Books); Maura Milan for *Ignite the Stars* (Albert Whitman and Company); Scott Westerfeld for *Impostors* (Scholastic); Courtney Alameda for *Pitch Dark* (Feiwel and Friends); Brandon Sanderson for *Skyward* (Delacorte); Gene Doucette for *The Spaceship Next Door* (John Joseph Adams Books); Sangu Mandanna for *A Spark of White Fire* (Sky Pony); Arwen Elys Dayton for *Stronger, Faster, and More Beautiful* (Delacorte); Kayla Olson for *This Splintered Silence* (HarperTeen); Adrianne Finlay for *Your One & Only* (Houghton Mifflin Harcourt).

Locus Awards. For science fiction writing. *Offered by:* Locus Publications. *Winners:* (science fiction) Mary Robinette Kowal for *The Calculating Start* (Tor); (fantasy) Naomi Novik for *Spinning Silver* (Del Rey); (horror) Paul Tremblay for *The Cabin at the End of the World* (William Morrow); (young adult) Justina Ireland for *Dread Nation* (Balzer+Bray); (first novel) Rebecca Roanhorse for *Trail of Lightning* (Saga); (novella) Martha Wells for *Artificial Condition*

(Tor.com); (novelette) Brooke Bolander for *The Only Harmless Great Thing* (Tor.com); (short story) Phenderson Djèlí Clark for "The Secret Lives of the Nine Negro Teeth of George Washington" (published by Fireside, February 2018); (anthology) Gardner Dozois (ed.) for *The Book of Magic* (Bantam); (collection) N. K. Jemisin for *How Long 'til Black Future Month* (Orbit US); (nonfiction) Ursula K. Le Guin and David Naimon for *Ursula K. Le Guin: Conversations on Writing* (Tin House); (art book) Ursula K. Le Guin (author) and Charles Vess (illustrator) for *The Books of Earthsea: The Complete Illustrated Edition* (Saga Press / Gollancz).

Elizabeth Longford Prize for Historical Biography (United Kingdom) (£5,000). *Sponsors:* Flora Fraser and Peter Soros. *Winner:* Julian Jackson for *A Certain Idea of France: The Life of Charles De Gaulle* (Allen Lane).

Los Angeles Times Book Prizes. To honor literary excellence. *Offered by: Los Angeles Times. Winners:* (Art Seidenbaum Award for First Fiction) Nafissa Thompson-Spires for *Heads of the Colored People* (Atria); (biography) David W. Blight for *Frederick Douglass: Prophet of Freedom* (Simon & Schuster); (Christopher Isherwood Prize for Autobiographical Prose) Kiese Laymon for *Heavy: An American Memoir* (Scribner); (current interest) Francisco Cantú for *The Line Becomes a River: Dispatches from the Border* (Riverhead Books); (fiction) Rebecca Makkai for *The Great Believers* (Viking); (graphic novel / comics) Tillie Walden for *On a Sunbeam* (First Second); (history) Julia Boyd for *Travelers in the Third Reich: The Rise of Fascism 1919–1945* (Pegasus Books); (mystery/thriller) Oyinkan Braithwaite for *My Sister, the Serial Killer* (Doubleday); (poetry) Carl Phillips for *Wild Is the Wind: Poems* (Farrar, Straus and Giroux); (science & technology) Beth Macy for *Dopesick: Dealers, Doctors, and the Drug Company That Addicted America* (Little, Brown and Company); (young adult literature) Elizabeth Acevedo for *The Poet X* (HarperTeen/HarperCollins).

Amy Lowell Poetry Traveling Scholarship. For one or two U.S. poets to spend one year outside North America in a country the recipients feel will most advance their work. *Offered by:* Amy Lowell Poetry Traveling Scholarship. *Winner:* Ann Pierson Wiese.

Walter & Lillian Lowenfels Criticism Award. *Offered by:* Before Columbus Foundation. *Winner:* Not awarded in 2019.

J. Anthony Lukas Awards. For nonfiction writing that demonstrates literary grace, serious research, and concern for an important aspect of American social or political life. *Offered by:* Columbia University Graduate School of Journalism and the Nieman Foundation for Journalism at Harvard. *Winners:* (Lukas Book Prize, $10,000) Shane Bauer for *American Prison: A Reporter's Undercover Journey into the Business of Punishment* (Penguin Publishing Group); (Mark Lynton History Prize, $10,000) (tie) Andrew Delbanco for *The War Before the War: Fugitive Slaves and the Struggle for America's Soul from the Revolution to the Civil War* (Penguin) and Jeffrey C. Stewart for *The New Negro: The Life of Alain Locke* (Oxford University Press); (Work-in-Progress Award, $30,000) (tie) Maurice Chammah for *Let the Lord Sort Them: Texas and the Death Penalty's Rise and Fall in America* (Crown) and Steven Dudley for *Mara: The Making of the MS13* (Hanover Square Press).

Macavity Awards. For excellence in mystery writing. *Offered by:* Mystery Readers International. *Winners:* (mystery novel) Lou Berney for *November Road* (William Morrow); (first mystery) John Copenhaver for *Dodging and Burning* (Pegasus Books); (nonfiction) Sarah Weinman for *The Real Lolita: The Kidnapping of Sally Horner and the Novel That Scandalized the World* (HarperCollins); (short story) Art Taylor for "English 398: Fiction Workshop" in *Ellery Queen's Mystery Magazine, July/August 2018*; (Sue Feder Historical Mystery Award) Sujata Massey for *The Widows of Malabar Hill* (Soho Crime).

McKitterick Prize (United Kingdom) (£4,000). To an author over the age of 40 for a first novel, published or unpublished. *Winner:* Kelleigh Greenberg-Jephcott for *Swan Song* (Hutchinson).

Man Booker International Prize (United Kingdom) (£60,000). To the author and translator of a work translated into English. *Offered by:* Man Group. *Winner:* Jokha Alharthi for *Celestial Bodies*, translated by Marilyn Booth (Sandstone Press).

Man Booker Prize for Fiction (United Kingdom) (£50,000). For the best novel written in English by a Commonwealth author. *Offered by:* Booktrust and the Man Group. *Winners:* (tie) Margaret Atwood for *The Testaments* (Chatto & Windus) and Bernardine Evaristo for *Girl, Woman, Other* (Hamish Hamilton).

Lenore Marshall Poetry Prize ($25,000). For an outstanding book of poems published in the United States. *Offered by:* Academy of American Poets. *Winner:* Kyle Dargan for *Anagnorisis* (TriQuarterly/Northwestern UP).

Somerset Maugham Awards (United Kingdom) (£2,500). For works in any genre except drama by a writer under the age of 35, to enable young writers to enrich their work by gaining experience of foreign countries. *Winners:* Raymond Antrobus for *The Perseverance* (Penned in the Margins); Damian Le Bas for *The Stopping Places: A Journey Through Gypsy Britain* (Vintage); Phoebe Power for *Shrines of Upper Austria* (Carcanet Press); and Nell Stevens for *Mrs Gaskell and Me: Two Women, Two Love Stories, Two Centuries Apart* (Picador).

Addison M. Metcalf Award in Literature ($2,000). Awarded biennially in alternation with the Addison M. Metcalf Award in Art. *Winner (2019):* Aracelis Girmay.

Vicky Metcalf Award for Literature for Young People (C$25,000) (Canada). To a Canadian writer of children's literature for a body of work. *Offered by:* Writers' Trust of Canada. *Sponsor:* Metcalf Foundation. *Winner:* Susin Nielsen.

Midwest Booksellers Choice Awards. *Offered by:* Midwest Independent Booksellers Association. *Winners:* (fiction) Rebecca Makkai for *The Great Believers* (Viking); (nonfiction) Sarah Smarsh for *Heartland: A Memoir of Working Hard and Being Broke in the Richest Country on Earth* (Scribner); (poetry) Heid E. Erdrich (ed.), *New Poets of Native Nations* (Graywolf Press); (young adult and middle grade) Adib Khorram for *Darius the Great Is Not Okay* (Dial Books); (children's picture book) Mary Casanova (writer) and Nick Wroblewski (illustrator) for *Hush Hush, Forest* (University of Minnesota Press).

William C. Morris YA Debut Award. To honor a debut book published by a first-time author writing for teens and celebrating impressive new voices in young adult literature. *Offered by:* American Library Association, Young Adult Library Services Association. *Donor:* William C. Morris Endowment. *Winner:* Adib Khorram for *Darius the Great Is Not Okay* (Dial Books).

Mythopoeic Fantasy Awards. To recognize fantasy or mythic literature for children and adults that best exemplifies the spirit of the Inklings, a group of fantasy writers that includes J. R. R. Tolkien, C. S. Lewis, and Charles Williams. *Offered by:* Mythopoeic Society. *Winners:* (adult literature) Naomi Novik for *Spinning Silver* (Del Rey); (children's literature) Wendy Mass and Rebecca Stead for *Bob* (Feiwel and Friends); (Mythopoeic Scholarship Award in Inklings Studies) Verlyn Flieger for *There Would Always Be a Fairy Tale: More Essays on Tolkien* (Kent State University Press); (Mythopoeic Scholarship Award in Myth and Fantasy Studies) Dimitra Fimi for *Celtic Myth in Contemporary Children's Fantasy: Idealization, Identity, Ideology* (Palgrave Macmillan).

National Book Awards. To celebrate the best in American literature. *Offered by:* National Book Foundation. *Winners:* (fiction) Susan Choi for *Trust Exercise* (Henry Holt); (nonfiction) Sarah M. Broom, *The Yellow House* (Grove Press); (poetry) Arthur Sze for *Sight Lines* (Copper Canyon Press); (translated literature) László Krasznahorkai for *Baron Wenckheim's Homecoming*, translated by Ottilie Mulzet (New Directions); (young people's literature) Martin Sandler for *1919: The Year That Changed America* (Bloomsbury Children's Books).

National Book Critics Circle Awards. For literary excellence. *Offered by:* National Book Critics Circle. *Winners:* (fiction) Edwidge Danticat for *Everything Inside* (Knopf); (nonfiction) Patrick Radden Keefe for *Say Nothing: A True Story of Murder and Memory in Northern Ireland* (Doubleday); (biography) Josh Levin for *The Queen: The Forgotten Life Behind an American Myth* (Little, Brown); (autobiography) Chanel Miller for *Know My Name: A Memoir* (Viking); Morgan Parker for *Magical Negro:*

Poems (Tin House) (criticism) Saidiya Hartman for *Wayward Lives, Beautiful Experiments: Intimate Histories of Social Upheaval* (W. W. Norton); (John Leonard Prize) Sarah M. Broom for *The Yellow House: A Memoir* (Grove); (Nona Balakian Citation for Excellence in Reviewing) Katy Waldman; (Ivan Sandrof Lifetime Achievement Award) Naomi Shihab Nye.

National Book Foundation Literarian Award for Outstanding Service to the American Literary Community. *Offered by:* National Book Foundation. *Winner:* Ann Patchett.

National Book Foundation Medal for Distinguished Contribution to American Letters ($10,000). To a person who has enriched the nation's literary heritage over a life of service or corpus of work. *Offered by:* National Book Foundation. *Winner:* Edmund White.

National Translation Awards ($5,000). To honor translators whose work has made a valuable contribution to literary translation into English. *Offered by:* American Literary Translators Association. *Winners:* (prose) Karen Emmerich, translator from Greek, for *What's Left of the Night* by Ersi Sotriopoulos (New Vessel Press); (poetry) Bill Johnston, translator from Polish, for *Pan Tadeusz: The Last Foray in Lithuania* by Adam Mickiewicz (Archipelago Books).

Nebula Awards. For science fiction writing. *Offered by:* Science Fiction and Fantasy Writers of America (SFWA). *Winners:* (novel) Mary Robinette Kowal for *The Calculating Stars* (Tor); (novella) Aliette de Bodard for "The Tea Master and the Detective" (Subterranean Press); (novelette) Brooke Bolander for "The Only Harmless Great Thing" (Tor.com); (short story) P. Djèlí Clark for "The Secret Lives of the Nine Negro Teeth of George Washington" (in *Fireside Magazine*); (Ray Bradbury Award for dramatic presentation) Phil Lord and Rodney Rothman (screenplay) for *Spider-Man: Into the Spider-Verse* (Sony); (Andre Norton Award for young adult science fiction and fantasy) Adeyemi for *Children of Blood and Bone* (Henry Holt).

John Newbery Medal. For the most distinguished contribution to literature for children. *Offered by:* American Library Association, Association for Library Service to Children. *Winner:* Meg Medina for *Merci Suarez Changes Gears* (Candlewick Press).

Nibbies (United Kingdom). See British Book Awards.

Nimrod Literary Awards ($2,000 plus publication). *Offered by: Nimrod International Journal of Prose and Poetry. Winners:* (Pablo Neruda Prize in Poetry) Robert Thomas for "Negligee and Hatchet: A Sonnet Crown"; (Katherine Anne Porter Prize in Fiction) Jonathan Wei for "Capybara."

Nobel Prize in Literature (Sweden). For the total literary output of a distinguished career. *Offered by:* Swedish Academy. *Winner:* Peter Handke.

Eli M. Oboler Memorial Award. Given biennially to an author of a published work in English or in English translation dealing with issues, events, questions, or controversies in the area of intellectual freedom. *Offered by:* Intellectual Freedom Round Table, American Library Association. *Winners (2018):* Robert P. Doyle for *Banned Books: Defending Our Freedom to Read* (Office for Intellectual Freedom, American Library Association).

Flannery O'Connor Awards for Short Fiction. For collections of short fiction. *Offered by:* University of Georgia Press. *Winners:* Patrick Earl Ryan for *If We Were Electric* (University of Georgia Press).

Oddest Book Title of the Year Award. See Bookseller/Diagram Prize for Oddest Title of the Year.

Scott O'Dell Award for Historical Fiction ($5,000). *Offered by: Bulletin of the Center for Children's Books,* University of Chicago. *Winner:* Lesa Cline-Ransome for *Finding Langston* (Holiday House).

Odyssey Award. To the producer of the best audiobook for children and/or young adults available in English in the United States. *Sponsors:* American Library Association, ALSC / Booklist / YALSA. *Winner:* Macmillan Audio for *Sadie* by Courtney Summers, narrated by Rebecca Soler, Fred Berman, Dan Bittner, Gabra Zackman, and more.

Seán Ó Faoláin Short Story Competition (€2,000 and publication in the literary journal *Southword*). *Offered by:* Munster Literature Centre, Cork, Ireland. *Winner:* Mike Allen for "Come Closer."

Dayne Ogilvie Prize (C$4,000) (Canada). To an emerging Canadian writer from the LGBT community who demonstrates promise through a body of quality work. *Offered by:* Writers' Trust of Canada. *Winner:* Lindsay Nixon.

Orbis Pictus Award for Outstanding Nonfiction for Children. *Offered by:* National Council of Teachers of English. *Winner:* Sandra Neil Wallace for *Between the Lines: How Ernie Barnes Went from the Football Field to the Art Gallery*, illustrated by Bryan Collier (Simon & Schuster).

Oxford-Weidenfeld Translation Prize. *Winners:* Celia Hawkesworth for her translation from Serbo-Croatian of *Omer Pasha Latas* by Ivo Andric (New York Review of Books).

PEN Award for Poetry in Translation ($3,000). For a book-length translation of poetry from any language into English, published in the United States. *Offered by:* PEN American Center. *Winner:* Richard Sieburth for his translation from French of *A Certain Plume* by Henri Michaux (New York Review of Books).

PEN/Saul Bellow Award for Achievement in American Fiction ($25,000). Awarded biennially to a distinguished living American author of fiction. *Offered by:* PEN American Center. *Winner (2018):* Edmund White.

PEN/Bellwether Prize for Socially Engaged Fiction ($25,000). Awarded biennially to the author of a previously unpublished novel that addresses issues of social justice and the impact of culture and politics on human relationships. *Founder:* Barbara Kingsolver. *Winner (2018):* Katherine Seligman for *If You Knew* (Algonquin).

PEN Beyond Margins Awards. See PEN Open Book Awards.

PEN/Robert W. Bingham Prize ($25,000). To a writer whose first novel or short story collection represents distinguished literary achievement and suggests great promise. *Offered by:* PEN American Center. *Winner:* Will Mackin for *Bring Out the Dog* (Random House).

PEN/Robert J. Dau Short Story Prize for Emerging Writers ($2,000 to 12 writers). To recognize 12 emerging fiction writers for their debut short stories. *Offered by:* PEN American Center. *Winners:* Sarah Curry for "The Rickies" in *Nimrod Journal*; Laura Freudig for "Mother and Child" in *The Sun*; Doug Henderson for "The Manga Artist" in *The Iowa Review*; Enyeribe Ibegwan for "Good Hope" in *Auburn Avenue*; Pingmei Lan for "Cicadas and the Dead Chairman" in *Epiphany*; John Paul Infante for "Without a Big One" in *Kweli Journal*; Tamiko Beyer for "Last Days, Part 1" in *Black Warrior Review*; Marilyn Manolakas for "Tornado Season" in *Alaska Quarterly Review*; Erin Singer for "Bad Northern Women" in *Conjunctions*; Kelsey Peterson for "The Unsent Letters of Blaise and Jacqueline Pascal" in *Conjunctions*; Jade Jones for "Today, You're a Black Revolutionary" in *The Rumpus*; A. B. Young for "Vain Beasts" in *Lady Churchill's Rosebud Wristlet*.

PEN/Diamonstein-Spielvogel Award for the Art of the Essay ($10,000). For a book of essays by a single author that best exemplifies the dignity and esteem of the essay form. *Winner:* Michelle Tea for *Against Memoir* (Feminist Press).

PEN/ESPN Award for Literary Sports Writing ($5,000). To honor a nonfiction book on the subject of sports. *Winner:* Rowan Ricardo Phillips for *The Circuit: A Tennis Odyssey* (Farrar, Straus and Giroux).

PEN/ESPN Lifetime Achievement Award for Literary Sports Writing ($5,000). For a writer whose body of work represents an exceptional contribution to the field. *Winner:* Jackie MacMullan.

PEN/Faulkner Award for Fiction ($15,000). To honor the year's best work of fiction published by an American. *Winner:* Azareen Van der Vliet Oloomi for *Call Me Zebra* (Houghton Mifflin Harcourt).

PEN/John Kenneth Galbraith Award for Nonfiction ($10,000). Given biennially for a distinguished book of general nonfiction. *Offered by:* PEN American Center. *Winner:* Bernice Yeung for *In a Day's Work* (The New Press).

PEN Grant for the English Translation of Italian Literature ($5,000). *Winner:* Not awarded in 2019.

PEN/Heim Translation Fund Grants ($2,000–$4,000). To support the translation of book-length works of fiction, creative nonfiction, poetry, or drama that have not previously appeared in English or have appeared only in an egregiously flawed translation. *Winners:*

Bruna Dantas Lobato, Hope Campbell-Gustafson, Stephen Epstein, Misha Hoekstra, Lucas Klein, Simon Leser, Emma Lloyd, Ottilie Mulzet, Catherine Nelson, Julia Powers, Lara Vergnaud.

PEN/Ernest Hemingway Foundation Award. For a distinguished work of first fiction by an American. *Offered by:* PEN New England. *Winner:* Tommy Orange for *There There* (Knopf).

PEN/O. Henry Prize. For short stories of exceptional merit, in English, published in U.S. and Canadian magazines. *Winners:* Tessa Hadley for "Funny Little Snake" in *The New Yorker*; John Keeble for "Synchronicity" in *Harper's Magazine*; Moira McCavana for "No Spanish" in *Harvard Review*; Rachel Kondo for "Girl of Few Seasons" in *Ploughshares Solos*; Sarah Shun-lien Bynum for "Julia and Sunny" in *Ploughshares*; Stephanie Reents for "Unstuck" in *Witness*; Alexia Arthurs for "Mermaid River" in *The Sewanee Review*; Valerie O'Riordan for "Bad Girl" in *LitMag*; Patricia Engel for "Aguacero" in *Kenyon Review*; Kenan Orhan for "Soma" in *The Massachusetts Review*; Sarah Hall for "Goodnight Nobody" in *One Story*; Bryan Washington for "610 North, 610 West" in *Tin House*; Isabella Hammad for "Mr. Can'aan" in *The Paris Review*; Weike Wang for "Omakase" in *The New Yorker*; Caoilinn Hughes for "Prime" in *Granta.com*; Souvankham Thammavongsa for "Slingshot" in *Harper's Magazine*; Liza Ward for "The Shrew Tree" in *Zyzzyva*; Doua Thao for "Flowers for America" in *Fiction*; Alexander MacLeod for "Lagomorph" in *Granta*; John Edgar Wideman for "Maps and Ledgers" in *Harper's Magazine.*

PEN/Nora Magid Award ($2,500). Awarded biennially to honor a magazine editor who has contributed significantly to the excellence of the publication he or she edits. *Winners (2019):* Alexandra Watson for *Apogee*.

PEN/Malamud Award. To recognize a body of work that demonstrates excellence in the art of short fiction. *Winner:* John Edgar Wideman.

PEN/Ralph Manheim Medal for Translation. Given triennially to a translator whose career has demonstrated a commitment to excellence. *Winner (2018):* Barbara Harshav.

PEN/Nabokov Award for Achievement in International Literature ($50,000). To a writer of any genre and of any nationality for their exceptional body of work. *Winner:* Sandra Cisneros.

PEN/Phyllis Naylor Working Writer Fellowship ($5,000). To a published author of children's or young adult fiction to aid in completing a book-length work in progress. *Offered by:* PEN American Center. *Winner:* Noni Carter for *Womb Talk* (work in progress).

PEN New England Awards. For works of fiction, nonfiction, and poetry by New England writers or with New England topics or settings. *Winners:* Not awarded in 2019.

PEN New England Henry David Thoreau Prize for Literary Excellence in Nature Writing. *Winner:* Mary Oliver.

PEN Open Book Award (formerly PEN Beyond Margins Award) ($5,000). For book-length writings by authors of color, published in the United States during the current calendar year. *Offered by:* PEN American Center. *Winner:* Nafissa Thompson-Spires for *Heads of the Colored People* (Atria).

PEN/Joyce Osterweil Award for Poetry ($5,000). A biennial award given in odd-numbered years to recognize a new and emerging American poet. *Offered by:* PEN American Center. *Winner (2019):* Jonah Mixon-Webster.

PEN/Laura Pels Foundation Awards for Drama ($7,500 and $2,500). To recognize a master American dramatist, an American playwright in midcareer, and an emerging American playwright. *Offered by:* PEN American Center. *Winners:* (master) Not awarded in 2019; (midcareer) Larissa FastHorse; (emerging) Not awarded in 2019.

PEN/Jean Stein Book Award ($75,000). To recognize a book-length work of any genre for its originality, merit, and impact. *Winner:* Nana Kwame Adjei-Brenyah for *Friday Black* (Mariner Books).

PEN/Jean Stein Grant for Literary Oral History ($10,000). For a literary work of nonfiction that uses oral history to illuminate an event, individual, place, or movement. *Winner:* Loida Maritza Pérez for *Beyond the Pale* (work-in-progress).

PEN Translation Prize ($3,000). To promote the publication and reception of translated world literature in English. *Winner:* Martin Aitken for his translation from the Norweigan of *Love* by Hanne Ørstavik (Archipelago Books).

PEN/Edward and Lily Tuck Award for Paraguayan Literature ($3,000 author and $3,000 to translator). Given in even-numbered years to the living author of a major work of Paraguayan literature. *Winner (2018):* Javier Viveros for *Fantasmario*, illustrated by Charles DaPonte (Tiempo Ediciones & Contenidos).

PEN/Voelcker Award for Poetry. Given in even-numbered years to an American poet at the height of his or her powers. *Offered by:* PEN American Center. *Winner (2018):* Kamau Brathwaite.

PEN/Jacqueline Bograd Weld Award for Biography ($5,000). To the author of a distinguished biography published in the United States during the previous calendar year. *Offered by:* PEN American Center. *Winner:* Imani Perry for *Looking for Lorraine: The Radiant and Radical Life of Lorraine Hansberry* (Beacon Press).

PEN/E. O. Wilson Literary Science Writing Award ($10,000). For a book of literary nonfiction on the subject of the physical and biological sciences. *Winner:* Ben Goldfarb for *Eager: The Surprising, Secret Life of Beavers and Why They Matter* (Chelsea Green).

Maxwell E. Perkins Award. To honor an editor, publisher, or agent who has discovered, nurtured, and championed writers of fiction in the United States. *Offered by:* Center for Fiction, Mercantile Library of New York. *Winner:* Lynn Nesbit.

Aliki Perroti and Seth Frank Most Promising Young Poet Award ($1,000). For a student poet 23 years old or younger. *Offered by:* Academy of American Poets. *Winner:* Jonathan Teklit for "Black Mythology."

Phoenix Awards. To the authors of English-language children's books that failed to win a major award at the time of publication 20 years earlier. *Winner:* Louise Erdrich for *The Birchbark House* (Hyperion Books for Children).

Edgar Allan Poe Awards. For outstanding mystery, suspense, and crime writing. *Offered by:* Mystery Writers of America. *Winners:* (novel) Walter Mosley for *Down the River Unto the Sea* (Mulholland Books); (first novel) James A. McLaughlin for *Bearskin* (Ecco Press); (paperback original) Alison Gaylin for *If I Die Tonight* (William Morrow); (fact crime) Robert W. Fieseler for *Tinderbox: The Untold Story of the Up Stairs Lounge Fire and the Rise of Gay Liberation* (Liveright); (critical/biographical) Leslie S. Klinger for *Classic American Crime Fiction of the 1920s* (Pegasus Books); (short story) Art Taylor for "English 398: Fiction Workshop" in *Ellery Queen Mystery Magazine* (Dell Magazines); (juvenile) Pete Hautman for *Otherwood* (Candlewick Press); (young adult) Courtney Summers for *Sadie* (Wednesday Books); (television episode) Matthew Weiner and Donald Joh (teleplay) for "The One That Holds Everything" in *The Romanoffs* (Amazon Prime Video); (Robert L. Fish Memorial Award) Nancy Novick for "How Does He Die This Time?" in *Ellery Queen Mystery Magazine* (Dell Magazines); (grand master) Martin Cruz Smith; (Raven Award) Marilyn Stasio, *The New York Times*; (Ellery Queen Award) Linda Landrigan, *Alfred Hitchcock Mystery Magazine*; (Mary Higgins Clark Award) Sujata Massey for *The Widows of Malabar Hill* (Soho Crime); (Sue Grafton Memorial Award) Sara Paretsky for *Shell Game* (William Morrow).

Poets Out Loud Prize ($1,000 and publication by Fordham University Press). For a book-length poetry collection. *Sponsor:* Fordham University. *Winners:* S. Brook Corfman for "Luxury, Blue Lace"; (editor's prize) Jose Felipe Alvergue for "gist : rift: drift : bloom."

Katherine Anne Porter Award ($20,000). Awarded biennially to a prose writer of demonstrated achievement. *Offered by:* American Academy of Arts and Letters. *Winner (2018):* Noy Holland.

Michael L. Printz Award. For excellence in literature for young adults. *Offered by:* American Library Association, Young Adult Library Services Association. *Winner*: Elizabeth Acevedo for *The Poet X* (HarperTeen/HarperCollins).

V. S. Pritchett Short Story Prize (United Kingdom) (£1,000). For a previously unpublished short story. *Offered by:* Royal Society of Literature. *Winner:* Ursula Brunetti for "Beetleboy."

Pritzker Military Library Literature Award ($100,000). To recognize a living author for a body of work that has profoundly enriched the public understanding of American military history. *Sponsor:* Tawani Foundation. *Winner:* Dr. John Morrow, Jr.

Prix Aurora Awards (Canada). For science fiction. *Offered by:* Canadian SF & Fantasy Association. *Winners:* (novel) Kate Heartfield for *Armed in Her Fashion* (ChiZine Publications); (young adult novel) Fonda Lee for *Cross Fire: An Exo Novel* (Scholastic); (short fiction) Kelly Robson for "Gods, Monsters, and the Lucky Peach" (Tor.com); (related work) Dominik Parisien and Elsa Sjunneson-Henry (eds.) for "Disabled People Destroy Science Fiction" (*Uncanny Magazine*); (graphic novel) Kari Maaren for *It Never Rains* (Webcomic); (poem/song) Sarah Tolmie for "Ursula Le Guin in the Underworld" in *On Spec*, issue 107 vol. 28.4; (artist) Samantha M. Beiko; (visual presentation) *Deadpool 2*.

Prix Goncourt (France). For "the best imaginary prose work of the year." *Offered by:* Société des Gens des Lettres. *Winner:* Jean-Paul Dubois for *Tous les hommes n'habitent pas le monde de la même façon*.

PROSE Awards. For outstanding professional and scholarly works. *Offered by:* Association of American Publishers. *Winners*: (biological and life sciences) Pantheon Books, a division of Penguin Random House, for *Who We Are and How We Got Here* by David Reich; (humanities) Oxford University Press for *Down Girl: The Logic of Misogyny* by Kate Manne; (physical sciences and mathematics) AGU and Wiley for *GeoHealth*, Gabriel Philippelli (editor-in-chief); (social sciences) Oxford University Press for *Cyberwar: How Russian Hackers and Trolls Helped Elect a President* by Kathleen Hall Jamieson.

Pulitzer Prizes in Letters ($10,000). To honor distinguished work dealing preferably with American themes. *Offered by:* Columbia University Graduate School of Journalism. *Winners:* (fiction) Richard Powers for *The Overstory* (W. W. Norton and Company); (drama) Jackie Sibblies Drury for *Fairview*; (history) David W. Blight for *Frederick Douglass: Prophet of Freedom* (Simon & Schuster); (biography/autobiography) Jeffrey C. Stewart for *The New Negro: The Life of Alain Locke* (Oxford University Press); (poetry) Forrest Gander for *Be With* (New Directions); (general nonfiction) Eliza Griswold, for *Amity and Prosperity: One Family and the Fracturing of America* (Farrar, Straus and Giroux).

Raiziss / De Palchi Translation Award ($10,000 book award and a $25,000 fellowship, awarded in alternate years). For a translation into English of a significant work of modern Italian poetry by a living translator. *Offered by:* Academy of American Poets. *Winner:* (fellowship) Will Schutt for *Selected Poems by Fabio Pusterla* (*Sewanee Review*).

RBC Bronwen Wallace Award for Emerging Writers (C$10,000) (Canada). For writers under the age of 35 who are unpublished in book form; award alternates each year between poetry and short fiction. *Offered by:* Writers' Trust of Canada. *Sponsor:* Royal Bank of Canada. *Winner:* John Elizabeth Stintzi.

Arthur Rense Poetry Prize ($20,000). Awarded triennially to an exceptional poet. *Offered by:* American Academy of Arts and Letters. *Winner (2017):* August Kleinzahler.

Harold U. Ribalow Prize. For Jewish fiction published in English. *Sponsor: Hadassah* magazine. *Winner:* Michael Lukas for *The Last Watchman of Old Cairo* (Spiegel & Grau).

Rita Awards. *Offered by:* Romance Writers of America. *Winners:* (first book) Marie Tremayne for *Lady in Waiting* (Avon Impulse); (short contemporary romance) Teri Wilson for *The Bachelor's Baby Surprise* (Harlequin); (mid-length contemporary romance) Susannah Nix for *Advanced Physical Chemistry* (self-published); (long contemporary romance) Kennedy Ryan for *Long Shot* (self-published); (erotic) Elia Winters for *Three-Way Split* (Entangled Publishing); (long historical) Mia Vincy for *A Wicked Kind of Husband* (self-published); (short historical) Kelly Bowen for *A Duke in the Night* (Grand Central Publishing); (mainstream) Sarah Morgan for *How to Keep a Secret* (Harlequin); (inspirational) Carla Laureano for *The Saturday Night Supper Club* (Tyndale House); (paranormal) J. R. Ward for *Dearest Ivie* (Ballantine Books); (novella) M. Malone for *Bad Blood* (self-published); (suspense) Elizabeth Dyer for *Fearless* (self-published); (young adult) Nisha Sharma for *My So-Called Bollywood Life* (Crown Books for Young Readers).

Rita Golden Heart Awards. For worthy unpublished romance manuscripts. *Offered by:* Romance Writers of America. *Winners:* (contemporary) Rosie Danan for "*Never Have I Ever*"; (short contemporary) Betsy Gray for "*Love on the Books*"; (historical) Emily Sullivan for "*Tempting the Heiress*"; (mainstream) Melissa Wiesner for "*Everything Comes Back to You*"; (paranormal) Heather Leonard for "*Bless Your Heart and Other Southern Curses*"; (religious or spiritual) Martha Hutchens for "*The Promise of Spring*"; (suspense) Angie Hockman for "The Hustler"; (young adult) Susan Lee for "Dragged!"

Sami Rohr Prize for Jewish Literature ($100,000). For emerging writers of Jewish literature. *Offered by:* Family of Sami Rohr. *Winner:* Michael Lukas for *The Last Watchman of Old Cairo* (Spiegel & Grau).

Rosenthal Family Foundation Award ($10,000). To a young writer of considerable literary talent for a work of fiction. *Offered by:* American Academy of Arts and Letters. *Winner:* Tommy Orange for *There There* (Knopf).

Royal Society of Literature Benson Medal (United Kingdom). To recognize meritorious works in poetry, fiction, history and belles letters, honoring an entire career. The recipient may be someone who is not a writer but has done conspicuous service to literature. *Winner:* Susheila Nasta.

Royal Society of Literature Giles St Aubyn Awards for Non-Fiction (United Kingdom). For first-time writers of nonfiction. *Offered by:* Royal Society of Literature. *Winners:* (£10,000) Harry Davies for *Operation Information* (The Bodley Head); (£5,000) Olive Heffernan for *The High Seas: The Race to Save the Earth's Last Wilderness* (Profile Books); (special commendation) Rebecca Fogg for *Beautiful Trauma* (Granta).

Royal Society of Literature Ondaatje Prize (United Kingdom) (£10,000). For a distinguished work of fiction, nonfiction, or poetry evoking the spirit of a place. *Offered by:* Royal Society of Literature. *Winner:* Aida Edemariam for *The Wife's Tale: A Personal History* (4th Estate).

Saltire Society Scotland Literary Awards. To recognize noteworthy work by writers of Scottish descent or living in Scotland, or by anyone who deals with the work or life of a Scot or with a Scottish problem, event, or situation. *Offered by:* Saltire Society. *Sponsors:* Creative Scotland, the National Library of Scotland, the Scottish Poetry Library, the Scottish Historical Review Trust, Tamdhu Speyside Single Malt Scotch Whisky. *Winners:* (book of the year £5,000, individual categories £2,000) Kirstie Blair for *Working Verse in Victorian Scotland: Poetry, Press, Community* (Oxford University Press); (fiction book of the year) Ewan Morrison for *Nina X* (Fleet); (nonfiction book of the year) Melanie Reid for *The World I Fell Out Of* (Fourth Estate); (research book of the year) Kirstie Blair for *Working Verse in Victorian Scotland: Poetry, Press, Community* (Oxford University Press); (poetry book of the year) Janette Ayachi for *Hand Over Mouth Music* (Pavilion Poetry); (history) Norman H Reid for *Alexander III: 1249–1286, First Among Equals* (published by Birlinn); (first book) (tie) Stephen Rutt for *The Seafarers: A Journey Among Birds* (Elliott & Thompson) and Clare Hunter for *Threads of Life* (Hodder & Stoughton); (lifetime achievement) Alasdair Gray.

Carl Sandburg Literary Awards. *Sponsor:* Chicago Public Library Foundation. *Winner:* George R. R. Martin; (21st Century Award, for significant recent achievement by a Chicago-area writer) Eve Ewing.

Schneider Family Book Awards ($5,000). To honor authors and illustrators for books that embody artistic expressions of the disability experience of children and adolescents. *Offered by:* American Library Association. *Donor:* Katherine Schneider. *Winners:* (young children) Jessica Kensky and Patrick Downes (authors) and Scott Magoon (illustrator) for *Rescue & Jessica: A Life-Changing Friendship* (Candlewick Press); (middle school) Leslie Connor for *The Truth as Told by Mason Buttle* (Katherine Tegen Books); (teen) Mark Oshiro for *Anger Is a Gift* (Tor Teen).

Scotiabank Giller Prize (Canada) (C$100,000 first place, C$10,000 to each of the finalists).

For the best Canadian novel or short story collection written in English. *Offered by:* Giller Prize Foundation and Scotiabank. *Winner:* Ian Williams for *Reproduction* (Random House Canada); (finalists) David Bezmozgis for *Immigrant City* (HarperCollins); Megan Gail Coles for *Small Game Hunting at the Local Coward Gun Club* (House of Anansi Press); Michael Crummey for *The Innocents* (Doubleday Canada); Alix Ohlin for *Dual Citizens* (Knopf); Steven Price for *Lampedusa* (McClelland & Stewart).

Shamus Awards. To honor mysteries featuring independent private investigators. *Offered by:* Private Eye Writers of America. *Winners:* (hardcover novel) Kristen Lepionka for *What You Want to See* (Minotaur Books); (first novel) Katrina Carrasco for *The Best Bad Things* (Farrar, Straus and Giroux); (original paperback) Max Wirestone for *The Questionable Behavior of Dahlia Moss* (Redhook Books); (short story) S. J. Rozan for "Chin Yong-Yun Helps a Fool" in *Ellery Queen's Mystery Magazine*.

Shelley Memorial Award ($6,000 to $9,000). To a poet or poets living in the United States, chosen on the basis of genius and need. *Offered by:* Poetry Society of America. *Winner:* Carl R. Martin.

Robert F. Sibert Medal. For the most distinguished informational book for children. *Offered by:* American Library Association, Association for Library Service to Children. *Winner:* Joyce Sidman for *The Girl Who Drew Butterflies: How Maria Merian's Art Changed Science* (Houghton Mifflin Harcourt).

Society of Authors Traveling Scholarships (United Kingdom) (£2,500). *Winners:* Kathryn Hughes, Damian Le Bas, Nadifa Mohamed, Johny Pitts, Gwendoline Riley.

Spur Awards. *Offered by:* Western Writers of America. *Winners:* Susan Henderson for *The Flicker of Old Dreams* (HarperCollins); (historical novel) G. K. Aalborg for *River of Porcupines* (Five Star Publishing); (traditional novel) Brad Smith for *The Return of Kid Cooper* (Arcade); (historical nonfiction) Brenden W. Rensink for *Native but Foreign: Indigenous Immigrants and Refugees in the North American Borderlands* (Texas A&M University Press); (contemporary nonfiction) Francisco Cantú for *The Line Becomes a River: Dispatches from the Border* (Riverhead Books); (nonfiction biography) Mark J. Nelson for *White Hat: The Military Career of Captain William Philo Clark* (University of Oklahoma Press); (original mass-market paperback novel) Reavis Z. Wortham for *Hawke's War* (Pinnacle); (romance novel) C. K. Crigger for *The Woman Who Built a Bridge* (Wolfpack); (juvenile fiction) Johnny D. Boggs for *Taos Lightning* (Center Point); (juvenile nonfiction) Francie M. Berg for *Buffalo Heartbeats across the Plains: The Last Great Hunts and Saving the Buffalo* (Dakota Buttes Visitors Council); (storyteller—illustrated children's book) Allen Morris Jones for *Montana for Kids: The Story of Our State* (Bangtail Press); (short fiction) Therese Greenwood for "Buck's Last Ride" in *Kill As You Go* (Coffin Hop Press); (short nonfiction) Peter H. Hassrick for "Art, Agency, and Conservation: A Fresh Look at Albert Bierstadt's Vision of the West" (*Montana the Magazine of Western History*); (poem) John D. Nesbitt for "Prairie Center" (R. R. Productions); (song) Mike Blakely for "The Outside Circle" (Quien Sabe Music); (drama script) Chloe Zhao for *The Rider* (Sony); (first nonfiction book) Francisco Cantú for *The Line Becomes a River: Dispatches from the Border* (Riverhead Books); (first novel) Ellen Notbohm for *The River by Starlight* (She Writes Press).

Wallace Stevens Award ($100,000). To recognize outstanding and proven mastery in the art of poetry. *Offered by:* Academy of American Poets. *Winner:* Rita Dove.

Bram Stoker Awards. For superior horror writing. *Offered by:* Horror Writers Association. *Winners (2019):* To be announced. *Winners (2018)*: (novel) Paul Tremblay for *The Cabin at the End of the World* (William Morrow); (first novel) Gwendolyn Kiste for *The Rust Maidens* (Trepidatio Publishing); (young adult novel) Kiersten White for *The Dark Descent of Elizabeth Frankenstein* (Delacorte Press); (graphic novel) Victor LaValle for *Victor LaValle's Destroyer* (BOOM! Studios); (long fiction) Rena Mason for *The Devil's Throat (Hellhole: An Anthology of Subterranean Terror)* (Adrenaline Press); (short fiction) Jess Landry for "Mutter" in *Fantastic Tales of Terror* (Crystal Lake

Publishing); (fiction collection) Eric J. Guignard for *That Which Grows Wild* (Cemetery Dance Publications); (screenplay) Meredith Averill for *The Haunting of Hill House: The Bent-Neck Lady (episode 01:05)* (Amblin Television, Flanagan Film, Paramount Television); (anthology) Ellen Datlow for *The Devil and the Deep: Horror Stories of the Sea* (Night Shade Books); (nonfiction) Joe Mynhardt and Eugene Johnson for *It's Alive: Bringing Your Nightmares to Life* (Crystal Lake Publishing); (poetry) Sara Tantlinger for *The Devil's Dreamland* (Strangehouse Books).

Stonewall Book Awards. *Offered by:* Gay, Lesbian, Bisexual, and Transgender Round Table, American Library Association. *Winners:* (Barbara Gittings Literature Award) Rebecca Makkai for *The Great Believers* (Viking); (Israel Fishman Nonfiction Award) Michael Amherst for *Go the Way Your Blood Beats* (Repeater); (Mike Morgan and Larry Romans Children's and Young Adult Literature Award) Jessica Love for *Julian Is a Mermaid* (Candlewick Press) and Kacen Callender for *Hurricane Child* (Scholastic/Scholastic Press).

Story Prize ($20,000). For a collection of short fiction. *Offered by: Story* magazine. *Winner:* Edwidge Danticat for *Everything Inside* (Knopf).

Flora Stieglitz Straus Awards. For nonfiction books that serve as an inspiration to young readers. *Offered by:* Bank Street College of Education and the Florence M. Miller Memorial Fund. *Winner:* (older readers) Bryan Stevenson for *Just Mercy* (Delacorte Press); (younger readers) Yuyi Morales for *Dreamers* (Holiday House).

Theodore Sturgeon Memorial Award. For the year's best short science fiction. *Offered by:* Gunn Center for the Study of Science Fiction. *Winner:* Annalee Newitz for "When Robot and Crow Saved East St. Louis" (*Slate.com).*

Sunburst Awards for Canadian Literature of the Fantastic (C$1,000). *Winners:* (adult) Andromeda Romano Lax for *Plum Rains* (Penguin Random House Canada); (young adult) Rachel Hartman for *Tess of the Road* (Penguin Random House Canada); (short story) Senaa Ahmad for "The Glow-in-the-Dark Girls" in *Strange Horizons, January 15, 2018.*

Sunday Times Audible Short Story Award (United Kingdom) (£30,000). To an author from any country for an English-language story of 6,000 words or less. *Winner:* Danielle McLaughlin for "A Partial List of the Saved."

Tanizaki Prize (Japan) (1 million yen, approximately $8,450). For a full-length work of fiction or drama by a professional writer. *Offered by:* Chuokoron-Shinsha, Inc. *Winner:* Not awarded in 2019.

RBC Taylor Prize (formerly the Charles Taylor Prize for Literary Nonfiction) (Canada) (C$25,000). To honor a book of creative nonfiction widely available in Canada and written by a Canadian citizen or landed immigrant. *Offered by:* Charles Taylor Foundation. *Winner:* Kate Harris for *Lands of Lost Borders: Out of Bounds on the Silk Roads* (Vintage Canada).

Sydney Taylor Book Awards. For a distinguished contribution to Jewish children's literature. *Offered by:* Association of Jewish Libraries. *Winners:* (younger readers) Emily Jenkins (author) and Paul O. Zelinsky (illustrator) for *All-of-a-Kind Family Hanukkah* (Schwartz & Wade); (older readers) Jonathan Auxier for *Sweep: The Story of a Girl and Her Monster* (Amulet); (teen readers) Vesper Stamper for *What the Night Sings* (Alfred A. Knopf).

Sydney Taylor Manuscript Award ($1,000). For the best fiction manuscript appropriate for readers ages 8–13, both Jewish and non-Jewish, revealing positive aspects of Jewish life, and written by an unpublished author. *Winner:* Jessica Littman for *A Corner of the World.*

Theatre Library Association Award. See Richard Wall Memorial Award.

Dylan Thomas Prize (United Kingdom) (£30,000). For a published or produced literary work in the English language, written by an author under 30. *Offered by:* Swansea University. *Winner:* Guy Gunaratne for *In Our Mad and Furious City* (Tinder Press).

Thriller Awards. *Offered by:* International Thriller Writers. *Winners:* (hardcover novel) Jennifer Hillier for *Jar of Hearts* (Minotaur Books); (first novel) C. J. Tudo for *The Chalk Man* (Crown); (paperback original)

Jane Harper for *The Lost Man* (Pan Macmillan Australia); (short story) Helen Smith for "Nana" in *Killer Women: Crime Club Anthology #2* (Killer Women, Ltd.); (young adult) Teri Bailey Black for *Girl at the Grave* (Tor Teen); (e-book original novel) Alan Orloff for *Pray for the Innocent* (Kindle Press); (master) John Sandford; (Silver Bullet) Harlan Coben; (legend) Margaret Marbury.

Thurber Prize for American Humor ($5,000). For a humorous book of fiction or nonfiction. *Offered by:* Thurber House. *Winner:* Simon Rich for *Hits and Misses* (Little, Brown and Company).

Tom-Gallon Trust Award (United Kingdom) (£1,000). For a short story. *Offered by:* Society of Authors. *Sponsor:* Authors' Licensing and Collecting Society. *Winner:* Dima Alzayat for "Once We Were Syrians."

Betty Trask Prize and Awards (United Kingdom). To Commonwealth writers under the age of 35 for "romantic or traditional" first novels. *Offered by:* Society of Authors. *Winners:* (Betty Trask Prize, £10,000) James Clarke for *The Litten Path* (Salt); (Betty Trask Awards, £2,700) Samuel Fisher for *The Chameleon* (Salt); Imogen Hermes Gowar for *The Mermaid and Mrs. Hancock* (Harvill Secker); Ruqaya Izzidien for *The Watermelon Boys* (Hoopoe); Daisy Lafarge for *Paul*; Rebecca Ley for *Sweet Fruit, Sour Land* (Sandstone Press); Sophie Mackintosh for *The Water Cure* (Hamish Hamilton).

Kate Tufts Discovery Award ($10,000). For a first or very early book of poetry by an emerging poet. *Offered by:* Claremont Graduate University. *Winner:* Diana Khoi Nguyen for *Ghost Of* (Omnidawn Publishing).

Kingsley Tufts Poetry Award ($100,000). For a book of poetry by a midcareer poet. *Offered by:* Claremont Graduate School. *Winner:* Dawn Lundy Martin for *Good Stock Strange Blood* (Coffee House Press).

21st Century Award. To honor recent achievement in writing by an author with ties to Chicago. See Carl Sandburg Literary Awards.

UKLA Children's Book Awards (United Kingdom). Sponsor: United Kingdom Literacy Association. *Winners:* (ages 3–6) Morag Hood for *I Am Bat* (Two Hoots); (ages 7–11) Katherine Rundell for *The Explorer, illustrated by Hannah Horn* (Bloomsbury); (ages 12–16) Jason Reynolds for *Long Way Down, illustrated by Chris Priestley* (Faber).

Ungar German Translation Award ($1,000). Awarded biennially for a distinguished literary translation from German into English that has been published in the United States. *Offered by:* American Translators Association. *Winner (2019):* Tim Mohr for his translation of *Sand* by Wolfgang Herrndorf (New York Review Books Classics).

John Updike Award ($10,000). Biennial prize to a writer in midcareer whose work has demonstrated consistent excellence. *Offered by:* American Academy of Arts and Letters. *Winner (2019):* D. A. Powell.

VCU/Cabell First Novelist Award ($5,000). For a first novel published in the previous year. *Offered by:* Virginia Commonwealth University. *Winner:* Ling Ma for *Severance* (Farrar, Straus and Giroux).

Harold D. Vursell Memorial Award ($20,000). To a writer whose work merits recognition for the quality of its prose style. *Offered by:* American Academy of Arts and Letters. *Winner:* John Keene.

Amelia Elizabeth Walden Award ($5,000). To honor a book relevant to adolescents that has enjoyed a wide teenage audience. *Sponsor:* Assembly on Literature for Adolescents, National Council of Teachers of English. *Winner:* Elizabeth Acevedo for *The Poet X* (HarperTeen/HarperCollins).

Richard Wall Memorial Award (formerly the Theatre Library Association Award). To honor an English-language book of exceptional scholarship in the field of recorded performance, including motion pictures, television, and radio. *Offered by:* Theatre Library Association. *Winner:* Maya Montanez Smukler for *Liberating Hollywood: Women Directors and the Feminist Reform of 1970s American Cinema* (Rutgers University Press).

George Washington Book Prize ($50,000). To recognize an important new book about America's founding era. *Offered by:* Washington College and the Gilder Lehrman Institute of American History. *Winner:* Colin Calloway for *The Indian World of George Washington: The First President, the First Americans, and the Birth of the Nation* (Oxford University Press).

Hilary Weston Writers' Trust Prize for Nonfiction (C$60,000) (Canada). *Offered by:* Writers' Trust of Canada. *Winner:* Jenny Heijun Wills for *Older Sister. Not Necessarily Related* (McClelland & Stewart).

E. B. White Award ($10,000). Biennial award to a writer for achievement in children's literature. *Offered by:* American Academy of Arts and Letters. *Winner (2019):* Katherine Patterson.

E. B. White Read-Aloud Awards. For children's books with particular appeal as read-aloud books. *Offered by:* American Booksellers Association / Association of Booksellers for Children. *Winners:* (picture book) Ryan T. Higgins for *We Don't Eat Our Classmates* (Disney Hyperion); (middle readers) Jewell Parker Rhodes for *Ghost Boys* (Little, Brown Books for Young Readers).

Whiting Writers' Awards ($50,000). For emerging writers of exceptional talent and promise. *Offered by:* Mrs. Giles Whiting Foundation. *Winners:* (poetry) Kayleb Rae Candrilli, Tyree Daye, and Vanessa Angélica Villarreal; (fiction) Hernan Diaz, Nafissa Thompson-Spires, Merritt Tierce; (nonfiction) Terese Marie Mailhot and Nadia Owusu; (drama) Michael R. Jackson and Lauren Yee.

Walt Whitman Award ($5,000). To a U.S. poet who has not published a book of poems in a standard edition. *Offered by:* Academy of American Poets. *Winner:* Leah Naomi Green for *The More Extravagant Feast* (Graywolf Press).

Richard Wilbur Award ($1,000 and publication by University of Evansville Press). For a book-length poetry collection. *Winner:* Jehanne Dubrow for "Simple Machines."

Laura Ingalls Wilder Award. See Children's Literature Legacy Award.

Thornton Wilder Prize for Translation ($20,000). To a practitioner, scholar, or patron who has made a significant contribution to the art of literary translation. *Offered by:* American Academy of Arts and Letters. *Winner (2018):* Bill Porter (aka Red-Pine).

Robert H. Winner Memorial Award ($2,500). To a midcareer poet over 40 who has published no more than one book of poetry. *Offered by:* Poetry Society of America. *Winner:* Nancy Chen Long.

George Wittenborn Memorial Book Awards. To North American art publications that represent the highest standards of content, documentation, layout, and format. *Offered by:* Art Libraries Society of North America (ARLIS/NA). *Winners (2018):* Naomi Beckwith and Valerie Cassel Oliver (eds.) for *Howardena Pindell: What Remains to Be Seen* (DelMonaco Books / Prestel).

Thomas Wolfe Prize and Lecture. To honor writers with distinguished bodies of work. *Offered by:* Thomas Wolfe Society and University of North Carolina at Chapel Hill. *Winner:* Dorothy Allison.

Thomas Wolfe Fiction Prize ($1,000). For a short story that honors Thomas Wolfe. *Offered by:* North Carolina Writers Network. *Winner:* Leslie Kirk Campbell for "City of Angels."

Helen and Kurt Wolff Translator's Prize ($10,000). For an outstanding translation from German into English, published in the United States. *Offered by:* Goethe Institut Inter Nationes, New York. *Winner:* Damion Searls for his translation of *Anniversaries: From the Life of Gesine Cresspahl* by Uwe Johnson (New York Review Books Classics).

Women's Prize for Fiction (United Kingdom) (formerly the Bailey's Women's Prize for Fiction) (£30,000). For the best novel written by a woman and published in the United Kingdom. *Winner:* Tayari Jones for *An American Marriage* (Algonquin Books).

World Fantasy Awards. For outstanding fantasy writing. *Offered by:* World Fantasy Convention. *Winners:* (novel) C. L. Polk for *Witchmark* (Tor.com); (novella) Kij Johnson for *The Privilege of the Happy Ending* (*Clarkesworld*, August 2018); (short fiction) (tie) Mel Kassel for "Ten Deals with the Indigo Snake" (*Lightspeed*, October 2018), and Emma Torzs for "Like a River Loves the Sky" (*Uncanny Magazine*, March–April 2018); (anthology) Irene Gallo (editor) for *Worlds Seen in Passing: The Years of Tor.com Short Fiction* (Tor.com); (collection) Paolo Bacigalupi and Tobias S. Buckell for *The Tangled Lands* (Saga Press / Head of Zeus UK); (best artist) Rovina Cai; (special award, professional) Huw Lewis-Jones for *The Writer's Map: An Atlas of Imaginary Lands* (University of Chicago Press);

(special award, nonprofessional) Scott H. Andrews for *Beneath Ceaseless Skies: Literary Adventure Fantasy*; (lifetime achievement) Hayao Miyazaki; Jack Zipes.

Writers' Trust Engel / Findley Award (C$25,000) (Canada). To a Canadian writer predominantly of fiction, for a body of work. *Offered by:* Writers' Trust of Canada. *Sponsors:* Writers' Trust Board of Directors, Pitblado Family Foundation, and Michael Griesdorf Fund. *Winner:* Rawl Hage.

Writers' Trust Fiction Prize (C$50,000) (Canada). To a Canadian author of a novel or short story collection. *Offered by:* Writers' Trust of Canada. *Winner:* Andre Alexis for *Days by Moonlight* (Coach House Books).

Writers' Trust/McClelland & Stewart Journey Prize (C$10,000) (Canada). To a new, developing Canadian author for a short story first published in a Canadian literary journal during the previous year. *Offered by:* Writers' Trust of Canada. *Sponsor:* McClelland & Stewart. *Winner:* Angelique Lalonde for "Pooka."

Writers' Trust Shaughnessy Cohen Prize for Political Writing (C$25,000) (Canada). For literary nonfiction that captures a political subject of relevance to Canadian readers. *Offered by:* Writers' Trust of Canada. *Winner (2018):* Rachel Giese for *Boys: What It Means to Become a Man* (Seal Press).

YALSA Award for Excellence in Nonfiction. For a work of nonfiction published for young adults (ages 12–18). *Offered by:* American Library Association, Young Adult Library Services Association. *Winner:* Don Brown for *The Unwanted: Stories of the Syrian Refugees* (Houghton Mifflin Harcourt).

Young Lions Fiction Award ($10,000). For a novel or collection of short stories by an American under the age of 35. *Offered by:* Young Lions of the New York Public Library. *Winner:* Ling Ma for *Severance* (Farrar, Straus and Giroux).

Young People's Poet Laureate ($25,000). For lifetime achievement in poetry for children. Honoree holds the title for two years. *Offered by:* Poetry Foundation. *Winner (2019):* Naomi Shihab Nye.

Morton Dauwen Zabel Award ($10,000). Awarded biennially, in rotation, to a progressive and experimental poet, writer of fiction, or critic. *Offered by:* American Academy of Arts and Letters. *Winner (2018):* Elaine Scarry.

Zoetrope Short Fiction Prizes. *Offered by: Zoetrope: All-Story. Winners:* (first, $1,000) Uzma Aslam Khan for "Plum Island"; (second, $500) Steve Trumpter for "You Would Set Your Jaws Upon My Throat"; (third, $250) Katheryn Soleil for "Our Lady of Recreation."

Charlotte Zolotow Award. For outstanding writing in a picture book published in the United States in the previous year. *Offered by:* Cooperative Children's Book Center, University of Wisconsin–Madison. *Winner:* Marla Frazee for *Little Brown* (Beach Lane).

Part 6
Directory of Organizations

Directory of Library and Related Organizations

Networks, Consortia, and Other Cooperative Library Organizations

This list is taken from the current edition of *American Library Directory* (Information Today, Inc.), which includes additional information on member libraries and primary functions of each organization.

United States

Alabama

Alabama Health Libraries Assn., Inc. (AL-HeLa), Lister Hill Lib., Univ. of Alabama, Birmingham 35294-0013. SAN 372-8218. Tel. 205-975-8313, fax 205-934-2230. *Pres.* Errica Evans.

Library Management Network, Inc. (LMN), 255 Grant Street SE, Ste 309, Decatur 35601. SAN 322-3906. Tel. 256-308-2529, fax 256-308-2533. *Secy.* Julia Everett.

Marine Environmental Sciences Consortium, Dauphin Island Sea Laboratory, 101 Bienville Blvd., Dauphin Island 36528. SAN 322-0001. Tel. 251-861-2141, fax 251-861-4646, e-mail disl@disl.org. *Admin. Asst.* Shelley Stevens.

Network of Alabama Academic Libraries, c/o Alabama Commission on Higher Education, Montgomery 36104. SAN 322-4570. Tel. 334-242-2211, fax 334-242-0270. *Exec. Dir.* Sheila Snow-Croft.

Alaska

Alaska Library Network (ALN), P.O. Box 230051, Anchorage 99523-0051. SAN 371-0688. Tel. 907-786-0618, e-mail info@aklib.net. *Exec. Dir.* Steve Rollins.

Arkansas

Northeast Arkansas Hospital Library Consortium, 223 E. Jackson, Jonesboro 72401. SAN 329-529X. Tel. 870-972-1290, fax 870-931-0839. *Dir.* Karen Crosser.

California

49-99 Cooperative Library System, c/o Southern California Lib. Cooperative, 248 E. Foothill Blvd., Suite 101, Monrovia 91016. SAN 301-6218. Tel. 626-359-6111, fax 626-283-5949. *Dir.* Diane R. Satchwell.

Bay Area Library and Information Network (BayNet), 1462 Cedar St., Berkeley 94702. SAN 371-0610. Tel. 415-355-2826, e-mail infobay@baynetlibs.org. *Pres.* Vacant.

Califa, 330 Townsend St., Ste. 133, San Francisco 94107. Tel. 888-239-2289, fax 415-520-0434, e-mail califa@califa.org. *Exec. Dir.* Paula MacKinnon.

Gold Coast Library Network, 3437 Empresa Dr., Suite C, San Luis Obispo 93401-7355. Tel. 805-543-6082, fax 805-543-9487. *Admin. Dir.* Maureen Theobald.

National Network of Libraries of Medicine–Pacific Southwest Region (NN/LM-PSR), Louise M. Darling Biomedical Lib., Los Angeles 90095-1798. SAN 372-8234. Tel. 310-825-1200, fax 310-825-5389, e-mail psr-nnlm@library.ucla.edu. *Dir.* Judy Consales.

Nevada Medical Library Group (NMLG), Barton Memorial Hospital Lib., 2170 South Ave., South Lake Tahoe 96150. SAN 370-0445. Tel. 530-543-5844, fax 530-541-4697. *Senior Exec. Coord.* Laurie Anton.

Northern California Assn. of Law Libraries (NOCALL), 268 Bush St., No. 4006, San Francisco 94104. SAN 323-5777. E-mail admin@nocall.org.

Northern and Central California Psychology Libraries (NCCPL), 2040 Gough St., San Francisco 94109. SAN 371-9006. Tel. 415-771-8055. *Pres.* Scott Hines.

Peninsula Libraries Automated Network (PLAN), 2471 Flores St., San Mateo 94403-4000. SAN 371-5035. Tel. 650-349-5538, fax 650-349-5089. *Dir., Information Technology* Monica Schultz.

San Bernardino, Inyo, Riverside Counties United Library Services (SIRCULS), 555 W. 6th St., San Bernadino 92410. Tel. 909-381-8257, fax 909-888-3171, e-mail ils@inlandlib.org. *Exec. Dir.* Vera Skop.

San Francisco Biomedical Library Network (SFBLN), San Francisco General Hospital UCSF/Barnett-Briggs Medical Lib., 1001 Potrero Ave., Bldg. 30, 1st Fl., San Francisco 94110. SAN 371-2125. Tel. 415-206-6639, e-mail fishbon@ucsfmedctr.org. *Lib. Dir.* Stephen Kiyoi.

Santa Clarita Interlibrary Network (SCILNET), Powell Lib., Santa Clarita 91321. SAN 371-8964. Tel. 661-362-2271, fax 661-362-2719. *Libn.* John Stone.

Serra Cooperative Library System, Serra c/o SCLC, 254 N. Lake Ave., Suite 874, Pasadena 91101. SAN 371-3865. Tel. 626-359-6111. *Dir.* Diane R. Satchwell.

Southern California Library Cooperative (SCLC), 254 N. Lake Ave., Suite 874, Pasadena 91101. SAN 371-3865. Tel. 626-359-6111. *Dir.* Diane R. Satchwell.

Colorado

Colorado Alliance of Research Libraries, 3801 E. Florida Ave., Suite 515, Denver 80210. SAN 322-3760. Tel. 303-759-3399, fax 303-759-3363. *Exec. Dir.* George Machovec.

Colorado Assn. of Law Libraries, P.O. Box 13363, Denver 80201. SAN 322-4325. Tel. 303-492-7535, fax 303-492-2707. *Pres.* Diane Forge Bauersfeld.

Colorado Council of Medical Librarians (CCML), c/o CU Strauss Health Sciences Library, 12950 E. Montview Blvd. A003, Aurora 80045. SAN 370-0755. Tel. 303-724-2124, fax 303-724-2154. *Pres.* Ben Harnke.

Colorado Library Consortium (CLiC), 7400 E. Arapahoe Rd., Suite 75, Centennial 80112. SAN 371-3970. Tel. 303-422-1150, fax 303-431-9752. *Exec. Dir.* Jim Duncan.

Connecticut

Bibliomation, 24 Wooster Ave., Waterbury 06708. Tel. 203-577-4070. *Exec. Dir.* Carl DeMilia.

Connecticut Library Consortium, 234 Court St., Middletown 06457-3304. SAN 322-0389. Tel. 860-344-8777, fax 860-344-9199, e-mail clc@ctlibrarians.org. *Exec. Dir.* Jennifer Keohane.

Council of State Library Agencies in the Northeast (COSLINE), Connecticut State Lib., 231 Capitol Ave., Hartford 06106. SAN 322-0451. Tel. 860-757-6510, fax 860-757-6503. *Exec. Dir.* Timothy Cherubini.

CTW Library Consortium, Olin Memorial Lib., Middletown 06459-6065. SAN 329-4587. Tel. 860-685-3887, fax 860-685-2661. *Libn. for Collaborative Projects* Lorri Huddy.

Hartford Consortium for Higher Education, 31 Pratt St., 4th Fl., Hartford 06103. SAN 322-0443. Tel. 860-702-3801, fax 860-241-1130. *Exec. Dir.* Martin Estey.

Libraries Online, Inc. (LION), 100 Riverview Center, Suite 252, Middletown 06457. SAN 322-3922. Tel. 860-347-1704, fax 860-346-3707. *Exec. Dir.* Alan Hagyard.

Library Connection, Inc., 599 Matianuck Ave., Windsor 06095-3567. Tel. 860-937-8261, fax 860-298-5328. *Exec. Dir.* George Christian.

District of Columbia

Association of Research Libraries, 21 Dupont Circle NW, Suite 800, Washington 20036. Tel. 202-296-2296, fax 202-872-0884. *Exec. Dir.* Mary Lee Kennedy.

Council for Christian Colleges and Universities, 321 8th St. N.E., Washington 20002.

SAN 322-0524. Tel. 202-546-8713, fax 202-546-8913, e-mail council@cccu.org. *Pres.* Shirley V. Hoogstra.

District of Columbia Area Health Science Libraries (DCAHSL). Disbanded 2019.

FEDLINK/Federal Library and Information Network, c/o Federal Lib. and Info. Center Committee, 101 Independence Ave. SE, Washington 20540-4935. SAN 322-0761. Tel. 202-707-4800, fax 202-707-4818, e-mail flicc@loc.gov. *Exec. Dir.* Laurie Neider.

Washington Theological Consortium, 487 Michigan Ave. N.E., Washington 20017-1585. SAN 322-0842. Tel. 202-832-2675, fax 202-526-0818, e-mail wtc@washtheocon.org. *Exec. Dir.* Larry Golemon.

Florida

Florida Library Information Network, R. A. Gray Bldg., State Library and Archives of Florida, Tallahassee 32399-0250. SAN 322-0869. Tel. 850-245-6600, fax 850-245-6744, e-mail library@dos.myflorida.com. *Bureau Chief* Cathy Moloney.

Library and Information Resources Network, 7855 126th Ave. N, Largo 33773. Tel. 727-536-0214, fax 727-530-3126.

Midwest Archives Conference (MAC), 2598 E Sunrise Blvd., Suite 2104, Fort Lauderdale 33304. E-mail membership@midwestarchives.org. *Pres.* Erik Moore.

Northeast Florida Library Information Network (NEFLIN), 2233 Park Ave., Suite 402, Orange Park 32073. Tel. 904-278-5620, fax 904-278-5625, e-mail office@neflin.org. *Exec. Dir.* Brad Ward.

Panhandle Library Access Network (PLAN), Five Miracle Strip Loop, Suite 8, Panama City Beach 32407-3850. SAN 370-047X. Tel. 850-233-9051, fax 850-235-2286. *Exec. Dir.* Charles Mayberry.

SEFLIN/Southeast Florida Library Information Network, Inc, Wimberly Lib., Office 452, Florida Atlantic Univ., 777 Glades Rd., Boca Raton 33431. SAN 370-0666. Tel. 561-208-0984, fax 561-208-0995. *Exec. Dir.* Jennifer Pratt.

Southwest Florida Library Network (SWFLN), 13120 Westlinks Terrace, Unit 3, Fort Myers 33913. Tel. 239-313-6338, fax 239-313-6329. *Exec. Dir.* Luly Castro.

Tampa Bay Library Consortium, Inc., 4042 Park Oaks Blvd., Suite 430, Tampa 33619. SAN 322-371X. Tel. 813-622-8252, fax 813-628-4425. *Exec. Dir.* Jim Walther.

Tampa Bay Medical Library Network, Medical Lib., Department 7660, 501 Sixth Ave. South, Saint Petersburg 33701. SAN 322-0885. Tel. 727-767-8557. *Chair* Susan Sharpe.

Georgia

Association of Southeastern Research Libraries (ASERL), c/o Robert W. Woodruff Library, 540 Asbury Circle, Suite 316, Atlanta 30322-1006. SAN 322-1555. Tel. 404-727-0137. *Exec. Dir.* John Burger.

Atlanta Health Science Libraries Consortium, Fran Golding Medical Lib. at Scottish Rite, 1001 Johnson Ferry Rd. NE, Atlanta 30342-1600. Tel. 404-785-2157, fax 404-785-2155. *Pres.* Kate Daniels.

Atlanta Regional Council for Higher Education (ARCHE), 141 E. College Ave., Box 1084, Decatur 30030. SAN 322-0990. Tel. 404-651-2668, fax 404-880-9816, e-mail arche@atlantahighered.org. *Exec. Dir.* Tracey Brantley.

Consortium of Southern Biomedical Libraries (CONBLS), Robert B. Greenblatt, MD Library, 1439 Laney Walker Blvd., Augusta, 30912. SAN 370-7717. Tel. 843-792-8839. *Chair* Brenda Seago.

Georgia Interactive Network for Medical Information (GAIN), c/o Mercer Univ. School of Medicine, 1550 College St., Macon 31207. SAN 370-0577. Tel. 478-301-2515, fax 478-301-2051, e-mail gain.info@gain.mercer.edu.

GOLD Georgia Resource Sharing for Georgia's Libraries (GOLD), c/o Georgia Public Lib. Service, 1800 Century Pl. NE, Suite 150, Atlanta 30345-4304. SAN 322-094X. Tel. 404-235-7128, fax 404-235-7201. *Project Mgr.* Elaine Hardy.

LYRASIS, 1438 W. Peachtree St. N.W., Suite 150, Atlanta 30309. SAN 322-0974. Tel. 800-999-8558, fax 404-892-7879. *CEO* Robert Miller.

Public Information Network for Electronic Services (PINES), 2872 Woodcock Blvd., Suite 250, Atlanta 30341. Tel. 404-235-7200. *Prog. Mgr.* Terran McCanna.

Hawaii

Hawaii-Pacific Chapter, Medical Library Assn. (HPC-MLA), Health Sciences Lib., Honolulu 96813. SAN 371-3946. Tel. 808-692-0810, fax 808-692-1244. *Chair* Kris Anderson.

Idaho

Canyon Owyhee Library Group (COLG), 203 E. Owyhee Ave., Homedale 83628. Tel. 208-337-4613, fax 208-337-4933.

Cooperative Information Network (CIN), 8385 N. Government Way, Hayden 83835-9280. SAN 323-7656. Tel. 208-772-5612, fax 208-772-2498.

Library Consortium of Eastern Idaho (LCEI), 113 S. Garfield, Pocatello 83204-3235. SAN 323-7699. Tel. 208-237-2192. *Pres.* Marilyn Kamoe.

LYNX Consortium, c/o Boise Public Lib., 715 S. Capitol Ave., Boise 83702-7195. SAN 375-0086. Tel. 208-384-4238, fax 208-384-4025. *Dir.* Kevin Booe.

Illinois

Areawide Hospital Library Consortium of Southwestern Illinois (AHLC), c/o St. Elizabeth Hospital Health Sciences Lib., 211 S. Third St., Belleville 62222. SAN 322-1016. Tel. 618-234-2120 ext. 2011, fax 618-222-4614.

Assn. of Chicago Theological Schools (ACTS), Univ. of St. Mary of the Lake, Mundelein 60060-1174. SAN 370-0658. Tel. 847-566-6401. *Coord.* Jennifer Oulds.

Big Ten Academic Alliance (formerly Committee on Institutional Cooperation), 1819 S. Neil St., Suite D, Champaign 61820-7271. Tel. 217-333-8475, fax 217-244-7127, e-mail btaa@staff.cic.net. *Exec. Dir.* Keith A. Marshall.

Center for Research Libraries, 6050 S. Kenwood, Chicago 60637-2804. SAN 322-1032. Tel. 773-955-4545, fax 773-955-4339. *Pres.* Gregory Eow.

Chicago Area Museum Libraries (CAML), c/o Lib., Field Museum, Chicago 60605-2496. SAN 371-392X. Tel. 312-665-7970, fax 312-665-7893. *Museum Libn.* Christine Giannoni.

Consortium of Academic and Research Libraries in Illinois (CARLI), 100 Trade Center Dr., Suite 303, Champaign 61820. SAN 322-3736. Tel. 217-244-4664, fax 217-244-7596, e-mail support@carli.illinois.edu. *Chair.* Taran Ley.

Council of Directors of State University Libraries in Illinois (CODSULI), Southern Illinois Univ. School of Medicine Lib., 801 N. Rutledge, Springfield 62702-4910. SAN 322-1083. Tel. 217-545-0994, fax 217-545-0988.

East Central Illinois Consortium, Booth Lib., Eastern Illinois Univ., 600 Lincoln Ave., Charleston 61920. SAN 322-1040. Tel. 217-581-7549, fax 217-581-7534. *Mgr.* Stacey Knight-Davis.

Heart of Illinois Library Consortium, 511 N.E. Greenleaf, Peoria 61603. SAN 322-1113. *Chair* Leslie Menz.

Illinois Heartland Library System, 1704 W. Interstate Dr., Champaign 61822. Tel. 217-352-0047. *Exec. Dir.* Leslie Bednar.

Illinois Library and Information Network (ILLINET), c/o Illinois State Lib., Gwendolyn Brooks Bldg. 300 S. Second St., Springfield 62701-1796. SAN 322-1148. Tel. 217-785-5600. *Dir.* Greg McCormick.

LIBRAS, Inc., North Park Univ., 3225 W. Foster Ave., Chicago 60625-4895. SAN 322-1172. Tel. 773-244-5584, fax 773-244-4891. *Pres.* Estevon Montano.

Metropolitan Consortium of Chicago, Chicago School of Professional Psychology, 325 N. Wells St., Chicago 60610. SAN 322-1180. Tel. 312-329-6630, fax 312-644-6075. *Coord.* Margaret White.

Network of Illinois Learning Resources in Community Colleges (NILRC), P.O. Box 120, Blanchardville, WI 53516-0120. Tel. 608-523-4094, fax 608-523-4072. *Bus. Mgr.* Lisa Sikora.

System Wide Automated Network (SWAN), 800 Quail Ridge Dr., Westmont 60559. Tel. 844-792-6542. *Exec. Dir.* Aaron Skog.

Indiana

Central Indiana Health Science Libraries Consortium, Indiana Univ. School of Medicine Lib., Indianapolis 46202. SAN 322-1245. Tel. 317-274-8358, fax 317-274-4056.

Consortium of College and University Media Centers (CCUMC), Indiana Univ., 306 N. Union St., Bloomington 47405-3888. SAN 322-1091. Tel. 812-855-6049, fax 812-855-2103, e-mail ccumc@ccumc.org. *Exec. Dir.* Aileen Scales.

Evergreen Indiana Consortium, Indiana State Lib., 315 W. Ohio St., Indianapolis 46202. Tel. 317-234-6624, fax 317-232-0002. *Coord.* Anna Goben.

Iowa

National Network of Libraries of Medicine–Greater Midwest Region (NN/LM-GMR), c/o Hardin Library for the Health Sciences, 600 Newton Road, Iowa City, 52242. SAN 322-1202. Tel. 319-353-4479. *Dir.* Linda Walton.

Polk County Biomedical Consortium, c/o Broadlawns Medical Center Lib., Des Moines 50314. SAN 322-1431. Tel. 515-282-2394, fax 515-282-5634. *Treas.* Elaine Hughes.

Quad City Area Biomedical Consortium, Great River Medical Center Lib., West Burlington 52655. SAN 322-435X. Tel. 319-768-4075, fax 319-768-4080. *Coord.* Judy Hawk.

Sioux City Library Cooperative (SCLC), c/o Sioux City Public Lib., Sioux City 51101-1203. SAN 329-4722. Tel. 712-255-2933 ext. 255, fax 712-279-6432. *Chair* Betsy Thompson.

State of Iowa Libraries Online (SILO), State Lib. of Iowa, Des Moines 50319. SAN 322-1415. Tel. 515-281-4105, fax 515-281-6191. *State Libn.* Michael Scott.

Kansas

Dodge City Library Consortium, c/o Comanche Intermediate Center, 1601 First Ave., Dodge City 67801. SAN 322-4368. Tel. 620-227-1609, fax 620-227-4862.

State Library of Kansas/Statewide Resource Sharing Div., 300 S.W. 10 Ave., Room 312-N., Topeka 66612-1593. SAN 329-5621. Tel. 785-296-3296, fax 785-368-7291. *Dir.* Jeff Hixon.

Kentucky

Assn. for Rural and Small Libraries, 201 E. Main St., Suite 1405, Lexington 40507. Tel. 859-514-9178, e-mail szach@amrms.com. *Pres.* Andrea Berstler.

Assn. of Independent Kentucky Colleges and Universities (AIKCU), 484 Chenault Rd., Frankfort 40601. SAN 322-1490. Tel. 502-695-5007, fax 502-695-5057. *Pres.* Gary S. Cox.

Eastern Kentucky Health Science Information Network (EKHSIN), c/o Camden-Carroll Lib., Morehead 40351. SAN 370-0631. Tel. 606-783-6860, fax 606-784-2178. *Lib. Dir.* Tammy Jenkins.

Kentuckiana Metroversity, Inc., 200 W. Broadway, Suite 800, Louisville 40202. SAN 322-1504. Tel. 502-897-3374, fax 502-895-1647.

Kentucky Medical Library Assn., VA Medical Center, Lib. Services 142D, Louisville 40206-1499. SAN 370-0623. Tel. 502-287-6240, fax 502-287-6134. *Head Libn.* Gene M. Haynes.

Theological Education Assn. of Mid America (TEAM-A), Southern Baptist Theological Seminary, Louisville 40280. SAN 377-5038. Tel. 502-897-4807, fax 502-897-4600. *Dir., Info. Resources* Ken Boyd.

Louisiana

Health Sciences Library Assn. of Louisiana (HSLAL), 433 Bolivar St., New Orleans 70112. SAN 375-0035. Tel. 504-568-5550. *Pres.* Rebecca Bealer.

Loan SHARK, State Lib. of Louisiana, 701 N. Fourth St., Baton Rouge 70802. SAN 371-6880. Tel. 225-342-4918, fax 225-219-4725, e-mail ill@state.lib.la.us. *Admin.* Kytara Christophe.

Louisiana Library Network (LOUIS), 1201 N. Third St., Suite 6-200, Baton Rouge 70802. E-mail louisresources@regents.la.gov. *Exec. Dir.* Terri Gallaway.

New Orleans Educational Telecommunications Consortium, 2045 Lakeshore Dr., Suite 541, New Orleans 70122. Tel. 504-524-0350, e-mail noetc@noetc.org. *Dir.* Michael Adler.

Southeastern Chapter of the American Assn. of Law Libraries (SEAALL), c/o Supreme Court of Louisiana, New Orleans 70130-2104. Tel. 504-310-2405, fax 504-310-2419. *Pres.* Michelle Cosby.

Maryland

Maryland Interlibrary Loan Organization (MILO), c/o Enoch Pratt Free Lib., Baltimore 21201-4484. SAN 343-8600. Tel. 410-396-5498, fax 410-396-5837, e-mail milo@prattlibrary.org. *Mgr.* Emma E. Beaven.

National Network of Libraries of Medicine (NNLM), National Lib. of Medicine, Bldg. 38, 8600 Rockville Pike, Room B1-E03, Bethesda 20894. SAN 373-0905. Tel. 301-496-4777, fax 301-480-1467. *Head, National Network Coordinating Office* Amanda J. Wilson.

National Network of Libraries of Medicine–Southeastern Atlantic Region (NN/LM-SEA), Univ. of Maryland Health Sciences and Human Services Lib., 601 W. Lombard S., Baltimore 21201-1512. SAN 322-1644. Tel. 410-706-2855, fax 410-706-0099, e-mail hshsl-nlmsea@hshsl.umaryland.edu. *Dir.* Mary Tooey.

U.S. National Library of Medicine (NLM), 8600 Rockville Pike, Bethesda 20894. SAN 322-1652. Tel. 301-594-5983, fax 301-402-1384, e-mail custserv@nlm.nih.gov. *Coord.* Martha Fishel.

Washington Research Library Consortium (WRLC), 901 Commerce Dr., Upper Marlboro 20774. SAN 373-0883. Tel. 301-390-2000, fax 301-390-2020. *Exec. Dir.* Mark Jacobs.

Massachusetts

Boston Library Consortium, Inc., 401 Edgewater Place, Suite 600, Wakefield 01880. SAN 322-1733. Tel. 781-876-8859, fax 781-623-8460, e-mail admin@blc.org. *Exec. Dir.* Susan Stearns.

Cape Libraries Automated Materials Sharing Network (CLAMS), 270 Communication Way, Unit 4E, Hyannis 02601. SAN 370-579X. Tel. 508-790-4399, fax 508-771-4533. *Exec. Dir.* Gayle Simundza.

Central and Western Massachusetts Automated Resource Sharing (C/W MARS), 67 Millbrook St., Suite 201, Worcester 01606. SAN 322-3973. Tel. 508-755-3323 ext. 30, fax 508-755-3721.

Cooperating Libraries of Greater Springfield (CLGS), Springfield Technical Community College, Springfield 01102. SAN 322-1768. Tel. 413-755-4565, fax 413-755-6315, e-mail lcoakley@stcc.edu.

Fenway Libraries Online, Inc. (FLO), c/o Wentworth Institute of Technology, 550 Huntington Ave., Boston 02115. SAN 373-9112. Tel. 617-989-5032. *Exec. Dir.* Walter Stein.

Massachusetts Health Sciences Libraries Network (MAHSLIN), Lamar Soutter Lib., Univ. of Massachusetts Medical School, Worcester 01655. SAN 372-8293. http://nahsl.libguides.com/mahslin/home. *Pres.* Stephanie Friree Ford.

Merrimack Valley Library Consortium, 4 High St., North Andover 01845. SAN 322-4384. Tel. 978-557-1050, fax 978-557-8101. *Exec. Dir.* Eric C. Graham.

Minuteman Library Network, 10 Strathmore Rd., Natick 01760-2419. SAN 322-4252. Tel. 508-655-8008, fax 508-655-1507. *Exec. Dir.* Susan McAlister.

National Network of Libraries of Medicine–New England Region (NN/LM-NER), Univ. of Massachusetts Medical School, 55 Lake Ave. N., Room S4-241, Worcester 01655. SAN 372-5448. Tel. 800-338-7657, fax 508-856-5977. *Dir.* Elaine Martin.

North Atlantic Health Sciences Libraries, Inc. (NAHSL), Hirsh Health Sciences Lib., 145 Harrison Ave., Boston 02111. SAN 371-0599. Tel. 617-636-3638, fax 617-636-3805. *Chair* Debra Berlanstein.

North of Boston Library Exchange, Inc. (NOBLE), 26 Cherry Hill Drive, Danvers 01923. SAN 322-4023. Tel. 978-777-8844, fax 978-750-8472. *Exec. Dir.* Ronald A. Gagnon.

Northeast Consortium of Colleges and Universities in Massachusetts (NECCUM), Merrimack College, 315 Turnpike St., North Andover 01845. SAN 371-0602. Tel. 978-556-3400, fax 978-556-3738. *Pres.* Richard Santagati.

Northeastern Consortium for Health Information (NECHI), Lowell General Hospital Health Science Lib., 295 Varnum Ave., Lowell 01854. SAN 322-1857. Tel. 978-937-6247, fax 978-937-6855. *Libn.* Donna Beales.

SAILS Library Network, 10 Riverside Dr., Suite 102, Lakeville 02347. SAN 378-0058. Tel. 508-946-8600, fax 508-946-8605, e-mail support@sailsinc.org. *Exec. Dir.* Deborah K. Conrad.

Southeastern Massachusetts Consortium of Health Science (SEMCO), Wilkens Lib., 2240 Iyannough Rd., West Barnstable 02668. SAN 322-1873. *Pub. Serv. Coord.* Tim Gerolami.

Western Massachusetts Health Information Consortium, Baystate Medical Center Health Sciences Lib., Springfield 01199. SAN 329-4579. Tel. 413-794-1865, fax 413-794-1974. *Pres.* Susan La Forter.

Michigan

Detroit Area Consortium of Catholic Colleges, c/o Wayne State Univ., Detroit 48202. SAN 329-482X. Tel. 313-883-8500, fax 313-883-8594. *Dir.* Chris Spilker.

Detroit Area Library Network (DALNET), 5150 Anthony Wayne Dr., Detroit 48202. Tel. 313-577-6789, fax 313-577-1231, info @dalnet.org. *Interim Dir.* Cathy Wolford.

Lakeland Library Cooperative, 4138 Three Mile Rd. N.W., Grand Rapids 49534-1134. SAN 308-132X. Tel. 616-559-5253, fax 616-559-4329. *Dir.* Carol Dawe.

The Library Network (TLN), 41365 Vincenti Ct., Novi 48375. SAN 370-596X. Tel. 248-536-3100, fax 248-536-3099. *Dir.* James Pletz.

Michigan Health Sciences Libraries Assn. (MHSLA), 1407 Rensen St., Suite 4, Lansing 48910. SAN 323-987X. Tel. 517-394-2774, fax 517-394-2675. *Pres.* Jill Turner.

Mideastern Michigan Library Cooperative, 503 S. Saginaw St., Suite 839, Flint 48502. SAN 346-5187. Tel. 810-232-7119, fax 810-232-6639. *Dir.* Eric Palmer.

Mid-Michigan Library League, 201 N Mitchell, Suite 302, Cadillac 49601-1835. SAN 307-9325. Tel. 231-775-3037, fax 231-775-1749. *Dir.* Sheryl L. Mase.

Midwest Collaborative for Library Services, 1407 Rensen St., Suite 1, Lansing 48910. Tel. 800-530-9019, fax 517-492-3878. *Exec. Dir.* Scott Garrison.

Southeastern Michigan League of Libraries (SEMLOL), Lawrence Technological Univ., 21000 W. Ten Mile Rd., Southfield 48075. SAN 322-4481. Tel. 810-766-4070, fax 248-204-3005. *Treas.* Gary Cocozzoli.

Southwest Michigan Library Cooperative, 401 Wix St., Ostego 49078. SAN 308-2156. Tel. 269-657-3800, e-mail aestelle@otsego library.org. *Dir.* Andrea Estelle.

Suburban Library Cooperative (SLC), 44750 Delco Blvd., Sterling Heights 48313. SAN 373-9082. Tel. 586-685-5750, fax 586-685-5750. *Dir.* Tammy Turgeon.

Upper Peninsula of Michigan Health Sciences Library Consortium, c/o Marquette Health System Hospital, 580 W. College Ave., Marquette 49855. SAN 329-4803. Tel. 906-225-3429, fax 906-225-3524. *Lib. Mgr.* Janis Lubenow.

Upper Peninsula Region of Library Cooperation, Inc., 1615 Presque Isle Ave., Marquette 49855. SAN 329-5540. Tel. 906-228-7697, fax 906-228-5627. *Treas.* Suzanne Dees.

Valley Library Consortium, 3210 Davenport Ave., Saginaw 48602-3495. Tel. 989-497-0925, fax 989-497-0918. *Exec. Dir.* Randall Martin.

Minnesota

Capital Area Library Consortium (CALCO), c/o Minnesota Dept. of Transportation, Lib. MS155, 395 John Ireland Blvd., Saint Paul 55155. SAN 374-6127. Tel. 651-296-5272, fax 651-297-2354. *Libn.* Shirley Sherkow.

Central Minnesota Libraries Exchange (CMLE), Miller Center, Room 130-D, Saint Cloud 56301-4498. SAN 322-3779. Tel. 320-308-2950, fax 320-654-5131, e-mail cmle@stcloudstate.edu. *Exec. Dir.* Mary Wilkins-Jordan.

Cooperating Libraries in Consortium (CLIC), 1619 Dayton Ave., Suite 204, Saint Paul 55104. SAN 322-1970. Tel. 651-644-3878. *Exec. Dir.* Ruth Dukelow.

Metronet, 1619 Dayton Ave., Suite 314, Saint Paul 55104. SAN 322-1989. Tel. 651-646-0475, fax 651-649-3169, e-mail information @metrolibraries.net. *Exec. Dir.* Ann Walker Smalley.

Metropolitan Library Service Agency (MELSA), 1619 Dayton Ave., No. 314, Saint Paul 55104-6206. SAN 371-5124. Tel. 651-645-5731, fax 651-649-3169, e-mail melsa @melsa.org. *Exec. Dir.* Ken Behringer.

MINITEX, Univ. of Minnesota–Twin Cities, 60 Wilson Library, 309 19th Ave. S., Minneapolis 55455-0439. SAN 322-1997. Tel. 612-624-4002, fax 612-624-4508. *Dir.* Valerie Horton.

Minnesota Library Information Network (MnLINK), Univ. of Minnesota–Twin Cities, Minneapolis 55455-0439. Tel. 800-462-5348, fax 612-624-4508. *Info. Specialist* Nick Banitt.

Minnesota Theological Library Assn. (MTLA), Luther Seminary Lib., 2375 Como Ave., Saint Paul 55108. SAN 322-1962. Tel. 651-641-3447. *Exec. Dir.* Sandra Oslund.

MNPALS, Minnesota State Univ. Mankato, 3022 Memorial Library, Mankato 56001. Tel. 507-389-2000, fax 507-389-5488. *Exec. Dir.* Johnna Horton.

Northern Lights Library Network (NLLN), 1104 7th Ave. S., Box 136, Moorhead 56563. SAN 322-2004. Tel. 218-477-2934. *Exec. Dir.* Kathy Brock Enger.

Prairielands Library Exchange, 109 S. 5th St., Marshall 56258. SAN 322-2039. Tel. 507-532-9013, fax 507-532-2039, e-mail info@sammie.org. *Exec. Dir.* Shelly Grace.

Southeastern Libraries Cooperating (SELCO), 2600 19th St. N.W., Rochester 55901-0767. SAN 308-7417. Tel. 507-288-5513, fax 507-288-8697. *Exec. Dir.* Ann Hutton.

Twin Cities Biomedical Consortium (TCBC), c/o Fairview Univ. Medical Center, 2450 Riverside Ave., Minneapolis 55455. SAN 322-2055. Tel. 612-273-6595, fax 612-273-2675. *Mgr.* Colleen Olsen.

Mississippi

Central Mississippi Library Council (CMLC), c/o Millsaps College Lib., 1701 N. State St., Jackson 39210. SAN 372-8250. Tel. 601-974-1070, fax 601-974-1082. *Chair* Justin Huckaby.

Mississippi Electronic Libraries Online (MELO), Mississippi State Board for Community and Junior Colleges, Jackson 39211. Tel. 601-432-6518, fax 601-432-6363, e-mail melo@colin.edu. *Dir.* Audra Kimball.

Missouri

Greater Western Library Alliance (GWLA), 5109 Cherry St., Kansas City 64110. Tel. 816-926-8765, fax 816-926-8790. *Exec. Dir.* Joni Blake.

Health Sciences Library Network of Kansas City (HSLNKC), Univ. of Missouri–Kansas City Health Sciences Lib., 2411 Holmes St., Kansas City 64108-2792. SAN 322-2098. Tel. 816-235-1880, fax 816-235-6570. *Pres.* Cindi Kerns.

Kansas City Library Service Program (KC-LSP), 14 W. 10 St., Kansas City 64105. Tel. 816-701-3520, fax 816-701-3401, e-mail kc-lspsupport@kclibrary.org. *Lib. Systems and Service Prog. Mgr.* Melissa Carle.

Mid-America Law Library Consortium (MALLCO), 800 N. Harvey Ave., Oklahoma City 73102. Tel. 405-208-5393, e-mail mallcoexecutivedirector@gmail.com. *Exec. Dir.* Susan Urban.

Mid-America Library Alliance/Kansas City Metropolitan Library and Information Network, 15624 E. 24 Hwy., Independence 64050. SAN 322-2101. Tel. 816-521-7257, fax 816-461-0966. *Exec. Dir.* Mickey Coalwell.

Mobius, 111 E. Broadway, Suite 220, Columbia 65203. Tel. 877-366-2487, fax 541-264-7006. *Exec. Dir.* Donna Bacon.

Saint Louis Regional Library Network, 1190 Meramec Station Rd., Suite 207, Ballwin 63021. SAN 322-2209. Tel. 800-843-8482, fax 636-529-1396, e-mail slrln@amigos.org. *Pres.* Nina O'Daniels.

Western Council of State Libraries, 1190 Meramec Station Rd., Suite 207, Ballwin 63021-6902. Tel. 972-851-8000, fax 636-529-1396.

Montana

Treasure State Academic Information and Library Services (TRAILS), Montana State Univ., P.O. Box 173320, Bozeman 59717. Tel. 406-994-4432, fax 406-994-2851. *Coord.* Pamela Benjamin.

Nebraska

ICON Library Consortium, McGoogan Lib. of Medicine, Univ. of Nebraska, Omaha 68198-6705. Tel. 402-559-7099, fax 402-559-5498. *Exec. Secy.* Cindy Perkins.

Nevada

Desert States Law Library Consortium, Wiener-Rogers Law Lib., William S. Boyd School of Law, 4505 Maryland Pkwy., Las Vegas 89154-1080. Tel. 702-895-2400, fax 702-895-2416. *Dir.* Jean Price.

Information Nevada, Interlibrary Loan Dept., Nevada State Lib. and Archives, 100 N. Stewart St., Carson City 89701-4285. SAN 322-2276. Tel. 775-684-3360, fax 775-684-3330. *Asst. Admin., Lib. and Development Svcs.* Tammy Westergard.

New Hampshire

GMILCS, Inc., 31 Mount Saint Mary's Way, Hooksett 03106. Tel. 603-485-4286, fax 603-485-4246, e-mail helpdesk@gmilcs.org. *Systems Admin.* Marilyn Borgendale.

Health Sciences Libraries of New Hampshire and Vermont, Breene Memorial Lib., 36 Clinton St., New Hampshire Hospital, Concord 03246. SAN 371-6864. Tel. 603-527-2837, fax 603-527-7197. *Admin. Coord.* Anne Conner.

Librarians of the Upper Valley Coop. (LUV Coop), c/o Converse Free Library, 38 Union St., Lyme 03768. SAN 371-6856. Tel. 603-795-4622. *Coord.* Judith G. Russell.

Merri-Hill-Rock Library Cooperative, c/o Sandown Public Lib., 305 Main St., P.O. Box 580, Sandown 03873. SAN 329-5338. E-mail director@sandownlibrary.us. *Chair* Deborah Hoadley.

New Hampshire College and University Council, 3 Barrell Court, Suite 100, Concord 03301-8543. SAN 322-2322. Tel. 603-225-4199, fax 603-225-8108. *Pres.* Thomas R. Horgan.

Nubanusit Library Cooperative, c/o Frost Free Lib., 28 Jaffrey Rd., Marlborough 03455. SAN 322-4600. *Chair* Kristin Readel.

Rochester Area Librarians, c/o Milton Free Public Lib., 13 Main St., Milton Mills 03852. E-mail mfpl@metrocast.net. *Dir.* Betsy Baker.

New Jersey

Basic Health Sciences Library Network (BHSL), Overlook Hospital Health Science Lib., 99 Beauvoir Ave., Summit 07902. SAN 371-4888. Tel. 908-522-2886, fax 908-522-2274. *Coord.* Pat Regenberg.

Bergen County Cooperative Library System, 810 Main St., Hackensack 07601. Tel. 201-498-7301, fax 201-489-4215, e-mail bccls@bccls.org. *Pres.* Kurt Hadeler.

Burlington Libraries Information Consortium (BLINC), 5 Pioneer Blvd., Westampton 08060. Tel. 609-267-9660, fax 609-267-4091, e-mail hq@bcls.lib.nj.us. *Dir.* Ranjna Das.

Health Sciences Library Association of New Jersey (HSLANJ), P.O. Box 12606, Wilmington, DE 19850-2606. Tel. 570-856-5952, fax 888-619-4432, e-mail communications@hslanj.org. *Exec. Dir.* Robb Mackes.

Libraries of Middlesex Automation Consortium (LMxAC), 27 Mayfield Ave., Edison 08837. SAN 329-448X. Tel. 732-750-2525, fax 732-750-9392. *Exec. Dir.* Eileen M. Palmer.

LibraryLinkNJ, New Jersey Library Cooperative, 44 Stelton Rd., Suite 330, Piscataway 08854. SAN 371-5116. Tel. 732-752-7720, fax 732-752-7785. *Interim Dir.* Juliet Machie.

Morris Automated Information Network (MAIN), 16 Wing Dr., Suite 212, Cedar Knolls 07927. SAN 322-4058. Tel. 973-862-4606, fax 973-512-2122. *Exec. Dir.* Phillip Berg.

Morris-Union Federation, 214 Main St., Chatham 07928. SAN 310-2629. Tel. 973-635-0603, fax 973-635-7827. *Exec. Dir.* Karen Brodsky.

New Jersey Health Sciences Library Network (NJHSN), Overlook Hospital Lib., 99 Beauvoir Ave., Summit 07902. SAN 371-4829. Tel. 908-522-2886, fax 908-522-2274. *Lib. Mgr.* Patricia Regenberg.

New Jersey Library Network, Lib. Development Bureau, 185 W. State St., Trenton 08608. SAN 372-8161. Tel. 609-278-2640 ext. 152, fax 609-278-2650. *Admin.* Ruth Pallante.

Virtual Academic Library Environment (VALE), NJEdge/NJIT, 218 Central Ave., GITC 3902, Newark 07102-1982. Tel. 855-832-3343. *Prog. Mgr.* Melissa Lena.

New Mexico

Estacado Library Information Network (ELIN), 509 N. Shipp, Hobbs 88240. Tel. 505-397-9328, fax 505-397-1508.

New Mexico Consortium of Academic Libraries, c/o Donnelly Library, 802 National Ave., Las Vegas. SAN 371-6872. *Pres.* Poppy Johnson-Renval.

New Mexico Consortium of Biomedical and Hospital Libraries, c/o Presbyterian Hospital, Robert Shafer Library, 1100 Central Ave., S.E., Santa Fe 87505. SAN 322-449X. Tel. 505-820-5218, fax 505-989-6478. *Pres.* Amanda Okandan.

New York

Academic Libraries of Brooklyn, Long Island Univ. Lib. LLC 517, One University Plaza, Brooklyn 11201. SAN 322-2411. Tel. 718-488-1081, fax 718-780-4057. *Dir.* Ingrid Wang.

Associated Colleges of the Saint Lawrence Valley, SUNY Potsdam, 288 Van Housen Extension, Potsdam 13676-2299. SAN 322-242X. Tel. 315-267-3331, fax 315-267-2389. *Admin. Coord.* Ben Dixon.

Brooklyn–Queens–Staten Island–Manhattan–Bronx Health Sciences Libns. (BQSIMB), 150 55th St., Brooklyn 11220. Tel. 718-630-7200, fax 718-630-8918. *Pres.* Sheryl Ramer Gesoff.

Capital District Library Council (CDLC), 28 Essex St., Albany 12206. SAN 322-2446. Tel. 518-438-2500, fax 518-438-2872. *Exec. Dir.* Kathleen Gundrum.

Central New York Library Resources Council (CLRC), 5710 Commons Park Dr., East Syracuse 13057. SAN 322-2454. Tel. 315-446-5446, fax 315-446-5590. *Exec. Dir.* Marc Wildman.

CONNECTNY, Inc., 6721 U.S. Highway 11, Potsdam 13676. Tel. 716-930-7752. *Exec. Dir.* Pamela Jones.

Consortium of Foundation Libraries, 32 Old Slip, 24th Fl., New York 10005-3500. SAN 322-2462. Tel. 212-620-4230, e-mail foundationlibraries@gmail.com. *Chair* Susan Shiroma.

Library Assn. of Rockland County (LARC), P.O. Box 917, New City 10956-0917. Tel. 845-359-3877. *Pres.* Carol Connell Connor.

Library Consortium of Health Institutions in Buffalo (LCHIB), Abbott Hall, SUNY at Buffalo, 3435 Main St., Buffalo 14214. SAN 329-367X. Tel. 716-829-3900 ext. 143, fax 716-829-2211, e-mail hubnet@buffalo.edu; ulb-lchib@buffalo.edu. *Exec. Dir.* Martin E. Mutka.

Long Island Library Resources Council (LILRC), 627 N. Sunrise Service Rd., Bellport 11713. SAN 322-2489. Tel. 631-675-1570. *Dir.* Tim Spindler.

Medical and Scientific Libraries of Long Island (MEDLI), c/o Palmer School of Lib. and Info. Science, Brookville 11548. SAN 322-4309. Tel. 516-299-2866, fax 516-299-4168. *Pres.* Claire Joseph.

Metropolitan New York Library Council (METRO), 599 Eleventh Ave., 8th Fl., New York 10036. SAN 322-2500. Tel. 212-228-2320, fax 212-228-2598, e-mail info@metro.org. *Exec. Dir.* Nate Hill.

New England Law Library Consortium (NELLCO), 756 Madison Ave., Suite 102, Albany 12208. SAN 322-4244. Tel. 518-694-3025, fax 518-694-3027. *Exec. Dir.* Corie Dugas.

Northern New York Library Network, 6721 U.S. Hwy. 11, Potsdam 13676. SAN 322-2527. Tel. 315-265-1119, fax 315-265-1881, e-mail info@nnyln.org. *Exec. Dir.* Meg Backus.

Rochester Regional Library Council, 390 Packetts Landing, Fairport 14450. SAN 322-2535. Tel. 585-223-7570, fax 585-223-7712, e-mail rrlc@rrlc.org. *Exec. Dir.* Laura Ousterhout.

South Central Regional Library Council, 108 N. Cayuga St., Clinton Hall, 3rd Floor, Ithaca 14850. SAN 322-2543. Tel. 607-273-9106, fax 607-272-0740, e-mail scrlc@scrlc.org. *Exec. Dir.* Mary-Carol Lindbloom.

Southeastern New York Library Resources Council (SENYLRC), 21 S. Elting Corners Rd., Highland 12528-2805. SAN 322-2551. Tel. 845-883-9065, fax 845-883-9483. *Exec. Dir.* Tessa Killian.

SUNYConnect, Office of Lib. and Info. Services, Office of Library & Information Services, SUNY Administration Plaza, 353 Broadway, Albany 12246. Tel. 518-443-5577, fax 518-443-5358. *Asst. Provost for Lib. and Info. Svcs.* Carey Hatch.

United Nations System Electronic Information Acquisitions Consortium (UNSEIAC), c/o United Nations Lib., New York 10017. SAN 377-855X. Tel. 212-963-3000, fax 212-963-2608, e-mail unseiac@un.org. *Coord.* Amy Herridge.

Western New York Library Resources Council, 4950 Genesee St., Buffalo 14225. SAN 322-2578. Tel. 716-633-0705, fax 716-633-1736. *Exec. Dir.* Sheryl Knab.

North Carolina

North Carolina Community College System, 200 W. Jones St., Raleigh 27603-1379. SAN 322-2594. Tel. 919-807-7100, fax 919-807-7165. *Pres.* Peter Hans.

Northwest AHEC Library at Hickory, Catawba Medical Ctr., 810 Fairgrove Church Rd., Hickory 28602. SAN 322-4708. Tel. 828-326-3662, fax 828-326-3484. *Dir.* Karen Lee Martinez.

Northwest AHEC Library Information Network, Wake Forest Univ. School of Medicine, Medical Center Blvd., Winston-Salem 27157-1060. SAN 322-4716. Tel. 336-713-7700, fax 336-713-7701.

Triangle Research Libraries Network, Wilson Lib., CB No. 3940, Chapel Hill 27514-8890. SAN 329-5362. Tel. 919-962-8022, fax 919-962-4452. *Exec. Dir.* Lisa Croucher.

Western North Carolina Library Network (WNCLN), c/o Appalachian State Univ., 218 College St., Boone 28608. SAN 376-7205. Tel. 828-262-2774, fax 828-262-3001. *Libn.* Ben Shirley.

North Dakota

Central Dakota Library Network, Morton Mandan Public Lib., Mandan 58554-3149. SAN 373-1391. Tel. 701-667-5365, e-mail mortonmandanlibrary@cdln.info.

Ohio

Assn. of Christian Librarians (ACL), P.O. Box 4, Cedarville 45314. Tel. 937-766-2255, fax 937-766-5499, e-mail info@acl.org. *Pres.* Denise Nelson.

Christian Library Consortium (CLC), c/o ACL, P.O. Box 4, Cedarville 45314. Tel. 937-766-2255, fax 937-766-5499, e-mail info@acl.org. *Coord.* Beth Purtee.

Consortium of Ohio Libraries, P.O. Box 38, Cardington 43315-1116. E-mail Info@info.cool-cat.org. *Chair* Lisa Murray.

Consortium of Popular Culture Collections in the Midwest (CPCCM), c/o Popular Culture Lib., Bowling Green 43403-0600. SAN 370-5811. Tel. 419-372-2450, fax 419-372-7996. *Head Libn.* Nancy Down.

Five Colleges of Ohio, 173 West Lorain Street, Room 208, Oberlin College, Oberlin 44074. Tel. 440-775-5500, e-mail info@ohio5.com. *Exec. Dir.* Sarah Stone.

Northeast Ohio Regional Library System (NEO-RLS), 1580 Georgetown Rd., Hudson 44236. SAN 322-2713. Tel. 330-655-0531, fax 330-655-0568. *Exec. Dir.* Catherine Hakala-Ausperk.

NORWELD (formerly Northwest Regional Library System), 181½ S. Main St., Bowling Green 43402. SAN 322-273X. Tel. 419-352-2903, fax 419-353-8310. *Exec. Dir.* Arline V. Radden.

OCLC Online Computer Library Center, Inc., 6565 Kilgour Place, Dublin 43017-3395. SAN 322-2748. Tel. 614-764-6000, fax 614-718-1017, e-mail oclc@oclc.org. *Pres./CEO* Skip Pritchard.

Ohio Health Sciences Library Assn. (OHSLA), Medical Lib., South Pointe Hospital, Warrensville Heights 44122. Tel. 216-491-7454, fax 216-491-7650. *Pres.* Mary Pat Harnegie.

Ohio Library and Information Network (OhioLINK), 1224 Kinnear Rd., Columbus 43215. SAN 374-8014. Tel. 614-485-6722, fax 614-228-1807, e-mail info@ohiolink.edu. *Interim Exec. Dir.* Amy Pawlowski.

OHIONET, 1500 W. Lane Ave., Columbus 43221-3975. SAN 322-2764. Tel. 614-486-2966, fax 614-486-1527. *Exec. Officer* Nancy S. Kirkpatrick.

Ohio Network of American History Research Centers, Ohio Historical Society Archives–Lib., Columbus 43211-2497. SAN 323-9624. Tel. 614-297-2510, fax 614-297-2546, e-mail reference@ohiohistory.org. *Exec. Dir.* Jackie Barton.

Ohio Public Library Information Network (OPLIN), 2323 W. 5 Ave., Suite 130, Columbus 43204. Tel. 614-728-5252, fax 614-728-5256, e-mail support@oplin.org. *Exec. Dir.* Don Yarman.

Serving Every Ohioan Library Center, SEO, 40780 Marietta Rd., Caldwell 43724. SAN 356-4606. Tel. 740-783-5705, fax 800-446-4804. *Dir.* Dianna Clark.

Southeast Ohio and Neighboring Libraries (SWON), 10250 Alliance Rd., Suite 112,

Cincinnati 45242. SAN 322-2675. Tel. 513-751-4422, fax 513-751-0463, e-mail info@swonlibraries.org. *Exec. Dir.* Cassondra Vick.

Southeast Regional Library System (SERLS), 252 W. 13 St., Wellston 45692. SAN 322-2756. Tel. 740-384-2103, fax 740-384-2106, e-mail dirserls@oplin.org. *Dir.* Jay Burton.

Southwestern Ohio Council for Higher Education (SOCHE), Miami Valley Research Park, 3155 Research Blvd., Suite 204, Dayton 45420-4015. SAN 322-2659. Tel. 937-258-8890, fax 937-258-8899, e-mail soche@soche.org. *Exec. Dir.* Cassie Barlow.

State Assisted Academic Library Council of Kentucky (SAALCK), 12031 Southwick Lane, Cincinnati 45241. SAN 371-2222. Tel. 800-771-1972, e-mail saalck@saalck.org. *Exec. Dir.* Anne Abate.

Theological Consortium of Greater Columbus (TCGC), Trinity Lutheran Seminary, Columbus 43209-2334. Tel. 614-384-4646, fax 614-238-0263. *Lib. Systems Mgr.* Ray Olson.

Oklahoma

Mid-America Law Library Consortium (MALLCO), 800 N. Harvey Ave., Oklahoma City 73102. Tel. 405-208-5393, e-mail mallcoexecutivedirector@gmail.com. *Exec. Dir.* Susan Urban.

Oklahoma Health Sciences Library Assn. (OHSLA), HSC Bird Health Science Lib., Univ. of Oklahoma, Oklahoma City 73190. SAN 375-0051. Tel. 405-271-2285 ext. 48755, fax 405-271-3297. *Exec. Dir.* Joy Summers-Ables.

Oregon

Chemeketa Cooperative Regional Library Service, 4000 Lancaster Dr. N.E., Rm. 9/136, Salem 97305-1453. SAN 322-2837. Tel. 503-399-5165, fax 503-399-7316, e-mail contact@cclrs.org. *Dir.* John Goodyear.

Library Information Network of Clackamas County (LINCC), 1810 Red Soils Court, #110, Oregon City 97045. SAN 322-2845. Tel. 503-723-4888, fax 503-794-8238. *Lib. System Analyst* Greg Williams.

Orbis Cascade Alliance, 2300 Oakmont Way, Eugene 97401. SAN 377-8096. Tel. 541-246-2470. *Exec. Dir.* Kim Armstrong.

Oregon Health Sciences Libraries Assn. (OHSLA), Oregon Health and Science Univ. Lib., 3181 S.W. Sam Jackson Park Rd., Portland 97239-3098. SAN 371-2176. Tel. 503-494-3462, fax 503-494-3322, e-mail library@ohsu.edu. *Pres.* Jackie Wirz.

Washington County Cooperative Library Services, 111 N.E. Lincoln St., MS No. 58, Hillsboro 97124-3036. SAN 322-287X. Tel. 503-846-3222, fax 503-846-3220.

Pennsylvania

Berks County Library Assn. (BCLA), c/o Berks County Public Libraries, 1040 Berks Rd., Leesport 19533. SAN 371-0866. Tel. 610-478-9035, 610-655-6350. *Pres.* Amy Resh.

Central Pennsylvania Consortium (CPC), c/o Franklin & Marshall College, Goethean Hall 101, Lancaster 17604. SAN 322-2896. Tel. 717-358-2896, fax 717-358-4455, e-mail cpc@dickinson.edu. *Exec. Asst.* Kathy Missildine.

Central Pennsylvania Health Sciences Library Assn. (CPHSLA), Office for Research Protections, Pennsylvania State Univ., 212 Kern Graduate Bldg., University Park 16802. SAN 375-5290. Fax 814-865-1775. *Pres.* Helen Houpt.

Eastern Mennonite Associated Libraries and Archives (EMALA), 2215 Millstream Rd., Lancaster 17602. SAN 372-8226. Tel. 717-393-9745, fax 717-393-8751. *Chair* John Weber.

Greater Philadelphia Law Library Assn. (GPLLA), P.O. Box 335, Philadelphia 19105. SAN 373-1375. *Pres.* Lori Strickler Corso.

HSLC/Access PA (Health Science Libraries Consortium), 3600 Market St., Suite 550, Philadelphia 19104-2646. SAN 323-9780. Tel. 215-222-1532, fax 215-222-0416, e-mail support@hslc.org. *Exec. Dir.* Maryam Phillips.

Interlibrary Delivery Service of Pennsylvania (IDS), c/o Bucks County IU, No. 22, 705 N Shady Retreat Rd., Doylestown 18901. SAN 322-2942. Tel. 215-348-2940 ext. 1625, fax

215-348-8315, e-mail ids@bucksiu.org. *Admin. Dir.* Pamela Dinan.

Keystone Library Network, 1871 Old Main Drive, Shippensburg 17257. Tel. 717-720-4088, fax 717-720-4211. *Interim Coord.* Ed Zimmerman.

Lehigh Valley Assn. of Independent Colleges, 1309 Main St., Bethlehem 18018. SAN 322-2969. Tel. 610-625-7888, fax 610-625-7891. *Exec. Dir.* Diane Dimitroff.

Montgomery County Library and Information Network Consortium (MCLINC), 301 Lafayette St., 2nd Fl., Conshohocken 19428. Tel. 610-238-0580, fax 610-238-0581, e-mail webmaster@mclinc.org. *Exec. Dir.* Sharon Moreland-Sender.

National Network of Libraries of Medicine–Middle Atlantic Region (NN/LM-MAR), Univ. of Pittsburgh, 3550 Terrace St., 200 Scaife Hall, Pittsburgh 15261. Tel. 412-684-2065, fax 412-648-1515, e-mail nnlmmar@pitt.edu. *Exec. Dir.* Renae Barger.

Northeastern Pennsylvania Library Network, c/o Marywood Univ. Lib., 2300 Adams Ave., Scranton 18509-1598. SAN 322-2993. Tel. 570-348-6260, fax 570-961-4769. *Exec. Dir.* Catherine H. Schappert.

Northwest Interlibrary Cooperative of Pennsylvania (NICOP), Mercyhurst College Lib., 501 E. 38th St., Erie 16546. SAN 370-5862. Tel. 814-824-2190, fax 814-824-2219. *Archivist/Libn.* Earleen Glaser.

Pennsylvania Academic Library Consortium, 1005 Pontiac Rd., Suite 330, Drexel Hill 19026. Tel. 215-567-1755. *Exec. Dir.* Jill Morris.

Pennsylvania Library Assn., 220 Cumberland Pkwy, Suite 10, Mechanicsburg 17055. Tel. 717-766-7663, fax 717-766-5440. *Exec. Dir.* Christi Buker.

Philadelphia Area Consortium of Special Collections Libraries (PACSCL), P.O. Box 22642, Philadelphia 19110-2642. Tel. 215-985-1445, fax 215-985-1446, e-mail lblanchard@pacscl.org. *Exec. Dir.* Laura Blanchard.

Southeastern Pennsylvania Theological Library Assn. (SEPTLA), c/o Biblical Seminary, 200 N. Main St., Hatfield 19440. SAN 371-0793. Tel. 215-368-5000 ext. 234. *Pres.* Patrick Milas.

State System of Higher Education Library Cooperative (SSHELCO), c/o Bailey Lib., Slippery Rock 16057. Tel. 724-738-2630, fax 724-738-2661. *Coord.* Mary Lou Sowden.

Susquehanna Library Cooperative (SLC), Stevenson Lib., Lock Haven Univ., 401 N. Fairview St., Lock Haven 17745. SAN 322-3051. Tel. 570-484-2310, fax 570-484-2506. *Interim Dir. of Lib. and Info. Svcs.* Joby Topper.

Tri-State College Library Cooperative (TCLC), c/o Rosemont College Lib., 1400 Montgomery Ave., Rosemont 19010-1699. SAN 322-3078. Tel. 610-525-0796, e-mail office@tclclibs.org. *Coord.* Mary Maguire.

Rhode Island

Ocean State Libraries (OSL), 300 Centerville Rd., Suite 103S, Warwick 02886-0226. SAN 329-4560. Tel. 401-738-2200, e-mail support@oslri.net. *Exec. Dir.* Stephen Spohn.

RILINK, 317 Market St., Warren 02885. SAN 371-6821. Tel. 401-245-4998. *Exec. Dir.* Dorothy Frechette.

South Carolina

Charleston Academic Libraries Consortium (CALC), P.O. Box 118067, Charleston 29423-8067. SAN 371-0769. Tel. 843-574-6088, fax 843-574-6484. *Chair* Charnette Singleton.

Partnership Among South Carolina Academic Libraries (PASCAL), 1122 Lady Street, Suite 300, Columbia 29201. Tel. 803-734-0900, fax 803-734-0901. *Exec. Dir.* Rick Moul.

South Carolina AHEC, c/o Medical University of South Carolina, 1 South Park Circle, Suite 203, Charleston 29407. SAN 329-3998. Tel. 843-792-4431, fax 843-792-4430. *Exec. Dir.* David Garr.

South Dakota

South Dakota Library Network (SDLN), 1200 University, Unit 9672, Spearfish 57799-9672. SAN 371-2117. Tel. 605-642-6835, fax 605-642-6472. *Dir.* Warren Wilson.

Tennessee

Appalachian College Assn., 7216 Jewel Bell Lane, Bristol 40475. Tel. 859-986-4584, fax 859-986-9549. *Pres.* Beth Rushing.

Knoxville Area Health Sciences Library Consortium (KAHSLC), Univ. of Tennessee Preston Medical Lib., 1924 Alcoa Hwy., Knoxville 37920. SAN 371-0556. Tel. 865-305-9525, fax 865-305-9527. *Pres.* Cynthia Vaughn.

Tennessee Health Science Library Assn. (THeSLA), Holston Valley Medical Center Health Sciences Lib., 130 W. Ravine Rd., Kingsport 37660. SAN 371-0726. Tel. 423-224-6870, fax 423-224-6014. *Pres.* Sandy Oelschlegel.

Tenn Share, P.O. Box 331871, Nashville 37203-7517. Tel. 615-669-8670, e-mail execdir@tenn-share.org. *Exec. Dir.* Jenifer Grady.

Tri-Cities Area Health Sciences Libraries Consortium (TCAHSLC), James H. Quillen College of Medicine, East Tennessee State Univ., Johnson City 37614. SAN 329-4099. Tel. 423-439-6252, fax 423-439-7025. *Dir.* Biddanda Ponnappa.

Texas

Abilene Library Consortium, 3305 N. 3 St., Suite 301, Abilene 79603. SAN 322-4694. Tel. 325-672-7081, fax 325-672-7082. *Exec. Dir.* Edward J. Smith.

Amigos Library Services, Inc., 4901 LBJ Freeway, Suite 150, Dallas 75244-6179. SAN 322-3191. Tel. 972-851-8000, fax 972-991-6061, e-mail amigos@amigos.org. *Chief Prog. Officer* Tracy Byerly.

Council of Research and Academic Libraries (CORAL), P.O. Box 6733, San Antonio 78212. SAN 322-3213. Tel. 210-710-4475. *Pres.* Michelea Mason.

Del Norte Biosciences Library Consortium, El Paso Community College, El Paso 79998. SAN 322-3302. Tel. 915-831-4149, fax 915-831-4639. *Coord.* Becky Perales.

Harrington Library Consortium, 413 E. 4 Ave., Amarillo 79101. SAN 329-546X. Tel. 806-378-6037, fax 806-378-6038. *Dir.* Amanda Barrera.

Health Libraries Information Network (Health LINE), 3500 Camp Bowie Blvd. LIB-222, Fort Worth 76107-2699. SAN 322-3299. E-mail dfwhealthline@gmail.com. *Pres.* Michele Whitehead.

Houston Area Library Automated Network (HALAN), Houston Public Lib., 500 McKinney Ave., Houston 77002. Tel. 832-393-1411, fax 832-393-1427, e-mail website@hpl.lib.tx.us. *Chief* Judith Hiott.

Houston Area Research Library Consortium (HARLiC), c/o Univ. of Houston Libs., 114 University Libraries, Houston 77204-2000. SAN 322-3329. Tel. 713-743-9807, fax 713-743-9811. *Pres.* Dana Rooks.

National Network of Libraries of Medicine–South Central Region (NN/LM-SCR), c/o UNT Health Science Center, Gibson D. Lewis Library, Room 310, 3500 Camp Bowie Blvd., Fort Worth 76107. SAN 322-3353. Tel. 713-799-7880, fax 713-790-7030, e-mail nnlm-scr@exch.library.tmc.edu. *Dir.* Brian Leaf.

South Central Academic Medical Libraries Consortium (SCAMeL), c/o Lewis Lib.-UNTHSC, 3500 Camp Bowie Blvd., Fort Worth 76107. SAN 372-8269. Tel. 817-735-2380, fax 817-735-5158. *Chair* Kelly Gonzalez.

Texas Council of Academic Libraries (TCAL), VC/UHV Lib., 2602 N. Ben Jordan, Victoria 77901. SAN 322-337X. Tel. 361-570-4150, fax 361-570-4155. *Chair* Cate Rudowsky.

TEXSHARE—Texas State Library and Archives Commission, 1201 Brazos St., Austin 78701. Tel. 512-463-5455, fax 512-936-2306, e-mail texshare@tsl.texas.gov. *Dir. and State Libn.* Mark Smith.

Utah

National Network of Libraries of Medicine–MidContinental Region (NN/LM-MCR), Spencer S. Eccles Health Sciences Lib., Univ. of Utah, Salt Lake City 84112-5890. SAN 322-225X. Tel. 801-587-3650, fax 801-581-3632. *Dir.* Catherine Soehner.

Utah Academic Library Consortium (UALC), Univ. of Utah, Salt Lake City 84112. SAN 322-3418. Tel. 801-581-7701, 801-581-3852, fax 801-585-7185, e-mail UALCmail@library.utah.edu. *Chair* Wendy Holliday.

Vermont

Catamount Library Network, 43 Main St., Springfield 05156. *Mailing Address:* Ten Court St., Rutland 05701-4058. *Pres.* Amy Howlett.

Vermont Resource Sharing Network, c/o Vermont Dept. of Libs., 109 State St., Montpelier 05609-0601. SAN 322-3426. Tel. 802-828-3261, fax 802-828-1481. *Ref. Libn.* Scott Murphy.

Virginia

American Indian Higher Education Consortium (AIHEC), 121 Oronoco St., Alexandria 22314. SAN 329-4056. Tel. 703-838-0400, fax 703-838-0388, e-mail info@aihec.org. *Pres./CEO* Carrie Billy.

Lynchburg Area Library Cooperative, c/o Sweet Briar College Lib., P.O. Box 1200, Sweet Briar 24595. SAN 322-3450. Tel. 434-381-6315, fax 434-381-6173. *Dir.* Nan B. Carmack.

Lynchburg Information Online Network (LION), 2315 Memorial Ave., Lynchburg 24503. SAN 374-6097. Tel. 434-381-6311, fax 434-381-6173. *Systems Admin.* Lisa Broughman.

Richmond Academic Library Consortium (RALC), James Branch Cabell Lib., Virginia Commonwealth Univ., 901 Park Ave., Richmond 23284. SAN 322-3469. Tel. 804-828-1110, fax 804-828-1105. *Pres.* Christopher Richardson.

Southside Virginia Library Network (SVLN), Longwood Univ., 201 High St., Farmville 23909-1897. SAN 372-8242. Tel. 434-395-2431, 434-395-2433, fax 434-395-2453. *Dean of Lib.* Suzy Szasz Palmer.

Southwestern Virginia Health Information Librarians, Sentara RMH Virginia Funkhouser Health Sciences Library, 2010 Health Campus Dr., Harrisonburg 22801. SAN 323-9527. Tel. 540-689-1772, fax 540-689-1770, e-mail mdkhamph@sentara.com. *Libn.* Megan Khamphavong.

Virginia Independent College and University Library Assn., c/o University Librarian, Washington and Lee University, 204 W. Washington St., Lexington 24450. SAN 374-6089. Tel. 540-458-8642. *Chair* John Tombarge.

Virginia Tidewater Consortium for Higher Education (VTC), 4900 Powhatan Ave., Norfolk 23529. SAN 329-5486. Tel. 757-683-3183, fax 757-683-4515, e-mail lgdotolo@aol.com. *Pres.* Lawrence G. Dotolo.

Virtual Library of Virginia (VIVA), George Mason Univ., 4400 University Dr., Fenwick 5100, Fairfax 22030. Tel. 703-993-4652, fax 703-993-4662. *Dir.* Anne Osterman.

Washington

National Network of Libraries of Medicine–Pacific Northwest Region (NN/LM-PNR), T-344 Health Sciences Bldg., Univ. of Washington, Seattle 98195. SAN 322-3485. Tel. 206-543-8262, fax 206-543-2469, e-mail nnlm@u.washington.edu. *Assoc. Dir.* Catherine Burroughs.

WIN Library Network, Gonzaga Univ., 502 E. Boone Ave., AD 95, Spokane 99258. Tel. 509-313-6545, fax 509-313-5904, e-mail winsupport@gonzaga.edu. *Pres.* Kathleen Allen.

West Virginia

Mid-Atlantic Law Library Cooperative (MALLCO), College of Law Lib., West Virginia Univ., Morgantown 26506-6135. SAN 371-0645. Tel. 304-293-7641, fax 304-293-6020. *Lib. Dir.* Lynn Maxwell.

Wisconsin

Fox River Valley Area Library Consortium (FRVALC), c/o Polk Lib., Univ. of Wisconsin–Oshkosh, 800 Algona Blvd., Oshkosh 54901. SAN 322-3531. Tel. 920-424-3348, 920-424-4333, fax 920-424-2175. *Coord.* Holly Egebo.

Fox Valley Library Council, c/o OWLS, 225 N. Oneida St., Appleton 54911. SAN 323-9640. Tel. 920-832-6190, fax 920-832-6422. *Pres.* Pat Exarhos.

NorthEast Wisconsin Intertype Libraries, Inc. (NEWIL), c/o Nicolet Federated Library System, 1595 Allouez Ave. Suite 4, Green Bay 54311. SAN 322-3574. Tel. 920-448-4410, fax 920-448-4420. *Coord.* Jamie Matczak.

Southeastern Wisconsin Health Science Library Consortium, Veterans Admin. Center

Medical Lib., Milwaukee 53295. SAN 322-3582. Tel. 414-384-2000 ext. 42342, fax 414-382-5334. *Coord.* Kathy Strube.

Southeastern Wisconsin Information Technology Exchange, Inc. (SWITCH), 6801 North Yates Rd., Milwaukee 53217. Tel. 414-382-6710. *Coord.* Jennifer Schmidt.

Wisconsin Library Services (WILS), 1360 Regent St., No. 121, Madison 53715-1255. Tel. 608-216-8399, e-mail information@wils.org. *Dir.* Stef Morrill.

Wisconsin Public Library Consortium (WPLC), c/o WILS, 1360 Regent St., No. 121, Madison 53715-1255. Tel. 608-216-8399, e-mail information@wils.org. *Dir.* Stef Morrill.

Wisconsin Valley Library Service (WVLS), 300 N. 1 St., Wausau 54403. SAN 371-3911. Tel. 715-261-7250, fax 715-261-7259. *Dir.* Marla Rae Sepnafski.

WISPALS Library Consortium, c/o Gateway Technical College, 3520 30th Ave., Kenosha 53144-1690. Tel. 262-564-2602, fax 262-564-2787. *Chair* Scott Vrieze.

Wyoming

WYLD Network, c/o Wyoming State Lib., 2800 Central Ave., Cheyenne 82002-0060. SAN 371-0661. Tel. 307-777-6333, e-mail support@wyldnetwork.com. *State Libn.* Jamie Marcus.

Canada

Alberta

The Alberta Library (TAL), # 700, 10707 – 100 Ave. N.W., Edmonton T5J 3M1. Tel. 780-414-0805, fax 780-414-0806, e-mail admin@thealbertalibrary.ab.ca. *CEO* Margaret Law.

Council of Prairie and Pacific University Libraries (COPPUL), c/o High Density Library, University of Calgary, 150 B – 11711 85th St. N.W., Calgary T3R 1J3. Tel. 403-220-2414. *Exec. Dir.* Vivian Stieda.

NEOS Library Consortium, Cameron Lib., 5th Fl., Edmonton T6G 2J8. Tel. 780-492-0075, fax 780-492-8302. *Mgr.* Anne Carr-Wiggin.

British Columbia

British Columbia Electronic Library Network (BCELN), WAC Bennett Lib., 7th Fl., Simon Fraser Univ., Burnaby V5A 1S6. Tel. 778-782-7003, fax 778-782-3023, e-mail office@eln.bc.ca. *Exec. Dir.* Anita Cocchia.

Center for Accessible Post-Secondary Education Resources, Langara College Library, 100 W. 49th Ave., Vancouver V5Y 2Z6. SAN 329-6970. Tel. 604-323-5639, fax 604-323-5544, e-mail caperbc@langara.bc.ca. *Dir.* Patricia Cia.

Electronic Health Library of British Columbia (e-HLbc), c/o Bennett Lib., 8888 University Dr., Burnaby V5A 1S6. Tel. 778-782-5440, fax 778-782-3023, e-mail info@ehlbc.ca. *Exec. Dir.* Anita Cocchia.

Northwest Library Federation, 12495 Budds Rd., Prince George V2N 6K7. Tel. 250-988-1860, e-mail director@nwlf.ca. *Dir.* Anna Babluck.

Public Library InterLINK, 5489 Byrne Rd., No 158, Burnaby V5J 3J1. SAN 318-8272. Tel. 604-517-8441, fax 604-517-8410, e-mail info@interlinklibraries.ca. *Exec. Dir.* Michael Burris.

Manitoba

Manitoba Library Consortium, Inc. (MLCI), c/o Lib. Admin., Univ. of Winnipeg, 515 Portage Ave., Winnipeg R3B 2E9. SAN 372-820X. Tel. 204-786-9801, fax 204-783-8910. *Chair* Heather Brydon.

Nova Scotia

Maritimes Health Libraries Assn. (MHLA-ABSM), W. K. Kellogg Health Sciences Lib., Halifax B3H 1X5. SAN 370-0836. Tel. 902-494-2483, fax 902-494-3750. *Libn.* Shelley McKibbon.

NOVANET, The Consortium of Nova Scotia Academic Libraries, 120 Western Pkwy., No. 202, Bedford B4B 0V2. SAN 372-4050. Tel. 902-453-2470, fax 902-453-2369, e-mail office@novanet.ca. *Mgr.* Bill Slauenwhite.

Ontario

Canadian Assn. of Research Libraries (Association des Bibliothèques de Recherche du Canada), 203-309 Cooper St., Ottawa K2P

0G5. SAN 323-9721. Tel. 613-482-9344, fax 613-562-5297, e-mail info@carl-abrc.ca. *Exec. Dir.* Susan Haigh.

Canadian Health Libraries Assn. (CHLA-ABSC), 468 Queen St. E., LL-02, Toronto M5A 1T7. SAN 370-0720. Tel. 416-646-1600, fax 416-646-9460, e-mail info@chla-absc.ca. *Exec. Dir.* Perry Ruehlen.

Canadian Heritage Information Network, 1030 Innes Rd., Ottawa K1B 4S7. SAN 329-3076. Tel. 613-998-3721, fax 613-998-4721, e-mail pch.rcip-chin.pch@canada.ca. *Dir*. Charlie Costain.

Canadian Research Knowledge Network (CRKN), 11 Holland Ave., Suite 301, Ottawa K1Y 4S1. Tel. 613-907-7040, fax 866-903-9094. *Exec. Dir.* Clare Appavoo.

Hamilton and District Health Library Network, 100 King Street W., Hamilton L8P 1A2. SAN 370-5846. Tel. 905-521-2100, fax 905-540-6504. *Coord.* Karen Dearness.

Health Science Information Consortium of Toronto, c/o Gerstein Science Info. Center, Univ. of Toronto, 9 King's College Circle, Toronto M5S 1A5. SAN 370-5080. Tel. 416-978-6359, fax 416-971-2637. *Exec. Dir.* Lori Anne Oja.

Ontario Council of University Libraries (OCUL), 130 Saint George St., Toronto M5S 1A5. Tel. 416-946-0578, fax 416-978-6755. *Exec. Dir.* John Barnett.

Ontario Library Consortium (OLC), c/o Brant Public Lib., 12 William St., Paris M3L 1K7. *Pres.* Kelly Bernstein.

Perth County Information Network (PCIN), c/o Stratford Public Lib., 19 St. Andrew St., Stratford N5A 1A2. Tel. 519-271-0220, fax 519-271-3843, e-mail webmaster@pcin.on.ca. *CEO* Sam Coglin.

Southwestern Ontario Health Libraries and Information Network (SOHLIN), London Health Sciences Centre, London N6A 5W9. Tel. 519-685-8500 ext. 56038. *Pres.* Jill McTavish.

Toronto Health Libraries Assn. (THLA), 3409 Yonge St., Toronto M4N 2L0. SAN 323-9853. Tel. 416-485-0377, fax 416-485-6877, e-mail medinfoserv@rogers.com. *Pres.* Zack Osborne.

Woodstock Hospital Regional Library Services, Woodstock General Hospital, 310 Juliana Dr., Woodstock N4V 0A4. SAN 323-9500. Tel. 519-421-4233 ext. 2735, fax 519-421-4236. *Contact* Bailey Urso.

Quebec

Assn. des Bibliothèques de la Santé Affiliées a l'Université de Montréal (ABSAUM), c/o Health Lib., Univ. of Montreal, Montreal H3C 3J7. SAN 370-5838. Tel. 514-343-6826, fax 514-343-2350. *Dir.* Monique St-Jean.

Federal Libraries Consortium (FLC), 550 de la Cité Blvd., Gatineau K1A 0N4. Tel. 613-410-9752, fax 819-934-7539, e-mail fedlibrariesconsortium.LAC@canada.ca.

Réseau BIBLIO de l'Ouatouais, 2295 Saint-Louis St., Gatineau, Quebec J8T 5L8. SAN 319-6526. Tel. 819-561-6008. *Exec. Gen.* Sylvie Thibault.

Saskatchewan

Consortium of Academic and Special Libraries of Saskatchewan (CASLS), Courthouse, 2425 Victoria Ave., Regina S4P 3M3. *Mailing address:* P.O. Box 5032, Regina S4P 3M3. *Chair* Melanie Hodges Neufeld.

Library and Information-Industry Associations and Organizations, U.S. and Canada

AIIM—The Association for Information and Image Management

Chair, Martin Birch
President and CEO, Peggy Winton
8403 Colesville Rd., Suite 1100, Silver Spring, MD 20910
800-477-2446, 301-587-8202, fax 301-587-2711, e-mail aiim@aiim.org
World Wide Web http://www.aiim.org
European Office: Broomhall Business Centre, Lower Broomhall Farm, Broomhall Ln., Worcester WR5 2NT, UK
Tel. 44-1905-727600, fax 44-1905-727609, e-mail info@aiim.org

Objective

AIIM is an international authority on enterprise content management, the tools and technologies that capture, manage, store, preserve, and deliver content in support of business processes. Founded in 1943.

Officers (2020)

Chair Martin Birch, ibml; *V.Chair* Dave Jones, AODocs; *Treas.* Kramer Reeves, IBM; *Past Chair* Ian Story, Microsoft.

Board Members

Daniel Abdul, Ron Cameron, Rikkert Engels, Karen Hobert, Shukra Kichambare, Stephen Ludlow, Riley McIntosh, Rand Wacker.

Publication

The AIIM Blog.

American Association of Law Libraries

Executive Director, Vani Ungapen
105 W. Adams St., Suite 3300, Chicago, IL 60603
312-939-4764, fax 312-431-1097, e-mail vungapen@aall.org
World Wide Web http://www.aallnet.org

Our Mission

The American Association of Law Libraries advances the profession of law librarianship and supports the professional growth of its members through leadership and advocacy in the field of legal information and information policy.

Membership

4,000 members. For law librarians and other legal information professionals of any professional sector. Dues (Indiv.) $263; (Ret.) $65; (Student) $65. Year. June–May.

Officers (2019–2020)

Pres. Michelle Cosby; *V.P.* Emily Florio; *Secy.* Luis Acosta; *Treas.* Cornell H. Winston; *Past Pres.* Femi Cadmus.

Board Members

Elizabeth G. Adelman; Emily M. Janoski-Haehlen, June Hsiao Liebert; Jean P. O'Grady; Karen Selden; Jason R. Sowards.

Publications

AALL eNewsletter (mo.).

AALL eBriefing.

AALL Spectrum (bi-mo.; free; nonmemb. $75).

Law Library Journal (q.; digital ed. memb. only; pdf, free; or print, memb. $35, nonmemb. $125).

AALL Biennial Salary Survey & Organizational Characteristics (biennial; memb. only online; print e-mail orders@aall.org).

Index to Foreign Legal Periodicals (print or online).

AALL White Papers (digital).

Universal Citation Guide.

American Indian Library Association

Executive Director, Heather Devine-Hardy (Eastern Shawnee)
E-mail hhdevine@gmail.com
World Wide Web https://ailanet.org

Objective

To improve library and information services for American Indians. Founded in 1979; affiliated with American Library Association in 1985.

Membership

Any person, library, or other organization interested in working to improve library and information services for American Indians may become a member. Dues (Inst.) $40; (Indiv.) $20; (Student) $10.

Officers (2019–2020)

Pres. George Gottschalk (Muscogee [Creek] Nation); *V.P./Pres.-Elect* Cindy Hohl; *Secy.* Aaron LaFromboise (Blackfeet); *Treas.* Liana Juliano; *Past Pres.* Lillian Chavez (Mescalero Apache Tribe); Naomi Bishop (Gila River); *Memb.-at-Large* Joy Bridwell (Chippewa-Cree), Carla Davis-Castro, Carlos Duarte, Rhiannon Sorrell (Diné), Ofelia "Liz" Zepeda (Tohono O'odham).

Editorial Board Chairs

Newsletter Editor. George Gottschalk.

Publication

AILA Newsletter (bi-ann., electronic and print). *Ed.* George Gottschalk.

American Library Association

Executive Director, Mary W. Ghikas
50 E. Huron St., Chicago, IL 60611
800-545-2433, fax 312-440-9374, e-mail mghikas@ala.org.
World Wide Web http://www.ala.org

Objective

The object of the American Library Association shall be to promote library service and librarianship. The mission of the American Library Association (ALA) is to provide leadership for the development, promotion, and improvement of library and information services and the profession of librarianship in order to enhance learning and ensure access to information for all. Founded 1876.

Membership

Memb. (Indiv.) 51,842; (Inst.) 5,189; (Corporate) 146; (Total) 57,177. Any person, library, or other organization interested in library service and librarians. Dues (Indiv.) 1st year, $74; 2nd year, $112; 3rd year and later, $148; (Trustee and Assoc. Memb.) $67; (Lib. Support Staff) $53; (Student) $39; (Foreign Indiv.) $89; (Nonsalaried/Unemployed/Ret.) $53; (Inst.) $175 and up, depending on operating expenses of institution.

Officers (2019–2020)

Pres. Wanda Kay Brown. Winston-Salem State Univ., Winston-Salem, NC 27110. Tel. 336-750-2446; *Pres.-Elect* Julius C. Jefferson, Jr. Lib. of Congress/Congressional Research Svc., Washington, D.C.; *Treas.* Maggie Farrell. Univ. of Nevada, Las Vegas, Las Vegas, NV 89001; *Past Pres.* Loida A. Garcia-Febo.

Divisions

See the separate entries that follow: American Assn. of School Libns.; Assn. for Lib. Collections and Technical Services; Assn. for Lib. Service to Children; Assn. of College and Research Libs.; Assn. of Specialized, Government, and Cooperative Lib. Agencies; Lib. and Info. Technology Assn.; Lib. Leadership and Management Assn.; Public Lib. Assn.; Reference and User Services Assn.; United for Libraries; Young Adult Lib. Services Assn.

Board Members

Tamika Barnes *(2018–2021)*; Trevor A. Dawes *(2017–2020)*; Ed Garcia *(2018–2021)*; Eboni M. Henry *(2019–2022)*; Maria McCauley, Ph.D. *(2018–2021)*; Less Kanani'opua Pelayo-Lozada *(2017–2020)*; Karen G. Schneider *(2019–2022)*; Patricia "Patty" M. Wong *(2017–2020)*.

Round Table Chairs

Ethnic & Multicultural Information Exchange (EMIERT). Tinamarie Vella.
Exhibits (ERT). David Lysinger.
Film and Media (FMRT). Gisele Tanasse.
Games and Gaming Round Table (GameRT). Jennifer Bartlett.
Gay, Lesbian, Bisexual, Transgender Round Table (GLBTRT). Megan Drake.
Government Documents Round Table (GODORT). Susanne Caro.
Graphic Novel and Comics (GNCRT). Amie Wright.
Intellectual Freedom (IFRT). Audrey Barbakoff.
International Relations (IRRT). Richard Sapon-White.
Learning (LearnRT, formerly CLENERT). Cheryl Wright.
Library History (LHRT). Anthony Bernier.
Library Instruction (LIRT). Mark Robison.
Library Research (LRRT). Audrey Church.
Library Support Staff Interests (LSSIRT). Nina Manning.
Map and Geospatial Information (MAGIRT). Iris Taylor.
New Members (NMRT). Nicole LaMoreaux.

Retired Members. Nann Hilyard.
Social Responsibilities (SRRT). Charles Kratz.
Sustainability. Uta Hussong-Christian.

Committee Chairs

Accreditation. Loretta Parham.
ALA-Children's Book Council Joint. April Roy.
American Libraries Advisory. Polos Susan.
Awards. Basco Buenaventura.
Budget Analysis and Review. Peter Hepburn.
Chapter Relations. Susan Jennings.
Committee on Appointments. Julius Jefferson, Jr.
Committee on Committees. Julius Jefferson, Jr.
Conference. Matt Beckstrom.
Constitution and Bylaws. Ben Hunter.
Council Orientation. Rodney Lippard.
Diversity. Shauntee Burns-Simpson.
Diversity, Literacy, and Outreach Services Advisory. Martin. Garnar.
Education. Xinyu Yu.
Election. Satia Orange.
Human Resource Development and Recruitment Advisory. Michael Crumpton.
Information Technology Advisory. George Stachokas.
Information Technology Policy Advisory. Sukrit Goswami.
Intellectual Freedom. Julia Warga.
International Relations. Emily Drabinski.
Legislation. Robert Banks.
Library Advocacy. Jeremy Johannesen.
Literacy. Kevin Reynolds.
Membership. Christina Rodrigues.
Membership Meetings. Michael Golrick.
Nominations. Candice Mack.
Organization. James Neal.
Policy Monitoring. Edward Sanchez.
Professional Ethics. Andrew Harant.
Public and Cultural Programs Advisory. Jeff Lambert.
Public Awareness. Eboni Henry.
Publishing. Nicole Spoor.
Research and Statistics. Melissa Cardenas-Dow.
Resolutions. Mike Marlin.
Rural, Native, and Tribal Libraries of All Kinds. John Sandstrom.
Scholarships and Study Grants. Hong Huang.
Status of Women in Leadership. Eileen Palmer.
Training, Orientation, and Leadership Development. Elisandro Cabada.

Publications

American Libraries (6 a year; memb.; organizations in U.S., Canada, and Mexico $74; elsewhere $84; single copy $7.50).
Booklist (22 a year, with digital edition access to current and past issues of *Book Links* and 24/7 access to *Booklist Online*; U.S. and Canada $169.50; foreign $188).
Library Studies, Issues & Trends report.
Library Technology Reports (8 a year, online and print $335, non-U.S. $379).
Smart Libraries Newsletter (mo., online, and print $99, non-U.S. $109).

American Library Association
American Association of School Librarians

Executive Director, Sylvia Knight Norton (ex officio)
50 E. Huron St., Chicago, IL 60611
312-280-4382, 800-545-2433 ext. 4382, e-mail snorton@ala.org
World Wide Web http://www.aasl.org, e-mail aasl@ala.org

Objective

The American Association of School Librarians empowers leaders to transform teaching and learning.

Established in 1951 as a separate division of the American Library Association, AASL understands the current realities and evolving dynamics of the school librarian professional environment and is positioned to help members transform learning through school libraries. AASL publishes standards for the profession *National School Library Standards for Learners, School Librarians, and School Libraries* (2018, its latest), providing a comprehensive approach through integrated frameworks consisting of four domains (Think, Create, Share, Grow) and six Shared Foundations (Inquire, Include, Collaborate, Curate, Explore, Engage).

Membership

Memb. 7,000+. Open to all school librarians, librarians, libraries, interested individuals, and business firms, with requisite membership in ALA.

Board of Directors (2019–2020)

Pres. Mary Keeling, Newport News Public Schools, Supervisor Lib. Svcs., VA; *Pres.-Elect* Kathy Carroll, Westwood HS, Lead Lib. Media Specialist, SC; *Treas.* Judy Deichman, Richmond Public Schools, Instructional Specialist, Lib. Media Svcs., VA; *Past Pres.* Kathryn Roots Lewis, Norman Public Schools, Dir. of Libs. and Instructional Tech., OK; *Div. Councilor* Diane R. Chen; Maria Cahill, Becky Calzada, Anita Cellucci, Sue Heraper, Laura Hicks, Blake Hopper, Kathy Lester, Courtney L. Lewis, Jennisen Lucas, Allison Mackley, Ann Morgester, Suzanna L. Panter, Sarah Searles, Ann Schuster, Holly Schwarzmann, Phoebe Warmack.

Section Leadership

AASL/ESLS. Elizabeth Burns, Angela Branyon, Maria Cahill, Daniella Smith.
AASL/ISS. Elizabeth Nelson, Anna Brannin, Sarah Ludwig, Bianca N. Spurlock, Phoebe Warmack.
AASL/SPVS. Susan Gauthier, Christina Shepard Norman, Maria Petropulos, Jenny Takeda.

Committee Chairs

AASL/ALSC/YALSA Joint Committee on School/Public Library Cooperation. Cynthia Zervos (AASL).
Association of American University Presses Book Selection. Dona Helmer.
Annual Conference. Allison Cline, Laura Hicks.
Awards. Susan Yutzey.
Best Digital Tools for Teaching and Learning. Mary Morgan Ryan.
Budget and Finance. Judy Deichman.
Bylaws and Organization. Devona Pendergrass.
CAEP Coordinating Committee. April Dawkins, Gail Dickinson.
Leadership Development. Kathryn Roots Lewis.
National Conference. Heather Jankowski, Alice Bryant.
Practice. Eileen Kern, Lori Donovan.
Professional Learning. Buffy Edwards.
School Library Month. Shannon DeSantis Gile.
Social Media Recognition. Marifran DeMaine.
Standards. Ann Vickman.

Editorial Board Chairs

Knowledge Quest Editorial Board. Karla Collins.

School Library Research Editorial Board. Audrey Church, Meg Subramaniam.

Social Media Editorial Board. Len Bryan.

Task Force Chairs

Crosswalk. Cynthia Zervos.

Instructional Role of the School Librarian Position Statement. Rachel Altobelli.

Presidential Initiative. Erika Long.

Reading Position Statements. Judi Moreillon.

School Librarian Job Description. Cherity Pennington.

Awards Committee Chairs

ABC-CLIO Leadership Grant. Michael-Brian Ogawa.

Affiliate of the Year Award. Mary Jo Richmond.

Collaborative School Library Award. Jennifer Powell.

Distinguished School Administrators Award. Susan Hess.

Distinguished Service Award. Liz Deskins.

Frances Henne Award. Martha Pangburn.

Innovative Reading Grant. Deb Sondall Saetveit.

Inspire Collection Development Grant. Nicolle Mazzola.

Inspire Disaster Recovery Grant. Donna Sullivan-Macdonald.

Inspire Special Event Grant. Rebecca Gordon.

Intellectual Freedom Award. Valerie Ayer.

National School Library of the Year Award. Priscille Dando.

Past-Presidents Planning Grant. Dorcas Hand.

Roald Dahl Miss Honey Social Justice Award. Lisa Koch.

Ruth Toor Grant for Strong Public Schools Libraries. Hilda Weisburg.

Publications

Knowledge Quest (bi-mo.; memb.; nonmemb. $12 per issue; https://knowledgequest.aasl.org). *Ed.* Meg Featheringham. E-mail mfeatheringham@ala.org.

School Library Research (electronic, free, at http://www.ala.org/aasl/slr). *Ed.* Meg Featheringham. E-mail mfeatheringham@ala.org.

American Library Association
Association for Library Collections and Technical Services

Executive Director, Keri Cascio
50 E. Huron St., Chicago, IL 60611
800-545-2433 ext. 5030, fax 312-280-5033, e-mail kcascio@ala.org
World Wide Web http://www.ala.org/alcts

Objective

The Association for Library Collections and Technical Services (ALCTS) envisions an environment in which traditional library roles are evolving. New technologies are making information more fluid and raising expectations. The public needs quality information anytime, anyplace. ALCTS provides frameworks to meet these information needs.

ALCTS provides leadership to the library and information communities in developing principles, standards, and best practices for creating, collecting, organizing, delivering, and preserving information resources in all forms. It provides this leadership through its members by fostering educational, research, and professional service opportunities. ALCTS is committed to quality information, universal access, collaboration, and lifelong learning.

Standards—Develop, evaluate, revise, and promote standards for creating, collecting, organizing, delivering, and preserving information resources in all forms.

Best practices—Research, develop, evaluate, and implement best practices for creating, collecting, organizing, delivering, and preserving information resources in all forms.

Education—Assess the need for, sponsor, develop, administer, and promote educational programs and resources for lifelong learning.

Professional development—Provide opportunities for professional development through research, scholarship, publication, and professional service.

Interaction and information exchange—Create opportunities to interact and exchange information with others in the library and information communities.

Association operations—Ensure efficient use of association resources and effective delivery of member services.

Established in 1957; renamed in 1988.

Membership

Memb. 3,800. Any member of the American Library Association may elect membership in this division according to the provisions of the bylaws.

Officers (2019–2020)

Pres. Jennifer B. Bowen; *Pres.-Elect* Christopher J. Cronin; *Past Pres.* Kristin E. Martin.

Board of Directors

Officers; Miranda Henry Bennett, Morag Boyd, Trevor A. Dawes, Leigh Ann DePope, Megan Dougherty, Lori Duggan, Thomas Ferren, Dracine Hodges, Katharine D. Leigh, Mary E. Miller, Brooke Morris-Chott, Julie Mosbo, Nathan B. Putnam, Julie Reese; Lori P. Robare, Sandra K. Roe. Chelcie Juliet Rowell, Abigail Sparling, Kerry Ward, Gabrielle Somnee Wiersma.

Committee Chairs

Advocacy and Policy. Patricia M. Dragon.

Affiliate Relations. Nathan B. Putnam.

ALCTS/LITA/LLAMA Exchange Working Group. Kristin E. Martin.

Budget and Finance. Miranda Henry Bennett.

Continuing Education. Jeremy J. Myntti, Amanda Ann Stone.

Fundraising. Rachel K. Fischer, Heath Martin.

International Relations. Kjerste Christensen.

Leadership Development. Laura N. Evans.

Library Materials Price Index Editorial Board. George J. Aulisio, Jr.

LITA/ALCTS Metadata Standards Committee. Darnelle O. Melvin, Scott A. Opasik.

Membership. Erin E. Boyd, Elyssa M. Gould.

Monographs Editorial Board. Susan E. Thomas.

Nominating. Mary Beth Thomson.

Organization and Bylaws. Morag Boyd.

Planning Committee. Katharine D. Leigh.

President's Program. Cynthia Marie Whitacre.

Program. Richard R. Guajardo, Sarah Wallbank.

Publications. Alison M. Armstrong, Treshani Perera.

Standards. Cynthia A. Romanowski.

Interest Group Chairs

Acquisitions Managers and Vendors. Beverly D. Charlot.

Authority Control (ALCTS/LITA). Lisa Robinson.

Bibliographic Conceptional Models. Thomas M. Dousa, Beth Guay.

Book and Paper. Kim Knox Norman.

CaMMS Catalog Management. Dan Tam Thi Do, Marina Morgan.

CaMMS Cataloging Norms. Liz Perlman Bodian, Keiko Suzuki.

CaMMS Competencies and Education for a Career in Cataloging. Daniel N. Joudrey, Erin Leach.

CaMMS Copy Cataloging. Heidy Berthoud, Joy DuBose.

CaMMS Faceted Subject Access. Nerissa Lindsey, Lucas (Wing Kau) Mak.

Cartographic Resources Cataloging IG (MAGIRT). Maggie Long.

Catalog Form and Function. Kelsey Diane George.
Cataloging and Classification Research. Amy Bailey, Jianying Shou.
Chief Collection Development Officers at Large Research Libraries. Christopher Palazzolo.
CMS Collection Development Librarians of Academic Libraries. James Galbraith.
CMS Collection Management in Public Libraries (RUSA Codes). Holly S. Blosser, Jessica Russell.
Collection Development Issues for the Practitioner. Julia M. Gelfand.
Collection Evaluation and Assessment. Natasha A. Cooper, Lisa Leyser Jochelson.
Collection Management and Electronic Resources. Meghan E. Burke.
College and Research Libraries. Danielle Lorraine Ostendorf.
Creative Ideas in Technical Services. Jennifer A. Maddox Abbott.
Digital Conversion. Virginia Dressler, Roger Smith.
Digital Preservation. Justin Lee Baumgartner, Angela Fritz.
Electronic Resources. Abigail Sparling.
Electronic Resources Management (ALCTS/LITA). Jenny Levine, Julie Reese.
FRBR. Michele Seikel.
Heads of Cataloging Departments. Renee Bu, David A. Van Kleeck.
Linked Library Data (ALCTS/LITA). Craig Allen Boman, Annamarie C. Klose.
MARC Formats Transition. Elizabeth J. Cox, Alexander DelPriore.
Metadata. Darnelle O. Melvin.
New Members. Sarah Faith Cruz, Kumiko Reichert.
Newspapers. Brian Geiger.
Preservation Administrators. Beth Doyle, Sabrena Johnson.
Preservation Metadata. Ilda Cardenas.
Promoting Preservation. Justin Carroll Bridges, Mark Coulbourne.
Public Libraries Technical Services. Yu-Lan Margaret Chou, Michael P. Santangelo.
Publisher-Vendor-Library Relations. Ellen Amatangelo, Ajaye Bloomstone, Carolyn Morris.
Role of the Professional Librarian in Technical Services. Christine Davidian, Sai Deng.
Scholarly Communication. Emma Molls.
Technical Services Directors of Large Research Libraries. Dracine Hodges.
Technical Services Managers in Academic Libraries. Lauren Elise DeVoe.
Technical Services Workflow Efficiency. Jesse A. Lambertson, Gina Solares.

Editorial Board Chair

Mary Beth Weber.

Publications

ALCTS News (q.; free; posted at https://alcts.ala.org/news/). E-mail alctsnews@ala.org.
Library Resources and Technical Services (LRTS) (q.; nonmemb. $100; international $100). Electronic only. *Ed.* Mary Beth Weber, Technical and Automated Services Dept., Rutgers Univ. Libs., 47 Davidson Rd., Piscataway, NJ 08854. E-mail lrseditor@lists.ala.org.

American Library Association
Association for Library Service to Children

Executive Director, Aimee Strittmatter
225 N. Michigan Ave., Suite 1300
800-545-2433 ext. 2163, fax 312-280-5271, e-mail alsc@ala.org
World Wide Web http://www.ala.org/alsc

Objective

The Association for Library Service to Children (ALSC) develops and supports the profession of children's librarianship by enabling and encouraging its practitioners to provide the best library service to our nation's children.

The Association for Library Service to Children is interested in the improvement and extension of library services to children in all types of libraries. It is responsible for the evaluation and selection of book and nonbook library materials and for the improvement of techniques of library service to children from preschool through the eighth grade of junior high school age, when such materials and techniques are intended for use in more than one type of library. ALSC has specific responsibility for

1. Continuous study and critical review of activities assigned to the division.
2. Conduct of activities and carrying on of projects within its area of responsibility.
3. Cooperation with all units of ALA whose interests and activities have a relationship to library service to children.
4. Interpretation of library materials for children and of methods of using such materials with children, to parents, teachers, and other adults, and representation of librarians' concern for the production and effective use of good children's books to groups outside the profession.
5. Stimulation of the professional growth of its members and encouragement of participation in appropriate type-of-library divisions.
6. Planning and development of programs of study and research in the area of selection and use of library materials for children for the total profession.
7. Development, evaluation, and promotion of professional materials in its area of responsibility. Founded in 1901.

Membership

Memb. 4,000. Open to anyone interested in library services to children. Dues in addition to ALA membership (Regular) $50; (Student) $20; (Nonsalaried/Ret.) $35; (Advocate) $25.

Address correspondence to the ALSC Office, http://www.ala.org/alsc/aboutalsc/contact.

Officers (2019–2020)

Pres. Cecilia P. McGowan. E-mail nmcgowanalsc@gmail.com; *V.P./Pres.-Elect* Kirby McCurtis. E-mail kirbyalsc@gmail.com; *Past Pres.* Jamie Campbell Naidoo. E-mail naidooalsc@gmail.com; *Div. Councilor* Julie Dietzel-Glair; *Fiscal Officer* Amber Lea Creger.

Board of Directors

Officers; Linda L. Ernst; Elisa Gall; Africa S. Hands, Maggie Jacobs; Sujei Lugo; April Mazza; Sue McCleaf Nespeca; Amy E. Sears; Aimee Strittmatter (Ex-Officio).

Committee Chairs

Advocacy and Legislation. Nathaniel D. Halsan, Erica M. Ruscio.

Arbuthnot Honor Lecture 2020. Lisa Von Drasek.

Budget. Gretchen Caserotti.

Building Partnerships. Jackie Cassidy, Hadeal Salamah.

Children and Libraries Editorial Advisory. Anna Haase Krueger.

Children and Technology. Angela Nolet.
Distinguished Service Award. Mary Beth Dunhouse.
Early Childhood Programs and Services. Kimberly Alberts, Stephanie C. Prato.
Education. Rachel Reinwald, Amanda Yother.
Excellence for Early Learning Digital Media. Katie A. Paciga.
Grants Administration. Ariana Augustine Sani Hussain.
Intellectual Freedom. Justin Azevedo, Betsy Boyce Brainerd.
Library Service to Underserved Children and Their Caregivers. Jason Miles Driver, Sr., Erin Lovelace.
Local Arrangements. Eboni R. Njoku.
Managing Children's Services. Laura Koenig.
Membership. Alyx Andrea Campbell.
Nominating and Leadership Development. Andrew Medlar.
Notable Children's Books. Melody R. Frese.
Notable Children's Digital Media. Laura Bos, Alec B. Chunn.
Notable Children's Recordings. Annamarie E. Carlson.
Oral History. Sharon McKellar.
Organization and Bylaws. Julie A. Corsaro, Joanna Ward.
Preconference Planning. Vicky Smith.
Program Coordinating. Michael P. Santangelo.
Public Awareness. Skye Corey, Mary Schreiber.
Quicklists Consulting. Amanda Yuk-Wah Choi, Kimberly Probert Grad.
Charlmae Rollins President's Program. Marianne Martens, Johanna Ulloa Giron.
Scholarships. Heather Acerro.
School-age Programs and Service. Alexa E. Newman.
Special Collections and Bechtel Fellowship. Allison G. Kaplan.
Website Advisory. Roxanne Hsu Feldman, Patrick J. Gall.

Task Force Chairs

Equity, Diversity, and Inclusion (EDI) within ALSC Implementation. Hanna Lee, Kirby McCurti.
National Institute Planning. Marge Loch-Wouters.
Research Agenda. Kathleen Campana, Brooke E. Newberry.
Student Gift Membership. Andrea Vaughn Johnson.
Summer/Out-of-School-Time Learning. Elsa D. Ouvrard-Prettol.

Awards Committee Chairs

Mildred L. Batchelder Award 2021. Lauren Aimonette Liang.
Pura Belpré Award 2021. Maria Xochitl Peterson.
Randolph Caldecott Award 2021. Julie F. Roach.
Theodor Seuss Geisel Award 2021. Jean B. Gaffney.
John Newbery Award 2020. Krishna Grady.
Odyssey Award 2021. Sharon Haupt.
Robert F. Sibert Informational Book Award 2021. Sally L. Miculek.

Publications

ALSC Matters! (q., electronic; open access).
Children and Libraries: The Journal of the Association for Library Service to Children (q.; print and online; memb.; nonmemb. $50; intl. $60).

American Library Association
Association of College and Research Libraries

Executive Director, Mary Ellen K. Davis
50 E. Huron St., Chicago, IL 60611-2795
312-280-2523, 800-545-2433 ext. 2523, fax 312-280-2520, e-mail acrl@ala.org
World Wide Web http://www.ala.org/acrl

Objective

The Association is a forum for and an advocate of academic and research librarians and library personnel. The object of the Association is to provide leadership for the development, promotion, and improvement of academic and research library resources and services, and to advance learning, research, and scholarly communication. Founded 1940.

Membership

Memb. 11,172. For information on dues, see ALA entry.

Officers (2019–2020)

Pres. Karen Munro; *Pres.-Elect* Jon E. Cawthorne; *Past Pres.* Lauren Pressley.

Board of Directors

Officers; Carolyn Henderson Allen, Jacquelyn A. Bryant, Faye A. Chadwell, Kim Copenhaver, April D. Cunningham, Emily Daly, Jeanne R. Davidson, Mary Ellen K. Davis (Ex-Officio), Caroline Fuchs, Cinthya Ippoliti, Kelly Gordon Jacobsma, Allison Payne, Elois Sharpe.

Committee Chairs

ACRL 2021 Coordinating. Beth McNeil.
ACRL 2021 Colleagues. Julia M. Gelfand, Damon E. Jaggars.
ACRL 2021 Contributed Papers. Faye A. Chadwell, Clara Llebot Lorente.
ACRL 2021 Innovations. Toni Anaya, Leila June Rod-Welch.
ACRL 2021 Invited Presentations. Erla P. Heyns, Willie Miller.
ACRL 2021 Keynote Speakers. John P. Culshaw, Janice D. Welburn.
ACRL 2021 Lightning Talks. Sarah Bankston, Heidi Steiner Burkhardt.
ACRL 2021 Local Arrangements. John Danneker, Christie J. Flynn.
ACRL 2021 Panel Sessions. Merinda Kaye Hensley, LeRoy Jason LaFleur.
ACRL 2021 Poster Sessions. Trevor A. Dawes, Martin L. Garnar.
ACRL 2021 Preconference Coordinating. Bill Gillis, Federico Martinez-Garcia, Jr.
ACRL 2021 Roundtable Discussions Committee. Amanda K. Nida, Kathy A. Parsons.
ACRL 2021 Scholarships. Twanna K. Hodge, Lisa M. Stillwell.
ACRL 2021 TechConnect Presentations. Shawn P. Calhoun, Adriene I. Lim.
ACRL 2021 Virtual Conference. Rachel Besara, Paul A. Sharpe.
ACRL 2021 Workshop Programs. Anne Marie Casey, Alexia Hudson-Ward.
Appointments. Meghan Elizabeth Sitar.
Budget and Finance. Carolyn Henderson Allen.
Equity, Diversity and Inclusion. Derrick Jefferson.
(Dr. E. J.) Josey Spectrum Scholar Mentor. Nikhat J. Ghouse.
External Liaisons. Susie A. Skarl.
Liaisons Assembly. Farzaneh Razzaghi.
Government Relations. Amy Bush, Peter L. Kraus.
Immersion Program. Anne Charlotte Behler.
Leadership Recruitment and Nomination. Sarah E. McDaniel.
Membership. Dawn Behrend.
Section Membership. Larayne J. Dallas.
New Roles and Changing Landscapes. Jolie O. Graybill.
Professional Development. Carrie E. Dunham-LaGree.
2021 President's Program Planning. Jon E. Cawthorne, Megan R. Griffin.

2020 President's Program Planning. Anne-Marie Deitering.
Professional Values. Peter Bremer.
Publications Coordinating. Kristen Grace Totleben.
Research Planning and Review. Allison Benedetti.
Research and Scholarly Environment. Nathan Frank Hall.
Standards. Willie Miller.
Information Literacy Frameworks and Standards. Amanda Nichols Hess.
Student Learning and Information Literacy. Nicole E. Brown.
Value of Academic Libraries. Jill Becker.

Editorial Board Chairs

Academic Library Trends and Statistics Survey. Adrian K. Ho.
ACRL/LLAMA Interdivisional Academic Library Facilities Survey. Anne Marie Casey, Eric A. Kidwell.
Choice. Amanda L. Folk.
College & Research Libraries. Wendi Arant Kaspar.
College & Research Libraries News. Heidi Steiner Burkhardt.
New Publications Advisory. Courtney McDonald.
Project Outcome for Academic Libraries. Tiffany Garrett.
Publications in Librarianship. Daniel Clark Mack.
RBM. Richard Saunders.
Resources for College Libraries. Tammera Marie Race.

Task Force Chairs

Academic Librarians Standards and Guidelines Review. Julia M. Gelfand.
ACRL/ALA/ARL IPEDS. Robert E. Dugan, Erik Mitchell.
ACRL/RBMS-ARLIS/NA-SAA Joint Task Force on Development of the Art and Rare Materials BIBFRAME Ontology Extension. Jason Kovari.
Diversity Alliance. Jon E. Cawthorne.
Impactful Scholarship and Metrics. Rachel Borchardt.
RBMS-SAA Joint Task Force to Revise the Statement on Access to Research Materials in Archives and Special Collections Libraries. Elizabeth Call, Michelle Aviva Ganz.

Discussion Group Conveners

Assessment. Nancy B. Turner.
Balancing Baby and Book. Laura Bornella.
Copyright. Sara R. Benson, Sandra Enimil.
First-Year Experience. Charissa Powell.
Global Library Services. Hong Cheng, Daniel Perkins.
Heads of Public Services. William H. Weare, Jr.
Hip Hop Librarian Consortium. Craig E. Arthur.
International Perspectives on Academic and Research Libraries. Raymond Pun.
Language and Linguistics. Katie E. Gibson, Dan Mandeville, Jennifer Nason
Leadership. Raymond Pun.
Learning Commons. Diane M. Fulkerson.
Library and Information Science Collections. Rachael Clark, Duncan R. Stewart.
Library Support for Massive Open Online Courses (MOOCs). Lauren Carlton.
MLA International Bibliography in Academic Libraries. Odile Harter.
Media Resources. Steven Dennis Milewski.
MLA International Biography. Daniel P. Coffey.
New Members. Ashley Rosener.
Personnel Administrators and Staff Development. Julie Brewer, Michael A. Crumpton.
Philosophical, Religious, and Theological Studies. Megan Welsh, Desirae Zingarelli-Sweet.
Scholarly Communication. Mel DeSart, Erin Elizabeth Owens.
Student Retention. Nicole Helregel.
Undergraduate Librarians. Jason Kruse.

Interest Group Conveners

Academic Library Services to Graduate Students. Mark Nathaniel Lenker.
Academic Library Services to International Students. Olga Hart, Kathryn Ruth Webb.
Access Services. Derek Dolby, Federico Martinez-Garcia, Jr.

African-American Studies Librarians. Tahirah Z. Akbar-Williams.
Asian, African, and Middle Eastern Studies. Qian Liu.
Contemplative Pedagogy. Matthew Thomas Regan.
Digital Badges. Kelsey O'Brien, Victoria Raish.
Health Sciences. John Siegel.
History Librarians. Rachel Bohlmann.
Image Resources. Jane Darcovich.
Librarianship in For-Profit Educational Institutions. Mary A. Snyder.
Library Marketing and Outreach. Kimberly Shotick, Stephanie Espinoza Villamor.
Research Assessment and Metrics. Robin Elise Champieux.
Residency. Twanna K. Hodge.
Systematic Reviews and Related Methods. Megan Kocher.
Technical Services. Cynthia A. Romanowski.
Universal Accessibility. Jill A. Power.
Virtual Worlds. Valerie J. Hill.

Awards Committee Chairs

Academic/Research Librarian of the Year Award. Jeannette E. Pierce.
Hugh C. Atkinson Memorial Award. Angela M. Gooden, Rebecca L. Mugridge, Dale Poulter, Holly A. Tomren.
Excellence in Academic Libraries Awards. Cheryl A. Middleton.

Publications

Choice (12 a year; $513; Canada and Mexico $551; other international $660). *Ed.* Mark Cummings. Tel. 860-347-6933 ext. 119, e-mail mcummings@ala-choice.org.

Choice Reviews-on-Cards (requires subscription to *Choice* or *Choice Reviews* $576; Canada and Mexico $618; other international $713).

College & Research Libraries (*C&RL*) (6 a year; open access online-only). *Ed.* Wendi Arant Kaspar. E-mail warant@tamu.edu.

College & Research Libraries News (*C&RL News*) (11 a year; memb.; nonmemb. $58; Canada and other PUAS countries $63; other international $68). *Ed.* David Free Tel. 312-280-2517, e-mail dfree@ala.org.

RBM: A Journal of Rare Books, Manuscripts, and Cultural Heritage (s. ann.; $52; Canada and other PUAS countries $58; other international $69). *Ed.* Richard Saunders. Southern Utah Univ., 351 W. University Blvd. Gerrald R. Sherratt Lib., Cedar City, UT 84720-2415. Tel. 435-865-7947, fax 435-865-8152, e-mail rsaunders@suu.edu.

American Library Association
Association of Specialized, Government, and Cooperative Library Agencies

Executive Director, Jeannette P. Smithee
50 E. Huron St., Chicago, IL 60611-2795
312-280-4399, e-mail ascla@ala.org
World Wide Web http://www.ala.org/asgcla

Vision

The Association of Specialized Government and Cooperative Library Agencies (ASGCLA), a division of the American Library Association, is the premier destination for ALA members to find information and build capacity to serve populations that are served by state library agencies, federal libraries, armed forces libraries, specialized libraries, library cooperatives, library networks and cooperatives, and library consultants, among others.

Mission

ASGCLA enhances the effectiveness of library service by advocating for and providing high-quality networking, enrichment, and educational opportunities for its diverse members. ASGCLA's members are

- Librarians, library agencies, and staff serving populations with special needs, such as those with sensory, physical, health, or behavioral conditions or those who are incarcerated or detained
- Librarians and staff of state library agencies, and state library consultants—organizations created or authorized by state governments to promote library services
- Library networks and cooperatives, organizations of one or more types of libraries—academic, public, special, or school—that collaborate to maximize the funds available for provision of library services to all citizens; they may serve a community, a metropolitan area, a region, or a statewide or multistate area
- Consultants, independent, or contract librarians, as well as those who work outside traditional library settings

Member activity is centered around interest groups.

Membership

Memb. 800+. For information on dues, see ALA entry.

Officers (2019–2020)

Pres. Sherry Machones; *Pres.-Elect* Carrie Scott Banks; *Secy.* Lily Sacharow; *Past Pres.* Adam S. Szczepaniak, Jr.; *Div. Councilor* Michael A. Golrick.

Interest Group Leaders

Alzheimer's and Related Dementias. Kayla Kuni, Heather Ogilvie.

Armed Forces Librarian. Lee Lipscomb, Virginia Sanchez.

Bridging Deaf Cultures @ your library. Alec McFarlane.

Collaborative Digitization. Sandra McIntyre.

Consortial eBooks. Veronda Pitchford, Stephen Spohn.

Consortium Management. Tracy Byerly, Brad Ward.

Consumer Health Information Librarians. Michael Balkenhol, Lydia Collins.

Library Consulting. Martha Kyrillidou.

LSTA Coordinators. Kathleen Peiffer.

Physical Delivery. Amanda (Mandy) Malikowski, Susan Palmer.

State Library Agencies—Library Development. Shannon White, Wendy Knapp.

State Library Agencies—Youth Services Consultants. Sharon Rawlins.

Tribal Librarians. Lillian Chavez.

Universal Access. Marti Goddard.

For more information on interest groups, see https://www.ascladirect.org/interest-groups.

Board of Directors

Officers; Carson Block, Tracy Byerly, Vicky L. Crone, Ed Garcia, Michael A. Golrick, Rhonda K. Gould, Martha Kyrillidou, Mike L. Marlin, Nancy C. Pack, Jeannette Smithee, Stephen H. Spohn, Jr., Reed W. Strege, Lance D. Wiscamb.

Committee Chairs

Accessibility Assembly. Reed W. Strege.

Awards. John H. Barnett.

Conference Programming. Allan Martin Kleiman.

Guidelines for Lib. and Information Services for the American Deaf Community. Martha L. Goddard.

Membership. Elizabeth A. Burns.

Nominating. Jules Shore.

Online Learning. Wendy Cornelisen.

Web Presence. Stephanie Irvin.

American Library Association
Library and Information Technology Association

Executive Director, Jenny Levine
50 E. Huron St., Chicago, IL 60611-2795
800-545-2433, x4270, fax 312-280-3257, e-mail lita@ala.org
World Wide Web http://www.lita.org

Objective

As the center of expertise about information technology, the Library and Information Technology Association (LITA) leads in exploring and enabling new technologies to empower libraries. LITA members use the promise of technology to deliver dynamic library collections and services.

LITA educates, serves, and reaches out to its members, other ALA members and divisions, and the entire library and information community through its publications, programs, and other activities designed to promote, develop, and aid in the implementation of library and information technology.

Membership

Memb. 2,900. Dues (Reg.) $60; (Nonsalaried/ Ret./Earning less than $30,000 per year) $30; (Student) $25; (Org./Corporate) $90.

Officers (2019–2020)

Pres. Emily Morton-Owens; *Pres.-Elect* Evviva R. Weinraub; *Past Pres.* Bohyun Kim.

Board of Directors

Officers; Mark A. Beatty. Tel. 312-280-4268, e-mail mbeatty@ala.org; Galen Charlton; Lindsay Anne Cronk; Tabatha Farney; Jodie Gambill; Amanda L. Goodman; Margaret Heller; Christopher Lawton; Jenny Levine. Tel. 312-280-4267, e-mail jlevine@ala.org; Hong Ma; Michael Rodriguez; Chrishelle M. Thomas; Berika Williams; *Div. Councilor* Aaron Dobbs.

Committee Chairs

Appointments. Evviva R. Weinraub.
Assessment and Research. Laura Costello.
Blog Subcommittee. Jessica D. Gilbert Redman.
Bylaws and Organization. Christopher Lawton.
Communications and Marketing. Cameron Cook.
Diversity and Inclusion. Paula Jharina Pascual.
Education. Steven W. Pryor, II.
Financial Advisory. Michael Rodriguez.
Forum Planning 2019. Berika Williams.
Fundraising. Bohyun Kim.
LITA/ALCTS Metadata Standards. Darnelle O. Melvin, Scott A. Opasik.
Membership Development. Leland Deeds.
Nominating. Frank J. Skornia.
Program Planning. John J. Hernandez.
Publications. Julie Housknecht.
Top Technology Trends. Louis Brooks.
Web Coordinating. Michael Joseph Paulmeno.

Interest Group Chairs

Altmetrics and Digital Analytics. Jennifer Chan, Tabatha Farney.
Authority Control. Lisa Robinson.
Drupal4Lib. Jenny Levine.
E-rate and CIPA Compliance Interest Group. Jenny Levine.
Electronic Resources Management (LITA/ ALCTS). Jenny Levine, Julie Reese.
E-rate CIPA. Victoria Teal Lovely, Rob Lee Nunez, II.
Heads of Library Technology. Jenny Levine.
Imagineering. Dena Heilik.
Instructional Technologies. Lilly Ramin.
Linked Library Data. Craig Allen Boman, Annamarie C. Klose.
Machine and Deep Learning Research. Jenny Levine.
Maker Technology. Erik Carlson.

MARC Formats Transition. Elizabeth J. Cox, Alexander DelPriore.

Mobile Computing. Jenny Levine.

New Members. Mark A. Beatty, Jenny Levine.

Open Source Systems. Jenny Levine.

Patron Privacy Technologies. Jenny Levine.

User Experience. Jenny Levine.

Women in Information Technology. Melissa A. Hofmann, Sharon M. Whitfield.

Editorial Board Chairs

LITA Acquisitions Editor Marta Deyrup.

ITAL Editor Ken Varnum.

Awards Committee Chairs

Hugh C. Atkinson Award. Angela M. Gooden, Rebecca L. Mugridge, Holly A. Tomren.

Frederick G. Kilgour Award. Emma Hill Kepron.

LITA / Christian Larew Memorial Scholarship. Dale Poulter.

LITA / Ex Libris Student Writing Award. Julia Bauder.

LITA / Library Hi Tech Award. Janet A. Crum.

LITA / Recognizing Excellence in Children's and Young Adult Science Fiction. Wendy Steadman Stephens.

Publication

Information Technology and Libraries (*ITAL*) (open source at https://ejournals.bc.edu/index.php/ital/index). *Ed.* Ken Varnum. For information or to send manuscripts, contact the editor.

American Library Association
Library Leadership and Management Association

Executive Director, Kerry Ward
50 E. Huron St., Chicago, IL 60611
312-280-5032, 800-545-2433 ext. 5036, fax 312-280-2169
e-mail kward@ala.org
World Wide Web http://www.ala.org/llama

Objective

The Library Leadership and Management Association (LLAMA) Strategic Plan sets out the following:

Mission: The Library Leadership and Management Association advances outstanding leadership and management practices in library and information services by encouraging and nurturing individual excellence in current and aspiring library leaders.

Vision: As the foremost organization developing present and future leaders in library and information services, LLAMA provides a welcoming community where aspiring and experienced library leaders and library supporters from all types of libraries can seek and share knowledge and skills in leadership, administration, and management in a manner that creates meaningful transformation in libraries around the world.

Core Values: LLAMA believes advancing leadership and management excellence is achieved by fostering the following values—exemplary and innovative service to and for our members, and leadership development and continuous learning opportunities for our members.

Established in 1957.

Membership

Memb. 3,900+. Dues (Indiv.) $50; (Org.) $65; (Student) $15.

Officers (2019–2020)

Pres. Anne Cooper Moore, Univ. of North Carolina at Charlotte; *Pres.-Elect* Tyler Dzuba, DeEtta Jones & Associates; *Treas.* Susan M. Considine, Fayetteville Free Lib.; *Past Pres.* Lynn Hoffman, Somerset County Lib. System; *Div. Councilor* Rivkah K. Sass, Univ. of Southern California.

Board of Directors

Officers; Audrey Barbakoff, King County Lib. System; Tamika Barnes; Karen Neurohr; Fred Reuland. Tel. 800-545-2433, ext. 5032, e-mail freuland@ala.org; Joseph A. Salem, Jr.; Kerry Ward. Tel. 800-545-2433, ext. 5036, e-mail kward@ala.org.

Committee Chairs

ACRL/LLAMA Interdivisional Committee on Building Resources. Anne Marie Casey, Eric A. Kidwell.
Competencies. Nancy A. Cunningham.
Content Coordinating. Lynn Hoffman.
Continuing Education Development. Christina Pryor.
Equity, Diversity and Inclusion. Crystal C. Miles.
Innovation Incubator. Cinthya Ippoliti.
Marketing and Communications. Cassandra J. Thompson.
Membership. Kerry Ward.
Mentoring. Mary Thornton Moser.
Nominating. Michelle Poston Osborne.
Project Management Project Team
Program. Sara Roberts.
Project Management Project Team. Anastasia G. Guimaraes.

Discussion Group Chairs

Circulation/Access Services. Brian C. Greene.
Fiscal and Business Issues. David Borycz.
LLAMA Dialogue with Directors. Sheila C. Crosby, Michael Hull.
LLAMA New Directors. Lusiella Fazzino, Erik Nordberg.
LLAMA Solo Practioners. Elspeth Olson, Raymond Pun.
LLAMA Women Administrators. Jennifer Renee Steinford.
Library Facilities Planning. Jill Friedmann.
Library Interiors. Gili Meerovitch.
Library Storage. Jay Forrest.

Address correspondence to the executive director.

Publication

Library Leadership and Management (*LL&M*) (open access at https://journals.tdl.org/llm/index.php/llm). *Ed.* Joe Salem, Michigan State Univ., e-mail jsalem@msu.edu.

American Library Association
Public Library Association

Executive Director, Barbara A. Macikas
50 E. Huron St., Chicago, IL 60611
312-280-5752, 800-545-2433 ext. 5752, fax 312-280-5029, e-mail pla@ala.org
World Wide Web http://www.pla.org

The Public Library Association (PLA) has specific responsibility for

1. Conducting and sponsoring research about how the public library can respond to changing social needs and technical developments
2. Developing and disseminating materials useful to public libraries in interpreting public library services and needs
3. Conducting continuing education for public librarians by programming at national and regional conferences, by pub-

lications such as the newsletter, and by other delivery means

4. Establishing, evaluating, and promoting goals, guidelines, and standards for public libraries
5. Maintaining liaison with relevant national agencies and organizations engaged in public administration and human services, such as the National Association of Counties, the Municipal League, and the Commission on Postsecondary Education
6. Maintaining liaison with other divisions and units of ALA and other library organizations, such as the Association for Library and Information Science Education and the Urban Libraries Council
7. Defining the role of the public library in service to a wide range of user and potential user groups
8. Promoting and interpreting the public library to a changing society through legislative programs and other appropriate means
9. Identifying legislation to improve and to equalize support of public libraries

PLA enhances the development and effectiveness of public librarians and public library services. This mission positions PLA to

- Focus its efforts on serving the needs of its members
- Address issues that affect public libraries
- Commit to quality public library services that benefit the general public

The goals of PLA are

- Advocacy and Awareness: PLA is an essential partner in public library advocacy.
- Leadership and Transformation: PLA is the leading source for learning opportunities to advance transformation of public libraries.
- Literate Nation: PLA will be a leader and valued partner of public libraries' initiatives to create a literate nation.
- Organizational Excellence: PLA is positioned to sustain and grow its resources to advance the work of the association.

Membership

Memb. 8,000+. Open to all ALA members interested in the improvement and expansion of public library services to all ages in various types of communities.

Officers (2019–2020)

Pres. Ramiro S. Salazar, San Antonio Public Lib. San Antonio, TX; *Pres.-Elect* Michelle Jeske, City Libn., Denver, CO; *Past Pres.* Monique le Conge Ziesenhenne, Palo Alto City Lib., Palo Alto, CA. E-mail monique.leconge@cityofpaloalto.org; *ALA Div. Councilor* Stephanie Chase, Hillsboro Public Lib; *Fiscal Officer* Clara Nalli Bohrer, West Bloomfield Township Public Lib.

Board of Directors

Officers; Cindy Fesemyer, Toby Greenwalt, Richard Kong, Amita Kaur Lonial, Pamela Smith, Kelvin Watson, Carrie Willson.

Committee Chairs

Advocacy and Strategic Partnerships. Stephanie L. Beverage.

Annual Conference 2020 Program. Michael Spelman.

Budget and Finance. Clara Nalli Bohrer.

Continuing Education Advisory Group. Sarah Campbell Tansley.

Digital Literacy. Monica Marie Dombrowski, Brandy A. McNeil.

Leadership Development. Meaghan O'Connor.

Measurement, Evaluation and Assessment. Linda Hofschire.

Membership Advisory Group. Helen Rigdon.

Nominating. Pamela Smith.

PLA 2020 Conference Committee. Felton Thomas, Jr.

PLA 2020 Annual Conference Program Subcommittee. Juliane Morian.

Public Libraries Advisory. Mary Rzepczynski.

Technology. Henry Miller Bankhead.

Web Content Working Group. Jennifer L. Ferriss.

Task Force Chairs

2020 Census Library Outreach and Education Task Force. Larra Clark.

Family Engagement. Ashley Janet Brown, Jo Giudice.

Social Worker. Jean Badalamenti, Ms. Leah Esguerra.

Task Force on Equity, Diversity, Inclusion and Social Justice. Christina Fuller-Gregory, Lois Langer Thompson.

Awards Committee Chairs

Baker & Taylor Entertainment Audio Music/ Video Product Award. Amy Hanaway.

Gordon M. Conable Award Jury. Erin Eileen Gray.

EBSCO Excellence in Rural Library Service Award Jury. Nyama Yvonne Reed.

John Iliff Award Jury. Abby Bloom Simpson.

Library Innovation Award Jury. Robin L. Doughty.

Allie Beth Martin Award Jury. Susan Wray.

New Leaders Travel Grant Jury. Peggy P. Tseng.

Charlie Robinson Award Jury. Brian K. Auger.

Romance Writers of America Library Grant Jury. Morgan Marie McMillian.

Singer Group Helping Communities Come Together Award Jury. Brian Hasbrouck.

Advisory Group Staff Liaisons

Continuing Education. Angela Maycock.

Membership. Samantha Lopez, Megan Stewart.

Public Libraries. Kathleen M. Hughes, Megan Stewart.

Publication

Public Libraries (6 a year; memb.; nonmemb. $65; Canada and Mexico $75; Int'l. $100). *Ed.* Kathleen Hughes, PLA, 50 E. Huron St., Chicago, IL 60611. E-mail khughes@ala.org.

American Library Association
Reference and User Services Association

Executive Director, Bill Ladewski
50 E. Huron St., Chicago, IL 60611
800-545-2433 ext. 4395, 312-280-4395, fax 312-280-5273, e-mail bladewski@ala.org or rusa@ala.org
World Wide Web http://www.ala.org/rusa

Objective

The Reference and User Services Association (RUSA) is responsible for stimulating and supporting excellence in the delivery of general library services and materials, and the provision of reference and information services, collection development, readers' advisory, and resource sharing for all ages, in every type of library.

The specific responsibilities of RUSA are

1. Conduct of activities and projects within the association's areas of responsibility
2. Encouragement of the development of librarians engaged in these activities, and stimulation of participation by members of appropriate type-of-library divisions
3. Synthesis of the activities of all units within the American Library Association that have a bearing on the type of activities represented by the association
4. Representation and interpretation of the association's activities in contacts outside the profession
5. Planning and development of programs of study and research in these areas for the total profession
6. Continuous study and review of the association's activities

Membership

Memb. 3,200+

Officers (2019–2020)

Pres. Elizabeth Marie German; *Pres.-Elect* Courtney McDonald; *Secy.* Bobray J. Bordelon, Jr.; *Past Pres.* Ann K. G. Brown; *ALA Div. Councilor* Alesia M. McManus.

Board of Directors

Officers; Greg Fleming, Ed Garcia, Melissa F. Gonzalez, Stephanie J. Graves, Patricia L. Gregory, Kathleen Kern, David Ketchum, Bill Ladewski, Cynthia Robin Levine, Rodney E. Lippard, Ninah Moore, Christina Pryor, Shuntai Sykes, Melissa Vanyek.

Committee Chairs

AFL-CIO/ALA Labor. Jane Billinger, Benjamin Scott Blake.
Budget and Finance. Courtney McDonald.
Conference Program Coordinating. Barry Trott.
Membership Engagement. Candice Townsend.
Nominating. Chris Le Beau.
President's Program Planning. Bill Ladewski.
Professional Development. Stephanie J. Graves.
Professional Resources. Elizabeth Malafi.
Volunteer Development. Lori Lysiak.

For more committee rosters, see http://www.ala.org/rusa/contact/rosters.

Awards Committee Chairs

Andrew Carnegie Medal for Excellence in Fiction and Nonfiction. William Patrick Kelly, Jr.
Awards Coordinating Committee. Jenny L. Presnell.
Excellence in Reference and Adult Services Award. Suzanne Odom.
Isadore Gilbert Mudge Award. Gary White.
Gail Schlachter Memorial Research Grant. David A. Tyckoson.

Publications

Reference & User Services Quarterly (online only at http://journals.ala.org/index.php/rusq) (memb.). Ed. M. Kathleen Kern, Miller Learning Ctr., Univ. of Georgia.
RUSA Update (q., online newsletter, at http://www.rusaupdate.org). *Ed.* Carol Schuetz.

American Library Association United for Libraries: Association of Library Trustees, Advocates, Friends, and Foundations

Executive Director, Beth Nawalinski
600 Eagleview Blvd., Suite 300, Exton, PA 19341
800-545-2433, ext. 2161, fax 215-545-3821, e-mail bnawalinski@ala.org or united@ala.org
World Wide Web http://www.ala.org/united

Objective

United for Libraries was founded in 1890 as the American Library Trustee Association (ALTA). It was the only division of the American Library Association (ALA) dedicated to promoting and ensuring outstanding library service through educational programs that develop excellence in trusteeship and promote citizen involvement in the support of libraries. ALTA became an ALA division in 1961. In 2008 the members of ALTA voted to expand the division to more aggressively address the needs of friends of libraries and library foundations, and through a merger with Friends of Libraries USA (FOLUSA) became the Association of Library Trustees, Advocates, Friends and Foundations (ALTAFF). In 2012 members voted to add "United for Libraries" to its title.

Memb. 5,000. Open to all interested persons and organizations. Dues (prorated to match ALA membership expiration) $55; (student with ALA membership) $20.

Officers (2019–2020)

Pres. Peter Pearson; *V.P./Pres.-Elect* David Paige; *Secy.* Kathleen McEvoy; *Past Pres.* Skip Dye; *Div. Councilor* Kathy Spindel.

Board of Directors

Officers, Gordon Baker, Ned Davis, Maura Deedy, Alan Fishel, Patricia Hofmann, Patricia M. Hogan, Luis Herrera, Gary Kirk, Amandeep Kochar, Steve Laird, Mark Miller, Sarah Jessica Parker, Kristi Pearson, Veronda Pitchford, Libby Post, Patricia Schuman, Mark Smith, Rocco Staino, Charity Tyler, Dick Waters.

Committee Chairs

Annual Conference Program. Robin Hoklotubbe.*

Awards. Camila Alire.*

Leaders Orientation. Steve Laird.*

Legislation, Advocacy, and Intellectual Freedom. Deborah Doyle.*

Newsletter and Website Advisory. Ned Davis.*

Nominating. Christine Hage.*

PLA Conference Program 2016–2018. Marcellus Turner.*

* Update not available.

Publications

The Good, The Great, and the Unfriendly: A Librarian's Guide to Working with Friends Groups

The Complete Library Trustee Handbook.

Even More Great Ideas for Libraries and Friends.

A Library Board's Practical Guide to Self-Evaluation.

A Library Board's Practical Guide to Hiring Outside Experts.

Getting Grants in Your Community.

Making Our Voices Heard: Citizens Speak Out for Libraries.

American Library Association
Young Adult Library Services Association

Executive Director, Tammy Dillard-Steels
50 E. Huron St., Chicago, IL 60611
312-280-4390, 800-545-2433 ext. 4390, fax 312-280-5276, e-mail yalsa@ala.org
World Wide Web http://www.ala.org/yalsa
YALSA blog http://yalsa.ala.org/blog, The Hub http://yalsa.ala.org/thehub,
Wiki http://wikis.ala.org/yalsa, Twitter http://twitter.com/yalsa
Facebook http://www.facebook.com/YALSA

Objective

In every library in the nation, high-quality library service to young adults is provided by a staff that understands and respects the unique informational, educational, and recreational needs of teenagers. Equal access to information, services, and materials is recognized as a right, not a privilege. Young adults are actively involved in the library decision-making process. The library staff collaborates and cooperates with other youth-serving agencies to provide a holistic, community-wide network of activities and services that support healthy youth development. To ensure that this vision becomes a reality, the Young Adult Library Services Association (YALSA)

1. Advocates extensive and developmentally appropriate library and information services for young adults ages 12 to 18
2. Promotes reading and supports the literacy movement
3. Advocates the use of information and digital technologies to provide effective library service
4. Supports equality of access to the full range of library materials and services, including existing and emerging information and digital technologies, for young adults
5. Provides education and professional development to enable its members to serve as effective advocates for young people
6. Fosters collaboration and partnerships among its individual members with the library community and other groups involved in providing library and information services to young adults
7. Influences public policy by demonstrating the importance of providing library and information services that meet the unique needs and interests of young adults
8. Encourages research and is in the vanguard of new thinking concerning the provision of library and information services for youth

Membership

Memb. 4,100. Open to anyone interested in library services for and with young adults. For information on dues, see ALA entry.

Officers

Pres. Todd Krueger. E-mail toddbcpl@gmail.com; *Div. Councilor* Abigail Leigh Phillips. E-mail Abigail.LeighPhillips@gmail.com; *Fiscal Officer* Jane Gov. E-mail jgov@cityofpasadena.net; *Pres.-Elect* Amanda F. Barnhart. E-mail amandabarnhart@kclibrary.org; *Secy.* Josephine Watanabe. E-mail Josie.Watanabe@spl.org; *Past Pres.* Crystle Martin. E-mail crystle.martin@gmail.com.

Board of Directors

Officers; Trixie Dantis, Kate Denier, Tammy Dillard-Steels, Tracy Glass, Karen Lemons, Gregory D. Lum, Melissa McBride, Maria McCauley, Charli Osborne, Colleen Seisser, Valerie Tagoe.

Committee Chairs

Advocacy and Activism. Josephine Watanabe.

Fund and Partner Development. Colleen Seisser.

Publications

Journal of Research on Libraries and Young Adults (q.) (online, open source, peer-reviewed). *Ed.* Dr. Robin Moeller. E-mail yalsaresearch@gmail.com.

Young Adult Library Services (YALS) (q.) (online only; member; nonmember $70; foreign $70). *Ed.* Yolanda Hood. E-mail yalseditor@gmail.com.

Archivists and Librarians in the History of the Health Sciences

President, Melissa Grafe
E-mail contact.alhhs@gmail.com
World Wide Web http://iis-exhibits.library.ucla.edu/alhhs/index.html

Objective

The association was established exclusively for educational purposes, to serve the professional interests of librarians, archivists, and other specialists actively engaged in the librarianship of the history of the health sciences by promoting the exchange of information and by improving the standards of service.

Membership

Memb. Approximately 150. Dues $15.

Officers (2019–2020)

Pres. Melissa Grafe, Medical Historical Lib., Harvey Cushing/John Hay Whitney Medical Lib., Yale Univ. New Haven, CT. E-mail melissa.grafe@yale.edu; *Pres.-Elect* Jennifer Nieves, Dittrick Medical History Ctr., Cleveland, OH. E-mail jks4@case.edu; *Secy.* Dawne Lucas, Health Sciences Lib., Univ. of North Carolina at Chapel Hill. E-mail dawne_lucas@unc.edu; *Treas.* Phoebe Evans Letocha, Alan Mason Chesney Medical Archives, Johns Hopkins Univ., Baltimore, MD. E-mail alhhs.treasurer@gmail.com; *Past Pres.* Rachel Ingold, History of Medicine Collections, Rubenstein Rare Book and Manuscript Lib., Duke Univ., 411 Chapel Dr., Durham, NC. Tel. 919-684-8549, e-mail rachel.ingold@duke.edu. *Memb.-at-Large* Beth DeFrancis Sun, Emily R. Novak Gustainis, Joel Klein, Melanie Sorsby.

Committee Chairs

Annual Meeting 2020 Local Arrangements. Melissa Grafe.
Annual Meeting 2020 Program. Rachel Ingold.
Archivist. Jodi Koste.
Nominating 2020. Arlene Shaner.
Recruiting. Jonathan Erlen.
Website. Sara Alger, Beth DeFrancis Sun.

Editorial Board Chairs

The Watermark Stephen E. Novak.

Awards Committee Chairs

Joan E. Klein Travel Scholarship 2020. Barbara Niss.
Publications Awards 2020. Polina Ilieva.
Recognition Awards 2020. Stephen Greenberg.
Watermark (q.; memb.). *Ed.* Stephen E. Novak. Augustus C. Long Health Sciences Library, Columbia University. E-mail sen13@cumc.columbia.org.

ARMA International

CEO, Mona Buckley
11880 College Blvd., Suite 450, Overland Park, KS 66210
913-444-9174, 844-565-2120, fax 913-257-3855, e-mail headquarters@armaintl.org.
World Wide Web http://www.arma.org

Objective

To advance the practice of records and information management as a discipline and a profession; to organize and promote programs of research, education, training, and networking within that profession; to support the enhancement of professionalism of the membership; and to promote cooperative endeavors with related professional groups.

Membership

Approximately 26,000 in more than 30 countries. Annual dues (Professional) $175; (Assoc.) $95. Chapter dues vary.

Officers

Pres. Bill Bradford, Jagged Peak Energy. Tel. 303-947-4119, e-mail bill.bradford@armaintl.org; *Pres.-Elect* Jason C. Stearns, BlackRock. E-mail jasonstearns.arma@gmail.com; *Treas.* Michael Haley, Cohasset Associates. Tel. 908-642-3582, e-mail michaelhaley.arma@gmail.com; *Past Pres.* Ryan Zilm, USAA. E-mail ryanzilm.arma@gmail.com.

Board of Directors

Officers; Susan Goodman, John J. Jablonski, Michelle Kirk, Garth Landers, Mark Levin, Wendy McLain.

Publications

inDEPTH newsletter (bi-mo. memb.)

ARMA Magazine or *Information Management (IM)* (bi-mo., memb., e-magazine https://magazine.arma.org). *Ed.* Nick Inglis. Tel. 913-312-5567, e-mail nick.inglis@armaintl.org.

RIM and IG Around the World (mo.)

Art Libraries Society of North America

Executive Director, Nancy Short
7044 South 13th St., Oak Creek, WI 53154
414-908-4954, 800-817-0621, fax 414-768-8001, e-mail n.short@arlisna.org
World Wide Web https://www.arlisna.org

Objective

The object of the Art Libraries Society of North America (ARLIS/NA) is to foster excellence in art librarianship and visual resources curatorship for the advancement of the visual arts. Established 1972.

Membership

Memb. 1,000+. Dues (Business Affiliate) $250; (Introductory) $100 (two-year limit); (Indiv.) $150; (Student) $50 (three-year limit); (Ret.) $75; (Unemployed/Bridge) $50. Year. Jan. 1–Dec. 31. Membership is open to all those interested in visual librarianship, whether they be professional librarians, students, library assistants, art book publishers, art book dealers, art historians, archivists, architects, slide and photograph curators, or retired associates in these fields.

Officers (2019–2020)

Pres. Laura Schwartz, Univ. of Calif., San Diego. Tel. 858-534-1267, e-mail l7schwartz@ucsd.edu; *V.P./Pres.-Elect* Amy Trendler, University Libraries, Ball State Univ., Muncie, IN. Tel. 765-285-5858, e-mail aetrendler@bsu.edu; *Secy.* Rachel Resnik, Massachusetts College of Art and Design, Boston, MA. Tel. 617-879-7115, e-mail rresnik@massart.edu; *Treas.* Doug Litts, Ryerson and Burnham Libs., The Art Institute of Chicago. Tel. 312-443-3671, e-mail dlitts@artic.edu; *Past Pres.* Kim Collins, Robert W. Woodruff Lib., Emory Univ., Atlanta, GA. Tel. 404-727-2997, e-mail kcolli2@emory.edu.

Board Members

Officers; Stefanie Hilles, Lindsay King, *Editorial Dir.* Roger Lawson, Lauren MacDonald, Suzanne Rackover.

Committee Chairs

Advocacy and Public Policy. Serenity Ibsen.
Awards. Karyn Hinkle.
Cataloging Advisory. Andrea Puccio.
Development. Gregory P. J. Most.
Diversity. Amanda Meeks.
Documentation. Samantha Deutch.
Finance. Matthew Gengler.
International Relations. Beverly Mitchell.
Membership. Laurel Bliss.
Nominating. Debbie Kempe.
Professional Development. Stephanie Grimm.
Strategic Directions. Emilee Mathews.

Editorial Board Chairs

Roger Lawson.

Awards Committee Chairs

Karyn Hinkle.
Distinguished Service. Maria Oldal.
Melva J. Dwyer Award. Suzanne Rackover
Research. Andi Back.
Student Advancement. Courtenay McLeland.
Travel. Katie Keller.
George Wittenborn Award. Jon Evans.

Publications

ARLIS/NA Multimedia & Technology Reviews (bi-mo.; memb.). *Eds.* Melanie Emerson, Gabriella Karl-Johnson, Alexandra Provo. E-mail arlisna.mtr@gmail.com.

ARLIS/NA Research & Reports.

ARLIS/NA Reviews (bi-mo.; memb.). *Eds.* Rebecca Price, e-mail rpw@umich.edu; Terrie Wilson, e-mail wilso398@msu.edu.

Art Documentation (2 a year; memb., subscription). *Ed.* Judy Dyki. E-mail jdyki@cranbrook.edu.

Miscellaneous others (request current list from headquarters).

Asian/Pacific American Librarians Association

Executive Director, Lessa Kanani'opua Pelayo-Lozada
P.O. Box 1598, San Pedro, CA, 90733
310-377-9584 x237, e-mail ed@apalaweb.org
World Wide Web http://www.apalaweb.org

Object

To provide a forum for discussing problems and concerns of Asian/Pacific American librarians; to provide a forum for the exchange of ideas by Asian/Pacific American librarians and other librarians; to support and encourage library services to Asian/Pacific American communities; to recruit and support Asian/Pacific American librarians in the library/information science professions; to seek funding for scholarships in library/information science programs for Asian/Pacific Americans; and to provide a vehicle whereby Asian/Pacific American librarians can cooperate with other associations and organizations having similar or allied interests. Founded in 1980; incorporated 1981; affiliated with American Library Association 1982.

Membership

Approximately 300. Dues (Corporate) $250; (Inst.) $70; (Lib. Support Staff) $20; (Life) $400; (Personal) $35 (one-year limit); (Ret.) $20 (one-year limit); (Student) $15 (Unemployed) $20. Open to all librarians and information specialists of Asian/Pacific descent working in U.S. libraries and information centers and other related organizations, and to others who support the goals and purposes of the association. Asian/Pacific Americans are defined as people residing in North America who self-identify as Asian/Pacific American.

Officers (2019–2020)

Pres. Alanna Aiko Moore; *V.P./Pres.-Elect* Candice Wing-Yee Mack; *Secy.* Melissa Cardenas-Dow; *Treas.* Peter Spyers-Duran; *Past Pres.* Paolo Gujilde; *Memb.-at-Large (2019–2021)* Michelle Lee, Camden Kimura; *(2018–2020)* Rose L. Chou, Anchalee (Joy) Panigabutra-Roberts.

Committee Chairs

Communications and Media. Jaena Rae Cabrera, Molly Higgins.
Constitution and Bylaws. Sheila Garcia.
Family Literacy Focus. Hadeal Salamah.
Finance and Fundraising. Kat Bell, Yen Tran.
Literature Awards. Dora Ho, Ven Basco, Helen Look.
Membership. Maria (Pontillas) Shackles.
Mentorship. Tarida Anantachai, Pearl Ly.
Nominating. Paolo Gujilde.
Program Planning. Ray Pun.
Scholarships and Awards. Rebecca Martin.

Publication

APALA Newsletter (2–3 a year).

Association for Information Science and Technology

Executive Director, Lydia Middleton
8555 16th St., Suite 850, Silver Spring, MD 20910
301-495-0900, e-mail asist@asist.org
World Wide Web http://www.asist.org

Objective

The Association for Information Science and Technology (ASIS&T, formerly the American Society for Information Science and Technology) provides a forum for the discussion, publication, and critical analysis of work dealing with the design, management, and use of information, information systems, and information technology.

Membership

Regular Memb. (Indiv.) 1,100; (Student) 500. Dues (Professional) $140; (Early Career) $75; (Student) $45.

Officers (2019–2020)

Pres. Clara Chu, Univ. of Illinois at Urbana-Champaign, Urbana, IL. E-mail cmchu@illinois.edu; *Pres.-Elect* Brian Detlor, McMaster Univ., Hamilton, ON, Canada; *Treas.* Ina Fourie, Univ. of Pretoria, Pretoria, South Africa; *Past Pres.* Elaine Toms, Univ. of Sheffield, Sheffield, UK. E-mail e.toms@sheffield.ac.uk.

Board of Directors

Officers; James Andrews; Michael Olsson; *Dirs.-at-large* Emily Knox, Agnes Mainka, Soo Young Rieh, Anna Maria Tammaro; *Parliamentarian* Steve Hardin.

Committee Chairs

Awards and Honors. Abebe Rorissa.
Budget and Finance. Ina Fourie.
Governance. Heidi Julien.
Membership. Iris Xie.
Professional Development. Crystal Fulton.
Publications. Chirag Shah.
Research Engagement. Howard Rosenbaum.
Standards. Mark Needleman, Timothy Dickey.

Publications

Inside ASIS&T newsletter (bi-mo.).

Periodicals

Journal of the Association for Information Science and Technology. (JASIST) (mo.). Available with ASIS&T membership or from Wiley Blackwell.

Bulletin of the Association for Information Science and Technology (bi-mo.; memb.; online only).

Proceedings of the ASIS&T Annual Meeting. Available from ASIS&T.

Association for Library and Information Science Education

Executive Director, Cambria Happ
ALISE Headquarters, 4 Lan Dr., Suite 310, Westford, MA 01886
978-674-6190, e-mail office@alise.org
World Wide Web http://www.alise.org

Objective

The Association for Library and Information Science Education (ALISE) is an independent nonprofit professional association whose mission is to promote excellence in research, teaching, and service for library and information science education through leadership, collaboration, advocacy, and dissemination of research. Its enduring purpose is to promote research that informs the scholarship of teaching and learning for library and information science, enabling members to integrate research into teaching and learning. The association provides a forum in which to share ideas, discuss issues, address challenges, and shape the future of education for library and information science. Founded in 1915 as the Association of American Library Schools, it has had its present name since 1983.

Membership

Memb. 700+ in four categories: Personal, Institutional, International Affiliate Institutional, and Associate Institutional. Dues (Indiv. full-time) $155; (Emerging Professional/Part-Time/Ret.) $85; (Student) $40; (Inst. varies, based on school budget) $400–$2,900 (Inst. Int'l./Assoc.) $350. Personal membership is open to anyone with an interest in the association's objectives.

Officers (2019–2020)

Pres. Stephen Bajjaly, Wayne State Univ. E-mail bajjaly@wayne.edu; *Pres.-Elect* Sandy Hirsh, San José State Univ.; *Secy.-Treas.* Heather Moulaison Sandy, Univ. of Missouri. E-mail moulaisonhe@missouri.edu; *Past Pres.* Heidi Julien, SUNY Buffalo, NY. E-mail heidijul@buffalo.edu.

Directors

Officers; Denice Adkins; Lilia Pavlovsky; Rong Tang.

Publications

Journal of Education for Library and Information Science (*JELIS*) (q.; online only; memb.; nonmemb. $139). *Eds.* John M. Budd and Denice Adkins. E-mail jelis editor@alise.org.

Library and Information Science Education Statistical Report (ann.; electronic; memb.; nonmemb. $135).

Knowledge, Skills, and Abilities Survey (KSAs).

Association for Rural and Small Libraries

Executive Director, Kate Laughlin
P.O. Box 33731, Seattle, WA, 98133. Tel. 206-453-3579 e-mail info@arsl.org
World Wide Web http://www.arsl.info
Twitter @RuralLibAssoc

Objective

The Association for Rural and Small Libraries (ARSL) was established in 1978, in the Department of Library Science at Clarion University of Pennsylvania, as the Center for Study of Rural Librarianship.

ARSL is a network of people throughout the United States dedicated to the positive growth and development of libraries. ARSL believes in the value of rural and small libraries, and strives to create resources and services that address national, state, and local priorities for libraries situated in rural communities.

Its objectives are

- To organize a network of members concerned about the growth and development of useful library services in rural and small libraries
- To provide opportunities for the continuing education of members
- To provide mechanisms for members to exchange ideas and to meet on a regular basis
- To cultivate the practice of librarianship and to foster a spirit of cooperation among members of the profession, enabling them to act together for mutual goals
- To serve as a source of current information about trends, issues, and strategies
- To partner with other library and non-library groups and organizations serving rural and small library communities
- To collect and disseminate information and resources that are critical to this network
- To advocate for rural and small libraries at the local, state, and national levels

Membership

Dues (Indiv. varies, based on salary) $15–$49; (Inst.) $150; (Business) $200; (Affiliate) $150.

Officers (2019–2020)

Pres. Jennifer Pearson, Marshall County Memorial Lib., 310 Old Farmington Rd., Lewisburg, TN 37091. E-mail mcmlib@bellsouth.net; *V.P./Pres.-Elect* Kathy Zappitello, Conneaut Public Lib., 304 Buffalo St., Conneaut, OH. E-mail kathy.zappitello AT conneaut.lib.oh.us; *Secy.* Jennie Garner, North Liberty Community Lib., P.O. Box 320, North Liberty, IA 52317. E-mail jgarner@northlibertyiowa.org; *Treas.* Lisa Lewis, 181 N 9th St., Show Low, AZ 85901. E-mail llewis@showlowaz.gov; *COSLA Appointee* Timothy Owens, North Carolina State Lib., 4640 Mail Svc. Ctr., Raleigh, NC 27699-4600, e-mail Timothy.Owens@ncdcr.gov; *Past Pres.* Lisa Lewis, 181 N. 9th St., Show Low, AZ 85901. E-mail llewis@showlowaz.gov.

Board of Directors

Officers; Julie Elmore, Bailee Hutchinson, Jane Somerville, Kathy Street, Sara Wright.

Committee Chairs

Advocacy and Partnerships. Lisa Shaw.
Conference. Connie Mitchell, Laura DeBaun.
Elections. Lisa Lewis.
Finance. Lisa Lewis.
Governance. Mary Soucie, Sara Wright.
Marketing and Communication. Lori Juhlin.
Membership. Erin Busbea.

Association of Academic Health Sciences Libraries

Executive Director, Shira Rosen
2150 N. 107 St., Suite 205, Seattle, WA 98133
206-209-5261, fax 206-367-8777, e-mail office@aahsl.org
World Wide Web http://www.aahsl.org

Objective

The Association of Academic Health Sciences Libraries (AAHSL) comprises the libraries serving the accredited U.S. and Canadian medical schools belonging to or affiliated with the Association of American Medical Colleges. Its goals are to promote excellence in academic health science libraries and to ensure that the next generation of health practitioners is trained in information-seeking skills that enhance the quality of health care delivery, education, and research. Founded in 1977.

Membership

Memb. 150+. Full membership is available to nonprofit educational institutions operating a school of health sciences that has full or provisional accreditation by the Association of American Medical Colleges. Full members are represented by the chief administrative officer of the member institution's health sciences library. Associate membership (and nonvoting representation) is available to organizations having an interest in the purposes and activities of the association. For dues information, contact the association.

Officers (2019–2020)

Pres. Sandra Franklin, Woodruff Health Sciences Ctr. Lib., Emory Univ. Tel. 404-727-0288, e-mail librsf@emory.edu; *Pres.-Elect* Chris Shaffer. UCSF Lib., Univ. of California, San Francisco, CA. Tel. 415-476-2336, e-mail chris.shaffer@ucsf.edu; *Secy./Treas.* Tania Bardyn, Health Sciences Lib., Univ. of Washington. Tel. 206-543-0422, e-mail bardyn@uw.edu; *Past Pres.* Judith Cohn, Health Sciences Libs., Rutgers, State Univ. of New Jersey. Tel. 973-972-4353, e-mail judith.s.cohn@rutgers.edu.

Board of Directors

Officers, Kelly Gonzalez, Gabe Rios, Debra Rand.

Committee Chairs

Assessment and Statistics. Matthew Wilcox.
Diversity, Equity and Inclusion. Cristina Pope.
Future Leadership. Janice Jaguszewski.
New and Developing Health Sciences Libraries. Nadine Dexter.
Program and Education. Shannon Jones.
Research Services. Gabe Rios.
Scholarly Communication. Emily McElroy.

Task Force Chairs

AHS library support to affiliated hospitals and health systems. Melissa DeSantis, Megan Von Isenburg.
Implementation. Amy Blevins.

Association of Christian Librarians

Executive Director, Janelle Mazelin
P.O. Box 4, Cedarville, OH 45314
937-766-2255, fax 937-766-5499, e-mail info@acl.org
World Wide Web http://www.acl.org
Facebook https://www.facebook.com/ACLibrarians
Twitter @ACLibrarians

Objective

The mission of the Association of Christian Librarians (ACL) is to strengthen libraries through professional development of evangelical librarians, scholarship, and spiritual encouragement for service in higher education. ACL is a growing community that integrates faith, ministry, and academic librarianship through development of members, services, and scholarship.

Founded 1957.

Membership

Memb. 500+ at about 150 institutions. Membership is open to those who profess the Christian faith as outlined by the association's statement of faith, and are employed at an institution of higher education. Associate memberships are available for nonlibrarians who both agree with ACL's statement of faith and are interested in libraries or librarianship. Dues (Indiv. 1st Year) $40; (Ret. Libn., Lib. School Student) $35; (Varies, based on income) $40–$120.

Officers (2019–2020)

Pres. (2016–2020) Denise Nelson, Point Loma Nazarene Univ.; *V.P. (2017–2021)* Nate Farley, Univ. of Northwestern–St. Paul; *Secy. (2017–2020)* Carol Reid; *Treas. (2019–2021)* Rodney Birch, Northwest Nazarene Univ.

Board of Directors

Officers; Janelle Mazelin; *Dirs.-at-Large* Andrea Abernathy, Robert Burgess, Mark Hanson, Alison Johnson, Jeremy Labosier, Leslie Starasta.

Section Chairs

Bible College. Pradeep Das.

Liberal Arts. Gail Heideman.

Publications

The Christian Librarian. (2 a year; memb.; nonmemb. $30). *Ed.* Garrett Trott. Corban Univ., Salem, OR.

Christian Periodical Index (q.; electronic).

The Librarian's Manual (English or Spanish; electronic or print; $40).

Library Guidelines for ABHE Colleges and Universities (memb.).

Association of Independent Information Professionals

President, Judith Binder
8550 United Plaza Blvd., Suite 1001, Baton Rouge, LA 70809
225-408-4400, e-mail office@aiip.org
World Wide Web http://www.aiip.org
Facebook https://www.facebook.com/officialaiip
Twitter @AIIP

Objective

Members of the Association of Independent Information Professionals (AIIP) are owners of firms providing such information-related services as online and manual research, document delivery, database design, library support, consulting, writing, and publishing.

The objectives of the association are

- To advance the knowledge and understanding of the information profession
- To promote and maintain high professional and ethical standards among its members
- To encourage independent information professionals to assemble to discuss common issues
- To promote the interchange of information among independent information professionals and various organizations
- To keep the public informed of the profession and of the responsibilities of the information professional

Membership

Memb. 200+. Dues (Full) $200; (Assoc.) $200; (Student) $50; (Supporting) $500; (Ret.) $75; (Emeritus) $50.

Officers (2019–2020)

Pres. Judith Binder, RBSC Corp., Research Group; *Pres.-Elect* Jennifer Pflaumer, Paroo; *Secy.* Phyllis Smith, ITK Vector Inc.; *Treas.* Beth Plutchak, Beth Plutchak Consulting LLC; *Past Pres.* Cindy Shamel, Shamel Information Svcs.

Board of Directors

Officers; George Puro, Cindy Romaine, Kirsten Smith.

Publications

AIIP Connections (blog).
Member Directory (ann.).
Professional papers series.

Association of Jewish Libraries

President, Kathleen Bloomfield
P.O. Box 1118, Teaneck, NJ 07666
201-371-3255, e-mail info@jewishlibraries.org
World Wide Web http://www.jewishlibraries.org
Facebook https://www.facebook.com/jewishlibraries
Twitter @JewishLibraries

Objective

The Association of Jewish Libraries (AJL) is an international professional organization that fosters access to information and research in all forms of media relating to all things Jewish. The association promotes Jewish literacy and scholarship and provides a community for peer support and professional development.

AJL membership is open to individuals and libraries, library workers, and library supporters. There are two divisions within AJL: RAS (Research Libraries, Archives, and Special Collections) and SSCPL (Synagogue, School Center and Public Libraries). The diverse membership includes libraries in synagogues, JCCs, day schools, yeshivot, universities, Holocaust museums, and the Library of Congress. Membership is drawn from North America and places beyond, including China, the Czech Republic, the Netherlands, Israel, Italy, South Africa, Switzerland, and the United Kingdom.

Goals

The association's goals are to

- Maintain high professional standards for Judaica librarians and recruit qualified individuals into the profession
- Facilitate communication and exchange of information on a global scale
- Encourage quality publication in the field in all formats and media, print, digital, and so forth, and to stimulate publication of high-quality children's literature
- Facilitate and encourage establishment of Judaica library collections
- Enhance information access for all through application of advanced technologies
- Publicize the organization and its activities in all relevant venues: stimulate awareness of Judaica library services among the public at large; promote recognition of Judaica librarianship within the wider library profession; and encourage recognition of Judaica library services by other organizations and related professions
- Ensure continuity of the association through sound management, financial security, effective governance, and a dedicated and active membership

AJL conducts an annual convention in the United States or Canada in late June.

Membership

Memb. 600. Year: Oct. 1–Sept. 30. Dues (Indiv.) $70; (First-year Lib. School Student) Free; (Second/third-year Lib. School Student) $35; (Ret.) $35; (Large Inst.) (Greater than 100 FTE / includes personal membership) $100; (Small Inst.) (100 or fewer FTE / includes 1 personal membership) $75; (Corporate) $70.

Officers

Pres. Kathleen Bloomfield, Adat Shalom Reconstructionist Congregation, 1240 Oakmont Rd., Unit 52-i, Seal Beach, CA 90740; *V.P./Pres.-Elect* Michelle Chesner, Columbia Univ.; *V.P. Development* Jackie Ben-Efraim, Ostrow Lib., American Jewish Univ., 15600 Mulholland Dr., Los Angeles, CA 90077. Tel. 818-383-9672, e-mail ajladmanager@gmail.com; *Secy.* Eitan Kensky, Stanford Univ. E-mail kensky@stanford.edu; *Treas.* Holly Zimmerman, AARP, 601 E. St. N.W., Washington, DC

20049. E-mail hzimmerman@aarp.org; *Past Pres.* Dina Herbert, National Archives and Records Admin., Alexandria, VA. E-mail dina.herbert@gmail.com; *Memb.-at-Large* Rebecca Levitan. E-mail ralevitan@gmail.com; Daniel A. Scheide. E-mail dascheide@gmail.com; *RAS Pres.* Amalia Levi; *SSCPL Pres.* Samara Katz.

Board Members

Officers; Sharon Benamou, Emily Bergman, Joy Kingsolver, Ellen Share.

Committee Chairs

Accreditation. Shaindy Kurzmann.

Advertising. Jackie Ben-Efraim.

Archivist. Joy Kingsolver.

Cataloging. Heidi G. Lerner.

Conference, Local. Rachel Kamin, Marcie Eskin.

Conference, Organization-Wide. Lisa Silverman.

Conference Stipend. Lenore M. Bell.

Continuing Education. Haim Gottschalk.

Librarianship and Education. Haim Gottschalk.

Member Relations. Heidi Rabinowitz.

Public Relations. Jessica Fink.

Publications. Laura Schutzman.

Web. Sheryl Stahl.

Editorial Board Chairs

AJL News and Reviews. Sally Stieglitz.

Judaica Librarianship. Rachel Leket-Mor.

Awards Committee Chairs

Groner-Wikler Scholarship. Emily Bergman.

Jewish Fiction Award. Jeremiah Aaron Taub.

Reference and Bibliography Award. Amalia S. Levi.

Student Scholarship. Tina Weiss.

Sydney Taylor Book Award. Rebecca Levitan.

Sydney Taylor Manuscript Competition. Fan and Hyman Jacobs Library.

Publications

AJL Conference Proceedings.

AJL News and Reviews (q., digital; memb.). *Ed.* Sally Stieglitz. Tel. 631-6751-570 ext. 2005, e-mail sstieglitz@lilrc.org.

Judaica Librarianship (annual, digital). *Ed.* Rachel Leket-Mor, Arizona State Univ. Libs. E-mail rachel.leket-mor@asu.edu.

Association of Research Libraries

Executive Director, Mary Lee Kennedy
21 Dupont Circle N.W., Suite 800, Washington, DC 20036
202-296-2296, fax 202-872-0884, e-mail webmgr@arl.org
World Wide Web http://www.arl.org

Objective

The Association of Research Libraries (ARL) is a nonprofit organization of 124 research libraries in Canada and the United States whose mission is to advance research, learning, and scholarly communication. The Association fosters the open exchange of ideas and expertise, promotes equity and diversity, and pursues advocacy and public policy efforts that reflect the values of the library, scholarly, and higher education communities. ARL forges partnerships and catalyzes the collective efforts of research libraries to enable knowledge creation and to achieve enduring and barrier-free access to information.

Membership

Memb. 124. Membership is institutional. Dues: $30,605 for 2020.

Officers

Pres. Lorraine Haricombe, Univ. of Texas at Austin; *V.P./Pres.-Elect* John Culshaw, Univ. of Iowa; *Past Pres.* Susan Gibbons, Yale Univ.; *Treas.* Diane Parr Walker, Univ. of Notre Dame.

Board of Directors

John Culshaw, Univ. of Iowa; K. Matthew Dames, Boston Univ.; Trevor Dawes, Univ. of Delaware; Bob Fox, Univ. of Louisville; Susan Gibbons, Yale Univ.; Lorraine Haricombe, Univ. of Texas at Austin; Mary Lee Kennedy (ex officio, nonvoting), ARL; Vivian Lewis, McMaster Univ.; Adriene Lim, Univ. of Maryland; Joe Lucia, Temple Univ.; Catherine Murray-Rust, Georgia Inst. of Technology; Sarah Pritchard, Northwestern Univ.; Diane Parr Walker, Univ. of Notre Dame.

Advisory Group Chairs

Advocacy and Public Policy Committee. Kornelia Tancheva, Univ. of Pittsburgh.
ARL Academy Advisory Committee. Simon Neame, Univ. of Massachusetts, Amherst.
Audit Committee. Sarah Pritchard, Northwestern Univ.
Diversity, Equity, and Inclusion Committee. Damon Jaggars, Ohio State Univ.
Finance Committee. Diane Parr Walker, Univ. of Notre Dame.
Governance Committee. Catherine Murray-Rust, Georgia Inst. of Technology.
Member Engagement and Outreach Committee. Lorelei Tanji, Univ. of California, Irvine.
Membership Committee. Adriene Lim, Univ. of Maryland.
Program Strategy Committee. Mary Lee Kennedy, ARL.
Research and Analytics Committee. Don Gilstrap, Univ. of Alabama.
Scholars and Scholarship Committee. David Carlson, Texas A&M Univ.

Publications

ARL Academic Health Sciences Library Statistics (ann.).
ARL Academic Law Library Statistics (ann.).
ARL Annual Salary Survey (ann.).
ARL Statistics (ann.).
Research Library Issues (4 a year).

ARL Membership

Nonuniversity Libraries

Boston Public Lib.; Center for Research Libs.; Lib. of Congress; National Agricultural Lib.; National Archives and Records Administration; National Lib. of Medicine; New York Public Lib.; Smithsonian Institution Libs.

University Libraries

Alabama; Albany (SUNY); Alberta; Arizona; Arizona State; Auburn; Boston College; Boston Univ.; Brigham Young; British Columbia; Brown; Buffalo (SUNY); Calgary; California, Berkeley; California, Davis; California, Irvine; California, Los Angeles; California, Riverside; California, San Diego; California, Santa Barbara; Case Western Reserve; Chicago; Cincinnati; Colorado, Boulder; Colorado State; Columbia; Connecticut; Cornell; Dartmouth; Delaware; Duke; Emory; Florida; Florida State; George Washington; Georgetown; Georgia; Georgia Inst. of Technology; Guelph; Harvard; Hawaii, Manoa; Houston; Howard; Illinois, Chicago; Illinois, Urbana-Champaign; Indiana, Bloomington; Iowa; Iowa State; Johns Hopkins; Kansas; Kent State; Kentucky; Laval; Louisiana State; Louisville; McGill; McMaster; Manitoba; Maryland; Massachusetts, Amherst; Massachusetts Inst. of Technology; Miami (Florida); Michigan; Michigan State; Minnesota; Missouri, Columbia; Nebraska, Lincoln; New Mexico; New York; North Carolina, Chapel Hill; North Carolina State; Northwestern; Notre Dame; Ohio; Ohio State; Oklahoma; Oklahoma State; Oregon; Ottawa; Pennsylvania; Pennsylvania State; Pittsburgh; Princeton; Purdue; Queen's (Kingston, Ontario); Rice; Rochester; Rutgers; Saskatchewan; Simon Fraser; South Carolina; Southern California; Southern Illinois, Carbondale; Stony Brook (SUNY); Syracuse; Temple; Tennessee,

Knoxville; Texas, Austin; Texas A&M; Texas Tech; Toronto; Tulane; Utah; Vanderbilt; Virginia; Virginia Commonwealth; Virginia Tech; Washington; Washington, Saint Louis; Washington State; Waterloo; Wayne State; Western; Wisconsin, Madison; Yale; York.

Association of Vision Science Librarians

Co-Chairs Leslie Holland, Dede Rios
World Wide Web http://www.avsl.org

Objective

To foster collective and individual acquisition and dissemination of vision science information, to improve services for all persons seeking such information, and to develop standards for libraries to which members are attached. Founded in 1968.

Membership

Memb. (Indiv.) 150+, (Inst.) 100+.

Leadership Team

Co-Chair Rudy Barreras, Western Univ. of Health Sciences, Pomona, California. E-mail rbarreras@westernu.edu; *Co-Chair* Dede Rios, Rosenberg School of Optometry, Univ. of the Incarnate Word, San Antonio. E-mail dmrios1@uiwtx.edu; *Secy.* Louise Collins, Massachusetts Eye and Ear Institute, Howe Lib., Boston, MA. E-mail Louise_Collins@MEEI.HARVARD.EDU; *Archivist* Gale Oren, Univ. of Michigan Kellogg Eye Ctr., John W. Henderson Lib., Ann Arbor. E-mail goren@umich.edu.

Meetings

Annual meeting held in the fall, midyear minimeeting with the Medical Library Association.

Atla

Executive Director, Brenda Bailey-Hainer
300 S. Wacker Dr., Suite 2100, Chicago, IL 60606-6701
888-665-2852 or 312-454-5100, fax 312-454-5505, e-mail bbailey-hainer@atla.com.
World Wide Web http://www.atla.com

Mission

The mission of Atla (formerly known as the American Theological Library Association) is to foster the study of theology and religion by enhancing the development of theological and religious libraries and librarianship.

Membership

Dues (Inst.) $100–$1,000; (Indiv. varies, based on income) $35–$181.50; (Student) $35; (Affiliates) $100.

Officers (2019–2020)

Pres. Stephen Sweeney, Saint John Vianney Theological Seminary, 1300 South Steele St., Denver, CO 80210-2599. E-mail stephen.sweeney@archden.org; *V.P.* Ellen Frost, Perkins School of Theology, Bridwell Lib., P.O. Box 750476, Dallas, TX 75275-0476. E-mail efrost@smu.edu; *Secy.* Christina Torbert. Univ. of Mississippi—Libs., P.O. Box 1848, University, MS 38655. E-mail ctorbert@olemiss.edu; Treas. Armin Siedlecki, Pitts Theological Lib., Emory Univ., 1531 Dickey Dr., Suite 560, Atlanta, GA 30322. E-mail asiedle@emory.edu.

Board of Directors

Officers; Jennifer Bartholomew, Susan Ebertz, Suzanne Estelle-Holmer, Jeremie LeBlanc, Shanee' Yvette Murrain, Matthew Ostercamp, Michelle Spomer, Matthew Thiesen.

Committee Chairs

Conference. Erica Durham.
Diversity, Equity, and Inclusion. Evan Boyd.
Endowment. Pat Graham.
Professional Development. Michael Bradford.
Scholarly Communication. Michael Hemenway.

Publications

Theological Librarianship (open access journal) http://theolib.atla.com/theolib.

Theology Cataloging Bulletin (open access journal): http://serials.atla.com/tcb/index.

Atla Annual Yearbook (online open access ann. serial) http://serials.atla.com/yearbook.

Atla Newsletter (mo.; online).

Atla Proceedings (online open access ann. serial) http://serials.atla.com/proceedings.

books@Atla Open Press (online open access monographs): https://books.atla.com/atlapress.

Beta Phi Mu (International Library and Information Studies Honor Society)

Executive Director, Alison M. Lewis
P.O. Box 42139, Philadelphia, PA 19101
267-361-5018, e-mail executivedirector@betaphimu.org or headquarters@betaphimu.org
World Wide Web http://www.betaphimu.org

Objective

To recognize distinguished achievement in and scholarly contributions to librarianship, information studies, or library education, and to sponsor and support appropriate professional and scholarly projects relating to these fields. Founded at the University of Illinois in 1948.

Membership

Memb. 40,000. Eligibility for membership in Beta Phi Mu is by invitation of the faculty from institutions where the American Library Association, or other recognized accrediting agency approved by the Beta Phi Mu Executive Board, has accredited or recognized a professional degree program. Candidates must be graduates of a library and information science program and fulfill the following requirements: complete the course requirements leading to a master's degree with a scholastic average of 3.75 where A equals 4 points, or complete a planned program of advanced study beyond the master's degree which requires full-time study for one or more academic years with a scholastic average of 3.75 where A equals 4.0. Each chapter or approved institution is allowed to invite no more than 25 percent of the annual graduating class, and the faculty of participating library schools must attest to their initiates' professional promise.

Officers

Pres. (2018–2021) Cecelia Brown, School of Lib. and Information Studies, Univ. of Oklahoma, 401 W Brooks, Rm. 120, Norman, OK 73019-6032. Tel. 405-325-3921, e-mail cbrown@ou.edu; *V.P./Pres.-Elect (2019–2022)* Emily Knox, School of Information Sciences, Univ. of Illinois, 501 E. Daniel St., Champaign, IL 61820. Tel. 217-300-0212, e-mail knox@illinois.edu; *Interim Treas. (2019–2020)* Vicki Gregory, School of Information, Univ. of South Florida, College of Arts and Sciences, 4202 E. Fowler Ave., CIS 2036, Tampa, FL 33620. Tel. 813-974-3520, e-mail gregory@usf.edu. *Past Pres. (2017–2020)* Elaine Yontz, Dept. of Interdisciplinary Professions, College of Education,

East Carolina Univ., Ragsdale 112-Mail Stop 172, Greenville, NC 27858-4353. Tel. 252-737-1150, e-mail yontzm@ecu.edu; *Dirs.-at-large* Michelle Demeter, Camille McCutcheon.

Directors

Gordon N. Baker, Sheri Ross, Heather Moulaison Sandy, Laura Sanders.

Publications

Beta Phi Mu Scholars Series. Available from Rowman & Littlefield, Publishers, 4501 Forbes Blvd., Suite 200, Lanham, MD 20706. *Ed.* Andrea Falcone. E-mail bpmseries@gmail.com.

Newsletter. *The Pipeline* (biennial; electronic only). *Ed.* Alison Lewis.

Chapters

Alpha. Univ. of Illinois at Urbana-Champaign, School of Info. Sciences; *Gamma.* Florida State Univ., College of Communication and Info.; *Epsilon.* Univ. of North Carolina at Chapel Hill, School of Info. and Lib. Science; *Theta.* c/o Pratt Inst., School of Info.; *Iota.* Catholic Univ. of America, Dept. of Lib. and Info. Science; Univ. of Maryland, College of Info. Studies; *Lambda.* Univ. of Oklahoma, School of Lib. and Info. Studies; *Xi.* Univ. of Hawaii at Manoa, Lib. and Info. Science Program; *Omicron.* Rutgers Univ., Grad. School of Communication, Info., and Lib. Studies; *Pi.* Univ. of Pittsburgh, School of Info. Sciences; *Sigma.* Drexel Univ., College of Computing and Informatics; *Psi.* Univ. of Missouri at Columbia, School of Info. Science and Learning Technologies; *Omega.* San José State Univ., School of Info.; *Beta Beta.* Simmons Univ., School of Lib. and Info. Science; *Beta Delta.* State Univ. of New York at Buffalo, Dept. of Lib. and Info. Studies; *Beta Epsilon.* Emporia State Univ., School of Lib. and Info. Management; *Beta Zeta.* Louisiana State Univ., School of Lib. and Info. Science; *Beta Iota.* Univ. of Rhode Island, Grad. School of Lib. and Info. Studies; *Beta Kappa.* Univ. of Alabama, School of Lib. and Info. Studies; *Beta Lambda.* Texas Woman's Univ., School of Lib. and Info. Sciences; *Beta Mu.* Long Island Univ., Palmer School of Lib. and Info. Science; *Beta Nu.* St. John's Univ., Div. of Lib. and Info. Science-*Beta Xi.* North Carolina Central Univ., School of Lib. and Info. Sciences; *Beta Pi.* Univ. of Arizona, School of Info.; *Beta Rho.* Univ. of Wisconsin at Milwaukee, School of Info. Science; *Beta Phi.* Univ. of South Florida, School of Lib. and Info. Science; *Beta Psi.* Univ. of Southern Mississippi, School of Lib. and Info. Science; *Beta Omega.* Univ. of South Carolina, College of Lib. and Info. Science; *Beta Beta Epsilon.* Univ. of Wisconsin at Madison, School of Lib. and Info. Studies; *Beta Beta Theta.* Univ. of Iowa, School of Lib. and Info. Science; *Pi Lambda Sigma.* Syracuse Univ., School of Info. Studies; *Beta Beta Mu.* Valdosta State Univ., Lib. and Info. Science Program; *Beta Beta Nu.* Univ. of North Texas, College of Info.; *Beta Beta Omicron.* East Carolina Univ., Dept. of Interdisciplinary Professions; *Beta Beta Xi.* St. Catherine Univ., Master of Lib. and Info. Science Program.

Bibliographical Society of America

Executive Director, Erin Schreiner
P.O. Box 1537, Lenox Hill Station, New York, NY 10021
212-452-2710, e-mail bsa@bibsocamer.org
World Wide Web http://www.bibsocamer.org

Objective

To promote bibliographical research and to issue bibliographical publications. Organized in 1904.

Membership

Dues (Partner) $80; (Sustaining) $125; (Leadership) $250; (Advancing) $500; (Lifetime) $1,250; (Emerging bibliographers, 35 and under) $25. Year. Jan.–Dec.

Officers

Pres. Barbara A. Shailor, Yale Univ.; *V.P.* Kenneth Soehner, The Watson Lib., Metropolitan Museum of Art; *Secy.* John T. McQuillen, Morgan Museum and Lib.; *Treas.* G. Scott Clemons, Brown Brothers Harriman. E-mail scott.Clemons@bbh.com. *Delegate to the ACLS* David Vander Meulen, Univ. of Virginia.

Council

(2023) Mary Crawford, Andrew T. Nadell, Elizabeth Ott, Douglas Pfeiffer; *(2022)* Caroline Duroselle-Melish, Mark Samuels Lasner, Alice Schreyer, Jackie Vossler; *(2021)* Thomas Goldwasser, Adam G. Hooks, Michael F. Suarez, Nick Wilding.

Committee Chairs

Audit. Joan Friedman.
Development. Barbara A. Shailor.
Digital Strategy Working Group. Erin Schreiner.
Fellowship. Hope Mayo.
Finance. Jackie Vossler.
International Development and Collaboration Working Group. Greg Prickman.
Membership Working Group. Elizabeth Ott.
New Scholars. Barbara Heritage.
Policy and Procedures Manual Working Group. Joan Friedman.
Program. Sonja Drimmer.
Publications. Nicholas Wilding.

Publication

Papers of the Bibliographical Society of America (q.; memb.). *Ed.* David L. Gants, Florida State Univ. E-mail editor.pbsa@bibsocamer.org.

Bibliographical Society of Canada (La Société Bibliographique du Canada)

President, Karen Smith
360 Bloor St. W., P.O. Box 19035 Walmer, Toronto, ON M5S 3C9
E-mail secretary@bsc-sbc.ca
World Wide Web http://www.bsc-sbc.ca

Objective

The Bibliographical Society of Canada is a bilingual (English/French) organization that has as its goal the scholarly study of the history, description, and transmission of texts in all media and formats, with a primary emphasis on Canada, and the fulfillment of this goal through the following objectives:

- To promote the study and practice of bibliography: enumerative, historical, descriptive, analytical, and textual
- To further the study, research, and publication of book history and print culture
- To publish bibliographies and studies of book history and print culture
- To encourage the publication of bibliographies, critical editions, and studies of book history and print culture
- To promote the appropriate preservation and conservation of manuscript, archival, and published materials in various formats
- To encourage the utilization and analysis of relevant manuscript and archival sources as a foundation of bibliographical scholarship and book history
- To promote the interdisciplinary nature of bibliography, and to foster relationships with other relevant organizations nationally and internationally
- To conduct the society without purpose of financial gain for its members, and to ensure that any profits or other accretions to the society shall be used in promoting its goal and objectives

Membership

The society welcomes as members all those who share its aims and wish to support and participate in bibliographical research and publication. Dues (Reg.) $80; (Student) $35; (Ret.) $50; (Inst.) $100; (Life) $1,000.

Executive Council (2019–2020)

Pres. Karen Smith. E-mail president@bsc-sbc.ca; *1st V.P.* Christopher Young. E-mail vice_president_1@bsc-sbc.ca; *2nd V.P.* Svetlana Kochkina. E-mail vice_president_2@bsc-sbc.ca; *Secy.* Alexandra Kordoski Carter. E-mail secretary@bsc-sbc.ca; *Assoc. Secy.* Marie-Claude Felton; *Treas.* Tom Vincent. E-mail treasurer@bsc-sbc.ca; *Assoc. Treas.* Meaghan Scanlon; *Past Pres.* Ruth-Ellen St. Onge.

Council

Executive Council; *(2017–2020)* Gwen Davies, Hannah McGregor, Annie Murray; *(2018–2021)* Billy Johnson, Ruth Panofsky, Alison Rukavina; *(2019–2022)* Susan Cameron, Scott Schofield, Myra Tawik.

Committee Chairs

Awards. Hannah McGregor.

Communications. Svetlana Kochkina.

Fellowships. Ruth Panofsky.

Publications. Geoffrey Little.

Publications

Bulletin (s. ann). *Ed.* Philippe Mongeau.

Papers of the Bibliographical Society of Canada/Cahiers de la Société Bibliographique du Canada (s. ann.). *Interim Ed.* Ruth-Ellen St. Onge.

Black Caucus of the American Library Association

President, Richard Ashby
P.O. Box 174, New York, NY 10159-0174
646-721-1358
World Wide Web http://www.bcala.org

Mission

The Black Caucus of the American Library Association (BCALA) serves as an advocate for the development, promotion, and improvement of library services and resources for the nation's African American community and provides leadership for the recruitment and professional development of African American librarians. Founded in 1970.

Membership

Membership is open to any person, institution, or business interested in promoting the development of library and information services for African Americans and other people of African descent and willing to maintain good financial standing with the organization. The membership is currently composed of librarians and other information professionals, library support staff, libraries, publishers, authors, vendors, and other library-related organizations in the United States and abroad. Dues (Lifetime) $500; (Corporate) $200; (Inst.) $60; (Reg.) $45; (Library Support Staff) $20; (Student) $10; (Ret.) $25.

Officers

Pres. Richard Ashby, Jr.; *V.P./Pres.-Elect* Shauntee Burns-Simpson; *Secy.* Brenda Johnson-Perkins; *Treas.* Brandy McNeil; *Past Pres.* Denyvetta Davis.

Board Members

Officers; *(2019–2021)* Latrice Booker, Vivian Bordeaux, Rudolph Clay, James Allen Davis, Jr., Tashia Munson, Ana Ndumu, Regina Renee Ward; *(2018–2020)* Elizabeth Jean Brumfield, Valerie Carter, Jina DuVernay, Nichelle Hayes, Tatanisha Love, Jasmine Simmons.

Committee Chairs

Affiliates. Andrew P. Jackson.
ALA Relations. Trevor Dawes.
Awards. John Page.
Budget and Finance. Sharon Mahaffey.
Constitution and Bylaws. Jos Holman.
Fundraising. BRIAN HART.
History. Sybyl Moses.
International Relations. Eboni M. Henry.
Marketing and Public Relations. Shaundra Walker.
Membership. Rudolph Clay, Jr.
National Conference. Tracey Hunter Hayes, Keith Jemison.
Nomination and Election. Denyvetta Davis.
President's Advisory. Richard E. Ashby, Jr.
Programs. Shauntee Burns-Simpson.
Publications. Nichelle Hayes.
Recruitment and Professional Development. Ana Ndumu.
Services to Children and Families of African Descent. Karen Lemmons.
Technology Advisory. Jerrod Moore, Roosevelt Weeks.

Awards Committee Chairs

Literary Awards. Gladys Smiley Bell.
Dr. E. J. Josey Scholarship. Sylvia Sprinkle-Hamlin.

Publication

BCALA News (3 a year; memb.). *Ed.* Jason Alston. E-mail jasonalston@gmail.com.

Canadian Association for Information Science (L'Association Canadienne des Sciences de l'Information)

President, Philippe Mongeon
World Wide Web http://www.cais-acsi.ca

Objective

To promote the advancement of information science in Canada and encourage and facilitate the exchange of information relating to the use, access, retrieval, organization, management, and dissemination of information.

Membership

Institutions and individuals interested in information science and involved in the gathering, organization, and dissemination of information (such as information scientists, archivists, librarians, computer scientists, documentalists, economists, educators, journalists, and psychologists) and who support Canadian Association for Information Science (CAIS) objectives can become association members.

Officers (2019–2020)

Pres. Philippe Mongeon, Aarhus Univ.; *Secy.* Fei Shu, Hangzhou Dianzi Univ.; *Treas.* Michael Ridley, Western Univ.; *Past Pres.* Heather Hill, Western Univ.; *Memb.-at-Large* Danica Pawlick-Potts.

Board Members

Officers; Roger Chabot, Western Univ.; Christina Parsons, Robyn Stobbs, Univ. of Alberta; Sam A. Vander Kooy, Western Univ.

Editorial Board Chairs

Canadian Journal of Info. and Lib. Science. Valerie M. Nesset.

Publication

Canadian Journal of Information and Library Science. (q.; memb.; print; online). For nonmember subscription information visit https://utpjournals.press/loi/cjils. *Ed.* Heather Hill, Information and Media Studies, Western Univ. E-mail cjils@cais-acsi.ca.

Canadian Association of Research Libraries (Association des Bibliothèques de Recherche du Canada)

Executive Director, Susan Haigh
309 Cooper St., Suite 203, Ottawa, ON K2P 0G5
613-482-9344 ext. 101, e-mail info@carl-abrc.ca
World Wide Web http://www.carl-abrc.ca
Twitter @carlabrc

Membership

The Canadian Association of Research Libraries (CARL), established in 1976, is the leadership organization for the Canadian research library community. The association's members are the 29 major academic research libraries across Canada together with Library and Archives Canada and the National Research Council Canada, National Science Library. Membership is institutional, open primarily to libraries of Canadian universities that have doctoral graduates in both the arts and the sciences. CARL is an associate member of the

Association of Universities and Colleges of Canada (AUCC) and is incorporated as a not-for-profit organization under the Canada Corporations Act.

Mission

The association provides leadership on behalf of Canada's research libraries and enhances their capacity to advance research and higher education. It promotes effective and sustainable scholarly communication, and public policy that enables broad access to scholarly information.

Officers (2019–2020)

Pres. Jonathan Bengtson, Univ. of Victoria, Victoria, BC; *V.P.* Vivian Lewis, McMaster Univ., Hamilton, ON; *Secy.* Loubna Ghaouti, Univ. Laval, Montréal, PQ; *Treas.* Susan Cleyle, Memorial Univ., St. John's, NL.

Board of Directors

Larry Alford, Univ. of Toronto, Toronto (Ontario Region Representative). Melissa Just, Univ. of Saskatchewan, Saskatoon (Western Region Representative).

Committee Chairs

Advancing Research. Catherine Steeves.
Assessment. Colleen Cook.
Policy. Carol Shepstone.
Strengthening Capacity. Brett Waytuck.

Member Institutions

National Members

Lib. and Archives Canada, National Research Council Canada, National Science Lib.

Regional Members

Univ. of Alberta, Univ. of British Columbia, Brock Univ., Univ. of Calgary, Carleton Univ., Concordia Univ., Dalhousie Univ., Univ. of Guelph, Univ. Laval, McGill Univ., McMaster Univ., Univ. of Manitoba, Memorial Univ. of Newfoundland, Univ. de Montréal, Univ. of New Brunswick, Univ. of Ottawa, Univ. du Québec à Montréal, Queen's Univ., Univ. of Regina, Ryerson Univ., Univ. of Saskatchewan, Université de Sherbrooke, Simon Fraser Univ., Univ. of Toronto, Univ. of Victoria, Univ. of Waterloo, Western Univ., Univ. of Windsor, York Univ.

Catholic Library Association

Executive Director, Melanie Talley
8550 United Plaza Blvd., Suite 1001, Baton Rouge, LA 70809
225-408-4417, e-mail cla2@cathla.org
World Wide Web http://www.cathla.org

Objective

The promotion and encouragement of Catholic literature and library work through cooperation, publications, education, and information. Founded in 1921.

Membership

Memb. 1,000. Dues $25–$500. Year. July–June.

Officers

Pres. Jack Fritts. 5700 College Rd., Lisle, IL 60532. Tel. 630-829-6060, e-mail jfritts@ben.edu; *V.P./Treas.* Kathryn Shaughnessy, e-mail shaughnk@stjohns.edu; *Past Pres.* N. Curtis LeMay. E-mail nclemay@stthomas.edu.

Board Members

Officers; Eva Gonsalves, Elyse Hayes, Pat Lawton, Cortney Schraut.

Section Chairs

Academic Libraries, Archives and Library Education. Bro. Andrew J. Kosmowski, SM.
High School and Young Adult Library Services. Eva Gonsalves.
Parish and Community Library Services. Phyllis Petre.

Publication

Catholic Library World (q.; memb.; nonmemb. $100 domestic, $125 international). *General Ed.* Sigrid Kelsey. E-mail sigridkelsey@gmail.com.

Chief Officers of State Library Agencies

Executive Director, Timothy Cherubini
201 E. Main St., Suite 1405, Lexington, KY 40507
859-514-9150, fax 859-514-9166, e-mail info@cosla.org
World Wide Web http://www.cosla.org
Twitter @COSLA_US

Objective

Chief Officers of State Library Agencies (COSLA) is an independent organization of the chief officers of state and territorial agencies designated as the state library administrative agency and responsible for statewide library development. Its purpose is to identify and address issues of common concern and national interest; to further state library agency relationships with federal government and national organizations; and to initiate cooperative action for the improvement of library services to the people of the United States.

COSLA's membership consists solely of these top library officers, variously designated as state librarian, director, commissioner, or executive secretary. The organization provides a continuing mechanism for dealing with the problems and challenges faced by these officers. Its work is carried on through its members, a board of directors, and committees.

Officers (2019–2020)

Pres. Stacey Aldrich, State Libn., Hawaii State Public Lib. System, 44 Merchant St. Honolulu. Tel. 808-586-3704, e-mail stacey.aldrich@librarieshawaii.org; *V.P./Pres.-Elect* Jennie Stapp, State Libn., Montana State Lib. Tel. 406-444-3116, e-mail jstapp2@mt.gov; *Secy.* Jennifer R. Nelson, Minnesota Dept. of Educ., State Libn. and Dir., Charter Ctr., 1500 Highway 36 West, Roseville, MN 55113. Tel. 651-582-8791, e-mail jennifer.r.nelson@state.mn.us; *Treas.* Karen Mellor, Rhode Island Office of Lib. and Information Svcs. One Capitol Hill, Providence. Tel. 401-574-9304, e-mail karen.mellor@olis.ri.gov; *Past Pres.* Sandra Treadway, Libn. of Virginia, Lib. of Virginia, 800 E. Broad St., Richmond, VA 23219. Tel. 804-692-3535, e-mail sandra.treadway@lva.virginia.gov.

Directors

Randy Riley, State Libn., Lib. of Michigan, 702 West Kalamazoo, P.O. Box 30007, Lansing, MI 48909. Tel. 517-373-5860, e-mail rileyr1@michigan.gov; Julie Walker, State Libn., Georgia Public Lib. Svcs. Tel. 404-406-4519, e-mail jwalker@georgialibraries.org.

Chinese American Librarians Association

Executive Director, Lian Ruan
E-mail lruan@illinois.edu
World Wide Web http://cala-web.org

Objective

To enhance communications among Chinese American librarians as well as between Chinese American librarians and other librarians; to serve as a forum for discussion of mutual problems and professional concerns among Chinese American librarians; to promote Sino-American librarianship and library services; and to provide a vehicle whereby Chinese American librarians can cooperate with other associations and organizations having similar or allied interests.

Membership

Memb. approximately 600. Membership is open to anyone interested in the association's goals and activities. Dues (Reg. $30; (International/Student/Nonsalaried/Overseas) $15; (Inst.) $100; (Affiliated) $100; (Life) $300.

Officers (2019–2020)

Pres. Fu Zhuo. E-mail zhuof@umkc.edu; *V.P./Pres.-Elect* Hong Yao. E-mail Hong.Yao@queenslibrary.org; *Treas.* Ying Liao. E-mail cairo_liao@hotmail.com; *Past Pres.* Ying Zhang. E-mail ying.zhang@ucf.edu; *Incoming V.P./Pres.-Elect* Wenli Gao. E-mail wgao5@central.uh.edu.

Board of Directors

Officers; *(2017–2020)* Ping Fu, Leping He, Weiling Liu, Ray Pun, Hong Yao; *(2018–2021)* Qi Chen, Michael Huang, Yuan Li, Guoying (Grace) Liu, Minhao Jiang; *(2019–2022)* Suzhen Chen, Jianye He, Hong Miao, Vincci Kwong, Xiaocan Wang.

Chapter Presidents (2019–2020)

NCA: Ray Pun; SCA: Kuei Chiu; GMA: Andrew Yanqing Lee; MW: Minhao Jiang; NE: Yuan Li; SE: Jia He; SW: Jingshan Xiao; Canada: Guoying (Grace) Liu, gliu@uwindsor.ca.

Committee Chairs

Assessment and Evaluation. Xiaoyin Zhang.
Conference Program. Hong Yao.
Constitution and Bylaws. Liya Deng.
Election Committee. Lian Ruan.
International Relations. Michael Huang, Jiaxun Wu.
Membership. Wenli Gao, Ya Wang.
Mentorship Program. Qi Chen.
Nominating. Ying Zhang.
Public Relations/Fundraising. Katherina Lee, Weiling Liu.
Publications. Lei Jin, Guoying Liu.
Web Committee. Minhao Jiang.

Editorial Board Chairs

CALA Newsletter. Ray Pun.
International Journal of Librarianship (IJOL) Guoying Liu.

Awards Committee Chairs

Best Book Award. Jie Huang, Xiaocan Wang.
Best Research. Li Sun, Feng-Ru Sheu.
Best Service Awards. Leping He, Wei Peng.
Conference Travel Grant. Yan He, Ya Wang.
Scholarship. Jen Woo.

Publications

CALA Newsletter (2 a year; memb.; online). *Eds.* Ray Pun. E-mail raypun101@gmail.com; Yingqi Tang. E-mail tang@jsu.edu.
International Journal of Librarianship (IJoL). *Ed.* Grace Liu. E-mail gliu@uwindsor.ca.

Coalition for Networked Information

Executive Director, Clifford A. Lynch
21 Dupont Circle, Suite 800, Washington, DC 20036
202-296-5098, fax 202-872-0884, e-mail clifford@cni.org
World Wide Web http://www.cni.org
Facebook https://www.facebook.com/cni.org
Twitter @cni_org
YouTube https://www.youtube.com/user/cnivideo/
Vimeo http://vimeo.com/cni

Mission

The Coalition for Networked Information (CNI) promotes the transformative promise of networked information technology for the advancement of scholarly communication and the enrichment of intellectual productivity.

Membership

Memb. 240+. Membership is institutional. Dues $8,450. Year. July–June.

Staff

Assoc. Exec. Dir. Joan K. Lippincott, 21 Dupont Cir., Suite 800, Washington, DC 20036. Tel. 202-296-5098, e-mail joan@cni.org; *Asst. Exec. Dir.* Diane Goldenberg-Hart. E-mail diane@cni.org; *Admin. Asst.* Sharon Adams. E-mail sharon@cni.org; *Systems Coord.* Maurice-Angelo F. Cruz. E-mail angelo@cni.org; *Office Mgr.* Jacqueline J. Eudell. E-mail jackie@cni.org; *Communications Coord.* Diane Goldenberg-Hart. E-mail diane@cni.org.

Steering Committee Members (2019–2020)

Kristin Antelman, Univ. of California–Santa Barbara; Daniel Cohen, Northeastern Univ.; P. Toby Graham, Univ. of Georgia; Mary Lee Kennedy *(ex officio)* ARL; Clifford A. Lynch *(ex officio)* CNI; Beth Sandore Namachchivaya, Univ. of Waterloo; John O'Brien, *(ex officio)* EDUCAUSE; Gina M. Siesing, Bryn Mawr College; Jenn Stringer, Univ. of California–Berkeley; Donald J. Waters.

Publications

CNI-Announce (online; subscribe by online form at https://www.cni.org/resources/follow-cni/cni-announce).

Periodic reports (https://www.cni.org/resources/publications/other-publications-by-cni-staff).

Council on Library and Information Resources

Chair, Christopher Celenza
2221 S. Clark St., Arlington, VA 22202
E-mail contact@clir.org
World Wide Web http://www.clir.org
Twitter @CLIRnews

Objective

In 1997 the Council on Library Resources (CLR) and the Commission on Preservation and Access (CPA) merged and became the Council on Library and Information Resources (CLIR). CLIR is an independent, nonprofit organization that forges strategies to enhance research, teaching, and learning environments in collaboration with libraries, cultural institutions, and communities of higher learning.

CLIR promotes forward-looking collaborative solutions that transcend disciplinary, institutional, professional, and geographic boundaries in support of the public good. CLIR identifies and defines the key emerging issues relating to the welfare of libraries and the constituencies they serve, convenes the leaders who can influence change, and promotes collaboration among the institutions and organizations that can achieve change. The council's interests embrace the entire range of information resources and services from traditional library and archival materials to emerging digital formats. It assumes a particular interest in helping institutions cope with the accelerating pace of change associated with the transition into the digital environment.

While maintaining appropriate collaboration and liaison with other institutions and organizations, CLIR operates independently of any particular institutional or vested interests. Through the composition of its board, it brings the broadest possible perspective to bear upon defining and establishing the priority of the issues with which it is concerned.

Officers

Chair Christopher Celenza, Georgetown Univ.; *V.Chair* Buhle Mbambo-Thata, AfLIA–African Lib. and Info. Assns. and Insts. *Treas.* Guy Berthiaume, Librarian and Archivist of Canada.

Board of Directors

Officers; Edward Ayers, Univ. of Richmond; Michele Casalini, Casalini Libri; Dan Cohen, Northeastern Univ.; Jill Cousins, Hunt Museum; Tess Davis, Antiquities Coalition; Kurt De Belder, Leiden Univ.; Kathlin Fitzpatrick, Michigan State Univ.; Fenella France, Library of Congress; Charles Henry, CLIR; Michael A. Keller, Stanford Univ.; W. Joseph King, Lyon College; Carol Mandel, New York Univ. Div. of Libs.; Max Marmor, Samuel H. Kress Fdn.; Richard Ovenden, Univ. of Oxford; Ingrid Parent, Univ. of British Columbia; Winston Tabb, Johns Hopkins Univ., Sohair Wastawy, The Information Guild.; John Price Wilkin, Univ. of Illinois at Urbana-Champaign.

Address correspondence to headquarters.

Publications

Annual Report.
CLIR Issues (bi-mo.; electronic).

EveryLibrary

Executive Director, John Chrastka
P.O. Box 406, 45 E. Burlington St., Riverside, IL. 60546
312-574-5098, e-mail info@everylibrary.org
World Wide Web http://www.everylibrary.org
Facebook https://www.facebook.com/EveryLibrary
LinkedIn https://www.linkedin.com/company/3801587/
Twitter @EveryLibrary

Objective

EveryLibrary is a national political action committee for libraries. Organized as a 501(c)4, the organization provides pro bono advising and consulting to libraries about their funding requests, either when it appears on a ballot or through a municipal funding partner. Its school library–focused digital activism platform SaveSchoolLibrarians.org works to support school librarian positions and budgets for school library programs. Their national network in 2019 included over 340,000 Americans. EveryLibrary's mission is to "build voter support for libraries" at all levels of government, and it works to fulfill that mission as a completely donor-supported organization.

Board Members

John Chrastka, Kyle Courtney, Trevor A. Dawes, Erica Findley, Britten Follett, Amy Garmer, Fran Glick, Kafi Kumasi, Steve Potter, MaryEllin Santiago, Rivkah Sass, Cal Shepard, Maureen Sullivan, Patrick "PC" Sweeney, Jill Hurst-Wahl, Ann Weeks.

Publication

The Political Librarian (irreg.; open access). (Transferred from EveryLibrary in 2019.) *Ed.* Christopher Stewart. E-mail stewart@everylibraryinstitute.org.

Federal Library and Information Network

Executive Director, Laurie Neider
Library of Congress, Washington, DC 20540-4935
202-707-4801, e-mail lneider@loc.gov
World Wide Web http://www.loc.gov/flicc
Twitter @librarycongress

Objective

The Federal Library and Information Network (FEDLINK) is an organization of federal agencies working together to achieve optimum use of the resources and facilities of federal libraries and information centers by promoting common services, coordinating and sharing available resources, and providing continuing professional education for federal library and information staff. FEDLINK serves as a forum for discussion of the policies, programs, procedures, and technologies that affect federal libraries and the information services they provide to their agencies, to Congress, to the federal courts, and to the public.

Membership

The FEDLINK voting membership is composed of representatives of the following U.S. federal departments and agencies: Each of the national libraries (the Library of Congress, National Agricultural Library, National Library of Education, National Library of Medicine, and the National Transportation Library); each cabinet-level executive department, as defined in 5 U.S.C. § 101; additional departments and agencies (the Defense Technical Information Center; departments of the Air Force, Army, and Navy; Executive Office of the President, Government Accountability Office, General Services Administration, Government Printing Office, Institute of Museum and Library Services, National Aeronautics and Space Administration, National Archives and Records Administration, National Technical Information Service [Department of Commerce], Office of Management and Budget, Office of Personnel Management, Office of Scientific and Technical Information [Department of Energy], Office of the Director of National Intelligence, and the Smithsonian Institution); the U.S. Supreme Court and the Administrative Office of the U.S. Courts; the District of Columbia; and other federal independent agencies and government corporations.

Address correspondence to the executive director.

Publication

FEDLINK Bulletin (bi-wk.; electronic).

Medical Library Association

Executive Director, Kevin Baliozian
225 West Wacker Dr., Suite 650, Chicago, IL 60606-1210
312-419-9094, fax 312-419-8950, e-mail websupport@mail.mlahq.org
World Wide Web http://www.mlanet.org
Twitter @MedLibAssn

Objective

The Medical Library Association (MLA) is a nonprofit professional education organization with nearly 4,000 health sciences information professional members and partners worldwide. MLA provides lifelong educational opportunities, supports a knowledge base of health information research, and works with a global network of partners to promote the importance of high-quality information for improved health to the health care community and the public.

Membership

Memb. (Inst.) 400+; (Indiv.) 3,200+, in more than 50 countries. Dues (Indiv.) $75–$225; (Student) $50; (Int'l.) $150; (Affiliate) $140; (Inst.) $325–$880. Year. Institutional members are medical and allied scientific libraries. Individual members are people who are (or were at the time membership was established) engaged in professional library or bibliographic work in medical and allied scientific libraries or people who are interested in medical or allied scientific libraries. Members can be affiliated with one or more of MLA's more than 20 special-interest sections and its regional chapters.

Officers

Pres. Julia Esparza, Louisiana State Univ. HSC; *Pres.-Elect* Lisa K. Traditi, Univ. of Colorado Anschutz Med. Campus; *Secy.* Gurpreet Kaur Rana, Taubman Health Sciences Lib., Univ. of Michigan; *Treas.* Shannon D. Jones, Med. Univ. of South Carolina; *Past Pres.* Beverly Murphy, Duke Univ. Med. Ctr.; *Exec. Dir.* Kevin Baliozian. Med. Lib. Assn.

Board of Directors

Officers; Marie T. Ascher, Donna R. Berryman, Stephanie Fulton, Sally Gore, Elizabeth R. Lorbeer, Sandra Irene Martin, Meredith I. Solomon.

Committee Chairs

Ad Hoc Committee to Review Core Clinical Journals. Andrea M. Ketchum, Michele S. Klein-Fedyshin.

Awards. Deborah L Lauseng.
Books Panel. Carolann Lee Curry.
Bylaws. Emily Ginier.
Communities Transition Team. Stephanie Fulton, Keith W. Cogdill.
Credentialing. Keydi Boss O'Hagan.
Education Steering. Merinda McLure.
Finance. Shannon D Jones.
Governmental Relations. Margaret Ansell.
Grants and Scholarships. Shalu Gillum.
Joseph Leiter NLM/MLA Lectureship. Stacey J. Arnesen.
Librarians Without Borders®. Irene (Rena) Machowa Lubker.
Membership. Karen Gau.
National Program. Janna C. Lawrence, Melissa De Santis.
Nominating. Beverly Murphy.
Oral History. Kathleen Amos.
Professional Recruitment and Retention. Jaclyn Vialet.
Scholarly Communications. Shirley Zhao.

Editorial Board Chairs

JMLA Editor-in-Chief. Katherine Goold Akers.
MLAConnect Christine Willis.

Task Force Chairs

Annual Meeting Innovation. Kevin Baliozian, Lisa K. Traditi.
Diversity and Inclusion. Sandra G. Franklin.
Joint MLA/AAHSL Legislative. Sandra L. Bandy.
Research Imperative. Mary M. Langman.

Awards Committee Chairs

Virginia L. and William K. Beatty Volunteer Service. Leila Ledbetter.
Estelle Brodman Award for the Academic Medical Librarian of the Year. Judith Smith.
Caucus Project of the Year. Erin Wentz.
Clarivate Analytics/Frank Bradway Rogers Information Advancement Award. Susan K. Kendall.
Lois Ann Colaianni Award for Excellence and Achievement in Hospital Librarianship. Lisa L. Habegger.
Consumer Health Librarian of the Year Award Jury. Lisa Huang.
Louise Darling Medal for Distinguished Achievement in Collection Development in the Health Sciences. Carolyn Schubert.
Janet Doe Lectureship. J. Dale Prince.
Ida and George Eliot Prize. Pamela R. Herring.
Fellows and Honorary Members. Heather N. Holmes.
Carla J. Funk Governmental Relations. Alice Jean Jaggers.
T. Mark Hodges International Service. Majid Anwar.
Majors/MLA Chapter Project of the Year. Jeanne M. Burke.
Lucretia W. McClure Excellence in Education. Jill M Tarabula.
Erich Meyerhoff Prize. Mary E. Helms.
Research Advancement in Health Sciences Librarianship Awards Jury. Kate Silfen.
Rising Stars. Norice Lee.
Rittenhouse. Sarah Senter.

Grants, Scholarships, and Fellowships Juries

Ysabel Bertolucci MLA Annual Meeting Grant. Susan M. Foster-Harper.
Naomi C. Broering Hispanic Heritage Grant. Elaina Vitale.
Clarivate Analytics/MLA Doctoral Fellowship Clarivate. Janice Swiatek.
Continuing Education. Emily Couvillon Alagha.
Cunningham Memorial International Fellowship. Mariana Lapidus.
Eugene Garfield Research Fellowship. Ellen Rothbaum.
David A. Kronick Traveling Fellowship. Nha Huynh.
Librarians Without Borders® Ursula Poland International Scholarship. Jeffrey Prock.
Donald A. B. Lindberg Research Fellowship. Emily B. Kean.
MLA/EBSCO Annual Meeting Grant. Chana Kraus-Friedberg.
MLA/HLS Professional Development Grant. Emily Lawson.
MLA Librarians Without Borders® Elsevier Foundation/Research4Life Grants. Jane Morgan-Daniel.

MLA/MIS Career Development Grant. Emily E Petersen.

MLA Research, Development, and Demonstration Project Grant. Bette Bissonnette.

MLA Scholarship. Molly Knapp.

MLA Scholarship for Underrepresented Students. Irma Singarella.

Research Training Institute Jury. Sandy De Groote.

Publications

Journal of the Medical Library Association (q.; electronic version, free to all through PubMed Central). *Ed.* Katherine G. Akers, Wayne State Univ. E-mail jmla@journals.pitt.edu.

MLAConnect (10 a year; electronic; memb.). *Ed.* Christine Willis, Children's Healthcare of Atlanta.

Music Library Association

President, Susannah Cleveland
1600 Aspen Commons Suite 100, Middleton, WI 53562
608-836-5825, fax 608-831-8200, e-mail mla@areditions.com
World Wide Web https://www.musiclibraryassoc.org
Facebook https://www.facebook.com/Music.Library.Association
Twitter @musiclibassoc
Vimeo https://vimeo.com/musiclibraryassoc

Objective

The Music Library Association provides a professional forum for librarians, archivists, and others who support and preserve the world's musical heritage. To achieve this mission, it

- Provides leadership for the collection and preservation of music and information about music in libraries and archives
- Develops and delivers programs that promote continuing education and professional development in music librarianship
- Ensures and enhances intellectual access to music for all by contributing to the development and revision of national and international codes, formats, and other standards for the bibliographic control of music
- Ensures and enhances access to music for all by facilitating best practices for housing, preserving, and providing access to music
- Promotes legislation that strengthens music library services and universal access to music
- Fosters information literacy and lifelong learning by promoting music reference services, library instruction programs, and publications
- Collaborates with other groups in the music and technology industries, government, and librarianship, to promote its mission and values

Membership

Memb. 1,200+. Dues (Inst.) $175; (Indiv.) $140; (Ret.) $105; (Paraprofessional) $75; (Student) $65. (Foreign, add $10.) Year. July 1–June 30.

Officers

Pres. Susannah Cleveland. E-mail Susannah.Cleveland@unt.edu; *V.P./Pres.-Elect* Liza Vick. E-mail lizavick@upenn.edu; *Recording Secy.* Misti Shaw. E-mail mistshaw@indiana.edu.

Board of Directors

Officers; *Admin. Officer* Tracey Rudnick, *Asst. Admin. Officer* Janelle West; *Memb.-at-Large (2019–2021)* Jonathan Sauceda, Anne Shelley, Kimmy Szeto; *(2020–2022)* Brian McMillan, Casey Mullin, Diane Steinhaus.

Committee Chairs

Archives and Special Collections. Maristella J. Feustle.
Awards: Best of Chapters. Carolyn A. Johnson.
Career Development and Services. Emma Dederick, Timothy Sestrick.
Cataloging and Metadata. Hermine Vermeij.
Development. Lindsay J. Brown.
Diversity. Joy M. Doan.
Education. Sonia Archer-Capuzzo.
Emerging Technologies and Services. Jonathan Manton.
Finance. Anne E. Shelley.
Joint Committee: MLA, MPA, and MOLA. Jane Gottlieb.
Legislation. Kyra Folk-Farber.
Membership. Mallory Sajewski.
Music Library Advocacy. Linda B. Fairtile.
Nominating. Gerald A. Szymanski II.
Oral History. Therese Z. Dickman.
Planning. Bruce J. Evans.
Preservation. Treshani Perera.
Program, 2020. Erin Conor.
Program, 2020. Kristina L. Shanton.
Public Libraries. Kristine E. Nelsen.
Public Services. Sara J. Manus.
Publications. Liza F. Vick.
Resource Sharing and Collection Development. Stephanie Bonjack.
Web. Kerry C. Masteller.

Awards Committee Chairs

Carol J. Bradley Award for Historical Research in Music Librarianship.
Lenore Coral IAML Travel Grant. Darwin F. Scott.
Diversity Scholarship. Treshani Perera.
Dena Epstein Award for Archival and Library Research in American Music. Charley Roush.
Kevin Freeman Travel Grant. Jason Imbesi.
Walter Gerboth Award. Molly O'Brien.
Publications. Allison McClanahan.

Publications

Basic Manual Series. *Series Ed.* Kathleen A. Abromeit.
Basic Music Library. *Ed.* Daniel Boomhower.
Index and Bibliography Series (irreg.; price varies). *Ed.* Maristella Feustle.
MLA Newsletter. (6 a year; memb.). *Ed.* Michelle Hahn.
Music Cataloging Bulletin (mo.; online subscription only, $35). *Ed.* Christopher Holden.
Notes (q.; memb.). *Ed.* Deborah Campana.
Technical Reports and Monographs in Music Librarianship (irreg.; price varies). *Ed.* Jonathan Sauceda.

NASIG

President, Kristen Wilson
PMB 305, 1902 Ridge Rd., West Seneca, NY 14224-3312
716-324-1859, e-mail info@nasig.org
World Wide Web http://www.nasig.org
Twitter: @NASIG
Facebook: https://www.facebook.com/groups/2399345882/
Instagram: https://www.instagram.com/nasig_official/
LinkedIn: https://www.linkedin.com/groups/149102/
YouTube: https://www.youtube.com/channel/UCVvnh_CzXS8YgftuvIypTiQ

Vision and Mission

Established in 1985, NASIG is an independent organization working to advance and transform the management of information resources. NASIG's goal is to facilitate and improve the distribution, acquisition, and long-term accessibility of information resources in all formats and business models. There are three key components to the organization's mission:

1. NASIG supports a dynamic community of professionals including, but not limited to, librarians, publishers, and vendors engaging in understanding one another's

perspectives and improving functionality throughout the information resources lifecycle with an emphasis on scholarly communications, serials, and electronic resources.

2. NASIG provides a rich variety of conference and continuing education programming to encourage knowledge sharing among its members and to support their professional and career development.
3. NASIG promotes the development and implementation of best practices and standards for the distribution, acquisition and long-term accessibility of information resources in all formats and business models throughout their lifecycle. In addition to developing best practices, NASIG supports the development of standards by NISO, an affiliated organization.

Membership

Memb. 596. For any person, library, or organization interested in information resources and scholarly communication. Dues (Indiv.) $75; (Ret.) $25; (Student) Free; (Lifetime) $1,000/ one time; (Inst.) $195.

Officers (2019–2020)

Pres. Kristen Wilson, Index Data; *Pres.-Elect* Betsy Appleton, Univ. of Texas at Austin; *Secy.* Beth Ashmore, North Carolina State Univ.; *Treas.* Jessica Ireland, Radford Univ.; *Treas. in Training* Cris Ferguson, Murray State Univ.; *Past Pres.* Angela Dresselhaus, Innovative Interfaces, Inc.; *Memb.-at-Large* Keondra Bailey, Duke Univ. Medical Center Lib.; Michael Fernandez, Yale Univ.; Shannon Keller, New York Public Lib.; Lisa Martincik, Univ. of Iowa; Marsha Seamans, Univ. of Kentucky; Steve Shadle, Univ. of Washington; Newsletter Editor-in-chief Lori Duggan, Indiana Univ. Bloomington; Marketing & Social Media Coord., Eugenia Beh (MIT); Coord. in Training, Chris Bulock, California State Univ., Northridge.

Board Members

Officers; *Newsletter Editor-in-chief* Lori Duggan, Indiana Univ. Bloomington; *Marketing and Social Media Coord.* Eugenia Beh (MIT).

Committee Chairs

Archivist. Peter Whiting, Univ. of Southern Indiana.

Awards and Recognition. Jamie Carlsone, Northwestern Univ.

Bylaws. Laurie Kaplan, ProQuest.

Communications. Alexis Linoski, Georgia Inst. of Tech. and Matthew Jabaily, Univ. of Colorado–Colorado Springs.

Conference Planning. Sion Romaine, Univ. of Washington and Lisa Barricella, East Carolina Univ.

Conference Proceedings Editors. Paul Moeller, Univ. of Colorado Boulder, Cecilia Genereux, Univ. of Minnesota Twin Cities, Sara Bahnmaier, Univ. of Michigan, and Courtney McAllister, Yale Univ.

Conference Coordinator. Anne Creech, Univ. of Richmond.

Continuing Education. Adele Fitzgerald, St. Joseph's College New York and Jennifer Pate, Univ. of North Alabama.

Digital Preservation. Ted Westervelt, Lib. of Congress.

Equity and Inclusion, Dana Tomlin, SUNY–Westbury.

Evaluation and Assessment. Esta Tovstiadi, SUNY–Potsdam.

Membership Services. Christine Radcliff, Texas A&M Univ.–Kingsville and Mandi Smith, Univ. of Arkansas.

Mentoring and Student Outreach. Xiaoyan Song, North Carolina State Univ. and Denise Williams, Univ. of Evansville.

Newsletter. Lori Duggan, Indiana Univ.

Nominations and Elections. Madeline Kelly, Western Washington Univ.

Open Initiatives. Andrew Wesolek, Vanderbilt Univ.

Program Planning. Wendy Roberston, Univ. of Iowa.

Registrar. Mary Ann Jones, Mississippi State Univ.

Standards. Fiona McNabb, PubMed Central.

Task Force Chairs

Vendor and Publisher Engagement. Anu Moorthy, Duke Univ. Medical Ctr. Lib.

Web-Based Infrastructure Implementation. David Macaulay, Univ. of Wyoming.

Publications

Conference Proceedings (currently published in two issues of *Serials Librarian*).

Core Competencies for Electronic Resources Librarians.

Core Competencies for Print Serials Management.

Core Competencies for Scholarly Communication Librarians.

NASIG Newsletter.

Various NASIGuides.

NASIG Blog.

NASIG Jobs Blog.

Meetings

Annual conference held in the summer. Continuing education events and webinars throughout the year.

National Association of Government Archives and Records Administrators

Executive Director, Johnny Hadlock
444 N. Capitol Street, N.W. Suite 237, Washington, DC 20001
202-508-3800, fax 202-508-3801, e-mail info@nagara.org
World Wide Web http://www.nagara.org
Twitter @InfoNAGARA

Objective

Founded in 1984, the National Association of Government Archives and Records Administrators (NAGARA) is a nationwide association of local, state, and federal archivists and records administrators, and others interested in improved care and management of government records. NAGARA promotes public awareness of government records and archives management programs, encourages interchange of information among government archives and records management agencies, develops and implements professional standards of government records and archival administration, and encourages study and research into records management problems and issues.

Membership

Most NAGARA members are federal, state, and local archival and records management agencies. Dues (Org.) $225–$750 dependent on number of contacts; (NARA Employees Indiv.) $40; (Students/Ret.) $50; (All other Indiv.) $89.

Officers (2019–2020)

Pres. Casey Coleman, U.S. Securities and Exchange Commission, Washington, D.C. E-mail colemanca@sec.gov; *V.P.* Patricia C. Franks, San José State Univ. E-mail patricia.franks@sjsu.edu; *Pres.-Elect* Caryn Wojcik, Michigan Records Management Svcs. E-mail wojcikc@michigan.gov; *Secy.* Marissa Paron, Lib. and Archives Canada. E-mail marissa.paron@canada.ca; *Treas.* Bethany Cron, National Archives and Records Admin., Ann Arbor, MI. E-mail bethany.cron@nara.gov; *Past Pres.* Rebekah Davis, Limestone County Archives, 102 W. Washington St., Athens, AL 35611. E-mail rebekah.davis@limestonecounty-al.gov.

Board of Directors

Officers; Tara Bell, Jen Haney Conover, Anne Frantilla, Jennifer Green, Angela Ossar, Kristopher Stenson, Kathleen Williams.

Committee Chairs

Advocacy. Mark Walsh.

Communications. Rebekah Davis.

Membership. Jen Haney Conover, Jennifer Green.

Professional Development. Pari Swift.

Publications

Newsletter (q.; memb.; electronic).

National Information Standards Organization

Executive Director, Todd Carpenter
3600 Clipper Mill Rd., Suite 302, Baltimore, MD 21211-1948
301-654-2512, e-mail nisohq@niso.org
World Wide Web http://www.niso.org

Objective

The National Information Standards Organization (NISO) fosters the development and maintenance of standards that facilitate the creation, persistent management, and effective interchange of information so that it can be trusted for use in research and learning. To fulfill this mission, NISO engages libraries, publishers, information aggregators, and other organizations that support learning, research, and scholarship through the creation, organization, management, and curation of knowledge. NISO works with intersecting communities of interest and across the entire lifecycle of an information standard. NISO standards apply both traditional and new technologies to the full range of information-related needs, including discovery, retrieval, repurposing, storage, metadata, business information, and preservation.

NISO also develops and publishes recommended practices, technical reports, white papers, and information publications. NISO holds regular educational programs on standards, technologies, and related topics where standards-based solutions can help solve problems. These programs include webinars, online virtual conferences, in-person forums, and teleconferences.

Experts from the information industry, libraries, systems vendors, and publishing participate in the development of NISO standards and recommended practices. The standards are approved by the consensus body of NISO's voting membership, representing libraries, publishers, vendors, government, associations, and private businesses and organizations. NISO is supported by its membership and grants.

NISO is a not-for-profit association accredited by the American National Standards Institute (ANSI) and serves as the U.S. Technical Advisory Group Administrator to ISO/TC 46 Information and Documentation as well as the secretariat for ISO/TC 46/SC 9, Identification and Description.

Membership

Voting Members: 80+. Open to any organization, association, government agency, or company willing to participate in and having substantial concern for the development of NISO standards. Library Standards Alliance Members: 60+. Open to any academic, public, special, or government-supported library interested in supporting the mission of NISO.

Officers

Chair Marian Hollingsworth, Clarivate Analytics, 1500 Spring Garden St., Philadelphia PA 19130. Tel. 215-386-0100, e-mail marian.hollingsworth@clarivate.com; *V.Chair* Peter

Simon, NewsBank, Inc.; *Treas.* Jabin White, ITHAKA JSTOR, 100 Campus Dr., Suite 100, Princeton, NJ 08154. Tel. 609-986-2224, e-mail jabin.white@ithaka.org; *Past Chair* Keith Webster, Dean of Univ. Libs., Carnegie Mellon Univ., 5000 Forbes Ave., Pittsburgh. Tel. 412-268-2447, e-mail kwebster@andrew.cmu.edu.

Directors

Ryan Bernier, Gregory Grazevich, Allan Lu, Wendy Queen, Rhonda Ross, Mary Sauer-Games, Chris Shillum, Maria Stanton, Wayne Strickland, Greg Suprock, Miranda Walker, Robert Wheeler.

Committee Chairs

Audit. Greg Suprock.

Finance. Jabin White.

Nominating. Todd Carpenter.

Staff

Assoc. Exec. Dir. Nettie Lagace; *Dir. of Content* Jill O'Neill; *Dir. of Strategic Initiatives* Jason Griffey.

Publications

Information Standards Quarterly (back issues available in open access from the NISO website).

NISO Newsline (free e-newsletter released on the first Wednesday of each month; distributed by e-mail and posted on the NISO website).

For additional NISO publications, see the article "NISO Standards" beginning on page 599 of this volume.

NISO's published standards, recommended practices, and technical reports are available free of charge as downloadable PDF files from the NISO website (http://www.niso.org). Hard-copy documents are available for sale from the website.

Patent and Trademark Resource Center Association

President, Jared Hoppenfeld
Reference Department. University of Delaware Library, Newark, DE 19717-5267
World Wide Web https://ptrca.org

Objective

The Patent and Trademark Resource Center Association (PTRCA) provides a support structure for the more than 80 patent and trademark resource centers (PTRCs) affiliated with the U.S. Patent and Trademark Office (USPTO). The association's mission is to discover the interests, needs, opinions, and goals of the PTRCs and to advise USPTO in these matters for the benefit of PTRCs and their users, and to assist USPTO in planning and implementing appropriate services. Founded in 1983 as the Patent Depository Library Advisory Council; name changed to Patent and Trademark Depository Library Association in 1988; became an American Library Association affiliate in 1996. In 2011 the association was renamed the Patent and Trademark Resource Center Association.

Membership

Open to any person employed in a patent and trademark resource center library whose responsibilities include the patent and trademark collection. Affiliate membership is also available. Dues (Reg.) $65; (Student) $10.

Officers (2019–2020)

Pres. Jared Hoppenfeld, College Station, TX; *V.P./Pres.-Elect* Rebecca M. (Missy) Murphey, Orlando, FL; *Secy.* Sara Butts, Wichita, KS; *Treas.* Jim Miller, McKeldin Lib., Univ. of Maryland, Library Lane, College Park. Tel. 301-405-9152, e-mail jmiller2@umd.edu; *Past Pres.* Dave Zwicky, West Lafayette, IN; *Div. Reps. (Academic) (2019–2021)* Suzanne

Reinman, Stillwater, OK; *(2018–2020)* Siu Min Yu, Houston, TX; *(Public) (2019–2021)* James Bettinger, Cleveland, OH; *(2018–2020)* Sharyl Overhiser, Philadelphia, PA.

Committee Chairs (2019–2020)

Bylaws. Marian Armour-Gemman.
Conferences. Jared Hoppenfeld.
Database. Jim Miller.

Election. Leena Lalwani.

Membership and Mentoring. Rebecca Murphey.

Publications. Suzanne Reinman.

Publication

PTRCA Journal. Electronic at https://ptrca.org/newsletters.

Polish American Librarians Association

President, Ewa Barczyk
P.O. Box 301061, Chicago, IL 60630-1061
World Wide Web http://palalib.org

Objective

The mission of the Polish American Librarians Association (PALA) is to positively affect services provided to library patrons of Polish descent and individuals interested in Polish culture.

The organization's vision is

- To enhance professional knowledge by developing forums for discussion and networks of communication among library staff working with Polish collections and patrons of Polish origin
- To promote understanding and respect among all cultures by expanding the means to access reliable, current information about Polish and Polish American culture
- To promote Polish American librarianship
- To provide opportunities for cooperation with other library associations

Founded in 2009.

Membership

Membership is open to librarians, students of library schools, library support staff, and others who support the vision of PALA. Dues $50 (one-time dues to support the goals of PALA).

Officers

Pres. Ewa Barczyk, Golda Meir Lib., Univ. of Wisconsin Milwaukee, 2311 E. Hartford Ave., Milwaukee. Tel. 414-412-5456, e-mail ewa@uwm.edu; *Secy.* Paulina Poplawska, New Ulm Public Lib., New Ulm, MN. E-mail ppoplawska@tds.lib.mn.us; *Treas.* Bernadetta Koryciarz, Niles-Maine District Lib., 6960 Oakton St., Niles, IL 60714. Tel. 847-663-6642, e-mail bkorycia@nileslibrary.org; *Past Pres.* Leonard Kniffel, PolishSon.com, 2743 N. Greenview Ave., Chicago. Tel. 773-935-3635, e-mail lkniffel@sbcglobal.net.

Board of Directors

Officers; *Dirs.-at-Large* Iwona Bozek, Krystyna Matusiak, Hanna Przybylski, Marianne Ryan, Ronald V. Stoch.

REFORMA (National Añssociation to Promote Library and Information Services to Latinos and the Spanish-Speaking)

President, Kenny Garcia
P.O. Box 832, Anaheim, CA 92815-0832
E-mail info@reforma.org
World Wide Web http://www.reforma.org

Objective

Promoting library services to the Spanish-speaking for nearly 40 years, REFORMA, an affiliate of the American Library Association, works in a number of areas to advance the development of library collections that include Spanish-language and Latino-oriented materials; the recruitment of more bilingual and bicultural professionals and support staff; the development of library services and programs that meet the needs of the Latino community; the establishment of a national network among individuals who share its goals; the education of the U.S. Latino population in regard to the availability and types of library services; and lobbying efforts to preserve existing library resource centers serving the interest of Latinos.

Membership

Memb. 800+. Membership is open to any person who is supportive of the goals and objectives of REFORMA. Dues (Indiv.) $10–$50; (Int'l.) Free; (Life) $450; (Inst.) $100–$250. Year.

Executive Committee (2019–2020)

Pres. Kenny Garcia, California State Univ., Monterey Bay Lib. E-mail president@reforma.org; *V.P./Pres.-Elect* Oscar Baeza, El Paso Community College. E-mail vice-president@reforma.org; *Secy.* Ana Campos, Los Angeles Public Lib. E-mail secretary@reforma.org; *Treas.* Denice Adkins, Univ. of Missouri. E-mail treasurer@reforma.org; *Past Pres.* Madeline Peña Feliz, Los Angeles Public Lib., 630 West 5th St., Los Angeles, CA 90071. Tel. 213-228-7496, e-mail past-president@reforma.org; *Memb.-at-Large* Alda Allina Migoni, Library of Congress. E-mail at-large-rep@reforma.org; *Chapter Reps.* Manny Figueroa, Queens Lib. E-mail chapter-east-region@reforma.org; David López, OC Public Libraries. E-mail chapter-west-region@reforma.org.

Committee Chairs

Awards. Haydee Hodis.
Education. Michele A. L. Villagran.
Finance. Tess Tobin.
Fundraising. Cynthia Bautista, Sonia Bautista.
International Relations. Ray Pun.
Legislative. Mario Ascencio.
Membership. Adriana Blancart-Hayward.
Mentoring. Antonio Apodaca.
Nominations. Maria Kramer.
Organizational Development and New Chapters. Gloria Grover.
Program. Kenny Garcia.
Public Relations. Jesus Espinosa.
Recruitment and Mentoring. Minerva Alaniz.
REFORMA National Conferences Coordinating Committee. Roxana Benavides, Abigail Morales.
Scholarship. Delores Carlito.
Technology. Edwin Rodarte.
Translations. Lupie Leyva.

Awards Committee Chairs

Pura Belpré Award. Ramona Caponegro.
Dr. Arnulfo D. Trejo Librarian of the Year. Haydee Hodis.

Publication

REFORMA (enewsletter). *Ed.* Chris Ortega.

Meetings

General membership and board meetings take place at the American Library Association Midwinter Meeting and Annual Conference and Exhibition.

Scholarly Publishing and Academic Resources Coalition

Executive Director, Heather Joseph
1201 Connecticut Ave. N.W., P.O. 607/608, Washington, DC 20036
202-630-5090, e-mail sparc@sparcopen.org
World Wide Web https://sparcopen.org
Twitter @SPARC_NA

Objective

SPARC, the Scholarly Publishing and Academic Resources Coalition, is a global organization that promotes expanded sharing of scholarship in the networked digital environment. It is committed to faster and wider sharing of outputs of the research process to increase the impact of research, fuel the advancement of knowledge, and increase the return on research investments.

Launched as an initiative of the Association of Research Libraries, SPARC has become a catalyst for change. Its pragmatic focus is to stimulate the emergence of new scholarly communication models that expand the dissemination of scholarly research and equip libraries for the inexorable growth in research output. Action by SPARC in collaboration with stakeholders—including authors, publishers, and libraries—builds on the unprecedented opportunities created by the networked digital environment to advance the conduct of scholarship.

SPARC's role in stimulating change focuses on

- Educating stakeholders about the problems facing scholarly communication and the opportunities for them to play a role in achieving positive change
- Advocating policy changes that advance scholarly communication and explicitly recognize that dissemination of scholarship is an essential, inseparable component of the research process
- Incubating demonstrations of new publishing and sustainability models that benefit scholarship and academe

SPARC is an advocate for changes in scholarly communication that benefit more than the academic community alone. Founded in 1997, now operating independently of ARL, SPARC has expanded to represent more than 800 academic and research libraries in North America, the United Kingdom, Europe, and Japan.

Membership

Memb. 240+ institutions. SPARC membership is open to international academic and research institutions, organizations, and consortia that share an interest in creating a more open and diverse marketplace for scholarly communication. Dues are scaled by membership type and budget. For more information, visit SPARC's website at https://sparcopen.org/become-a-member, SPARC Europe at https://sparcopen.org/people/sparc-europe/, SPARC Japan at http://www.nii.ac.jp/sparc, or SPARC Africa at https://sparcopen.org/people/sparc-africa/.

Staff

Dir., Open Education Nicole Allen. E-mail nicole@sparcopen.org; *Open Education Coord.* Hailey Babb. E-mail hailey@sparcopen.org; *Senior Consultant* Raym Crow. E-mail crow@sparcopen.org; *Chief Operating Officer* Val Hollister. E-mail val@sparcopen.org; *Exec. Dir.* Heather Joseph. E-mail heather@sparcopen.org; *Programs and Operations Assoc.* Stacie Lemick. E-mail stacie@sparcopen.org; *Asst. Dir., Right to Research Coalition* Joseph McArthur. E-mail joe@righttoresearch.org; *Open Educ. Coord.* Mo Nyamweya. E-mail mo@sparcopen.org; *Dir. of Programs and Engagement* Nick Shockey. E-mail nick@sparcopen.org; *Instructor, Open Educ. Leadership Program* Tanya Spilovoy. E-mail leadership@sparcopen.org; *Consultant* Greg Tananbaum. E-mail greg@sparcopen.org.

Steering Committee

H. Austin Booth, Boyoung Chae, Christopher Cox, Carrie Gits, Jennifer Grayburn, Rachel Harding, Heather Joseph, Joy Kirchner, Vivian Lewis, Beth McNeil, Carmelita Pickett, Shilpa Rele, Judy Ruttenberg, Steven Escar Smith, Virginia Steel.

Publications

OER State Policy Playbook (2020) (https://sparcopen.org/our-work/oer-state-policy-playbook/).

SPARC Roadmap for Action: Academic Community Control of Data Infrastructure (November 2019) (https://sparcopen.org/our-work/roadmap-for-action/).

SPARC Landscape Analysis: The Changing Academic Publishing Industry—Implications for Academic Institutions (March 2019) by Claudio Aspesi (lead author), Nicole Allen, Raym Crow, Shawn Daugherty, Heather Joseph, Joseph McArthur, and Nick Shockey. (https://sparcopen.org/our-work/landscape-analysis/).

Society for Scholarly Publishing

Executive Director, Melanie Dolechek
1120 Route 73, Suite 200, Mount Laurel, NJ 08054
856-439-1385, fax 856-439-0525, e-mail info@sspnet.org
World Wide Web http://www.sspnet.org
Twitter @ScholarlyPub

Objective

To draw together individuals involved in the process of scholarly publishing. This process requires successful interaction of the many functions performed within the scholarly community. The Society for Scholarly Publishing (SSP) provides the leadership for such interaction by creating opportunities for the exchange of information and opinions among scholars, editors, publishers, librarians, printers, booksellers, and all others engaged in scholarly publishing.

Membership

Memb. 1,000+. Open to all with an interest in the scholarly publishing process and dissemination of information. Dues (New Member) $185; (Indiv. Renewal) $200; (Libn.) $85; (Early Career New) $60; (Ret. Renewal) $75; (Student) $40; (Supporting Organization) $2,195; (Sustaining Organization) $5,747; (Intl. Indiv.) $50; (Intl. Early Career) $25; (Intl. Libn.) $25; (Intl. Student); $10. Year. Jan.–Dec.

Officers

Pres. Angela Cochran, American Society of Civil Engineers; *Pres.-Elect* Lauren Kane, DeltaThink; *Secy./Treas.* Byron Laws, Nova Techset; *Past Pres.* Adrian Stanley, Digital Science; *Memb.-at-Large* Elizabeth R. Lorbeer.

Board of Directors

Officers; *Membs.-at-Large* Hillary Corbett, David Crotty, Robert Harington, Lisa Hinchliffe, Elizabeth R. Lorbeer, Rebecca McLeod, Alison Mudditt, Laura Ricci, Isabel Thompson, Miranda Walker; *Exec. Dir.* Melanie Dolechek.

Committee Chairs

Annual Meeting Program. Lori Carlin, Yael Fitzpatrick, Cason Lynley.

Career Development. Kelly J. Denzer, Barrett A. Winston.

Community Engagement. Thomas A. Ciavarella, Byron A. Russell.

Development. Richard Kobel, Paul Yeager.
Education. Stephanie F. Decouvelaere, Ben Mudrak, Greg Suprock.
Finance. Ted Bakamjian, Byron Laws.
Marketing. Marianne Calilhanna, Josh Lancette, Nicola Poser.
Membership. Janice E. Kuta, Timothy Lamkins, Keith L. Layson.
Nominating and Awards. Adrian Stanley.
Scholarly Kitchen Cabinet. Susan Kesner.

Task Force Chairs

Funder. Adrian Stanley.

Publication

Learned Publishing (memb.). Published by the Association of Learned and Professional Society Publishers (ALPSP) in collaboration with SSP. *Ed.* Pippa Smart.
The Scholarly Kitchen (Moderated blog). *Ed.* David Crotty.

Meetings

An annual meeting is held in late May/early June. SSP also conducts a Librarian Focus Group (January) and the Fall Seminar Series (October).

Society of American Archivists

Executive Director, Nancy P. Beaumont
17 N. State St., Suite 1425, Chicago, IL 60602
312-606-0722, toll-free 866-722-7858, fax 312-606-0728, e-mail saahq@archivists.org
Twitter @archivists_org

Object

Founded in 1936, the Society of American Archivists (SAA) is North America's oldest and largest national archival professional association. Representing more than 6,000 individual and institutional members, SAA promotes the value and diversity of archives and archivists and is the preeminent source of professional resources and the principal communication hub for American archivists.

Membership

Memb. 6,200+. Dues (Indiv.) $80 to $325, graduated according to salary; (Assoc. domestic) $115; (Ret.) $77; (Student/Bridge) $55; (Inst.) $340; (Sustaining Inst.) $595.

Officers

Pres. Meredith Evans, Jimmy Carter Presidential Lib. and Museum; *V.P.* Michelle Light, Univ. of Nevada, Las Vegas; *Treas.* Amy Fitch, Rockefeller Archive Ctr.

SAA Council

Members Steven Booth, Courtney Chartier, Melissa Gonzales, Brenda Gunn, Petrina Jackson, Erin Lawrimore, Bertram Lyons, Ricardo Punzalan, Audra Yun; *Ex Officio* Nancy P. Beaumont; *Staff Liaisons* Matt Black, Teresa Brinati, Peter Carlson, Felicia Owens, Rana Salzmann.

Committee Chairs

Appointments. Rachel Onuf.
Awards. Christina Zamon, Jennifer Kinniff.
Diversity. Harrison Inefuku.
Education. Erin Faulder.
Ethics and Professional Conduct. Sarah Keen, Polina Ilieva.
Finance. Amy Fitch.
Host. Jennifer Hecker, Kristy Sorensen.
Membership. Michelle Sweetser.
Nominating. Dominique Luster.
Program. Joyce Gabiola, Rachel Winston.
Public Awareness. Caryn Radick.
Public Policy. Sarah Quigley.

Research, Data, and Assessment. Paul Conway, Jennifer King.

Selection of SAA Fellows. Danna Bell.

Standards. John Bence, Rebecca Wiederhold.

Working Groups Chairs

Dictionary. Rosemary Flynn.

Intellectual Property. Aprille McKay.

Editorial Board Chairs

American Archivist Christopher Lee.

Publications Board. Christopher Prom.

Task Force Chairs

Research/Data and Evaluation. Melissa Gonzales.

Tragedy Response Initiative. Lisa Calahan.

Publications

American Archivist (s. ann.; memb.; nonmemb. "premium," print and online edition $289, online only $239, print only $239). *Ed.* Christopher Lee. Tel. 919-962-7024, e-mail AmericanArchivist@archivists.org; *Reviews Ed.* Bethany Anderson. Tel. 217-300-0908, e-mail ReviewsEditor@archivists.org.

Archival Outlook (bi-mo.; memb.).

In the Loop e-newsletter (bi-wk.).

Software and Information Industry Association

President, Jeff Joseph
1090 Vermont Ave. N.W. Sixth Floor, Washington, DC 20005-4905
202-289-7442, fax 202-289-7097
World Wide Web http://www.siia.net
Twitter @SIIA

The Software and Information Industry Association (SIIA) was formed January 1, 1999, through the merger of the Software Publishers Association (SPA) and the Information Industry Association (IIA).

Membership

Memb. 800+ companies. Open to companies that develop software and digital information content. For details on membership and dues, see the SIIA website, http://www.siia.net.

Officers

Pres. Jeff Joseph. Tel. 202-789-4440.

Senior Staff

Managing Dir., Educ. Tech. Industry Network Jill Abbott; *Managing Dir., Software and Svcs. Div.* Jennifer Carl; *Managing Dir., SIPA* Amanda McMaster; *Senior V.P. and Managing Dir., FISD* Tom Davin; *Managing Dir., Connectiv* Mike Marchesano; *Senior V.P., Global Public Policy* Carl Schonander; *V.P., Marketing and Membership* Michelle Harris; *V.P., Finance and Operations* Carl Walker; *SIIA Pres.* Jeff Joseph.

Board of Directors

Kerry Baker-Relf, Refinitiv; Steve Dickey, Cboe Global Markets, Steven M. Emmert, RELX Group; Kate Friedrich, Thomson Reuters; Meg Hargreaves, CQ Roll Call Group; Jace Johnson, Adobe Systems, Inc.; Chuck Melley, Pearson; Heath Morrison, McGraw-Hill Education; Kevin Novak, 2040 Digital; Morris Panner, Ambra Health; Marcy V. Pike, FIA, Fidelity Investments; Brandon Pinette, Cengage Learning; Johanna Shelton, Google, Inc.; Sallianne Taylor, Bloomberg L.P.; Trip Wadleigh, FIA, TRG Screen.

Special Libraries Association

Executive Director, Amy Lestition Burke
7918 Jones Branch Drive, Suite 300, McLean, VA 22102
703-647-4900, fax 703-506-3266, e-mail aburke@sla.org.
World Wide Web https://www.sla.org
Twitter @SLAhq

Mission

The Special Libraries Association (SLA) promotes and strengthens its members through learning, advocacy, and networking initiatives.

Strategic Vision

SLA is a global association of information and knowledge professionals who are employed in every sector of the economy. Its members thrive where data, information, and knowledge intersect, and its strategic partners support SLA because they believe in the association's mission and the future of its members. SLA's goal is to support information professionals as they contribute, in their varied and evolving roles, to the opportunities and achievements of organizations, communities, and society.

Membership

Memb. 9,000+ in 75 countries. Dues (Org.) $750; (Indiv.) $100–$200; (Student/Intl./Salary less than $18,000 income per year) $50; (Ret.) $100.

Officers (2020)

Pres. Tara Murray, Pennsylvania State Univ., University Park, PA. E-mail tem10@psu.edu; *Pres.-Elect* Catherine Lavallée-Welch, Bishop's Univ., Sherbrooke, PQ. E-mail clw@ubishops.ca; *Treas.* Bill Noorlander, BST America, New York, NY. E-mail bill.noorlander@bstamerica.com; *Past Pres.* Hal Kirkwood, Univ. of Oxford, Oxford, U.K. E-mail kirkwoodhal@gmail.com.

Board of Directors

Directors; Officers; *Chapter Cabinet Chair* Robin Dodge; *Chapter Cabinet Chair-Elect* Elaine Lasda; *Past Chapter Cabinet Chair* Valerie Perry; *Division Cabinet Chair* Jill Konieczko; *Division Cabinet Chair-Elect* Julie Snyder; *Past Division Cabinet Chair* Emma Davidson.

Directors

Hildy Dworkin, P. K. Jain, Amy Jankowski, Jim Miller.

Committee Chairs

Annual Conference Advisory Council. Tina Franks.

Awards and Honors. Roberto Sarmiento.

Finance. Willem Noorlander.

Governance and Strategy. Catherine Lavallée-Welch.

Information Outlook Advisory Council. Elizabeth Price.

Membership Advisory Council. Kim Bloedel.

Nominating. Niamh Tumelty.

Professional Development Advisory Council. Tina Budzise-Weaver.

Public Policy Advisory Council. Kevin Adams.

Public Relations Advisory Council. Connie Crosby.

Students and New Professionals Advisory Council. Laura Walesby.

Technology Advisory Council. James King.

Workplace Preparedness and Response Advisory Council (PREP). Eugene Michael Giudice.

Publication

Information Outlook (bi-mo.; memb.; nonmemb. $240/yr.). *Ed.* Stuart Hales. E-mail shales@sla.org.

Theatre Library Association

President, Francesca Marini
c/o New York Public Library for the Performing Arts
40 Lincoln Center Plaza, New York, NY 10023
E-mail theatrelibraryassociation@gmail.com
World Wide Web http://www.tla-online.org/
Twitter @theatrelibassn

Objective

To further the interests of collecting, preserving, and using theater, cinema, and performing arts materials in libraries, museums, and private collections. Founded in 1937.

Membership

Memb. 300. Dues (Indiv.) $50; (Student/Nonsalaried) $25; (Inst.) $75; (Sustaining) $150. Year. Jan.–Dec.

Officers

Pres. Francesca Marini, Cushing Lib., Texas A&M Univ. E-mail fmarini@library.tamu.edu; *V.P.* Diana King, Univ. of California, Los Angeles. E-mail diking@library.ucla.edu; *Treas.* Beth Kattelman, Ohio State Univ. E-mail kattelman.1@osu.edu; *Past Pres.* (ex officio) Colleen Reilly, Houston Community College. E-mail colleen.reilly@hccs.edu.

Board of Directors

(2018–2020) Suzanne Lipkin, David Nochimson, Joseph Tally; *(2019–2021)* Matt DiCintio, Rachel Smiley, Dale Stinchcomb, Scott Stone; *(2020–2022)* William Daw, Sophie Glidden-Lyon, Karin Suni.

Committee Chairs

Conference Planning. Diana King.
Membership. Matt DiCintio.
Nominating. Helice Koffler.
Publications. Joseph Tally.
Strategic Planning. Diana King.
Website Editorial. Eric Colleary, Charlotte Price.

Awards Committee Chairs

Book Awards. Suzanne Lipkin, Annemarie van Roessel.

Publications

Broadside Archive (digital back issues). *Ed.* Angela Weaver *(2008–2014).*

Performing Arts Resources (occasional) see http://www.tla-online.org/publications/performing-arts-resources/performing-arts-resources-volumes/ for links to subscription and https://www.proquest.com/products-services/iipa_ft.html for database from ProQuest.

Urban Libraries Council

President and CEO, Susan Benton
1333 H St. N.W., Suite 1000 West, Washington, DC 20005
202-750-8650, e-mail info@urbanlibraries.org
World Wide Web http://www.urbanlibraries.org
Facebook https://www.facebook.com/UrbanLibrariesCouncil/
Twitter @UrbanLibCouncil

Objective

Since 1971 the Urban Libraries Council (ULC) has worked to strengthen public libraries as an essential part of urban life. A member organization of North America's leading public library systems, ULC serves as a forum for research widely recognized and used by public- and private-sector leaders. Its members are thought leaders dedicated to leadership, innovation, and the continuous transformation of libraries to meet community needs.

ULC's work focuses on helping public libraries to identify and utilize skills and strategies that match the challenges of the 21st century.

Membership

Membership is open to public libraries and to corporate partners specializing in library-related materials and services. The organization also offers associate memberships. Annual membership dues for libraries are based on the size of a library's operating budget (local + state).

Officers (2019–2020)

Chair Vickery Bowles; *V.Chair/Chair-Elect* Richard Reyes-Gavilan; *Secy./Treas.* Brandon Neal; *Past Chair* Rhea Brown Lawson; *Memb.-at-Large* Mary J. Wardell-Ghirarduzzi.

Board Members

Jill Bourne, Karl Dean, Janet Hutchinson, John W. Laney, Michael Meyer, C. Mary Okoye, Skye Patrick, Mary Blankenship Pointer, Jesus Salas, Rebecca Stavick, Michelle VonderHaar.

State, Provincial, and Regional Library Associations

The associations in this section are organized under three headings: United States, Canada, and Regional. Both the United States and Canada are represented under Regional associations.

United States

Alabama

Memb. 1,200. Publication. *ALLA COMmunicator* (q.).

Pres. Jessica Hayes, Auburn Univ. at Montgomery, P.O. Box 244023, Montgomery 36124-4023. Tel. 334-244-3814, e-mail jhayes11@aum.edu; *Pres.-Elect* Daniel Tackett, Vestavia Hills Library in the Forest. Tel. 205-978-3683, e-mail dtackett@bham.lib.al.us; *Secy.* Paula Webb, Univ. of South Alabama, 5901 USA Dr. North, Mobile 36688. Tel. 251-461-1933, e-mail pwebb@southalabama.edu; *Treas.* Karen Preuss, Montgomery City-County Public Lib., P.O. Box 1950, Montgomery 36102-1950. Tel. 334-240-4300, e-mail kpreuss@mccpl.lib.al.us; *Memb.-at-Large* (Central Alabama) Jeff Graveline, Univ. of Alabama at Birmingham, Mervyn H. Sterne Lib., SL 172, 1720 2nd Ave S., Birmingham 35294-0014. Tel. 205-934-6364, e-mail jgraveli@uab.edu; (North Alabama) Ashley Cummins, Russellville Public Lib. Tel. 256-332-1535, e-mail ruslib110@yahoo.com; (South Alabama) Wendy Congairdo, Thomas B. Norton Public Lib., 221 W. 19th Ave., Gulf Shores 36542. Tel. 251-968-1176, e-mail wcongiardo@hotmail.com. *Past Pres.* Carrie Steinmehl, Hoover Public Lib., 200 Municipal Dr., Hoover 35216. Tel. 205-444-7748, e-mail carries@bham.lib.al.us; *Assn. Admin.* (ex-officio) Angela Moore, Alabama Lib. Assn., 6030 Monticello Dr., Montgomery 36117. Tel. 334-414-0113, e-mail allaadmin@allanet.org.

Address correspondence to administrator. Alabama Lib. Assn., 6030 Monticello Dr., Montgomery 36117. Tel. 334-414-0113, e-mail allibraryassoc@gmail.com.

World Wide Web http://allanet.org.

Alaska

Memb. 450+. Publication. *Newspoke* (q.) (online at http://akla.org/newspoke).

Pres. Deborah Rinio. E-mail northernlightslibrarian@gmail.com; *Pres.-Elect* Jonas Lamb; *Secy.* Paul Adasiak. E-mail pfadasiak@alaska.edu; *Treas.* Samantha Blanquart; *Conference Coords.* Robert Barr. E-mail Robert.Barr@juneau.org, Freya Anderson. E-mail freya.anderson@alaska.gov; *ALA Rep.* Lorelei Sterling. E-mail lsterling@alaska.edu; *PNLA Rep.* Julie Niederhauser. E-mail Julie.niederhauser@alaska.gov; *Past Pres.* Robert Barr. E-mail Robert.Barr@juneau.org.

Address correspondence to the secretary, Alaska Lib. Assn., P.O. Box 81084, Fairbanks 99708. E-mail akla@akla.org.

World Wide Web https://akla.org.

Arizona

Memb. 1,000. Term of Office. Nov.–Nov. Publication. *AzLA Newsletter* (6x yearly).

Pres. Corey Christians; *Pres.-Elect* John Walsh; *Secy.* Amber Kent, Casa Grande Public Lib., 449 N. Drylake St., Casa Grande 85122. Tel. 520 421-8710, e-mail AKent@casagrandeaz.gov; *Treas.* Rene Tanner, Arizona State Univ., Tempe. Tel. 480-965-7190, e-mail rene.tanner@asu.edu; *Northern Regional Rep.* Martha Baden; *Central Regional Rep.* Rachel Martinez; *Southern Regional Rep.* Carrie Dawson; *ALA Councilor* Dan Stanton; *MPLA Rep.* Amadee Ricketts; *Past Pres.* Michelle Simon, Pima County Public Lib., 101 N. Stone Ave., Tucson 85701. Tel. 520-594-5654, e-mail michesimon54@gmail.com.

Address correspondence to Arizona Lib. Assn., 1645 W. Valencia Rd. #109-432. Tucson 85746. Tel. 602-614-2841, e-mail admin@azla.org.

World Wide Web http://www.azla.org.

Arkansas

Memb. 600. Publication. *Arkansas Libraries* (4x yearly).

Pres. Crystal Gates, William F. Laman Public Libr. System, 2801 Orange St., North Little Rock 72114. Tel. 501-771-1995, e-mail crystal.gates@lamanlibrary.org; *Pres.-Elect* Philip Shackelford, South Arkansas Community College, El Dorado, AR 71730. Tel. 870-864-7116, e-mail pshackelford@southark.edu; *Secy.* Jessica Riedmueller, Univ. of Central Arkansas, 201 Donaghey Ave., Conway 72035. Tel., 501-450-5233, e-mail jriedmueller@uca.edu; *Treas.* Lynn Valetutti, National Park College, 101 College Dr., Hot Springs, AR 71913, e-mail lvaletutti@np.edu; *ALA Councilor* Lacy Wolfe, Henderson State Univ., 1100 Henderson St., Box 7541, Arkadelphia 71999. Tel. 870-230-5322, e-mail wolfel@hsu.edu; *Non-Voting: SELA State Rep.* Emily Rozario, William F. Laman Public Lib., 2801 Orange St., North Little Rock, AR 72114. E-mail emily.rozario@lamanlibrary.org; *Past Pres.* Jil'Lana Heard, Lake Hamilton Junior High, 281 Wolf St., Pearcy 72035. Tel. 501-767-2731, e-mail jillana.heard@lhwolves.net.

Address correspondence to Arkansas Lib. Assn., P.O. Box 3821, Little Rock 72203. Tel. 501-313-1398, e-mail info@arlib.org.

World Wide Web http://arlib.org.

California

Memb. 2,500. Publication. CLA *Insider* (memb.; online).

Pres. Michelle Perera, Pasadena Public Lib. E-mail mperera@cityofpasadena.net; *V.P./Pres.-Elect* Hillary Theyer, Torrance Public Lib. E-mail HTheyer@torranceca.gov; *Secy.* Stephanie Beverage, Huntington Beach Public Lib. E-mail Stephanie.Beverage@surfcity-hb.org; *Treas.* Derek Wolfgram, Redwood City Public Lib., E-mail dwolfgram@redwoodcity.org; *Past Pres.* Dolly Goyal, San Mateo County Libs. E-mail goyal@smcl.org.

Address correspondence to California Lib. Assn., 1055 E. Colorado Blvd., 5th Floor, Pasadena 91106. Tel. 626-204-4071, e-mail info@cla-net.org.

World Wide Web http://www.cla-net.org.

Colorado

Pres. Ryan F. Buller, Univ. of Denver. E-mail Ryan.Buller@du.edu; *Pres.-Elect* Tiah Frankish, Adams 12 Five Star Schools. E-mail tfrankish@gmail.com; *Secy.* Anne Holland, Space Science Institute. E-mail aholland@spacescience.org; *Treas.* Nanette Fisher, Anythink Libs. E-mail nfisher@anythinklibraries.org; *Membs.-at-Large* Tiffanie Wick, Western Colorado Univ. E-mail twick@western.edu, Haley Justine Baker, Bemis Public Lib. E-mail hbaker@littletongov.org; *Past Pres.* Tammy Sayles, Pikes Peak Lib. District. E-mail tjsmlis@gmail.com.

Address correspondence to Colorado Assn. of Libs., P.O. Box 740905, Arvada 80006-0905. Tel. 303-463-6400, fax 303-458-0002, e-mail cal@cal-webs.org.

World Wide Web World Wide Web http://www.cal-webs.org.

Connecticut

Memb. 1,000+. Term of Office. July–June. Publication. *CLA Today* (6x yearly; online). E-mail editor@ctlibrarians.org.

Pres. Lisa Karim, Simsbury Public Lib., 725 Hopmeadow St., Simsbury. Tel. 860-658-7663, fax 860-658-6732, e-mail lkarim@simsburylibrary.info; *V.P./Pres.-Elect* Thomas Piezzo, Brainerd Memorial Lib. E-mail tpiezzo@brainerdlibrary.org; *Recording Secy.* Danielle Duffy Valenzano, Milford Public Lib. E-mail dvalenzano@milfordct.gov; *Treas.* Kristina Edwards, Central Connecticut State Univ. E-mail kristina.edwards@uconn.edu; *Past Pres.* Kate Byroade, Cragin Memorial Lib., 8 Linwood Ave., Colchester 06415. Tel. 860-537-5752, e-mail kbyroade@colchesterct.gov.

Address correspondence to Connecticut Lib. Assn., 234 Court St., Middletown 06457. Tel. 860-346-2444, fax 860-344-9199, e-mail cla@ctlibrarians.org.

World Wide Web http://ctlibraryassociation.org.

Delaware

Memb. 200+. Publication. *DLA Bulletin* (q.; online). E-mail Nicole.Ballance@lib.de.us.

Pres. Alison Wessel, DHSS Lib., Delaware Dept. of Health and Social Svcs., Herman M. Holloway Sr. Health and Social Svcs. Campus,

1901 N. DuPont Hwy., New Castle 19720. Tel. 302-255-2986, e-mail alisonwessel.dla@gmail.com; *V.P./Conference Chair* Catherine Wimberley, New Castle County Libs., 2020 W. 9th St., Wilmington 19805. Tel. 302-571-7425, e-mail catherinewimberley@newcastlede.gov; *Secy.* Marlowe Bogino, Wilmington Univ. Lib., 320 N. DuPont Hwy., New Castle 19720. Tel. 302-327-4892, e-mail marlowe.b.bogino@wilmu.edu; *Treas.* Jaclyn Hale, Dover Public Lib., 35 Loockerman Plz., Dover 19901. Tel. 302-736-7185, e-mail jaclynhaledla@gmail.com; *ALA Councilor* Lauren Wallis, Univ. of Delaware Morris Lib. Tel. 302-831-3763, e-mail lwallis@udel.edu; *Delaware State Libn.* Annie Norman, Delaware Div. of Libs., 121 Martin Luther King Jr. Blvd. N., Dover 19901. Tel. 302-257-3001, fax 302-739-6787, e-mail annie.norman@state.de.us; *Pres., Friends of Delaware Libs.* Kay Bowes. E-mail kaybowes@gmail.com; *Past Pres.* Sarah Katz, Univ. of Delaware, Morris Lib., 181 S. College Ave., Newark 19717. Tel. 302-831-6306, e-mail sekatz@udel.edu.

Address correspondence to Delaware Lib. Assn., c/o Delaware Division of Libs., 121 Martin Luther King Jr. Blvd. N., Dover 19901. E-mail dla@lib.de.us.

World Wide Web http://dla.lib.de.us.

District of Columbia

Memb. 300+. Term of Office. July–June. Publication. *Capital Librarian* (mo., online).

Pres. Tracy Sumler. E-mail president@dcla.org; *V.P.* Meg Metcalf. E-mail vice_president@dcla.org; *Secy.* Leah Castaldi. E-mail secretary@dcla.org; *Treas.* Heather Wiggins. E-mail treasurer@dcla.org; *ALA Councilor* Erica Harbeson. E-mail ala_councilor@dcla.org; *Past Pres.* Nicholas Brown. E-mail past_president@dcla.org.

Address correspondence to District of Columbia Lib. Assn., Union Station, 50 Massachusetts Ave. N.E., P.O. Box 1653 Washington, DC 20002.

World Wide Web http://www.dcla.org.

Florida

Memb. (Indiv.) 1,000+. Publication. *Florida Libraries* (s. ann.).

Pres. Eric Head, Citrus County Lib. System. E-mail eric.head@citruslibraries.org; *V.P./Pres.-Elect* Laura Spears, Univ. of Florida; *Secy.* Sarah Divine, Nova Southeastern Univ., Alvin Sherman Lib.; *Treas.* Donna Vazquez, Florida Gulf Coast Univ. E-mail devazque@fgcu.edu; *State Libn.* Amy Johnson, Division of Lib. and Info. Svcs. E-mail Amy.Johnson@dos.myflorida.com; *ALA Councilor* Sara Gonzalez, Orange County Lib. System; *Past Pres.* Sarah Hammill, Florida Intl. Univ. E-mail hammills@fiu.edu; *Exec. Dir.* Lisa O'Donnell. Tel. 850-270-9205, e-mail lisa@flalib.org.

Address correspondence to the executive director. Florida Lib. Assn., 541 E. Tennessee St., #103, Tallahassee 32308. Tel. 850-270-9205, e-mail admin@flalib.org.

World Wide Web http://www.flalib.org.

Georgia

Memb. 800+. Publication. *Georgia Library Quarterly* (q., online). *Ed.* Virginia Feher, Univ. of North Georgia. E-mail virginia.feher@ung.edu.

Pres. Laura Burtle, Georgia State Univ. Lib., 100 Decatur St. S.E., Atlanta 30303. Tel. 404-413-2706, e-mail lburtle@gsu.edu; *1st V.P./Pres.-Elect* Oscar Gittemeier, Atlanta-Fulton Public Lib. Tel. 404-730-1826, e-mail oscar.gittemeier@fultoncounty.gov; *2nd V.P.* Janice Shipp, Savannah State Univ., 2200 Savannah State Univ., Savannah 31404. Tel. 912-358-4339, e-mail shippj@savannahstate.edu; *V.P. Marketing and Branding* Jacqueline Radebaugh, Columbus State Univ., 4225 University Ave., Columbus 31907. Tel. 706-507-8693, e-mail radebaugh_jacqueline@columbusstate.edu; *Secy.* Scott Piper. Georgia State Univ. Lib. Tel. 678-891-2587, e-mail spieper1@gsu.edu; *Treas.* Ben Bryson, Marshes of Glynn Libs., 208 Gloucester St., Brunswick 31520. Tel. 912-279-3735, e-mail bbryson@glynncounty-ga.gov. *Past Pres.* Jennifer Lautzenheiser, Middle Georgia Regional Lib., 1180 Washington St., Macon 31208. Tel. 478-744-0880, e-mail lautzenheiserj@bibblib.org.

Address correspondence to the president. Georgia Lib. Assn., P.O. Box 30324, Savannah 31410. Tel. 912-999-7979, e-mail membership.gla@gmail.com.

World Wide Web http://gla.georgialibraries.org.

Hawaii

Memb. 250. Publication. *HLA Newsletter* (q., online).

Pres. Michael Aldrich, BYU Hawaii. E-mail michael.aldrich@byuh.edu; *V.P./Pres.-Elect* Joyce Tokuda, Kapi olani Community Coll. E-mail jtokuda@hawaii.edu; *Secy.* Alicia Yanagihara, Nanakuli Public Lib. E-mail alicia.yanagihara@librarieshawaii.org; *Treas.* Joy Oehlers, Kapi'olani Community College Lib., 4303 Diamond Head Rd., Honolulu 96816. Tel. 808-734-9352, e-mail aichin@hawaii.edu; *Past Pres.* Sharrese Castillo, Wahiawa Public Lib. E-mail sharrese.c.c@gmail.com.

Address correspondence to Hawai'i Lib. Assn., P.O. Box 4441, Honolulu 96812-4441. E-mail hawaii.library.association@gmail.com.

World Wide Web http://hawaiilibrary association.weebly.com.

Idaho

Memb. 420. Term of Office. Oct.–Oct.

President Katherine Lovan, Middleton Public Library, Middleton. E-mail klovan@mymiddletonlibrary.org and LeAnn Gelskey, Hailey Public Lib., Hailey. E-mail leanngelskey@gmail.com; *V.P./Pres.-Elect* Erin Downey, Boise School District. Tel. 208-854-4110, e-mail erindowney.ila@gmail.com; *Secy.* Beverley Richmond, Priest Lake Public Lib., 28769 Idaho 57, Priest Lake 83856. Tel. 208-443-2454, e-mail plplibrary@hotmail.com; *Treas.* Jane Clapp, Boise State Univ. E-mail janeclapp.ila@gmail.com; *Membership Committee Chair* Cindy Bigler, Soda Springs Public Lib. E-mail sspl@sodaspringsid.com.

Address correspondence to Idaho Lib. Assn., 4911 N. Shirley Ave., Boise 83703.

World Wide Web http://idaholibraries.org.

Illinois

Memb. 3,500. Publication. *ILA Reporter* (bi-mo.; online).

Pres. Molly Beestrum, Northwestern Univ. Libs.; *V.P./Pres.-Elect* Veronica De Fazio, Plainfield Public Lib. Dist.; *Treas.* Brian Shepard, Indiana Trails Public Lib. District; *ALA Councilor* Jeannie Dilger, Palatine Public Lib. District; *Past Pres.* Cynthia L. Fuerst, Vernon Area Public Lib. District; *Exec. Dir.* Diane Foote. E-mail dfoote@ila.org.

Address correspondence to the executive director. Illinois Lib. Assn., 33 W. Grand Ave., Suite 401, Chicago 60654-6799. Tel. 312 644-1896, fax 312 644-1899, e-mail ila@ila.org.

World Wide Web http://www.ila.org.

Indiana

Indiana Lib. Federation. Memb. 2,000+. Publications. *Focus on Indiana Libraries* (mo.; memb.). *Communications Mgr.* Tisa M. Davis, 941 E. 86th St., Suite 260, Indianapolis 46240. Tel. 317-257-2040, ext. 104, fax 317-257-1389, e-mail askus@ilfonline.org.

Pres. Leslie Sutherlin, South Dearborn Community Schools, 5770 Highlander Pl., Aurora 47001. Tel. 812-926-3772; *Pres.-Elect* Latrice Booker, Indiana Univ. Northwest, 3400 Broadway, Gary 46408; *Secy.* Kristi Howe, Vigo County Public Lib., 1 Library Sq., Terre Haute, IN 47807; *Treas.* Michael Williams, Indianapolis Public Lib., 40 E. Saint Clair St., Indianapolis 46204. Tel. 317 275-4302; *ALA Councilor* Beth Munk, Kendallville Public Lib., 221 S. Park, Kendallville 46755 Tel. 260-343-2022; *Past Pres.* Susie Highley, Indiana Middle Level Education Assn., 11025 E. 25th St., Indianapolis 46229. Tel. 317-894-2937; *Exec. Dir.* Lucinda Nord. Tel. 317-257-2040, ext. 101, e-mail exec@ilfonline.org.

Address correspondence to Indiana Lib. Federation, 941 E. 86 St., Suite 260, Indianapolis 46240. Tel. 317-257-2040, fax 317-257-1389, e-mail askus@ilfonline.org.

World Wide Web http://www.ilfonline.org.

Iowa

Memb. 1,500. Publication. *Catalyst* (bi-mo., online).

Pres. Mara Strickler. E-mail mstrickler@cityofpella.com; *Pres.-Elect* Stacy Goodhue. E-mail sgoodhue@carlisle.lib.ia.us; *Secy. Parliamentarian* Jennifer Sterling. E-mail *Treas.* Genevieve McCleeary. E-mail gnmccleeary@dmpl.org; *ALA Councilor* Samantha Helmick, Burlington Public Lib. Tel. 319-753-1647, e-mail shelmick@burlington.lib.ia.us; *Past Pres.* Dan Chibnall, Drake Univ., 2507 University Ave., Des Moines 50311. Tel. 515-271-2112, e-mail dan.chibnall@drake.edu.

Address correspondence to Iowa Lib. Assn., 6919 Vista Dr., West Des Moines 50266. Tel. 515-282-8192.

World Wide Web http://www.iowalibraryassociation.org.

Kansas

Kansas Lib. Assn. Memb. 1,500. Term of Office. July–June. Publication. *Kansas Libraries!* (6x yearly; online). E-mail kilbmag@gmail.com.

Pres. Robin Newell, Emporia Public Lib., 110 E. Sixth Ave., Emporia 66801. Tel. 620-340-6464, e-mail newellr@emporialibrary.org; *1st V.P.* Meagan Zampieri, Hays Public Lib. E-mail mzampieri@hayslibrary.org; *2nd V.P.* Holly Mercer, Southwest Kansas Lib. System; *Secy.* Bethanie O'Dell, Emporia State Univ. E-mail bodell1@emporia.edu; *Treas.* Diedre Lemon, Dodge City Public Lib.; *ALA Councilor* Marie Pyko, Topeka and Shawnee County Lib. E-mail mpyko@tscpl.org; *Exec. Secy.* George Seamon, Northwest Kansas Lib. System, #2 Washington Sq.; Norton 67654. Tel. 785-877-5148, e-mail director@nwkls.org; *Parliamentarian* Dan Ireton Kansas State Univ. E-mail dli6873@k-state.edu. *Past Pres.* Laura Littrell, Kansas State Univ., Lib. Planning and Assessment, 1117 Mid-Campus Drive North, 314A Hale Lib., Manhattan 66506. Tel. 785-532-5467, e-mail laurlit@k-state.edu.

Address correspondence to the president. Kansas Lib. Assn., Northwest Kansas Lib. System, 2 Washington Sq., Norton 67654. Tel. 785-877-5148.

World Wide Web http://www.kslibassoc.org.

Kentucky

Memb. 1,600. Publication. *Kentucky Libraries* (q.). *Ed.* Robin Harris, Law Lib., Brandeis School of Law, Univ. of Louisville, Louisville, 40292-0001. Tel. 502-852-6083, e-mail robin.harris@louisville.edu.

Pres. Kandace Rogers, Sullivan Univ., 2355 Harrodsburg Rd., Lexington 40504. Tel. 859-514-3359, e-mail krogers@sullivan.edu; *Pres.-Elect* Mark Adler, Paris-Bourbon County Lib., 701 High St., Paris 40361. Tel. 859-987-4419, x103, e-mail madler@bourbonlibrary.org; *Secy.* Adele Koch, Sacred Heart Model School, 3107 Lexington Rd., Louisville 40206. Tel. 502-896-3931, e-mail akoch@shslou.org; *Past Pres.* Debbra Tate, Kentucky State Univ., Blazer Lib., 400 E. Main St., Frankfort 40601. Tel. 502-597-6862, e-mail debbra.tate@gmail.com; *Exec. Dir.* John Tom Underwood, Kentucky Lib. Assn., 5932 Timber Ridge Drive, Unit 101, Prospect 40059. Tel. 502-223-5322, fax 502-223-4937, e-mail info@kylibasn.org.

Address correspondence to the executive director. Kentucky Lib. Assn., 5932 Timber Ridge Dr., Suite 101, Prospect 40059. Tel. 502-223-5322, fax 502-223-4937, e-mail info@kylibasn.org.

World Wide Web http://www.klaonline.org.

Louisiana

Memb. 1,000+. Term of Office. July–June. Publication. *Louisiana Libraries* (q.). *Ed.* Celise Reech-Harper, Assoc. Dir., Beauregard Parish Lib., 205 South Washington Ave., DeRidder 70634. Tel. 337-463-6217 ext. 22, e-mail celise@beau.org.

Pres. Sonnet Ireland. Tel. 504-390-6834, e-mail sonnet.ireland@yahoo.com; *2nd V.P.* Julie Champagne. E-mail julie.champagne@stmarylibrary.org; *Secy.* Erin Chesnutt. E-mail echesnut@beau.org; *ALA Councilor* Vivian McCain. Tel. 318-513-5508, e-mail vmccain@mylpl.org; *Parliamentarian* Chris Achee. E-mail cachee@state.lib.la.us; *Past Pres.* Catherine A. Smith. Tel. 318-603-6374, e-mail catlib2000@yahoo.com.

Address correspondence to Louisiana Lib. Assn., 1190 Meramec Station Rd., Suite 207, Ballwin, MO 63021. Tel. 972-851-8000, fax 972- 991-6061, e-mail lla@amigos.org.

World Wide Web http://www.llaonline.org.

Maine

Maine Lib. Assn. Memb. 950. Publication. *MLA to Z* (q., online). E-mail mlatozeditor@gmail.com.

Pres. Jennifer Alvino, Windham Public Lib., 217 Windham Center Rd., Windham 04062. Tel. 207-892-1908, e-mail jaalvino@windhammaine.us; *V.P.* Wynter Giddings, Curtis Memorial Lib., 23 Pleasant St., Brunswick 04011. Tel. 207-725-3542, e-mail giddingswynter@gmail.com; *Secy.* Courtney Sparks, Freeport Community Lib., 10 Library Dr., Freeport 04032. Tel. 207-865-3307, e-mail freeportlibrary.org;

Treas. Nissa Flanagan, Merrill Memorial Lib., 215 Main St., Yarmouth 04096. Tel. 207-846-4763, e-mail nflanagan@yarmoughlibrary.org; *Membs.-at-Large* Cadence Atchinson. E-mail catchinson@une.edu, Kate Wing. E-mail katemwing@gmail.com; *ALA Councilor* Kara Reiman, Walker Memorial Lib., 800 Main St., Westbrook 04092. Tel. 207-854-0630 ext. 4, kreiman@westbrook.me.us; *NELA Rep.* Michelle Sampson, York Public Lib., 15 Long Sands Rd., York 03909. Tel. 207-363-2818, e-mail msampson@york.lib.me.us; *Exec. Dir.* Jenna Blake Davis. Tel. 207-730-3028, e-mail mainelibrary@gmail.com.

Address correspondence to executive director, Maine Lib. Assn., 93 Saco Ave., Old Orchard Beach 04064. Tel. 207-730-3028, e-mail mainelibrary@gmail.com.

World Wide Web http://mainelibraries.org.

Maryland

Maryland Lib. Assn. Memb. 1,000+. Term of Office. July–July. Publication. *The Crab* (q., memb., online). *Ed.* Annette Haldeman. E-mail annette.haldeman@mlis.state.md.us.

Pres. Andrea Berstler, Carroll County Public Lib., 1100 Green Valley Rd., New Windsor 21776. Tel. 443-293-3136, e-mail aberstler@carr.org; *V.P./Pres.-Elect* Morgan Miller, Cecil County Public Lib. 301 Newark Ave., Elkton 21921. Tel. 410-996-1055, e-mail mmiller@ccplnet.org; *Secy.* Mary Anne Bowman, St. Mary's County Public Lib., 23250 Hollywood Rd., Leonardtown 20650. Tel. 301-475-2846 ext. 1015, fax 410-884-4415, e-mail mabowman@stmalib.org; *Treas.* Carl Olson, Towson Univ., Cook Lib., 8000 York Rd., Towson 21252. Tel. 410-704-3267, e-mail colson@towson.edu; *ALA Councilor* David Dahl, Univ. of Maryland. Tel. 301-314-0395, e-mail ddahl1@umd.edu; *Conference Dir.* Naomi Keppler, Baltimore County Public Lib., 6105 Kenwood Ave., Rosedale 21237. Tel. 410-887-0521, e-mail nkeppler@bcpl.net; *Past Pres.* Joseph Thompson, Carroll County Public Lib., 1100 Green Valley Rd., New Windsor 21776. Tel. 443-293-3131, e-mail jthompson@carr.org; *Exec. Dir.* Margaret Carty, Maryland Lib. Assn., 1401 Hollins St., Baltimore 21223. Tel. 410-947-5090, e-mail mcarty@mdlib.org.

Address correspondence to Maryland Lib. Assn., 1401 Hollins St., Baltimore 21223. Tel. 410-947-5090, fax 410-947-5089, e-mail mla@mdlib.org.

World Wide Web http://www.mdlib.org.

Massachusetts

Massachusetts Lib. Assn. Memb. (Indiv.) 1,000; (Inst.) 100.

Pres. Esmé E. Green, Goodnow Lib., 21 Concord Rd., Sudbury 01776. Tel. 978-440-5515, e-mail president@masslib.org; *V.P.* Nora Blake, Emily Williston Memorial Lib., Easthampton. E-mail vicepresident@masslib.org; *Secy.* Noelle Boc, Tewksbury Lib., 300 Chandler St., Tewksbury 01876. Tel. 978-640-4490, e-mail secretary@masslib.org; *Treas.* Bernadette Rivard, Bellingham Public Lib., Bellingham. E-mail treasurer@masslib.org; *Past Pres.* William L. Adamczyk, Milton Public Lib., 476 Canton Ave., Milton 02186. Tel. 617-698-5757, e-mail pastpresident@masslib.org.

Address correspondence to Massachusetts Lib. Assn., P.O. Box 404, Malden 02148. Tel. 781-698-7764, e-mail manager@masslib.org.

World Wide Web http://www.masslib.org.

Michigan

Memb. 1,200+.

Pres. Kristin Shelley, East Lansing Public Lib.; *Pres.-Elect* Julia Eisenstein, Univ. of Detroit Mercy; *Treas.* Richard Schneider; *ALA Councilor* Jennifer Dean; *State Librarian* (ex-officio) Randy Riley; *Past Pres.* Steven Bowers, Wayne State Univ. Lib. System; *Exec. Dir.* Deborah E. Mikula. Tel. 517-394-2774, ext. 224, e-mail dmikula@milibraries.org.

Address correspondence to the executive director. Michigan Lib. Assn., 3410 Belle Chase Way, Suite 100, Lansing 48911. Tel. 517-394-2774, e-mail MLA@milibraries.org.

World Wide Web http://www.milibraries.org.

Minnesota

Memb. 1,100. Term of Office. (*Pres., Pres.-Elect*) Jan.–Dec. Publication. *Roundup* (mo., online).

Pres. Patti Bross, Lake City Public Lib.; *Pres.-Elect* Stacey Hendren, Anoka County Lib.; *Secy.* Lisa Motschke, St. Paul Public Lib.; *Treas.* Sarah Ethier, Scott County Lib.; *Memb.-at-Large* Katie Sundstrom, Two Harbors

Public Lib.; *ALA Chapter Councilor* Hannah Buckland, Minnesota Dept. of Education; *Past Pres.* Kirsten Clark, Univ. of Minnesota Libs.; *Exec. Dir.* Jen Newberg. E-mail jen.newberg@management-hq.com.

Address correspondence to the executive director. Minnesota Lib. Assn., 400 S. 4th St., Suite 754E, Minneapolis 55415. Tel. 612-294-6549, e-mail mla@management-hq.com.

World Wide Web http://www.mnlibraryassociation.org.

Mississippi

Memb. 625. Term of Office. Jan.–Dec. Publication. *Mississippi Libraries* (q.). *Ed.* Tina Harry. E-mail tharry@olemiss.edu.

Pres. Mary Beth Applin, Hinds Community College. Tel. 601-857-3380; *V.P.* Mara Polk, Central Mississippi Regional Lib. System. Tel. 601-825-0100; *Secy.* Tamara Blackwell, Bolivar Lib. System. Tel. 662-843-2774; *Treas.* Lori Barnes, Jackson-George Regional Lib. System. Tel. 228-769-3227; *ALA Councilor* Meredith Wickham, First Regional Lib. System. Tel. 662-429-4439; *Parliamentarian* Patsy C. Brewer, Waynesboro-Wayne County Lib. Tel. 601-735-2268; *Past Pres.* Sarah Crisler-Ruskey, Harrison County Public Lib. System. Tel. 228-539-0110; *Admin.* Paula Bass, P.O. Box 13687, Jackson 39236-3687. Tel. 601-981-4586, e-mail info@misslib.org.

Address correspondence to administrator. Mississippi Lib. Assn., P.O. Box 13687, Jackson 39236-3687. Tel. 601-981-4586, e-mail info@misslib.org.

World Wide Web http://www.misslib.org.

Missouri

Memb. 800+. Term of Office. Jan.–Dec. Publication. *MO INFO* (bi-mo.).

Pres. Cindy Dudenhoffer, Central Methodist Univ. E-mail mlapresident@molib.org; *Pres.-Elect* Cindy Thompson, UMKC Univ. Libs.; *Secy. and Memb.-at-Large* Shannon Midyett, Poplar Bluff Municipal Lib.; *Treas. and Memb.-at-Large* Steve Campbell, Scenic Regional Lib.; *Memb.-at-Large* Jenny Bossaller, Meredith McCarthy, Jennifer Parsons, Christina Prucha. *Treas.-Elect and Member-at-Large* Katie Hill, Cape Girardeau Public Lib.; *ALA Councilor* Margaret Conroy, Daniel Boone Regional Lib.; *Past Pres.* Erin Gray, Amigos Lib. Svcs.

Address correspondence to the president. Missouri Lib. Assn., 1190 Meramec Station Rd., Suite 207, Ballwin, 63021-6902. E-mail mlapresident@molib.org.

World Wide Web http://www.molib.org.

Montana

Memb. 600. Term of Office. July–June. Publication. *Focus* (bi-mo.). *Eds.* Star Bradley and Sarah Creech. E-mail mlaFOCUSeditor@gmail.com.

Pres. Mary Anne Hansen, MSU-Bozeman Lib., P.O. Box 173320, Bozeman 59717; *V.P./Pres.-Elect* Gavin Woltjer, Billings Public Lib., 510 North Broadway, Billings 59101; *Secy./Treas.* Megan Stark, UM-Missoula Lib., 32 Campus Dr., Missoula 59812; *ALA Rep.* Matt Beckstrom, Lewis & Clark Lib., 120 S. Last Chance Gulch, Helena 59601; *Past Pres.* Elizabeth Jonkel, Missoula Public Lib., 301 E. Main, Missoula 59802. Tel. 406-721-2665, e-mail ejonkel@missoula.lib.mt.us; *Exec. Dir.* Debbi Kramer, Montana Lib. Assn., Inc., 33 Beartooth View Dr., Laurel 59044. Tel. 406-579-3121, e-mail debkmla@hotmail.com.

Address correspondence to the executive director. Montana Lib. Assn. E-mail debkmla@hotmail.com.

World Wide Web http://www.mtlib.org.

Nebraska

Term of Office. Jan.–Dec.

Pres. Michael Straatmann. E-mail nlapresident@nebraskalibraries.org; *Pres.-Elect* Laura England-Biggs. E-mail nlapresidentelect@nebraskalibraries.org; *Secy.* Bailey Halbur. E-mail nlasecretary@nebraskalibraries.org; *Treas.* Denise Harders. E-mail nlatreasurer@nebraskalibraries.org; *ALA Councilor* Micki Dietrich. E-mail mdietrich@omahalibrary.org; *Past Pres.* Rebecca McCorkindale. E-mail nlapastpresident@nebraskalibraries.org; *Exec. Dir.* Creative Association Management. E-mail nlaexecutivedirector@nebraskalibraries.org.

Address correspondence to the executive director. Nebraska Lib. Assn., P.O. Box 21756, Lincoln 68542-1756. E-mail nlaexecutivedirector@nebraskalibraries.org.

World Wide Web https://nebraskalibraries.org.

Nevada

Memb. 450. Term of Office. Jan.–Dec. Publication. *Nevada Libraries* (q.).

Pres. Forrest Lewis, North Las Vegas Lib. District. E-mail lewisf@cityofnorthlasvegas.com; *Pres.-Elect* Tod Colegrove, Carson City Lib., E-mail tcolegrove@carson.org; *Exec. Secy.* Carla Land, Las Vegas–Clark County Lib. District; *Treas.* Joy Gunn, Henderson Libs. E-mail jgunn@hendersonlibraries.com; *Finance* Morgan Tiar, Washoe County Library System. E-mail matiar@washoecounty.us; *State Libn.* Tammy Westergard, Nevada State Lib., Archives and Public Records. E-mail twestergard@admin.nv.gov; *ALA Delegate* Amy Geddes, Lyon County Lib. District. E-mail ageddes@lyon-county.org; *Past Pres.* Jeff Scott, Washoe County Lib. System. E-mail jscott@washoecounty.us.

Address correspondence to the executive secretary.

World Wide Web http://www.nevadalibraries.org.

New Hampshire

Memb. 700.

Pres. Amy Lappin, Lebanon Public Libs., 80 Main St., West Lebanon 03784. Tel. 603-298-8544, e-mail president@nhlibrarians.org; *V.P./Pres.-Elect* Yvette Couser, Merrimack Public Lib., 470 Daniel Webster Hwy., Merrimack 03784. Tel. 603-424-5021 ext. 108, e-mail ycouser@merrimacklibrary.org; *Secy.* Sarah St. Martin, Manchester City Lib., 405 Pine St., Manchester 03104. Tel. 603-624-6550, ext. 3343, e-mail secretary@nhlibrarians.org; *Treas.* Kim Gabert, Wadleigh Memorial Lib., 49 Nashua St., Milford 03055. Tel. 603-249-0645, e-mail treasurer@nhlibrarians.org; *ALA Councilor* Lori Fisher, New Hampshire State Lib., 20 Park St., Concord 03301. Tel. 603-271-2393, e-mail lori.fisher@dncr.nh.gov; *Past Pres.* Christine Friese, Portsmouth Public Library, 175 Parrott Avenue, Portsmouth 03801. Telephone 603-766-1703, e-mail pastpresident@nhlibrarians.org.

Address correspondence to New Hampshire Lib. Assn., c/o New Hampshire State Lib., 20 Park St., Concord 03301-6314. E-mail nhlaexecutive@googlegroups.com.

World Wide Web http://nhlibrarians.org.

New Jersey

Memb. 1,800. Term of Office. July–June. Publication. *New Jersey Libraries NEWSletter* (q.). E-mail newsletter_editor@njlamembers.org.

Pres. Jen Schureman, Gloucester County Lib. System. E-mail schubacca2@yahoo.com; *1st V.P./Pres.-Elect* Amy Babcock-Landry, Livingston Public Lib. E-mail babcock-landry@livingston.bccls.org; *2nd V.P.* Susanne Sacchetti, Cumberland County Library. E-mail susannesa@cclnj.org; *Secy.* Kate Jaggers, Highland Park Public Library. E-mail kjaggers@piscatawaylibrary.org; *Treas.* Judah Hamer, Rutherford Public Lib. E-mail hamer@rutherford.bccls.org; *ALA Councilor* Eileen Palmer, LMXAC. E-mail empalmer@lmxac.org; *Past Pres.* Leah Wagner, Monroe Township Library (Middlesex). E-mail lwagner@monroetwplibrary.org *Exec. Dir.* Patricia Tumulty, New Jersey Lib. Assn., P.O. Box 1534, Trenton 08607. Tel. 609-394-8032, fax 609-394-8164, e-mail ptumulty@njla.org.

Address correspondence to the executive director. New Jersey Lib. Assn., P.O. Box 1534, Trenton 08607. Tel. 609-394-8032, fax 609-394-8164.

World Wide Web http://www.njla.org.

New Mexico

Memb. 550. Term of Office. Apr.–Apr. Publication. *NMLA Newsletter* (bi-mo., online). *Ed.* Robyn Gleasner. E-mail newsletter@nmla.org.

Pres. David Cox. E-mail president@nmla.org; *V.P./Pres.-Elect* Melanie Templet. E-mail vicepresident@nmla.org; *Secy.* Sarah Obenauf. E-mail secretary@nmla.org; *Treas.* Kelli Murphy. E-mail treasurer@nmla.org; *Membs.-at-Large* Ellen Bosman. E-mail ebosman@nmsu.edu, Kate Alderete. E-mail kalderete@taosgov.com, Sharon Jenkins. E-mail djenkins@nmsu.edu, Anne Lefkosfsky. E-mail alefkofsky@cabq.gov; *ALA-APA Councilor* Elizabeth Titus. E-mail etitus@lib.nmsu.edu.

Address correspondence to New Mexico Lib. Assn., P.O. Box 26074, Albuquerque 87125. Tel. 505-400-7309, fax 505-544-5740, e-mail contact@nmla.org.

World Wide Web http://nmla.org.

New York

Memb. 4,000. Term of Office. Nov.–Nov. Publication. *The eBulletin* (6x yearly, online).

Pres. Jen Cannell, St. John Fisher College; *Pres.-Elect* Claudia Depkin, Haverstraw King's Daughters Public Lib.; *Treas.* Roger Reyes, Suffolk Cooperative Lib. System; *Treas.-Elect* Grace Riario, Ramapo Catskill Lib. System; *ALA Chapter Councilor* Cassie Guthrie, Greece Public Lib.; *Past Pres.* Michelle Young, Clarkson Univ.; *Exec. Dir.* Jeremy Johannesen, New York Lib. Assn., 6021 State Farm Rd., Guilderland 12084. Tel. 518-432-6952, fax 518-427-1697, e-mail director@nyla.org.

Address correspondence to the executive director. New York Lib. Assn., 6021 State Farm Rd., Guilderland 12084. Tel. 518-432-6952, fax 518-427-1697, e-mail info@nyla.org.

World Wide Web http://www.nyla.org.

North Carolina

Memb. 1,100. Term of Office. Oct.–Oct. Publication. *North Carolina Libraries* (1–2x yearly, online). *Ed.* Ralph Scott. E-mail scottr@ecu.edu.

Pres. Lorrie Russell, High Point Public Lib., 901 Main St., High Point 27262. Tel. 336-883-3644, e-mail president@nclaonline.org; *V.P./Pres.-Elect* Libby Stone. E-mail vicepresident@nclaonline.org; *Secy.* Julie Raynor, e-mail secretary@nclaonline.org; *Treas.* Amy Harris, Univ. of North Carolina–Greensboro, P.O. Box 26170, Greensboro 27412-0001. Tel. 336-256-0275, e-mail treasurer@nclaonline.org; *Treas.-Elect* Lara Luck. E-mail luckla@forsyth.cc; *ALA Councilor* Siobhan Loendorf. E-mail sloendorf@catawbacountync.gov; *State Libn. (Ex Officio)* Timothy Owens. E-mail timothy.owens@ncdcr.gov; *Past Pres.* Michael A. Crumpton, Walter Clinton Jackson Lib., Univ. of North Carolina–Greensboro, 320 College Ave., Greensboro 27412. Tel. 336-256-1213, e-mail macrumpt@uncg.edu.

Address correspondence to the executive assistant. North Carolina Lib. Assn., 265 Eastchester Dr., Suite 133, #364, High Point 27262. Tel. 919-839-6252, fax 888-977-3143, e-mail nclaonline@gmail.com.

World Wide Web http://www.nclaonline.org.

North Dakota

Memb. (Indiv.) 300+. Term of Office. Sept.–Sept. Publication. *The Good Stuff* (q.). *Ed.* Marlene Anderson, Bismarck State College Lib., P.O. Box 5587, Bismarck 58506-5587. Tel. 701-224-5578, e-mail marlene.anderson@bismarckstate.edu.

Pres. Traci Lund, Divide County Public Lib. E-mail president@ndla.info; *Pres.-Elect* Amy Soma, Fargo Public Schools. E-mail somaa@fargo.k12.nd.us; *Treas.* Aaron Stefanich, Grand Forks Public Lib., 2110 Lib. Cir., Grand Forks 58201. Tel. 701-772-8116, e-mail aaron.stefanich@gflibrary.com; *ALA Councilor* Laurie L. McHenry, Univ. of North Dakota–Thormodsgard Law Lib. E-mail laurie.mchenry@und.edu; *State Libn.,* Mary J. Soucie, North Dakota State Lib. E-mail msoucie@nd.gov; *Past Pres.* Margaret (Maggie) Townsend, Legacy High School. E-mail maggie_townsend@bismarckschools.org.

Address correspondence to the president. North Dakota Lib. Assn., 604 E. Boulevard Ave., Bismarck 58505.

World Wide Web http://www.ndla.info.

Ohio

Memb. 2,700+. Term of Office. Jan.–Dec. Publication. *OLC News* (online).

Chair Cheryl Kuonen, Mentor Public Lib. Tel. 440-255-8811, e-mail cheryl.kuonen@mentorpl.org; *V.Chair/Chair-Elect* Jennifer Slone, Chillicothe and Ross County Public Lib. Tel. 740-702-4103, e-mail jslone@crcpl.org; *Secy./Treas.* Aimee Fifarek, Public Lib. of Youngstown and Mahoning County. Tel. 330-744-8636, e-mail afifarek@libraryvisit.org; *Immediate Past Chair* Kacie Armstrong, Euclid Public Lib. Tel. 216-261-5300, e-mail kacie.armstrong@euclidlibrary.org; *ALA Councilor* Meg Delaney, Toledo Lucas County Public Lib. Tel. 419-259-5333, e-mail meg.delaney@toledolibrary.org; *Exec. Dir.* Michelle Francis, Ohio Lib. Council, 1105 Schrock Rd., Ste. 440, Columbus, OH 43229. Tel. 614-410-8092 ext. 105, e-mail mfrancis@olc.org.

Address correspondence to the executive director. Ohio Lib. Council, 1105 Schrock Rd., Suite 440, Columbus 43229. Tel. 614-410-8092.

World Wide Web http://www.olc.org.

Oklahoma

Memb. (Indiv.) 1,000; (Inst.) 60. Term of Office. July–June. Publication. *Oklahoma Librarian* (bi-mo.).

Pres. Lisa Wells; *V.P./Pres.-Elect* Cathy Blackman; *Secy.* Jennifer Ballard; *Treas.* Susan Urban; *ALA Councilor* Sarah Robbins; *Past Pres.* Stacy Schrank.

Address correspondence to Oklahoma Lib. Assn., 1190 Meramec Station Rd., Suite 207, Ballwin, MO 63021-6902. Tel. 800-843-8482, fax 636-529-1396, e-mail ola@amigos.org.

World Wide Web http://www.oklibs.org.

Oregon

Memb. (Indiv.) 1,000+. Publications. *OLA Hotline.* (bi-w.). E-mail olahotline@olaweb.org; *OLA Quarterly.* (q.) *Ed.* Charles Wood. E-mail wuchakewu@gmail.com.

Pres. Elaine Hirsch, Lewis and Clark College, Watzek Lib. E-mail olapresident@olaweb.org; *V.P./Pres.-Elect* Kate Lasky, Josephine Community Lib. District. E-mail olavp@olaweb.org; *Secy.* Laura Baca, Cedar Mill Community Lib. E-mail olasecretary@olaweb.org; *Treas.* Lori Wamsley, Mt. Hood Community College Lib. E-mail olatreasurer@olaweb.org; *Memb.-at-Large* Star Khan, Driftwood Public Lib. E-mail skhan@lincolncity.org; *ALA Rep.* Kirsten Brodbeck-Kenney, Driftwood Public Lib. E-mail olachaptercouncilor@olaweb.org; *Past Pres.* Esther Moberg, Seaside Public Lib. E-mail olapastpresident@olaweb.org.

Address correspondence to Oregon Lib. Assn., P.O. Box 3067, La Grande 97850. Tel. 541-962-5824, e-mail ola@olaweb.org.

World Wide Web http://www.olaweb.org.

Pennsylvania

Memb. 1,900+. Term of Office. Jan.–Dec. Publication. *PaLA Bulletin* (q.).

Pres. Michele Legate; *1st V.P.* Tom Reinsfelder; *2nd V.P. (2020 Kalahari)* Slyvia Orner; *2nd V.P. (2021 Monroeville)* Nicole Henline; *3rd V.P.* Sheli Pratt-McHugh, Univ. of Scranton. E-mail michelle.mchugh@scranton.edu; *Treas.* Kate Boyle; *ALA Councilor* Barbara McGary; *Past Pres.* Denise Sticha, Berks Co. Public Libs. E-mail denise.sticha@berks.lib.pa.us; *Exec. Dir.* Christi Buker. Pennsylvania Lib. Assn., 220 Cumberland Pkwy., Suite 10, Mechanicsburg 17055. Tel. 717-766-7663, e-mail christi@palibraries.org.

Address correspondence to the executive director. Pennsylvania Lib. Assn., 220 Cumberland Parkway, Suite 10, Mechanicsburg 17055. Tel. 717-766-7663, fax 717-766-5440.

World Wide Web http://www.palibraries.org.

Rhode Island

Memb. (Indiv.) 350+; (Inst.) 50+. Term of Office. June–June. Publication. *RILA Bulletin* (6x yearly). *Ed.* Deb Estrella, Tiverton Public Lib. Tel. 401-625-6796. E-mail communications@rilibraries.org.

Pres. Julie Holden, Cranston Public Lib. E-mail president@rilibraries.org; *V.P.* Rachael Juskuv, Bryant Univ. Tel. 401-232-6299, e-mail vicepresident@rilibraries.org; *Secy.* Celeste Dyer, Cumberland Public Lib. Tel. 401-333-2552, e-mail secretary@rilibraries.org; *Treas.* Beatrice Pulliam, Providence Public Lib. E-mail treasurer@rilibraries.org; *Memb.-at-Large* Bohyun Kim, Univ. of Rhode Island. Tel. 401-874-4607, Megan Hamlin-Black, Rhode Island State Libn. Tel. 401-330-3184, e-mail mblack@sos.ri.gov; *ALA Councilor* Jack Martin, Providence Public Lib. E-mail jmartin@provlib.org; *Past Pres.* Kieran Ayton, Rhode Island College, 600 Mt. Pleasant Ave., Providence, 02908. Tel. 401-456-9604, e-mail kayton@ric.edu.

Address correspondence to Rhode Island Lib. Assn., P.O. Box 6765, Providence 02940.

World Wide Web http://www.rilibraries.org.

South Carolina

Memb. 350+. Term of Office. Jan.–Dec. Publication. *South Carolina Libraries* (s.-ann., online). *Eds.* April Akins, Lander Univ. Tel. 864-388-8184, e-mail aakins@lander.edu; Megan Palmer, Clemson Univ. Tel. 864-656-5179, e-mail mpalme4@clemson.edu.

Pres. Nathan Flowers, Francis Marion Univ., 4822 E. Palmetto St., Florence 29506. Tel. 843-661-1306, e-mail nflowers@fmarion.edu; *1st V.P.* Megan Palmer, Clemson Univ. Tel. 864-656-5179, e-mail mpalme4@clemson.edu; *2nd V.P.* Sara DeSantis, Univ. of South Carolina–Upstate. Tel. 864-503-5006, e-mail sarabd@uscupstate.edu; *Secy.* Jade Geary, Univ. of South Carolina, Thomas Cooper Lib. Tel. 803-777-9944, e-mail gearyja@mailbox.sc.edu. *Treas.* Steven Sims, Francis Marion Univ., 4822 E. Palmetto St., Florence 29506. Tel. 843-661-1299, e-mail ssims@fmarion.edu; *ALA Councilor* Jonathan Newton, Univ. of South Carolina–Upstate. E-mail jdn3@uscupstate.edu; *Past Pres. Exec. Secy.* Donald Wood, South Carolina Lib. Assn., P.O. Box 1763, Columbia 29202. Tel. 803-252-1087, fax 803-252-0589, e-mail scla@capconsc.com.

Address correspondence to the executive secretary. South Carolina Lib. Assn., P.O. Box 1763, Columbia 29202. Tel. 803-252-1087, e-mail scla@capconsc.com.

World Wide Web http://www.scla.org.

South Dakota

Memb. (Indiv.) 450+; (Inst.) 60+. Publication. *Book Marks* (q.). *Ed.* Kelly Henkel Thompson, McGovern Lib., Dakota Wesleyan Univ., Mitchell 57301. E-mail bookmarkssd@gmail.com.

Pres. Ashia Gustafson, Brookings Public Lib., Brookings. E-mail agustafson@cityofbrookings.org *V.P./Pres.-Elect* Julie Erickson, TIE, Rapid City. E-mail jerickson@tie.net; *Recording Secy.* Kim Bonen, K. O. Lee Aberdeen Public Lib., Aberdeen. E-mail kbonen@g.emporia.edu; *Exec. Secy./Treas.* Audrea Buller, Lennox Community Lib., Lennox. E-mail SDLibraryAssociation@gmail.com; *ALA Councilor* Lisa Brunick, Augustana Univ., Sioux Falls. E-mail lisa.brunick@augie.edu; *Past Pres.* Maria Gruener, Watertown Regional Lib., Watertown. E-mail mgruener@watertownsd.us.

Address correspondence to the executive secretary. South Dakota Lib. Assn., P.O. Box 283, Lennox 57039. Tel. 605-214-8785.

World Wide Web http://www.sdlibraryassociation.org.

Tennessee

Memb. 600+. Term of Office. July–June. Publications. *Tennessee Libraries* (q.; online). *Ed.* Sharon Holderman, Tennessee Tech Univ. Lib. E-mail sholderman@tntech.edu; *TLA Newsletter* (q.; online). *Ed.* Holly Mills. E-mail hcmills@tntech.edu.

Pres. Jill Rael. E-mail tnlapresident2019@gmail.com; *V.P./Pres.-Elect* Erika Long. E-mail erikalong.lib@gmail.com; *Recording Secy.* Holly Hebert. E-mail holly.hebert@mtsu.edu; *Past Pres.* Jeffie Nicholson. E-mail jeffie.nicholson@williamsoncounty-tn.gov. *Exec. Dir.* Cathy Farley. E-mail exdirtla@gmail.com.

Address correspondence to the executive director. Tennessee Lib. Assn., P.O. Box 6297, Sparta 38583. Tel. 931-607-1182, e-mail exdirtla@gmail.com.

World Wide Web http://tnla.org.

Texas

Memb. 6,500+. Term of Office. Apr.–Apr. Publications. *Texas Library Journal* (q.), *Ed.* Wendy Woodland. E-mail wendyw@txla.org, *TLACast* (6–8x yearly; online).

Pres. Cecilia Barham, North Richland Hills Public Lib.; *Pres.-Elect* Christina Gola, Univ. of Houston; *Treas.* Edward Melton, Harris County Public Lib.; *ALA Councilor* Mary Woodard, Mesquite ISD; *Past Pres.* Jennifer LaBoon, Fort Worth ISD; *Exec. Dir.* Shirley Robinson, Texas Lib. Assn., 3355 Bee Cave Rd., Ste. 401, Austin 78746-6763. Tel. 512-328-1518 ext. 151, e-mail shirleyr@txla.org.

Address correspondence to the executive director. Texas Lib. Assn., 3355 Bee Cave Rd., Suite 401, Austin 78746-6763. Tel. 512-328-1518, fax 512-328-8852, e-mail tla@txla.org.

World Wide Web http://www.txla.org.

Utah

Memb. 650. Publication. *Utah Libraries News* (q.; online). *Ed.* Mindy Hale. E-mail mehale@slcolibrary.org.

Pres. Vern Waters, South Jordan Lib. E-mail vwaters@slcolibrary.org; *Pres.-Elect* Daniel Mauchley, Duchesne 84021. E-mail dmauchley@duchesne.utah.gov; *Treas.* Javaid Lal, 15 N. Temple, Salt Lake City 84150. E-mail JLal@ula.org; *ALA Chapter Councilor* Pamela Martin. E-mail pamela.martin@usu.edu; *Past Pres.* Rebekah Cummings, J. Willard Marriott Lib., Univ. of Utah. Tel. 801-581-7701, e-mail rebekah.cummings@utah.edu; *Exec. Dir.* Barbara Hopkins-Winters, Canyons School District, 9150 S. 500 W., Sandy 84070. Tel. 801-826-5095, e-mail barbaraw.hopkins@gmail.com.

Address correspondence to the executive director.

World Wide Web http://www.ula.org.

Vermont

Memb. 400. Publication. *VLA News* (q.). *Ed.* Janet Clapp, Rutland Free Lib., 10 Court St., Rutland. Tel. 802-773-1860, e-mail jclappmls@gmail.com or vermontlibrariesnews@gmail.com.

Pres. Amy Olsen, Lanpher Memorial Lib., 141 Main St., Hyde Park 05655. Tel. 802-888-4628, e-mail vermontlibrariespresident@gmail.com; *Secy.* Marie A. Schmukal, Warren Public Lib., 413 Main St., Warren 05674. Tel. 802-496-3913, e-mail director@warrenlibrary.com; *Treas.* Susan Smolinsky, Peacham Lib., 656 Bayley Hazen Rd., Peacham 05862. Tel. 802-592-3216, e-mail vermontlibrariestreasurer@gmail.com; *Past Pres.* Cindy Weber, Stowe Free Lib., 90 Pond St., Stowe 05672. Tel. 802-253-6145, e-mail vermontlibrariespastpresident@gmail.com.

Address correspondence to Vermont Lib. Assn., P.O. Box 803, Burlington 05402.

World Wide Web http://www.vermontlibraries.org.

Virginia

Memb. 950+. Term of Office. Oct.–Oct. Publication. *Virginia Libraries* (ann.). *Ed.* Virginia (Ginny) Pannabecker, Virginia Tech. E-mail vpannabe@vt.edu.

Pres. Jennifer Resor-Whicker, Radford University, McConnell Lib., P.O. Box 6881, Radford 24142. Tel. 540-831-5691, e-mail jrwhicker@radford.edu; *Pres.-Elect* Joslyn Bowling Dixon, Prince William Lib. System *2nd V.P.* Regina Sierra Carter, U.S. Army; *Secy.* Kayla Payne, Staunton Public Library. *Treas.* Bill Edwards-Bodmer, Suffolk Public Lib.; *ALA Councilor* Lucy Rush Wittkower, Old Dominion Univ.; *Past Pres.* Jessica Scalph, Haymarket Gainesville Community Lib., 14870 Lightner Rd., Haymarket. Tel. 703-792-8702, e-mail jscalph@pwcgov.org; *Exec. Dir.* Lisa Varga, Virginia Lib. Assn., P.O. Box 56312, Virginia Beach 23456. Tel. 757-689-0594, e-mail vla.lisav@cox.net.

Address correspondence to the executive director. Virginia Lib. Assn., P.O. Box 56312, Virginia Beach 23456. Tel. 757-689-0594, fax 757-447-3478, e-mail vla.lisav@cox.net.

World Wide Web http://www.vla.org.

Washington

Memb. (Indiv.) 742, (Inst.) 47. Publications. *Alki: The Washington Library Association Journal* (3x yearly, online). *Ed.* Johanna Jacobsen Kiciman, Univ. of Washington. E-mail alkieditor@wla.org.

Pres. Emily Keller, Univ. of Washington Libs. Tel. 206-685-2660, e-mail emkeller@uw.edu; *V.P./Pres.-Elect* Danielle Miller, Washington Talking Book and Braille Lib. E-mail danielle.miller@sos.wa.gov; *Treas.* Joy Neal, La Conner Regional Lib. E-mail joyzneal@yahoo.com; *ALA Councilor* Steven Bailey, King County Lib. System; *Past Pres.* Rhonda Gould, Walla Walla County Rural Lib. District. E-mail rhondag@wwrurallibrary.com; *Exec. Dir.* Brianna Hoffman, Washington Lib. Assn., P.O. Box 33808, Seattle 98133. Tel. 206-823-1138, e-mail brianna@wla.org.

Address correspondence to the executive director. Washington Lib. Assn., P.O. Box 33808, Seattle 98133. Tel. 206-823-1138, e-mail info@wla.org.

World Wide Web http://www.wla.org.

West Virginia

Memb. 650+.

Pres. Heather Campbell-Shock. West Virginia Lib. Commission, 1900 Kanawha Blvd., Charleston 25305. Tel. 304-558-2069, e-mail Heather.S.Campbell@wv.gov; *1st V.P./Pres.-Elect* Todd Duncan, South Charleston Public Lib., 312 4th Ave., South Charleston 25303. Tel. 304-744-6561, e-mail todd@scplwv.org; *2nd V.P.* Breana Bowen, Cabell County Public Lib., 455 9th St., Huntington 25701. Tel. 304-528-5700, fax 304-528-5701, e-mail breana.bowen@cabell.lib.wv.us; *Treas.* Sarah Mitchell, Kanawha County Public Lib., 123 Capitol St., Charleston 25301. Tel. 304-343-4646, e-mail sarah.mitchell@kanawhalibrary.org; *ALA Councilor* Majed Khader, Marshall Univ., 1625 Campbell Dr., Huntington 25705. Tel. 304-696-3121, fax 304-696-5219, e-mail khader@marshall.edu; *Past Pres.* Megan Hope Tarbett, Putnam County Lib., 4219 State Route 34, Hurricane 25526. Tel. 304-757-7308, e-mail megan.tarbett@putnam.lib.wv.us; *Exec. Dir.* Kelly Funkhouser, Morgantown Public Lib., West Virginia Lib. Assn., P.O. Box 1432, Morgantown 26507. Tel. 304-291-7425, e-mail wvlaexdir@gmail.com.

Address correspondence to the president.

World Wide Web http://www.wvla.org.

Wisconsin

Memb. 1,900. Term of Office. Jan.–Dec. Publication. *WLA eNewsletter* (3–4x yearly; online). *Ed.* Jill Fuller. E-mail jfuller@bridgeslibrarysystem.org.

Pres. Sherry Machones. E-mail sherrymachones@gmail.com; *V.P.* Nyama Reed. E-mail n.reed@wfblibrary.org; *Secy.* Desiree Bongers, Ripon Public Lib., Ripon. Tel. 920-748-6160, e-mail dbongers@riponlibrary.org; *Treas.* Katharine Clark. E-mail kclark@mcfarlandlibrary.org; *ALA Councilor* Sherry Machones. E-mail smachones@northernwaters.org; *Past Pres.* Scott Vrieze. E-mail scott@melsa.org; *Exec. Dir.* Plumer Lovelace III, Wisconsin Lib. Assn., 4610 S. Biltmore Ln., Madison 53718. Tel. 608-245-3640, e-mail lovelace@wisconsinlibraries.org.

Address correspondence to Wisconsin Lib. Assn., 4610 S. Biltmore Ln., Madison 53718. Tel. 608-245-3640, e-mail wla@wisconsinlibraries.org.

World Wide Web http://wla.wisconsinlibraries.org.

Wyoming

Memb. 450+. Term of Office. Oct.–Oct. Publication. Newsletter (ann.; August).

Pres. Abby Beaver, Wyoming State Lib. Tel. 307-777-5913, e-mail abby.beaver@wyo.gov; *V.P.* Jacob Mickelsen, Carbon County Lib. System. Tel. 307-328-2623, e-mail director@carbonlibraries.org; *ALA Councilor* Janice Grover-Roosa, Western Wyoming Community College. E-mail librarian@westernwyoming.edu; *State Libn. (ex officio)* Jamie Markus, Wyoming State Lib. Tel. 307-777-5914, e-mail jamie.markus@wyo.gov; *Past Pres.* Kate Mutch, Natrona County Lib. Tel. 307-237-4935 ext. 111, e-mail kmutch@natronacountylibrary.org; *Exec. Secy.* (ex-officio) Laura Grott, P.O. Box 1387, Cheyenne 82003. Tel. 307-632-7622, e-mail lauragrott@gmail.com.

Address correspondence to the executive secretary. Wyoming Lib. Assn., 1190 Meramac Station Rd., Suite 207, Ballwin, MO 63201.

World Wide Web http://www.wyla.org.

Canada

Alberta

Memb. 800+. Term of Office. May–April.

Pres. Briana Ehnes, Red Deer Public Lib. E-mail president@laa.ca; *1st V.P.* Kirk MacLeod, Alberta Law Libs. E-mail 1stvicepresident@laa.ca; *2nd V.P.* Céline Gareau-Brennan, Univ. of Alberta. E-mail 2ndvicepresident@laa.ca; *Treas.* Louisa Robison, Service Alberta. E-mail treasurer@laa.ca; *Past Pres.* Norene Erickson, MacEwan Univ. E-mail pastpresident@laa.ca; *Exec. Dir.* Christine Sheppard, 80 Baker Cres. N.W., Calgary T2L 1R4. Tel. 403-284-5818, 877-522-5550, e-mail info@laa.ca.

Address correspondence to the executive director. Lib. Assn. of Alberta, 80 Baker Cres. N.W., Calgary T2L 1R4. Tel. 403-284-5818, 877-522-5550.

World Wide Web http://www.laa.ca.

British Columbia

Memb. 750+. Term of Office. April–April. Publication. *BCLA Perspectives* (q.; online). E-mail perspectives@bcla.bc.ca.

Pres. Chris Middlemass, Vancouver Public Lib.; *V.P./Pres.-Elect* Todd Mundle, Kwantlen Polytechnic Univ. Lib.; *Recording Secy.* Danielle LaFrance, Vancouver Public Lib.; *Treas.* Lilian Pintos, Vancouver Public Lib.; *Asst./Incoming Treas.* Adam Farrell, New Westminster Public Lib.; *Past Pres.* Shirley Lew, Vancouver Community College Lib.; *Exec. Dir.* Annette DeFaveri, British Columbia Lib. Assn., 900 Howe St., Suite 150, Vancouver V6Z 2M4. Tel. 604-683-5354 or 888-683-5354, e-mail execdir@bcla.bc.ca.

Address correspondence to the executive director. British Columbia Lib. Assn., 900 Howe St., Suite 150, Vancouver V6Z 2M4. Tel. 604-683-5354, e-mail bclaoffice@bcla.bc.ca.

World Wide Web http://www.bcla.bc.ca.

Manitoba

Memb. 500+. Term of Office. May–May.

Pres. Kerry Macdonald. (Acting) E-mail president@mla.mb.ca; *Secy.* Camille Fitch-Kustcher. E-mail secretary@mla.mb.ca; *Treas.* Kelly Murray; *Past Pres.* Kerry Macdonald.

Address correspondence to Manitoba Lib. Assn., 606-100 Arthur St., Winnipeg R3B 1H3. Tel. 204-943-4567, e-mail secretary@mla.mb.ca.

World Wide Web http://www.mla.mb.ca.

Ontario

Memb. 5,000+. Publications. *Open Shelf* (mo., multimedia). *Ed.* Martha Attridge Bufton; *The Teaching Librarian* (3x yearly; memb.). *Ed.* Caroline Freibauer. E-mail teachinglibrarian@outlook.com.

Pres. Andrea Cecchetto, Markham Public Lib. E-mail acecch@markham.library.on.ca; *V.P./Pres.-Elect* Sabrina Saunders, The Blue Mountains Public Lib.; *Treas.* Janneka Guise, Univ. of Toronto. E-mail jan.guise@utoronto.ca; *Past Pres.* Richard Reid, Durham District School Board. E-mail richard.reid@ddsb.ca; *Exec. Dir.* Shelagh Paterson, Ontario Lib. Assn. E-mail spaterson@accessola.com.

Address correspondence to Ontario Lib. Assn., 2 Toronto St., Toronto M5C 2B6. Tel. 416-363-3388 or 866-873-9867, fax 416-941-9581 or 800-387-1181, e-mail info@accessola.com.

World Wide Web http://www.accessola.com.

Quebec

Memb. (Indiv.) 100+. Term of Office. May–April. Publication. *ABQLA Bulletin* (3x yearly). *Ed.* Maria Ressina.

Pres. Eamon Duffy; *V.P.* Sandy Hervieux; *Treas.* Anne Wade. E-mail wada@education.concordia.ca; *Past Pres.* Katherine Hanz. E-mail katherine.hanz@mcgill.ca.

Address correspondence to the president. Assn. des Bibliothecaires du Quebec/Quebec Lib. Assn., C.P. 26717, CPS Beaconsfield H9W 6G7.

World Wide Web http://www.abqla.qc.ca.

Saskatchewan

Memb. 200+.

Pres. Amy Rankin, CMP Resource Centre, P.O. Box 6500, Regina. Tel. 639-625-3537, e-mail amy.rankin@rcmp-grc.gc.ca; *V.P. Membership and Pubns.* Linda Winkler, Univ. of Regina. E-mail linda.winkler@uregina.ca; *V.P. Advocacy and Development* Anthony Woodword, Regina Public Lib.; *Treas.* Darrel Yates. 1302 101 St., North Battleford S9A 2C3. Tel. 306-445-6108, e-mail director@lakeland.lib.sk.ca; *Past Pres.* Alison Jantz, Saskatoon Theological Union, Univ. of Saskatchewan, Saskatoon. Tel. 306-270-1532, e-mail akj175@campus.usask.ca or Alison.Jantz@usask.ca; *Exec. Dir.* Dorothea Warren Saskatchewan Lib. Assn., #15 – 2010 7th Ave. Regina S4R 1C3. Tel. 306-780-9413, fax 306-780-9447, e-mail slaexdir@sasktel.net.

Address correspondence to the executive director. Saskatchewan Lib. Assn., 10 – 2010 7th Ave., Regina S4R 1C3. Tel. 306-780-9413, fax 306-780-3633, e-mail slaexdir@sasktel.net.

World Wide Web http://www.saskla.ca.

Regional

Atlantic Provinces: N.B., N.L., N.S., P.E.I.

Memb. (Indiv.) 320+; (Inst.) Publication. *APLA Bulletin* (4x yearly). *Eds.* Marc Harper, Kathryn Rose. E-mail bulletin@apla.ca.

Pres. Trecia Schell, Pictou-Antigonish Regional Lib. E-mail president-elect@apla.ca; *V.P./Pres.-Elect* Ann Smith, Acadia Univ., Wolfville, NS. E-mail president-elect@apla.ca *V.P. Membership* Erin Alcock. E-mail membership@apla.ca; *V.P. Nova Scotia* Cate Carlyle. E-mail ns@apla.ca; *V.P. New Brunswick* Ruth Cox. E-mail nb@apla.ca; *V.P. Newfoundland and Labrador* Andrew Wood. E-mail nfl@apla.ca; *V.P. Prince Edward Island* Beth Clinton. E-mail pei@apla.ca; *Secy.* Amy Lorencz, St. Mary's Univ. Tel. 902-420-5174, e-mail secretary@apla.ca; *Treas.* Terri Winchcombe, Patrick Power Lib., St. Mary's Univ. Halifax, NS. Tel. 902-420-5535, e-mail treasurer@apla.ca; *Past President* Patricia Doucette, Holland College, Prince Edward

Island. Tel. 902-566-9350, e-mail president@apla.ca.

Address correspondence to Atlantic Provinces Lib. Assn., Kenneth C. Rowe Mgt. Bldg., Dalhousie Univ., 6100 University Ave., Suite 4010, P.O. Box 15000, Halifax, NS B3H 4R2. E-mail president@apla.ca or secretary@apla.ca.

World Wide Web http://www.apla.ca.

Mountain Plains: Ariz., Colo., Kans., Mont., Neb., Nev., N.Dak., N.Mex., Okla., S.Dak., Utah, Wyo.

Memb. 700. Term of Office. Oct.–Oct. Publications. *MPLA Newsletter* (6x yearly, online). *Ed.* Melanie Argo, Madison Public Lib., 209 E. Center, Madison, SD 57042. Tel. 605-256-7525, e-mail editor@mpla.us.

Pres. Stephen Sweeney, St. John Vianney Seminary, Cardinal Stafford Lib., 1300 South Steele St., Denver, CO 80210. Tel. 303-715-3192, fax 303-715-2037, e-mail president@mpla.us; *V.P./Pres.-Elect* Robin Newell, Emporia Public Lib., 110 E. Sixth Ave., Emporia, KS 66801. Tel. 620-340-6464, e-mail vicepresident@mpla.us; *Recording Secy.* Whitney Vitale, Oklahoma State Univ., Edmon Low Lib., Stillwater, OK 74078. Tel. 405-744-7142, e-mail secretary@mpla.us; *Past Pres.* Leslie H. Langley, Southeastern Public Lib. System, Wister Public Lib., 101 Caston Ave., Wister, OK 74966. Tel. 918-655-7654, fax 918-655-3267, e-mail pastpresident@mpla.us; *Exec. Secy.* Judy Kulp, 14293 West Center Dr., Lakewood, CO 80228. Tel. 303-985-7795, e-mail execsecretary@mpla.us.

Address correspondence to the executive secretary. Mountain Plains Lib. Assn., 14293 West Center Dr., Lakewood, CO 80228. Tel. 303-985-7795, e-mail execsecretary@mpla.us.

World Wide Web http://www.mpla.us.

New England: Conn., Maine, Mass., N.H., R.I., Vt.

Memb. (Indiv.) 650+. Term of Office. Nov.–Oct. Publication. *NELA News* (blog).

Pres. Jennifer Bruneau, Boylston Public Lib., Boylston, MA. Tel. 413-323-5925, ext. 102, e-mail president@nelib.org; *V.P.* Mike Zeller, Shrewsbury Public Lib., Shrewsbury, MA. Tel. 413-323-5925, ext 103, e-mail vicepresident@nelib.org; *Secy.* Lucinda Walker, Norwich Public Lib., Norwich, VT. Tel. 413-323-5925, ext. 106. E-mail secretary@nelib.org; *Treas.* Bernie Prochnik, Bath Public Lib., Bath, NH. Tel. 413-323-5925, ext. 105, e-mail treasurer@nelib.org; *Past Pres.* Susan Edmonds, Milford Town Lib., Milford, MA. Tel. 413-323-5925, ext. 104, e-mail pastpresident@nelib.org; *Admin.* Robert Scheier. NELA Office, 55 N. Main St., Unit 49, Belchertown, MA 01007. Tel. 413-323-5925, ext. 100, e-mail library-association-administrator@nelib.org.

Address correspondence to the administrator. New England Lib. Assn., 55 N. Main St., Unit 49, Belchertown, MA 01007. Tel. 413-323-5925, e-mail rlibrary-association-administrator@nelib.org.

World Wide Web http://www.nelib.org.

Pacific Northwest: Alaska, Idaho, Mont., Ore., Wash., Alberta, B.C.

Memb. 170+. Term of Office. Aug.–Aug. Publication. *PNLA Quarterly. Eds.* Robert Perret, Jennifer Ward. E-mail pqeditors@gmail.com.

Co-Pres. Honore Bray, Missoula Public Lib. Missoula, MT. Tel. 406-721-2665; Rick Stoddart, Eugene, OR; *V.P./Pres.-Elect* Pam Henley, Montana State Lib., Helena (and Bozeman). Tel. 406-461-9049; *2nd V.P./Membership Chair* Ilana Kingsley, Univ. of Alaska–Fairbanks, Rasmuson Lib., Fairbanks, AK. Tel. 907-474-7518; *Secy.* Erin Hvizdak, Washington State Univ., Pullman, WA. Tel. 509-335-9514; *Treas.* Lisa Fraser, PNLA, P.O. Box 1032, Bothell WA 98041. Tel. 425-369-3458, e-mail lgfraser@kcls.org; *Past Pres.* Jenny Grenfell, North Mason Timberland Lib., Belfair, WA. Tel. 360-275-3232, e-mail ktfjen@gmail.com.

Address correspondence to Pacific Northwest Lib. Assn., P.O. Box 1032, Bothell WA 98041.

World Wide Web http://www.pnla.org.

Southeastern: Ala., Ark., Fla., Ga., Ky., La., Miss., N.C., S.C., Tenn., Va., W.Va.

Memb. 500. Publication. *The Southeastern Librarian (SELn)* (q.). *Ed.* Perry Bratcher, 263

Steely Lib., Northern Kentucky Univ., Highland Heights, KY 41099. Tel. 859-572-6309, fax 859-572-6181, e-mail bratcher@nku.edu.

Pres. Tim Dodge, Auburn Univ. Libs., Auburn, AL. E-mail president@selaonline.org; *Pres.-Elect* Melissa Dennis, Univ. of Mississippi, University, MS. E-mail president.elect@selaonline.org; *Secy.* Crystal Gates, William F. Laman Public Lib., North Little Rock, AR. E-mail secretary@selaonline.org; *Treas.* Beverly James, Greenville County Lib. System, Greenville, SC. E-mail treasurer@selaonline.org; *Archivist* Camille McCutcheon, Univ. of South Carolina Upstate, Spartanburg, SC. E-mail archivist@selaonline.org; *Past Pres.* Linda Suttle Harris, Univ. of Alabama at Birmingham.

Address correspondence to Southeastern Lib. Assn., Admin. Services, P.O. Box 30703, Savannah, GA 31410. Tel. 912-999-7979, e-mail selaadminservices@selaonline.org.

World Wide Web http://selaonline.org.

State and Provincial Library Agencies

The state library administrative agency in each of the U.S. states will have the latest information on its state plan for the use of federal funds under the Library Services and Technology Act (LSTA). The directors and addresses of these state agencies are listed below.

United States

Alabama

Nancy Pack, Dir., Alabama Public Lib. Svc., 6030 Monticello Dr., Montgomery 36117. Tel. 334-213-3900, fax 334-213-3993, e-mail npack@apls.state.al.us. World Wide Web http://statelibrary.alabama.gov.

Alaska

Patience Frederiksen, Dir., Alaska State Lib., P.O. Box 110571, Juneau 99811-0571. Tel. 907-465-2911, fax 907-465-2151, e-mail patience.frederiksen@alaska.gov. World Wide Web http://library.state.ak.us.

Arizona

Holly Henley, State Libn. and Dir. of Lib. Svcs., Arizona State Lib., Archives and Public Records, 1901 W. Madison St., Phoenix 85009. Tel. 602-542-6200. World Wide Web http://www.azlibrary.gov.

Arkansas

Carolyn Ashcroft, State Libn., Arkansas State Lib., 900 W. Capitol, Suite 100, Little Rock 72201. Tel. 501-682-1526, e-mail carolyn@library.arkansas.gov. World Wide Web http://www.library.arkansas.gov.

California

Greg Lucas, State Libn., California State Lib., P.O. Box 942837, Sacramento 94237-0001. Tel. 916-323-9759, fax 916-323-9768, e-mail csl-adm@library.ca.gov. World Wide Web http://www.library.ca.gov.

Colorado

Nicolle Davies, Asst. Commissioner, Colorado State Lib., 201 E. Colfax Ave., Denver 80203-1799. Tel. 303-866-6733, fax 303-866-6940, e-mail davies_n@cde.state.co.us. World Wide Web http://www.cde.state.co.us/cdelib.

Connecticut

Kendall F. Wiggin, State Libn., Connecticut State Lib., 231 Capitol Ave., Hartford 06106. Tel. 860-757-6510, fax 860-757-6503, e-mail kendall.wiggin@ct.gov. World Wide Web http://www.ctstatelibrary.org.

Delaware

Annie Norman, Dir., Delaware Division of Libs., 121 Martin Luther King Jr. Blvd. N., Dover 19901. Tel. 302-257-3001, fax 302-739-6787, e-mail annie.norman@delaware.gov. World Wide Web http://libraries.delaware.gov.

District of Columbia

Richard Reyes-Gavilan, Exec. Dir., District of Columbia Public Lib., 1990 K St. N.W., Washington, DC 20006. Tel. 202-727-1101, fax 202-727-1129, e-mail rrg@dc.gov. World Wide Web http://www.dclibrary.org.

Florida

Amy L. Johnson, Div. Dir., Division of Lib. and Info. Svcs., R.A. Gray Bldg., 500 S. Bronough St., Tallahassee 32399-0250. Tel. 850-245-6600, fax 850-245-6622, e-mail info@dos.myflorida.com. World Wide Web http://dos.myflorida.com/library-archives/.

Georgia

Julie Walker, State Libn., Georgia Public Lib. Svc., 2872 Woodcock Boulevard, Suite 250, Atlanta 30341. Tel. 404-235-7200, e-mail jwalker@georgialibraries.org. World Wide Web http://www.georgialibraries.org.

Hawaii

Stacy Aldrich, State Libn., Hawaii State Public Lib. System, Office of the State Libn., 44 Merchant St., Honolulu 96813. Tel. 808-586-3704, fax 808-586-3715, e-mail stlib@libraries hawaii.org. World Wide Web http://www.librarieshawaii.org.

Idaho

Stephanie Bailey-White, State Libn., Idaho Commission for Libs., 325 W. State St., Boise 83702. Tel. 208-639-4145, fax 208-334-4016, e-mail stephanie.bailey-white@libraries.idaho.gov. World Wide Web http://libraries.idaho.gov.

Illinois

Greg McCormick, Dir., Illinois State Lib., 300 S. Second St., Springfield 62701-1796. Tel. 217-785-5600, fax 217-785-4326, e-mail islinfo@ilsos.net. World Wide Web http://www.cyberdriveillinois.com/departments/library/home.html.

Indiana

Jacob Speer, State Libn., Indiana State Lib., 315 W. Ohio St., Indianapolis 46202. Tel. 317-232-3675, e-mail jspeer@library.in.gov. World Wide Web http://www.in.gov/library.

Iowa

Michael Scott, State Libn., State Lib. of Iowa, 1112 E. Grand Ave., Des Moines 50319-0233. Tel. 800-248-4483, fax 515-281-6191, e-mail Michael.Scott@iowa.gov. World Wide Web http://www.statelibraryofiowa.org.

Kansas

Eric Norris, State Libn., Kansas State Lib., Capitol Bldg., 300 S.W. 10th Ave., Rm. 312-N, Topeka 66612. Tel. 785-296-5466, e-mail eric.norris@ks.gov. World Wide Web http://www.kslib.info.

Kentucky

Terry Manuel, Commissioner, Kentucky Dept. for Libs. and Archives, 300 Coffee Tree Rd., P.O. Box 537, Frankfort 40602-0537. Tel. 502-564-8303, e-mail terry.manuel@ky.gov. World Wide Web http://www.kdla.ky.gov.

Louisiana

Rebecca Hamilton, State Libn., State Lib. of Louisiana, 701 N. 4th St., P.O. Box 131, Baton Rouge 70821-0131. Tel. 225-342-4923, fax 225-219-4804, e-mail rhamilton@crt.la.gov. World Wide Web http://www.state.lib.la.us.

Maine

James Ritter, State Libn., Maine State Lib., 64 State House Sta., Augusta 04333-0064. Tel. 207-287-5600, fax 207-287-5615, e-mail james.ritter@maine.gov. World Wide Web http://www.maine.gov/msl/.

Maryland

Irene M. Padilla, State Libn., Maryland State Lib., 22 S. Calhoun St., Baltimore 21223. Tel. 667-219-4800, fax 667-219-4798, e-mail elizabeth.fletcher@maryland.gov. World Wide Web https://www.marylandlibraries.org/.

Massachusetts

James Lonergan, Dir., Massachusetts Board of Lib. Commissioners, 98 N. Washington St., Suite 401, Boston 02114-1933. Tel. 617-725-1860, ext. 222, fax 617-725-0140, e-mail james.lonergan@state.ma.us. World Wide Web http://mblc.state.ma.us.

Michigan

Randy Riley, State Libn., Lib. of Michigan, 702 W. Kalamazoo St., P.O. Box 30007, Lansing 48909-7507. Tel. 517-335-1517, e-mail rileyr1@michigan.gov. World Wide Web http://www.michigan.gov/libraryofmichigan.

Minnesota

Jennifer R. Nelson, Dir. of State Lib. Services, Minnesota State Lib. Agency, Div. of State Lib. Svcs., MN Dept. of Educ., 1500 Hwy. 36 W., Roseville 55113. Tel. 651-582-8791, fax 651-582-8752, e-mail mde.lst@state.mn.us. World Wide Web https://education.mn.gov/MDE/dse/Lib/sls/index.htm.

Mississippi

Hulen Bivins, Exec. Dir., Mississippi Lib. Commission, 3881 Eastwood Dr., Jackson 39211. Tel. 601-432-4039, e-mail hbivins@mlc.lib.ms.us. World Wide Web http://www.mlc.lib.ms.us.

Missouri

Robin Westphal, State Libn., Missouri State Lib., 600 W. Main St., P.O. Box 387, Jefferson City 65101. Tel. 573-526-4783, e-mail robin.westphal@sos.mo.gov. World Wide Web http://www.sos.mo.gov/library.

Montana

Jennie Stapp, State Libn., Montana State Lib., 1515 E. 6th Ave., P.O. Box 201800, Helena, 59620-1800. Tel. 406-444-3116, fax 406-444-0266, e-mail jstapp2@mt.gov. World Wide Web http://msl.mt.gov.

Nebraska

Rodney G. Wagner, Dir., Nebraska Lib. Commission, 1200 N St., Suite 120, Lincoln 68508-2023. Tel. 402-471-4001, fax 402-471-2083, e-mail rod.wagner@nebraska.gov. World Wide Web http://www.nlc.nebraska.gov.

Nevada

Tammy Westergard, Admin., Nevada State Lib. and Archives, 100 N. Stewart St., Carson City 89701. Tel. 775-684-3306, fax 775-684-3311, e-mail twestergard@admin.nv.gov. World Wide Web http://nsla.nv.gov/.

New Hampshire

Michael York, State Libn., New Hampshire State Lib., 20 Park St., Concord 03301. Tel. 603-271-2397, e-mail michael.york@dncr.nh.gov. World Wide Web http://www.state.nh.us/nhsl.

New Jersey

Mary Chute, State Libn., New Jersey State Lib., an affiliate of Thomas Edison State Univ., P.O. Box 520, Trenton 08625-0520. Tel. 609-278-2640 ext. 101, fax 609-278-2652, e-mail mchute@njstatelib.org. World Wide Web http://www.njstatelib.org.

New Mexico

Eli Guinnee, State Libn., New Mexico State Lib., 1209 Camino Carlos Rey, Santa Fe 87507-5166. Tel. 505-476-9762, e-mail Eli.Guinnee@state.nm.us. World Wide Web http://www.nmstatelibrary.org.

New York

Lauren Moore, State Libn., New York State Lib., Cultural Educ. Ctr., 222 Madison Ave., Albany 12230. Tel. 518-474-5930, fax 518-474-5786, e-mail statelibrarian@nysed.gov. World Wide Web http://www.nysl.nysed.gov/.

North Carolina

Timothy G. Owens, State Libn., State Lib. of North Carolina, Administrative Section, 4640 Mail Svc. Ctr., Raleigh 27699-4600; 109 E. Jones St., Raleigh 27601. Tel. 919-814-6784, fax 919-733-8748, e-mail timothy.owens@ncdcr.gov. World Wide Web http://statelibrary.ncdcr.gov.

North Dakota

Mary J. Soucie, State Libn., North Dakota State Lib., 604 E. Boulevard Ave., Dept. 250, Bismarck 58505-0800. Tel. 701-328-4654, fax 701-328-2040, e-mail msoucie@nd.gov. World Wide Web http://ndsl.lib.state.nd.us/.

Ohio

William Morris, Interim Exec. Dir., State Lib. of Ohio, 274 E. First Ave., Suite 100, Columbus 43201. Tel. 616-644-6843, e-mail wmorris@library.ohio.gov. World Wide Web http://www.library.ohio.gov/.

Oklahoma

Melody Kellogg, Dir., Oklahoma Dept. of Libs., 200 N.E. 18th St., Oklahoma City 73105-3298. Tel. 405-521-2502, fax 405-525-7804, World Wide Web http://www.odl.state.ok.us.

Oregon

Jennifer Patterson, State Libn., State Lib. of Oregon, 250 Winter St., N.E., Salem 97301. Tel. 503-378-4367, fax 503-585-8059, e-mail jennifer.l.patterson@state.or.us. World Wide Web https://www.oregon.gov/Library.

Pennsylvania

Glenn Miller, Deputy Secy. of Educ., Commissioner of Libs., and State Libn., State Lib. of Pennsylvania, Commonwealth Keystone Bldg., Plaza Lib. (Museum Plaza Wing), 400 North St., Harrisburg, PA 17120-0211. Tel. 717-787-2646, fax 717-772-3265, e-mail ra-edocldepty secty@pa.gov. World Wide Web http://www.statelibrary.pa.gov.

Rhode Island

Karen Mellor, Chief of Lib. Services, Rhode Island Office of Lib. and Info. Svcs., One Capitol Hill, Providence 02908. Tel. 401-574-9304, fax 401-574-9320, e-mail karen.Mellor@olis.ri.gov. World Wide Web http://www.olis.ri.gov.

South Carolina

Leesa M. Aiken, Dir., South Carolina State Lib., 1500 Senate St., Columbia 29201. Tel. 803-734-8668, fax 803-734-8676, e-mail laiken@statelibrary.sc.gov. World Wide Web http://www.statelibrary.sc.gov.

South Dakota

Daria Bossman, State Libn., South Dakota State Lib., MacKay Bldg., 800 Governors Dr., Pierre 57501. Tel. 605-773-3131, option 6, fax 605-773-6962, e-mail daria.bossman@state.sd.us. World Wide Web http://library.sd.gov/.

Tennessee

Charles A. Sherrill, State Libn. and Archivist, Tennessee State Lib. and Archives, 403 7th Ave. N., Nashville 37243. Tel. 615-741-7996, fax 615-532-9293, e-mail chuck.sherrill@tn.gov. World Wide Web http://www.tennessee.gov/tsla/.

Texas

Mark Smith, Dir. and Libn., Texas State Lib. and Archives Commission, 1201 Brazos St., Austin 78701; P.O. Box 12927, Austin 78711-2927. Tel. 512-463-6856, fax 512-463-5436, e-mail msmith@tsl.state.tx.us. World Wide Web http://www.tsl.state.tx.us.

Utah

Colleen Eggett, State Libn., Utah State Lib. Div., 250 N. 1950 W., Suite A, Salt Lake City 84116-7901. Tel. 801-715-6770, fax 801-715-6767, e-mail ceggett@utah.gov. World Wide Web http://library.utah.gov/.

Vermont

Jason Broughton, State Libn., Vermont State Lib., 60 Washington St., Suite 2, Barre, VT 05641. Tel. 802-636-0040, e-mail jason.broughton@vermont.gov. World Wide Web https://libraries.vermont.gov/state_library.

Virginia

Sandra Gioia Treadway, Libn. of Virginia, Lib. of Virginia, 800 E. Broad St., Richmond 23219-8000. Tel. 804-692-3535, fax 804-692-3556, e-mail sandra.treadway@lva.virginia.gov. World Wide Web http://www.lva.virginia.gov/.

Washington

Cindy Aden, State Libn., Washington State Lib., Office of the Secretary of State, Point Plaza E., 6880 Capitol Blvd., Tumwater 98501; P.O. Box 42460, Olympia 98504-2460. Tel. 360-704-5276, e-mail cindy.aden@sos.wa.gov. World Wide Web http://www.sos.wa.gov/library.

West Virginia

Karen Goff, Exec. Secy., West Virginia Lib. Commission Cultural Ctr., Bldg. 9, 1900 Kanawha Blvd. E., Charleston 25305. Tel. 304-558-2041 ext. 2084, fax 304-558-2044, e-mail karen.e.goff@wv.gov. World Wide Web http://www.librarycommission.wv.gov/.

Wisconsin

Kurt Kiefer, Asst. State Superintendent, Div. for Libs. and Tech., Wisconsin Dept. of Public Instruction, 125 S. Webster St., Madison 53703; P.O. Box 7841, Madison 53707-7841.

Tel. 608-266-2205, fax 608-267-9207, e-mail Kurt.Kiefer@dpi.wi.gov. World Wide Web http://dpi.wi.gov.

Wyoming

Jamie Markus, State Libn., Wyoming State Lib., 2800 Central Ave., Cheyenne 82002. Tel. 307-777-5914, e-mail jamie.markus@wyo.gov. World Wide Web http://library.wyo.gov/.

American Samoa

Justin H. Maga, Territorial Libn., Feleti Barstow Public Lib., Box 997687, Pago Pago 96799. Tel. 684-633-5816, fax 684-633-5823, e-mail justinmaga@gmail.com. World Wide Web https://www.americansamoa.gov/feleti-barstow-public-library.

Federated States of Micronesia

Augustine Kohler, Acting Dir., Office of National Archives, Culture, and Historic Preservations, PS175, Palikir, Pohnpei State 96941. Tel. 691-320-2343, fax 691-320-5632, e-mail hpo@mail.fm. World Wide Web http://www.fsmgov.org.

Guam

Sandra Stanley, Admin. Officer, Guam Public Lib. System, 254 Martyr St., Hagatna 96910-5141. Tel. 671-475-4765, fax 671-477-9777, e-mail sandra.stanley@guampls.guam.gov. World Wide Web http://gpls.guam.gov/.

Northern Mariana Islands

Erlinda Naputi, State Lib. Dir., CNMI Joeten-Kiyu Public Lib., P.O. Box 501092, Saipan 96950. Tel. 670-235-7322, fax 670-235-7550, e-mail ecnaputi@gmail.com. World Wide Web http://cnmilib.org.

Palau

Sinton Soalalai, Chief, Div. of School Mgt., Palau Ministry of Educ., P.O. Box 7080, Koror 96940. Tel. 680-488-2570, fax 680-488-2380, e-mail ssoalablai@palaumoe.net. World Wide Web https://www.palaugov.pw/executive-branch/ministries/education.

Puerto Rico

Mary Jean Haver, Acting Dir., Lib. and Info. Svcs. Program, Puerto Rico Dept. of Educ., P.O. Box 190759, San Juan 00919-0759. Tel. 787 773 3570, fax 787-753-6945, e-mail haverbmj@de.pr.gov. World Wide Web website not available.

Republic of the Marshall Islands

Melvin Majmeto, Exec. Dir., Alele Museum, Lib. and National Archives, P.O. Box 629, Majuro 96960. Tel. 011-692-625-3372, fax 011-692-625-3226, World Wide Web https://www.alele.org.

U.S. Virgin Islands

Arlene Pinney-Benjamin, Acting Dir., The Division of Libraries, Archives and Museums, c/o Florence Williams Public Lib., 1122 King St. Christiansted, St. Croix 00820. Tel. 340-773-5715, fax 340-773-5327, e-mail arlene.benjamin@dpnr.vi.gov. World Wide Web http://www.virginislandspubliclibraries.org/usvi/.

Canada

Alberta

Diana Davidson, Dir., Alberta Public Lib. Svcs., Municipal Affairs, 8th fl., 10405 Jasper Ave., Edmonton T5J 4R7. Tel. 780-415-0284, fax 780-415-8594, e-mail diana.davidson@gov.ab.ca or libraries@gov.ab.ca. World Wide Web http://www.municipalaffairs.alberta.ca/alberta_libraries.cfm.

British Columbia

Mari Martin, Dir., Libs. Branch, Ministry of Educ., P.O. Box 9831, Stn. Prov. Govt., Victoria V8W 9T1. Tel. 250-886-2584, fax 250-953-4985, e-mail Mari.Martin@gov.bc.ca. World Wide Web https://www2.gov.bc.ca/gov/content/education-training/administration/community-partnerships/libraries.

Manitoba

Dir., Public Lib. Services, Public Lib. Services Branch, B10 - 340 9th St., Brandon R7A 6C2. Tel. 204-726-6590, fax 204-726-6868, e-mail pls@gov.mb.ca. World Wide Web http://www.gov.mb.ca/chc/pls/index.html.

New Brunswick

Kevin Cormier, Exec. Dir., New Brunswick Public Libs., Provincial Office, 570 Two Nations Crossing, Suite 2, Fredericton E3A 0X9. Tel. 506-453-2354, fax 506-444-4064, e-mail kevin.cormier@gnb.ca. World Wide Web http://www2.gnb.ca/content/gnb/en/departments/nbpl.html.

Newfoundland and Labrador

Andrew Hunt, Exec. Dir., Provincial Info. and Lib. Resources Board, 48 St. George's Ave., Stephenville A2N 1K9. Tel. 709-643-0900, fax 709-643-0925, e-mail ahunt@nlpl.ca. World Wide Web http://www.nlpl.ca.

Northwest Territories

Brian Dawson, Territorial Libn., Northwest Territories Public Lib. Services, 75 Woodland Dr., Hay River X0E 1G1. Tel. 867-874-6531, fax 867-874-3321, e-mail brian_dawson@gov.nt.ca. World Wide Web http://www.nwtpls.gov.nt.ca.

Nova Scotia

Dir., Provincial Lib., Nova Scotia Provincial Lib., 6016 University Ave., 5th fl., Halifax B3H 1W4. Tel. 902-424-2457, fax 902-424-0633, e-mail nspl@novascotia.ca. World Wide Web https://library.novascotia.ca.

Nunavut

Ron Knowling, Mgr., Nunavut Public Lib. Svcs., P.O. Box 270, Baker Lake X0C 0A0. Tel. 867-793-3353, fax 867-793-3360, e-mail rknowling@gov.nu.ca. World Wide Web http://www.publiclibraries.nu.ca.

Ontario

Rod Sawyer, Ontario Government Ministry of Heritage, Sport, Tourism, and Culture Industries, 401 Bay St., Suite 1700, Toronto M7A 0A7. Tel. 416-314-7627, fax 416-212-1802, e-mail rod.sawyer@ontario.ca. World Wide Web http://www.mtc.gov.on.ca/en/libraries/contact.shtml.

Prince Edward Island

Kathleen Eaton, Dir., Education, Early Learning and Culture, Public Lib. Svc., Public Lib. Svc. of Prince Edward Island, 89 Red Head Rd., Morell C0A 1S0. Tel. 902-368-4784, fax 902-894-0342, e-mail keeaton@gov.pe.ca. World Wide Web http://www.library.pe.ca.

Quebec

Jean-Louis Roy, CEO, Bibliothèque et Archives Nationales du Québec (BAnQ), 2275 rue Holt, Montreal H2G 3H1. Tel. 800-363-9028 or 514-873-1100, e-mail pdg@banq.qc.ca. World Wide Web http://www.banq.qc.ca/portal/dt/accueil.jsp.

Saskatchewan

Alison Hopkins, Provincial Libn./Exec. Dir., Provincial Lib. and Exec. Dir., Ministry of Educ., 409A Park St., Regina S4N 5B2. Tel. 306-787-2972, fax 306-787-2029, e-mail alison.hopkins@gov.sk.ca. World Wide Web http://www.education.gov.sk.ca/provincial-library/public-library-system.

Yukon Territory

Melissa Yu Schott, Dir., Public Libs., Community Development Div., Dept. of Community Svcs., Government of Yukon, P.O. Box 2703, Whitehorse Y1A 2C6. Tel. 867-335-8600, e-mail Melissa.YuSchott@gov.yk.ca. World Wide Web https://yukon.ca.

State School Library Associations

Alabama

Youth Services and School Libns. Div., Alabama Lib. Assn. (ALLA). Memb. 600+.

Chair Jennifer Powell, Tarrant High School. E-mail powell.jennifer@tarrant.k12.11.us; *Chair-Elect* Daniel Tackett, Vestavia Hills Library in the Forest. Tel. 205-978-3683, e-mail dtackett@bham.lib.al.us; *Secy.* Caitlin Rogers, the Altamont School. E-mail crogers@altamontschool.org.

Address correspondence to the Youth Services and School Libns. Div., ALLA, 6030 Monticello Dr., Montgomery 36117. Tel. 334-414-0113, e-mail allibraryassoc@gmail.com.

World Wide Web https://www.allanet.org/youth-services-and-school-library-division-yssld-.

Alaska

Alaska Assn. of School Libns. (AKASL). Memb. 100+. Publication. *The Puffin* continuing basis online at http://akasl.org/puffin-news. Submissions e-mail akasl.puffin@gmail.com.

Pres.-Elect Pam Verfaille. E-mail akasl.representative4@gmail.com; *Secretary* Jessica Tonnies; *Treas.* Laura Guest. E-mail akasl treasurer@gmail.com; *Past Pres.* Janet Madsen.

Address correspondence to AKASL, P.O. Box 81084, Fairbanks 99708.

World Wide Web http://www.akasl.org.

Arizona

Teacher-Libn. Div., Arizona Lib. Assn. (AZLA). Memb. 1,000. Term of Office. Jan.–Dec.

Co-Chair Jean Kilker, Maryvale High School, 3415 N. 59th Ave., Phoenix 85033. Tel. 602-764-2134, e-mail jkilker@phoenixunion.org; *Co-Chair* Judi Moreillon, Tel. 520-603-4868, e-mail info@storytrail.com.

Address correspondence to the chairpersons, AZLA, c/o Arizona Lib. Assn., 1645 W. Valencia Rd., Suite 109-432, Tucson 85746.

World Wide Web https://www.azla.org/page/TLD.

Arkansas

Arkansas Assn. of School Libns. (ARASL), div. of Arkansas Lib. Assn.

Chair Rachel Shankles, 891 Hwy. 7, Bismarck 71929. Tel. 501-276-4949, e-mail arasl.chair@gmail.com; *Past Chair* Daniel Fouts II, Osceola High School, 2800 W. Semmes Ave., Osceola 72370. Tel. 870-563-1863, e-mail dfouts@glaucus.org.

Address correspondence to the chairperson via e-mail.

World Wide Web https://arasl.weebly.com.

California

California School Lib. Assn. (CSLA). Memb. 1,200+. Publications. *CSLA Journal* (2x yearly). *Ed.* Mary Ann Harlan, San José State Univ. E-mail maryann.harlan@sjsu.edu; *CSLA Newsletter* (10x yearly, memb., via e-mail).

(State Board)

Pres. Katie McNamara, Bakersfield Unified School Dist., Fresno Pacific Univ. E-mail Katie_McNamara@kernhigh.org; *Pres.-Elect* Lisa Bishop, Aptos Middle School; *Secy.* Terri Brown, Fort Miller Middle, Fresno Unified School Dist., 2847 Beverly Ave., Clovis 93611. E-mail tbrown411@gmail.com; *Treas.* Lori Stevens, Riverside Poly High School, 5450 Victoria Ave., Riverside 92506. E-mail lstevens@rusd.k12.ca.us; *Past Pres.* Kathleen Sheppard, Los Angeles Unified School Dist. E-mail krsheppard814@gmail.com.

Address correspondence to CSLA, 6444 E. Spring St., No. 237, Long Beach 90815-1553. Tel./fax 888-655-8480, e-mail info@csla.net.

World Wide Web http://www.csla.net.

Colorado

Colorado Assn. of School Libs. (CASL). Memb. 250+.

Co-Pres. Terri Brungardt, Widefield School Dist. 3. E-mail brungardtt@wsd3.org; *Co-Pres.* Tiah Frankish, Adams 12 Five Star Schools. E-mail fra008000@adams12.org; *Co-Secy.* Katherine Kates, Academy Dist. 20.

E-mail k_kates@hotmail.com; *Membs.-at-Large* Rachel Budzynski, University Schools. E-mail rbudzynski@universityschools.com; Amy Hawkins-Keeler, Widefield High School. E-mail keelera@wsd3.org; *Legislative Rep.* David Sanger, CAL Legislative Committee. E-mail dsanger401@aol.com.

Address correspondence to CASL, c/o Colorado Assn. of Libs., P.O. Box 740905, Arvada 80006-0905. Tel. 303-463-6400.

World Wide Web https://cal-webs.org/Colorado_Association_of_School_Libraries.

Connecticut

Connecticut Assn. of School Libns. (CASL). Memb. 500+. Term of Office. July–June.

Pres. Barbara Johnson. E-mail bjohnson@ctcasl.org; *V.P.* Melissa Thom. E-mail joyfullearning@melissathom.com; *Recording Secy.* Jenny Lussier. E-mail jlussier13@gmail.com; *Treas.* Jody Pillar. E-mail treasurer@ctcasl.org.

Address correspondence to the president. CASL, P.O. Box 166, Winchester Center 06094.

World Wide Web https://casl.wildapricot.org.

Delaware

Delaware Assn. of School Libns. (DASL), div. of Delaware Lib. Assn. Memb. 100+. Publications. *DASL Newsletter* (online; irreg.); column in *DLA Bulletin* (2x yearly).

Pres. Alison Wessel, Univ. of Delaware, Morris Lib., 181 S. College Ave., Newark 19717. Tel. 302-831-1730, e-mail allisonwessel.dla@gmail.com. *V.P.* Catherine Wimberley, New Castle County Libs., 2020 W. 9th St., Wilmington 19805. Tel. 302-571-7425, e-mail catherinewimberley@newcastlede.gov. *Secy.* Marlowe Bogino, Wilmington Univ. Lib., 320 N. DuPont Hwy., New Castle 19720. Tel. 302-327-4892, e-mail Marlowe.b.bogino@wilmu.edu. *Treas.* Jaclyn Hale, Dover Public Lib., 35 Loockerman Plz., Dover 19901. Tel. 302-736-7185, e-mail jaclynhaledla@gmail.com. *Past Pres.* Sarah Katz, Univ. of Delaware, Morris Lib., 181 S. College Ave., Newark 19717. Tel. 302-831-6306, e-mail sekatz@udel.edu.

Address correspondence to the president, DASL, c/o Delaware Lib. Assn., Delaware Division of Libs., 121 Martin Luther King, Jr. Blvd. N., Dover 19901.

World Wide Web http://dla.lib.de.us/divisions/dasl/.

District of Columbia

District of Columbia Assn. of School Libns. (DCASL). Memb. 8. Publication. *Newsletter* (4x yearly).

Address correspondence to DCASL, 330 10th St. N.E., Washington, DC 20002. Tel. 301-502-4203, e-mail contactdcasl@gmail.com.

World Wide Web http://dcasl.weebly.com.

Florida

Florida Assn. for Media in Educ. (FAME). Memb. 1,400+. Term of Office. Nov.–Oct. Publication. *Florida Media Quarterly* (q.; memb.). *Ed.* Okle Miller. E-mail okle.miller@gmail.com.

Pres. Lorraine Stinson. E-mail Lorraine.Stinson@stjohns.k12.fl.us; *Pres.-Elect* Ashlee Cornett. E-mail noblebeach@gmail.com; *Secy.* Debbie Tanner; *Treas.* Amelia Zukoski. E-mail Amelia.Zukoski@stjohns.k12.fl.us; *Past Pres.* Julie Hiltz. E-mail juliehiltz@gmail.com.

Address correspondence to FAME, P.O. Box 941169, Maitland 32794-1169. Tel. 863-585-6802, e-mail FAME@floridamediaed.org.

World Wide Web http://www.floridamediaed.org.

Georgia

Georgia Lib. Media Assn. (GLMA). Memb. 700+.

Pres. Holly Frilot. E-mail president@glma-inc.org; *Pres.-Elect* Martha Bongiorno; *Secy.* Julie Pszczola; *Treas.* Lora Taft. E-mail treasurer@glma-inc.org; *Past Pres.* Jennifer Helfrich.

Address correspondence to GLMA, P.O. Box 148, Waverly Hall 31831. E-mail info@glma-inc.org.

World Wide Web http://www.glma-inc.org.

Hawaii

Hawaii Assn. of School Libns. Memb. (HASL). 145. Term of Office. June–May. Publication. *HASL Newsletter* (3x yearly). *Newsletter Chair*

Jenny Yamamoto, Leilehua High School. E-mail myhaslnews@gmail.com.

Co-Pres. Imelda Amano, Manoa Elementary (Ret.); *Co-Pres.* Meera Garud, Hawai'i P-20 Partnerships for Education; *V.P. Programming* Caitlin Ramirez, Mokapu Elementary; *V.P. Membership* Laurel Oshiro, Sacred Hearts Academy; *Recording Secy.* Elodie Arellano, Ahuimanu Elementary; *Treas.* Danielle Fujii, Kalaheo High School.

Address correspondence to HASL, P.O. Box 29691 Honolulu. E-mail hasl.contactus@gmail.com.

World Wide Web https://haslhawaii.weebly.com.

Idaho

School Libs. Services and Consulting, Idaho Commission for Libs. (ICfL).

School Library Action Planning Committee: School Library Consultant Jeannie Standal. Tel. 208-639-4139, e-mail jeannie.standal@libraries.idaho.gov; Kit Anderson, Teton High School, Teton School Dist.; Dennis Hahs, West Ada School Dist.; Lynn Johnson, Mountain View School Dist.; Kiersten Kerr, Coeur d'Alene School Dist.; Susan Tabor-Boesch, Wood River Middle School, Blaine County Schools.

Address correspondence to Jeannie Standal, Idaho Commission for Libs., 325 W. State St., Boise 83702. Tel. 208-639-4139, fax 208-334-4016, e-mail jeannie.standal@libraries.idaho.gov.

World Wide Web http://guides.lili.org/survival_guide/school_library.

Illinois

Assn. of Illinois School Lib. Educators (AISLE). Memb. 1,000. Term of Office. July–June. Publications. Newsletter (4x yearly). *Ed.* David P. Little. E-mail dplittleretired@gmail.com.

Pres. Anna Kim, Chappell Elementary, Chicago. E-mail president@aisled.org; *Pres.-Elect* Christy Semande, Canton USD #66, Canton. E-mail preselect@aisled.org; *Secy.* Joanna Marek, La Grange School Dist. 105. E-mail secretary@aisled.org; *Treas.* Jacob Roskovensky, Charleston High School. E-mail; treasurer@aisled.org; *Past Pres.* Mary Morgan Ryan, Northern Suburban Special Education Dist., Highland Park. E-mail pastpres@aisled.org; *Exec. Secy.* Becky Robinson. E-mail execsecretary@aisled.org.

Address correspondence to Assn. of Illinois School Lib. Educators. P.O. Box 110, Seneca 61360. Tel./fax 815-357-6023, e-mail execsecretary@aisled.org.

World Wide Web https://www.aisled.org.

Indiana

Assn. of Indiana School Library Educators (AISLE), affiliation of the Indiana Lib. Federation.

Advisory Board Diane Rogers, Ben Davis 9th Grade Ctr. Tel. 317-988-7577; Chad Heck, MSD Pike Township. Tel. 317-347-8673; JoyAnn Boudreau, Hamilton Southeastern Intermediate/Junior High. Tel. 317-594-4120; Jennifer Longgood, Northwestern High School. Tel. 765-438-7151; Sarah Bardwell, Southwest Dubois School Corp. Tel. 812-683-2217; Stacey Kern, Clark-Pleaasant Middle School. Tel. 317-535-7121; *Exec. Dir. ILF* Lucinda Nord, 941 East 86th St., Suite 260, Indianapolis 46240. Tel. 317-257-2040, ext. 101.

Address correspondence to AISLE, c/o Indiana Lib. Federation, 941 E. 86 St., Suite 260, Indianapolis 46240. Tel. 317-257-2040, fax 317-257-1389, e-mail askus@ilfonline.org.

World Wide Web https://www.ilfonline.org/page/AISLE.

Iowa

Iowa Assn. of School Libns. (IASL), div. of the Iowa Lib. Assn. Memb. 180+. Term of Office. Jan.–Jan.

Pres. Jenahlee Chamberlain, Cedar Rapids. E-mail jenahlee.chamberlain@gmail.com. *Secy./Treas.* Jen Keltner. E-mail kaseyjenkeltner@gmail.com; *Membs.-at-Large* Michelle Kruse, Miranda Kral, Diana Geers; *Past Pres.* Katy Kauffman, Ankeny. E-mail TLkatykauffman@gmail.com.

Address correspondence to the president, IASL, c/o the Iowa Lib. Assn., 6919 Vista Dr., W. Des Moines 50266.

World Wide Web http://www.iasl-ia.org.

Kansas

Kansas Assn. of School Libns. (KASL). Memb. 600.

Pres. Martha House. E-mail mhouse@cgrove417.org; *Pres.-Elect* Tonya Foster. E-mail tonya_foster@cox.net; *Secy.* Rachel Hodges. E-mail hodgesrac@gmail.com; *Treas.* Amanda Harrison. E-mail amanda.harrison@mcpherson.com; *Past Pres.* Marla Wigton. E-mail marla.wigton510@gmail.com.

Address correspondence to the president, KASL, c/o Kansas Library Assn., 2 Washington Sq., Norton 67654.

World Wide Web http://www.ksschoollibrarians.org.

Kentucky

Kentucky Assn. of School Libns. (KASL), section of Kentucky Lib. Assn. Memb. 600+. Publication. *KASL Blog.* (blog) http://www.kaslblog.com/.

Pres. Emily Northcutt. E-mail emilynorthcutt@shelby.kyschools.us; *Pres.-Elect* Sam Northern. E-mail samuel.northern@simpson.kyschools.us; *Secy.* Deidra Bowling-Meade. E-mail deidra.bowlingmeade@ashland.kyschools.us; *Treas.* Fred Tilsley. E-mail ftilsley@windstream.net; *Past Pres.* Lori Hancock. E-mail lhancock@thelexingtonschool.org.

Address correspondence to the president, KASL, c/o Kentucky Lib. Assn., 5932 Timber Ridge Drive, Suite 101, Prospect 40059.

World Wide Web http://www.kasl.us.

Louisiana

Louisiana Assn. of School Libns. (LASL), section of the Louisiana Lib. Assn. Memb. 230. Term of Office. July–June. Publication. *LASL Newsletter* (3x yearly).

Pres. Kimberly Adkins. E-mail kwadkins@caddoschools.org; *1st V.P./Pres.-Elect* Amanda Blanco. E-mail arblanco@lpssonline.com; *Secy.* Stephanie Wilkes. E-mail stephaniecwilkes@gmail.com.

Address correspondence to LASL, c/o Louisiana Lib. Assn., 8550 United Plaza Blvd., Suite 1001, Baton Rouge 70809. Tel. 225-922-4642, fax 225-408-4422, e-mail office@llaonline.org.

World Wide Web http://laslonline.weebly.com.

Maine

Maine Assn. of School Libs. (MASL). Memb. 200+.

Pres. Amanda Kozaka, Cape Elizabeth Middle School. E-mail akozaka@capeelizabethschools.org; *Pres.-Elect* Jennifer Stanbro, Skillin Elementary, South Portland; *Secy.* Cathy Potter, Falmouth Middle School, Falmouth; *Treas.* Megan Blakemore, Dyer Elementary School, South Portland; *Past Pres.* Tina Taggart, Foxcroft Academy, 975 W. Main St., Dover-Foxcroft 04426. E-mail tina.taggart@staff.foxcroftacademy.org.

Address correspondence to the president, MASL, c/o Maine State Lib. Assn., 64 State House Station, Augusta 04333-0064. E-mail maslibraries@gmail.com.

World Wide Web http://www.maslibraries.org.

Maryland

Maryland Assn. of School Libns (MASL). Publication. Newsletter (mo.; online).

Pres. April Wathen, G. W. Carver Elementary, St. Mary's County Public Schools. E-mail aawathen@smcps.org; *Pres.-Elect* Jen Sturge, Calvert County Public Schools. E-mail presidentelect@ maslmd.org; *Secy.* Kimberly Johnson, Westminster High School, Carrol County Public Schools. E-mail secretary@maslmd.org; *Treas.* Jenifer Lavell, Thomas Johnson Middle School, Prince George's County Public Schools. E-mail treasurer@maslmd.org; *Membs.-at-Large* Margaret Gaudino, Timothy Steelman, Kyra Kreinbrook; *Delegate* Tanishia Love, Loch Raven Technical Academy. E-mail delegate@maslmd.org; *MSDE Rep.* Laura Hicks. E-mail laura.hicks@maryland.gov; *Past Pres.* Brittany Tignor, Snow Hill High School, Worcester County Public Schools. E-mail BDHulme-Tignor@worcesterk12.org.

Address correspondence to the secretary via e-mail to secretary@maslmd.org.

World Wide Web http://maslmd.org.

Massachusetts

Massachusetts School Lib. Assn. (MSLA). Memb. 800. Publication. *MSLA Forum* (irreg.; online). *Eds.* Katherine Steiger, Reba Tierney.

Pres. Laura Luker, Pioneer Valley Immersion Charter, Hadley. E-mail lluker@maschoolibraries.org; *Past Pres.* Carrie Tucker, East Bridgewater Jr./Sr. High School. E-mail ctucker@maschoolibraries.org; *Secy.* Jennifer Dimmick, Newton South High School. E-mail jdimmick@maschoolibraries.org; *Treas.* Jennifer Varney, MLKing, Jr. School, Cambridge. E-mail jvarney@maschoolibraries.org; *Exec. Dir.* Kathy Lowe, Massachusetts School Lib, Assn., P.O. Box 658, Lunenburg 01462. E-mail klowe@maschoolibraries.org.

Address correspondence to the executive director, MSLA, P.O. Box 658, Lunenburg 01462.

World Wide Web http://www.maschoolibraries.org.

Michigan

Michigan Assn. for Media in Educ. (MAME). Memb. 1,200. Publication. *Media Matters!* newsletter (mo.). *Eds.* Beverly Banks. E-mail beverlybanks@wlcsd.org and Jonathan Richards. E-mail jrichards@vanburenschools.net.

Pres. Cat Kerns, Saginaw Township Community Schools, 3460 N. Center Rd., Saginaw 48603. Tel. 989-799-5790 ext. 8080, e-mail ckerns@mimame.org; *Pres.-Elect* Shannon Torres, Northville Public Schools. E-mail torressh@mimame.org; *Secy.* Alexa Hirsh Lalejini. E-mail ahirsch@mimame.org; *Treas.* Lisa Kelley, Rochester Community Schools, University Hills, 600 Croydon, Rochester Hills 48309. Tel. 248-726-4404, e-mail lkelley@mimame.org; *Past Pres.* Cynthia Zervos, F., Bloomfield Hills Schools, Way Elementary, 765 W. Long Lake, Bloomfield Hills 48302. E-mail cynthia.zervos@mimame.org; *Exec. Secy.* Teri Belcher. E-mail tbelcher@mimame.org.

Address correspondence to MAME, 1407 Rensen, Suite 3, Lansing 48910. Tel. 517-394-2808, fax 517-492-3878, e-mail mame@mimame.org.

World Wide Web http://www.mimame.org.

Minnesota

Info. and Technology Educators of Minnesota (ITEM) (formerly Minnesota Educ. Media Organization). Memb. 400+. Term of Office. July–June.

Co-Pres. Sara Florin, Centennial Public Schools; *Co-Pres.* Kim Haugo, Osseo Public Schools; *Co-Pres.-Elect* Ashley Krohn, Minneapolis Public Schools; *Co-Pres.-Elect* Dana Woods, Bemidji Public Schools; *Secy.* Sarah Rose, Minneapolis Public Schools; *Treas.* Dawn French, Saint Paul Public Schools; *Past Co-Pres.* Lisa Gearman, Chaska High School; *Past Co-Pres.* Tammi Wilkins, Duluth Public Schools.

Address correspondence to ITEM, P.O. Box 130555, Roseville 55113. Tel. 651-771-8672, e-mail admin@mnitem.org.

World Wide Web http://mnitem.org.

Mississippi

School Lib. Section, Mississippi Lib. Assn. (MLA). Memb. 1,300.

School Library Section Chair Angela Mullins, Simpson Central School / Simpson County School Dist. Tel. 601-847-2630, e-mail angelamullins39073@gmail.com.

Address correspondence to School Lib. Section, MLA, P.O. Box 13687, Jackson 39236-3687. Tel. 601-981-4586, e-mail info@misslib.org.

World Wide Web http://www.misslib.org/page-1818448.

Missouri

Missouri Assn. of School Libns. (MASL). Memb. 1,000. Term of Office. July–June.

Pres. Amy Hertzberg, Nevada Middle School, Nevada R-V School Dist. E-mail ahertzberg@nevada.k12.mo.us; *1st V.P.* Kirsten Shaw, Martin Warren Elementary School, Warrensburg School Dist. E-mail kshaw@warrensburgr6.org; *2nd V.P.* Kris Baughman, Eastwood Hills Elementary School, Raytown C-2 School Dist. E-mail kris.baughman@raytownschools.org; *Secy.* Jill Williams, McDonald County High School, McDonald County R-1 School Dist. E-mail jwilliams@mcdonaldco.k12.mo.us; *Treas.* Melissa Corey, Robidoux Middle School, St. Joseph School

Dist. E-mail treasurer@maslonline.org; *AASL Affiliate Assembly Delegate* Victoria Jones, Wydown Middle School, School Dist. of Clayton. E-mail victoriajones@claytonschools.net; *Past Pres.* Jennifer Millikan, St. Joseph's Academy. E-mail jmillikan@stjosephacademy.org.

Address correspondence to MASL, P.O. Box 2107, Jefferson City 65102. Tel. 573-893-4155, fax 573-635-2858, e-mail info@maslonline.org.

World Wide Web http://www.maslonline.org.

Montana

School Lib. Div., Montana Lib. Assn. (MLA). Memb. 200+.

Co-Chair Brittany Alberson, Bozeman High School Lib., 205 N. 11th Ave, Bozeman; *Co-Chair* Erin Regele, Billings West HS Lib., 2201 St. Johns Ave., Billings 59102; *MLA Exec. Dir.* Debbi Kramer, 5176 N. Valle Dorado, Kingman, AZ 86409. Tel. 406-579-3121, e-mail debkmla@hotmail.com.

Address correspondence to the MLA executive director.

World Wide Web http://www.mtlib.org/governance/sld.

Nebraska

Nebraska School Libns. Assn. (NSLA). Memb. 300+. Term of Office. July–June. Publication. *NSLA News* (blog; mo.).

Pres. Cynthia Stogdill. E-mail cynstogdill@gmail.com; *Pres.-Elect* Angela Blankenship. E-mail angieklimek2715@gmail.com; *Secy.* Crys Bauermeister. E-mail cbauermeister@gmail.com; *Treas.* Jackie Harris. E-mail readerharris30@gmail.com; *Past Pres.* Courtney Pentland. E-mail mrspentland@gmail.com; *Exec. Secy.* Kim Gangwish. E-mail contactnsla@gmail.com.

Address correspondence to the executive secretary via e-mail.

World Wide Web http://www.neschoollibrarians.org.

Nevada

Nevada School and Children Libns., section of the Nevada Lib. Assn. (NLA). Memb. 120.

Chair Susan Thurnbeck, Las Vegas–Clark County Lib. Dist. E-mail thurnbecks@lvccld.org; *Past Chair* Larry Johnson, Las Vegas–Clark County Lib. Dist.; *Exec. Secy. NLA* Sue (Seungyeon) Yang-Peace, Las Vegas-Clark County Lib. Dist. E-mail sueyangpeace@gmail.com.

Address correspondence to the executive secretary, NLA School and Children Libns. Section, 4905 Chennault St., Papillion 68133.

World Wide Web http://nevadalibraries.org/Handbook-NSCLS.

New Hampshire

New Hampshire School Lib. Media Assn. (NSHLMA). Memb. 250+. Term of Office. July–June. Publication. *NHSLMA Newsletter* (irreg.; online).

Pres. Karen Abraham, Laconia High School. E-mail president@nhslma.org; *V.P.* Justine Thain, Hooksett School Dist., Hooksett. E-mail vice-president@nhslma.org; *Recording Secy.* Audra Lewis, Nottingham School, Nottingham. E-mail secretary@nhslma.org; *Treas.* Helen Burnham, Lincoln Street School, Exeter. E-mail treasurer@nhslma.org; *Past Pres.* Caitlin Bennett, Londonderry Middle School, Londonderry. E-mail past-president@nhslma.org.

Address correspondence to the president, NHSLMA, P.O. Box 418, Concord 03302-0418. E-mail nhslma@gmail.com.

World Wide Web http://nhslma.org.

New Jersey

New Jersey Assn. of School Libns. (NJASL). Memb. 1,000+. Term of Office. Aug. 1–July 31. Publication. *Bookmark Newsletter* (mo.; memb.). *Ed.* Casey Schaffer. E-mail bookmark@njasl.org.

Pres. Jill Mills. E-mail president@njasl.org; *Pres.-Elect.* Beth Thomas. E-mail presidentelect@njasl.org; *V.P.* Amy Gazaleh. E-mail vp@njasl.org; *Recording Secy.* Casey Jane Schaffer. E-mail secretary@njasl.org; *Treas.* Jean Stock, Larchmont Elementary, 301 Larchmont Blvd., Mt. Laurel 08054. Tel. 856-273-3700 ext.17508, e-mail treasurer@njasl.org; *Memb.-at-Large* Beth Raff. E-mail membersatlarge@njasl.org. *Past Pres.* Christina Cucci. E-mail pastpresident@njasl.org;

Address correspondence to the recording secretary, NASL, P.O. Box 1460, Springfield 07081.

World Wide Web http://www.njasl.org.

New York

Section of School Libns., New York Lib. Assn. (NYLA). Memb. 800+. Term of Office. Nov.–Oct. Publication. *School Library Update* (3x yearly; memb.; online).

President Tara Thibault-Edmonds. E-mail tthibault-edmonds@rondout.k12.ny.us; *Pres.-Elect* Dawn Pressimone. E-mail dpressimone@waynecsd.org; *Secy.* Gail Brisson. E-mail Gail.brisson@gmail.com; *Treas.* Anne Paulson. E-mail anneppaulson@gmail.com; *V.P. of Conferences* Michelle Miller. E-mail mmiller@mwcsd.org; *V.P. of Communications* Heather Turner. E-mail hturner@fabiuspompey.org; *Past Pres.* Charlie Jennifer Kelly. E-mail charlieakajennykelly@gmail.com.

Address correspondence to the Section of School Libns., NYLA, 6021 State Farm Rd., Guilderland 12084. Tel. 518-432-6952, fax 518-427-1697, e-mail info@nyla.org.

World Wide Web https://www.nyla.org/4DCGI/cms/review.html?Action=CMS_Document&DocID=136&MenuKey=ssl.

North Carolina

North Carolina School Lib. Media Assn. (NCSLMA). Memb. 1,000+. Term of Office. Nov.–Oct.

Pres. Laura Long. E-mail lauralong@nclsma.org; *Pres.-Elect* Cindy Sturdivant. E-mail cindysturdivant@ncslma.org; *Secy.* Joanie Williams. E-mail joaniewilliams@ncslma.org; *Treas.* Jennifer Abel, North Henderson High School, 35 Fruitland Rd., Hendersonville 28792. Tel. 828-697-4500, e-mail jenniferabel@ncslma.org; *Past Pres.* Bitsy Griffin, Old Town Global Academy, 3930 Reynolda Rd., Winston-Salem 27106. Tel. 336-703-4283, e-mail bitsygriffin@ncslma.org.

Address correspondence to the president, NCSLMA, 151 NC Hwy. 9, Suite B-188, Black Mountain, 28711.

World Wide Web http://www.ncslma.org.

North Dakota

School Lib. and Youth Svcs. section of the North Dakota Lib. Assn. (NDLA). Memb. 100.

Chair Carmen Redding, North Dakota State Library. E-mail carmen.redding@k12.nd.us; *Chair-Elect* Leslie Allan, Williston Public Schools. E-mail librarylesley@gmail.com; *Secy.* Amber Emergy, Fargo Public Library. E-mail aelibrary@fargolibrary.org; *Past Chair* Allison Radermacher, Ellendale Public School. E-mail aradermacher@ellendale.k12.nd.us.

Address correspondence to the School Lib. and Youth Svcs. Section, NDLA, 604 E. Boulevard Ave., Bismarck 58505.

World Wide Web https://ndla.info/SLAYS.

Ohio

Ohio Educ. Lib. Media Assn. (OELMA). Memb. 1,000.

Pres. Brandi Young, South-Western City School Dist., Westland High School. E-mail b.nicole.young@gmail.com; *V.P.* Karen Gedeon, Cuyahoga Falls City Schools. E-mail kgedeon2@gmail.com; *Secy.* Jamie Davies, Dublin City Schools, Eli Pinney Elementary. E-mail jdaviesoelma@gmail.com; *Past Pres.* Deb Logan, Pleasant Local Schools. E-mail deb.jd3logan@gmail.com.

Address correspondence to OELMA, 1737 Georgetown Rd., Suite B, Hudson 43236. Tel. 330-615-2409, fax 1-800-373-9594, e-mail OELMA@neo-rls.org.

World Wide Web http://www.oelma.org.

Oklahoma

Oklahoma School Libns. Div., Oklahoma Lib. Assn. (OLA). Memb. 200+.

Chair Amanda Kordeliski. E-mail oksl@oklibs.org; *Chair-Elect* Ashleigh Dautermann; *Treas.* Angela Risch.

Address correspondence to the chairperson, School Libs. Div., OLA, 1190 Meramec Station Rd., Suite 207, Ballwin, MO 63021-6902. Tel. 800-843-8482, fax 636-529-1396.

World Wide Web https://www.oklibs.org/page/OKSL.

Oregon

Oregon Assn. of School Libs. (OASL). Memb. 600. Publication. *Interchange* (3x yearly). *Co-ord. Ed.* Dana Berglund. E-mail interchange@oasl.olaweb.org.

Pres. Laurie Nordahl. E-mail president@oasl.olaweb.org; *Pres.-Elect* Kate Weber. E-mail presidentelect@oasl.olaweb.org; *Secy.* Jenny Takeda. E-mail secretary@oasl.olaweb.org; *Treas.* Jennifer Maurer. E-mail treasurer@oasl.olaweb.org; *Membs.-at-Large* Ayn Frazer, Elaine Ferrell-Burns. E-mail region2@oasl.olaweb.org; *Past Pres.* Stuart Levy. E-mail pastpresident@oasl.olaweb.org.

Address correspondence to the president, OASL, c/o Oregon Lib. Assn., P.O. Box 3067, La Grande 97850. Tel. 541-962-5824, e-mail president@oasl.olaweb.org.

World Wide Web http://www.olaweb.org/oasl-home.

Pennsylvania

Pennsylvania School Libns. Assn. (PSLA). Memb. 800+. Publication. *PSLA Pulse* (blog).

Pres. Cathi Fuhrman, Hempfield School Dist. E-mail cfuhrman@psla.org; *Pres.-Elect.* Robin Burns, Salisbury Township School Dist. E-mail rburns@psla.org; *V.P.* Laura Ward, Fox Chapel Area School Dist. E-mail lward@psla.org; *Secy.* Jane Farrell, Dallastown Area School Dist. E-mail secretary@psla.org; *Treas.* Sandy Reilly, Pleasant Valley School Dist. E-mail treasurer@psla.org; *Past Pres.* Allison Mackley, Derry Township School Dist. E-mail allisons21@gmail.com.

Address correspondence to the president, PSLA, Hershey Square #125, 1152 Mae St., Hummelstown 17036.

World Wide Web http://www.psla.org.

Rhode Island

School Libns. of Rhode Island, section of the Rhode Island Library Assn. (RILA). Memb. 350+. Publication. *SLRI Update* (irreg.; online).

Pres. Deanna Brooks. E-mail SLRI.prez@gmail.com; *V.P.* Joan Mouradjian. E-mail SLRI.viceprez@gmail.com; *Secy.* Lisa Casey. E-mail SLRI.secretary@gmail.com; *Treas.* Jillian Waugh. E-mail SLRI.treasurer@gmail.com; *Past Pres.* Lisa Girard.

Address correspondence to the president, School Libns. of Rhode Island, RILA, P.O. Box 6765, Providence 02940.

World Wide Web https://rilibraries.org/slri.

South Carolina

South Carolina Assn. of School Libns. (SCASL). Memb. 900. Term of Office. July–June. Publication *The SCASL Messenger* (q., online, memb.). *Ed.* Anya Bonnette. E-mail anya.bonnette@ocsd5.net.

Pres. Pamela Williams. E-mail president@scasl.net; *Pres.-Elect* Linda Waskow. E-mail president.elect@scasl.net; *Secy.* Susan Myers. E-mail secretary@scasl.net; *Treas.* Camillia Harris; *Past Pres.* Heather Thore.

Address correspondence to SCASL, P.O. Box 2442, Columbia 29202. Tel./fax 803-492-3025.

World Wide Web http://www.scasl.net.

South Dakota

South Dakota School Lib. Media Section, South Dakota Lib. Assn. (SDLA). Memb. 140+. Term of Office. Oct.–Sept.

Chair Korey Erickson, Sioux Falls Public Schools, Sioux Falls. E-mail korey.erickson@k12.sd.us; *Past Chair* Kimberly Darata, Douglas School Dist. E-mail kimberly.darata@k12.sd.us.

Address correspondence to the chairperson. South Dakota School Lib. Media Section, SDLA, P.O. Box 283, Lennox 57039. Tel. 605-214-8785.

World Wide Web http://www.sdlibraryassociation.org/page/Sections.

Tennessee

Tennessee Assn. of School Libns. (TASL). Memb. 450. Term of Office. Jan.–Dec. Publication. *TASL Talks* (wk.; blog).

Pres. Vicki Winstead, Vance Middle School, 815 Edgemont Ave., Bristol 37620. E-mail vcwinstead.tasl@gmail.com; *Pres.-Elect* Lindsey Kimery, Woodland Middle School, 1500 Volunteer Pkwy., Brentwood 37027. E-mail lindskanderson@gmail.com; *Secy.* Elizabeth Shepherd, Discovery School, 1165 Middle TN

Blvd., Murfreesboro 37130. E-mail eshepherd 78@gmail.com; *Treas.* Ginny Britt, Robertson County Schools. E-mail ginny.britt@rcstn.net; *Past Pres.* Jennifer Sharp, Overton High School, 4820 Franklin Rd., Nashville 37220. E-mail jennifer.sharp.tasl@gmail.com.

Address correspondence to the president, TASL, P.O. Box 11185, Murfreesboro 37129.

World Wide Web http://www.tasltn.org.

Texas

Texas Assn. of School Libns. (TASL), div. of Texas Lib. Assn. Memb. 4,500+. Term of Office. Apr.–Mar.

Chair Richelle O'Neil. E-mail rgoneil@garlandisd.net; *Chair-Elect* Kristi Starr. E-mail kristi.starr@lubbockisd.org; *Secy.* Liza Zinkie. E-mail librarianzee6@gmail.com; *Councilor* Nicole Cruz; *Alternate Councilor* Jen Hampton; *Past Chair* Nancy Jo Lambert. E-mail Lambertn@friscoisd.org; *TLA Exec. Dir.* Shirley Robinson. E-mail shirleyr@txla.org.

Address correspondence to the chairperson, TASL, c/o Texas Lib. Assn., 3355 Bee Cave Rd., Suite 401, Austin 78746. Tel. 512-328-1518, fax 512-328-8852.

World Wide Web http://www.txla.org/groups/tasl.

Utah

Utah Educ. Lib. Media Assn. (UELMA). Memb. 500+. Publication. *UELMA Works* (q.). *Ed.* Liz Petty. E-mail elisabethapetty@outlook.com.

Pres. Ann Riding, North Davis Junior High, 835 S. State St., Clearfield 84015. Tel. 801-402-6500, e-mail board@uelma.org; *Pres.-Elect* Emily DeJong, Salt Lake School Dist. E-mail board@uelma.org; *Secy.* Stephanie MacKay, Centennial Jr. High; *Past Pres.* Lorraine Wyness, Taylorsville High School, 5225 S. Redwood Rd., Taylorsville 84123. Tel. 385-646-8949, e-mail board@uelma.org; *Exec. Dir.* Davina Sauthoff. Tel. Wasatch Junior High, 3750 South 3100 E., Salt Lake City 84109. Tel. 435-512-6809, e-mail executivedirector@uelma.org.

Address correspondence to the executive director.

World Wide Web http://www.uelma.org.

Vermont

Vermont School Lib. Assn. (VSLA). Memb. 220+. Term of Office. May–May.

Pres. Deb Ehler-Hansen. E-mail vermonthan1@gmail.com; *Pres.-Elect* Peter Langella; *Secy.* Caitlin Classen. E-mail vslasecretary@gmail.com; *Treas.* Megan Sutton. E-mail msutton@acsdvt.org; *Past Pres.* Martine Larocque Gulick. E-mail mgulick@ewsd.org.

Address correspondence to the president via e-mail.

World Wide Web https://vsla.wildapricot.org.

Virginia

Virginia Assn. of School Libns. (VAASL) (formerly Virginia Educ. Media Assn. [VEMA]). Memb. 1,200. Term of Office. Nov.–Nov. Publication. *VAASL Voice* (q.; memb.).

Pres. Patrice Lambusta. E-mail president@vaasl.org; *Pres.-Elect* Jennifer Cooper. E-mail presidentelect@vaasl.org; *Secy.* Heather Balsley. E-mail secretary@vaasl.org; *Treas.* Trish Branscome. E-mail Treasurer@vaasl.org; *Past Pres.* Kendel Lively. E-mail pastpresident@vaasl.org; *Exec. Dir.* Margaret Baker. E-mail executive@vaasl.org.

Address correspondence to the executive director, VAASL, P.O. Box 2015, Staunton 24402-2015. Tel. 540-416-6109, e-mail executive@vaasl.org.

World Wide Web http://vaasl.org.

Washington

School Lib. Div., Washington Lib. Assn. (WLA). Memb. 700+. Term of Office. Apr.–Apr.

Chair Hillary Marshall. E-Mail hillary.marshall@washougalsd.org; *V.Chair/Chair-Elect* Sam Harris. E-mail sharris@charleswright.org; *Secy.* Elizabeth Roberts. E-mail elizabeth.k.roberts@gmail.com; *Past Chair* Ann Hayes-Bell. E-mail ann.hayes.bell@k12.shorelineschools.org.

Address correspondence to WLA School Lib. Div., P.O. Box 33808, Seattle 98133. Tel. 206-823-1138, e-mail info@wla.org.

World Wide Web http://www.wla.org/school-libraries.

West Virginia

School Lib. Div., West Virginia Lib. Assn. (WVLA). Memb. 50. Term of Office. Nov.–Nov.

Chair Leigh Ann Hood, East Park Elementary, 805 Pittsburgh Ave., Fairmont 26554. Tel. 304-534-0927, e-mail lahood@k12.wv.us; *Past Chair* Lynda Suzie Martin, Brookhaven Elementary, 147 Estate Dr., Morgantown 26508. Tel. 304-282-0147, e-mail librarynbct@gmail.com.

Address correspondence to the chairperson, WVLA School Lib. Div., P.O. Box 1432, Morgantown 26507.

World Wide Web http://www.wvla.org.

Wisconsin

Wisconsin Educ. Media and Technology Assn. (WEMTA). Memb. 800+.

Pres. Micki Uppena. E-mail president@wemta.org; *V.P.* Raquel Rand; *Pres.-Elect* Rachel Schemelen; *Secy.* Dawn Totzke; *Treas.* Pamela Hansen; *Past Pres.* Michele Green.

Address correspondence to WEMTA, 5329 Fayette Ave., Madison 53713. Tel. 608-588-6006, e-mail wemta@wemta.org.

World Wide Web http://www.wemta.org.

Wyoming

School Lib. Interest Group, Wyoming Lib. Assn. (WLA). Memb. 100+.

Chair Connie Hollin, Guernsey-Sunrise School (K–12). Tel. 307-836-2733, e-mail chollin@gsviking.org.

Address correspondence to the chairperson, SLIG, c/o WLA, 1190 Meramac Station Rd., Suite 207, Ballwin MO 63201.

World Wide Web https://wyla.org/School-Library-Interest-Group.

International Library Associations

International Association of Law Libraries

Kurt Carroll, President
P.O. Box 5709, Washington, DC 20016
E-mail president@iall.org
World Wide Web http://www.iall.org

Objective

The International Association of Law Libraries (IALL) is a worldwide organization of librarians, libraries, and other persons or institutions concerned with the acquisition and use of legal information emanating from sources other than their jurisdictions and from multinational and international organizations.

IALL's purpose is to facilitate the work of librarians who acquire, process, organize, and provide access to foreign legal materials. IALL has no local chapters but maintains liaison with national law library associations in many countries and regions of the world.

Membership

More than 400 members in more than 50 countries on five continents.

Officers

Pres. Kurt Carroll, Library of Congress, Washington, DC 20550. Tel. 202-707-1494, e-mail president@iall.org; *V.P.* Kerem Kahvecioglu, Haciahment Mahellesi, Pir Hüsamettin Sokak 20, 34440 Beyoğlu, Istanbul. Tel: 90 212 311 5157, e-mail vicepresident@iall.org; *Secy.* David Gee, Institute of Advanced Legal Studies, Univ. of London, 17 Russell Sq., London. Tel. 44 (0)20 7862 5822, fax 44 (0)20 7862 5770, e-mail David.Gee@sas.ac.uk; *Treas.* Barbara Garavaglia, Univ. of Michigan Law Lib., Ann Arbor 48109-1210. Tel. 734-764-9338, fax 734-764-5863, e-mail bvaccaro@umich.edu; *Past Pres.* Jeroen Vervliet, The Hague. Tel. 31-70-302-4242, e-mail j.vervliet@ppl.nl.

Board of Directors

Kristina J. Alayan, Howard Univ. School of Law, Washington, D.C. Tel. 202-806-8047, e-mail kristina.alayan@law.howard.edu; Rebecca J. Five Bergstrøm, Univ. of Oslo Law Lib. Tel. 4722859306, e-mail r.j.f.bergstrom@ub.uio.no; Heather Casey, Georgetown Univ. Law Lib., Washington, D.C. Tel. 202-661-6573, e-mail hec29@georgetown.edu; François Desseilles, Univ. of Liège Lib., Liège (Sart-Tilman). E-mail fdesseills@uliege.be; Mark D. Engsberg, MacMillan Law Lib., Emory School of Law, Atlanta, GA. Tel. 404-727-6983, e-mail mengsbe@emory.edu; Michel Fraysse, Université Toulouse, FR. Tel. 00 33 (5) 34 61 34, e-mail michel.fraysse@ut-capitole.fr; Trung Quach, Melbourne Law School, Univ. of Melbourne, Victoria. Tel. 61 3 9035 3061, e-mail trung.quach@unimelb.edu.au; Jean M. Wenger, Chicago-Kent College of Law, Chicago, IL 60661. Tel. 312-906-5610, e-mail jwenger@kentlaw.iit.edu.

Publications

International Journal of Legal Information (*IJLI*) (3x yearly; memb.).

IALL Newsletter (3x yearly; memb.).

International Association of Music Libraries, Archives, and Documentation Centres

Anders Cato, Secretary-General
Gothenburg University Library, P.O. Box 210, SE 405 30 Gothenburg, Sweden
Tel. 46-31-786-4057, cell 46-703-226-092, fax 46-31-786-40-59, e-mail secretary@iaml.info
World Wide Web http://www.iaml.info

Objective

The objective of the International Association of Music Libraries, Archives, and Documentation Centres (IAML) is to promote the activities of music libraries, archives, and documentation centers and to strengthen the cooperation among them; to promote the availability of all publications and documents relating to music and further their bibliographical control; to encourage the development of standards in all areas that concern the association; and to support the protection and preservation of musical documents of the past and the present.

Membership

Memb. approximately 1,700 in about 40 countries worldwide.

Officers

Pres. Stanislaw Hrabia, Uniwersytet Jagiellonski, Kraków. E-mail president@iaml.info; *V.P.s* Jane Gottlieb, The Juilliard School, New York; Rupert Ridgewell, British Lib., London; Jürgen Diet, Bayerische Staatsbibliothek, Munich; Anna Pensaert, Cambridge Univ. Lib. and the Pendlebury Lib. of Music; *Secy.-Gen.* Pia Shekhter, Gothenburg Univ. Lib., Box 210, SE 405 30 Gothenburg. Tel. 46-31-786-40-57, e-mail secretary@iaml.info; *Treasurer* Thomas Kalk, Stadtbüchereien Düsseldorf. E-mail treasurer@iaml.info; *Past Pres.* Barbara Dobbs Mackenzie, *Répertoire International de Littérature Musicale* (*RILM*), New York.

Publication

Fontes Artis Musicae (q.; memb.). *Ed.* James P. Cassaro, Univ. of Pittsburgh, B-30 Music Bldg., Pittsburgh, PA 15260. Tel. 412-624-4131, e-mail fontes@iaml.info.

Professional Branches

Archives and Music Documentation Centres. *Chair* Marie Cornaz, Bibliothèque Royale de Belgique, Brussels. E-mail archives@iaml.info.

Broadcasting and Orchestra Libraries. *Chair* Sabina Benelli, Teatro alla Scala, Milan. E-mail broadcasting-orchestra@iaml.info.

Libraries in Music Teaching Institutions. *Chair* Charles Peters, William & Gayle Cook Music Lib., Indiana Univ., Bloomington. E-mail teaching@iaml.info.

Public Libraries. *Chair* vacant. *V.Chair* Carolyn Dow, Polley Music Lib., Lincoln City Libs., Lincoln, NE. E-mail public-libraries@iaml.info.

Research Libraries. *Chair* Thomas Leibnitz. Musiksammlung der Österreichischen Nationalbibliothek, Vienna. E-mail research-libraries@iaml.info.

Subject Sections

Audio-Visual Materials. *Chair* Jonathan Manton, Yale University, New Haven. E-mail ajustice@usc.edu.

Bibliography. *Chair* Stefan Engl, Österreichische Nationalbibliothek, Vienna. E-mail bibliography@iaml.info.

Cataloguing and Metadata. *Chair* Frédéric Lemmers, Bibliothèque royale de Belgique, Brussels. E-mail cataloguing@iaml.info.

Service and Training. *Chair* Anna Pensaert, Cambridge Univ. Lib., Cambridge. E-mail service@iaml.info.

International Association of School Librarianship

Jill Hancock, Executive Director
P.O. Box 684, Jefferson City, MO 65102
Tel. 573-635-2173, e-mail iasl@c2pro.solutions
World Wide Web http://www.iasl-online.org

Mission and Objectives

The mission of the International Association of School Librarianship (IASL) is to provide an international forum for those interested in promoting effective school library programs as viable instruments in the education process. IASL also provides guidance and advice for the development of school library programs and the school library profession. IASL works in cooperation with other professional associations and agencies.

Membership is worldwide and includes school librarians, teachers, librarians, library advisers, consultants, education administrators, and others who are responsible for library and information services in schools. The membership also includes professors and instructors in universities and colleges where there are programs for school librarians, and students who are undertaking such programs.

The objectives of IASL are to advocate the development of school libraries throughout all countries; to encourage the integration of school library programs into the instruction and curriculum of the school; to promote the professional preparation and continuing education of school library personnel; to foster a sense of community among school librarians in all parts of the world; to foster and extend relationships between school librarians and other professionals in connection with children and youth; to foster research in the field of school librarianship and the integration of its findings with pertinent knowledge from related fields; to promote the publication and dissemination of information about successful advocacy and program initiatives in school librarianship; to share information about programs and materials for children and youth throughout the international community; and to initiate and coordinate activities, conferences, and other projects in the field of school librarianship and information services.

Founded 1971.

Membership

Approximately 825.

Officers

Pres. Katy Manck, Independent Book Reviewer, Gilmer, Tex. E-mail katyroo@gmail.com or Katy.Manck@gmail.com; *V.P. Assn. Operations* Mihaela Banek Zorica, Univ. of Zagreb, Faculty of Humanities and Social Sciences, Dept. of Information Sciences, Zagreb, Croatia. E-mail mbanek@ffzg.hr; *V.P. Assn. Relations* Albert Boekhorst, Brasil, Netherlands. E-mail albertkb@gmail.com; *V.P. Advocacy and Promotion* Annie Tam, the Independent Schools Foundation Academy, Hong Kong, China. E-mail atam@isf.edu.hk; *Treas.* Jennifer Branch-Mueller, Univ. of Alberta, Canada. E-mail jbranch@ualberta.ca.

Regional Board of Directors

Jerry Mathema, Africa; Shyh-Mee Tan, Asia; Kacy Song, East Asia; Meghan Harper, North America; Laura Vilela Rodriges Rezende, Latin America/Caribbean; Vanja Jurilj, Europe; Sevgi Arioglu, North Africa/Middle East; Susan La Marca, Oceania; Zakir Hossain, International Schools.

Publications

School Libraries Worldwide (http://www.iasl-online.org/publications/slw/index.html), the association's refereed research and professional journal (online only; 2x yearly; memb.).

IASL Newsletter (http://www.iasl-online.org/publications/newsletter.html) (print; 3x yearly; memb.).

International Association of Scientific and Technological University Libraries (IATUL)

Anne Horn, President
World Wide Web http://www.iatul.org

Objective

The main objective of the International Association of Scientific and Technological University Libraries (IATUL) is to provide a forum where library directors and senior managers can meet to exchange views on matters of current significance and to provide an opportunity for them to develop a collaborative approach to solving problems. IATUL also welcomes into membership organizations that supply services to university libraries, if they wish to be identified with the association's activities.

Membership

260 in 60 countries.

Officers

Pres. Anne Horn, Univ. of Sheffield, UK. E-mail a.horn@sheffield.ac.uk; *V.P.* Charles Eckman, Univ. of Miami, USA. E-mail ceckman@miami.edu; *Secy.* Lucille Webster, Durban Univ. of Technology, South Africa. E-mail webster@dut.ac.za; *Treas.* Howard Amos, Univ. of Otago Lib., New Zealand. E-mail howardamos@otago.ac.nz.

Board Members

Officers: Jill Benn, Univ. of Western Australia, Perth. Donna Bourne-Tyson, Dalhousie Univ., Canada. Lars Egeland, Oslo Metropolitan Univ., Norway; J. K. Vijaykumar, King Abdullah University of Science and Technology, Saudi Arabia. Anna Walek, Gdańsk University of Technology, Poland.

Publication

IATUL Conference Proceedings (https://www.iatul.org/publications/proceedings).

International Council on Archives

Anthea Seles, Secretary-General
60 rue des Francs-Bourgeois, 75003 Paris, France
Tel. 33-1-40-27-63-06, fax 33-1-42-72-20-65, e-mail ica@ica.org
World Wide Web http://www.ica.org

Objective

The mission of the International Council on Archives (ICA) is to establish, maintain, and strengthen relations among archivists of all lands, and among all professional and other agencies or institutions concerned with the custody, organization, or administration of archives, public or private, wherever located. Established 1948.

Membership

Approximately 1,900 in nearly 200 countries and territories

Officers

Pres. David Fricker, Australia; *V.P.s* M. Normand Charbonneau, Canada; Henri Zuber, France; *Secy.-Gen.* Anthea Seles, France.

Board Members

Emma De Ramon Acevedo, Chile; Hamad Bin Mohammed Al-Dhawyani, Oman; Opeta Alefaio, Fiji; Azemi Abdul Aziz, Malaysia; Françoise Banat-Berger, France; Avril Belfon, Trinidad and Tobago; Alexander Lukas Bieri, Switzerland; Caroline Brown, UK; Margaret Crockett, France; Yonten Dargye, Bhutan; Abdulla A. Kareem El Reyes, UAE; Charles Farrugia, Malta; Emilie Gagnet Leumas, USA; Tim Harris, UK; Jeff James, UK; Takeo Katoh, Japan; Gustavo Castaner Marquadt, Belgium; Matthias Massode, Benin; Jean-Paul Nenga Mukanya, Congo; Yolanda Cagigas Ocejo, Spain; Vilde Ronge, Norway; Fina Sola I Gasset, Spain; David Sutton, UK; Rita Tjien-Fooh, Suriname; Ian E. Wilson, Canada; Atakilty Assefa Asgedom (ex officio), Ethiopia.

Publications

Comma (print and online; 2x yearly, memb.).

Flash (online only; 2x yearly; memb.).

ICA e-newsletter (online only; mo.).

Conference Papers and Proceedings.

International Federation of Film Archives (Fédération Internationale des Archives du Film)

Michael Loebenstein , Secretary-General
Secretariat, 42 rue Blanche, B-1060 Brussels, Belgium
Tel. 32-2-538-30-65, fax 32-2-534-47-74, e-mail info@fiafnet.org
World Wide Web http://www.fiafnet.org

Objective

Founded in 1938, the International Federation of Film Archives (FIAF) brings together not-for-profit institutions dedicated to rescuing films and any other moving-image elements considered both as cultural heritage and as historical documents.

FIAF is a collaborative association of the world's leading film archives whose purpose has always been to ensure the proper preservation and showing of motion pictures. Almost 90 member archives in more than 50 countries collect, restore, and exhibit films and cinema documentation spanning the entire history of film.

FIAF seeks to promote film culture and facilitate historical research, to help create new archives around the world, to foster training and expertise in film preservation, to encourage the collection and preservation of documents and other cinema-related materials, to develop cooperation between archives, and to ensure the international availability of films and cinema documents.

Officers

Pres. Frédéric Maire; *Secy.-Gen.* Michael Loebensten; *Treas.* Jon Wengström. *V.P.s* Cecilia Cenciarelli, Michal Bregant, Iris Elezi.

Address correspondence to Christophe Dupin, Senior Administrator, FIAF Secretariat. E-mail c.dupin@fiafnet.org.

Publications and Databases

FIAF Bulletin Online.

FIAF Directory.

FIAF International Index to Film Periodicals database. (ProQuest).

International Index to Film Periodicals database. (OVID).

International Index to Television Periodicals database.

Journal of Film Preservation. Ed. Elaine Burrows. E-mail jfp.editor@fiafnet.org.

Treasures from the Film Archives database.

Extensive selection of books through the FIAF Bookshop.

International Federation of Library Associations and Institutions

P.O. Box 95312, 2509 CH The Hague, Netherlands
Tel. 31-70-314-0884, fax 31-70-383-4827, e-mail ifla@ifla.org
World Wide Web http://www.ifla.org

Objective

The objective of the International Federation of Library Associations and Institutions (IFLA) is to promote international understanding, cooperation, discussion, research, and development in all fields of library activity, including bibliography, information services, and the education of library personnel, and to provide a body through which librarianship can be represented in matters of international interest. IFLA is the leading international body representing the interests of library and information services and their users. It is the global voice of the library and information profession. Founded 1927.

Officers

Pres. Christine Mackenzie, Australia; *Pres.-Elect* Barbara Lison, Stadtbibliothek Bremen, Germany; *Treas.* Antonia Arahova, Athens, Greece; *Past Pres.* Glòria Pérez-Salmerón, Federación Española de Sociedades de Archivística, Biblioteconomía, Documentación y Museística, Spain; *Secy.-Gen.* Gerald Leitner (ex officio), Netherlands.

Governing Board

Huanwen Cheng (China), Michael Dowling (USA), Marwa El Sahn (Egypt), Jonathan Hernández Pérez (Mexico), Sueli Mara Soares Pinto Ferreira (Brazil), Ai Cheng Tay (Singapore), Minna von Zansen (Finland), Knud Schulz (Denmark), plus the chairs of the IFLA Professional Committee and divisions.

Publications

IFLA Annual Report.
IFLA Journal (4x yearly).
IFLA Trend Reports.
IFLA Professional Reports.
IFLA Publications Series.
IFLA Series on Bibliographic Control.
Global Studies in Libraries and Information (irreg. series).
Access and Opportunity for All: How Libraries Contribute to the United Nations 2030 Agenda.

American Membership

Associations

American Lib. Assn., Assn. for Lib. and Info. Science Educ., Assn. of Research Libs., Chief Officers of State Lib. Agencies, Medical Lib. Assn., Special Libs. Assn., Urban Libs. Council, Chinese American Libns. Assn., Polish American Lib. Assn.

Institutional Members

More than 100 libraries and related institutions are institutional members or consultative bodies and sponsors of IFLA in the United States (out of a total of more than 1,000 globally), and more than 100 are individual affiliates (out of a total of more than 300 affiliates globally).

International Organization for Standardization

Sergio Mujica, Secretary-General
ISO Central Secretariat, Chemin de Blandonnet 8, CP 4011214 Vernier, Geneva, Switzerland
Tel. 41-22-749-01-11, fax 41-22-733-34-30, e-mail central@iso.org
World Wide Web http://www.iso.org

Objective

Founded in 1947, the International Organization for Standardization (ISO) is a worldwide federation of national standards bodies that currently comprises members from 164 countries and 785 technical committees and subcommittees working on various aspects of standards development. The objective of ISO is to promote the development of standardization and related activities in the world with a view to facilitating international exchange of goods and services, and to developing cooperation in the spheres of intellectual, scientific, technological, and economic activity. The scope of ISO covers international standardization in all fields except electrical and electronic engineering standardization, which is the responsibility of the International Electrotechnical Commission (IEC). The results of ISO technical work are published as international standards.

Officers

Pres. Eddy Njoroge, Kenya; *V.P.s* Scott Steedman, UK *(Policy)*, Sauw Kook Choy, Singapore *(Technical Management)*, Mitsuo Matsumoto, Japan *(Finance)*; *Treas.* Dominique Christin, Switzerland; *Secy.-Gen.* Sergio Mujica, Chile.

Technical Work

The technical work of ISO is carried out by groups of experts collaborating worldwide, representing every imaginable sector, from soaps to spacecraft, from MP3 to coffee. Among its technical committees are

ISO/TC 46—Information and documentation (Secretariat, Association Française de Normalization, 11 ave. Francis de Pressensé, 93571 La Plaine Saint-Denis, Cedex, France). Scope: Standardization of practices relating to libraries, documentation and information centers, indexing and abstracting services, archives, information science, and publishing.

ISO/TC 37—Language and terminology (Secretariat, Standardization Administration of China, No. 9 Madian Donglu, Haidian District, Beijing 100088, China). Scope: Standardization of descriptions, resources, technologies, and services related to terminology, translation, interpreting, and other language-based activities in the multilingual information society.

ISO/IEC JTC 1—Information technology (Secretariat, American National Standards Institute, 1899 L St. NW, 11th Fl., Washington, DC 20036). Scope: Standardization in the field of information technology.

ISO Annual Report.

ISOfocus (6x yearly).

Extensive selection of titles on the ISO website (https://www.iso.org/publication-list.html).

Foreign Library Associations

The following is a list of regional and national library associations around the world. A more complete list can be found in *International Literary Market Place* (Information Today, Inc.).

Regional

Africa

Standing Conference of Eastern, Central, and Southern African Lib. and Info. Assns. (SCECSAL), c/o General-Secretary, Uganda Library and Information Association, P.O. Box 5894, Kampala, Uganda. Tel. +256-772-488937, +256-782-617623, +256-782-42204, e-mail info@ulia.or.ug, World Wide Web https://www.scecsal.org/.

The Americas

Assn. of Caribbean Univ., Research, and Institutional Libs. (ACURIL), P.O. Box 21337, San Juan, Puerto Rico 00931. Tel. 787-612-9343, e-mail executivesecretariat@acuril.org, World Wide Web https://acuril.org. *Pres.* Anne Pajard; *Exec. Secy.* Luisa Vigo-Cepeda.

Seminar on the Acquisition of Latin American Lib. Materials (SALALM), c/o SALALM Secretariat, Latin American Lib., 422 Howard Tilton Memorial Lib., Tulane Univ., 7001 Freret St., New Orleans, LA 70118-5549. Tel. 504-247-1366, fax 504-247-1367, e-mail salalm@tulane.edu, World Wide Web https://salalm.org. *Exec. Dir.* Hortensia Calvo. E-mail hcalvo@tulane.edu.

Asia

Congress of Southeast Asian Libns. (CONSAL), # Razathingaha Road, Nearby Razathingaha Circle, Uottra Thiri TSP, Naypyitaw, Myanmar. Tel. 95 67 418427, fax 95 67 418426, e-mail info@consalxvii.org, World Wide Web https://www.facebook.com/consal.sec/.

The Commonwealth

Commonwealth Lib. Assn. (COMLA), c/o University of the West Indies, Bridgetown Campus, Learning Resource Center, P.O. Box 64, Bridgetown, Barbados. Tel. 246-417-4201, fax 246-424-8944, e-mail watsone@uwichill.edu.bb, World Wide Web https://uia.org/s/or/en/1100024839.

U.K. Library and Archives Group on Africa (SCOLMA), c/o Sarah Rhodes, Bodleian Social Science Lib., Univ. of Oxford, Manor Rd. Bldg., Manor Rd., Oxford OX1 3UQ, England. Tel. 01865-277162, World Wide Web http://scolma.org. *Chair* Lucy McCann; *Secy.* Sarah Rhodes.

Europe

European Bureau of Library, Information and Documentation Associations (EBLID), c/o EBLIDA Secretariat, Koninklijke Bibliotheek (National Library of the Netherlands), Prins Willem-Alexanderhof 5, 2595 BE, The Hague. Tel. 31 (0) 70 3140137, e-mail eblida@eblida.org, World Wide Web http://www.eblida.org.

Ligue des Bibliothèques Européennes de Recherche (LIBER) (Assn. of European Research Libs.), P.O. Box 90407, 2509 LK The Hague, Netherlands. Tel. 31-70-314-07-67, fax 070-314-01-97, e-mail liber@kb.nl, World Wide Web http://www.libereurope.eu. *Pres.* Jeannette Frey; *V.P.* Julien Roche; *Secy.-Gen.* John MacColl; *Exec. Dir.* Astrid Verheusen.

National

Argentina

ABGRA (Asociación de Bibliotecarios Graduados de la República Argentina) (Assn. of Graduate Libns. of Argentina), Paraná 918, 2do Piso, C1017AAT Buenos Aires. Tel. 54-11-4811-0043, fax 54-11-4816-3422, e-mail info@abgra.org.ar, World Wide Web http://www.abgra.org.ar.

Australia

Australian Lib. and Info. Assn., Box 6335, Kingston, ACT 2604. Tel. 61-2-6215-8222, fax 61-2-6282-2249, e-mail enquiry@alia.org.au, World Wide Web http://www.alia.org.au. *CEO* Sue McKerracher. E-mail sue.mckerracher@alia.org.au.

Australian Society of Archivists, P.O. Box 576, Crows Nest, NSW 1585. Tel. 612-9431-8644, e-mail office@archivists.org.au, World Wide Web http://www.archivists.org.au. *Pres.* Julia Mant; *V.P.* Nicola Laurent.

National and State Libs. Australia (NSLA), State Lib. Victoria, 328 Swanston St., Melbourne VIC 3000. Tel. 03 8664 7512, e-mail nsla@slv.vic.gov.au, World Wide Web https://www.nsla.org.au. *Chair* Marie-Louise Ayers.

Austria

Österreichische Gesellschaft für Dokumentation und Information (Austrian Society for Documentation and Info.), c/o Österreichische Computer Gesellschaft OCG, Wollzeile 1, 1010 Vienna. E-mail office@oegdi.at, World Wide Web http://www.oegdi.at. *Chair* Gerhard Frohlich.

Vereinigung Österreichischer Bibliothekarinnen und Bibliothekare (VOEB) (Assn. of Austrian Libns.), Universitätsbibliothek Graz, Universitätsplatz 3, 8010 Graz. E-mail voeb@ub.tuwein.ac.at, World Wide Web http://www.univie.ac.at/voeb/php. *President* Mag. Bruno Bauer. E-mail bruno.bauer@meduniwien.ac.at.

Bangladesh

Bangladesh Assn. of Libns., Info. Scientists and Documentalists (BALID), House # 67/B (3rd floor), Road # 9/A, Dhanmondi, Dhaka-1209, Bangladesh. E-mail balidbd@gmail.com, info@balidbd.org, World Wide Web https://www.balid.org.

Belgium

Archief- en Bibliotheekwezen in België (Belgian Assn. of Archivists and Libns.), Royal Library of Belgium, Boulevard de l'Empereur 2, 1000 Brussels. Tel. 2-519-53-93, fax 2-519-56-10, e-mail abb@kbr.be, World Wide Web http://www.archibib.be.

Assn. Belge de Documentation/Belgische Vereniging voor Documentatie (Belgian Assn. for Documentation), 4 Boulevard de l'Empereur, 1000 Bruxelles. Tel. 2-675-58-62, fax 2-672-74-46, e-mail abdbvd@abd-bvd.be, World Wide Web http://www.abd-bvd.be. *Pres.* Guy Delsaut. E-mail guy.delsaut@skynet.be; *Secy.-Gen.* Michele Orban. E-mail michele.orban@gmail.com.

Association des Professionales des Bibliothèques Francophones de Belgique (APBFB), Rue Nanon 98, 5002 Namur. Tel. 32-472-94-12-05, e-mail info@apbfb.be, World Wide Web http://www.apbfb.be. *Pres.* Françoise Dury.

Association Professionnelle des Bibliothécaires et Documentalistes. See Association des Professionales des Bibliothèques Francophones de Belgique (APBFB).

Vlaamse Vereniging voor Bibliotheek-, Archief-, en Documentatiewezen (Flemish Assn. of Libns., Archivists, and Documentalists), Statiestraat 179, B-2600 Berchem, Antwerp. Tel. 3-281-44-57, e-mail vvbad@vvbad.be, World Wide Web http://www.vvbad.be. *Coord.* Jessica Jacobs. E-mail jessica.jacobs@vvbad.be.

Belize

Belize National Lib. Service and Info. System (BNLSIS), P.O. Box 287, Princess Margaret Dr., Belize City. Tel. 501-223-4248, fax 501-223-4246, e-mail nls@btl.net, World Wide Web http://www.nlsbze.bz.

Bolivia

Centro Nacional de Documentación Científica y Tecnológica (National Scientific and Technological Documentation Center), Av. Mariscal Santa Cruz 1175, Esquina c Ayacucho, La Paz. Tel. 02-359-583, fax 02-359-586, e-mail iiicndct@huayna.umsa.edu.bo, World Wide Web http://www.bolivian.com/industrial/cndct.

Bosnia and Herzegovina

Drustvo Bibliotekara Bosne i Hercegovine (Libns. Society of Bosnia and Herzegovina),

Zmaja od Bosne 8B, 71000 Sarajevo. Tel. 33-275-301, e-mail nubbih@nub.ba, World Wide Web http://www.nub.ba. *Pres.* Ismet Ovcina. E-mail ured.direktora@nub.ba.

Botswana

Botswana Lib. Assn., Box 1310, Gaborone. Tel. 267-732-31047, e-mail secretary@bla.org.bw, World Wide Web http://www.bla.org.bw. *Pres.* Lynn Jabril. E-mail president@bla.org.bw.

Brunei Darussalam

Persatuan Perpustakaan Negara Brunei Darussalam (National Lib. Assn. of Brunei), c/o Class 64 Lib., SOASC, Jalan Tengah, Bandar Seri Begawan BS8411. Fax 2-222-330, e-mail pobox.bla@gmail.com, World Wide Web http://bruneilibraryassociation.wordpress.com.

Cameroon

Assn. des Bibliothécaires, Archivistes, Documentalistes et Muséographes du Cameroun (Assn. of Libns., Archivists, Documentalists, and Museum Curators of Cameroon), BP 12092, Yaoundé. Tel. 237-2-22-22-28-98, e-mail abadcameroun@gmail.com, World Wide Web http://www.abadcam.sitew.com. *Pres.* Alim Garga. E-mail a_garga@yahoo.fr.

Chile

Colegio de Bibliotecarios de Chile (Chilean Lib. Assn.), Avda. Diagonal Paraguay 383, Torre 11, Oficina 122, 6510017 Santiago. Tel. 2-222-5652, e-mail cbc@bibliotecarios.cl, World Wide Web http://www.bibliotecarios.cl. *Pres.* Gabriel Díaz Morales.

China

China Society for Lib. Science, 33 Zhongguancun Nandajie, Hai Dian District, Beijing 100081. Tel. 86-10-8854-4114, fax 86-10-6841-7815, e-mail webmaster@nlc.gov.cn, World Wide Web http://www.nlc.cn/newen/.

Colombia

Asociación Colombiana de Bibliotecólogos y Documentalistas (Colombian Assn. of Libns. and Documentalists), Calle 21, No. 6-58, Oficina 404, Bogotá D.C. Tel. 1-282-3620, fax 1-282-5487, e-mail secretaria@ascolbi.org, World Wide Web http://www.ascolbi.org. *Pres.* Leonardo Ramírez O.

Congo (Republic of)

Assn. des Bibliothécaires, Archivistes, Documentalistes et Muséologues du Congo (ABADOM) (Assn. of Librarians, Archivists, Documentalists, and Museologists of Congo), BP 3148, Kinshasa-Gombe. E-mail bernardakondzo72@gmail.com.

Croatia

Hrvatsko Knjiznicarsko Drustvo (Croatian Lib. Assn.), c/o National and Univ. Lib., Hrvatske bratske zajednice 4, 10 000 Zagreb. Tel./fax 1-615-93-20, e-mail hkd@nsk.hr, World Wide Web http://www.hkdrustvo.hr. *Pres.* Dijana Machala; *Secy.* Andreja Tominac.

Cuba

Asociación Cubana de Bibliotecarios (ASCUBI) (Lib. Assn. of Cuba), P.O. Box 6670, Havana. Tel. 7-555-442, fax 7-816-224, e-mail ascubi@bnjm.cu, World Wide Web http://ascubi.blogspot.com/. *Chair* Margarita Bellas Vilariño. E-mail ascubi@bnjm.cu.

Cyprus

Kypriakos Synthesmos Vivliothicarion (Lib. Assn. of Cyprus), c/o Pedagogical Academy, P.O. Box 1039, Nicosia. E-mail kebepcy@gmail.com, World Wide Web http://kebep.blogspot.com.

Czech Republic

Svaz Knihovniku a Informacnich Pracovniku Ceske Republiky (SKIP) (Assn. of Lib. and Info. Professionals of the Czech Republic), National Library of the Czech Republic, Mariánské náměstí 190/5, 110 00 Prague 1.

Tel. 420-221-663-379, fax 420-221-663-175, e-mail skip@nkp.cz, World Wide Web https://www.skipcr.cz/. *Chair Mgr.* Roman Giebisch.

Denmark

Arkivforeningen (Archives Society), Ingrid Nostberg, Vestfoldmuseene IKS, Department Vestfoldarkivet, 3205 Sandefjord. Tel. 958 21 501, e-mail post@arkivarforeningen.no, World Wide Web http://www.arkivarforeningen.no. *Deputy Chair* Ingrid Nostberg.

Danmarks Biblioteksforening (Danish Lib. Assn.), Vartov, Farvergade 27D, 1463 Copenhagen K. Tel. 3325-0935, fax 3325-7900, e-mail db@db.dk, World Wide Web http://www.db.dk. *Director* Michel Steen-Hansen. E-mail msh@db.dk.

Danmarks Forskningsbiblioteksforening (Danish Research Lib. Assn.), c/o University of Southern Denmark, Studiestræde 6, 1455 Copenhagen K. Tel. 45-4220-2177, e-mail secretariat@dfdf.dk, World Wide Web http://www.dfdf.dk. *Pres.* Bertil Dorch. E-mail bfd@bib.sdu.dk.

Dansk Musikbiblioteks Forening (Assn. of Danish Music Libs.), c/o Helene Olsen, Sundby Library, Jemtelandsgade 3, Copenhagen S. E-mail sekretariat@dmbf.nu, World Wide Web http://www.dmbf.nu. *Chair* Emilie Wieth-Knudsen. E-mail emwk@ltk.dk.

Kommunernes Forening for Paedagogiske Laeringscentre (Municipal Association of Educational Learning Centers—KFPLC), The Old Town Hall, Industrivej 2, 4683 Ronnede. Tel. 33-11-13-91, e-mail kfplc@kfplc.dk, World Wide Web http://www.kfplc.dk. *Chair* Michael Nohr; *Mgr.* Gitte Frausing. E-mail gf@ksbf.dk.

Ecuador

Asociación Ecuatoriana de Bibliotecarios (Ecuadoran Lib. Assn.), c/o Casa de la Cultura Ecuatoriana, Casillas 87, Quito. E-mail asoecubiblio@gmail.com, World Wide Web http://aeb-nacional.blogspot.com/.

El Salvador

Asociación de Bibliotecarios de El Salvador (ABES) (Assn. of Salvadorian Libns.), Járdines de la Hacienda Block D pje, 19 No. 158, Ciudad Merliot, Antiguo Cuscatlán, La Libertad. Tel. 503-2534-8924, fax 523-2228-2956, e-mail abeselsalvador@gmail.com, World Wide Web https://www.facebook.com/AbesAsociacionDeBibliotecariosDeElSalvador/. *Pres.* Claudia Oviedo.

Finland

Suomen Kirjastoseura (Finnish Lib. Assn.), Runeberginkatu 15 A 6, 00100 Helsinki. Tel. 44-522-2941, e-mail info@fla.fi, World Wide Web http://www.fla.fi. *Exec. Dir.* Rauha Maarno. E-mail rauha.maarno@fla.fi.

France

Association des Archivistes Français (Assn. of French Archivists), 8 rue Jean-Marie Jego, 75013 Paris. Tel. 1-46-06-39-44, fax 1-46-06-39-52, e-mail secretariat@archivistes.org, World Wide Web http://www.archivistes.org.

Association des Bibliothécaires Français (Assn. of French Libns.), 31 rue de Chabrol, F-75010 Paris. Tel. 1-55-33-10-30, fax 1-55-30-10-31, e-mail info@abf.asso.fr, World Wide Web http://www.abf.asso.fr. *Chair* Alice Bernard; *Gen. Secy.* Chantal Ferreux.

Association des Professionnels de l'Information et de la Documentation (Assn. of Info. and Documentation Professionals), 25 rue Claude Tillier, 75012 Paris. Tel. 06-81-39-82-14, e-mail adbs@adbs.fr, World Wide Web http://www.adbs.fr. *Pres.* Danielle DuFour-Coppolani.

Germany

Arbeitsgemeinschaft der Spezialbibliotheken (Assn. of Special Libs.), c/o Wissenschaftskolleg zu Berlin—Bibliothek, Wallotstr. 19, 14193 Berlin. Tel. 030-89001-144, fax 030-89001-400, e-mail geschaeftsstelle@aspb.de, World Wide Web http://aspb.de. *Chair*

Kirsten Schoof. E-mail kirsten.schoof@aesthetics.mpg.de.

Berufsverband Information Bibliothek (Assn. of Info. and Lib. Professionals), Geschäftsstelle, Postfach 13 24, D-72703 Reutlingen. Tel. 7121-3491-0, fax 7121-3491-34, e-mail mail@bib-info.de, World Wide Web http://www.bib-info.de.

Deutsche Gesellschaft für Informationswissenschaft und Informationspraxis eV (German Society for Information Science and Practice eV), Windmühlstr. 3, 60329 Frankfurt-am-Main. Tel. 69-43-03-13, fax 69-490-90-96, e-mail mail@dgi-info.de, World Wide Web http://www.dgi-info.de. *Pres.* Margarita Reibel-Felten.

Deutscher Bibliotheksverband eV (German Lib. Assn.), Fritschestr. 27–28, 10585 Berlin. Tel. 30-644-98-99-10, fax 30-644-98-99-29, e-mail dbv@bibliotheksverband.de, World Wide Web http://www.bibliotheksverband.de. *Dir.* Barbara Schleihagen.

VdA—Verband Deutscher Archivarinnen und Archivare (Assn. of German Archivists), Woerthstr. 3, 36037 Fulda. Tel. 661-29-109-72, fax 661-29-109-74, e-mail info@vda.archiv.net, World Wide Web http://www.vda.archiv.net. *Chair* Ralf Jacob.

Verein Deutscher Bibliothekare eV (Society of German Libns.), Univ. Lib. Erlangen-Nürnberg, Universitatsstrasse 4, 91054 Erlangen. Tel. 09131-85-22150, e-mail geschaeftsstelle@vdb-online.org, World Wide Web http://www.vdb-online.org. *Chair* Konstanze Söllner. E-mail chairman@vdb-online.org.

Ghana

Ghana Lib. Assn., Box GP 4105, Accra. Tel. 244-17-4930, e-mail info@gla-net.org, World Wide Web http://gla-net.org. *Pres.* Samuel B. Aggrey.

Greece

Enosis Hellinon Bibliothekarion (Association of Greek Librarians), Akadimias 84, PC 106 78, Athens. Tel./fax 210-330-2128, e-mail info-eebep@eebep.gr, World Wide Web http://www.eebep.gr. *Pres.* Alexandra Papazoglou; *Secy.* Eva Semertaki.

Guyana

Guyana Lib. Assn., c/o Department of Public Information, Area 'B' Homestretch Ave., D'Urban Park, Georgetown. Tel. 592-226-6715, fax 592-227-4052, e-mail info@dpi.gov.gy, World Wide Web https://dpi.gov.gy/tag/guyana-library-association/.

Hong Kong

Hong Kong Lib. Assn., GPO Box 10095, Hong Kong, China. E-mail hkla@hkla.org, World Wide Web http://www.hkla.org. *Pres.* Owen Man Lik Tam. E-mail president@hkla.org. *Secy.* Wong Hoi Yan Wendy. E-mail membership@hkla.org.

Hungary

Magyar Könyvtárosok Egyesülete (Assn. of Hungarian Libns.), H-1054, Hold u 6, Budapest. Tel./fax 1-311-8634, e-mail mke@oszk.hu, World Wide Web http://www.mke.info.hu. *Chair* Dr. Ágnes Hajdu; *Secy. Gen.* Judit Gerencsér.

Iceland

Upplysing—Felag bokasafns-og upplysingafraeoa (Information—The Icelandic Lib. and Info. Science Assn.), Mailbox 8865, 128 Reykjavík. Tel. 354-864-6220, e-mail upplysing@upplysing.is, World Wide Web http://www.upplysing.is. *Chair* Oddfrídur Steinunn Helgadóttir. E-mail formadur@upplysing.is.

India

Indian Assn. of Special Libs. and Info. Centres, P-291, CIT Scheme 6M, Kankurgachi, Kolkata 700-054. Tel. 33-2362-9651, e-mail iaslic@vsnl.net, World Wide Web http://www.iaslic1955.org.in. *President* Narendra Lahkar; *Gen. Secy.* Abhijit Kumar.

Indian Lib. Assn., A/40-41, Flat 201, Ansal Bldg., Mukerjee Nagar, New Delhi 110009. Tel./fax 11-2765-1743, e-mail dvs-srcc@rediffmail.com, World Wide Web http://www.ilaindia.net. *Pres.* B. D. Kumbar; *Gen. Secy.* O. N. Chaubey.

Indonesia

Ikatan Pustakawan Indonesia (Indonesian Lib. Assn.), Jl. Salemba Raya, RT.8 / RW.8, Kramat Senen, Kota Jakarta Pusat, DKI Jakarta 10430. Tel. (021) 3900944, World Wide Web http://ipi.web.id.

Ireland

Cumann Leabharlann na hEireann (Lib. Assn. of Ireland), c/o 138–144 Pearse St., Dublin 2. E-mail honsecretary@libraryassociation.ie, World Wide Web http://www.libraryassociation.ie. *Pres.* Philip Cohen. E-mail president@libraryassociation.ie. *Hon. Secy.* Eimear McGinn. E-mail honsecretary@libraryassociation.ie.

Israel

Israeli Center for Libs., 22 Baruch Hirsch St., P.O. Box 801, 51108 Bnei Brak. Tel. 03-6180151, fax 03-5798048, e-mail meida@gmail.com or icl@icl.org.il, World Wide Web http://www.icl.org.il. *CEO* Zvika Mier. E-mail zvika@icl.org.il.

Italy

Associazione Italiana Biblioteche (Italian Lib. Assn.), Biblioteca Nazionale Centrale, Viale Castro Pretorio 105, 00185 Rome RM. Tel. 6-446-3532, fax 6-444-1139, e-mail segreteria@aib.it, World Wide Web http://www.aib.it.

Jamaica

Lib. and Info. Assn. of Jamaica, P.O. Box 125, Kingston 5. Tel./fax 876-927-1614, e-mail liajapresident@yahoo.com, World Wide Web http://www.liaja.org.jm.

Japan

Info. Science and Technology Assn., 1-11-14, Shinkawa, Chuo-ku, Tokyo 104-0033. Tel. 81-3-6222-8506, fax 81-3-6222-8107, e-mail infosta@infosta.or.jp, World Wide Web http://www.infosta.or.jp.

Nihon Toshokan Kyokai (Japan Lib. Assn.), 1-11-14 Shinkawa, Chuo-ku, Tokyo 104 0033. Tel. 3-3523-0811, fax 3-3523-0841, e-mail info@jla.or.jp, World Wide Web http://www.jla.or.jp.

Senmon Toshokan Kyogikai (Japan Special Libs. Assn.), c/o Japan Lib. Assn., Bldg. F6, 1-11-14 Shinkawa Chuo-ku, Tokyo 104-0033. Tel. 3-3537-8335, fax 3-3537-8336, e-mail jsla@jsla.or.jp, World Wide Web http://www.jsla.or.jp.

Jordan

Jordan Lib. and Info. Assn., P.O. Box 6289, Amman 11118. Tel./fax 00962-64629412, World Wide Web http://jlia.org/component/content/en. *Pres.* Naguib Al-Sharbaji.

Kenya

Kenya Assn. of Lib. and Info. Professionals (formerly Kenya Lib. Assn.), Buruburu, P.O. Box 49468-00100 Nairobi. Tel. 20-733-732-799, e-mail info@kenyalibraryassociation.or.ke, World Wide Web http://www.kenyalibraryassociation.or.ke.

Korea (Democratic People's Republic of)

Lib. Assn. of the Democratic People's Republic of Korea, c/o Grand People's Study House, P.O. Box 200, Pyongyang. E-mail korea@korea-dpr.com.

Korea (Republic of)

Korean Lib. Assn., San 60-1, Banpo-dong, Seocho-gu, Seoul 137-702. Tel. 2-535-4868, fax 2-535-5616, e-mail license@kla.kr, World Wide Web http://www.kla.kr. *Pres.* Nam Young-joon.

Laos

Association des Bibliothécaires Laotiens (Lao Lib. Assn.), c/o Direction de la Bibliothèque Nationale, Ministry of Educ., BP 704, Vientiane. Tel. 21-21-2452, fax 21-21-2408, e-mail bailane@laotel.com.

Latvia

Latvian Libns. Assn., c/o Latvian National Lib., Mukusalas iela 3, Riga, LV-1423. Tel.

67806100, fax 67280851, e-mail lnb@lnb.lv, World Wide Web http://www.lnb.lv.

Lebanon

Lebanese Lib. Assn., P.O. Box 13-5053, Beirut 1102 2801. Tel. 1-786-456, e-mail kjaroudy@lau.edu.lb, World Wide Web http://www.lebaneselibraryassociation.org/. *Pres.* Fawz Abdallah. E-mail fabdallas@gmail.com.

Lesotho

Lesotho Lib. Assn., 988782, Our Street, L.A. Tel. +266 6212 1281 | 6300 2119, e-mail info@lla.co.ls, World Wide Web https://lla.org.ls. *Pres.* Kubelo Tsiki.

Lithuania

Lietuvos Bibliotekininkų Draugija (Lithuanian Libns. Assn.), Gedimino pr. 51, Vilnius, LT-01504. Tel. 370-5-231-8585, e-mail lbd.sekretore@gmail.com, World Wide Web http://www.lbd.lt. *Chair* Jolita Stephonaitiene. E-mail jolita.stephonaitiene@lnb.lt.

Luxembourg

Association Luxembourgeoise des Bibliothécaires, Archivistes, et Documentalistes (ALBAD) (Luxembourg Assn. of Libns., Archivists, and Documentalists), c/o National Lib. of Luxembourg, BP 295, L-2012 Luxembourg. Tel. 352-621-46-14-15, World Wide Web http://www.albad.lu. *Pres.* Estelle Beck. E-mail presidence@albad.lu. *Secy. Gen.* Bernard Linster. E-mail secretarie@albad.lu.

Malaysia

Persatuan Pustakawan Malaysia (Libns. Assn. of Malaysia), P.O. Box 12545, 50782 Kuala Lumpur. Tel./fax 3-2694-7390, e-mail pustakawan55@gmail.com, World Wide Web http://ppm55.org. *Pres.* Dato 'Nafisah binti Ahmad. E-mail nafisah@pnm.gov.my.

Mali

Association Malienne des Bibliothécaires, Archivistes et Documentalistes (Mali Assn. of Libns., Archivists, and Documentalists) (AMBAD), BP E4473, Bamako. Tel. 20-29-94-23, fax 20-29-93-76, e-mail dnambko@afribone.net.ml.

Malta

Malta Lib. and Info. Assn. (MaLIA), c/o Univ. of Malta Lib., Msida MSD 2080. E-mail info@malia-malta.org, World Wide Web https://www.facebook.com/malia.malta/. *CEO* Cheryl Falzon.

Mauritania

Association Mauritanienne des Bibliothécaires, Archivistes, et Documentalistes (Mauritanian Assn. of Libns., Archivists, and Documentalists), c/o Bibliothèque Nationale, BP 20, Nouakchott. Tel. 525-18-62, fax 525-18-68, e-mail bibliothequenationale@yahoo.fr.

Mauritius

Mauritius Lib. Assn., Quatre Bornes, Mauritius 230. Tel. 230 5769 7392, fax 454-9553, e-mail mauritiuslibassociation@gmail.com, World Wide Web https://www.facebook.com/Mauritius-Library-Association-MLA-142991592578201/.

Mexico

Asociación Mexicana de Bibliotecarios (Mexican Assn. of Libns.), Angel Urraza 817-A, Colonia Del Valle, Benito Juárez, Mexico DF, CP 03100. Tel. 55-55-75-33-96, e-mail correo@ambac.org.mx, World Wide Web http://www.ambac.org.mx. *Pres.* Marisela Castro Moreno; *V.P.* Brenda Cabral Vargas.

Myanmar

Myanmar Lib. Assn., Room 003, Diamond Jubilee Hall, Yangon University, Yangon, Myanmar. Tel. 95-9-420728446, e-mail libraryassociation@mlamyanmar.org, World Wide Web http://myanmarlibraryassociation.org. *Pres.* Daw Ah Win.

Namibia

Namibia Information Workers Assn., P.O. Box 308, Windhoek. Tel. 264-8148-10713, e-mail niwaassociation@gmail.com, World

Wide Web http://www.niwa-namibia.org. *Chair* Elizabeth Matheus.

Nepal

Nepal Lib. Assn., KVPL, Bhrikuti Mandap, Kathmandu. Tel. 01-4221163, e-mail nepal libraryassociation@gmail.com, World Wide Web https://nla.org.np/. *Pres.* Indraprasad Adhikari. *Secy.* Reshma Dangol.

The Netherlands

KNVI—Koninklijke Nederlandse Vereniging van Informatieprofessionals (Royal Dutch Association of Information Professionals), Ambachtsstraat 15, 3861 RH Nijkerk. Tel. 033-2473427, e-mail info@knvi.nl, World Wide Web http://knvi.nl. *Co-Chairs* Paul Baak, Wouter Bronsgeest.

New Zealand

New Zealand Lib. Assn. (LIANZA), 70 Molesworth St., Wellington 6140. Tel. 027-347-5326, e-mail officeadmin@lianza.org.nz, World Wide Web http://www.lianza.org.nz. *Pres.* Rachel Esson.

Nicaragua

Asociación Nicaraguense de Bibliotecarios y Profesionales Afines (ANIBIPA) (Nicaraguan Assn. of Libns.), Bello Horizonte, Tope Sur de la Rotonda 1/2 cuadra abajo, J-11-57, Managua. Tel. 277-4159, e-mail anibipa@hotmail.com. World Wide Web https://www.facebook.com/ANIBIPA.

Nigeria

National Lib. of Nigeria, Central Business District, P.M.B. 1 Garki—Abuja, 900001. Tel. 09-234-6773, e-mail info@nln.gov.ng, World Wide Web https://www.nln.gov.ng/. *Chair* Zaynab Alkhali.

Norway

Arkivar Foreningen (Assn. of Archivists), Vestfoldmuseene IKS. department Vestfoldarkivet, 3205 Sandefjord. Tel. 936 56 026, e-mail post@arkivarforeningen.no, World Wide Web http://www.arkivarforeningen.no/. *Deputy Chair* Ingrid Nostberg.

Norsk Bibliotekforening (Norwegian Lib. Assn.), Universitetsgata 14, 0164 Oslo. Tel. 23 24 34 30, e-mail nbf@norskbibliotekforening.no, World Wide Web https://norskbibliotekforening.no/. *Dir.* Mariann Schjeide. *Gen. Secy.* Ann Berit Hulthin. E-mail abh@norskbibliotekforening.no.

Panama

Asociación Panameña de Bibliotecarios (Lib. Assn. of Panama), c/o Biblioteca Interamericana Simón Bolivar, Estafeta Universitaria, Panama City. E-mail biblis2@arcon.up.ac.pa, Tel. 507-6527-1904, e-mail ocastillos@hotmail.com, World Wide Web https://www.facebook.com/asociacionpanamenabibliotecarios/info.

Paraguay

Asociación de Bibliotecarios Graduados del Paraguay (Assn. of Paraguayan Graduate Libns.), Facultad Politécnica, Universidad Nacional de Asunción, 2160 San Lorenzo. Tel. 21-585-588, e-mail abigrap@pol.una.py, World Wide Web http://www.pol.una.py/abigrap. *Chair* Emilce Sena Correa, e-mail esena@pol.una.py.

Peru

Asociación Peruana de Archiveros y Gestores de la Información (Peruvian Assn. of Archivists and Info. Managers), Av. Manco Capac No. 1180, Dpto 201, La Victoria, Lima. Tel. 51-934-182079, e-mail contacto@archiverosdelperu.org, World Wide Web http://archiverosdelperu.org/. *Pres.* Ricardo Arturo Moreau Heredia.

Philippines

Assn. of Special Libs. of the Philippines, c/o Goethe-Institut Philippinen, G/4-5/F Adamson Centre, 121 Leviste St., Salcedo Village, 1227 Makati City. Tel. 2-840-5723, e-mail aslplibrarians@gmail.com, World Wide Web https://aslplibrarians.org/home. *Pres.* Brian Lloyd Dayrit.

Philippine Libns. Assn., Room 301, National Lib. Bldg., T. M. Kalaw St., 1000 Ermita, Manila. Tel. 525-9401. World Wide Web http://plai.org.ph. *Pres.* Emma Rey.

Poland

Stowarzyszenie Bibliotekarzy Polskich (Polish Libns. Assn.), al Niepodleglosci 213, 02-086 Warsaw. Tel. 22-608-28-24, e-mail biuro@sbp.pl, World Wide Web http://www.sbp.pl. *Dir.* Anna Grzecznowska. E-mail a.grzecznowska@sbp.pl; *Secy.* Małgorzata Dargiel-Kowalska. E-mail m.dargiel-kowalska@sbp.pl.

Portugal

Associação Portuguesa de Bibliotecários, Arquivistas e Documentalistas (Portuguese Assn. of Libns., Archivists, and Documentalists), Praça Dr. Nuno Pinheiro Torres 10-A, 15500 246 Lisbon. Tel. 21-816-19-80, fax 21-815-45-08, e-mail bad@bad.pt, World Wide Web http://www.apbad.pt.

Puerto Rico

Sociedad de Bibliotecarios de Puerto Rico (Society of Libns. of Puerto Rico), Apdo 22898, San Juan 00931-2898. Tel./fax 787-764-0000, World Wide Web http://www.sociedadbibliotecarios.org. *Pres.* Milady Pérez Gerana.

Russia

Rossiiskaya Bibliotechnaya Assotsiatsiya (Russian Lib. Assn.), 18 Sadovaya St., St. Petersburg 191069. Tel./fax 812-110-5861, e-mail rba@nlr.ru, World Wide Web http://www.rba.ru. *Exec. Secy.* Trushina Irina Aleksandrovna.

Senegal

Association Sénégalaise des Bibliothécaires, Archivistes et Documentalistes (Senegalese Assn. of Libns., Archivists, and Documentalists), BP 2006, Dakar RP, Université Cheikh Anta Diop, Dakar. Tel. 77-651-00-33, fax 33-824-23-79, e-mail asbadsn@gmail.com, World Wide Web http://www.twitter.com/asbadsn.

Serbia

Jugoslovenski Bibliografski Informacijski Institut, Terazije 26, 11000 Belgrade. Tel. 11-2687-836, fax 11-2687-760.

Sierra Leone

Sierra Leone Assn. of Archivists, Libns., and Info. Scientists, 7 Percival Street, Freetown. Tel. 022-220-758.

Singapore

Lib. Assn. of Singapore, National Lib. Board, 100 Victoria St., No. 14-01, Singapore 188064. Tel. 6332-3255, fax 6332-3248, e-mail lassec@las.org.sg, World Wide Web http://www.las.org.sg. *Pres.* Tan Chui Peng. E-mail president@las.org.sg.

Slovenia

Zveza Bibliotekarskih Društev Slovenije (Union of Assns. of Slovene Libns.), Turjaöka 1, 1000 Ljubljana. Tel. 1-2001-176, fax 1-4257-293, e-mail info@zbds-zveza.si, World Wide Web http://www.zbds-zveza.si. *Pres.* Sabina Fras Popovic. E-mail sabina.fras-popovic@mb.sik.si.

South Africa

Lib. and Info. Assn. of South Africa, P.O. Box 1598, Pretoria 0001. Tel. 27 (0) 12-328-2010, 27 (0) 12-323-4912, fax 27 (0) 12-323-1033, e-mail liasa@liasa.org.za, World Wide Web http://www.liasa.org.za. *Pres.* Nikki Crowster. E-mail nikki.crowster@uct.ac.za.

Spain

Federación Española de Archiveros, Bibliotecarios, Arqueólogos, Museólogos y Documentalistas (ANABAD) (Spanish Federation of Assns. of Archivists, Libns., Archaeologists, Museum Curators, and Documentalists), de las Huertas, 37, 28014 Madrid. Tel. 91-575-1727, fax 91-578-1615, e-mail anabad@anabad.org, World Wide Web http://www.anabad.org. *Pres.* José María Nogales Herrera.

Sri Lanka

Sri Lanka Lib. Assn., Sri Lanka Professional Centre 275/75, Stanley Wijesundara Mawatha, Colombo 7. Tel./fax 11-258-9103, e-mail slla@slltnet.lk, World Wide Web http://www.slla.org.lk. *Pres.* N. D. Wijayasundara, e-mail nayanaw@sjp.ac.lk;

Gen. Secy. Ms. Lilamani Amerasekara lila amerasekera@gmail.com.

Sweden

Foreningen for Archiv & Informationsforvaltening (Society of Archives and Records Management in Sweden—FAI), c/o Foreningshuset Sedab AB, Virkesvägen 26, 120 30 Stockholm. Tel. 08-121 513 21, e-mail info@fai.nu, World Wide Web https://fai.nu. *Pres.* Katarina Ekelof.

Svensk Biblioteksförening (Swedish Lib. Assn.), Oxtorgsgrand 2, 111 57 Stockholm. Tel. 08-545-132-30, fax 8-545-132-31, e-mail info@svbib.se, World Wide Web http://www.biblioteksforeningen.se. *Secy. Gen.* Karin Linder.

Svensk Förening för Informationsspecialister (Swedish Assn. for Info. Specialists), Box 2001, 135 02 Tyresö. E-mail info@sfis.nu, World Wide Web http://www.sfis.nu. *Chair* Elisabeth Hammam Lie.

Svenska Arkivsamfundet (Swedish Archival Society). See Foreningen for Archiv & Informationsforvaltening (Society of Archives and Records Management in Sweden—FAI).

Switzerland

Verein Schweizer Archivarinnen und Archivare (Assn. of Swiss Archivists), Schweizerisches Bundesarchiv, Büro Pontri GmbH, Solohurnstr. 13, Postfach CH-3322, Urtenen Schönbühl. Tel. 41-31-312-26-66, fax 41-31-312-26-68, e-mail info@vsa-aas.ch, World Wide Web http://www.vsa-aas.org. *Pres.* Alain Dubois.

Taiwan

Lib. Assn. of the Republic of China (LAROC), 20 Zhongshan South Rd., Taipei 10001. Tel. 2-2361-9132, fax 2-2370-0899, e-mail lac@msg.ncl.edu.tw, World Wide Web http://www.lac.org.tw.

Tanzania

Tanzania Lib. Assn., P.O. Box 33433, Dar es Salaam. Tel./fax 255-744-296-134, e-mail info@tla.or.tz, World Wide Web http://www.tla.or.tz.

Thailand

Thai Lib. Assn., 1346 Songkhon 5 Road (between Sri Burapha Road 8-9), Klong Chan, Bang Kapi, Bangkok 10240. Tel. 02-734-9022, fax 02-734-9021, e-mail tla2497@gmail.com, World Wide Web http://tla.or.th.

Trinidad and Tobago

Lib. Assn. of Trinidad and Tobago, P.O. Box 1275, Port of Spain. Tel. 868-687-0194, e-mail latt46@gmail.com, World Wide Web https://www.facebook.com/latt46.

Tunisia

Association Tunisienne des Documentalistes, Bibliothécaires et Archivistes (Tunisian Assn. of Documentalists, Libns., and Archivists), c/o Directorate General of Communication, Prime Minister, Casbah, 1020 Tunis.

Turkey

Türk Kütüphaneciler Dernegi (Turkish Libns. Assn.), Necatibey Cad Elgun Sok 8/8, 06440 Kizilay, Ankara. Tel. 312-230-13-25, fax 312-232-04-53, e-mail tkd.dernek@gmail.com, World Wide Web http://www.kutuphaneci.org.tr. *Pres.* Ali Fuat Kartal.

Uganda

Uganda Lib. and Info. Assn., P.O. Box 25412, Kampala. Tel. 256-704-885-246, e-mail secretariat@ulia.org.ug. World Wide Web https://www.ulia.org.ug.

Ukraine

Ukrainian Lib. Assn., a/c 62, Kiev, 03057. Tel. 380-44-383-14-32, e-mail info@ula.org.ua, World Wide Web http://www.uba.org.ua. *Exec. Dir.* Soshynska Yaroslava.

United Kingdom

Archives and Records Assn., UK and Ireland (formerly the Society of Archivists), Prioryfield House, 20 Canon St., Taunton TA1 1SW, England. Tel. 1823-327-077, fax 1823-271-719, e-mail societyofarchivists@archives.org.uk, World Wide Web http://www.archives.org.uk. *Chief Exec.* John Chambers; *Chair* Karl Magee.

Bibliographical Society, Institute of English Studies, Senate House, Malet St., London WC1E 7HU, England. E-mail admin@bibsoc.org.uk, World Wide Web http://www.bibsoc.org.uk. *Pres.* Margaret Ford. E-mail president@bibsoc.org.uk.

Chartered Institute of Lib. and Info. Professionals (CILIP), 7 Ridgmount St., London WC1E 7AE, England. Tel. 20-7255-0500, fax 20-7255-0501, e-mail info@cilip.org.uk, World Wide Web http://www.cilip.org.uk.

School Lib. Assn., 1 Pine Court, Kembrey Park, Swindon SN2 8AD, England. Tel. 1793-530-166, fax 1793-481-182, e-mail info@sla.org.uk, World Wide Web http://www.sla.org.uk. *Pres.* Chris Riddell; *Chief Exec.* Allison Tarrant.

Scottish Lib. and Info. Council, 175 W. George St., Glasgow G2 2LB, Scotland. Tel. 141-202-2999, e-mail info@scottishlibraries.org, World Wide Web http://www.scottishlibraries.org. *Chair* Ian Ruthven.

Society of College, National, and Univ. Libs. (SCONUL) (formerly Standing Conference of National and Univ. Libs.), 94 Euston St., London NW1 2HA, England. Tel. 20-7387-0317, fax 20-7383-3197, e-mail info@sconul.ac.uk, World Wide Web http://www.sconul.ac.uk. *Exec. Dir.* Ann Rossiter.

Uruguay

Agrupación Bibliotecológica del Uruguay (Uruguayan Lib. and Archive Science Assn.) and Asociación de Bibliotecólogos del Uruguay (Uruguayan Libns. Assn.), Eduardo V. Haedo 2255, CP 11200, Montevideo. Tel. 2409-9989, e-mail abu@adinet.com.uy, World Wide Web http://www.abu.net.uy.

Vietnam

Hôi Thu-Vien Viet Nam (Vietnam Lib. Assn.), National Lib. of Vietnam, 31 Trang Thi, Hoan Kiem, 10000 Hanoi. Tel. 43-9366596, e-mail info@nlv.org.vn, World Wide Web https://www.facebook.com/VietnameseLibraryAssociation.

Zambia

Lib. and Info. Assn. of Zambia, P.O. Box 50183 Ridgeway, Lusaka. Tel. 260-965-024914, e-mail liaz@zambia.co.zm, World Wide Web https://zambia.co.zm/.

Zimbabwe

Zimbabwe Lib. Assn., ZimLA Midlands Branch, P.O. Box 1521, Gweru. Tel. 263-773-568-837, e-mail information@zimla.org.zw, World Wide Web http://zimla.org.zw.

Directory of Book Trade and Related Organizations

Book Trade Associations, United States and Canada

For more extensive information on the associations listed in this section, see the annual edition of *Literary Market Place* (Information Today, Inc.).

AIGA—The Professional Assn. for Design, 222 Broadway, New York, NY 10038. Tel. 212-807-1990, fax 212-807-1799, e-mail general@aiga.org, World Wide Web http://www.aiga.org. *Exec. Dir.* Bennie F. Johnson; *Interim CFO* Anthony Graziano; *Senior Dir. of Admin.* Amy Chapman.

American Book Producers Assn. (ABPA), 23 Waverly Place, Suite 6-B, New York, NY 10003. Tel. 917-620-9440, fax 212-675-1364, e-mail office@ABPAonline.org, World Wide Web http://www.abpaonline.org. *Pres.* Richard Rothschild; *V.P./Treas.* Nancy Hall; *Admin.* Michael Centore.

American Booksellers Assn., 333 Westchester Ave. Suite S202, White Plains, NY 10604. Tel. 800-637-0037, fax 914-417-4013, e-mail info@bookweb.org, World Wide Web http://www.bookweb.org. *Pres.* Jamie Fiocco, Flyleaf Books, 752 Martin Luther King Blvd., Chapel Hill, NC 27514. Tel. 919-942-7936, e-mail jamie@flyleafbooks.com; *V.P./Secy.* Bradley Graham, Politics and Prose Bookstore, 5015 Connecticut Ave. NW, Washington, DC 20008. E-mail bgraham@politics-prose.com. *CEO* Allison Hill. E-mail allisonhill@bookweb.org.

American Literary Translators Assn. (ALTA), University of Arizona, Esquire Building #205, 1230 N. Park Ave., Tucson, AZ 85721. World Wide Web https://literarytranslators.org/. *Exec. Dir.* Elisabeth Jaquette. E-mail elisabeth@literarytranslators.org.

American Printing History Assn., Box 4519, Grand Central Sta., New York, NY 10163-4519. World Wide Web http://www.printinghistory.org. *Pres.* Haven Hawley; *Treas.* David Goodrich; *Board Secy.* Virginia Bartow; *Exec. Secy.* Lyndsi Barnes. E-mail secretary@printinghistory.org.

American Society for Indexing, 1628 E. Southern Ave., No. 9-223, Tempe, AZ 85282. Tel. 480-245-6750, e-mail info@asindexing.org, World Wide Web http://www.asindexing.org. *Pres.* Jennifer Spanier. E-mail president@asindexing.org; *V.P./Pres.-Elect.* Michelle Combs. E-mail presidentelect@asindexing.org; *Exec. Dir.* Gwen Henson. E-mail gwen@asindexing.org.

American Society of Journalists and Authors, 355 Lexington Ave., 15th Fl., New York, NY 10017-6603. Tel. 212-997-0947, fax 212-937-2315, e-mail asjaoffice@asja.org, World Wide Web http://www.asja.org. *Pres.* Milt Toby. E-mail president@asja.org; *V.P.* Laura Laing. E-mail vicepresident@asja.org; *Exec. Dir.* Tim Bennett.

American Society of Media Photographers, P.O. Box 1810, Traverse City, MI 49685-1810. Tel. 877-771-2767, fax 231-946-6180, e-mail asmp@vpconnections.com, World Wide Web http://www.asmp.org. *Chair* Marianne Lee. E-mail president@asmp.org; *V.Chair* Michael Shay. E-mail shay@asmp.org; *Exec. Dir.* Tom Kennedy. E-mail kennedy@asmp.org.

American Society of Picture Professionals, 201 E. 25 St., No. 11C, New York, NY 10010. Tel. 516-500-3686, e-mail director@aspp.com, World Wide Web http://www.aspp.com.

Pres. Cecilia de Querol. E-mail president@aspp.com; *Exec. Dir.* Darrell Perry. E-mail director@aspp.com.

American Translators Assn., 225 Reinekers Lane, Suite 590, Alexandria, VA 22314. Tel. 703-683-6100, fax 703-683-6122, e-mail ata@atanet.org, World Wide Web http://www.atanet.org. *Pres.* Ted R. Wozniak; *Secy.* Karen Tkaczyk; *Treas.* John M. Milan; *Exec. Dir.* Walter W. Bacak, Jr. E-mail walter@atanet.org.

Antiquarian Booksellers Assn. of America, 20 W. 44 St., No. 507, New York, NY 10036-6604. Tel. 212-944-8291, fax 212-944-8293, World Wide Web http://www.abaa.org. *Pres.* Brad Johnson; *V.P.* Sheryl Jaeger; *Secy.* Elizabeth Svendsen; *Treas.* Peter Blackman; *Exec. Dir.* Susan Benne. E-mail sbenne@abaa.org.

Assn. Media and Publishing, 1090 Vermont Ave., N.W., 6th Fl., Washington, DC 20005-4905. Tel. 646-568-1309, e-mail ExecutiveDirector@associationmediaandpublishing.org, World Wide Web http://www.siia.net/amp. *President* Christina Folz; *V.P.* Diane Rusignola.

Assn. of American Publishers, 455 Massachusetts Ave. N.W., Suite 700, Washington, DC 20001. Tel. 202-347-3375, fax 202-347-3690, World Wide Web http://www.publishers.org. *Pres./CEO* Corinne Burton. E-mail ceo@publishers.org. *Chair* John Sargent; *V.Chair* Brian Napack; *Treas.* Jeremy North.

Assn. of American University Presses, 1412 Broadway, Suite 2135, New York, NY 10018. Tel. 212-989-1010, fax 212-989-0275, e-mail info@aaupnet.org, World Wide Web http://aaupnet.org. *Pres.* Kathryn Conrad, Univ. of Arizona Press; *Pres.-Elect* Niko Pfund, Oxford Univ. Press; *Treas.* Jean Kim, Stanford Univ. Press; *Exec. Dir.* Peter Berkery. Tel. 917-288-5594, e-mail pberkery@aaupnet.org.

Assn. of Canadian Publishers, 174 Spadina Ave., Suite 306, Toronto, ON M5T 2C2. Tel. 416-487-6116, fax 416-487-8815, e-mail admin@canbook.org, World Wide Web http://www.publishers.ca. *Pres.* Melissa Pitts, University of British Columbia Press, Vancouver; *V.P.* Ruth Linka, Orca Book Publishers, Victoria; *Treas.* Katherine Boersma, OwlKids Books, Toronto; *Exec. Dir.* Kate Edwards. Tel. 416-487-6116 ext. 2340, e-mail kate_edwards@canbook.org.

Audio Publishers Assn., 333 Hudson Street Suite 503, New York, NY 10013. Tel. 646-688-3044, e-mail info@audiopub.org; World Wide Web http://www.audiopub.org. *Pres.* Ana Maria Allessi; *V.P.* Amy Metsch; *Secy.* Natalie Fedewa *Treas.* Anthony Goff; *Exec. Dir.* Michele Cobb. E-mail mcobb@audiopub.org.

Authors Guild, 31 E. 32 St., 7th Fl., New York, NY 10016. Tel. 212-563-5904, fax 212-564-5363, e-mail staff@authorsguild.org, World Wide Web http://www.authorsguild.org. *Pres.* Doug Preston; *V.P.* Monique Truong; *Secy.* Rachel Vail; *Treas.* Peter Petre. *Exec. Dir.* Mary Rasenberger.

Book Industry Study Group, 232 Madison Ave., Suite 1400, New York, NY 10016. Tel. 646-336-7141, e-mail info@bisg.org, World Wide Web http://bisg.org. *Chair* Andrew Savikas, getAbstract; *V.Chair* Kathleen Reid, Elsevier; *Secy.* David Hetherington, knk Software; *Treas.* Dennis E. Abboud, Jr., ReaderLink; *Exec. Dir.* Brian O'Leary. Tel. 646-336-7141 ext. 12. e-mail brian@bisg.org.

Book Manufacturers' Institute (BMI), P.O. Box 731388, Ormand Beach, FL 32173. Tel. 386-986-4552, fax 386-986-4553, World Wide Web http://www.bmibook.org. *Pres.* Joseph H. Upton, Above the Treeline; *Exec. Dir./Secy.* Matthew J. Baehr; *V.P./Pres.-Elect* David McCree, LSC Communications; *Treas.* Suzanne Wiersma, Wallaceburg Bookbinding.

Bookbuilders of Boston, 115 Webster Woods Lane, North Andover, MA 01845. Tel. 781-378-1361, fax 419-821-2171, e-mail office@bbboston.org, World Wide Web http://www.bbboston.org. *Pres.* James Taylor. E-mail james.taylor@bbboston.org; *1st V.P.* Margaret Rosewitz. E-mail margaret.rosewitz@bbboston.org; *2nd V.P.* Michele DeVenuto. E-mail michelle.devenuto@bbboston.org; *Treasurer* Isabel Tran. E-mail isabel.tran@bbboston.org; *Clerk* Laura Rodriguez. E-mail laura.rodriguez@bbboston.org.

Bookbuilders West. See Publishing Professionals Network.

Canadian International Standard Numbers (ISNs) Agency, c/o Lib. and Archives Canada, 395 Wellington St., Ottawa, ON K1A 0N4. Tel. 866-578-7777 (toll-free) or 613-996-5115, World Wide Web http://www.bac-lac.gc.ca/eng/services/isbn-canada/Pages/isbn-canada.aspx.

Canadian Printing Industries Assn., 3-1750 The Queensway, Suite 135, Toronto, ON M9C 5H5, World Wide Web http://www.cpia-aci.ca. *Chair* Richard Kouwenhoven. E-mail rkouwenhoven@hemlock.com; *Admin.* Tracey Preston. Tel. 866-244-3311, e-mail tpreston.opia@on.aibn.com.

Children's Book Council, 54 W. 39 St., 14th Fl., New York, NY 10018. Tel. 917-890-7416, e-mail cbc.info@cbcbooks.org, World Wide Web http://www.cbcbooks.org. *Exec. Dir.* Carl Lennertz.

Community of Literary Magazines and Presses, 154 Christopher St., Suite 3C, New York, NY 10014. Tel. 212-741-9110, e-mail info@clmp.org, World Wide Web http://www.clmp.org. *Co-chairs* Nicole Dewey, Gerald Howard; *Exec. Dir.* Mary Gannon. E-mail mgannon@clmp.org.

Copyright Society of the USA, 1 E. 53 St., 8th Fl., New York, NY 10022. Tel. 212-354-6401, World Wide Web http://www.csusa.org. *Pres.* Glenn Pudelka; *V.P./Pres.-Elect* Naomi Jane Gray; *Secy.* Theodore Cheng; *Treas.* Casey M. Chisick; *Exec. Dir.* Kaitland E. Kubat.

Educational Book and Media Assn. (formerly Educational Paperback Assn.), P.O. Box 3363, Warrenton, VA 20188. Tel. 540-318-7770, e-mail info@edupaperback.org, World Wide Web http://www.edupaperback.org. *Pres.* Nancy Stetzinger; *V.P.* Lisa Maisonneuve; *Treas.* Bryan Thompson; *Exec. Dir.* Brain Gorg.

Evangelical Christian Publishers Assn., 9633 S. 48 St., Suite 140, Phoenix, AZ 85044. Tel. 480-966-3998, fax 480-966-1944, e-mail info@ecpa.org, World Wide Web http://www.ecpa.org. *Pres./CEO* Stan Jantz; *Chair* Jeff Crosby; *V.Chair and Secy.* Dan Kok; *Treas.* Dan Baker.

Graphic Artists Guild, 31 West 34th St., 8th Fl., New York, NY 10001. Tel. 212-791-3400, e-mail admin@graphicartistsguild.org, World Wide Web http://www.graphicartistsguild.org. *Pres.* Lara Kisielewska. E-mail president@graphicartistsguild.org; *Admin. Dir.* Paula Hinkle. E-mail membership@graphicartistsguild.org.

Great Lakes Independent Booksellers Assn., c/o Exec. Dir., 250 Woodstock Ave, Clarendon Hills, IL 60514. Tel. (630) 841-8129, e-mail larry@gliba.org, World Wide Web http://www.gliba.org. *Pres.* Susan Thomas, Coffee Tree Books, 159 E Main St., Morehead, KY 40351. Tel. 606-784-8364, e-mail coffeetreebooks@hotmail.com. *Exec. Dir.* Larry Law.

Guild of Book Workers, 521 Fifth Ave., New York, NY 10175. Tel. 212-292-4444, e-mail communications@guildofbookworkers.org, World Wide Web http://www.guildofbookworkers.org. *Pres.* Bexx Caswell. E-mail president@guildofbookworkers.org; *V.Pres.* Brien Beidler. E-mail vicepresident@guildofbookworkers.org; *Secy.* Rebecca Smyrl. E-mail secretary@guildofbookworkers.org; *Treas.* Laura Bedford. E-mail treasurer@guildofbookworkers.org.

Horror Writers Assn., P.O. Box 56687, Sherman Oaks, CA 91413. E-mail hwa@horror.org, World Wide Web http://www.horror.org. *Pres.* John Palisano. E-mail president@horror.org; *V.P.* Meghan Arcuri. E-mail vp@horror.org; *Secy.* Becky Spratford. E-mail secretary@horror.org; *Treas.* Leslie Klinger. E-mail treasurer@horror.org; Admin. Brad Hodson. E-mail admin@horror.org.

Independent Book Publishers Assn., 1020 Manhattan Beach Blvd., Suite 204, Manhattan Beach, CA 90266. Tel. 310-546-1818, fax 310-546-3939, e-mail info@ibpa-online.org, World Wide Web http://www.ibpa-online.org. *Chair* Brook Warner, She Writes Press; *Treas.* Richard Lena, Brattle Publishing; *Secy.* Kathy Strahs, Burnt Cheese Press; *CEO* Angela Bole. E-mail angela@ibpa-online.org.

International Standard Book Numbering U.S. Agency, 630 Central Ave., New Providence, NJ 07974. Tel. 877-310-7333, fax 908-219-0188, e-mail isbn-san@bowker.com, World Wide Web http://www.isbn.org. *Dir., Identifier Svcs.* Beat Barblan.

Jewish Book Council, 520 Eighth Ave., 4th Fl., New York, NY 10018. Tel. 212-201-2920, fax 212-532-4952, e-mail jbc@jewishbooks.

org, World Wide Web http://www.jewishbookcouncil.org. *Pres.* Jane Weitzman; *V.P.s* Joy Greenberg, Carol Levin, Lenore J. Weitzman; *Secy.* Elisa Spungen Bildner; *Treasurer* Alan Kadish; *Exec. Dir.* Naomi Firestone-Teeter.

Midwest Independent Publishers Assn. (MIPA), P.O. Box 580475, Minneapolis, MN 55458-0475. Tel. 651-917-0021, World Wide Web http://www.mipa.org. *Pres.* Suzzanne Kelley, North Dakota State Univ. Press, Tel. 701-231-6848, e-mail president@mipa.org; *V.P.* Peter Liptak, Exile Press. Tel. 612-392-2805, e-mail vicepresident@mipa.org; *Treas.* Jennifer Baum, Scribe Publishing. Tel. 248-259-0090, e-mail treasurer@mipa.org.

Miniature Book Society. Tel. 619-226-4441, e-mail member@mbs.org, World Wide Web http://www.mbs.org. *Pres.* Tony Firman; *V.P.* Ron Wood; *Secy.* Gail Faulkner; *Treas.* Kim Herrick.

Minnesota Book Publishers' Roundtable. E-mail information@publishersroundtable.org, World Wide Web http://www.publishersroundtable.org. *Pres.* Carla Valdez, Coffee House Press, 837 Glenwood Avenue, Minneapolis, MN 55405. E-mail laura@wiseinkpub.com; *V.P.* Lauren Kukla. E-mail lauren@mightymedia.com; *Secy.* Elizabeth Dingmann Schneider. E-mail e.schneider@redlineeditorial.com; *Treas.* Erik Gilg, 401 2nd Ave. N., Suite 310, Minneapolis, MN 55401. E-mail erik.gilg@quarto.com.

Mountains and Plains Independent Booksellers Assn., 2105 Union Drive, Lakewood, CO 80215. Tel. 720-272-0805, fax 970-484-0037, e-mail info@mountainsplains.org, World Wide Web http://www.mountainsplains.org. *Pres.* Christopher Green; *Vice Pres.* Allison Senecal; *Treas.* Amanda Sutton; *Secy.* Stephanie Schindhelm; *Exec. Dir.* Heather Duncan. E-mail heather@mountainsplains.org.

MPA—The Assn. of Magazine Media (formerly Magazine Publishers of America), 757 Third Ave., 11th Fl., New York, NY 10017. Tel. 212-872-3700, e-mail mpa@magazine.org, World Wide Web http://www.magazine.org. *Chair* Tom Harty. *Pres./CEO.* Brigitte Schmidt Gwyn. E-mail bsgywn@magazine.org.

National Assn. of College Stores, 500 E. Lorain St., Oberlin, OH 44074-1294. Tel. 800-622-7498, 440-775-7777, fax 440-775-4769, e-mail info@nacs.org, World Wide Web http://www.nacs.org. *Pres. and Treas.* Steve Westenbroek; *Pres.-Elect and Secy.* Adam Hustwitt; *CEO* Eric Schlechenmayer. E-mail eschlichenmayer@nacs.org.

National Book Foundation, 90 Broad St., Suite 604, New York, NY 10004. Tel. 212-685-0261, fax 212-213-6570, e-mail nationalbook@nationalbook.org, World Wide Web http://www.nationalbook.org. *Chair* David Steinberger, Perseus Books Group; *V.Chair* Fiona McCrea, Graywolf Publishing; *Secy.* Calvin Sims; *Treas.* W. Drake McFeely; *Exec. Director* Lisa Lucas. E-mail llucas@nationalbook.org.

National Coalition Against Censorship (NCAC), 19 Fulton St., Suite 407, New York, NY 10038. Tel. 212-807-6222, fax 212-807-6245, e-mail ncac@ncac.org, World Wide Web http://www.ncac.org. *Dirs.* Jon Anderson, Michael Bamberger, Joan E. Bertin, Judy Blume, Susan Clare, Chris Finan, Eric M. Freedman, Robie Harris, Phil Harvey, Michael Jacobs, Emily Knox, Chris Peterson, Julie Samuels, Larry Siems, Emily Whitfield; *Exec. Dir.* Chris Finan. E-mail chris@ncac.org.

New Atlantic Independent Booksellers Assn. (NAIBA), 2667 Hyacinth St., Westbury, NY 11590. Tel. 516-333-0681, fax 516-333-0689, e-mail naibabooksellers@gmail.com, World Wide Web http://www.newatlanticbooks.com. *Pres.* Bill Reilly, The River's End Bookstore; *V.P.* Rebecca Fitting, Greenlight Bookstores; *Secy.-Treas.* Donna Fell, Sparta Books; *Exec. Dir.* Eileen Dengler. E-mail NAIBAeileen@gmail.com.

New England Independent Booksellers Assn. (NEIBA), One Beacon Street, 15th Floor, Boston, MA 02108. Tel. 617-547-3642, fax 617-830-8768, e-mail beth@neba.org, World Wide Web http://www.newenglandbooks.org. *Pres.* Beth Wagner, Phoenix Books, Essex Junction, VT; *V.P.* Emily Russo, Print: A Bookstore, Portland, ME; *Treas.* Emily Crow, An Unlikely Story, Plainville, MA; *Exec. Dir.* Beth Ineson. E-mail beth@neba.org.

Northern California Independent Booksellers Assn., 651 Broadway, 2nd Fl., Sonoma, CA 95476. Tel. 415-561-7686, fax 415-561-7685, e-mail info@nciba.com, World Wide Web http://www.nciba.com. *Pres.* Michael Barnard; *Treas.* Melinda Powers; *Secy.* Carolyn Hutton. *Exec. Dir.* Calvin Crosby. E-mail calvin@nciba.com.

PEN American Center, Div. of International PEN, 588 Broadway, Suite 303, New York, NY 10012. Tel. 212-334-1660, fax 212-334-2181, e-mail pen@pen.org, World Wide Web http://www.pen.org. *Pres.* Jennifer Egan; *Exec. V.P.* Markus Dohle; *V.P.s* Masha Gessen, Tracy Higgins; *Secy.* Ayad Ahktar; *Treas.* Yvonne Marsh; *CEO* Susanne Nossel. E-mail snossel@pen.org.

Publishing Professionals Network (formerly Bookbuilders West), c/o Postal Annex, 274 Redwood Shores Parkway, Box 129, Redwood City, CA 94065-1173. E-mail operations@pubpronetwork.org, World Wide Web http://pubpronetwork.org. *Pres.* David Zielonka. E-mail david.zielonka@cengage.com; *V.P.* Brenda Ginty. E-mail gintybrenda@gmail.com; *Secy.* Mimi Heft. E-mail mimi.heft.design@gmail.com; *Treas.* Barbara Fuller. E-mail barbara@editcetera.com.

Romance Writers of America, 14615 Benfer Rd., Houston, TX 77069. Tel. 832-717-5200, e-mail info@rwa.org, World Wide Web http://www.rwa.org. *Pres.* Alyssa Day. E-mail president@rwa.org; *Secy.* C. Chilove. E-mail secretary@rwa.org; *Treasurer* E. J. Russell. E-mail treasurer@rwa.org; *Interim Exec. Dir.* Leslie Scantlebury. E-mail leslie.scantlebury@rwa.org.

Science Fiction and Fantasy Writers of America, P.O. Box 3238, Enfield, CT 06083-3238. World Wide Web http://www.sfwa.org. *Pres.* Mary Robinette Kowal. E-mail president@sfwa.org; *V.P.* Erin M. Hartshorn. E-mail erin.hartshorn@sfwa.org; *Secy.* Curtis C. Chen. E-mail curtis.chen@sfwa.org; *CFO* Nathan Lowell. E-mail cfo@sfwa.org; *Exec. Dir.* Kate Baker. E-mail office@sfwa.org.

SIBA (formerly Southern Independent Booksellers Alliance), 51 Pleasant Ridge, Asheville, NC 28805. Tel. 803-994-9530, e-mail siba@sibaweb.com, World Wide Web http://www.sibaweb.com. *Exec. Dir.* Wanda Jewell. E-mail wanda@sibaweb.com; *Asst. Exec. Dir.* Linda-Marie Barrett, E-mail lindamarie@sibaweb.com.

Society of Children's Book Writers and Illustrators (SCBWI), 4727 Wilshire Blvd., Suite 301, Los Angeles, CA 90010. Tel. 323-782-1010, e-mail scbwi@scbwi.org, World Wide Web http://www.scbwi.org. *Exec. Dir.* Lin Oliver. E-mail linoliver@scbwi.org; *Assoc. Exec. Dir.* Sarah Baker, E-mail sarahbaker@scbwi.org.

Society of Illustrators (SI), 128 E. 63 St., New York, NY 10065. Tel. 212-838-2560, fax 212-838-2561, e-mail info@societyillustrators.org, World Wide Web http://www.societyillustrators.org. *Pres.* Tim O'Brien; *Exec. Secy.* Leslie Cober-Gentry; *Exec. Dir.* Anelle Miller. E-mail anelle@societyillustrators.org.

Southern Independent Booksellers Alliance. See SIBA.

Western Writers of America, c/o Candy Moulton, 271 CR 219, Encampment, WY 82325 Tel. 307-329-8942, e-mail wwa.moulton@gmail.com, World Wide Web http://www.westernwriters.org. *Pres.* Nancy Plain; *V.P.* Chris Enss; *Exec. Dir., Secy./Treas.* Candy Moulton.

Women's National Book Assn., P.O. Box 237, FDR Sta., New York, NY 10150. Tel. 866-610-WNBA (9622), e-mail info@wnba-books.org, World Wide Web http://www.wnba-books.org. *Pres.* Rachelle Yousuf; e-mail nationalpresidentWNBA@gmail.com; *V.P.s* Natalie Obando-Desai, Bebe (Sarah) Brechner; *Secy.* Linda Rosen; *Treasurer* Christine Sikule.

International and Foreign Book Trade Associations

For Canadian book trade associations, see the preceding section, "Book Trade Associations, United States and Canada." For a more extensive list of book trade organizations outside the United States and Canada, with more detailed information, consult *International Literary Market Place* (Information Today, Inc.), which also provides extensive lists of major bookstores and publishers in each country.

International

African Publishers' Network, c/o Ghana Book Publishers Assn., Bureau of Ghana Languages Building, Kawukudi Culture, P.O. Box Lt 471, Laterbiokorshie, Accra, Ghana. Tel. 233-302-912764, 233-209-115191, e-mail info.africanpublishers@gmail.com, World Wide Web http://www.african-publishers.net/. *Acting Exec. Dir.* Ernest Oppong.

Afro-Asian Book Council, 212, Shahpur Jat, New Delhi—110 049, India. Tel. 91-11-26493326, fax 91-11-41752055, e-mail info@aabookcouncil.org, World Wide Web http://www.aabookcouncil.org/. *Secretary-General* Ramesh Mittal. E-mail rkmittal@dkagencies.com; *Dir.* Pranav Gupta. E-mail pgprintsindia@gmail.com.

Centro Regional para el Fomento del Libro en América Latina y el Caribe (CERLALC) (Regional Center for Book Promotion in Latin America and the Caribbean), Calle 70, No. 9-52, Bogotá, Colombia. Tel. 571-518-70-70, e-mail cerlalc@cerlalc.com, World Wide Web http://www.cerlalc.org. *Dir.* Andrés Ossa.

Federation of European Publishers, Chaussee d'Ixelles 29/35, Box 4, 1050 Brussels, Belgium. Tel. 32-2-770-11-10, fax 32-2-771-20-71, e-mail info@fep-fee.eu, World Wide Web http://www.fep-fee.eu. *Pres.* Rudy Vanschoonbeek; *Dir.* Anne Bergman-Tahon.

International Board on Books for Young People (IBBY), Nonnenweg 12, Postfach CH-4009, Basel, Switzerland. Tel. 41-61-272-29-17, fax 41-61-272-27-57, e-mail ibby@ibby.org, World Wide Web http://www.ibby.org. Pres. Mingzhou Zhang. *Exec. Dir.* Elizabeth Page.

International League of Antiquarian Booksellers (ILAB), c/o Rue Toepffer 5, Case postale 499, 1211 Geneva 12, Switzerland. E-mail secretariat@ilab.org, World Wide Web http://www.ilab.org. *Pres.* Sally Burdon; *Gen. Secy.* Stewart Bennett.

International Publishers Assn. (Union Internationale des Editeurs), 23 ave. de France, CH-1202 Geneva, Switzerland. Tel. 41-22-704-1820, fax 41-22-704-1821, e-mail info@internationalpublishers.org, World Wide Web http://www.internationalpublishers.org. *Pres.* Hugo Setzer; *Secy.-Gen.* José Borghino.

STM: The International Assn. of Scientific, Technical, and Medical Publishers, Prama House, 267 Banbury Road, Oxford OX2 7HT, England. Tel. 44-0-1865-339-321, fax 44-0-1865-339-325, e-mail info@stm-assoc.org, World Wide Web http://www.stm-assoc.org. *CEO* Ian Moss; Chair James Milne.

National

Argentina

Cámara Argentina del Libro (Argentine Book Assn.), Av. Belgrano 1580, 4 piso, C1093AAQ Buenos Aires. Tel. 54-11-4381-8383, fax 54-11-4381-9253, e-mail cal@editores.org.ar, World Wide Web http://www.editores.org.ar.

Fundación El Libro (Book Foundation), Yrigoyen 1628, 5 piso, C1089AAF Buenos Aires. Tel. 54-11-4370-0600, fax 54-11-4370-0607, e-mail fundacion@el-libro.com.ar, World Wide Web http://www.el-libro.org.ar. *Pres.* Gabriel Waldhuter; *Admin. Dir.* José Gutiérrez Brianza.

Australia

Australian and New Zealand Assn. of Antiquarian Booksellers (ANZAAB), P.O. Box 590, Carindale, Brisbane, QLD 4152. E-mail admin@anzaab.com, World Wide Web http://www.anzaab.com. *Pres.* Douglas Stewart.

Australian Booksellers Assn., 828 High St., Unit 9, Kew East, Vic. 3102. Tel. 3-9859-7322, fax 3-9859-7344, e-mail mail@aba.org.au, World Wide Web http://www.booksellers.org.au. *CEO* Robbie Egan.

Australian Publishers Assn., 60/89 Jones St., Ultimo, NSW 2007. Tel. 2-9281-9788, e-mail apa@publishers.asn.au, World Wide Web http://www.publishers.asn.au. *Pres.* Lee Walker.

Austria

Hauptverband des Österreichischen Buchhandels (Austrian Publishers and Booksellers Assn.), Grünangergasse 4, A-1010 Vienna. Tel. 43-1-512-15-35, fax 43-1-512-84-82, e-mail office@hvb.at, World Wide Web http://www.buecher.at. *Mgr.* Gustav Soucek.

Verband der Antiquare Österreichs (Austrian Antiquarian Booksellers Assn.), Grünangergasse 4, A-1010 Vienna. Tel. 1-512-1535-14, e-mail sekretariat@hvb.at, World Wide Web http://www.antiquare.at.

Belarus

National Book Chamber of Belarus, 31a V Horuzhei Str., Rm. 707, 220002 Minsk. Tel. 375-17-288-67-15, fax 375-17-283-29-60, e-mail palata@natbook.org.by, World Wide Web http://natbook.org.by. *Dir.* Ivanova Elena Vitalievna. E-mail elvit@natbook.org.by.

Belgium

Boek.be (formerly Vlaamse Boekverkopersbond, Flemish Booksellers Assn.), Te Buelaerlei 37, 2140 Borgerhout. Tel. 03-230-89-23, fax 3-281-22-40, World Wide Web http://www.boek.be/over-boekbe. Vlaamse Uitgevers Vereniging (Flemish Publishers Assn.).

Brazil

Câmara Brasileira do Livro (Brazilian Book Assn.), Rua Cristiano Viana 91, Pinheiros-São Paulo-SP, CEP: 05411-000. Tel./fax 11-3069-1300, e-mail cbl@cbl.org.br, World Wide Web http://www.cbl.org.br. *Pres.* Vitor Tavares da Silva Filho.

Sindicato Nacional dos Editores de Livros (Brazilian Publishers Assn.), Rue da Ajuda 35-18 andar, 20040-000 Rio de Janeiro-RJ. Tel. 21-2533-0399, fax 21-2533-0422, e-mail snel@snel.org.br, World Wide Web http://www.snel.org.br. *Pres.* Marcos de Veiga Pereira.

Chile

Cámara Chilena del Libro AG (Chilean Assn. of Publishers, Distributors, and Booksellers), Av. Libertador Bernardo O'Higgins 1370, Oficina 501, Santiago. Tel. 2-672-0348, fax 2-687-4271, e-mail prolibro@tie.cl, World Wide Web https://camaradellibro.cl/. *Pres.* Eduardo Castillo.

Colombia

Cámara Colombiana del Libro (Colombian Book Assn.), Calle 35, No. 5A 05, Bogotá. Tel. 57-1-323-01-11, fax 57-1-285-10-82, e-mail camlibro@camlibro.com.co, World Wide Web http://www.camlibro.com.co. *Exec. Chair* Enrique González Villa; *Secy.-Gen.* Manuel José Sarmiento Ramírez.

Czech Republic

Svaz ceských knihkupcu a nakladatelu (Czech Publishers and Booksellers Assn.), Fugnerovo nameisti 1808/3, Prague 2, 120 00. Tel. 420-227-660-644, e-mail sckn@sckn.cz, World Wide Web http://www.sckn.cz. *Dir.* Marcela Turečková. E-mail tureckova@sckn.cz.

Denmark

Danske Boghandlerforening (Danish Booksellers Assn.), Slotsholmsgade 1 B, 1216 Copenhagen K. Tel. 45-32-54-2255, fax 45-32-54-0041, e-mail info@boghandlerne.dk, World Wide Web http://www.boghandlerforeningen.dk. *Chair* Helle Busck Fensvig; *Dir.* Bo Dybkær

Danske Forlæggerforening (Danish Publishers Assn.), Stock Exchange, Slotsholmsgade 1, 1217 Copenhagen K. Tel. 45-33-15-66-88, e-mail info@danskeforlag.dk, World Wide Web http://www.danskeforlag.dk. *Chair* Lars Boesgaard.

Ecuador

Cámara Ecuatoriana del Libro, N29-61 Eloy Alfaro and England, 9th Floor, Quito. Tel. 593-2-2553311, fax 593-2-2553314, e-mail info@celibro.org.ec, World Wide Web http://celibro.org.ec. *Pres.* Oswaldo Almeida Mora.

Egypt

General Egyptian Book Organization (GEBO), P.O. Box 235, Cairo 11511. Tel. 2-257-75367, e-mail walaakotb@gebo.gov.eg, World Wide Web https://www.facebook.com/pages/General-Egyptian-Book-Organization/.

Estonia

Estonian Publishers Assn., Roosikrantsi 6-207, 10119 Tallinn. Telephone 372-644-9866, fax 372-617-7550, e-mail kirjastusteliit@eki.ee, World Wide Web http://www.estbook.com. *Managing Dir.* Kaidi Urmet. E-mail kirjastusteliit@eki.ee.

Finland

Kirjakauppaliitto Ry (Booksellers Association of Finland), Eteläranta 10, 00130 Helsinki. Tel. 040-689-9112, e-mail toimisto@kirjakauppaliitto.fi, World Wide Web http://www.kirjakauppaliitto.fi. *Managing Director* Laura Karlsson. E-mail laura.karlsson@kirjakauppaliitto.fi.

Suomen Kirjasaatio (Finnish Book Foundation). Eteläranta 10, FI-00130 Helsinki. Tel. 358 9 228 77 255, World Wide Web https://kustantajat.fi/&lang=en-gb. *Secy. Gen.* Sanna-Maaria Tornivaara.

France

Bureau International de l'Edition Française (BIEF) (International Bureau of French Publishing), 115 blvd. Saint-Germain, F-75006 Paris. Tel. 01-44-41-13-13, fax 01-46-34-63-83, e-mail info@bief.org, World Wide Web http://www.bief.org. Pres. Vera Michalski-Hoffmann. *Dir. Gen.* Nicolas Roche. *New York Branch* French Publishers Agency, 30 Vandam Street, Suite 5A, New York, NY 10013. Tel./fax 212-254-4540, World Wide Web https://www.frenchrights.com/.

Cercle de la Librairie (Circle of Professionals of the Book Trade), 35 rue Grégoire-de-Tours, F-75006 Paris. Tel. 01-44-41-28-00, fax 01-44-41-28-65, e-mail support@electre.com, World Wide Web http://www.electre.com.

Syndicat de la Librairie Française, Hotel Massa, 38 rue du Faubourg Saint-Jacques, F-75014 Paris. Tel. 01-53-62-23-10, fax 01-53-62-10-45, e-mail contact@syndicat-librarie.fr, World Wide Web http://www.syndicat-librairie.fr. *Admin. Secy.* Anne Criulanscy. E-mail a.criulanscy@syndicat-librairie.fr.

Syndicat National de la Librairie Ancienne et Moderne (SLAM) (National Assn. of Antiquarian and Modern Booksellers), 4 rue Gît-le-Coeur, F-75006 Paris. Tel. 01-43-29-46-38, fax 01-43-25-41-63, e-mail slam-livre@wanadoo.fr, World Wide Web http://www.slam-livre.fr. *Pres.* Herve Valentin; *Secy.-Gen.* Pierre Prevost.

Syndicat National de l'Edition (SNE) (National Union of Publishers), 115 blvd. Saint-Germain, F-75006 Paris. Tel. 01-44-41-40-50, fax 01-44-41-40-77, World Wide Web http://www.sne.fr. *Pres.* Vincent Montagne.

Germany

Börsenverein des Deutschen Buchhandels e.V. (Stock Exchange of German Booksellers), Braubachstr. 16, 60311 Frankfurt-am-Main. Tel. 49-69-1306-0, fax 49-69-1306-201, e-mail info@boev.de, World Wide Web http://www.boersenverein.de. *Gen. Mgr.* Alexander Skipis.

Verband Deutscher Antiquare e.V. (German Antiquarian Booksellers Assn.), Geschäftsstelle, Seeblick 1, 56459 Elbingen. Tel. 49-0-6435-90-91-47, fax 49-0-6435-90-91-48, e-mail buch@antiquare.de, World Wide Web http://www.antiquare.de. *Chair* Sibylle Wieduwilt. E-mail s.wieduwilt@antiquare.de.

Hungary

Magyar Könyvkiadók és Könyvterjesztök Egyesülése (Assn. of Hungarian Publishers and Booksellers), Kertész u. 41. I / 4, 1073 Budapest. Tel. 06-1-343-2538, e-mail mkke@mkke.hu, World Wide Web http://www.mkke.hu. *Pres.* Gál Katalin.

Iceland

Félag Islenskra Bókaútgefenda (Icelandic Publishers Assn.), Brautarholti 8, 105 Reykjavik. Tel. 517-7200, e-mail fibut@fibut.is, World Wide Web http://www.fibut.is. *Chair* Heidar Ingi Svannsson.

India

Federation of Indian Publishers, Federation House, 18/1C Institutional Area, Aruna Asaf Ali Marg, New Delhi 110067. Tel. 11-2696-4847, fax 11-2686-4054, e-mail fippresident@gmail.com, World Wide Web http://www.fiponline.org. *Exec. Dir.* Shri. Ramesh K. Mittal.

Indonesia

Ikatan Penerbit Indonesia (Assn. of Indonesian Book Publishers), Jl. Kalipasir 32, Cikini Jakarta Pusat 10330. Tel. 21-3141-907, e-mail sekretariat@ikapi.org, World Wide Web http://www.ikapi.org. *Secy.* Novi Arsianti.

Ireland

Publishing Ireland/Foilsiu Eireann (formerly CLÉ: The Irish Book Publishers' Assn.), 63 Patrick St., Dun Laoghaire, Co Dublin. Tel. 353-1-639-4868, e-mail info@publishingireland.com, World Wide Web http://www.publishingireland.com. *Manager* Stephanie Lawless. E-mail stephanie@publishingireland.com.

Israel

Book Publishers' Assn. of Israel, 29 Carlebach St., 67132 Tel Aviv. Tel. 3-561-4121, fax 3-561-1996, e-mail info@tbpai.co.il, World Wide Web http://www.tbpai.co.il. *Chair* Benjamin Trivaks.

Italy

Associazione Italiana Editori (Italian Publishers Assn.), Corso di Porta Romana 108, 20122 Milan. Tel. 2-89-28-0800, fax 2-89-28-0860, e-mail info@aie.it, World Wide Web http://www.aie.it. *Pres.* Ricardo Franco Levy.

Associazione Librai Antiquari d'Italia (Antiquarian Booksellers Assn. of Italy), via Discipilini 32, Riva del Garda (TN) 38066. E-mail alai@alai.it, World Wide Web http://www.alai.it. *Pres.* Mario Giupponi.

Japan

Antiquarian Booksellers Assn. of Japan, Kokusai Hamamatsucho Bldg., 9th Floor, 1-9-18 Kaigan, Minato-ku, Tokyo, 105-0022. Tel. 81-3-6367-6070, fax 81-3-6367-6196, e-mail abaj@abaj.gr.jp, World Wide Web http://www.abaj.gr.jp.

Japan Assn. of International Publications (formerly Japan Book Importers Assn.), 1-1-13-4F Kanda, Jimbocho, Chiyodak-ku, Tokyo 101-0051. Tel. 3-5479-7269, fax 3-5479-7307, e-mail office@jaip.jp, World Wide Web http://www.jaip.jp. *Exec. Dir.* Mark Gresham.

Japan Book Publishers Assn., 5th Fl., Shuppan-Club Building 1-32, Kanda-Jimbocho, Chiyoda-ku, Tokyo,101-0051. Tel. 81-0-3-6273-7065, fax 81-0-3-6811-0959, e-mail research@jbpa.or.jp, World Wide Web http://www.jbpa.or.jp. *Pres.* Masahiro Oga.

Kenya

Kenya Publishers Assn., P.O. Box 42767, Nairobi 00100. Tel. 254-020-2635498, e-mail info@kenyapublishers.org, World Wide Web http://www.kenyapublishers.org. *Chair* Lawrence Njagi.

Korea (Republic of)

Korean Publishers Assn., Samchungro 6, Sogang-dong, Jongro-gu, Seoul 03062. Tel. 2-733-8402, fax 2-738-5414, e-mail webmaster@kpa21.or.kr, World Wide Web http://eng.kpa21.or.kr. *Chair* Yoon Chul-ho.

Latvia

Latvian Publishers' Assn., Baznicas iela 37-3, LV-1010 Riga. Tel./fax 67-217-730, e-mail lga@gramatizdeveji.lv, World Wide Web http://www.gramatizdeveji.lv. *Exec. Dir.* Dace Pugacha.

Lithuania

Lithuanian Publishers Assn., Germany 18A, LT 01130, Vilnius. Tel. 370-675-75692, fax 370-670-32287, e-mail info@lla.lt, World Wide Web http://www.lla.lt. *Pres.* Remigijus Jokubauskas; *Exec. Dir.* Rūta Elijošaityte-Kaikarė.

Malaysia

Malaysian Book Publishers' Assn., No. 7-6, Block E2, Jl PJU 1/42A, Dataran Prima, 47301 Petaling Jaya, Selangor. Tel. 3-7880-5840, fax 3-7880-5841, e-mail info@mabopa.com.my, World Wide Web http://www.mabopa.com.my. *Pres.* Arief Hakim Sani Rahmat.

Mexico

Cámara Nacional de la Industria Editorial Mexicana (Mexican Publishers' Assn.), Holanda No. 13, Col. San Diego Churubusco, Deleg. Coyoacán, 04120 Mexico DF. Tel. 155-56-88-20-11, fax 155-56-04-31-47, e-mail contacto@caniem.com, World Wide Web http://www.caniem.com. *Pres.* Juan Luis Arzoz Arbide. E-mail presidencia@caniem.com.

The Netherlands

KVB—Koninklijke Vereeniging van het Boekenvak (Royal Society for the Book Trade), P.O. Box 12040, AA Amsterdam-Zuidoost. Tel. 20-624-02-12, fax 20-620-88-71, e-mail info@kvb.nl, World Wide Web http://www.kvb.nl. *Dirs.* M. K. J. David and A. Schroën.

Nederlands Uitgeversverbond (Royal Dutch Publishers Assn.), Postbus 12040, 1100 AA Amsterdam. Tel. 20-430-9150, fax 20-430-9199, e-mail info@mediafederatie.nl, World Wide Web https://mediafederatie.nl. *Chair* Derk Haank; *Dir.* Peter Stadhouders. E-mail pstadhouders@mediafederatie.nl.

Nederlandsche Vereeniging van Antiquaren (Netherlands Assn. of Antiquarian Booksellers), Notendijk 7, 4583 SV Terhole. Tel. 31-0-114-3142-09, fax 31-0-114-e-mail info@nvva.nl, World Wide Web http://www.nvva.nl. *Chair* Gert Jan Bestebreurtje; *Secy.* Peter Everaers.

Nederlandse Boekverkopersbond (Dutch Booksellers Assn.), Arnhemse Bovenweg 100, 3708 AG Zeist. Tel. 088-600-9500, e-mail info@boekbond.nl, World Wide Web http://www.boekbond.nl. *Chair* Rob Haans.

New Zealand

Booksellers New Zealand, P.O. Box 25033, Featherston Street, Wellington 6146. Tel. 4-472-1908, fax 4-472-1912, e-mail info@booksellers.co.nz, World Wide Web http://www.booksellers.co.nz. *CEO* Lincoln Gould. E-mail lincoln.gould@booksellers.co.nz. *Assoc. Mgr.* Dan Slevin. E-mail dan.slevin@booksellers.co.nz.

Nigeria

Nigerian Publishers Assn., 1st Floor Premium House, Opp. Evans Brothers (Nig. Publishers) Ltd., Jericho, GPO Box 2541, Dugbe, Ibadan, Oyo States. Tel. 234-803-917-7779, e-mail nigerianpublishers@ymail.com, World Wide Web http://www.nigerianpublishers.com. *Pres.* Adedapo Gbadega.

Norway

Norske Bokhandlerforening (Norwegian Booksellers Association), Sehesteds gate 6, 0164 Oslo. Tel. 47-22-39-68-00, e-mail firmapost@bokhandlerforeningen.no, World Wide Web http://www.bokhandlerforeningen.no. *Chief Executive Officer* Trine Stensen. E-mail trine@bokhandlerforeningen.no.

Norske Forleggerforening (Norwegian Publishers Assn.), Sehesteds gate 6, 0164 Oslo. Tel. 22-00-75-80, fax 22-33-38-30, e-mail dnf@forleggerforeningen.no, World Wide Web http://www.forleggerforeningen.no. *Chair* Edmund Austigard; *Managing Dir.* Kristenn Einarsson.

Peru

Cámara Peruana del Libro (Peruvian Publishers Assn.), Av. Cuba 427, Jesús María, Apdo. 10253, Lima 11. Tel. (511) 265-0735, fax (511) 265-0735, e-mail cp-libro@cpl.org.pe, World Wide Web http://www.cpl.org.pe. *Pres.* José Wilfredo Del Pozo Alarcón.

Philippines

Philippine Educational Publishers Assn., Phoenix Building, 927 Quezon Ave., Quezon City. Tel. (632) 376-4041 local 334, fax (632) 376-4031, e-mail pepasecretariat@gmail.com. World Wide Web http://www.pepa.org.ph. *Pres.* Jose Paolo M. Sibal.

Poland

Władze Stowarzyszenie Księgarzy Polskich (Assn. of Polish Booksellers), ul. Świętokrzyska 14, 00-050 Warsaw. Tel./fax 0-22-827-93-81, e-mail skp@ksiegarze.org.pl, World Wide Web http://www.ksiegarze.org.pl. *Chair* Tadeusz Prześlakiewicz; *Gen. Secy.* Katarzyna Balicka-Więckowska.

Portugal

Associação Portuguesa de Editores e Livreiros (Portuguese Assn. of Publishers and Booksellers), Av. dos Estados Unidas da America 97, 6 Esq., 1700-167 Lisbon. Tel. 21-843-51-80, e-mail geral@apel.pt, World Wide Web http://www.apel.pt. Exec. Dir. João Alvim.

Russia

Assn. of Book Publishers of Russia, 101000, Lubyanka, Luchnikov per., D.4, p. 1, Moscow. Tel. 7-926-900-85-27, e-mail askibook@gmail.com, World Wide Web http://www.aski.ru.

Rossiiskaya Knizhnaya Palata (Russian Book Chamber), Zvezdny boulevard 17, building 1, 129085, Moscow. Tel. 495-688-96-89, fax 495-688-99-91, e-mail info@bookchamber.ru, World Wide Web http://www.bookchamber.ru.

Singapore

Singapore Book Publishers Assn., 9 Jurong Town Hall Road, 02-02 Trade Association Hub, Jurong Town Hall, Singapore 609431. Tel. 65-6957-7093, e-mail info@singaporebookpublishers.sg, World Wide Web http://www.singaporebookpublishers.sg. *President* Peter Schoppert. E-mail schoppert@nus.edu.sg. *Exec. Dir.* Cecilia Woo.

Slovenia

Zdruzenie Zaloznikov in Knjigotrzcev Slovenije Gospodarska Zbornica Slovenije (Assn. of Publishers and Booksellers of Slovenia), Dimičeva 13, SI-1504 Ljubljana. Tel. 386-1-5898-000, fax 386-1-5898-100, e-mail info@gzs.si, World Wide Web https://www.gzs.si/zbornica_knjiznih_zaloznikov_in_knjigotrzcev.

South Africa

Publishers Assn. of South Africa (PASA), P.O. Box 18223, Wynberg 7824. Tel. 21-762-9083, fax 21-762-2763, e-mail pasa@publishsa.co.za, World Wide Web http://www.publishsa.co.za. *Chair* Steve Cilliers; *Exec. Dir.* Mpuka Radinku.

South African Booksellers Assn. (formerly Associated Booksellers of Southern Africa), Regus Business Centre, 2 Fir Street, Observatory, 7925, Cape Town. Tel. 27 21 003 8098, e-mail saba@sabooksellers.com, World Wide Web http://sabooksellers.com. *Pres.* Melvin Kaabwe. E-mail melvin.kaabwe@vanschaik.com.

Spain

Federación de Gremios de Editores de España (Federation of Spanish Publishers Assns.), Calle de Cea Bermúdez 44, 28003 Madrid. Tel. 91-534-51-95, fax 91-535-26-25, e-mail fgee@fge.es, World Wide Web http://www.federacioneditores.org. *Pres.* Miguel Barrero; *Secy.* Antonio María Ávila.

Sri Lanka

Sri Lanka Book Publishers Assn., No. 3G 12C, BMICH Office Complex, Block 04, Bauddhaloka Mawatha, Colombo. Tel. 0094-112-696-821, e-mail bookpub@sltnet.lk, World Wide Web https://www.facebook.com/SLBPA.

Sweden

Svenska Förläggareföreningen (Swedish Publishers Assn.), c/o Svenska Publisher AB, Kungstensgatan 38, 2 tr, 113 59 Stockholm. Tel. 8-736-19-40, e-mail info@forlaggare.se, World Wide Web http://www.forlaggare.se. *Chair* Eva Gedin.

Switzerland

Swiss Booksellers and Publishers Association (SBVV), Limmatstrasse 111, Postfach 8031, Zürich. Tel. 44-421-36-00, fax 44-421-36-18, e-mail info@sbvv.ch, World Wide Web https://www.sbvv.ch. *Dir.* Daniel Waser. E-mail daniel.waser@sbvv.ch.

Thailand

Publishers and Booksellers Assn. of Thailand, 83/159 Moo Chinnakhet 2, Ngam Wong Wan Rd., Tungsonghong Lak Si, Bangkok 10210. Tel. 2-954-9560-4, fax 02-954-9565-6, e-mail info@pubat.or.th, World Wide Web http://www.pubat.or.th. *Pres.* Chonrungsri Chalermchaikit.

Uganda

Uganda Publishers Assn., P.O. Box 7732, Kampala. Tel. 256-752-707327. World Wide Web https://www.facebook.com/UgandaPublishers/.

United Kingdom

Antiquarian Booksellers Assn., 21 John Street, London WC1N 2BF, England. Tel. 44-0-20-8004-9512, e-mail admin@aba.org.uk, World Wide Web http://www.aba.org.uk.

Assn. of Learned and Professional Society Publishers, Egale 1, 80 St Albans Road, Watford, Hertfordshire WD17 1DL England. Tel. 44 (0)1245 260571, e-mail admin@alpsp.org, World Wide Web http://www.alpsp.org. *Chair* Niamh O'Connor; *Chief Exec.* Wayne Sime.

Booktrust, G8 Battersea Studios, 80 Silverthorne Rd., Battersea, London SW8 3HE, England. Tel. 020 7801 8800, e-mail query@booktrust.org.uk, World Wide Web http://www.booktrust.org.uk. *Pres.* Michael Morpurgo; *Chief Exec.* Diana Gerald.

Publishers Assn., 50 Southwark Street, London SE1 1UN, England. Tel. 44 0 20 7378 0504, e-mail mail@publishers.org.uk, World Wide Web http://www.publishers.org.uk. *Pres.* Stephen Lotinga.

Scottish Book Trust, Sandeman House, Trunk's Close, 55 High St., Edinburgh EH1 1SR, Scotland. Tel. 131-524-0160, e-mail info@scottishbooktrust.com, World Wide Web http://www.scottishbooktrust.com. *CEO* Mark Lambert.

Welsh Books Council (Cyngor Llyfrau Cymru), Castell Brychan, Aberystwyth, Ceredigion SY23 2JB, Wales. Tel. 1970-624-151, fax 1970-625-385, e-mail info@wbc.org.uk, World Wide Web http://www.cllc.org.uk. *Chief Exec.* Helgard Krause.

Uruguay

Cámara Uruguaya del Libro (Uruguayan Publishers Assn.), Colón 1476, Apdo. 102, 11000 Montevideo. Tel. 2-916-93-74, fax 2-916-76-28, e-mail gerencia@camaradellibro.com.uy, World Wide Web http://www.camaradellibro.com.uy. *Pres.* Alvaro Risso.

Venezuela

Cámara Venezolana del Libro (Venezuelan Publishers Assn.), Av. Andrés Bello, Centro Andrés Bello, Torre Oeste 11, piso 11, of. 112-0, Caracas 1050. Tel. 212-793-1347, fax 212-793-1368, e-mail cavelibro@gmail.com, World Wide Web https://www.facebook.com/CamaradelLibro/.

Zambia

Booksellers and Publishers Assn. of Zambia, P.O. Box 51109, 10100 Lusaka. E-mail dongo.banda@gmail.com.

Zimbabwe

Zimbabwe Book Publishers Assn., P.O. Box 3041, Harare. Tel. 4-773-236, fax 4-754-256.

National Information Standards Organization (NISO)

NISO, the National Information Standards Organization, a nonprofit association accredited by the American National Standards Institute (ANSI), identifies, develops, maintains, and publishes technical standards to manage information in today's continually changing digital environment. NISO standards apply to both traditional and new technologies and to information across its whole lifecycle, from creation through documentation, use, repurposing, storage, metadata, and preservation. The following listing includes NISO standards of interest to readers of *Library and Book Trade Almanac.*

Content and Collection Management

ANSI/NISO Z39.2-1994 (R2016)	Information Interchange Format ISBN 978-1-937522-70-4
ANSI/NISO Z39.14-1997 (R2015)	Guidelines for Abstracts ISBN 978-1-937522-44-5
ANSI/NISO Z39.18-2005 (R2010)	Scientific and Technical Reports—Preparation, Presentation, and Preservation ISBN 978-1-937522-21-6
ANSI/NISO Z39.19-2005 (R2010)	Guidelines for the Construction, Format, and Management of Monolingual Controlled Vocabularies ISBN 978-1-937522-22-3
ANSI/NISO Z39.23-1997 (S2015)	Standard Technical Report Number Format and Creation ISBN 978-1-937522-45-2
ANSI/NISO Z39.29-2005 (R2010)	Bibliographic References ISBN 978-1-937522-26-1
ANSI/NISO Z39.32-1996 (R2012)	Information on Microfiche Headers ISBN 978-1-937522-29-2
ANSI/NISO Z39.41-1997 (S2015)	Placement Guidelines for Information on Spines ISBN 978-1-937522-46-9

ANSI/NISO Z39.43-1993 (R2017) — Standard Address Number (SAN) for the Publishing Industry
ISBN 978-1-937522-75-9

ANSI/NISO Z39.48-1992 (R2009) — Permanence of Paper for Publications and Documents in Libraries and Archives
ISBN 978-1-937522-30-8

ANSI/NISO Z39.71-2006 (R2011) — Holdings Statements for Bibliographic Items
ISBN 978-1-937522-31-5

ANSI/NISO Z39.73-1994 (R2012) — Single-Tier Steel Bracket Library Shelving
ISBN 978-1-937522-32-2

ANSI/NISO Z39.74-1996 (R2012) — Guides to Accompany Microform Sets
ISBN 978-1-937522-40-7

ANSI/NISO Z39.78-2000 (R2018) — Library Binding
ISBN 978-1-937522-86-5

ANSI/NISO Z39.84-2005 (R2010) — Syntax for the Digital Object Identifier
ISBN 978-1-937522-34-6

ANSI/NISO Z39.85-2012 — The Dublin Core Metadata Element Set
ISBN 978-1-937522-14-8

ANSI/NISO Z39.86-2005 (R2012) — Specifications for the Digital Talking Book
ISBN 978-1-937522-35-3

ANSI/NISO Z39.96-2019 — JATS: Journal Article Tag Suite, version 1.2
ISBN 978-1-937522-89-6

ANSI/NISO Z39.98-2012 — Authoring and Interchange Framework for Adaptive XML Publishing Specification
ISBN 978-1-937522-07-0

ANSI/NISO Z39.102-2017 — STS: Standards Tag Suite
ISBN 978-1-937522-78-0

ANSI/NISO/ISO 12083-1995 (R2009) — Electronic Manuscript Preparation and Markup
ISBN 978-1-880124-20-8

Standards for Discovery to Delivery

ANSI/NISO Z39.19-2005 (R2010) — Guidelines for the Construction, Format, and Management of Monolingual Controlled Vocabularies
ISBN 978-1-937522-22-3

ANSI/NISO Z39.50-2003 (S2014) — Information Retrieval (Z39.50) Application Service Definition and Protocol Specification
ISBN 978-1-937522-42-1

ANSI/NISO Z39.83-1-2012	NISO Circulation Interchange Part 1: Protocol (NCIP), version 2.02 ISBN 978-1-937522-03-2
ANSI/NISO Z39.83-2-2012	NISO Circulation Interchange Protocol (NCIP) Part 2: Implementation Profile 1, version 2.02 ISBN 978-1-937522-04-9
ANSI/NISO Z39.85-2012	The Dublin Core Metadata Element Set ISBN 978-1-937522-14-8
ANSI/NISO Z39.87-2006 (R2017)	Data Dictionary—Technical Metadata for Digital Still Images ISBN 978-1-937522-76-6
ANSI/NISO Z39.88-2004 (R2010)	The OpenURL Framework for Context-Sensitive Services ISBN 978-1-937522-38-4
ANSI/NISO Z39.89-2003 (S2014)	The U.S. National Z39.50 Profile for Library Applications ISBN 978-1-937522-43-8
ANSI/NISO Z39.99-2017	ResourceSync Framework Specification ISBN 978-1-937522-73-5

Business Information

ANSI/NISO Z39.7-2013	Information Services and Use: Metrics and Statistics for Libraries and Information Providers—Data Dictionary ISBN 978-1-937522-15-5
ANSI/NISO Z39.93-2014	The Standardized Usage Statistics Harvesting Initiative (SUSHI) Protocol ISBN 978-1-937522-47-6

Preservation and Storage

ANSI/NISO Z39.32-1996 (R2012)	Information on Microfiche Headers ISBN 978-1-937522-29-2
ANSI/NISO Z39.48-1992 (R2009)	Permanence of Paper for Publications and Documents in Libraries and Archives ISBN 978-1-937522-30-8
ANSI/NISO Z39.73-1994 (R2012)	Single-Tier Steel Bracket Library Shelving ISBN 978-1-937522-32-2
ANSI/NISO Z39.78-2000 (R2018)	Library Binding ISBN 978-1-937522-86-5

In Development / NISO Initiatives

NISO develops new standards, reports, and best practices on a continuing basis to support its ongoing standards development program. NISO working groups are currently developing or exploring the following:

- Collection Description Specification (NISO Z39.91-200x)
- Criteria for Indexes (NISO Z39.4-201x)
- Digital Bookmarking and Annotation (NISO Z39.97-201x)
- Information Retrieval Service—Description Specification (NISO Z39.92-200x)
- Information Services and Use Metrics & Statistics for Libraries and Information Providers—Data Dictionary (NISO Z39.7-201x)
- Permanence of Paper for Publications and Documents in Libraries and Archives (ANSI/NISO Z39.48-201x)
- Scientific and Technical Reports—Preparation, Presentation, and Preservation (ANSI/NISO Z39.18-2005 [R201x])
- Standard Interchange Protocol (SIP) (NISO Z39.100-201x)
- Standards-Specific Ontology (SSOS) (NISO Z39.103-201x)

NISO Recommended Practices

A Framework of Guidance for Building Good Digital Collections, 3rd ed., 2007
ISBN 978-1-880124-74-1

NISO RP-2005-01	Ranking of Authentication and Access Methods Available to the Metasearch Environment ISBN 978-1-880124-89-5
NISO RP-2005-02	Search and Retrieval Results Set Metadata ISBN 978-1-880124-88-8
NISO RP-2005-03	Search and Retrieval Citation Level Data Elements ISBN 978-1-880124-87-1
NISO RP-2006-01	Best Practices for Designing Web Services in the Library Context ISBN 978-1-880124-86-4
NISO RP-2006-02	NISO Metasearch XML Gateway Implementers Guide ISBN 978-1-880124-85-7
NISO RP-6-2012	RFID in U.S. Libraries ISBN 978-1-937522-02-5
NISO RP-7-2012	SERU: A Shared Electronic Resource Understanding ISBN 978-1-937522-08-7
NISO RP-8-2008	Journal Article Versions (JAV) ISBN 978-1-880124-79-6

NISO RP-9-2014	KBART: Knowledge Bases and Related Tools ISBN 978-1-937522-41-4
NISO RP-10-2010	Cost of Resource Exchange (CORE) Protocol ISBN 978-1-880124-84-0
NISO RP-11-2011	ESPReSSO: Establishing Suggested Practices Regarding Single Sign-On ISBN 978-1-880124-98-7
NISO RP-12-2012	Physical Delivery of Library Resources ISBN 978-1-937522-01-8
NISO RP-14-2014	NISO SUSHI Protocol: COUNTER-SUSHI Implementation Profile ISBN 978-1-937522-45-2
NISO RP-15-2013	Recommended Practices for Online Supplemental Journal Article Materials ISBN 978-1-937522-12-4
NISO RP-16-2013	PIE-J: The Presentation and Identification of E-Journals ISBN 978-1-937522-05-6
NISO RP-17-2013	Institutional Identification: Identifying Organizations in the Information Supply Chain ISBN 978-1-937522-11-7
NISO RP-19-2014	Open Discovery Initiative: Promoting Transparency in Discovery ISBN 978-1-937522-42-1
NISO RP-20-2014	Demand Driven Acquisition of Monographs ISBN 978-1-937522-44-5
NISO RP-21-2013	Improving OpenURLs Through Analytics (IOTA): Recommendations for Link Resolver Providers ISBN 978-1-937522-18-6
NISO RP-22-2015	Access License and Indicators ISBN 978-1-937522-49-0
NISO RP-23-2015	Protocol for Exchanging Serial Content (PESC) ISBN 978-1-937522-66-7
NISO RP-24-2019	Transfer Code of Practice, version 4.0 ISBN 978-1-937522-90-2
NISO RP-25-2016	Outputs of the NISO Alternative Assessment Project ISBN 978-1-937522-71-1
NISO RP-26-2019	KBART Automation: Automated Retrieval of Customer Electronic Holdings ISBN 978-1-937522-91-9
NISO RP-27-2019	Resource Access in the 21st Century ISBN 978-1-937522-99-5

NISO Technical Reports

NISO TR-01-1995 Environmental Guidelines for the Storage of Paper Records
by William K. Wilson
ISBN 978-1-800124-21-5

NISO TR-02-1997 Guidelines for Indexes and Related Information Retrieval Devices
by James D. Anderson
ISBN 978-1-880124-36-X

NISO TR-03-1999 Guidelines for Alphabetical Arrangement of Letters and Sorting of Numerals and Other Symbols
by Hans H. Wellisch
ISBN 978-1-880124-41-6

NISO TR-04-2006 Networked Reference Services: Question/Answer Transaction Protocol
ISBN 978-1-880124-71-0

NISO TR-05-2013 IOTA Working Group Summary of Activities and Outcomes
ISBN 978-1-937522-17-9

NISO TR-06-2017 Issues in Vocabulary Management
ISBN 978-1-937522-79-7

Other NISO Publications

The Case for New Economic Models to Support Standardization
by Clifford Lynch
ISBN 978-1-880124-90-1

The Exchange of Serials Subscription Information
by Ed Jones
ISBN 978-1-880124-91-8

The Future of Library Resource Discovery
by Marshall Breeding
ISBN 978-1-937522-41-4

Information Standards Quarterly (*ISQ*) [NISO quarterly open access magazine]
ISSN 1041-0031

Internet, Interoperability and Standards—Filling the Gaps
by Janifer Gatenby
ISBN 978-1-880124-92-5

Issues in Crosswalking Content Metadata Standards
by Margaret St. Pierre and William P. LaPlant
ISBN 978-1-880124-93-2

Making Good on the Promise of ERM: A Standards and Best Practices Discussion Paper
by the ERM Data Standards and Best Practices Review Steering Committee
ISBN 978-1-9357522-00-1

Metadata Demystified: A Guide for Publishers
by Amy Brand, Frank Daly, and Barbara Meyers
ISBN 978-1-880124-59-8

The Myth of Free Standards: Giving Away the Farm
by Andrew N. Bank
ISBN 978-1-880124-94-9

NISO Newsline [free monthly e-newsletter]
ISSN 1559-2774

NISO Working Group Connection (free quarterly supplement to *Newsline*)

Patents and Open Standards
by Priscilla Caplan
ISBN 978-1-880124-95-6

The RFP Writer's Guide to Standards for Library Systems
by Cynthia Hodgson
ISBN 978-1-880124-57-4

Streamlining Book Metadata Workflow
by Judy Luther
ISBN 978-1-880124-82-6

Understanding Metadata: What Is Metadata, and What Is It For?: A Primer
by Jenn Riley
ISBN 978-1-937522-72-8

Up and Running: Implementing Z39.50: Proceedings of a Symposium Sponsored by the State Library of Iowa
edited by Sara L. Randall
ISBN 978-1-880124-33-8

Z39.50: A Primer on the Protocol
ISBN 978-1-880124-35-2

Z39.50 Implementation Experiences
ISBN 978-1-880124-51-2

NISO standards are available at http://www.niso.org/publications/standards.

Recommended Practices, Technical Reports, White Papers, and other publications are available on the NISO website at http://www.niso.org/publications.

For more information, contact NISO, 3600 Clipper Mill Rd., Suite 302, Baltimore, MD 21211. Tel. 301-654-2512, fax 410-685-5278, e-mail nisohq@niso.org, World Wide Web http://www.niso.org.

Calendar, 2020–2028

This listing contains information on association meetings and promotional events that are, for the most part, national or international in scope. State and regional library association meetings are also included.

For information on additional book trade and promotional events, see *Literary Market Place* and *International Literary Market Place*, published by Information Today, Inc., and other library and book trade publications such as *Library Journal*, *School Library Journal*, and *Publishers Weekly*. The American Library Association (ALA) keeps an online calendar at http://www.ala.org/conferencesevents/planning-calendar. An Information Today events calendar can be found at http://www.infotoday.com/calendar.shtml.

[Due to the COVID-19 pandemic, a number of conferences scheduled for mid-2020 have been cancelled, moved to an online virtual format, or were being rescheduled for later in the year when *Library and Book Trade Almanac* went to press. To confirm the status as well as the starting or ending date of any meeting listed, contact the association directly. Addresses of library and book trade associations are listed in Part 6 of this volume.—*Ed.*]

2020

June

1–3	Specialized Information Publishers Assn.	Washington, DC
8–11	Assn. of Christian Librarians	Wichita, KS
13–15	Assn. of American University Presses	Seattle, WA
21–26	IEEE International Symposium on Information Theory	Los Angeles, CA
22–24	Assn. of Canadian Publishers Annual Meeting	Montreal, QC
24–26	Assn. of European Research Libraries (LIBER)	Belgrade, Serbia
24–28	Seoul International Book Fair	Seoul, South Korea
25–30	American Library Assn. Annual Conference	Chicago, IL
25–30	American Assn. of School Librarians @ ALA	Chicago, IL
29–July 1	Assn. of Jewish Libraries	Evanston, IL

July 2020

7–11	National Assn. of Government Archives and Records Administrators (NAGARA)	Denver, CO
11–14	American Assn. of Law Libraries (AALL)	New Orleans, LA
14–21	Hong Kong Book Fair	Hong Kong
16–17	Computing Conference	London, UK
23–26	Comic-Con International	San Diego, CA

August

3–8	Society of American Archivists	Chicago, IL
4–7	Alaska Library Assn.	Juneau, AK
4–7	Pacific Northwest Library Assn.	Juneau, AK
15–21	International Federation of Library Assns. (IFLA) General Conf. and Assembly	Dublin, Ireland
15–31	Edinburgh International Book Festival	Edinburgh, UK
20–22	International Symposium on Information Management and Big Data	Lima, Peru
26–30	Beijing International Book Fair	Beijing, China

September

2–6	Moscow International Book Fair	Moscow, Russia
10–11	Colorado Library Assn.	Loveland, CO
16–19	North Carolina Library Assn.	Black Mountain, NC
24–27	Gothenburg Book Fair	Gothenburg, Sweden
30–Oct. 2	Missouri Library Assn.	Springfield, MO
30–Oct. 2	North Dakota Library Assn.	Bismarck, ND
30–Oct. 2	South Dakota Library Assn.	Aberdeen, SD

October

1–2	Minnesota Library Assn.	Duluth, MN
1–3	Assn. of Library Service to Children (ALSC) National Institute	Minneapolis, MN
7–9	Georgia Libraries / Southeastern Library Assn.	Macon, GA
7–9	Nebraska Library Assn.	Kearney, NE
7–9	South Carolina Library Assn.	Columbia, SC
7–9	West Virginia Library Assn.	Davis, WV
7–10	Washington Library Assn.	Spokane, WA
8–9	Wyoming Library Assn.	Casper, WY
13–14	Internet Librarian International	London, UK
14–16	Iowa Library Assn.	Dubuque, IA

14–16	Kentucky Library Assn.	Lexington, KY
14–17	Arizona Library Assn.	Prescott, AZ
14–18	Frankfurt Book Fair	Frankfurt, Germany
15–18	International Literacy Assn.	Columbus, OH
15–19	Special Libraries Assn.	Charlotte, NC
16–18	Arkansas Library Assn.	Fort Smith, AR
18–21	Pennsylvania Library Assn.	Mount Pocono, PA
19–23	International Conference on Information and Knowledge Management (CIKM)	Galway, Ireland
20–22	Illinois Library Assn.	Springfield, IL
20–22	Internet Librarian	Monterey, CA
21–23	New Mexico Library Assn.	Albuquerque, NM
22–24	California Library Assn.	Pasadena, CA
22–25	Helsinki Book Fair	Helsinki, Finland
22–25	Krakow International Book Fair	Krakow, Poland
23–28	Assn. for Information Science and Technology (ASIS&T)	Pittsburgh, PA
24–Nov. 1	Belgrade International Book Fair	Belgrade, Serbia
25–27	New England Library Assn.	Manchester, NH
25–27	New Hampshire Library Assn.	Manchester, NH
27–30	Wisconsin Library Assn.	Green Bay, WI
28–30	Ohio Library Council	Columbus, OH
28–30	Virginia Library Assn.	Hot Springs, VA
28–30	Kansas Library Assn.	Wichita, KS
31–Nov. 8	Istanbul Book Fair	Istanbul, Turkey

November

4–7	New York Library Assn.	Saratoga Springs, NY
11–15	Buch Wein International Book Fair	Vienna, Austria
16–19	KM World	Washington, DC
25–30	Salon du Livre de Montreal	Montreal, QC
28–Dec. 6	Guadalajara International Book Fair	Guadalajara, Mexico
30–Dec. 1	Bibliographical Society of Australia and New Zealand	Adelaide, Australia
30–Dec. 2	International Conference of Indigenous Archives, Libraries, and Museums	Washington, DC

December

13–16	International Conference on Information Systems (ICIS)	Hyderabad, India

2021

January

5–8	Hawaii International Conference on System Sciences	Kauai, HI
22–26	American Library Assn. Midwinter Meeting	Indianapolis, IN
22–26	American Assn. of School Librarians (AASL) @ ALA Midwinter Meeting	Indianapolis, IN

March

9–11	London Book Fair	London, UK
23–25	Computers in Libraries	Arlington, VA

April

6–8	Tennessee Library Assn.	Memphis, TN
14–17	Assn. of College and Research Libraries	Seattle, WA
20–23	Texas Library Assn.	San Antonio, TX

June

15–17	Assn. of American University Presses	Montreal, PQ
24–29	American Library Assn. Annual Conference	Chicago, IL
24–29	American Assn. of School Librarians @ ALA	Chicago, IL

July

12–16	International Assn. of School Librarianship (IASL)	Denton, TX
17–20	American Assn. of Law Libraries (AALL)	Cleveland, OH

August

19–26	International Federation of Library Assns. (IFLA) General Conf. and Assembly	Rotterdam, Netherlands

September

29–Oct. 1	South Dakota Library Assn.	Pierre, SD

October

6–8	North Dakota Library Assn.	Grand Forks, ND
12–14	Illinois Library Assn.	Peoria, IL
17–20	Pennsylvania Library Assn.	Monroeville, PA
20–24	Frankfurt Book Fair	Frankfurt, Germany

21–23	American Assn. of School Librarians (AASL) National Conference	Salt Lake City, UT
29–Nov. 3	Assn. for Information Science and Technology (ASIS&T)	Salt Lake City, UT

November

3–6	New York Library Assn.	Syracuse, NY

December

12–15	International Conference on Information Systems (ICIS)	Austin, Texas

2022

January

21–25	American Library Assn. Midwinter Meeting	San Antonio, TX
21–25	American Assn. of School Librarians (AASL) @ ALA Midwinter Meeting	San Antonio, TX

March

22–26	Public Library Assn.	Portland, OR
29–31	Computers in Libraries	Arlington, VA

April

25–28	Texas Library Assn.	Fort Worth, TX

June

18–20	Assn. of American University Presses	Washington, DC
23–28	American Library Assn. Annual Conference	Washington, DC
23–28	American Assn. of School Librarians @ ALA	Washington, DC

July

16–19	American Assn. of Law Libraries (AALL)	Denver, CO

August

13–19	International Federation of Library Assns. General Conf. and Assembly	Auckland, (IFLA) New Zealand

September

28–30	South Dakota Library Assn.	Brookings, SD

October 2022

16–19	Pennsylvania Library Assn.	Harrisburg, PA
19–23	Frankfurt Book Fair	Frankfurt, Germany

November

2–5	New York Library Assn.	Saratoga Springs, NY

December

11–14	International Conference on Information Systems (ICIS)	Copenhagen, Denmark

2023

January

27–31	American Library Assn. Midwinter Meeting	New Orleans, LA
27–31	American Assn. of School Librarians (AASL) @ ALA Midwinter Meeting	New Orleans, LA

March

15–18	Assn. of College and Research Libraries	Pittsburgh, PA

April

19–22	Texas Library Assn.	Austin, TX

June

22–27	American Library Assn. Annual Conference	Chicago, IL
22–27	American Assn. of School Librarians @ ALA	Chicago, IL

July

15–19	American Assn. of Law Libraries	Boston, MA

October

18–22	Frankfurt Book Fair	Frankfurt, Germany
19–21	American Assn. of School Librarians (AASL) National Conference	Tampa, FL

November

1–4	New York Library Assn.	Saratoga Springs, NY

December

10–13	International Conference on Information Systems (ICIS)	Bangkok, Thailand

2024

April

16–19	Texas Library Assn.	San Antonio, TX

June

27–July 2	American Library Assn. Annual Conference	San Diego, CA
27–July 2	American Assn. of School Librarians @ ALA	San Diego, CA

July

17–20	American Assn. of Law Libraries (AALL)	Cleveland, OH

2025

April

1–4	Texas Library Assn.	Dallas, TX
2–5	Assn. of College and Research Libraries	Minneapolis, MN

June

26–July 1	American Library Assn. Annual Conference	Philadelphia, PA
26–July 1	American Assn. of School Librarians @ ALA	Philadelphia, PA

July

19–22	American Assn. of Law Libraries (AALL)	Portland, OR

October

16–19	American Assn. of School Librarians (AASL) National Conference	St. Louis, MO

2026

March

30–Apr. 2	Texas Library Assn.	Houston, TX

June 2026

25–30	American Library Assn. Annual Conference	Chicago, IL
25–30	American Assn. of School Librarians @ ALA	Chicago, IL

2027

March

30–Apr. 2	Texas Library Assn.	Dallas, TX

April

7–10	Assn. of College and Research Libraries	Portland, OR

June

24–29	American Library Assn. Annual Conference	New Orleans, LA
24–29	American Assn. of School Librarians @ ALA	New Orleans, LA

2028

April

24–27	Texas Library Assn.	San Antonio, TX

Acronyms

A

AACR2. Anglo-American Cataloging Rules
AAHSL. Association of Academic Health Sciences Libraries
AALL. American Association of Law Libraries
AAP. Association of American Publishers
AASL. American Association of School Librarians
AAU. Association of American Universities
AAUP. Association of American University Presses
ABA. Acquisitions and Bibliographic Access Directorate
ABA. American Booksellers Association
ABFE. American Booksellers for Free Expression
ABOS. Association of Bookmobile and Outreach Services
ABPA. American Book Producers Association
ACL. Association of Christian Librarians
ACM. Association of Children's Museums
ACRL. Association of College and Research Libraries
AFSIC. Alternative Farming Systems Information Center
AgLaw. Agricultural Law Information Partnership
AGLINET. Agricultural Libraries Network
AgNIC. Agriculture Network Information Collaborative
AGRICOLA. AGRICultural On-Line Access
AIGA. Professional Association for Design (formerly American Institute of Graphic Arts)
AIIM. Association for Information and Image Management
AIIP. Association of Independent Information Professionals
AILA. American Indian Library Association
AILI. FEDLINK American Indian Libraries Initiative
AJL. Association of Jewish Libraries
ALA. American Library Association
ALCTS. Association for Library Collections and Technical Services
ALD. *American Library Directory*
ALHHS. Archivists and Librarians in the History of the Health Sciences
ALIC. Archives Library Information Center
ALISE. Association for Library and Information Science Education
ALS. Academic Libraries Survey
ALSC. Association for Library Service to Children
ALTA. American Literary Translators Association
ANSI. American National Standards Institute
APALA. Asian/Pacific American Librarians Association
APP. Accelerating Promising Practices
ARL. Association of Research Libraries
ARLIS/NA. Art Libraries Society of North America
ARMA International (formerly the Association of Records Managers and Administrators)
ARSL. Association for Rural and Small Libraries
ASGCLA. Association of Specialized, Government, and Cooperative Library Agencies
ASI. American Society for Indexing
ASIS&T. Association for Information Science and Technology
ATALM. Association of Tribal Archives, Libraries, and Museums
Atla (formerly the American Theological Library Association)

AUPresses (Association of University Presses)
AVSL. Association of Vision Science Librarians
AWIC. Animal Welfare Information Center

B

BARD. Braille and Audio Reading Download
BCALA. Black Caucus of the American Library Association
BISAC. Book Industry Systems Advisory Committee
BMI. Book Manufacturers' Institute
BSA. Bibliographical Society of America
BSC-SCB. Bibliographical Society of Canada
BSIG. Book Industry Study Group

C

CAIS. Canadian Association for Information Science
CALA. Chinese American Librarians Association
CALL. Canadian Association of Law Libraries
CAP. Collections Assessment for Preservation
CARL. Canadian Association of Research Libraries
CASE. Copyright Alternative in Small-Claims Enforcement Act
CBC. Children's Book Council
CDO. Collection Development Office
CGP. Catalog of U.S. Government Publications
C&I. Cataloging and indexing
CIKM. International Conference on Information and Knowledge Management
CIP. Cataloging in Publication
CLA. Catholic Library Association
CLENERT. See LearnRT
CLIR. Council on Library and Information Resources
CMO. Communications and Marketing Office (ALA)
CNI. Coalition for Networked Information
CONAN. Constitution Annotated
COSLA. Chief Officers of State Library Associations
CRDP. Cataloging Record Distribution Program
CRO. Chapter Relations Office (ALA)
CRS. Congressional Research Service
CUI. Controlled unclassified information

D

DAMS. Digital Asset Management System
DDC. Dewey Decimal Classification
DEL. Documenting Endangered Languages
DHCP. Documentary Heritage Community Program
DLF. Digital Library Federation
DLME. Digital Library of the Middle East
DMCA. Digital Millennium Copyright Act
DPLA. Digital Public Library of America
DTIC. Defense Technical Information Center

E

ECIP. Electronic Cataloging in Publication Program
ECLS. Early Childhood Longitudinal Study
EDI. Equity, diversity and inclusion
ELS. Education Longitudinal Study
EMIERT. Ethnic and Multicultural Information and Exchange Round Table
ERA. Electronic Records Archives
ERIC. Education Resources Information Center
ERT. Exhibits Round Table

F

FAB. FEDLINK Advisory Board
FDLP. Federal Depository Library Program
FEDLINK. Federal Library and Information Network
FESABID. Federación Española de Sociedades de Archivística, Biblioteconomía, Documentación y Museística

FIAF. International Federation of Film Archives
FMRT. Film and Media Round Table
FNIC. Food and Nutrition Information Center
FOIA. Freedom of Information Act
FRCs. Federal Records Centers
FSRIO. Food Safety Research Information Office
FTRF. Freedom to Read Foundation

G

GLBTRT. Gay, Lesbian, Bisexual, and Transgendered Round Table
GNCRT. Graphic Novel and Comics Round Table
GODORT. Government Documents Round Table
GPO. Government Publishing Office
GREAT. Grant Reporting Efficiency and Agreements Transparency Act

H

HBCU. Historically Black Colleges and Universities
HRDR. Office for Human Resource Development and Recruitment (ALA)

I

IACs. Information Analysis Centers
IAL. Innovative Approaches to Literacy
IALL. International Association of Law Libraries
IAML. International Association of Music Libraries, Archives and Documentation Centres
IASL. International Association of School Librarianship
IATUL. International Association of Scientific and Technological University Libraries
IBBY. International Board on Books for Young People
IBD. Independent Bookstore Day
IBPA. Independent Book Publishers Association
ICA. International Council on Archives
ICIS. International Conference on Information Systems
IFLA. International Federation of Library Associations and Institutions
IFRT. Intellectual Freedom Round Table
IIPC. International Internet Preservation Consortium
ILA. International Literacy Association
ILAB. International League of Antiquarian Booksellers
ILL. Interlibrary loan
IMLS. Institute of Museum and Library Services
INALJ. Information professionals finding and sharing jobs
IPA. International Publishers Association
IPEDS. Integrated Postsecondary Education Data System
IRO. International Relations Office (ALA)
IRRT. International Relations Round Table
ISBD. International Standard Bibliographical Description
ISBN. International Standard Book Number
ISNs. Canadian International Standard Numbers
ISO. International Organization for Standardization
ISOO. Information Security Oversight Office
ISSN. International Standard Serial Number

J

JCLC. National Joint Conference of Librarians of Color
JELIS. *Journal of Education for Library and Information Science*

K

KHI. Kurdish Heritage Institute

L

LAC. Library and Archives Canada
LARC. Library and Research Center (ALA)
LC. Library of Congress
LCA. Library Copyright Alliance

LCI. Leading Change Institute
LearnRT. Learning Round Table (formerly CLENERT)
LHC. Lister Hill Center for Biomedical Communications
LHRT. Library History Round Table
LIBER. Association of European Research Libraries
LIR. Library Instruction Round Table
LIS. Library and information science
LITA. Library and Information Technology Association
LJ. *Library Journal*
LLAMA. Library Leadership and Management Association
LMPI. Library Materials Price Index
LPC. Library Publishing Coalition
LRRT. Library Research Round Table
LRS. Lawyers referral service
LRTS. *Library Resources and Technical Services*
LSCM. Library Services and Content Management
LSSIRT. Library Support Staff Interests Round Table
LSTA. Library Services and Technology Act

M

MAGIRT. Map and Geospatial Information Round Table
MAP. Museum Assessment Program
METRO. Metropolitan New York Library Council
MFA. Museums for America
MLA. Medical Library Association
MLA. Music Library Association
MLIS. Master of Library and Information Science
MLSA. Museum and Library Services Act
MMLIS. Master of Management in Library and Information Science
MOOCs. Massive Open Online Courses
MPA. Association of Magazine Media (formerly Magazine Publishers of America)

N

NAABPI. North American Academic Books Price Index
NAC. National Archives Catalog
NAGARA. National Association of Government Archives and Records Administrators
NAIBA. New Atlantic Independent Booksellers Association
NAL. National Agricultural Library
NALDC. National Agricultural Library Digital Collection
NALT. National Agricultural Library Thesaurus
NANP. National Digital Newspaper Program
NARA. National Archives and Records Administration
NASIG (formerly North American Serials Interest Group)
NCAC. National Coalition Against Censorship
NCBI. National Center for Biotechnology Information
NCES. National Center for Education Statistics
NCTE. National Council of Teachers of English
NDC. National Declassification Center
NDNP. National Digital Newspaper Program
NDSA. National Digital Stewardship Alliance
NEH. National Endowment for the Humanities
NFAIS. National Federation of Advanced Information Services
NHPRC. National Historical Publications and Records Commission
NIH. National Institutes of Health
NISIC. National Invasive Species Information Center
NISO. National Information Standards Organization
NLE. National Library of Education
NLM. National Library of Medicine
NLS. National Library Service for the Blind and Physically Handicapped
NLWD. National Library Workers Day
NMLSB. National Museum and Library Services Board
NMRT. New Members Round Table
NNLM. National Network of Libraries of Medicine
NTIS. National Technical Information Service

NTPS. National Teacher and Principal Survey
NTRL. National Technical Reports Library
NUWC. Naval Undersea Warfare Center

O

OCIO. Office of the Chief Information Officer (LC)
OCLC. Online Computer Library Center
ODLOS. Office for Diversity, Literacy and Outreach Services (ALA)
OFR. National Archives' Office of the Federal Register
OGIS. Office of Government Information Services
OIB. USSBY Outstanding International Books
OIF. Office for Intellectual Freedom
OLOS. Office for Literacy and Outreach Services

P

PALA. Polish American Librarians Association
PCC. Program for Cooperative Cataloging
PLA. Public Library Association
PPAO. Public Policy and Advocacy Office (ALA)
PPO. Public Programs Office (ALA)
PRD. Preservation Reformatting Division

R

RBMS. Rare Books and Manuscripts Section
RDA. Resource Description and Access
REFORMA. National Association to Promote Library and Information Services to Latinos and the Spanish-Speaking
RIC. Rural Information Center
RMS. Research Management and Support
RtC. Libraries Ready to Code
RUSA. Reference and User Services Association

S

SAA. Society of American Archivists
SAN. Standard Address Number
SASS. Schools and Staffing Survey
SCBWI. Society of Children's Book Writers and Illustrators
SIBA (formerly Southern Independent Booksellers Alliance)
SIIA. Software and Information Industry Association
SLA. Special Libraries Association
SLAA. State Library Administrative Agency
SPARC. Scholarly Publishing & Academic Resources Coalition
SRA. Sequence Read Archive
SRRT. Social Responsibilities Round Table
SSP. Society for Scholarly Publishing
STEAM. Science, Technology, Engineering, Arts, and Math
STEM. Science, Technology, Engineering, and Mathematics

T

TOME. Toward an Open Monograph Ecosystem
TPS. Teaching with Primary Sources
TRAIL. Technical Report Archive & Image Library
TRD. Trustworthy Digital Repository certification

U

UKSG (formerly the United Kingdom Serials Group)
ULC. Urban Libraries Council
USAIN. United States Agricultural Information Network
USBBY. United States Board on Books for Young People
USMA. U.S. Military Academy
USPPI. U.S. Periodical Price Index

V

VHP. Veterans History Project

W

WAIC. Water and Agriculture Information Center
WIPO. World Intellectual Property Organization
WLIC. World Library and Information Congress
WNBA. Women's National Book Association

Y

YALSA. Young Adult Library Services Association

Index

Note: Page numbers followed by "f" and "t" represent figures and tables respectively. The Directory of Organizations (Part 6) is not included in the index.

F

G

J

K

M

O

P